Further praise for HUBERT HARRISC

"Perry's significant biography lives up to the promise of its title. Finally, the voice of this major Harlem Renaissance progressive is to be heard again loud and clear."

—DAVID LEVERING LEWIS, NEW YORK UNIVERSITY, AUTHOR OF
A TWO-VOLUME BIOGRAPHY OF W.E.B. DU BOIS

"For decades a brilliant and critical voice of the Harlem Renaissance has been practically ignored by historians. At last that serious gap will be filled by Jeffrey B. Perry, who has thoroughly researched and carefully crafted a two-part definitive biography of the "Father of Harlem Radicalism," Hubert H. Harrison. These volumes, along with his previously published collection of Harrison's writings, are a significant contribution because they reveal in rich detail and masterful treatment the life of one of the most unusual and influential African American thinkers of that time. The people of Harlem flocked to Harrison's "university level" street orations on a wide range of topics, but few knew of his numerous journal articles on society, science, and socialism. Perry was driven to conduct extensive research when he discovered Harrison's clarity of writing and perceptiveness of analysis. Surely his own clarity of writing, meticulous attention to events and other activists, and masterful analysis will prove in time to be essential for understanding the political movements of the period."

—JOYCE MOORE TURNER, AUTHOR OF *CARIBBEAN CRUSADERS
AND THE HARLEM RENAISSANCE*, AND COEDITOR, WITH W. BURGHARDT
TURNER, OF *RICHARD B. MOORE: CARIBBEAN MILITANT IN HARLEM*

"This monumental and acute biography becomes the best point of entry into the whole history of modern radicalism in the United States."

—DAVID ROEDIGER, UNIVERSITY OF ILLINOIS, AND THE AUTHOR
OF *HOW RACE SURVIVED U.S. HISTORY*

"Hubert Harrison was one of the most gifted and creative intellectuals in the American Left and within Black America in the twentieth century. Perry's book presents a comprehensive analysis of the first phase of Harrison's remarkable public career. Before Marcus Garvey came to Harlem in 1916, Harrison had blazed the trail as the leading voice of Black radicalism. He founded the New Negro Movement and was a central antiwar leader during WWI. Perry captures Harrison's brilliance, energy, and leadership during a remarkable period in African-American history. The outstanding scholarship of his study will re-awaken popular interest in this remarkable figure."

—MANNING MARABLE, DIRECTOR, CENTER FOR CONTEMPORARY
BLACK HISTORY, COLUMBIA UNIVERSITY

"[A] brilliant masterpiece."

—WILLIAM J. MOSES, *AMERICAN HISTORICAL REVIEW*

"A magisterial piece of scholarship."

—*JOURNAL OF AMERICAN HISTORY*

"Perry's detailed research brings to life a transformative figure who has been little recognized for his contributions to progressive race and class politics."

—*BOOKLIST*

"Perry's clear prose allows access to a three-dimensional picture of Harrison's life."

—*LIBRARY JOURNAL*

"An excellent work and a great contribution to scholarship. . . . Perry must be applauded."

—*Z MAGAZINE*

"Offers profound insights on race, class, religion, immigration, war, democracy, and social change in America."

—*INDUSTRIAL WORKER*

"Through Perry's prodigious research Harrison's brilliance can once more engage a generation eager to find inspiration and renewed political spirit."

—HERB BOYD, *NEWORLD REVIEW*

"This critically important book will do for Harrison what David Levering Lewis did for Du Bois. . . . Essential."

—*CHOICE*

"This meticulously researched book fills an enormous gap in the knowledge of Black activist intellectuals in the U.S."

—CAROL BOYCE DAVIES, *WORKING USA*

"Rich and exhaustively researched."

—CLARENCE LANG, *AGAINST THE CURRENT*

"Perry has made a significant contribution to the history of Black radicalism through his biography of Hubert Harrison. With thorough research and compelling analysis, Perry offers the reader insight into a brilliant and under-studied activist and intellectual who played a major role in helping to shape the Black radical tradition. *Hubert Harrison* reads with a draw like that of a study of a long lost city, rediscovered and offering answers to an incomplete history."

—BILL FLETCHER, JR., EXECUTIVE EDITOR, BLACKCOMMENTATOR.COM, COAUTHOR OF *SOLIDARITY DIVIDED*

"Entrusted with the remains of Hubert Harrison's papers, Perry favors us with this meticulous chronicle of one of the century's most influential voices for democracy and freedom. Harrison, island-born, colonial subject, and immigrant, stirred the masses in Harlem, at the time the center of Black radical thought, to a 'new race-consciousness' and an apprehension of 'their powers and destiny' in the United States and world. *Hubert Harrison* testifies to the remarkable durability of lives well lived and truths told straight."

—GARY Y. OKIHIRO, COLUMBIA UNIVERSITY, AUTHOR OF *ISLAND WORLD: A HISTORY OF HAWAI'I AND THE UNITED STATES*

"Hubert Harrison was in his lifetime the leading American Black intellectual socialist, but he receded from memory after his death. We are all in debt to Perry for his devoted and fastidious recuperation of Harrison's memory. This assiduously researched biography, an extraordinary feat of scholarship, restores Harrison to his proper standing in the pantheon of other Afro-Caribbeans, from Marcus Garvey to C. L. R. James, who contributed to reshaping American political thought in the twentieth century."

—CHRISTOPHER PHELPS, OHIO STATE UNIVERSITY

"One of the most significant twentieth-century African American philosophers, Perry finally accords Harrison his place among the forebears of modern African American political and cultural thought and also suggests the sweeping scope of Harrison's life and achievement."

—PORTIA JAMES, CULTURAL RESOURCES MANAGER AND SENIOR CURATOR, ANACOSTIA COMMUNITY MUSEUM

"*Hubert Harrison* is not simply an archaeological uncovering of a century-old Black icon. Harrison's life and his insights on race and class, especially during wartime, leap off the page. They particularly resonate today. Harrison challenged the government's hypocritical notion of sending Black men to fight and die to make 'the world safe for democracy' in World War I while they were being lynched, segregated, and disenfranchised at home. I see Harrison's ghost on a

Harlem soapbox today exposing the links between the destructive wars abroad and the need to expand the fight for civil liberties and civil rights and to forge a new global partnership with the world's people. This is a ghost that needs to be listened to."

—GENE BRUSKIN, NATIONAL CO-CONVENER,
U.S. LABOR AGAINST THE WAR

"A groundbreaking biography and act of historical recovery that restores Hubert Harrison's vital importance to African American history and politics during the New Negro era. Meticulously written and painstakingly researched, *Hubert Harrison* is a major work of scholarship that will transform understanding of Black life during the early twentieth century."

—PENIEL E. JOSEPH, BRANDEIS UNIVERSITY, AUTHOR OF
*WAITING 'TIL THE MIDNIGHT HOUR: A NARRATIVE HISTORY
OF BLACK POWER IN AMERICA*

Hubert Harrison

The Voice of Harlem Radicalism, 1883–1918

Jeffrey B. Perry

Columbia University Press
New York

To
Charles Richardson, Ilva Harrison, Yvette Richardson,
Becky Hom, and Perri Hom

and to the memory of
Aida Harrison Richardson, William Harrison,
and Theodore W. Allen

Columbia University Press
Publishers Since 1893
New York   Chichester, West Sussex
Copyright © 2009 Jeffrey B. Perry
Paperback edition, 2011
All rights reserved

Library of Congress Cataloging-in-Publication Data

Perry, Jeffrey Babcock.
Hubert Harrison : the voice of Harlem radicalism, 1883–1918 /
Jeffrey B. Perry
p.   cm.
Includes bibliographical references and index.
ISBN 978-0-231-13910-6 (cloth : alk. paper) — ISBN 978-0-231-13911-3 (pbk. : alk. paper)
— ISBN 978-0-231-51122-3 (e-book)
1. Harrison, Hubert H. 2. Harrison, Hubert H.—Political and social views.
3. African American intellectuals—Biography. 4. Radicalism—United States—
History. 5. African Americans—Intellectual life. 6. Harlem Renaissance.
7. Harlem (New York, N.Y.)—Intellectual life. 8. New York (N.Y.)—Intellectual life.
9. United States—Social conditions—1865–1918. 10. United States—Race relations.
I. Title.

E185.97.H367P47   2009
973'.0496073—dc22
[B]
2008016976

∞

Columbia University Press books are printed on permanent and durable acid-free paper.

Printed in the United States of America

Politically, the Negro is the touchstone of the modern democratic idea. The presence of the Negro puts our democracy to the proof and reveals the falsity of it.... [True democracy and equality implies] a revolution ... startling even to think of.

—HUBERT HARRISON, *NEW YORK CALL*

As long as the Color Line exists, all the perfumed protestations of Democracy on the part of the white race must be simply downright lying. The cant of "Democracy" is intended as dust in the eyes of white voters.... It furnishes bait for the clever statesmen.

—HUBERT HARRISON, *NEW NEGRO*

During the war the idea of democracy was widely advertised, especially in the English-speaking world, mainly as a convenient camouflage behind which competing imperialists masked their sordid aims.... those who so loudly proclaimed and formulated the new democratic demands never had the slightest intention of extending the limits or the applications of "democracy."

—HUBERT HARRISON, *WHEN AFRICA AWAKES*

[America is a] great experiment in democracy ... unique in the history of the world.... And the great American experiment is to determine for the future whether we can make out of the welter of races and nations one people, one culture, one democracy. It is confessedly a hard task, but it can be done, and the grounds of that faith rest on the known facts of the present and the past.

—HUBERT HARRISON, *AMSTERDAM NEWS*

That individuals of genuine worth and immense potentialities who dedicate their lives to the advancement of their fellow men are permitted to pass unrecognized and unrewarded from the scene, while others, inferior to them in ability and altruism, receive acclaim, wealth, and distinction is common—yet it never ceases to shock all but the confirmed cynic. Those with a sense of right and wrong, ... will forever feel that this ought not to be....

Hubert Henry Harrison is the case in point. Harrison was not only the foremost Afro-American intellect of his time, but one of America's greatest minds. No one worked more seriously and indefatigably to enlighten his fellow men; none of the Afro-American leaders of his time had a saner and more effective program—but others, unquestionably his inferiors, received the recognition that was his due. Even today but a very small proportion ... has ever heard of him.

—J. A. ROGERS, *WORLD'S GREAT MEN OF COLOR*

Hubert Harrison, 1918. *Source:* Photo courtesy of the Hubert H. Harrison Papers, Rare Book and Manuscript Library, Butler Library, Columbia University, New York.

Contents

Illustrations

Preface and Acknowledgments

*During the 1960s, like millions of other people, I was deeply affected by the move-*ments for social change in the United States inspired by the civil rights struggle. As a student in that period I was afforded opportunity to study, to research, and to interact with scholars. My ancestral roots, as far back as identifiable, are entirely among working people. These factors, and many related experiences, have led me toward a life in which I have tried to mix worker- and community-based organizing with historical research and writing. My major preoccupation has been with the successes and failures of efforts at social change in the United States. In that context, I have focused on the role of white supremacy in under-mining efforts at social change and on the importance of struggle against white supremacy to social change, and it is this focus that has led me to write this biography of Hubert Harrison, of which this book is the first of two.

These influences and interests have provided me with a certain openness to the contributions of working-class and anti-white-supremacist writers and intel-lectuals. It was in this context, in the early 1980s, while researching a proposed Columbia University doctoral dissertation on approaches to the struggle against white supremacy, that I first encountered the work of Hubert Harrison. When I first read microfilm copies of Harrison's two published books I was arrested by the clarity of his writing and the perceptiveness of his analysis. I knew that I had encountered a writer of great importance, and, within a short while, I decided to change my dissertation topic to a biography of Harrison. I searched for what I could find on him and was several hundred pages into his biography when, through the help of two Virgin Islanders—G. James Fleming, professor emeri-tus of Morgan State University in Baltimore, and June A. V. Lindqvist, librarian at the Enid M. Baa Library and Archives in Charlotte Amalie, St. Thomas (and a relative of Harrison's wife)—I was put in contact with Harrison's daughter, Aida Harrison Richardson, and son, William Harrison.

I met Aida and William for the first time in 1983. Aida was a former school teacher and principal, William was a former attorney, and both were very bright, socially aware, race-conscious individuals who knew the value of their father's work. They, along with their mother, the late Irene Louise Horton Harrison, had preserved the remains of Hubert Harrison's once vast collection of papers and books in a series of Harlem apartments. After several meetings and discussions of their father's work, they very generously (before William's death in 1984) granted me access to some of their father's materials, which were in a room in William's Harlem apartment. At subsequent periods over the years I was provided access to additional materials by Aida and then (after she passed in 2001) by her son Charles Richardson. I proceeded to preserve and inventory the Hubert H. Harrison Papers (many of which were in fragile condition). The papers were always the property of the family, they had authorized me to use them for my work, I felt responsible for their preservation, and I had no further authorization. When the family requested, I worked with them to place the papers with the Rare Book and Manuscript Library of Columbia University. I have since that time worked with Columbia staff to develop a finding aid (http://www.columbia.edu/cu/libraries/inside/projects/findingaids/scans/pdfs/Harrison_Hubert_H.pdf) and a Hubert Harrison Web site. To Aida, William, and Charles, to William's daughter, Ilva Harrison, and to Charles's daughter, Yvette Richardson, I am forever grateful. Their generous spirit, human kindness, and willingness to help in support of my efforts as biographer and chronicler of Hubert Harrison's life have left a lasting impression on me and inspired my work.

I was influenced toward serious study of matters of race and class in America through personal experiences and through the insightful and seminal work of an independent scholar and close personal friend, the late Theodore William Allen (author of the two-volume work *The Invention of the White Race*), whose papers I am similarly preserving and inventorying. Allen's writings on the role of white supremacy in U.S. history and on the centrality of the struggle against white supremacy to efforts at social change have attracted increased, and well deserved, attention. Familiarity with Allen's life and work disposed me to be receptive to the life and work of Harrison, another independent, autodidactic, anti-white-supremacist, working-class intellectual.

As a doctoral student at Columbia University in the 1980s my principal advisors, Nathan I. Huggins and Hollis R. Lynch, offered the encouragement, support, and constructive critical comments that strengthened my research in its early stages; emphasized Harrison's importance; and encouraged a deeper understanding of the individuals, social forces, and ideas that influenced his life. Their assistance included helping me to put together an exceptional team of dissertation readers that included Eric Foner, Charles V. Hamilton, and Elliot Skinner. These scholars critically read my manuscript and offered constructive suggestions and encouragement that pushed me to seek to further improve my work on Harrison.

Subsequent drafts of my writings on Harrison were read, commented on, and encouraged by Sean Ahern, Ernest Allen Jr., Theodore William Allen, Lois Katz Brown, Gene Bruskin, Peter Dimock, Robert Fitch, Bill Fletcher Jr., Henry Louis Gates Jr., Geoffrey Jacques, Portia James, Winston James, Jack O'Dell, Michael Spiegel, and George F. Tyson. Winston James was always extremely knowledgeable, helpful, and encouraging, and his efforts greatly facilitated the publication of the two-volume Harrison biography. Manning Marable encouraged further work on Harrison by helping to publish an earlier version of the introduction in *Souls*, the critical journal of Black studies that he edits at Columbia. Encouragement was similarly extended by Victor Wallis and Yusuf Nuruddin who published a version of the introduction in *Socialism and Democracy* and by Tom Radko and Suzanna Tamminen of Wesleyan University Press who published a version in A Hubert Harrison Reader. The historian Joyce Moore Turner, daughter of Harrison's friend Richard B. Moore, and Sean Ahern, a New York City school teacher and close personal friend, have also offered important support, encouragement, and insights.

Winston James and Manning Marable, along with Jean Ashton, former director of Columbia University's Rare Book and Manuscript Library; Peter Dimock, senior editor at Columbia University Press; James Neal, director of Columbia University Libraries; the appraiser Wyatt Day; the attorney David Snipe; and Charles Richardson (on behalf of the Harrison/Richardson families) all helped to place the Harrison Papers with Columbia's Rare Book and Manuscript Library, where they are supported by the finding aid and Web site projects in an effort to make Harrison's writings freely and easily available to scholars and the general public. The work on the Harrison Papers, the finding aid, and the Web site at Columbia have benefited greatly from the expertise and support of Michael T. Ryan, director of Columbia's Rare Book and Manuscript Library. Aspects of the work have also benefited from the skilled professionalism of Stephen P. Davis, director of Columbia University Libraries Digital Program Division; Patrick T. Lawlor, technical services coordinator; Joanna diPasquale, Web page designer; and archivists Benjamin Heller and April Holm.

Readers of my earlier writings on Harrison who offered comments and encouragement applied toward this work in addition to those already mentioned include Norman Allen, Eric Arnesen, Marilyn Bailey, Rosalyn Baxandall, Jon Bekken, Peter Bohmer, Chris Booker, Herb Boyd, Alexis Buss, Mary Katherine Calloway, Margaret Fisher Dalrymple, James P. Danky, Ossie Davis, Ruby Dee,

Howard Dodson, Steve Early, Dan Georgakas, Ted Glick, Don Hazen, Maureen Hewitt, Robert A. Hill, Gerald Horne, Kazu Iijima, Donna Katzin, Yuri Kochiyama, David Lawyer, Lester P. Lee Jr., Alan J. Mancuso, Mike Merrill, Carole Mihalko, Reverend Kay Osborn, Michael Nash, Christopher Phelps, Tom Radko, Allen Ruff, Angelica Santamauro, David Slavin, Lenny and Helene Smollett, Ann Sparanese, Leslie Starr, Suzanna Tamminen, Clarence Taylor, Nigel Thomas, Andres Torres, Timothy B. Tyson, Burghardt Turner, Michael Votichenko, Irma Watkins-Owens, Kam Williams, Stella Winston, and Komozi Woodard. Important encouragement, feedback, and constructive criticisms were also offered by brothers and sisters active in Local 300 of the National Postal Mail Handlers Union and in the working-class movement.

Throughout my research I have found librarians and library workers to be consistently helpful and generous with their time and expertise. (I note, however, that a great gap usually exists between the compensation in wages and benefits that they receive and the value of the service that they provide.) I am particularly thankful to the staffs at the Schomburg Center for Research in Black Culture; the New York Public Library); Columbia University Libraries; the Tamiment Library, New York University; Moorland-Spingarn Research Center at Howard University); the Library of Congress; the National Archives in Washington, D.C., New York City (formerly in Bayonne, New Jersey), and East Point, Georgia; Florence Williams Public Library, Christiansted, St. Croix; Frederiksted, St. Croix, Public Library; Landarskivet, Archives of Sealand, Lolland-Falster and Bornholm, Copenhagen, Denmark; Royal Library/National Library, Copenhagen; the Marx Memorial Library, London; the British Library, London; the Hoover Institution of War, Revolution, and Peace, Stanford University; the Municipal Archives and Records Center, New York; United States District Court, Southern District, New York; Office of the New York County Clerk; Magistrates Court of New York City; the United States Postal Record Center, St. Louis, Missouri; the Research Department at the James A. Farley Postal Facility in New York; the Brooklyn Public Library; the Paterson, New Jersey, Public Library; the Free Library of Philadelphia; the Westwood, New Jersey, Public Library; Rutgers University libraries; Firestone Library at Princeton University; Lenin State Library, Moscow; Amistad Research Center, Tulane University, New Orleans; Minnesota Historical Society, St. Paul, Minnesota; and the University of Minnesota Library in Minneapolis.

The Harrison research developed over many years, and virtually everyone I asked for help responded positively. Among those librarians, curators, and records administrators I would like to thank are: Terrie Albano, *People's Weekly World*; Eleanor Alexander, Morgan State University, Baltimore; Otis D. Alexander, Frederiksted Public Library; Jorgen H. Anderson, Landarskivet; Marina Ayzenberg, Brooklyn Public Library; Joellen El Bashir, MSRC; Jeanette Allis

Bastian, Simmons College; David A. Benjamin, government of the Virgin Islands of the United States; J. Scott Blackman, Immigration and Naturalization Service, New York; J. Donald Blevins, U.S. Department of State, Washington, D.C.; Lisbeth W. Borgesen, Royal Library, Copenhagen; Thomas Bourke, NYPL; Jacqueline Brown, Wilberforce University, Wilberforce, Ohio; Margaret J. Brink, Swarthmore College, Swarthmore, Pennsylvania; Karen W. Brown, Thomas Cooper Library, University of South Carolina; Joel Buchwald, NA, Bayonne and New York; Karsten Bundgaard, Royal Library, Copenhagen; Teresa M. Burk, Robert W. Woodruff Library, Emory University; Carol Butler, Brown Brothers; James G. Cassedy, NA, Washington, D.C.; Kevin J. Chandler, Mary McLeod Bethune Council House, Washington, D.C.; Mary Ellen Chijoke, Swarthmore College; Kenneth R. Cobb, Municipal Archives, City of New York; Anna L. Cook, Lane College, Jackson, Tennessee; Robert Cox, W.E.B. Du Bois Library, University of Massachusetts, Amherst; Debra E. Cribbs, St. Louis Mercantile Library; Carter Cue, Winston-Salem State University; Betty M. Culpepper, MSRC, Howard University; Charles Cummings, Newark, New Jersey, Public Library; Cynthia Czesak, Paterson, N.J., Free Public Library; Rev. Wilford Daniel, St. John's Episcopal Church, Christiansted; James P. Danky, Wisconsin Historical Society; Susan E. Davis, NYPL; Timur Davis, Newark, N.J., Public Library; Jennifer Dellava, Johns Hopkins University Press; Lynn E. Eaton, Perkins Library, Duke University; Eppie D. Edwards; National Library of Jamaica, Kingston; Denise English, Carter G. Woodson Regional Library, Chicago; Peter J. Filardo, Tamiment Library, NYU; Martha Foley, NYPL; Erike Gottfried, Tamiment Library, NYU; Dagmar L. Greenaway, *Virgin Islands Daily News*; Charlie Hall, Marx Memorial Library, London; James K. Hall, U.S. Department of Justice, Washington, D.C.; Linda K. Harvey, Tuskegee University, John Earl Haynes, Library of Congress, Tuskegee, Alabama; Mary E. Herbert, Maryland Historical Society; Julio L. Hernandez-Delgado, Hunter College Libraries; Rachel Hertz, Harry Ransome Center, University of Texas; Reverend A. Ivan Heyliger, St. John's Episcopal Church, Christiansted, St. Croix; Beth Howse, John Hope and Aurelia Elizabeth Franklin Library, Fisk University; Megan Hurst, "Open Collections Program: Women Working, 1800–1930," Harvard University Library; Jean Blackwell Hutson, SCRBC; Jessica Ingram, Pixel Press; Diane M. Johnston, NYPL; Karl Kabelac, University of Rochester; Ernest D. Kaiser, SCRBC; Harvey Klehr, Emory University; Danielle Kovacs, W. E. B. Du Bois Library, University of Massachusetts, Amherst; G. Kürti, Hungarian Academy of Sciences, Budapest, Hungary; Diana Lachatanare, SCRBC; Bonnie Lange, *Truth Seeker* Magazine; Jennifer Lee, Rare Book and Manuscript Library, Columbia University; John Littlefield, Allen/Littlefield Collection; Ethel Lobomon, Tamiment Library, NYU; David Loerke, Oral History Project, Butler Library, Columbia University, Marilyn N. Loesch, Hampton University, Hampton, Virginia; William R. Massa, Yale University, New Haven; Linda M. Matthews, Emory University, Atlanta; Gene McAfee, Harvard Divinity School, Cambridge, Massachusetts; Brian McCartin, Thomas Paine National Historical Society; Douglas McDonald, Boston University; Joseph D. McDonald, publications clerks, U.S. House of Representatives, Committee on the Judiciary; Susan McElrath, Mary McLeod Bethune National Historic Site, Washington, D.C.; Mary R. McGee, *Christian Science Monitor*, Boston; Genna Rae McNeil, NYPL; R. Michael McReynolds, NA, Washington, D.C.; Kelly Meier, Lovejoy Library, Southern Illinois University, Edwardsville; Robert Moron, Enid M. Baa Library, St. Thomas, U.S. Virgin Islands; James Morris, Butler Library, Columbia University; Alan Moss, University of the West Indies, Cave Hill, Barbados; Ardie S. Myers, LOC; Michael Nash, Tamiment Library, NYU; James G. Neal, Columbia University Libraries; Peggy Norris, Ridgewood, New Jersey, Public Library; Charles G. Palm, Hoover Institution; Barry Pateman, Emma Goldman Papers Project, University of California, Berkeley; Warner W. Pflug, Wayne State University, Detroit; Terry L. Propes, Lee Davis Library, San Jacinto College, Pasadena, Texas; Mary Jo Pugh, University of Michigan; Ralph A. Pugh, Chicago Historical Society; Wendy Wick Reaves, National Portrait Gallery, Washington, D.C.; John Reeves, Bethune-Cookman University; Anne Rocklein, Indiana University Press; Alan Saltman, LOC; Angelo Salvo, Archivist, Bethune-Cookman University; Susan Sampietro, Westwood, New Jersey, Public Library; Angelica Santamauro, Botto House-American Labor Museum, Haledon, New Jersey; Oswald Schjang, Recorder of Deeds, Christiansted, St. Croix; Burtin R. Scholl, Board of Education of the City of New York; Linda Seidman, University of Massachusetts, Amherst; John H. Sengstacke, *Chicago Daily Defender*; Ann Allen Shockley, Fisk University Library, Nashville, Tennessee; Janet L. Sims-Wood, MSRC; Charles A. Shaughnessy, NA, Washington, D.C.; Robert Sink, NYPL; Donald Skemer, Princeton University; Betty Smith, International Publishers; Beverly Smith, Enid M. Baa Library, St. Thomas, U.S. Virgin Islands; Sister Marguerita Smith, Archdiocese of New York, Yonkers, New York; J. Alex Speer, Mineralogical Society of America; Leslie Starr, Wesleyan University Press; David Stivers, Nabisco Company, Parsippany, New Jersey; Ronald E. Swerczak, NA, Washington, D.C.; Marguerite Symonette, Mary McLeod Bethune Foundation, Daytona, Florida; Anastacio Teodoro, NYPL; Robert H. Terte, New York City Board of Education; Wendy Thomas, Radcliffe College, Cambridge, Massachusetts; Ellen B. Thomasson, Missouri Historical Museum, St. Louis; Anthony Toussaint, SCRBC; Shy Tuba, Westwood, New Jersey, Public Library; Ernest C. Wagner, College of the Virgin Islands, St. Thomas, United States Virgin Islands; William J. Walsh, NA, Washington, D.C.; Brooke Watkins, Butler Library, Columbia University; Neal Adam Watson, State Archives of Florida; Daoud-David Williams, Jersey City, New Jersey, Public Library; Deborah Willis-Thomas, SCRBC; Michael R. Winston, MSRC; Lucinda Wong, Pacifica

Foundation Radio Archives, Universal City, California; and Mary Yearwood, SCRBC. Thanks also to Laura Gottesman, LOC.

Others who assisted in the search for material and information include Norman Allen, Tomie Arai, Neil Arlin, Thabiti Asukile, Sol Auerbach, Mirel Bercovici, Camille Billops, Henry Black, Soren Black, Lloyd Brown, Randall K. and Nancy H. Burkett, Carola Burroughs, Norris Burroughs, Mercer Cook, Carl Cowl, John Crocitti, Sam and Emma Darcy, Ralph Dumain, Raya Dunayevskaya, Sheila Fleming-Hunter, William French, Gilberto Freyre Neto, David J. Garrow, Walter Goldwater, Gilbert Green, June Gunn, Jack Handler, George Hutchinson, Louis R. Harlan, James V. Hatch, John E. Haynes, Winston James, Janis M. Jaynes, Bernard K. Johnpoll, Gloria Joseph, Harvey Klehr, Ivan Lorand, Polly E. McLean, Joseph McDonald, Arlette Millard, Ani Mukherji, Jim Murray, Helen K. Nearing, Guishard Parris, Louise Thompson Patterson, Polly E. McLean, Evelyn Richardson, Helga Rogers, Franklin Rosemont, Mark D. Solomon, Romy Taylor, Joyce Moore Turner, Pat Tyrer, Ted Vincent, Hope McKay Virtue, Ella G. Wolfe, and Lionel Yard. Gregory Grazevich and Eric Wirth of the Modern Language Association helped at various times with questions on usage.

My deepest appreciation is extended to George F. Tyson, director of the St. Croix African Roots Project, for sharing with me the fruits of his important research on Harrison's family history and on St. Croix.

A very heartfelt special thanks is extended to Peter Dimock of Columbia University Press for supporting this work; for approaching Harrison with a profound understanding of his importance; for responding thoughtfully, professionally, and promptly to my questions; for offering very sound suggestions; and for being pleasant, encouraging, and consistently helpful. Peter dared to tread where others wouldn't and firmly supported a full, two-volume, Harrison biography. He understood that Harrison's voice needed to be brought fully into the discussion of early-twentieth-century America, and he has been singularly instrumental in facilitating that effort.

I also extend special thanks and gratitude to the Columbia University Press staff under the direction of James D. Jordan for their support and efforts in helping to bring Harrison to a twenty first-century audience. In particular, I thank my manuscript and production editor, Michael Haskell, whose expertise, professionalism, diligence, and understanding (particularly when last-minute information became available) were a joy to work with and allowed me to concentrate on what I was trying to say. I was truly fortunate to work with Michael and thank him for his many contributions. Similarly, Kabir Dandona, Anne Routon, and Marisa Pagano were extraordinarily helpful. Whenever I asked, they responded promptly and helpfully with thoughtful and professional assistance that contributed to making the entire publication process a writer's delight. I thank them very much for their deeply appreciated efforts.

To my sisters, Pamela and Debra, to my in-laws, Paul, Billy, Eddie, and Blanche, and to the Giblin, Buco, and Fong families, I extend special thanks with much love for their patience and support.

To my wife Becky Hom and to my daughter Perri Lin Hom go my deepest and most special thanks and love. They have been enormously supportive, and their freely and frequently offered "suggestions" have sustained this project and always made it fun while recognizing that the work was important. Without Becky's love, support, and encouragement and Perri's love and Harrison-like critical independence, this project would never have been the joyous labor that it has been.

A Note on Usage

Hubert Harrison used the word "Negro" with a capital "N" (as opposed to such words as "colored" and "negro"), and he struggled to have others do the same. He founded the New Negro Movement, presided over the Liberty League of Negro-Americans, and edited the *New Negro* monthly, the *Negro World*, the *Embryo of the Voice of the Negro*, and the *Voice of the Negro*. Results of the capitalization struggles included the change to the capital "N" by the *International Socialist Review* in 1912 and by the *New York Times* in 1930 (after Harrison's death).

In the 1960s, however, there was a shift from that usage, and today "Negro" has generally been replaced in the United States by "Black," "African American," or "Afro-American."

In this text, "Negro" is retained in titles, names, and quoted passages. When Harrison uses the term it is always capitalized, since that is how he always wrote it. In other cases, capitalization depends on the policy of the source document. When the term is contextually appropriate, it is enclosed in quotation marks. In general discussions, "African American" and "Black" are used.

Because Harrison and others struggled to capitalize the "N" in "Negro" as both a statement of pride *and* as a challenge to white supremacy, when the word "Black" is used as its equivalent it is used with a capital "B." There is no similarly compelling basis for capitalizing the "w" in "white." In addition, it should be noted, Harrison did not capitalize the "w" in "white."

HUBERT HARRISON

Figure 0.1. Hubert Harrison's unmarked gravesite (center) in Woodlawn Cemetery, Bronx, New York, April, 1990. Hubert Harrison lies buried in an unmarked shared plot in Woodlawn Cemetery in the Bronx. The absence of any memorial plaque or stone reflects the poverty that Harrison and his family endured and suggests the insufficient recognition that his life has received. *Source:* Courtesy of Jeffrey B. Perry.

Introduction

The brilliant writer, orator, educator, critic, and political activist Hubert Harrison (1883–1927) is one of the truly important yet little known figures of early-twentieth-century America. The historian Joel A. Rogers, in *World's Great Men of Color*, describes him as "the foremost Afro-American intellect of his time" and "one of America's greatest minds." Rogers adds (amid insightful chapters on the early-twentieth-century Black leaders Booker T. Washington, William Monroe Trotter, W. E. B. Du Bois, and Marcus Garvey), "No one worked more seriously and indefatigably to enlighten his fellow-men" and "none of the Afro-American leaders of his time had a saner and more effective program."[1]

Variants of Rogers's lavish praise were offered by other contemporaries. The author Henry Miller, a socialist in his youth, remembered Harrison on a soapbox as his "quondam idol." "There was no one in those days . . . who could hold a candle to Hubert Harrison," explained Miller. "With a few well-directed words he had the ability to demolish any opponent. He did it neatly and smoothly too, 'with kid gloves' so to speak. . . . He was a man who electrified by his mere presence."[2] William Pickens, field secretary of the National Association for the Advancement of Colored People, a former college dean, and an oratory prize winner at Yale, described Harrison as "a plain black man who can speak more easily, effectively, and interestingly on a greater variety of subjects than any other man I have ever met in the great universities." Pickens added that Harrison was a "'walking cyclopedia' of current human facts," especially history and literature, and it made "no difference" whether he spoke about "*Alice in Wonderland* or the most extensive work of H. G. Wells; about the lightest shadows of Edgar Allen Poe or the heaviest depths of Kant; about music, or art, or science, or political history."[3]

Bertha Washburn Howe, active with the freethought-influenced, interracial, Sunrise Club, would always "seek a seat" at the "jolly" and very approachable Harrison's table at club dinners and recollected that "anything you wanted to discuss, he could talk about it. He knew all the facts" and he "had one of the most marvelous memories of any man I ever knew."[4] Eugene O'Neill, playwright and Nobel Prize winner, lauded Harrison's ability as a writer and critic, considered his review of the ground-breaking play *The Emperor Jones* to be "one of the very few intelligent criticisms of the piece that have come to my notice," and assured Harrison that he would have a place as critic in "any theatre with which I have connection." O'Neill insightfully added, "You know what you are writing about . . . the only propaganda that ever strikes home is the truth about the human soul, black or white. Intentional uplift plays never amount to a damn—especially as uplift. To portray a human being, that is all that counts.[5]

The acclaim was similar in Harlem, the "symbol of Black America" and "Capital of the Black World," where Harrison was loved, respected, and deeply rooted.[6] Montserrat-born Hodge Kirnon, a freethinker, editor of the *The Promoter*, and a race- and class-conscious community activist, explained that Harrison (who lived on Harlem's most densely populated block) "lived with and amongst his people; not on the fringes of their social life" and he "taught the masses" and "drew much of his inspiration from them." Kirnon added that Harrison was "the first Negro whose radicalism was comprehensive enough to include racialism, politics, theological criticism, sociology and education in a thorough-going and scientific manner."[7] The British Guiana–born office worker and communist Hermie Dumont Huiswoud considered Harrison without peer as a street corner orator. She described how, when he spoke in Harlem, "it was not long before the crowd swelled . . . and even children ceased romping, keeping quiet as he developed his subject. His audience was always spell-bound and attentive as his address was so simply presented that his listeners had no difficulty understanding the subject and were also amused at the subtle humor he injected."[8] Virginia-born Williana Jones Burroughs, a teacher, union activist, and communist emphasized Harrison's role in the research and teaching of Black history. She explained that his research demonstrated "a rich heritage of [Black] revolt" and that his work and that of Du Bois helped to put an end to the charge that African Americans "would not resist oppression."[9]

Jamaica-born W. A. Domingo, a socialist and the first editor of Marcus Garvey's *Negro World*, called attention to Harrison as a radical and as a major influence on twentieth-century Black radicalism. He explained that Harrison "was a brilliant man, a great intellectual, a Socialist and highly respected" and "Garvey like the rest of us [A. Philip Randolph, Chandler Owen, Cyril Briggs, Grace Campbell, Richard B. Moore, and other "New Negro" militants] followed Hubert Harrison."[10] Taking a somewhat longer view, the Puerto Rico–born lay historian

Arthur A. Schomburg, Harrison's friend and pallbearer and the foremost book collector of the African diaspora, presciently pointed to Harrison's importance for future generations when he eulogized that the influential and popular Harrison was "ahead of his time."[11]

Despite such high praise from his contemporaries and despite being rated "one of the 20th century's major thinkers" by the double Pulitzer Prize–winning Du Bois biographer, David Levering Lewis, and "one of the most creative, wide-ranging, biting and perceptive students of race and race relations in the United States" by the historian Eric Arnesen, Harrison is, as Harvard University's Henry Louis Gates Jr., writes, "a major but neglected figure in our history." The historian Gerald C. Horne refers to him as "a scandalously ignored thinker and activist," and Winston James observes that "seldom has a person been so influential, esteemed, even revered in one period of history and [then become] so thoroughly unremembered."[12]

These appraisals are accurate. Harrison has never been the subject of a full-length biography, and his life and work have drawn far less general attention and scholarly analysis than those of figures such as Du Bois, Washington, Garvey, or Trotter. There is great loss in this since his writings and oratory offer a unique and extraordinarily articulate, bottom-up, race- and class-conscious analysis of issues, events, and individuals of early-twentieth-century America; since his life so greatly influenced a generation of activists and "common people"; and since his ideas had such an important, though often unacknowledged shaping influence on Black social activism throughout the century. Neither the significance and influence of his activism nor the brilliance and intellectual potential of his ideas concerning race and class in America has been given sufficient recognition.[13]

The life story of this freethinking, Black, Caribbean-born, race- and class-conscious, working-class intellectual-activist is a story that needs to be told. It offers a missing vision and voice that fill major gaps in the historical record and enable us to significantly reshape our understanding and interpretation of the first three decades of the twentieth century. Most important, perhaps, his life story offers profound insights for thinking about race, class, religion, immigration, war, democracy, and social change in America.

———

Hubert Henry Harrison was born to a poor, laboring-class, Afro-Caribbean, immigrant mother at Estate Concordia, St. Croix, Danish West Indies, on April 27, 1883. The color line was drawn differently in St. Croix than in the United States, and despite his family's poverty and his having to work at an early age, Hubert was also able to spend his early years in youthful exploration and educational pursuits. He grew up with a feeling of oneness with the downtrodden and with the belief that he was the equal of any other. He also learned important lessons about African customs, interactions and solidarity between immigrant and native working people, and the Crucian people's rich history of direct-action mass struggle. After his mother's death, he emigrated to the United States as a seventeen-year-old orphan in 1900.[14]

He arrived in New York with the clothes on his back, his Crucian roots, and an extraordinarily fertile and inquiring mind. His arrival coincided with the period of intense racial oppression of African Americans known as the "nadir," with the growth of what he described as the "imperialist tendencies of American capitalism," and with the era of critical writing and muckraking journalism that, according to the social commentator Daniel Bell, produced "the most concentrated flowering of criticism in the history of American ideas." Those three factors were important shaping influences on the remainder of his life.[15]

Over the next twenty-seven years, until his unexpected, appendicitis-related death at age forty-four, Harrison made his mark in the United States by struggling against class and racial oppression, by helping to create a remarkably rich and vibrant intellectual life among African Americans, and by working for the enlightened development of the lives of "the common people." He consistently emphasized the need for working-class people to develop class consciousness; for "Negroes" to develop race consciousness, self-reliance, and self-respect; and for all those he reached to challenge white supremacy and develop modern, scientific, critical, and independent thought as a means toward liberation.[16]

Harrison, who referred to himself as a "radical internationalist," was extremely well versed in history and events in Africa, Asia, the Middle East, the Americas, and Europe, and, according to Richard B. Moore, he was "above all" the militant Black socialists in his steady emphasis on "the liberation of the oppressed African and colonial peoples" as being a "vital aim." He opposed capitalism and maintained that white supremacy was central to capitalist rule in the United States, and, more than any other political leader of his era, he combined class consciousness and anti-white-supremacist race consciousness in a coherent political radicalism. Harrison also understood both the abuse of and the potential of "democracy" in America. He emphasized that "politically, the Negro is the touchstone of the modern democratic idea"; that "as long as the Color Line exists, all the perfumed protestations of Democracy on the part of the white race" were "downright lying"; that "the cant of 'Democracy'" was "intended as dust in the eyes of white voters"; and that true democracy and equality for "Negroes" implied "a revolution . . . startling even to think of."[17]

Working from this theoretical framework, he was active with a wide variety of movements and organizations, and he played signal roles in the development of what were, up to that time, the largest class-radical movement (socialism) and the largest race-radical movement (the "New Negro"/Garvey movement) in

U.S. history. His ideas on the centrality of the struggle against white supremacy anticipated the profound transformative power of the Civil Rights/Black Liberation struggles of the 1960s, and his thoughts on "democracy in America" offer penetrating insights on the limitations and the potential of America in the twenty-first century.

Harrison served as the foremost Black organizer, agitator, and theoretician in the Socialist Party of New York during its 1912 heyday; as the founder and leading figure of the militant, World War I–era New Negro movement; and as the editor of the *Negro World* and principal radical influence on the Garvey movement (described by the historian Randall K. Burkett as "the largest mass-based protest movement in Black American history") during its radical high point in 1920. His views on race and class profoundly influenced a generation of New Negro militants, including the class-radical socialists A. Philip Randolph and Chandler Owen, the future communists Cyril Briggs and Richard B. Moore, and the race-radical Marcus Garvey. Considered more race conscious than Randolph and Owen and more class conscious than Garvey, Harrison is the key link in the ideological unity of the two great trends of the Black Liberation Movement—the labor and civil rights trend associated with Martin Luther King Jr., and the race and nationalist trend associated with Malcolm X. (Randolph and Garvey were, respectively, the direct links to King marching on Washington, with Randolph at his side, and to Malcolm, whose father was a Garveyite preacher and whose mother was a writer for Garvey's *Negro World*, speaking militantly and proudly on Harlem's Lenox Avenue.)[18]

As the center of national Black leadership shifted from Booker T. Washington's Tuskegee, Alabama, headquarters to New York City in the era of the First World War, Harlem increasingly became an "international Negro Mecca" and "the center of radical Black thought."[19] In this period, Harrison earned the title, ascribed to him by A. Philip Randolph and others, "the father of Harlem radicalism."[20] During the 1910s and 1920s he was either the creator, or among the founders, of "almost every important development originating in Negro Harlem—from the Negro Manhood Movement to political representation in public office, from collecting Negro books to speaking on the streets, from demanding Federal control over lynching to agitation for Negroes on the police force." He was also a key figure in developing Caribbean radicalism; he exhibited a rare willingness to learn from the peoples and cultures of Africa; and his (often unattributed) ideas and writings from this period significantly shaped the contours of radical Black thought on matters of race and class in the twentieth century.[21]

Harrison was not only a political radical, however. Rogers described him as an "Intellectual Giant and Free-Lance Educator," whose contributions were wide-ranging, innovative, and influential. He was an immensely skilled and popular orator and educator who spoke or read six languages; a highly praised journalist, critic, and book reviewer (reportedly the first regular Black book reviewer in history); a pioneer Black activist in the freethought and birth-control movements; a bibliophile, library builder, and library popularizer who helped develop the 135th Street Public Library into an international center for research in Black culture; and a promoter and aid to Black writers and artists, including the authors J. A. Rogers and Solomon Tshekisho Plaatje (the first secretary-general of the South African Native National Congress, the forerunner of the African National Congress); the poets Claude McKay, Andy Razaf, Walter Everette Hawkins, and Lucian B. Watkins; the sculptor Augusta Savage; the actor Charles Gilpin; and the musician Eubie Blake. In his later years he was the leading Black lecturer for the New York City Board of Education and one of its foremost orators. Though he was a trailblazing literary critic in Harlem during the period known as the Harlem Renaissance, he questioned the "Renaissance" concept on the grounds of its willingness to take "standards of value ready-made from white society" and on its claim to being a significant new rebirth. (He maintained that "there had been an uninterrupted," though ignored, "stream of literary and artistic products" flowing "from Negro writers from 1850" into the 1920s.)[22]

Soon after his arrival in New York, Harrison began working low-paying jobs and attending high school at night. He finished school, read constantly, and started writing letters to the editor, which, beginning at age twenty, were published in the *New York Times*. In his first decade in New York, his insatiable thirst for knowledge, willingness to consider opposing views, critical mind, and desire to face the world with "eyes wide open" led him to develop an agnostic philosophy of life stressing rationalism, modern science, and evolution and placing humanity at the center of his worldview. He enhanced his self-education efforts through involvement in church lyceums and other Black intellectual circles, workers' groups, community organizations, the freethought movement, and the world of letters and ideas. Toward the end of his first decade in New York, he obtained postal employment, married his wife, Lin, and started to raise a family that eventually grew to seven.[23]

In this vibrant intellectual environment and with a developing self-confidence, Harrison boldly put forth his views, and this soon cost him his postal employment. After writing two letters that criticized Booker T. Washington, the most powerful Black leader in America, Harrison was fired from his postal job through the efforts of Washington's powerful "Tuskegee Machine." It was a devastating blow, and the resultant loss of income and security seriously affected his remaining years.[24]

Shortly after losing his postal job, Harrison turned to full-time work with the Socialist Party. From 1911 to 1914 he was America's leading Black Socialist—a prominent party speaker and campaigner (especially in the 1912 presidential campaign of Eugene V. Debs), an articulate and popular critic of capitalism, the leading Black Socialist organizer in New York, and (influenced by work by women and foreigners) the initiator of the Colored Socialist Club (CSC)—an unprecedented effort by U.S. socialists at organizing African Americans. He made major theoretical contributions on the subject of "The Negro and Socialism" by emphasizing that "the Negro" as "a group is more essentially proletarian than any other group" and by advocating that socialists champion the cause of African Americans as a revolutionary doctrine, that they develop a special appeal to and for African Americans, and that they affirm the duty of all socialists to oppose race prejudice. His proposal that "the crucial test of Socialism's sincerity" was its duty to champion the cause of the African American anticipated by more than a year Du Bois's dictum that the "Negro Problem . . . [is] the great test of the American Socialists." (Some of his writings from this period appeared in his first book, *The Negro and the Nation* [1917].) Such efforts were of little avail, however. Socialist Party theory and practice—including segregated locals in the South, the party's refusal to route the campaign of the 1912 presidential candidate, Eugene V. Debs (who insisted that his audiences be integrated), in Southern states, white-supremacist positions on Asian immigration at the 1912 national convention, and the failure to politically and economically support the CSC—led Harrison to conclude that Socialist Party leaders, like organized labor, put the white "race first and class after."[25]

Harrison moved away from the Socialists and turned his efforts toward the more egalitarian, militant, direct-action-oriented Industrial Workers of the World. He was a featured speaker (along with the IWW leaders "Big Bill" Haywood, Elizabeth Gurley Flynn, Carlo Tresca, and Patrick Quinlan) and the only Black speaker at the historic 1913 Paterson silk strike. He also publicly defended Haywood against attack by the right wing of the Socialist Party on the issue of "sabotage." SP leaders restricted his speaking, however. As their attacks on both his political views and his principal means of livelihood intensified, his disenchantment grew, and he left the party.

After leaving the Socialist Party, Harrison founded the "Radical Forum," taught at the Modern School, and lectured indoors and out on a variety of subjects including birth control and the racial aspects of the First World War. He was also involved in, and arrested in, free-speech struggles. His outdoor lectures pioneered the tradition of militant street-corner oratory in Harlem. As a soap-box orator he was brilliant and unrivaled. Factual and interactive, logical and playful, he exhibited wonderful mastery of language, humor, and irony, and, when appropriate, he employed a biting sarcasm. J. A. Rogers described how "crowds flocked to hear him" and "would stand hours at a time" as he presented "the most abstract matter in a clear and lively fashion." Claude McKay emphasized how he spoke "precisely and clearly," with "fine intelligence and masses of facts." A. Philip Randolph stressed that he was "far more advanced" than any other speaker, that he "made an enduring and valuable contribution to the life of the negro . . . and the world in general," and that he was "analytical" and "a good logician," with a "fine mind" that "reached in all areas of human knowledge." Henry Miller remembered his "broad, good-natured grin," "easy assurance," "self-possession," and "dignity" as he playfully worked a crowd. With his enlightening, crowd-engaging, popular, memorable, witty, and, at times, militant oratory, Harrison paved the way for those who followed—including Randolph and Garvey—and, much later, Malcolm X.[26]

By late 1916, his experiences with white supremacy within the socialist and labor movements convinced him of the need for a "race-first" political perspective for Black Americans. The final steps in this direction were made through the frontier of art as Harrison wrote several theater reviews in which he described how the "Negro Theatre" revealed the "social mind" of the race and offered a glimpse of "the Negro's soul as modified by his social environment." With his new "race-first" approach Harrison served over the next few years as the founder and intellectual guiding light of the "New Negro Manhood Movement," better known as the "New Negro Movement"[27]—the race-conscious, internationalist, mass-based, autonomous, militantly assertive movement for "political equality, social justice, civic opportunity, and economic power," which laid the basis for the Garvey movement and contributed so significantly (especially with his book reviews and "poetry for the people") to the social and literary climate leading to the 1925 publication of Alain Locke's well-known *The New Negro*. Harrison's mass-based political movement, however, was qualitatively different from the more middle-class, arts-based, apolitical movement associated with Locke.[28]

In 1917, as the "Great War" raged abroad, along with race riots, lynching, segregation, discrimination, and white-supremacist ideology at home, Harrison founded the Liberty League and *The Voice*. They were, respectively, the first organization and the first newspaper of the "New Negro Movement,"[29] and they were soon followed by A. Philip Randolph and Chandler Owen's *Messenger*, Cyril Briggs's *Crusader*, and Marcus Garvey's *Negro World*. The Liberty League was called into being, Harrison explained, by "the need for a more radical policy" than that of existing civil rights organizations such as the W. E. B. Du Bois–influenced National Association for the Advancement of Colored People. He felt that the NAACP too often limited itself to paper protests and repeatedly stumbled over the problem of what to do "if these ['white'] minds at which you are aiming remain unaffected" and refuse "to grant guarantees of life and liberty."[30]

In contrast to the NAACP, the Liberty League was not dependent on white supporters, and it aimed beyond the "Talented Tenth" at "the common people" of the "Negro race." Its program emphasized internationalism, political independence, and class and race consciousness. In response to white supremacy, *The Voice* called for a "race first" approach, full equality, federal antilynching legislation, enforcement of the Fourteenth and Fifteenth Amendments, labor organizing, support of socialist and anti-imperialist causes, political independence, and armed self-defense in the face of white-supremacist attacks. It stressed that new Black leadership would emerge from the masses, and it was "under [the Liberty League's] banner [that] the West Indians and American Negroes first cooperated on anything like a large scale."[31]

Contemporaries readily acknowledged that Harrison's work prepared the ground for the Garvey movement. From the Liberty League and *The Voice* (whose weekly circulation reportedly reached 11,000 and estimated readership 55,000) came the core progressive ideas and leaders later used by Marcus Garvey in the Universal Negro Improvement Association and the *Negro World*. Harrison himself claimed, with considerable basis, that from the Liberty League "Garvey appropriated every feature that was worthwhile in his movement" and that the secret of Garvey's success was that he "[held] up to the Negro masses those things which bloom in their hearts—racialism, race-consciousness, racial solidarity—things taught first in 1917 by *The Voice* and The Liberty League."[32]

After *The Voice* ceased publication in early 1918, Harrison briefly served as an organizer for the American Federation of Labor and then chaired the Negro-American Liberty Congress. The June 1918 Liberty Congress (co-headed by the long-time activist William Monroe Trotter) was the major wartime protest effort of African Americans and an important precursor to subsequent protests during World War II and the Vietnam War. The Liberty Congress issued demands against discrimination and segregation and petitioned the U.S. Congress for federal antilynching legislation. The Liberty Congress's wartime demands for equality and thoroughgoing democracy were forerunners of the March on Washington Movement led by A. Philip Randolph during World War II and the August 28, 1963, March on Washington during the Vietnam War led by Randolph and Martin Luther King Jr. As an elderly Randolph knowingly pointed out in 1972, with Harrison undoubtedly in mind, "The black militants of today are standing upon the shoulders of the New Negro radicals of my day."[33]

The autonomous and militant Liberty Congress effort was undermined by the U.S. Army's antiradical Military Intelligence Bureau in a campaign that was spearheaded by the NAACP founder Joel E. Spingarn and involved W. E. B. Du Bois. Following the Liberty Congress, Harrison criticized Du Bois for urging African Americans to forget justifiable grievances, for "closing ranks" behind President Woodrow Wilson's war effort, and for following Spingarn's lead and seeking a captaincy in Military Intelligence, the branch of government that monitored radicals and the African American community. Harrison's exposé, "The Descent of Dr. Du Bois," was a principal reason that Du Bois was denied the captaincy he sought in Military Intelligence, and more than any other document it marked the significant break between the "New Negroes" and the older leadership.[34]

This first volume of Harrison's biography concludes after he has been recognized as a major national protest figure and as the founder and prominent leader of the growing New Negro Movement. Though only thirty-five years old he had earned the title "the Father of Harlem Radicalism." He had challenged the powers of capitalism and white supremacy, offered articulate and insightful criticisms of the leadership of Booker T. Washington and W. E. B. Du Bois, served as the leading Black activist in the Socialist Party, founded *The Voice* and the Liberty League, and been a radicalizing influence on the next generation of class and race radicals. Harlem was establishing itself as the international center of radical Black thought and Hubert Harrison was the leading voice of Harlem radicalism.

The second volume of this biography, *Hubert Harrison: Race Consciousness and the Struggle for Democracy, 1918–1927* begins in 1918 after the Liberty Congress. Harrison attempted to take his race-conscious message into the Deep South, but illness caused him to return to New York. Then, after a series of bloody "race riots" in 1919, he edited the militant *New Negro* magazine, which was "intended as an organ of the international consciousness of the darker races—especially of the Negro race." In January 1920 he became the principal editor of the *Negro World*, the organ of Marcus Garvey's UNIA, as that paper swept the globe with its race-conscious and internationalist message. In one of the important chapters in the history of Black journalism, he reshaped and developed that paper—changed its style, format, content, and editorial page—and was primarily responsible for turning it into the preeminent radical, race-conscious, political, and literary publication of that time. (Many of his most important editorials and reviews from this period [as well as from the earlier Liberty League period] were reprinted in his book *When Africa Awakes* [1920].) Over the first eight months of 1920, he was the *Negro World*'s chief radical propagandist, and in August he was the one who gave radical tone to the UNIA's "Declaration of the Rights of the Negro Peoples of the World."[35]

By the UNIA's August 1920 convention, however, Harrison was highly critical of Garvey. His criticisms, articulated over the next few years, concerned the extravagance of Garvey's claims, his ego, his organizational leadership, the conduct of his stock selling and financial schemes, and his politics and practices. Though Harrison continued to write columns and book reviews for the *Negro World* into 1922, their political differences grew, and Harrison worked against and sought to develop political alternatives to Garvey. In particular, Harrison urged political action in terms of electoral politics: he attempted to build an all-Black Liberty Party; he argued that African Americans' principal struggle was in the United States (and that they should not seek to develop a state or empire in Africa); and he stressed that Africans, not African Americans, would lead struggles in Africa.[36]

In the 1920s, after breaking with Garvey, Harrison continued his full schedule of race-conscious activities. He lectured for the New York City Board of Education's elite "Trends of the Times" series, which included prominent professors from the city's foremost universities, as well as for its "Literary Lights of Yesterday and Today" series. Through his lectures, book donations, reviews, recommendations, and active involvement he helped to develop the 135th St. Public Library's "Negro literature and history" collection into what became the world-famous Schomburg Center for Research in Black History, which stands as a living connection between Black people and their history. His book and theater reviews and other writings appeared in many of the leading periodicals of the day—including the *New York Times*, *New York Tribune*, *New York World*, *Nation*, *New Republic*, *Modern Quarterly*, *Pittsburgh Courier*, *Chicago Defender*, *Amsterdam News*, *Boston Chronicle*, and *Opportunity* magazine. He also spoke out against the revived Ku Klux Klan and the white-supremacist attacks on the African American community of Tulsa, Oklahoma, and he worked with numerous groups, including the Virgin Island Congressional Council, the Democratic Party, the Farmer-Labor Party, the Single Tax Party, the Sunrise Club, the American Friends Service Committee, the Urban League, the Institute for Social Study, the Harlem Education Forum, the American Negro Labor Congress, the Workers School, and the Workers (Communist) Party.

One of his most important activities in this period was the founding of the International Colored Unity League and its organ, *The Voice of the Negro*. The ICUL was Harrison's most broadly unitary effort and attempted "to do for the Negro the things which the Negro needs to have done without depending upon or waiting for the co-operative action of white people." It urged Black people to develop "race consciousness" as a defensive measure —to be aware of their racial oppression and to use that awareness to unite, organize, and respond as a group. The 1924 ICUL platform had political, economic, and social planks urging protests, self-reliance, self-sufficiency, and collective action and included as its "central idea" the founding of "a Negro state, not in Africa, as Marcus Garvey would have done, but in the United States" as an outlet for "racial egoism." It was a plan for "the harnessing" of "Negro energies" and for "economic, political and spiritual self-help and advancement."[37] It preceded a somewhat similar plan by the Communist International by four years.[38] In addition, the ICUL, with

Schomburg on its executive committee, took major steps in promoting the study of Black history by hosting Harrison's 1926 series of lectures on "World Problems of Race."[39]

————————

Overall, in his writing and oratory, Harrison's appeal was both mass and individual. He focused on the man and woman in the street, those whom he referred to with love and respect as "the common people," and emphasized the importance of each individual's development of an independent, critical attitude. His work was encouraged, sustained, and developed by his intimate involvement with the Black community. By encouraging the development of strong individuals working with "unity of purpose," he was instrumental in awakening and nurturing the growing strength and consciousness of that community.[40]

The period during and after the First World War was one of intense racial oppression and great Black migration from the South and the Caribbean into urban centers, particularly in the North. Harrison's (working-class and Black-community-based) race-conscious mass appeal used newspapers, popular lectures, and street-corner talks and marked a major shift in style and substance from the leadership approaches of Booker T. Washington and W. E. B. Du Bois, the paramount Black leaders of Harrison's youth. He rejected Washington's reliance on powerful white patrons and an internal Black patronage and pressure machine (which deemphasized outward political struggle) and Du Bois's reliance on left or liberal white support and the "Talented Tenth of the Negro Race." Harrison's affective appeal, later identified with that of Garvey, was aimed directly at the urban masses and, as the Harlem activist Richard B. Moore explained, "More than any other man of his time, he [Harrison] inspired and educated the masses of Afro-Americans then flocking into Harlem."[41]

Though he lived amid and was extremely popular among the masses that "flocked to hear him," Harrison, according to Rogers, was often overlooked by "the more established conservative Negro leaders, especially those who derived support from wealthy whites." Others, "inferior . . . in ability and altruism, received acclaim, wealth, and distinction" that were his due. When he died on December 17, 1927, the Harlem community, in a major show of affection, turned out by the thousands for his funeral. A church was (ironically) named in his honor, and his portrait was to be placed prominently on the main floor of the 135th Street Public Library, which he, along with bibliophile Arthur Schomburg and others, had helped to develop.[42]

Despite these manifestations of love and respect from his contemporaries, Harrison was quickly "unremembered" in death. He lies buried in an unmarked, shared plot in Woodlawn Cemetery in the Bronx; the church named in his honor was abandoned; his portrait donated to the library cannot be found; and his life story and contributions are little known.

Some reasons for this "unremembrance" are readily apparent. Harrison was poor, Black, foreign born, and from the Caribbean. Each of these groups has suffered from significant discrimination in the United States and limited inclusion in the historical record. He opposed capitalism, white supremacy, and the Christian church—dominant forces of the most powerful society in the world. He supported socialism, "race consciousness," racial equality, women's equality, freethought, and birth control. The forces arrayed against the expression of such ideas were, and continue to be, formidable. Others, most notably (the similarly poor, Black, Caribbean-born) Garvey, who challenged the forces of white supremacy, only began to receive increased attention with the increase in Black studies and popular history, which were by-products of the civil rights and Black power struggles of the 1960s.[43] Even then, however, Harrison did not draw similar attention. In part this was undoubtedly due to his "radicalism" on issues other than race—particularly on matters of class and religion.

Age (and what one does over time) is another factor. Harrison died young, much younger than Washington, Du Bois, or Garvey. He was not martyred like King and Malcolm, who also died young. His prolific pen and exhilarating oratory did not continue into the 1930s or any later decades.

There are also other additional factors that have served to keep Harrison's achievements and ideas from the prominence they deserve. He lived in poverty, had major family financial responsibilities, and handled money poorly; these factors limited the success and promotion of some activities. He was more of a freelance activist than many of his better known contemporaries. He was not "somebody's man, whether that somebody was a Vesey Street Liberal, or Northern millionaire or a powerful politician" who would promote him and his ideas. He would not, as he said, "bow the knee to Baal, because Baal is in power." As a leader, he generally disdained flattery and would not wheedle or cajole followers or supporters. He found it difficult, in his words, "to suffer fools gladly." Though he worked with many organizations and played important roles in several key ones, he had no long-term, sustaining, and identifying relationship with any organization or institution, and so lacked the recognition and support that would have come with such a tie. As he explained in a 1922 letter, "I haven't any group. I always go alone, and find this much more productive of internal peace than the contrary process. And, of course, I have no chieftains—well meaning or other."[44]

Importantly, Harrison was also an inveterate critic whose style was candid and, at times, bitingly sarcastic. He criticized the ruling classes, white supremacists, organized religion, organized labor, politicians, journalists, historians, scientists, civil rights and race leaders, socialists and communists. Though his comments were usually perceptive, well researched, and without malice, they often challenged the established order and existing leaders and engendered reaction. As Rogers explains:

> Most of the enmity against Harrison was incurred by his devastating candor. . . . He spoke out freely what he thought, and more often than not it was with such annihilating sarcasm and wit, that those whom he attacked never forgave him. Before he began his attacks, he usually collected "the evidence" as he called it, consisting of verbatim utterances, verbal or printed, of the prospective victim. . . . There was, however, no personal malice in Harrison's shafts. Like a true sportsman, he was willing to shake hands with an opponent as soon as he had descended from the platform, and was surprised and hurt that others were not.[45]

In particular, Harrison's willingness to directly challenge prominent leaders and organizations in left and African American circles stung many of the individuals (Booker T. Washington, Mary White Ovington, Oswald Garrison Villard, Ernest Untermann, Kate Richards O'Hare, Charles W. Anderson, Fred R. Moore, Joel E. Spingarn, W. E. B. Du Bois, Chandler Owen, Kelly Miller, George E. Haynes, Emmett Scott, Robert Russa Moton, Marcus Garvey, James Weldon Johnson, Carl Van Vechten, and William Z. Foster) and groups (the American Federation of Labor, Socialist Party, Communist Party, Urban League, NAACP, *New York Age, Amsterdam News, New Review,* and *Nation*) most likely to keep his memory alive.

Also of great importance is the fact that his freethought and agnostic views and scientific approach posed serious challenges for many religious leaders and distanced him from the Black church, the most powerful institution in the Black community. Harrison was fully aware that "those who live by the people must needs be careful of the people's gods," but it was advice he did not often heed.[46] He was often more candidly critical than calculatingly cautious, and "leaders" and organizations that might have publicly preserved his memory made little effort to do so. Some actually led in the great neglect that followed.

In February 1928, less than two months after his massive funeral, Hodge Kirnon, the influential grassroots Harlem activist, ominously observed in a letter to the editor of the Black weekly *New York News*:

> It has now become a subject of popular discussion among thoughtful people as to the reason for the absence of any mention of the late Hubert Harrison in the columns of the three leading Negro monthly periodicals in this country. *The Messenger*—"a journal of scientific radicalism" [edited by the socialist A. Philip

Figure 0.2. J. A. Rogers, Ethiopia, 1935. Jamaica-born and self-educated Joel Augustus Rogers (1880–1966) was a Pullman porter, journalist, and prolific researcher and writer of Black history. In *World's Great Men of Color*, Rogers describes Hubert Harrison as "the foremost Afro-American intellect of his time" and claims that "none of the Afro-American leaders of his time had a saner and more effective program." *Source:* Courtesy of Thabiti Asukile and Special Collections, John Hope and Aurelia Elizabeth Franklin Library, Fisk University, Nashville, Tenn.

Randolph] has not a word to say concerning the death of the first and ablest Negro exponent of scientific radicalism. *The Crisis*—"A Record of the Darker Races" [edited by the NAACP's W. E. B. Du Bois] laments the passing of [the boxer] "Tiger" Flowers, but omits to record the services of a man who was a lecturer for the Board of Education, and of whom William Pickens says "can speak more easily, effectively and interestingly on a greater variety of subjects than any other man I have met, even in the great Universities." *Opportunity*—"a Journal of Negro Life" [edited by the Urban League's Charles S. Johnson] is equally silent over the demise of an acknowledged first rate thinker—one who gave liberally to the intellectual life of the Negro, and whose writings have appeared in that journal.

This concerted silence is ominous. It does appear that there is something wrong somewhere.[47]

There was indeed something wrong. A major figure, compared to Socrates by his peers, was being ignored.[48] The tragedy in this lies in the fact that Harrison's life story has so very much to offer. His journey from the depths of plantation poverty to political and intellectual achievements of great influence is a powerful testament to human potential. He was, according to Rogers, one of those "individuals of genuine worth and immense potentialities who dedicate their lives to the advancement of their fellow-men." His life was lived in poverty, yet he struggled relentlessly for knowledge, understanding, and the uplift of common people. According to the *Pittsburgh Courier*, Harrison, "despite the handicap of poverty, . . . became one of the most learned men of his day and was able to teach the wide masses of his race how to appreciate and enjoy all the finer things of life, to glance back over the whole history of mankind, and to look forward [in the words of George Bernard Shaw] 'as far as thought can reach.'"[49]

Harrison's life story is made much more personal and human by the survival of his papers, which include writings, books, photos, scrapbooks, memorabilia, and a diary that detail his intimate thoughts on a wide range of subjects, personal matters, and relations with organizations and individuals. These more intimate aspects of his biography further open the way for newer and deeper understanding of the social and intellectual milieu of the early twentieth century.

In recounting this story, certain personal characteristics and limitations are important to recognize. Harrison focused more on intellectual, educational, and agitational matters than organizational ones, and this fact, coupled with his often critical approach, his disdain for flattery, and his unwillingness to "suffer fools gladly," somewhat limited his organizational leadership. He was an intellectual whose message was more rational than emotional, and this limited the breadth of his appeal, particularly in comparison to Garvey. He was an autodidact who ventured where his interests led, and he often did not tend to practical matters well. He repeatedly underestimated the value of money and handled it poorly, and, since he lived in poverty, money problems constantly beset his efforts and caused severe hardship for his wife and five children. He sought to apply science and rationality to social problems during a period when the sciences (like the rest of society) contained many racist views, and he encountered contradictions (such as those pertaining to the concept and "shifting reality" of race)[50] that affected the work he did. He advocated rationalist freethought and severely distanced himself (particularly in the early years) from the Black church—the most important institution in the African American community. His political independence and willingness to openly challenge existing leaders and leadership often resulted in financial difficulties, circumscribed some political options, and at times put pressure on him to move in less desired political directions. His views on women and gender oppression were, at times, as Bill Fletcher Jr. of the Black Radical Congress suggests, not up to the level of "his otherwise radical approach to life and politics." He also was a man of amorous affairs (including interracial affairs and one with Garvey's first wife, Amy Ashwood), and he, at times, practiced a sexual double standard. These more personal matters hurt his home life and, despite his great love for his children, caused his relationship with his wife, Lin, to suffer some particularly difficult times.[51]

Harrison, however, had strengths that were remarkable. He faced the world with a critical mind, intellectual honesty, and "eyes wide-open." His radicalism was grounded in his study, his analysis of society, and his practical work. He was not rhetorical, utopian, or dogmatic. He stressed modern and historical knowledge, critical and scientific approaches to problems, political independence while working with different groups and parties, and concern with the great democratic issues of the day. His approach was eminently sane, and he worked tirelessly and indefatigably for the "common people." The radicalism in all this stems from the fact that it came from an African American who would not deny that race and class divided America. Then, as now, the basic demands for economic justice premised on true racial equality struck at the very heart of the existing social order and were inherently radical.[52]

This last point suggests a principal reason why Harrison's life story is important. In the period of the First World War, Harrison was the most class conscious of the race radicals, and the most race conscious of the class radicals. This seeming incongruity was made possible by the political-economic system of the United States, a system in which, according to the historian Theodore W. Allen, racial oppression was central to capitalist rule. An exploration of how Harrison was radical on both issues sheds considerable light on the nature of U.S. society and the essence of racial oppression. It also sheds considerable light, as Harrison explained, on the radical implications of true democracy and equality for African Americans.[53]

The observations of journalist Oscar J. Benson offered at the time of Harrison's death are instructive. Benson recognized both the importance of Harrison's life story and the key to capturing its essence when he explained:

> [There are those] in every generation whose knowledge is not hoarded: whose intellect is practical; and whose services are unlimited in the community in which they live, and naturally no one knows of their community without knowing of them. To this class of preceptors Hubert Harrison belongs.
>
> Literary men of this class are seldom honored by posterity . . . their philosophy must be caught on a fly. Like the plain "old uncle" Socrates they go about teaching here and there, their audiences are vast, and they are always in popular demand . . . Harrison was of this type. But he was more. He was original. . . . he instituted a new school of social thought, packed a new forum, dignified the soap-box orator; blocked Lenox and Seventh Avenue traffic; sent

humble men to libraries and book stores; sent them about to day and night schools; taught Negroes to think for themselves; taught them that in spite of all the handicaps of slavery and propaganda of anthropologists and sociologists, who said that the Negro was an imitator, that no one knew what the Negro could do until he tried. . . .

He . . . made great men his teachers, but not his masters. He was always willing to help or encourage a young writer or speaker. He saw the present condition of the Negro but anticipated a brighter future. . . .

His biography . . . [cannot be written], unless it be culled from the influence his teachings had upon the lives of others.[54]

Intellectual Growth
and Development

CHAPTER

1

Crucian Roots
(1883–1900)

Hubert Harrison, the son of plantation-working, Afro-Caribbean parents—an un-
married Barbadian immigrant mother and a formerly enslaved, absentee Crucian father—lived his first seventeen years on the Caribbean island of St. Croix,
a colony of Denmark, where he worked as a servant, knew poverty, and developed an empathy with the poor. He was also able to pursue opportunities for
study and self-study; to receive a good basic education; to be influenced by an
exemplary Black teacher; and to obtain work as an assistant teacher. As a youth,
living among immigrant and native laboring people, he grew up with an identifiable drive and a breadth to his perspective. He also developed an awareness of
his African roots and of the Crucian people's rich history of direct-action mass
struggle. Overall, it was a period in which, despite obstacles, he had a loving
family life and he was able to cultivate a love of learning, nurture his dreams,
and grow with the belief that he was the equal of any other.

When he moved to New York City at the turn of the twentieth century, Harrison brought a multicultural Crucian background, reading and writing skills,
intellectual curiosity, and a feeling of oneness with the downtrodden—all of
which would be important in his future work. In the United States, however, he
confronted the harsh realities of class exploitation and racial oppression quite
unlike anything he knew at home. While his U.S. experiences enabled him to
pursue his intellectual interests in a manner that was not possible in St. Croix;
they also increasingly pushed him in the direction of class and race radicalism.

His early years in the Caribbean set the stage for later developments. Unfortunately, biographical documentation from the island that Harrison and others
referred to as "Santa Cruz" was, for most of the last century, extremely difficult
to locate and to access. Vast quantities of historical documents and government

records were removed from St. Croix to the national archives of Denmark and the United States after the American government purchased the Danish West Indies in 1917. Serious research efforts confronted the difficult problem of trying to locate and access materials that were widely scattered on two continents and in the Virgin Islands. This situation is now in the process of being addressed through digitization efforts by the national archives of Denmark and the United States, and also through the extraordinary research and documentation efforts of the internationally coordinated St. Croix African Roots Project.[1]

In Harrison's case, the historical particulars that have been located come from his "diary" and family; from church, census, immigration, and other archival records; and from newspapers and other published sources. The published items, many of which Harrison undoubtedly influenced, were at times contradictory. This was likely because of occasional efforts to embellish in order to obtain employment and because for most of his life in America he was not a citizen of the United States[2] and was possibly subject to arrest and deportation.[3] It is reasonable to treat many of the published sources with caution.

Nevertheless, by selecting salient factors in the history, political economy, class structure, and social relations of St. Croix and combining these with the known particulars of Harrison's family life and youth, a picture does emerge. We see how the colonial, class, race, and social relations on the island shaped his thinking; how he was nurtured in a caring support network; why he took the bold step of emigrating from the Virgin Islands to New York in 1900; and how he had developed, in embryo, the core characteristics—race and class consciousness, sensitivity to human suffering, and an independent and wide-ranging intellect—that so marked his later life.

———

The island of St. Croix offers a pleasant natural environment, which cloaks an identifiably violent history of human development. It occupies eighty-four square miles in the northern Leeward chain of the Lesser Antilles, about seventeen hundred miles south of New York and sixty-five miles southeast of Puerto Rico. Its diverse terrain includes broken ranges of hills rising to twelve hundred feet in the northwest corner and a well-watered flat coastal plain in the center and south. The coastline, for the most part, is low-lying, and there are good natural harbors. Temperatures average close to eighty degrees Fahrenheit, with little seasonal variation, and rainfall, chiefly comprising brief but heavy showers, averages slightly over forty inches a year. Despite occasional drought, a variety of food from both land and sea has traditionally been available. Commenting on the climate, with words that could apply more generally to the island's natural environment, and perhaps with a touch of island pride, the historian Erik J. Lawaetz has claimed that, excluding hurricanes (which on occasion have been devastating), "the worst day in St. Croix . . . is better than the best days in most other places."[4]

The island's pre-Columbian inhabitants came from elsewhere in the Americas and found their new home hospitable. The first to arrive were small groups of hunters and gatherers around 300 to 400 B.C. They gave way to the agricultural Arawaks or Taino (who named the island "Ay-Ay") around 100 to 200 A.D. The Arawaks were subsequently displaced by Carib migrants, from northern South America, who arrived between 1350 and 1400. All of these indigenous peoples lived relatively comfortably off the natural resources of the island.[5]

Estate Concordia, where Hubert was born, is located near the Salt River estuary—a focal point of St. Croix's early history and the place where that Caribbean island's subordination to European domination literally began. On November 14, 1493, the essentially self-sufficient social order of the island's Carib inhabitants was jolted by the arrival of Christopher Columbus with seventeen ships, and twelve hundred armed men under the Spanish flag at the river's mouth. Columbus's men made a brief incursion onto land and seized some children and women (at least one of whom was raped), attempted to overtake a canoe at a place subsequently called Cabo de Fleches ("Cape of the Arrows"), and then met with resistance from the canoe's Carib warriors. In the ensuing skirmish— the first recorded fight between Europeans and Caribs—one Carib warrior and one Spaniard were killed. Within hours Columbus and his fleet left for a chain of islands visible to the north, which would prove both less hostile and more suitable to their needs. Columbus named these islands "las Virgenes" (the Virgins) after St. Ursula and the eleven thousand martyred virgins alleged to have been murdered by the Huns at Cologne.[6]

During the ensuing sixteen years, the Spanish left the aggressive Caribs of Ay-Ay, which Columbus had renamed "Sancta Crux" (Latin for Holy Cross), largely untouched, while they concentrated on conquering the larger, Taino-occupied islands of Hispaniola and Puerto Rico (Borinquen). The calm on St. Croix was broken in 1509, when Spanish slave traders from Puerto Rico (acting in the spirit of a royal *cedula* that allowed for the enslavement of Caribs on the grounds that they were heathens and practiced cannibalism) raided the island and took 150 captives. In 1511, the enraged Crucian Caribs joined forces with the Borinquen Tainos in an attempt to drive the Spaniards from Puerto Rico. The Spanish then forcefully attacked St. Croix, driving those island Caribs who were not taken captive into the northern Virgin Islands and then eastward into the northern Leeward Islands.[7]

By 1515, European military might had depopulated St. Croix. The Spanish Empire showed little interest in the mineral-deprived island (which had little potential for use as a major colony or a military installation), and St. Croix remained essentially uninhabited for over a century. Then, in the 1630s, small groups of English, French, and Dutch settled at different locations on the island. These new occupants fought among themselves, and against the Spanish, and by 1650, the French emerged triumphant and began to colonize St. Croix. Small numbers of French planters, using European servants and enslaved Africans, established a precarious agricultural economy, which was supplemented by smuggling with the neighboring islands of St. Thomas and Puerto Rico. St. Croix was far from the center of French power in the region, and its new occupants were unruly, hard to govern, defiant of authority, and given to marronage. The cost of controlling and defending these recalcitrants outweighed any meager returns they generated for the mother country, and the French government consequently decided to shut down the colony. In January 1696 a French fleet removed the free and enslaved inhabitants (excepting some who went maroon) to the fledgling colony of St. Dominique (later Haiti).[8]

Between 1696 and 1733, St. Croix, though nominally French, was essentially free from colonial dominion. It was frequented by people marginalized by capitalistic development in the region including maroons, freebooters, debtors, and deserters. Developing capitalism would tolerate a vacuum in the region for only so long, however, and in 1733, Denmark, which had established colonies in nearby St. Thomas and St. John, purchased St. Croix from France with the expectation of turning it into a producer of sugar cane. The island, which contained 150 English settlers, 456 enslaved African inhabitants, and an unknown number of maroons, was then turned over to the Danish West India and Guinea Company, which began its colonization in 1734. The company imposed an ordered plan that divided the island into nine quarters, which were subdivided into estates that were sold at low cost to the already resident foreigners and to immigrant planters from the neighboring English, French, and Dutch sugar islands. As a result of these developments, St. Croix's population was characterized by ethnic heterogeneity. While Danes took most jobs in government administration, few became planters. In 1755 company rule came to an end, and the Danish West Indies (comprising St. Croix, St. Thomas, St. John, and some inlets and cays) became a royal colony of Denmark with its capital at Christiansted, St. Croix's main seaport.[9]

In an attempt to develop St. Croix's sugar economy on a profitable basis, Denmark actively increased its participation in the transatlantic slave trade. Captured Africans were imported from four Danish forts maintained along the coast of modern day Ghana, from three factories in Africa, and from a wide trading area that stretched from Sierra Leone to Angola. Between 1755 and 1792, an estimated 22,000 Africans were sold into slavery on St. Croix. In that period, the island's enslaved population, which because of harsh conditions could not sustain itself through natural reproduction, increased from 8,285 to 22,240. The Moravian missionary C. G. A. Oldendorp visited the Danish West Indies between 1767 and 1769 and reported interviews with Fulani, Mandigoes, Amina, Akims, Popos, Ibos, and Yorubas. Of these African peoples it is believed that Akan-Amina speakers of Twi were the most numerous. While most enslaved newcomers came from Africa, a large number (many of whom were Creoles), were also imported from neighboring Caribbean islands. By 1792 the diverse, enslaved population on St. Croix plantations was 54 percent Creole and 46 percent African.[10]

The oppressive slavery established on St. Croix was maintained by severe repression. Pursuant to laws passed under Governor Philip Gardelin in 1733 (called "Gardelin's Code") activities such as dancing, feasts, plays, and drumming were prohibited. Punishments included use of hot irons, severing of limbs, branding, whipping and torture, and their severity has led the Virgin Island social scientist Malik Sekou to conclude that the "Danish slave codes were among the most brutal."[11]

Such repression led to various forms of resistance. In 1745 three hundred people escaped their slavery by fleeing to Puerto Rico. In 1746 and 1759 major conspiracies to organize mass rebellion were discovered and thwarted. Marronage, including mass desertions to Puerto Rico, persisted until slavery was ended by the collective action of those enslaved in 1848.[12]

In the three and a half decades before Hubert's birth, Crucians undertook two major direct-action mass struggles—one an enslaved-led rebellion to end slavery and the other an armed rebellion followed by a general strike for better working conditions. Crucian working people referred to these two struggles as "the first free" and "the second free."[13]

On July 3, 1848, several thousand "slaves," reputedly led by the legendary Black liberator "Buddhoe" (born John Gottliff, aka "Buddho," "Budhoe," "Buddo," "Burdeaux," or "Moses Gottlieb"), staged an essentially nonviolent demonstration in Frederiksted (the island's second-largest town) demanding their freedom. This determined collective action forced Governor Peter Karl Frederik von Scholten to decree an end to slavery in the Danish West Indies. This struggle, as the historian Neville Hall points out, was "the Caribbean's second successful slave uprising" (after Haiti).[14]

Though some 17,000 people had won freedom from slavery in 1848, the ensuing repressive Labor Act of 1849 established year-long labor contracts, five-day sunrise-to-sunset workweeks, prohibitions against refusal of work (including refusals by children), requirements to give notice before termination of work, and fixed (nonnegotiable) wages for three classes of workers of five, ten, and fifteen cents a day. The emancipation victory and subsequent restrictive labor law led Crucian workers to seek to terminate their contracts and leave the plantations, resulted in a growing labor shortage, and prompted a postemancipation influx of immigrant laborers (some 5,000 arrived between 1859 and 1870). Many of these immigrants were unemployed, hungry, and desperate Barbadians who, lured by recruiting agents, began arriving in great numbers in the 1860s and were subsequently described by planters as "troublemakers." By 1880 the census would list 1,023 Barbadians (329 women and 694 men) on St. Croix.[15]

Thirty years after the 1848 emancipation victory, workers of the island, chanting the watchword "our side"—and inspired by rebel leader "Queen Mary" Thomas (a thirty-year-old Antiguan immigrant and "canefield worker with a genius for leadership"), "Queen Agnes," "Queen Matilda," and others—conducted a week-long militant labor rebellion known as the "Fireburn." It was the beginning of the second great labor struggle in island history. The 1878 struggle opposed the oppressive labor contracts, low wages, wage inequalities, unequal employment opportunities, vagrancy laws, lack of upward mobility, and reduced medical services. During that struggle laborers expressed "profound dissatisfaction" with their conditions, foreign-born and native-born workers demonstrated class solidarity, and immigrants "played a prominent, even decisive role." Fifty-three sugar plantations and fifteen stock estates out of seventy-nine estates on the island were severely damaged. At least 84 Black laboring-class people (and possibly as many as 250) were killed, however, as groups of plantation owners, managers, and overseers known as the "Volunteers," engaged in murders, beatings, and arrests. A year later, some real gains in working conditions were consolidated through an islandwide general strike that gained workers freedom of movement and the right to negotiate terms of their employment. The "Fireburn" and general strike occurred only a few years before Hubert's birth.[16]

Despite such struggle, at the time of Hubert's birth in 1883 island life for the majority of the population continued to be shaped by outside domination and capitalist greed. St. Croix had a declining population of eighteen to nineteen thousand and a political economy centered on sugar (and related rum) production based on the owner-laborer, owner-renter-laborer, and tenant forms of capitalist relations of production. Continuing planter dominance was assured through their control of the legislative and land body, the Colonial Council, and it was further facilitated by a generally sympathetic governing Danish

Figures 1.1, 1.2, 1.3. (opposite page) In the three and a half decades before Harrison's birth, Crucians undertook major direct-action mass struggles, referred to by laboring people as "the first free" and "the second free." In 1848 the legendary Black liberator "Buddhoe" reportedly played a leading role in the successful enslaved-led emancipation struggle, the second such victorious struggle (after Haiti) in the Caribbean. In 1878, workers of the island, inspired by "Queen Mary" Thomas and other insurgents, and chanting the watchword "our side," sparked the militant, week-long labor rebellion known as the "Fireburn," which grew and matured into an October 1879 general strike that won major gains for working people. Harrison, influenced by such roots, would become a leading proponent of militant, direct-action mass struggle.

Figure 1.1. (left) "Buddhoe," from a woodcut rendering by Charles E. Taylor, c. 1888. *Source:* Courtesy of the Enid M. Baa Public Library, St. Thomas, United States Virgin Islands.
Figure 1.2. (right) "Queen Mary" Thomas, undated, sketch by Charles E. Taylor. *Source:* Courtesy of the Enid M. Baa Public Library, St. Thomas, United States Virgin Islands.

Figure 1.3. The Fireburn, 1878. *Source:* Courtesy of the Department of Prints and Photographs, the Royal Library, Copenhagen.

bureaucracy in both the mother country and the colonies. All important legislation for the island had to be approved in Denmark and implemented through generally autocratic colonial governors. For the propertyless laborers and their kin, daily existence was a constant struggle to meet the necessities of food, clothing, and shelter under an economic system in which others owned the principal means of making a living and in which true freedom was little more than a wish. This would continue to be the case after the United States purchased the Virgin Islands for $25 million and they were formally transferred on March 31, 1917, six days before the United States entered the First World War.[17]

One of the more significant political aspects of St. Croix's colonial history was the general lack of democratic institutions. The right to vote was restricted by a colonial law of 1863 to males who had property yielding $75 annually or who received a yearly income of $300 or more. In the 1880s the average wage for a field laborer was about $60 per year and, as late as 1921, four years after the island became a U.S. possession, only 475 males out of a population of 23,000 people on the island had the franchise. The voting laws were not significantly changed in Harrison's lifetime, including the years after the U.S. purchase, and he never forgot his time as a colonial subject and this lack of democracy. Decades later he explained that a subject is one "who owes allegiance to a government, its laws and officials without having, as a right, the power to make or remake that government or these laws" while a citizen is "the source of that government" to whom allegiance is owed.[18]

While the colonial status shaped the island's political economy during Harrison's youth, the day in, day out, economic conditions bore most directly on the majority of the Crucian population. They faced a constant struggle for bare subsistence. According to author Valdemar A. Hill Sr., "The name of the game was human exploitation" and "black people, . . . [though] 'promoted' from slaves to 'Danish subjects' remained a landless proletariat still dependent upon white colonists for economic survival."[19]

During Harrison's years on the island the consequences of the exploitation and oppression were manifest in various ways. Wages remained low, fluctuating between twenty and fifty cents per day for agricultural workers. Insufficient wages and difficult work conditions were further aggravated by droughts and low sugar prices, which prompted planters to cut back on housing, sanitation, and health care. Such conditions resulted in exceptionally high mortality rates, as well as in an increase in emigration, two factors that combined to reduce St. Croix's population from 22,760 in 1870 to 14,901 in 1917. Overall, the conditions during Harrison's St. Croix years are well described by Florence Lewisohn, who writes that "a widespread sense of uncertainty was the keynote of the whole second half of the 19th Century on St. Croix." The historian Isaac Dookhan, focusing on the mass of laborers, emphasizes that their plight in particular was "increasingly grave."[20]

Despite the economic uncertainty and hardship during Harrison's youth, colonial St. Croix's oppressive economic conditions were, for a while, mitigated by West African traditions. These traditions were reinforced by a climate similar to that found in parts of West Africa, by the preponderance of people of African descent in the population, and by what the historian Neville A. T. Hall refers to as "the socially learned and transmitted" patterns of the community that were developed by descendants of people from the African region between Upper Guinea and Angola.[21]

Harrison recollected some of these customs in an article on the Virgin Islands. He pointed out that the "black people of the Virgin Islands are almost entirely of African extraction," and their social characteristics are only "adequately understood and appreciated by similar reference to characteristics to be found in the West African Negroes from among whom the slaves for the Danish islands were mainly drawn—the locale extending from the Upper Gold Coast to the south-eastern limits of Nigeria." Among customs "rooted in the African communal system" that he noted were

a free public garden on every plantation which was stocked with fruit trees: mangoes, mammy-apples, sour-sops, avocados, sugar-apples, and bananas. These were to be had for the picking not only by every person resident on such plantations (or "estates," as they were called) but also by any strangers who happened to pass by. The fishes and shrimps in any "gut" or stream were just as free to everyone and the most popular method of taking them was that of throwing buckets of lees or liquid sugar-cane refuse into a small stream and picking out the intoxicated fish as they floated helplessly to the shore. Every family of agricultural laborers (like the English white slaves of the 13th century) had its own half-acre of provision land on which yams, tannias, okra, sago and potatoes were produced as additions to the regular dietary, the surplus being regularly disposed of in the towns on Saturday (which was a weekly holiday) in markets that exactly reproduced those to be found today in the hinterlands of Sierra Leone, Liberia, the Cameroons and Yoruba.[22]

Harrison added that these "communal extensions of individual economics" had enabled the agricultural laborer under Danish rule to "keep himself and his family healthy and well-dressed, and send some of the children to private school on 20 cents a day."[23]

Nevertheless, on St. Croix (where, by 1930, twenty families and one foreign industrial group owned 80 percent of the land) the trend was "always," according to a Hampton-Tuskegee study, "to reduce the standards of labor to the cheapest possible." Harrison maintained that after the United States expressed interest in the Danish West Indies in 1867 "the sugar industry . . . shrunk disastrously, and the black West Indian laborers . . . [began] to pour into the cities of our North Atlantic states in numbers that steadily increased as the years rolled by."[24] The African communal traditions could not counterbalance the capitalist greed of the European colonialism or the economic pressure of the declining sugar and rum industries that continually forced families below the subsistence level. It was this economic pressure that was one of the important factors pushing Harrison and others to emigrate.

———

The economic pressure on laboring people weighed ever more heavily because, despite the island's history of struggle, there was an effective system of social control in place. The roots and maintenance of that system are essential to understanding how and why the color line was drawn differently in St. Croix than in the United States. The differently drawn color line is also instructive in explaining the subsequent development of race consciousness in Harrison.

The Crucian economy, like the U.S. economy, was one in which the rich owners of capital dominated the poor and propertyless. For the ruling class this domination involved two principal tasks: first, social control had to be maintained; second, efforts were made to maximize profits. As in any system in which the poor greatly outnumber the rich, a method of social control had to be devised—a method to enlist support of other groups on the side of the rich. Such groups serve a buffer social control function in that they deflect and shield direct attacks on the rich and they act as agents for the rich among and against the poor. In both St. Croix and the United States the color line was the key to social control, but, because of different historical particulars and history of class struggle, the color line was drawn differently in each place. How it was drawn in St. Croix, where "free colored" were the key, influenced Harrison's youth, while how it was drawn in the United States, where the "white race" was the key, greatly influenced his adult years.[25]

In St. Croix, color and class tended to coincide. Using statistics from the 1917 census, the "white" (or "unmixed" European-descended) population was only 4–5 percent of the total population, and it was the prime constituent of the upper class. The 80 percent or greater "Negroes" (of "unmixed" African descent) constituted the primary laboring or lower class. An intermediate buffer social control middle stratum of perhaps 13 percent of the whole was composed primarily of "colored" (the offspring of European- and African-descended people).[26]

This social-control structure was particularly affected by the fact that, in contrast to England's peopling of Virginia, Maryland, and other plantation colonies to the north with surplus English laborers, few laborers from Denmark went to its island colonies. (According to William W. Boyer, "the proportion of slaves in the Virgin Islands exceeded 88 percent in 1789.") In St. Croix during slavery, free people of color served in the militia, were sometimes promoted into the middle class, and, if of acceptable behavior and standing, were allowed to register as "white." The historian Theodore W. Allen, whose work focuses on racial oppression, the historical particulars of class struggle and social control in Virginia, and the invention of the "white race" as a ruling-class social-control formation, offers important insights. While taking into consideration the history of the class struggle, geography, and other factors, Allen stresses that "the key to understanding the difference between [the] Virginia ruling-class policy of 'fixing a perpetual brand'" on African Americans and "the policy of the West Indian planters of formally recognizing the middle-class status 'colored' descendant (and other Afro-Caribbeans who earned special merit by their service to the regime)" was "rooted in the objective fact that in the West Indies there were *too few* laboring-class Europeans to embody an adequate petit bourgeoisie, while in the continental colonies there were *too many* to be accommodated in the ranks of that class." In St. Croix, as the historian Eric Williams explains, "the free people of color . . . served as a convenient buffer between whites and blacks" and under the Danes "was established the Caribbean tradition of race relations" in which "emphasis was on color, not race; and color was closely associated with class, and even determined by class." Neville A. T. Hall adds that "incipient class formation" was emphasized and coloreds were systematically promoted into intermediate positions.[27]

These two developments—promotion of people of African ancestry into the militia and the fostering of class development among African peoples—were, by the eighteenth century, noticeably lacking in the plantation colonies to the north. There, as Allen points out, "whites" of all classes made up the slave patrols (a principal instrument of social control), and African Americans were denied "the normal social distinctions characteristic of class systems."[28] In Virginia, for example, the key to social control was not "coloreds," but the "white race," a social-control formation comprising European Americans and excluding African Americans, including "free colored." "Whites" of all classes performed the social-control function and were the principal support of the existing order, despite the fact that the great majority were laboring people, not promoted out of their class, who were acting against their own class interests. In addition, not only were free people of African descent excluded from the buffer social control formation but, both pre- and postemancipation (and during Harrison's entire life), those of African descent constantly faced severe racial proscriptions.[29]

A related difference between the two societies concerned the organization and racial policy of whites. On top of the Crucian political and economic class structure, the white group maintained its dominance without the more starkly organized racial policy of its U.S. counterpart. This was in part because of Denmark's reliance on what Neville Hall calls a "'colonization by invitation'" that introduced other Europeans into the population, and in part because of the relative shortage of European laborers and the ruling class's need for other, nonwhite support. It was this need for additional support that led to the use of "free coloreds" in the militia and to the 1834 Edict of Full Equality between whites and free coloreds that was sponsored by Peter Carl Frederik von Scholten, the governor-general of the Danish West Indies in Christiansted. The psychologist Albert A. Campbell points out that the white ruling elite "fostered the development" of the "free-colored" buffer group, and, in so doing, "they yielded a considerable degree of equality to the favored members of the colored group, but they succeeded in maintaining their own minority in a position of social and political domination."[30]

The historian Gwendolyn Midlo Hall emphasizes the important fact that white supremacy was "more powerful in the United States than elsewhere in the Americas." Legalized segregation and lynching terror in the United States were but two of many major contrasts with St. Croix. Throughout Harrison's lifetime, as he and another West Indian–born leader, Marcus Garvey, would observe, organized white supremacy (and concomitant race consciousness among Blacks) was far more pronounced in the United States than in St. Croix or elsewhere in the West Indies. This difference would lead Jamaica-born Claude McKay to explain, after coming to the United States, "It was the first time I had ever come face to face with such manifest, implacable hatred of my race, and my feelings were indescribable." While he "had heard of prejudice in America, he "never dreamed of it being so intensely bitter."[31]

The social-control system that developed in St. Croix was an important factor in the earlier emancipation on the island. During the first part of the nineteenth century, the Crucian free coloreds' resistance to their oppression and unequal status intensified. They also mingled socially and sexually with the enslaved population. Consequently, the ruling elite in St. Croix were less sure of their loyalty than their counterpart elite in the United States were of the support of the laboring "white race" population. In St. Croix, there was, according to Neville Hall, a "demystification of whiteness as a mechanism of social control," which "hastened the slaves' disposition to confront the structures that oppressed them."[32]

By the time of Hubert's birth there was a clear and distinct racial shaping of the economic structure of Crucian society. Though the island's economy was based on agriculture, farm owners were a tiny portion of the population, and the majority of the working "Negro" population was engaged in agricultural labor or tenancy. Of those who did own farms, approximately one-third were "Negroes" and another one-sixth Colored (including the two co-owners of Estate Concordia, where Harrison was born). Very few of the farms in "Negro" hands were large. Importantly, however, "Negro" landholding and some concomitant upward social mobility were possible. A comparison between the 1917 U.S. census of the Virgin Islands and the 1920 U.S. census statistics from Black Belt counties in the Deep South (in Alabama, Mississippi, Florida, Georgia, and Louisiana) is revealing. It shows that the rate of "Negro" and "colored" farm ownership in St. Croix was almost 80 percent higher than that of "Negro" ("colored" included) farm ownership in the selected U.S. Black Belt counties.[33]

Under St. Croix's tripartite social structure, class differences among those of African descent were more pronounced than in the United States, and there were opportunities during Harrison's years on the island for some Black Crucians to achieve upward class mobility. In addition, Black people were limited far less by racial proscription in St. Croix, where formal "race discriminating rules of law did not exist."[34]

This was particularly true in the area of education. Schooling was compulsory for those age six to thirteen, and, as Harrison explained, the "similarly situated" Crucian was "furnished . . . with a more thorough and competent intellectual equipment than race-prejudiced America has given to the Negro American." Nevertheless, in the West Indies as in the United States, the educational system was controlled by "whites." Training for whites was in general superior to that for Blacks, and instruction emphasized notions of white superiority and Black inferiority. As Harrison later described, "The Negro boy and girl, getting the same (though worse) instruction, also get from it the same notion of the Negro's [inferior] place and part in life which the white children get."[35]

Still, in such a situation, in which a talented Black person was able to excel and whites were not as "race conscious" as in the United States, Harrison, a precocious youth, was able to stand out and grow with the belief that he was the equal of any other. This would seem to explain, in part, his recollection of racial relations in his homeland in contrast to his U.S. experience. In 1923, in the midst of the U.S. naval occupation of St. Croix that political scientist Gordon K. Lewis has depicted as marked by "American white racist contempt for the Negro population," Harrison described the U.S. navy (which was officially racially segregated in 1920) as an occupation force "in which 'Southernism' runs riot."[36] He contrasted its racial practices with the racial experiences of his youth:

During the Danish days there were "superior" and "inferior" people on the islands; but in no instance were they made so by the color of their skin. This doctrine of chromatic inferiors and superiors has been violently thrust upon the islanders by the personnel of the naval administration. . . . If the lines of social and economic cleavage had at any time followed those of chromatics . . . I knew of no such thing.[37]

Harrison added that Virgin Islanders "had no previous acquaintance with the psychology of race-prejudice and the harsh superciliousness of the Navy officials" did "much to disillusion them."[38]

Overall, the broad, shaping influences of St. Croix are clear. The monocultural economy centered on sugar and the pressures of capitalism weighed heavily on the laboring people who, as colonial subjects, had no formal say in island governance. Some African communal customs helped to lessen the pressure, but the main force that had historically checked exploitation and oppression was mass struggle by those at the bottom of society—Black laborers, both native born and foreign born. While Black people were, in general, at the bottom and white people were on top, the color line was drawn differently in St. Croix than in the United States. There was a conscious policy of promotion, not strict proscription, for a significant sector of the African-descended population. Because, in large part, of the history of struggle and the social-control needs of the ruling elite, St. Croix had no history of lynch terror and no formal segregation, class development among people of African descent was fostered, and white supremacy was not as virulent or as organized as in the United States. The young Black youth on St. Croix could grow with experiences and expectations significantly different than those of a counterpart youth in the United States. Harrison's early years are a case in point.

———————

Those early years are better understood when the specific details of Harrison's family history are added to the broad shaping influences of St. Croix history. These specifics, drawn from a wide variety of original sources, from the work of island historian George F. Tyson, and from the St. Croix African Roots Project, are particularly instructive in depicting Harrison's laboring class and immigrant roots and aspects of his family life and his family's living conditions.

A July 7, 1883, baptism record in St. John's Episcopal Church in Christiansted states that "Hubert Henry" was born to Cecilia Elizabeth Haines (sometimes elsewhere spelled as Haynes or Hynes) on April 27 on Estate Concordia. His godparents were listed as Elizabeth Hendricks, Charles Hendricks, and Catherine Cornelius. The estate, located in Queen's Quarter, was co-owned by Robert McCormick and William H. Heyliger, two men of color. It focused on sugar production, and, according to the 1880 St. Croix census, it included one hundred residents and fifty-seven households. (In 1859 Heyliger, a wealthy Christiansted merchant, united Estate Concordia with Estate Salt River, and they were operated jointly under his ownership until 1890.) The baptism record noticeably leaves blank both the spaces for listing the baby's father (a common practice regarding unwed parents in the Anglican Church) and that for his mother's occupation. This suggests that Cecilia was not married and that she was not working under

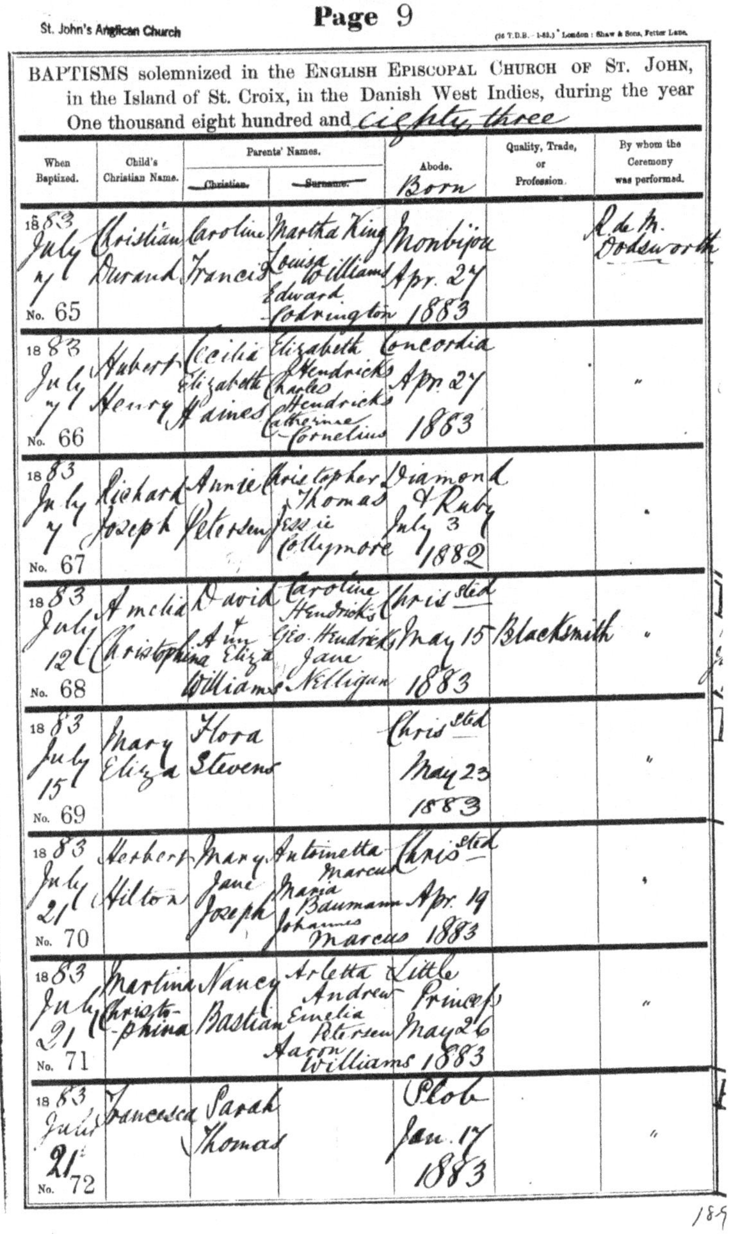

St. John's Anglican Church

Page 9

(26 T.D.B. · 1-83.) London: Shaw & Sons, Fetter Lane.

BAPTISMS solemnized in the ENGLISH EPISCOPAL CHURCH OF ST. JOHN, in the Island of St. Croix, in the Danish West Indies, during the year One thousand eight hundred and eighty three

When Baptized.	Child's Christian Name.	Parents' Names. Christian.	Parents' Names. Surname.	Abode. Born	Quality, Trade, or Profession.	By whom the Ceremony was performed.
1883 July 7 No. 65	Christian Durand	Caroline Francis	Martha King Louisa Williams Edward Codrington	Monbijou Apr. 27 1883		R de M. Dodsworth
1883 July 7 No. 66	Hubert Henry	Cecilia Elizabeth Haines	Elizabeth Hendricks Charles Hendricks Catherine Cornelius	Concordia Apr. 27 1883		"
1883 July 7 No. 67	Richard Joseph	Annie Petersen	Christopher Thomas Jessie Collymore	Diamond & Ruby July 3 1882		"
1883 July 12 No. 68	Amelia Christophina	David & Ann Eliza Williams	Caroline Hendricks Geo. Hendricks Jane Nelligun	Christsted May 15 1883	Blacksmith	"
1883 July 15 No. 69	Mary Eliza	Flora Stevens		Christsted May 23 1883		"
1883 July 21 No. 70	Herbert Hilton	Mary Jane Joseph	Antoinetta Marcus Maria Baumann Johannes Marcus	Christsted Apr. 19 1883		"
1883 July 21 No. 71	Martina Christophina	Nancy Bastian	Arletta Andrew Emelia Petersen Aaron Williams	Little Princess May 26 1883		"
1883 July 21 No. 72	Francesca	Sarah Thomas		Slob Jan. 17 1883		"

189

Figure 1.4. Baptism Record of Hubert Harrison in St. John's Episcopal Church, Christiansted, 1992. The baptism record of Hubert Henry (no last name given) indicates that he was born to Cecilia Elizabeth Haines (no father is listed) on April 27, 1883, and was baptized on July 7, 1883. Cecilia was an unmarried, Barbadian immigrant field laborer. Between 1870 and 1883 she gave birth to at least six children. Like other poor women on the island she labored in the fields and had principal responsibility for her children. *Source:* Courtesy of St. John's Episcopal Church, Christiansted, St. Croix, U.S. Virgin Islands.

a formal labor contract. Like other poor women on the island, she probably did agricultural work and had principal responsibility for her children.[39]

Information relating to Cecilia's personal background is limited and somewhat contradictory. According to the 1880 St. Croix census return, she was born in Barbados. However, the 1890 census return lists her birthplace (probably incorrectly) as St. Croix. In the 1920 U.S. census, Harrison's family reported that she was born in Barbados, and this is consistent with information passed on orally to his children. It appears that Cecilia was among the several thousand Bajan contract workers who were brought, lured to, or came to St. Croix during the 1860s and 1870s, a number of whom were employed in Queen's Quarter, where Estate Concordia is located. It is likely that she was the "Elizabeth Hynes" who, according to immigrant records, arrived in St. Croix in late September or early October 1866, and first went to work at Estate La Reine in King's Quarter.[40]

The date of Cecilia's birth and her age at death are also not precise. Her birth record has not been found among the rather complete set of church records that exist for St. Croix during the second half of the nineteenth century, and this lends credence to her Bajan ancestry. In the St. Croix census of 1880, she is listed as thirty-three years of age. Her marriage record of 1889 lists her as thirty-six, whereas the census return for 1890 gives her age as forty-four. Her St. John's Church death record indicates that she was fifty-one years old when she died on January 30, 1899; the Christiansted Probate Court "Register of Reported Deaths" says that she was forty-two; and a "Register of Deaths" in Christiansted indicates that the cause of death was consumption.[41]

Cecilia's St. Croix residences provide further information. She apparently lived her adult life in St. Croix in the Christiansted area. Church documents place her nearby at Estate Libanon Hill (sometimes Lebannon Hill) in King's Quarter in 1870, 1872, and 1875, at Estate Judith's Fancy in 1880 and 1881, at Concordia in 1878 and 1883, in Christiansted in 1890, and at Orange Grove in 1899.[42]

Records indicate that Cecilia, while unmarried, gave birth to at least five other children, in addition to Hubert. There is no indication that any of the children had the same biological father or that she lived with any of the men. Life was not easy for an unmarried, Black, female, immigrant field worker, however, and in many respects her life had much in common with other women.

A first daughter, Mary Rotilda Ann, was born on July 20, 1870, to "Cecilia Haynes," an Anglican of Estate Libanon Hill. The child was baptized in St. John's Episcopal Church on November 19, 1870, in a ceremony witnessed by her godparents, Lawrence James, Suzanna James, and Elizabeth Prince. Mary was later referred to as Mrs. May Francis in a 1927 newspaper article, but Harrison's children, Aida and William, knew her as Mary C. Francis, called her "Aunt Mamie," said that she remained especially close to Hubert and his family throughout her life, and remembered that her birthday was July 20. Mary preceded Hubert to New York (arriving in 1893) and lived on West Sixty-second St. in Manhattan when he arrived. Mamie (Mary or May) was always referred to by Harrison and his family in the United States as his sister (though technically she was probably his half sister), and this undoubtedly reflects Harrison's sense of his own family.[43]

Cecilia's second daughter, "Cecilia Ann Esther," was born on December 17, 1872. "Cecilia Haynes," an Anglican of Estate Libanon Hill, was listed in church records as the mother, the father was not listed, and the baby was baptized in the Anglican Church the same day, suggesting that she was probably sickly. The godparents were Lawrence James and Susanna James (who were also Mary's godparents) and Ann Plaskett (who was later identified as traveling on the same ship as Harrison when he emigrated to New York). It is most probable that baby Cecilia died young and that Hubert never knew her.[44]

A third daughter, Emily Frances ("Emma"), was born to "Cecilia Haynes" in Libanon Hill on March 2, 1875, and baptized on June 5 of that year. Though her father was not named in the church record, her godparents were listed as Mary Haynes, James Brathwaite, and Ann Plaskett (baby Cecilia's godparent). Emma (listed later as Emily Perry or Parry), had at least three daughters: Carmelita Maria Parris born on June 14, 1893, at Mt. Pleasant (Colquohoun) in King's Quarter, listed in church records as Ann Rebecca, and baptized at St. John's on September 16, 1893; June Elizabeth Samuel, known as "Sophy"; and Mary Eliza Samuel. "Emma Parry" appears in the 1901 census as a first-class laborer (a field worker) on Estate Mt. Pleasant living with her daughter Calamaria Parris, age eight. Hubert mentioned "Emma" and her three daughters in his diary, and his children knew of them.[45]

A first son, Alexander Conton (also Canton), was born to Cecilia, listed as "Elizabeth Hinds" of Estate Concordia in the St. John Church baptism records, on June 23, 1878. The father was not listed, but from the 1901 census he can be identified as Alexander Conton, born c. 1860 (he also fathered James Conton, the half brother of Cecilia's son, Alexander Conton). Young Alexander's September 7, 1878, baptism in St. John's Church was witnessed by "Wilfred Harrison," Mary Harrison, and Elizabeth James. Shortly thereafter, in the 1880 census, Barbados-born "Cecilia Haines" was listed as unmarried and living with her two children, Emily Perry (age five) and Alexander Canton (age two), on Estate Judiths Fancy, where she worked as a first-class laborer. Though the 1901 and 1911 St. Croix censuses indicate that Alexander was still alive in those years, no mention of him is found in Harrison's papers and Harrison's children never indicated that they knew of him.[46]

Cecilia's second son, David Elias, was born on June 2, 1881, on Estate Judith's Fancy. David may have died shortly thereafter, or perhaps in the yellow fever epidemic that hit St. Croix in 1886, since no further mention of him has been found in any records. His birth was followed twenty-three months later by that of Hubert, who is believed to have been Cecilia's last-born child.[47]

After giving birth to "Hubert Henry" in 1883, Cecilia moved back onto Estate Concordia. Six years later, she was living in Christiansted when she married Robert Collins, a forty-year-old laborer, in St. John Episcopal Church on December 12 1889. Her husband was likely the immigrant "Robert Collins" who arrived in St. Croix in September 1881 and worked at Estate Mon Bijou in King's Quarter until March 1884. In the 1890 census, "Cecilia Collin," age forty-four, Anglican, with no occupation listed, was living with her husband "Robert Collin," forty-four, born in Barbados, Anglican, a "squatter" (someone who legitimately rented and farmed a small parcel of land) at King's Cross St. 32 (actually 31 E), on the shoreline of the harbor in the "Watergut" section of Christiansted. Living with them were three of her children, all Anglicans, born in St. Croix—Hubert Harrison, age seven, a servant (probably a domestic working in someone's house); Emily Perry (sister Emma), age sixteen, a porter (a day laborer living in town who hired out to a plantation or other employer); and Alexander Conton, age thirteen, a servant. Records suggest that Hubert likely worked for another resident at his address, possibly Elizabeth Pelton, forty-one, a seller (probably a market woman) with three unemployed children ages eleven to seventeen, or possibly Ole Hansen, a forty-one-year-old Danish overseer, who lived with his wife and four children (none of whom were employed). According to Christiansted cemetery burial records, "Robert Collin," age fifty, died of jaundice in Peters Farm Hospital on June 26, 1901 (a year and a half after the death of his wife, Cecilia). Christiansted probate records indicate that he left behind no land or property of value and the Christiansted "Register of Deaths" states that he was unemployed and died of "miseries."[48]

For years there was no confirmed information on Harrison's biological father, who was reported in marriage and death certificates and government and biographical documents, by Harrison, his family, and others, as William Adolphus Harrison or Adolphus Harrison. Harrison's friend Richard B. Moore reported that he lived in Concordia; beyond that, none of Harrison's children or grandchildren could offer any additional information.[49]

It now appears, however, that the mystery of Harrison's father has been resolved. He is believed to have been "Adolphus" or "Adolphus Harrison." Although his birth records have not been located, it appears that he was born enslaved to an enslaved woman named "Philis" (aka "Eliza Marcus") c. 1844, probably on Estate Rattan. The 1857 census indicates that Adolphus, age sixteen, Lutheran, moved to Estate Salt River with his mother (and his brother Wilford, age twelve), in order to live with his stepfather, Ned Harrison, and to work as a second-class laborer. Census records indicate that Adolphus then lived on either Estate Salt River or Estate Concordia (which, beginning in 1859, were jointly owned and operated), working as a second-class laborer until 1890.[50]

In the 1870s and 1880s Adolphus Harrison fathered three children with Madalene (sometimes Magdalene, Madlane, or Madlene) Cornelius. On August 3, 1878, Adolphus Harrison, Lutheran, unmarried of Estate Concordia, and Magdalene Cornelius, thirty-one, of Estate Concordia, had a son, Wilford Adolphus Harrison. Young Willford, age six years and seven months, died on April 29, 1885, at Estate Salt River and was buried that same day on Estate Concordia, where he was born. He was probably visiting his father when he died. On March 2, 1881, Adolphus and "Madlane Cornelius" of Christiansted had a son, Henry Augustus Harrison, who died on July 14, 1881, of teething. On June 22, 1883, Adolphus Harrison, Lutheran, unmarried of Estate Concordia, and "Madlene Cornelius" of Christiansted had a daughter, Jessica Eliza Harrison. This was less than two months after Adolphus apparently fathered Hubert Henry (Harrison) with Cecilia Elizabeth Haines. Then, only five months after Jessica's birth, Madlane died of "natural causes" at age thirty-nine on November 19, 1883. Jessica apparently soon followed her mother, as she does not appear in either the 1890 or the 1901 censuses.[51]

For most of his adult life it appears that Adolphus Harrison worked as a field laborer and lived with his mother, Philis. In the 1870 census Adolphus Harrison, twenty-six, Lutheran, unmarried, a first-class laborer, was living on Estate Salt River with (his mother) Philis, forty-eight, Lutheran, unmarried, not working, and with (his brother) Wilford, twenty-two, Lutheran, unmarried, a first-class laborer. In the 1880 census Adolphus Harrison, thirty-one, Lutheran, unmarried, was living on Estate Salt River with Philis Harrison, fifty, Lutheran, widow, identified as "his mother" In the 1890 census Adolphus Harrison is listed as forty-eight, Lutheran, unmarried, laborer, living on Estates Salt River–Concordia, with the following family members: Philis Harrison, eighty, Lutheran, widow, invalid (his mother), and her two grandsons (probably the children of his brother) William Harrison, nine, Lutheran, and Wilford Harrison, four. On September 4, 1891, Adolphus, who was working on Estate Rust (or Twist) in the Northside B. Quarter, died of jaundice at age fifty. Christiansted cemetery records indicate he died a Moravian in Peters Farm Hospital, while Probate Court records indicate he died a Roman Catholic in Richmond Hospital.[52]

"Philis," Hubert Harrison's grandmother and Adolphus Harrison's mother, was born enslaved on Estate Rattan, probably in 1815, but definitely between 1811 and 1816. She first appears in records as an enslaved girl under age twelve in Estate Rattan inventories of 1815, 1817, 1819, and 1820, and as nine years of age in the Estate Rattan Vaccination List of 1824. She does not appear, however, on the Estate Rattan Slave List of 1811. She was freed on Estate Rattan by the general emancipation that took place on July 3, 1848. Philis had two male children, Adolphus and his younger brother, Wilford, with an unnamed man, in the 1840s. Census records indicate that she was unmarried and living on Estate Rattan with her two sons, Adolphus, eleven, a Moravian, and Wilford, eight, a Lutheran, in 1855. The sons do not appear with those names in any earlier census or in any baptismal record for the 1840s. They were probably born enslaved and baptized under different names.[53]

On September 13, 1857, Philis, thirty, a laborer first class, using the name "Eliza Marcus," married Ned Harrison (it was his first marriage), thirty-six, a Roman Catholic driver on Estate Salt River, in a Lutheran ceremony. That year she also moved onto Estate Salt River with her two children, Adolphus Harrison, age sixteen, and Wilford, age twelve. Based on census information, it appears that "Eliza Marcus" and Philis are the same person. In the 1860 St. Croix census Adolphus Harrison, sixteen, now a Roman Catholic and second-class laborer on Estate Salt River, was living with Ned, thirty-eight, Roman Catholic, married, a driver; with Philis, sixty-one, now a Roman Catholic, second-class laborer married to Ned; and with Wilford, thirteen, now a Roman Catholic, second-class laborer. Philis lived on either Estate Salt River or Estate Concordia until at least 1890. There is no record of her on St. Croix in 1901 and no death record has been found. It is likely that Philis died between 1890 and 1901.[54]

Ned Harrison, Philis's husband, was the son of a woman named "Brigit," who was born enslaved on Estate Salt River. He was baptized as "Edmund" in the Holy Trinity Roman Catholic Church on February 18, 1821. Absent the birth records, we cannot be certain if Ned Harrison was the biological father of either Adolphus Harrison or of his brother, Wilford Harrison. Estate Rattan is several miles east of Estate Salt River, and until about 1850, the owners of Estate Rattan operated a seventy-five-acre livestock estate next to Estate Salt River, so it is possible that Philis and Ned had opportunity to meet and to conceive children.[55] Ned Harrison, quite possibly Hubert Harrison's grandfather and at least his stepgrandfather, the born-enslaved son of the formerly enslaved Brigit, and the husband of Harrison's formerly enslaved grandmother Philis, died of consumption on May 28, 1865, at age forty-two.[56]

There is no substantiation that Hubert's biological parents, Adolphus Harrison and Cecilia Elizabeth Haines, were ever married, ever lived together, or ever had other children together. One questionable newspaper account (which contained a number of inaccuracies) from the January 19, 1924, *Chicago Defender* said that Harrison's father owned a large riverside estate. Such an estate, if it existed in the Concordia region, might have been in the 150- to 400-acre range. (If that were the case, the article may actually refer to Estate Concordia, owned until 1890 by William H. Heyliger, who was not Harrison's father.) It is much more likely, however, that if owned at all, it would have been one of the lesser parcels of land created as a result of the land distribution carried out after

General Christian Henrik Arendrup became governor in 1881 and the government implemented a "parceling-out" of plantation subdivisions to laborers. The parceling-out in 1882 and 1883 was a by-product of the labor struggles of 1878 and 1879 and resulted in some workers obtaining small plots in the one- to ten-acre range and later, after the program proved popular, in the eight- to twenty-eight-acre range. According to Isaac Dookhan, in an effort "to promote social and economic stability," such plots often went to "some of the most enterprising and industrious workers," though the land was often "the less valuable portions of . . . plantations which lay in bush or were on steep hills." When Arendrup broke up the large 700-acre Estate Work and Rest in Queen's Quarter (Estate Concordia was in both Queen's Quarter and West End Quarter) into forty sections, he parceled them out to "reliable" "Negro overseers." Then, "other government properties were divided under a so-called 'squatters' rights' system." Based on the fact that "Robert Collin" was listed as a "squatter" living with Hubert, Cecilia, Emily, and Alexander in the 1890 census, there is the possibility that Robert Collins, who rented, is the "father" referred to in the embellished story and the property was not large. Robert Collins, however, is not listed as one the "parcellists" who acquired Danish Government land at Work and Rest/Retreat/Humbug outside of Christiansted, and his probate record indicates that he did not own land when he died. There is also the possibility that the "father" was Harrison's biological father, Adolphus, who, by that time, may have been sick and unable to maintain any property. This is highly unlikely, however, since there is no indication that Adolphus, a laborer his entire adult life, ever owned, or even rented, land.[57]

At Harrison's death newspaper clippings reported a possible stepbrother named Wilford who lived in New York. Wilford, in fact, may have been Hubert's cousin (Adolphus's brother, Wilford's son). The elder Wilford may have been the "Wilfred Harrison" listed in 1878 as a witness at Alexander Conton's birth and in the 1880 census as a thirty-two-year-old Lutheran and driver on Estate Concordia.[58]

In sum, based on existing records, it appears that Hubert Henry Harrison was the son of Cecilia Elizabeth Haines (later Collins), a Barbadian immigrant to St. Croix who probably worked under contract and as field laborer. Cecilia had six children, three boys and three girls, two of whom probably died young. There is no indication that any of the children had the same biological father or that she was ever married to any of the biological fathers. As a youth, Hubert worked as a servant, as did his brother (actually his half brother), Alexander. A sister (actually a half sister), Emma, worked as a porter and later as a field laborer. Robert Collins, the Barbadian immigrant that Cecilia married when Hubert was six, was a laborer and then a squatter. Hubert's biological father, the field laborer Adolphus Harrison, was the born-enslaved son of an enslaved St. Croix woman, Philis, and

Figure 1.5. (top left) Paradise and Concordia Estates in St. Croix, 1869. *Source:* Photo courtesy of Arlette Millard, St.-Germain-en-laye, France.

Figure 1.6. (top right) Manager's House, Concordia, 1869. *Source:* Photo courtesy of Arlette Millard, St.-Germain-en-laye, France.

Figure 1.7. (bottom left) Manager's House, Concordia, 1869. *Source:* Photo courtesy of Arlette Millard, St.-Germain-en-laye, France.

Figure 1.8. (bottom right) Concordia Village, 1869. *Source:* Photo courtesy of George F. Tyson, St. Croix African Roots Project, and Arlette Millard, St.-Germain-en-laye, France.

he was very possibly the son of Philis's husband, the born-enslaved Ned Harrison, a driver. Adolphus had three children (siblings of Hubert) with Magdalen Cornelius, and each child appears to have died young. Among all these relatives, it was oldest sister, Mary, who remained close to Hubert for the remainder of his life. Overall, Hubert Harrison's Crucian and Bajan family history was deeply rooted in slavery, contract labor, servitude, plantation work, and poverty.

———

Other particulars of Hubert Harrison's life on St. Croix are sketchy. J. A. Rogers commented that his parents were of "apparently unmixed African descent" (and Harrison described himself as of "undiluted Negro blood"). His Barbadian mother and step-father were English speakers, as were 99 percent of St. Croix's inhabitants—despite the fact that St. Croix was a Danish possession, English was the predominant tongue. Danish, however, was also commonly spoken, and it is possible that members of Harrison's family were familiar with the language. Years later, Harrison, who had a facility with languages, still retained a Danish-language newspaper clipping in one of his scrapbooks.[59]

There is one interesting story related to Harrison's April 27 birthday. April 27 was coincidentally the birthday of the internationally famous British philosopher and sociologist Herbert Spencer, who, in 1883, a year after his trip to the United States, was at the height of his popularity in the Americas. Years later it was reported, with no substantiation, that Harrison was named Herbert at birth, after Spencer, and then, before his baptism, his father changed his name to Hubert. Curiously, as Harrison grew to adulthood he developed a great interest in Spencer's life and work and claimed to find personality characteristics in himself similar to those in Spencer. Perhaps Harrison was the source of the Spencer tale.[60]

Figures 1.5–1.8. (page 42) Estate Concordia, Hubert Harrison's 1883 birthplace, was owned by Robert McCormick and William H. Heyliger (two "men of color"), focused on sugar production, and employed approximately one hundred laborers, including an increasing number of poor Barbadian immigrants. Harrison's parents were plantation workers, his mother was an immigrant and his father and at least two of his grandmothers formerly enslaved. He later wrote that "contact with the stern realities of poverty . . . kept my heart open to the call of those who are down and has kept me from giving myself such airs as might make a chasm between myself and my people."

The fact that the owners of Estate Concordia and of some other Crucian plantations were "men of color" reflects the fact that the color line was drawn differently in St. Croix than in the United States. In St. Croix, class differentiation among those of African descent proceeded along lines more typical of capitalist society; Black people were limited far less by racial proscription; and formal "race discriminating rules of law did not exist." In the United States, African Americans were regularly denied "the normal social distinctions characteristic of class systems," and white supremacy was more virulent and powerfully organized. The existence of legalized segregation and lynching terror were two of many major contrasts with St. Croix.

Existing accounts indicate that Hubert was an eager and exceptional young student. This may be related, in part, to the fact that his mother and stepfather were from Barbados, an island noted throughout the Caribbean for its emphasis on education. The historian Winston James has explained that though Barbadians were "confined and politically inhibited at home," their children living elsewhere in the Caribbean tended to do well in school. He attributes this to several factors: since the eighteenth century "Barbadians have been among the most literate and educated black population in the world"; their emphasis on education was often passed on to their children; and, as immigrants elsewhere in the Caribbean, they often had the "ambition of the immigrant" to "perform well" in a new setting. It is quite possible that while living in Crucian society, Harrison's Bajan roots and multicultural experience contributed both to his eagerness and exceptional talent as a student and to his understanding of, and empathy with, different cultures and people.[61]

In Harrison's case, his eagerness as a student was reflected in several anecdotes recollected by his sister Mary. In one, a hurried attempt to rush back to class resulted in a fall that caused him to develop a speech impediment, a lisp. This lisp only disappeared with the help of Father Thomas M. O'Keefe of St. Benedict the Moor Roman Catholic Church in New York over a decade later. A second recollection, still vivid to Mary after sixty years, was of a precocious eight-year-old Hubert writing to her asking her to send a copy of *Tom Brown's School Days* and, later, a dictionary. *Tom Brown's School Days* was written by the English Christian Socialist, trade unionist, abolitionist, and cooperative society founder, Thomas Hughes. Young Squire Brown, according to a *New York Times* article, was "brave, helpful, truth-telling," "a gentleman and a Christian," and a "stout-hearted" defender "of the underdog."[62]

Harrison benefited, up to a point, from the Crucian education system. In St. Croix there was no formal segregation in the schools, and instruction was free, compulsory to age thirteen, and, since 1850, in English.[63] Most school records no longer exist, but the *Chicago Defender* reported that Hubert started private school at age six and in 1890 attended an Anglican School. His education then reportedly continued in a Danish government school, where he advanced very rapidly and where one of his schoolmates may have been David Hamilton Jackson, one year younger than Harrison. When Hubert was attending school, each of the six public country schools established under a May 7, 1884, ordinance had a teacher, a seamstress who taught the girls, and a student teacher for helping small children. The schools were each divided into three classes with the older boys and girls being taught separately. A tenth-grade education was not made available in St. Croix until 1933, so it is doubtful that Harrison went any higher than the equivalent of ninth grade on the island.[64]

Figure 1.9. David Hamilton Jackson (in the center on steps), undated. D. Hamilton Jackson (1884–1946), was likely Harrison's schoolmate and was a lifelong friend. On November 1, 1915, Jackson began publishing *The Herald*, a voice of the laboring and poor people of St. Croix, and in 1916 he led an islandwide "general strike," which led to St. Croix's first labor union and to the U.S. purchase of the Virgin Islands from Denmark in 1917. Jackson's efforts helped to establish November 1 as "Liberty Day," a national holiday in the Virgin Islands. *Source:* Courtesy of the St. Croix Landmarks Society.

Hubert also studied in St. Thomas, probably around 1892, when he was on that neighboring island. That was undoubtedly a very exciting year for him since thousands of Crucians journeyed to St. Thomas on March 11 in order to partake in the four-hundredth-anniversary celebrations of the Columbus voyage. All was not celebratory that year, however, for on September 1, 1892, in St. Thomas, a major, women-led labor protest headed by the coal worker and bamboula dancer "Queen Coziah," confronted armed soldiers at Market Square in Charlotte Amalie, the capital.[65]

D. (David) Hamilton Jackson was likely one of Harrison's schoolmates, and they would remain lifelong friends. Jackson became a school teacher, a crusading journalist, a delegate of working people to Copenhagen in 1915, the editor of the *Herald* (founded November 1, 1915), and the inspirational labor leader of the St. Croix Labor Union. Known as the "Black Moses" of St. Croix, he also led a January 1916 "general strike" of an estimated 6,000 workers who demanded higher wages, the right to free association, and better working conditions.[66] The strike, which was an important factor in the U.S. decision to finally purchase the islands,[67] also led to an increase in wages to twenty cents a day and, later, to thirty-five cents a day.[68]

Jackson's father, Wilford, was the schoolmaster of the government school at East Hill on the east end of St. Croix. After that school was closed in the 1890s, he taught in Christiansted. Harrison later described the senior Jackson as "the most prominent teacher, white or black, in the three [Danish West Indies] islands." He likely taught Harrison (perhaps together with his own son), and he was probably an important figure in Harrison's early intellectual growth.[69]

While still attending school, Harrison also continued his religious training. He was admitted to Holy Communion at St. John's Church in Christiansted on March 18, 1896. Though, as Neville Hall points out, religious education had been used in St. Croix as an instrument of social control, and though Harrison would soon criticize organized religion for encouraging servility and quiescence in the oppressed, the church did play an important part in his early education. His sister Mary remembered Harrison befriending a pastor on St. Croix, who granted him access to the institution's library to nurture his reading appetite. That person was possibly the Ceylon-born Anglican minister, Ralph De Mayne Dodsworth (who arrived in 1896), or W. Cloatson (the rector whose parish covered St. John's Church).[70]

The *Chicago Defender* article that described Harrison's family loss of its land and being forced into poverty offered additional insight on his life in these years. The *Defender* described how the fact that young Hubert was faced with poverty deepened his awareness of class and taught him a major lesson which stayed with him for the rest of his life. As Harrison explained:

> Up to that time we were well off, as West Indian families go, but from that time on we became and remained poor. I have often thought that this contact with the stern realities of poverty was good for me. It has kept my heart open to the call of those who are down and has kept me from giving myself such airs as might make a chasm between myself and my people.[71]

On January 30, 1899, at age fifteen, Hubert lost his mother, Cecilia Collins (née Haines), whom he apparently loved very much. Her death affected the fifteen-year-old deeply, and he noted the exact minute (7:57 A.M.) in the diary he started seven years later. In 1901, shortly after arriving in the United States, he penned a moving poem, "To My Mother":

> How melancholy, yet how sweet
> The thought that, after years
> Of separation we shall meet

Again, but not in tears!
For God shall wipe each teardimmed eye
And smooth all cares away
When we shall meet him in the sky
On the Resurrection Day.[72]

The poem's references to God take on added interest since Harrison's political-intellectual growth over the next decade would be influenced by his break from God and religion and his turn toward freethought and science.

Immediately after his mother's death, Harrison's sister Mary sent for him. Like a number of other West Indian women who were the first in their families to travel to the United States, she paved the way for a male relative. Mary was living in New York, and Harrison attempted to join her. According to Mary, though, his efforts met with delay because of immigration quotas. While it is quite possible that his trip was delayed, or that Harrison as a Black Crucian had encountered difficulties, his sister may have read a little back into history on this matter. Formal immigration quotas were not established by the United States until the 1920s, and they did not apply to all.[73]

It is likely that Harrison contemplated traveling abroad for some time. He had apparently developed excellent reading and writing skills on St. Croix, but additional educational opportunities were limited. He had lived among other immigrants and near Christiansted's waterfront, and he very likely knew people who had traveled abroad. He was also likely in contact with his sister Mary, who had been in New York since 1893.

What happened after Harrison's mother's death is questionable. During 1899, economic conditions on St. Croix were oppressive: sugar production and sales were extremely low, rainfall was down, and a major hurricane on August 7 and 8 devastated much of the island, destroying or forcing the closure of most of the smaller sugar and rum plantations. It is most likely that Harrison spent the next year and a half either working or traveling before coming to the United States in September 1900. He was likely among those he described as being "ambitious enough to be discontented with conditions at home and eager to improve their lot by seeking success in the land of Uncle Sam."[74]

Existing accounts suggest that Harrison secured employment on St. Croix around 1899. The *Chicago Defender* reported that he obtained a job in a Danish government school as a student teacher (D. Hamilton Jackson obtained similar work). Harrison wrote that he taught at the island's largest rural school at Friedensfeldt (probably at the government school, formerly the Moravian School, on Midland Road near Mon Bijou), and his sister Mary also maintained that he taught in St. Croix. If he did teach, he was probably a student teacher working with the smaller children. Such a job would have been a notable achievement,

Figure 1.10. View of Christiansted, c. 1850. This view looks down on historic Christiansted harbor, the island's largest port and center of commerce and the place from which Harrison left for America. *Source:* From the painting *A View from Bulows Minde,* by Frederik Von Scholten. Courtesy of the St. Croix Landmarks Society.

especially for one so young. There were only six public country schools on the island (in addition to bigger schools in Christiansted and Frederiksted), and "Negroes" were underrepresented in the teaching field, being 24 percent of the island's teachers though constituting 80 percent of the population. According to a boyhood associate, James Glasgow, Harrison also worked in Auguste Bough's grocery store (which also employed D. Hamilton Jackson around that time).[75]

It is possible that Harrison undertook a world tour as a cabin boy, a seaman, or a member of a student group as was reported by the *Chicago Defender,* the *Pittsburgh Courier,* the *Amsterdam News,* and J. A. Rogers. According to the *Defender,* on the prodding of a rich Danish druggist on St. Thomas, (Valdemar?) Riise, who had taken an interest in him, sixteen-year-old Hubert made his "Wanderjahre" ("grand tour") around the world with a yachting party of science students. The *Courier* reported that such a trip did occur and that Harrison "touched London, Paris, Berlin, Russia, Hongkong, Shanghai, Tokyo, Yokohama, Sierra Leone, Gold Coast, Liberia and Nigeria." The *Amsterdam News* referred to the trip as a significant turning point in his life, asserting that it "deepened his interest in mankind and developed in him a love for sociology, history, and anthropology."[76] Though teenagers as young as fourteen did serve as cabin boys, a search for documentation of the trip has not produced any corroborating facts.

While a "Wanderjahre" or some student travel may have occurred, there is also the possibility that this story is an embellishment of Harrison's early years.[77]

There is one item saved by Harrison that sheds some light on this period. It is an article identified as from the *Journal* in 1899. The article, "Peter Jackson Dying," is about the championship-caliber, St. Croix–born boxer known as "the Black Prince" and described by boxing historian Nat Fleisher as "the most feared fighter of his time." This is the only newspaper clipping from circa 1900 that remains in any of Harrison's scrapbooks and, since he was not a noted fight fan, the clipping suggests probable national or racial awareness in the teenage Harrison.[78]

Whether or not he made his "Wanderjahre," it appears that Hubert was in St. Croix in 1900 and, on September 15 of that year, aided by his sister Mary, who was working as a domestic, sailed for New York to join her. He later stated that he arrived in Manhattan on September 21 aboard the ship *Roraima*. The *Roraima* was a Canadian steamship under the British flag that sailed between the Caribbean Islands and the United States and primarily transported Caribbean immigrants and cargo. The *Roraima* was in New York harbor in September 1900 and on the twenty-fifth it departed for Bermuda. No confirming passenger lists or ship manifests for the *Roraima*, and no confirming immigration records for that period, have been located. The best available information concerning his travel to New York appears in the September 19, 1900, *Danish West-Indian*, published in Christiansted by Hermann Lawaetz. That newspaper indicates that "Hubert Harrison" left for New York on September 15, 1900, on the S.S. *Madiana*, traveling in steerage along with Annie Plaskett (probably the godmother of Cecilia's daughters Emily Frances and Cecilia Ann Esther) and Elizabeth James (probably the godmother to Cecilia's son Alexander Conton.) The *New York Times* indicates that the *Madiana* left St. Croix on September 15 and arrived with passengers in New York on September 21 at 10:45 A.M. Since the dates of the *Madiana* travel exactly match the dates Harrison subsequently offered, it is likely that it, not the *Roraima,* was the ship on which he traveled. In either case, such a trip entailed a certain degree of courage since it was hurricane season in the Caribbean, and, only a week before the indicated departure date, a devastating hurricane had hit Galveston, Texas, killing more than 6,000 people. It also took courage because few Black West Indians were coming to the United States at that time, and the immigration would, in many ways, be a lonely one. In 1900 only 703 Black West Indians (and only 714 Black people from throughout the world) immigrated to the United States, a number that represented only .1 percent of total U.S. immigration that year.[79]

Harrison's arrival coincided with the opening of school in New York. The seventeen-year-old arrived, unannounced, at his sister's apartment in San Juan

Hill (at that time a major New York "Negro District"), but she was not home. The determined Harrison, map in hand, wearing a blue suit and a Theodore Roosevelt badge and carrying a bag of fruit, had, upon his arrival in lower Manhattan, walked several miles to her apartment on W. Sixty-second St. He apparently came to the United States pro-Republican (the Republicans were the party of Abraham Lincoln, Frederick Douglass, Emancipation, and Reconstruction) and pro-Roosevelt, who had accepted the Republican nomination for vice president six days earlier. Roosevelt was extremely popular, and he had supported "equal and exact justice to all" as a member of the Civil Service Commission, had worked successfully to outlaw segregation in New York public schools, and had supported U.S. efforts to buy the Virgin Islands. Harrison's support for Roosevelt would prove relatively short-lived, however, and within a few years, particularly after the 1906 Brownsville, Texas, incident involving the dishonorable discharge of Black troops, Harrison would become a most bitter opponent of Roosevelt, of his presidential successor William Howard Taft, and of the Republican Party.[80]

In migrating from St. Croix, Harrison was part of a trend caused, in large part, by limited labor opportunities, which had led to a 30 percent decrease in the island's population over the previous sixty-five years. As the son of an immigrant, he was leaving his homeland, like his mother (and his stepfather and elder sister) before him. As a colonial subject he was making a move to a center of capitalism and to a country that, in general, offered greater political rights to its citizens. As a brilliant student he was motivated, as was fellow Virgin Island intellectual Edward Wilmot Blyden fifty years earlier, by a desire to pursue further educational opportunities in the United States.[81]

Despite his personal and familial experience with poverty, the intellectually oriented Harrison probably saw his own emigration from St. Croix as part of the student and labor exodus. In a 1923 article on "The Virgin Islands" he explained that during the "years [1869–1913] between [Andrew] Johnson and [Woodrow] Wilson the sugar-industry in the West Indies under the fierce competition of German and American sugar, had shrunk disastrously; and the black West Indian laborers had begun to pour into the cities of our North Atlantic states in numbers that steadily increased as the years rolled by." Later, in a 1927 article, he explained that in "the first period of West Indian immigration, . . . those who came here were mainly students and scholars seeking wider fields of usefulness," then, in the second period (especially after 1905), "came the slump in West Indian sugar, caused by German and American competition and the impoverished islands began to decant upon the mainland their working population, laborers, mechanics, [and] peasants," who were both "discontented" and "ambitious."[82]

It is clear that Harrison was driven by a desire to pursue further education. To do this he had little choice but to leave the island. The Virgin Island activist and legislator Valdemar Hill Sr. explains that at that time, "for the black Danish West Indian to get an adequate education and equal opportunities in life, he had to be fortunate enough to leave the Islands at an early age. Many natives were able to do this, and did not return to the Islands." So it was with Harrison.[83]

In a sense Harrison was like many other West Indians who came to the United States at that time: young, male, and literate; thwarted by limited educational, political, and occupational opportunities at home; in search of a better life; and with a desire for more education and a propensity for self-education. In a larger sense he was like many of the millions of immigrants coming to the United States at the turn of the century—men and women who left their homelands and ventured to a new land demonstrating a certain boldness of character that would mark so much of the immigrant contribution to U.S. history. Like virtually all of these immigrants, Harrison would face discrimination and class oppression. Like many of these immigrants, he would actively participate in movements that challenged such oppression and antiforeigner sentiment. Yet, Harrison, typical of most West Indians and other immigrants, was unfamiliar with the organized racial oppression of the United States, and he, like many other Black West Indians, would soon defiantly challenge assumptions of Black racial inferiority.[84]

Harrison stood out in other areas. He had exhibited an exceptional intellect; he was bold enough to come to the United States at age seventeen; he was sensitized to class oppression; and he was racially aware. Perhaps his friend, fellow West Indian J. A. Rogers, knew more deeply the significance of the talents that Harrison brought with him to the United States. After several decades of dealing with the racial, class, and political realities of the United States, Rogers sketched Harrison more somberly: "Destiny sent him into this world very poor. And if this were not enough, she gave him a critical mind, a candid tongue . . . a passion for knowledge; on top of all that a black skin, and sent him to America. Surely, a more formidable string of handicaps would be hard to conceive." Curiously, however, as Harrison implicitly recognized, these "handicaps" suited him well for the future roles he would play.[85]

2

Self-Education, Early Writings, and the Lyceums (1900–1907)

When Hubert Harrison arrived in lower Manhattan in September 1900, he was truly moving from the nineteenth century to the twentieth. The contrast between Concordia, a rural estate on the small agricultural island of St. Croix, and New York, the symbol of the new metropolis and one of the world's leading urban industrial centers, was dramatic. Harrison would never again return to St. Croix, and it was in this new and extraordinarily different setting that he would live the remainder of his life.

Now fully a young man, he was about five feet, seven inches in height, and his muscular body would fill out to a compact 170 pounds. He was, as later described by his friends J. A. Rogers, Claude McKay, and Richard B. Moore, of "dark hue" with "full lips," "ample nose," and a high forehead. His "head immediately attracted attention" since it "was unusually large," fully rounded, and gave "the appearance of bulging from within." Though Harrison was "very black," his forehead was of a lighter shade and appeared almost illuminated. His color took on importance during his life as he was victimized by (and, in turn, criticized) white-supremacist discrimination against "Negroes" and "within-race" color discrimination against dark-skinned people. The high forehead would become an occasional topic of conversation since contemporary pseudo-scientific racist theories held that large anterior regions of the brain were a measure of intelligence. Harrison did not believe such theories, and he and his friends occasionally joked about them.[1]

The racial climate Harrison encountered was inhospitable. In August 1900, a month before his stated arrival, the "fourth great race riot" in New York's history "burst in full fury." More than seventy Black people were injured by white mobs or police in the first four hours of rioting, and any Black person was

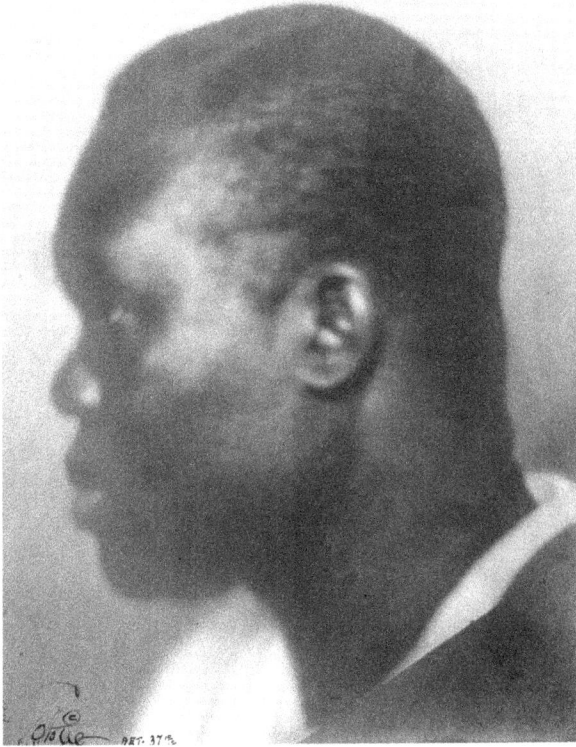

Figure 2.1. Hubert Harrison, February, 1921. This photograph, one of the oldest known Harrison portraits in the Hubert H. Harrison Papers, was displayed in Harrison family apartments for years after his death. *Source:* E. O. Hoppe, photographer. Courtesy of the Hubert H. Harrison Papers, Rare Book and Manuscript Library, Butler Library, Columbia University, New York.

subject to attack. According to the author, educator, and civil rights activist James Weldon Johnson, "Negroes were seized wherever they were found, and brutally beaten" as a white "mob of several thousand raged up and down Eighth Avenue and through the side streets from Twenty-seventh to Forty-second" Streets. The socially and politically oriented *Harper's Weekly* added that mobs of "whites" "attacked Negroes in the streets without much, if any, restraint from the police," who were themselves accused of extreme brutality. After the riot of August 12 through 16, *Harper's* declared that "at this time the opportunities of Negroes are less in New York than they have ever been, and there does not seem any likelihood that present conditions will be immediately changed."[2]

White supremacy was rampant throughout the city. Black people faced racial segregation in social activities and housing (which was overpriced and inferior).

Economic power was controlled by whites, and even educated Blacks found employment generally available only in the most menial occupations. Though there were 36,000 Black people in Manhattan, some 2 percent of the total population, they were excluded from political power. In politics, like everything else, segregation was the rule. There were no African American elected officials. Republicans were in power nationally, and federal appointments of African Americans were dispensed by white politicians through Black Republican Clubs. Locally, Tammany Democrats were in power, and Black Democrats had a newly established, segregated, citywide Democratic political organization, the United Colored Democracy. The UCD, like its Republican counterpart, took orders from white party leaders.[3]

Housing for Black people in Manhattan was confined to the meanest tenements, particularly in the run-down Sixty-second St. area where Harrison lived. This San Juan Hill district (between Sixtieth St. and Sixty-fourth St. and Amsterdam Ave. and the Hudson River) was part of the largest Black community in Manhattan, and it was noted for frequent race fights on the upgrade leading to Sixtieth Street. The area's name reportedly derived from its many racially charged street brawls and from the fact that many veterans of the all-Black Tenth Cavalry, which had fought valiantly at a similarly named battle site in the Spanish American War, lived in the area. The five blocks between Sixtieth and Sixty-fourth Streets and Amsterdam (Tenth) and West End (Eleventh) Avenues, in particular, was one of the densest Black concentrations in the city, housing more than 3,500 people. Apartment buildings there often had twenty to twenty-two family units per building, many with no access to outer air. In general the buildings were described as among the "worst examples of dilapidation, deprivation, and crime" in New York City. West Indians and other Black people rented these apartments at about fourteen dollars per week, three to six dollars more per week than what whites paid for similar housing.[4]

Employment opportunities for Black people in New York City were effectively limited to service occupations and to work as unskilled laborers. Over 60 percent of Black males were engaged in service jobs, and, as late as 1915, over 80 percent of Black women worked in domestic or personal service. Such jobs provided subsistence wages at best, and entire families only averaged between $12 and $15 per week in income. Seventy percent of single Black males earned under $6, and ninety percent of single Black females under $5 per week. In 1900 approximately 95 percent of the city's Black workers were not unionized.[5]

The employment opportunities for West Indian immigrants, in particular, were severely limited. Years later Harrison accurately depicted how, when this "working population" of "ambitious" "laborers, mechanics, and peasants" came to the United States they, at first, "furnished the elevator operators, bellboys and porters, maids and washerwomen of upper Manhattan almost exclusively, with

Figure 2.2. Interior court of an early-twentieth-century apartment house in the West Sixty-second St. area of Manhattan, photo taken April 1990. After his arrival in New York, Hubert and his sister Mary lived in this neighborhood, in which apartments, rented mostly to West Indians and Black Americans, were described as among the "worst" in New York City. *Source:* Courtesy of Jeffrey B. Perry.

a few tradesmen and skilled workers thrusting themselves forward into better positions and breaking the trail for the Negro-Americans to follow."[6]

Educational opportunities were similarly minimal. Only in 1884 and 1900 did New York City and state, respectively, outlaw segregated schools. New York was reportedly the last major city in the United States to open high schools, and it was not until 1905 that an evening high school was established in the "Negro district." Opportunities to enter a racially mixed high school were minimal, and by 1913 fewer than two hundred Black high school students attended racially mixed high schools.[7]

Despite these oppressive conditions, the orphaned Hubert was, if anything, a determined young man. His sister Mary recounted how, shortly after his arrival at her apartment, he visited a white school at Sixty-eighth St. and spoke with the principal for several hours. The principal was impressed and gave him a letter of introduction and advised him to go to high school. According to Mary, Harrison then enrolled in an almost exclusively white evening high school and attended classes at night while working as an elevator operator by day. Over the next few years he also picked up other jobs as a bellhop, a messenger, and, beginning around 1902, a stock clerk in a Japanese-fan company.[8]

Harrison excelled as a student. On April 5, 1903, the *World*, a major New York daily, ran an article headlined "Speaker's Medal to Negro Student: The Board of Education Finds a Genius in a West Indian Pupil." The "genius" was Harrison, who spoke on March 31 on "Verres Denounced." The talk was probably based on the denunciation of the Roman magistrate Gaius Verres for his misgovernment of Sicily by the famous first-century B.C. orator Cicero. For his efforts Harrison received the Board of Education's second-place, bronze prize for oratory at the New York Evening High School on West Forty-sixth St. All other finalists were second-year students, while Harrison was a first-year student who had only taken up oratory that semester. Harrison was described as "exceptionally thorough in Latin, English literature, and ancient history."[9]

These educational accomplishments were achieved despite his poverty and despite the fact that he was one of the few Black students in the school. The *World* noted that Harrison worked a job that took all day each weekday and two nights each week. His achievements were praised since he often had to miss night classes and had little time to study, other than late at night. Professor Henry Carr, who taught English literature at the New York Evening High School, said that in the final exams for a diploma, which were "rigid," Harrison "was passed perfect at 100 per cent, the only student in the class having that rating." Carr went on to say that Harrison was "the most remarkable Negro that I have ever met," and he predicted that "he will be heard from if learning has anything to do with success."[10]

During 1903 Harrison still lived with his sister Mary at 220 W. Sixty-second St. in the San Juan Hill area of Manhattan. Then, in the summer of 1904, he moved uptown to 63 W. Eighty-seventh St. Mary had gone away for two weeks, and when she returned she found that her brother, owing two weeks rent, had left quickly and moved uptown. This was the first of many incidents in which Harrison would either fail to meet his financial responsibilities or change his living quarters. Poor handling of money was, and remained, a serious Harrison fault, and several years later, on his twenty-fifth birthday he acknowledged in his diary that his "one great vice" was "the vice of borrowing money." It was, he wrote, "as a curse."[11]

While Harrison remained busy with self-study, it is not clear how much more he continued his formal education. He did attend DeWitt Clinton Evening High School (for Men) at Tenth Avenue and Fifty-ninth Street. Though school records on Harrison no longer exist, one account from the *New York News* held that he completed his high school education at Clinton at night, "at a time when it was a curiosity to find a colored boy at that institute of learning." (As late as 1913, only fifteen Black male students and no female students [who attended

Wadleigh] were registered at Clinton.) The paper went on to say that Harrison won interscholastic prizes for excellence in Latin and history in 1906 and that Dr. Joseph Thorne of the New York Board of Education, who presented him an award, declared that, "this young man has been a revelation to me in respect to the capabilities of his race, and I expect to hear from him in the future."[12]

On June 7, 1908, Harrison's diary entry revealed that he was again studying Latin and planned "to keep it up till September (together with my French) for the Regents" exam—the precollege competitive exam given throughout New York State. As late as November of that year he still discussed college with his friends. In later years, in order to secure work as a traveling lecturer, as a teacher at the Cosmopolitan College of Chiropractic, as a lecturer for the New York City Board of Education, and as a columnist for the *Boston Chronicle*, he would claim that he spent the years from 1907 to 1909 studying in Germany and Denmark and earned a doctor of science degree in Copenhagen. This was not true, and it likely reflected more economic necessity than ego pretension on his part since he was openly critical of those who put on false academic airs.[13]

At various times Harrison expressed a desire to go to college, but he never did. The fact that he never attended college is of interest, particularly since he was so intellectually oriented, since he was personally resourceful, and since other Caribbean immigrants of his generation did pursue higher education. While no instances have been found where he specifically addresses this matter, his friend J. A. Rogers said that he was "unable financially to enter college." Money was certainly an important factor—Harrison had to support himself; he was unemployed for "a long time"; he soon had responsibility for a growing family; he rarely was remunerated fairly; and he never handled money well. It was not, however, the only factor. Of great importance is the fact that Harrison was a true autodidact—self-motivated and purposefully self-directed in his study, inspired by other autodidacts, and free to roam. As he explained in his diary, "[I] range wherever I please." He also, over time, developed criticisms of what was being taught in most colleges and of the failure of many college-"educated" leaders "to come down from their Sinais and give it [real knowledge] to the common people." In addition, and of great significance, he viewed his developing political activism and educational work as important and personally fulfilling. While a college education might have helped him financially and brought a certain type of discipline and attention to his work, such an education would have had its costs. It is likely that Harrison (as Rogers suggests) saw the financial burden of college (both in costs and in wages lost) as impractical and that given his ongoing intellectual, political, and educational work, college was not the choice he chose to make.[14]

It is clear that the search for knowledge increasingly consumed young Hubert, and his early study habits demonstrate a purposeful organization. He was an omnivorous reader of newspapers and books, and years later it was reported, perhaps with some exaggeration, that he frequently finished as many as six books a day by staying up all night reading. Ernestine Rose, the community-oriented librarian and promoter of Black studies at the 135th St. Public Library, later told the Virgin Island–born Harlem activist and socialist Ivan Lorand that there was no one who borrowed more books from the library than Harrison. The journalist Oscar Benson described him as "bookish, but not of the sort classed as a bookworm." He read "assiduously," and "when he grabbed a book he knew just what parts to digest, what passages to mark, what dogma to criticize and whether any book was worth a second reading." Harrison's friend Hodge Kirnon, explained that he "took pains with whatever he planned to do in his educational efforts to an extraordinary degree; yet he would often times say that he memorized assimilated and transposed his wide range of reading upon technical subjects into their simplest and most understandable forms with but little or no effort." Kirnon added that Harrison

> spent a great deal of his time in reading a great number and variety of books, but he was able to preserve his intellectual individuality and hold his critical ability intact. He was always the master, never the pedant. He always found time to do his own thinking. He carried many social and philosophical problems in his mind for years, during which he would examine and probe them for hours; then he would shelve them for a short period, take them out again and again to be subjected to his rigid tests of critical inquiry, until he felt assured that he had reached some satisfactory solution. If none was forthcoming, he at least was made more aware of the difficulties and subtleties which surrounded such problems.[15]

Soon after his arrival in the United States, Harrison began to clip newspaper articles. These clippings were marked, commented on, and dated. Then, beginning in 1910, he pasted them in meticulously maintained scrapbooks, which were simply cardboard covered copies of magazines such as the *Literary Digest*, *Cosmopolitan*, and *Hearst's*. These scrapbooks served as a factual resource during the remainder of his life and reflect much about his thought process. Harrison was intellectually methodical, and his writings and thousands of clippings were classified according to a plan. When he began work on a subject he would pull his file or scrapbook and begin to subclassify according to need. His mind was not so much concerned with trivia or arbitrary relations as with understanding logical relations, and he constantly worked at internal system building and hypothesis testing.[16]

The forty scrapbooks that remain suggest his interests during these early years in New York. There are, for example, many numbered scrapbooks on

"The Negro-American." In addition, for the years 1900 through 1905, there are scrapbooks on: "The Negro in Africa," "Biographica," and a general "Clippings: Early 1901–1910" scrapbook with subheadings such as "History," "Biography," "Politics," "Literature," "Religion," and "The State of Society." In these scrapbooks are newspaper clippings on Negro affairs, myths about women, philosophy, Herbert Spencer, the rise of Japan as a world power, Africa, China, Russia, India, Panama, U.S. history, and the activities of the white-supremacist Mississippi congressman James K. Vardaman. Most of these general clippings for the first five years came from the "white" press: the *New York Times, Evening Post, Sun, Globe and Commercial Advertiser, Evening Journal, Press*, and *Literary Digest*. There are also several articles from New York's leading Black weekly, the *New York Age*. Such diverse sources give clear indication of Harrison's broad reading habits and his interest in current events.[17]

The most revealing document from Harrison's early years in New York is his diary. He first started a diary shortly after arriving in the United States but did not continue it, and that copy has not been located. He started a new diary on September 18, 1907, after securing work as a postal clerk. He would often make entries in it in the early-morning hours after working a late-night shift and returning to his apartment to read and write. When Harrison restarted his diary at age twenty-four he wrote down his thoughts on why he made that decision:

> It must surely be instructive to look back after long years on one's past thoughts and deeds and form new estimates of ourselves and others. Seen from another perspective large things grow small, small ones large and the lives of relative importance are bound to change position. At any rate it must be instructive to compare the impression of the moment, laden as it may be with the bias of feeling and clouded by partisan or personal prejudice, with the more broad and impartial review which distance in time or space makes possible.
>
> This may serve me in some sort as a history of myself twisted of two threads—what I do, and what I think. I hope I shall not make any conscious effort to impress upon it a character of any sort. So far as life is concerned as it comes so must it be set down. And if I omit any one phase of my life's experience I do so for judicial reasons and not for the sake of seeming better in my own eyes when memory has ceased to testify.[18]

While Harrison wrote his diary first for himself, there is no doubt from its content and occasional marginal comments that it was also written for those who would come after him—an indication that even as a young man he both had a strong sense of self-worth and was aware of the importance of the work he undertook.[19]

Harrison's first great intellectual transformation occurred around 1901, when he broke from his previously held religious views. He had been reared as a Christian in the Protestant Episcopal faith. His diary of May 20, 1908, describes in great detail the tremendous intellectual turmoil he underwent circa 1901 as he "divorced" himself "from orthodox and institutional Christianity" and became an "Agnostic." This break "was not effected at once"; it came in stages. Harrison emphasized that this "divorce" from the church represented "neither a proof of depravity nor of indifference."[20]

In the course of his study he read Thomas Paine's *Age of Reason*, written in 1794 during the French Revolution. Paine believed in a personal god distinct from the universe and apart from its affairs, not the traditional God of Christian revelation. He also maintained that "the Bible and the Testament are impositions and forgeries" and organized religion was "set up to terrify and enslave mankind, and monopolize power and profit."[21]

The eighteen-year-old Hubert was deeply influenced by Paine and felt that if his own "untried faith had first encountered the purely intellectual *non possumus* [we cannot (know)] which deism presented it would have survived." The deism advocated by thinkers such as Jean Jacques Rousseau, (François-Marie Arouet) Voltaire, and (Constantin François de Chasseboeuf, comte de) Volney, was "intellectually barren" and a "sterile hybrid" and would not have posed a serious intellectual challenge to his religious views. But, Paine, whom Harrison described as "the least learned of the 18th century deistic writers," presented "rationalistic results which bore their own proof on their face." Paine's "*reductio ad absurdum*" (reduction to the absurd) arguments were, at the time, irresistible."[22]

In a lecture he delivered years later, Harrison explained that Paine "popularized the arguments against Christianity and brought them down to the level of democracy." He considered Paine's significance to be the "dual aspect of . . . —militant unbelief and democratic dissent," two characteristics that were "truly representative" of "the thought of our time." Interestingly, Harrison would encourage "militant unbelief" and "democratic dissent" for the remainder of his life.[23]

The actual process of breaking with religion brought with it emotional pain, and Harrison used this as a spur to system building. His diary entry of May 20, 1908, details this break:

> I was not one of those who did not care: I suffered. Oh, how my poor wounded soul cried out in agony! I saw the whole fabric of thought and feeling crumbling at its very foundations, and in those first fearful weeks of stern reaction I could not console myself as so many have done with the husks of a superior

braggadocio. [So] I began with feverish anxiety to pick from the ruins those pieces that would serve for the building of another fabric. What *had* gone was the authenticity of the Bible, that which I had been taught was the word of God. For my God was the Bible God, the Jahveh of Hebrew tradition plus the tribune God fused from four centuries of Persian, Babylonian and Hindu teaching and the Alexandrine cobwebs of Porphyry, Plotinus and the Neo-Platonists. So when my Bible went my God went also. But I had to get one to worship, and I proceeded to build me a God of what was left. Do you remember [Alexander] Pope[']s *Universal Prayer*?

> "Father of all, in every age
> In every clime adored,
> By saint, by savage & by sage
> Jehovah, Jove, or Lord."

It was what I came to.[24]

Then, as he gathered himself together, he also developed a new philosophy of life. He wrote: "Time, the great healer, closed the wound and I began again to live—internally. But I now had a new belief—Agnosticism. I said belief: what I did mean was philosophy-of life, point-of-observation, attitude-toward-things. You *must* have one you know, or you will cease to live."[25]

In developing his philosophy of life, Harrison's first "great stumbling block" was "the personality of Jesus." For a long time the power of Jesus' personality "haunted" him. He did not consider Jesus a "pious fraud" as had the French historian and philosopher Volney. Harrison "lived in the 20th century when comparative mythology had more rational explanations to offer." In the end, however, the stumbling block of Jesus went also.[26] He explained:

> Now I am an Agnostic; not a dogmatic *dis*believer nor a bumptious and narrow infidel. I am not at all of Col. [Robert] Ingersoll's school and it gives me the keenest pleasure to engage in dialectic with the vulgarian infidels who assume the name of Agnostic without knowing what it means. If I am to explain myself by another I would say that I am (in my mental attitude) such an Agnostic as [Thomas] Huxley was and my principles are the same.[27]

Harrison was influenced by the scientific approach of the largely self-educated British biologist Huxley and, over the years, would include works by him on his recommended reading lists. Huxley, a leading exponent of evolutionary theory and defender of Charles Darwin, coined the word and popularized the concept of being "agnostic." "Agnosticism," he said, was "not a creed but a method," the essence of which was "the fundamental axiom of modern science"; "in matters of intellect," you "follow your reason as far as it will take you without regard to any other consideration" and "do not pretend that conclusions are certain which are not demonstrated or demonstrable." Like Huxley, Harrison "refuse[d] to put faith in that which does not rest on sufficient evidence." He chose instead to "look the universe in the face," to believe in "the sanctity of human nature," and to develop "a deep sense of . . . responsibility" for his actions. In his diary Harrison concluded that he would never "be anything but an honest Agnostic" because, as he wrote, "I prefer . . . to go to the grave with my eyes open."[28]

Harrison went through much of this intellectual struggle in "inner loneliness." In his diary he commented that since his boyhood he had turned to "Sorrow" as his heritage, though he knew not why. In one of his more personally revealing passages he wrote:

> The infinite sorrow in the face of the Christ-man, deeper than unfathomable seas, the face of [Thomas] Carlyle, ridged with the furrows of travail and turmoil; the fire-chastened face of Dante [Alighieri] that bearer of an immortal grief to the regions of underlying woe—these have always had a strange attraction for me. The things that sadden are more to me than the things that gladden.[29]

As he pondered his loneliness and his understanding of life, he concluded that God was "Unknown and Unknowable" and humanity was "more than life." With such understanding he placed the burden of human actions squarely on human shoulders: "For every man who *does* is God and in his work he lives, as God, forever." To those, "who think," he added, there was assured "an immortality more precious than that of their own individual existence."[30]

Harrison's grappling with a "philosophy-of-life" and his decision to put humanity at the center of his worldview took its toll. He did not have the rituals, institutions, or certainty of faith often provided by organized religion. The depths of his inner struggle may have left a mark on his later life. In 1903 he undertook research and started writing an essay on suicide, which he referred to as "the mightiest of my poor projections!"[31] He also started a suicide scrapbook. At several points later in life he would suffer from depression. Most revealingly, in 1908, pondering the "problem of existence," he wrote in his diary: "I wonder what the majority of the people find to live for. They eat and sleep and rise again to procure the wherewithal to eat and sleep—just like so many oxen. If I had no more than they have to live for I wouldn't hesitate two hours to put an end to my life. The soulless brutes!"[32]

Painful as it was, Harrison's break from religion made possible a healthy, critical approach to all other matters. The step had a certain logic, as had been noted in 1844 by a young Karl Marx, who, at that time, was similarly developing critical talents and a worldview. Marx pithily concluded that "criticism of religion is the premise of all criticism." So it was for Harrison.[33]

While he struggled inwardly, Harrison also began to extend his views outward to the larger world of letters and ideas. In the period from 1903 through 1910 he had twelve letters to the editor published in the *New York Times*, the influential newspaper of record. These wide-ranging letters give clear evidence of his developing race and class consciousness, socialist and freethought beliefs, and familiarity with current events, history, politics, literature, science, and evolutionary theory. They also reflect his beliefs that the intellectual arena was the one area of life where white supremacy would not totally proscribe his activities or deny his self-worth, that it was an area in which he could challenge notions of Black inferiority and white supremacy, and that "when the Negro enters fully into the intellectual life of the white American the customary barriers based on the assumption of his inferiority tend to break down."[34]

Not surprisingly, the first of these letters, published in the *Times* of June 28, 1903, when he was only twenty years old, took up lynching—the horror, unknown in St. Croix, that so marked the virulent white-supremacist nature of racial oppression in the U.S. The *Times* reported that from January 1 to June 22, 1903, eighteen of twenty lynching victims in the county were "negroes." It was the June 22 lynching of the African American laborer George White and a letter writer's white-supremacist support of the action that prompted Harrison to action.[35]

On June 15, Wilmington, Delaware, authorities apprehended White for the assault and rape of Helen Bishop, a seventeen-year-old white woman, who died the following day. Lynching hysteria grew among whites, and on June 21, as reported on the front page of the *Times*, armed mobs twice gathered outside the state workhouse where White was being held awaiting trial. That evening, Reverend Robert Ellwood of the Wilmington Olivet Presbyterian Church, delivered a sensationalized sermon arousing whites to seize the prisoner. The following evening a mob of over two thousand seized him in a carefully planned operation that faced virtually no resistance from the authorities. With the crowd shouting loudly, White was then tied to a stake, burned, and shot by several men as he begged for his life.[36]

In "A Negro on Lynching," written on June 24, Harrison responded to a letter to the *Times* by "S.H.B." that gave him "quite a shock" as it argued "that the tardiness of the legal and judicial machinery was a sufficient justification" for lynching. "Shock" was an understandable response both on human grounds and because public support for such behavior was far different than anything

Figure 2.3. The lynching of four unidentified African Americans, c. 1900, location unknown. In 1900, the year of Harrison's stated arrival in America, at least 107 African Americans were lynched nationwide, including, it is believed, these four unidentified victims. Lynching, which so marked the virulent white-supremacist nature of racial oppression in the United States, was a horror unknown in St. Croix, and it truly "shocked" Harrison, as it did many others. After the 1903 lynching of the African American laborer George White, Harrison wrote "A Negro on Lynching," the first of his many letters to the editor published in the *New York Times. Source:* Courtesy of Allen/Littlefield Collection.

he knew in St. Croix. Harrison then challenged S.H.B.'s "fallacious reasoning," which he said would result in the overthrow of all government, in "anarchy." He emphasized that the law assumes innocence until guilt is proven and noted that a "heavy part of the burden of responsibility" fell on the minister of God, Ellwood, whom he described as "one of those giddy enthusiasts . . . filled with the notion that they are God's specially chosen representatives." He also challenged descriptions of the victim as a "black wild beast" and "brute" and pointed out that contemporary biologists and ethnologists agreed that "the Negro . . . is a man—member of the genus homo." Harrison made it a point to call readers' attention to the list of lynchings in the *Times*, and he expressed doubt as to "whether Russia, with her Jew-baiting, can surpass this country in cold-blooded cruelty and barbarous brutality." He then closed by explaining—"this is the opinion of a Negro who feels the injustice and veiled oppression under which his race struggles in this 'home of the brave and the free.'"[37]

While the twenty-year-old Harrison's first published letter in the *Times* displayed his opposition to lynching and racial oppression, his next letter indicated his support for labor, free speech, and what he at the time referred to as "socialism." (A decade later Harrison explained that when he first read Single Tax literature he thought it was socialist.) The matter concerned the English labor agitator, organizer, and self-described "philosophic anarchist" John Turner, who, on October 23, 1903, was arrested in New York and imprisoned on Ellis Island in preparation for deportation. The action was taken under provisions of the Immigration Act of March 3, 1903 (32 Statutes-at-Large 1213), which provided for the exclusion of "anarchists, or persons who believe in, or advocate, the overthrow by force or violence of the government of the United States, or of all government, or of all forms of law, or the assassination of public officials." While Turner did not believe in or advocate the use of force or violence, he also did not believe in organized government, and he was being prosecuted and deported for what he did not believe in.[38]

Turner was defended on freethought and free speech grounds by *The Truth Seeker* (a freethought publication), the Manhattan Liberal Club, and the Free Speech League (a predecessor of the American Civil Liberties Union), and these groups organized a December 3 meeting at Cooper Union in New York. Former Democratic congressman John DeWitt Warner and the Single Taxers Ernest H. Crosby (president of the Anti-Imperialist League of New York) and Robert Baker (congressman and founder of the Citizen's Union) spoke. Letters of support were read from William Lloyd Garrison Jr., the literary editor of *The Nation* magazine and son of the famed abolitionist, and Edward M. Shepard, the 1901 Democratic mayoral candidate. Other supporters included Dr. Felix Adler, the rationalist founder of the Ethical Culture movement; Henry George Jr., son of the Single Tax movement founder; and Oswald Garrison Villard, the pacifist editor of *The Nation*.[39]

After a December 5 *Times* editorial defended the government's right to exclude Turner and criticized his supporters, Harrison entered the fray, explaining that "in this age of so-called free thought and free speech it is the duty of every man to aid the weaker side when that side seems . . . to be in the right." He realized that this was "a perilous undertaking" (in part, perhaps, because he was not a citizen), but he nevertheless declared, "I must follow where my convictions lead" and focus on "the importance of the principle involved." Acknowledging that Turner was detained legally under the 1903 law, Harrison countered: "I have yet to learn that legality and justice are interchangeable terms"; "slavery was once very legal . . . but we are by no means sure that it was ever just." He added that "to deport a man for exercising the right of free speech when the exercise of that right limits none of the natural rights of any one else, was unjust, tyrannical, and therefore undemocratic."[40]

Harrison went further in his letter and declared, "I am merely a Socialist, and I do not believe in Anarchy, philosophical or homicidal; yet I hold with the speakers at Cooper Union that if free speech is to be suppressed by unjust legalities, then we had better knock Liberty off her pedestal and erect a more typical symbol." He also took the *Times* to task for its zeal in attacking Turner, which led it to make "very indiscreet statements," such as, "there is no such thing as government based on force in this country." Surely, countered Harrison, "the protection of property, . . . the maintenance of the Monroe Doctrine, and a strenuous foreign policy" were examples to the contrary. He challenged the *Times* "to convince any intelligent person that the element of force is not a prerequisite of every present system of government." He then concluded, "I believe, as many do, that force is the necessary basis of government. The philosophical Anarchist believes otherwise, and it is for this belief that the dictators of the Republic would deport Mr. Turner after the farce of 'a trial without witness and without counsel.' And this is the sort of liberty we boast! Why, they do these things better in Russia."[41]

After his concluding references to czarist Russia in his first two letters to the *Times*, Harrison addressed "The Russian Menace" directly in a letter published on January 4, 1904. He claimed that his letter was prompted by the imminence of a serious war between Russia and Japan, which he viewed more broadly as "a world-drama, with England, Japan, China, and Russia as the principal actors." He began curiously, with a statement imbued with assumptions of racial superiority similar to those dominant in the United States and similar to those that he would regularly challenge. He wrote, "By superior force the nobler races have impressed their civilization . . . on the baser peoples, and so made for the elevation of humanity," although "sometimes the advance of civilization has been seriously checked by the force of barbaric hordes and the fate of humanity has trembled in the balance until the nobler races reasserted their superiority." Working from these general premises, he argued that "the Slavonic race, or, to be more exact, the Russian nation, is the most serious menace to advancing civilization." With its "political system based on the groveling subservience of the people, and the entrenched despotism of their rulers," it was attempting to extend dominion over eastern Asia toward the "final absorption of China" and the creation of "a Cossack world."[42]

Harrison's solution was to "look to the German races" for relief from this peril, and he urged that the "three great Germanic nations should exert their combined commercial and military powers to defeat the arms of Russia." In the meantime, the ominous storm clouds in the East portended "an approaching struggle, not merely between two nations, . . . but between two races; not merely between Russia on the one side and Japan supported by England on the other, but between the Slavonic and Germanic civilizations, to decide for the coming generations whether this shall be a world of bureaucratic despotism or of free institutions." Harrison hoped that "when the decisive struggle comes . . . God grant that the sceptre of civilization may remain in the hands of the Germanic race!"[43]

Aspects of this letter—a battle within the white race, white (Russia's) defeat in a war with nonwhite (Japan), and opposition to Russian despotism—foreshadow future Harrison writings. Other aspects do not fit in very well with his previously and subsequently expressed anti-white-supremacist and freethought-influenced views. Though Harrison was still developing his worldview, it appears that this letter includes some of his earliest use of irony. Harrison later described irony as "the weapon which enters the armor of complacence where other weapons far more intellectual are blunted," and he discussed the "need to put forth a book pretending to be written by a Caucasian which handles the racial situation either as [Jonathan] Swift did in his 'Modest Proposal' or more naively like the younger Henry Dodwell [Jr.]'s ironical essay, 'Christianity Not Founded on Argument.'" Swift's 1729 pamphlet, "A Modest Proposal: For Preventing the Children of Poor People in Ireland from Being a Burden to Their Parents or Country, and for Making Them Beneficial to the Publick," is one of the great ironic works in English literature. Written in the first person and with a self-righteous moral stance, the author proposes solving Irish problems by fattening Irish children and serving them as food (he even suggests cooking recipes). This approach, Swift argued, would address such matters as overpopulation, starvation, poverty, unemployment, and childrearing expenses and would also improve morality by leading to better treatment of wives and remaining children among the Irish. In this case, the freethought-influenced and anti-white-supremacist Harrison, writing in the first person, invokes God's goodwill and posits a superiority of the Germanic race in order to argue for struggle within the white race and for the defeat of despotic white Russia by non-white Japan.[44]

Harrison continued his social commentary in the *Times* with a February 4, 1904, response to comments from Mississippi's newly installed white-supremacist governor, James K. Vardaman, who had proclaimed "that the Negro as a race is 'deteriorating morally every day'"; that "['Negroes'] are more criminal as freemen than as slaves"; and that "['Negroes'] who can read and write are more criminal than the illiterate." Harrison considered this "the same old Southern superstition that if the Negro is educated he will become more wicked than he would be if steeped in ignorance." He explained that Southerners were "very rash and illogical" regarding the "Negro question" and during the Civil War they maintained "that the Negro would not work without physical compulsion." Then, after the success of Tuskegee, Hampton, and other African American industrial schools, they declared, like Vardaman, "that education makes the Negro a criminal." The "fallacy" of this was "evident," he added, since by such reasoning, such prominent African Americans as W. E. B. Du Bois, Paul Laurence Dunbar,

Booker T. Washington, Kelly Miller, Charles W. Chesnutt, and John E. Bruce, as well as the "talented tenth," would "constitute a class of deep-dyed criminals."[45]

Harrison also challenged Vardaman's claim that "an unmentionable crime committed by a Negro" was the manifestation of "the Negroes' aspiration for social equality." That view, put forth in similar fashion by South Carolina senator Benjamin R. Tillman (whom Harrison described as "the mobocrat, chief of the blue-jean aristocracy of the South"), was, he wrote, "the crux of the matter!" It was this "fear of 'social equality,' . . . bugaboo which converts Southern cavaliers into fiendish, murder-mad lynchers." Harrison explained that "Negroes do not desire this 'social equality:' the intelligent, because they know that no government can legislate one man to the table of another; and the unintelligent because they cannot raise their thoughts so high." It was "only the pitchfork politicians of South Carolina, Mississippi, and such places" who would invent such an improbable tale, and "only their illiterate and gullible myrmidons" who would believe it. Harrison concluded by "point[ing] with pride to our property holdings and other real estate to the amount of tens of millions of dollars; to our black doctors, lawyers, inventors, artists, mathematicians, sociologists; and, last but not least, to our army of industrial laborers" to show that "no people struggling against such adverse circumstances have advanced so rapidly in such a short time."[46]

Harrison's next letter to the *Times* concerned racist stereotypes. During the summer of 1904 the Hell's Kitchen area of New York, which included the San Juan Hill area where Harrison had lived, suffered another "race riot" and several near riots. Harrison believed that the press was largely responsible for inflaming racial tensions, and, after one particularly offensive *Times* editorial, he boldly wrote a letter to the editor that appeared in the December 11 edition. The *Times* regularly reflected Southern sentiment on the race question, and the earlier editorial had stereotyped Black people as "chicken-stealers," claiming that "Africans of any age, sex, or previous condition of servitude, . . . [have an] affinity for chicken overriding all conditions of ownership and ethics, . . . attested in an unbroken line of violated hen roosts dating back quite authentically to Noah's ark, and . . . to . . . Ham." "Stealing," according to historian Rayford Logan, "was the [derogatory] characteristic most frequently attributed to Negroes."[47]

The twenty-one-year-old Harrison's response exhibited the reasoned and forceful historical knowledge and race pride that so marked his efforts for the remainder of his life. It also exhibited a familiarity with evolutionary thought and a critical attitude toward the use of religion and religious myth to justify specious, pseudoscientific arguments.

His letter explained, "I, sir, am a Negro, and, strange as it may appear, I am proud of it. In the name of my race I resent the indignity which your editorial has put upon us." Harrison was using "Negro," as he would throughout the remainder of his life, as a term of racial pride. He challenged the assumption "that Africans (Negroes) . . . had been wont to steal chickens since the days of Ham and Noah's ark" and added, citing Thomas Huxley, that the ark story was "an impossible myth." Using his knowledge of biblical history Harrison stated that any man of ordinary intelligence could prove from the Christian Bible "that Ham (if there ever was a Noah) was not a Negro at all." Having narrowed the chicken-stealing period, he then pointed out that under the tribal governments of Africa, chicken culture was unknown and that in the West Indies, where fowls were plentiful, "chicken stealing [was] much less common than suicide is here." Thus, he reasoned, "it cannot be true that all Negroes are prone to steal fowls, nor that some Negroes have been wont to do so since the days of the wine-bibbing Noah." Harrison concluded that "as a Negro" he strongly objected to "the sweeping opinion of any newspaper that we are a race of thieves—either of fowls or of anything else."[48]

In yet another letter to the *Times*, several years later, Harrison countered the core white-supremacist argument that race prejudice is innate (and therefore little can be done about it) with the argument that race prejudice is a learned sentiment (and can, presumably, be unlearned or changed). In the July 20, 1907, *Times* he responded to a letter on "The Fate of the Negro" by "H.L.B.," whom, he said, started with "a prejudiced mind" and then "sought to enlist the support of science." H.L.B. relied on the science of philosophy professor William B. Smith of Tulane University in New Orleans (author of a recently published white-supremacist book *The Color Line: A Brief in Behalf of the Unborn*), who claimed that race prejudice was "a beneficent natural instinct—an instinct of self-preservation." Harrison challenged that assertion, citing the work of the late Harvard professor of paleontology, geology, and "cultural geography," Nathaniel Southgate Shaler, who, he said, argued that an "instinctive distrust and suspicion of the alien" had been "an instinct of self-preservation in the pre-human and early-human stages of . . . development." But, as contact continued, it "became less instinctive and less acute," similar to how an organ or instinct declines when the need no longer exists. Harrison added that H.L.B.'s "elimination of sentiment" placed him "far behind Du Bois" in understanding. Race prejudice, explained Harrison, was "a sentiment," as was "justice." Justice was "very different," however, and that sentiment played a role in the War of Independence, the War of Rebellion, English abolition, and the "granting of the franchise in the United States." Finally, Harrison challenged H.L.B.'s assertion that "race instinct" kept "the [white] race from fatal mongrelization" by pointing to "the increasing millions of mulattoes" in the nation (who were largely the result of white men taking liberties with Black women).[49]

These early social-commentary letters in the *Times* provided an outlet for Harrison's views, but this was clearly not enough for his searching intellect.

Harrison was determined to deepen his study and to share and develop his ideas through increased involvement in the Black community—to get, as he explained, "in full-touch with the *life* of my people." It was a course of action that provided an extraordinarily rich, varied, and vibrant intellectual life, and nowhere was this more the case than in the lyceums.[50]

––––––––––

In his first decade in New York, Harrison's community-based intellectual work began in the heart of Manhattan's Black community at the lyceums of two West Fifty-third Street churches, St. Benedict's and St. Mark's. The churches, which also had literary societies, were significant as central meeting places where West Indian immigrants and U.S.-born African Americans could meet and exchange ideas. The cooperative spirit of the lyceums was relatively unique in New York City, where tensions between these groups often ran high. The lyceums served other functions also. They were educational; they offered entertainment (to a community with limited access to the theater); they offered an element of "glamour" for a good orator; and they provided the talented an opportunity to develop friendships and skills and to receive constructive feedback and group recognition (opportunities not easily available in the larger society).[51]

St. Benedict the Moor Roman Catholic Church at 256 West Fifty-third Street (between Seventh and Eighth Avenues) was named after the famous sixteenth-century Black saint born in Sicily of African parents. The church served an interracial congregation, had a larger number of Black parishioners than any other Catholic Church in New York, and was especially concerned with the welfare of the African American community. Headed by Father Thomas M. O'Keefe and Father O'Mahoney, it held classes of instruction on Mondays and its lyceum on Wednesday nights. St. Benedict's also had a paper, the *Messenger*, which had a large circulation among the parishioners.[52]

Associated with St. Benedict's Lyceum were a number of very talented Black working-class intellectuals, including the journalist, customs messenger, and lay historian John E. Bruce; the clerk and bibliophile Arthur Schomburg; and a younger fellow West Indian, Samuel Duncan, who was a porter and a future

Figures 2.4–2.5. (opposite page) The Maryland-born, formerly enslaved journalist, customs messenger, and lay historian John E. Bruce (1856–1924) and the Puerto Rico–born, Afro-Caribbean bibliophile, lay historian, and clerk Arturo Alfonso Schomburg (1874–1938) were among a number of very talented Black working-class intellectuals associated, as was Harrsion, with St. Benedict's Lyceum, "the intellectual center of Negro New York." Years later Harrison referred to St. Benedict's as the "germ" of Black racial consciousness, and he recalled how the lyceums nurtured personal friendships and insistence on "the right to differ . . . , to criticize . . . and to dissent from . . . [that] which we believe to be wrong," and "to do this openly and publicly."

Figure 2.4. (top) John E. Bruce, c. 1911. *Source:* Courtesy of the Schomburg Center for Research in Black Culture, New York Public Library, Astor, Lenox, and Tilden Foundations.
Figure 2.5. (bottom) Arturo Alfonso Schomburg, c. 1904. *Source:* Courtesy of the Schomburg Center for Research in Black Culture, New York Public Library, Astor, Lenox, and Tilden Foundations.

president of the Universal Negro Improvement Association, editor of the Harlem newspaper the *Pilot-Gazette*, and chairperson of the Pioneer Development Corporation (which would seek to develop a "Colored Bank" in New York). At St. Benedict's, discussions ranged widely in politics, history, literature, and the arts, and the lyceum became known as "the intellectual center of the New York Negro." Years later Harrison referred to St. Benedict's as the "germ" of Black racial consciousness.[53]

Harrison's lyceum participation as listener, lecturer, and debater provided a true scholarly training for his developing intellect. It also exposed him to his first major organizational experience and to a group of people who would critically challenge "white" norms and standards. Harrison afterward recalled, with justifiable pride, what he termed "the days of our apprenticeship at old St. Benedict's [and] St. Mark's lyceum," where "the fiercest opposition in debate, could not take from the cordiality of personal friendship." From such training Harrison and others learned to "insist on the right to differ . . . , to criticise . . . and to dissent from . . . [that] which we believe to be wrong. And . . . [to] do this openly and publicly, without beating the devil around the stump."[54]

Of particular interest in Harrison's educational development in this period was the growth of his oratorical skills. He was able to overcome his lisp and become a formidable speaker. This was done, as his sister Mary recounted, through the painstaking efforts and assistance of Father O'Keefe of St. Benedict's.[55]

At St. Benedict's Harrison was exposed to independent and strong-minded intellectuals. Some years later Arthur Schomburg mentioned him and his St. Benedict's days in a letter to John E. Bruce, pointing out that "Harrison is clean cut in public life and can cut and nip things right and left. He has a mind of his own—He is a product of St. Benedicts Church" and is "determined in seeing things" in his "own way." Over time, Harrison's independent and direct manner would sometimes be misinterpreted, and individuals who became subjects of his forceful comments would frequently draw offense, though, as J. A. Rogers later explained, "no personal malice" was intended.[56]

Some of Harrison's earliest public speaking in this period probably grew out of his work with St. Benedict's Lyceum. On Wednesday, April 19, 1905, he delivered a speech after the meeting of the Manhattan Council, Catholic Benevolent Legion, on Columbus Avenue. His talk reviewed the work of Paul Laurence Dunbar, America's leading Black poet. Harrison contended that "poetry as an art ranks second only to music, and that men are decidedly deficient in culture if unable to appreciate either." The *Catholic News* reported that the audience commended him for his "grace," "charm," and "admirable discourse." Harrison's lecture was so well received that a second one was scheduled for St. Ignatius Council No. 151 of the Catholic Benevolent Legion on June 12. He was now described as "the well-known (colored) orator," and his next scheduled lecture, on "Dunbar as Poet and Author," was predicted to be "an intellectual treat." Such public work may have had wider implications, since shortly afterward St. Benedict's Father O'Keefe was nominated (and later nationally selected) to lead a proposed Catholic "Bureau of negro missions" to develop work in the Black community.[57]

The second lyceum that Harrison frequented was that of St. Mark's Methodist Episcopal Church at 316 West Fifty-third Street off Eighth Avenue. St. Mark's was the largest African Methodist Episcopal church in Manhattan and was led by the activist minister Rev. William Henry Brooks, considered among the "most influential" and "ablest" Black ministers in New York. Brooks attracted considerable attention after the west side of Manhattan suffered two race riots on July 9 and 12, 1905, and he delivered an August 6 sermon on "Race Riots" before an overflow crowd at St. Mark's.[58]

St. Mark's Lyceum began in 1883 and was held on Thursday evenings and Sunday afternoons from September through June or July. Lyceum participants over the years included the journalists John E. Bruce, Cleveland G. Allen, and John E. Robinson; the community activists Arthur W. Handy, W. T. R. Richardson, and Irene L. Moorman; the Columbia University student activist John Dotha Jones; bibliophile and bookseller George Young; the educator Dr. E. O. Roberts; the actor, elocutionist, and postal worker Charles Burroughs; and the White Rose Home superintendent Mrs. Frances Reynolds Keyser. The lyceum had special events such as "Newspaper Night," "Women's Night," and "Educational Day," and it held discussions on wide-ranging subjects including Dunbar, John Brown, Abraham Lincoln, women's suffrage, "Race Loyalty," and "Modern Science." Featured speakers over the years included Pixley Ka Isaka Seme (a future founder and president of the African National Congress of South Africa); Addie W. Hunton, a national organizer of Women's Clubs; William English Walling and Mary White Ovington of the Socialist Party; Rev. Adam Clayton Powell of Abyssinian Baptist Church; Ferdinand Q. Morton of the United Colored Democracy; and Kelly Miller, a sociology professor at Howard University.[59]

Around 1906 Harrison edited the *St. Mark's Mirror*, the lyceum's monthly paper. The *Mirror*, which focused on lyceum developments, began around September 1905 under editors Luther H. Smith and E. B. Wright. In 1907 John E. Robinson, who later became managing editor of the *Amsterdam News*, assumed the editorship. Though at various times the lyceum held programs on the *Mirror*, no extant copies have been located.[60]

On Wednesday, February 14, 1906, St. Mark's held a tribute to Paul Laurence Dunbar, who had died on February 9. Invited to the event was William Dean Howells, the dean of American letters, whose 1896 review of Dunbar's *Majors and Minors* in *Harper's* had been a significant contributing factor in bringing the twenty-four-year-old Dunbar's poetry to national critical acclaim and a wider audience. Though unable to attend, Howells did write to the editor of *The Union of St. Mark's Lyceum*, apologizing for missing the tribute. In the letter, which was received and kept by Harrison (who was apparently the editor), Howells added that Dunbar "will not be forgotten, in any progress his race is destined to make." Following the February activity, St. Mark's held a March 1 Dunbar memorial service at which Harrison, Rev. Brooks, Rev. Charles S. Morris of Abyssinian Baptist Church, Lewis H. Latimer (the poet and inventor), Dora Cole (the future actress and director), and the lyceum president John E. Robinson spoke.[61]

Harrison's interest in Dunbar would continue over the years. In October 1907 he purchased a copy of Dunbar's first novel, *The Uncalled* (1898), and confided in his diary that he didn't think much of it—he described it as "crude and immature," though "marred in many places by rhetoric and fine writing." Nevertheless, wrote Harrison, "it gets the heart," and the three principal characters "really live and are not mere caricatures." He considered the sermon delivered by the protagonist, the minister Frederick Brent, as "a splendid piece of work in form and spirit and a powerful antidote to much of our religious hypocrisy and uncharitableness." Overall, Harrison applauded "Good old Dunbar!" who, "with all his faults," still "struck a blow or two for the Right."[62]

While reading *The Uncalled* Harrison also read *The Life and Works of Paul Laurence Dunbar* by Lida Keck Wiggins, and on October 23, 1907, he began a long-projected essay on Dunbar, which was finished on March 13, 1908. He judged his essay "far behind [Thomas] Carlyle's 'Burns,'" despite the fact that he "had meant it as an American equivalent." Robert Burns, the former tenant farmer who became the Scottish national poet and voice of the common folk, was a personal favorite of Harrison. Carlyle's 1828 "Burns" essay had long been considered one of the finest pieces by the renowned Scottish critic, historian, and philosopher, and in it he describes how Burns "has insight into the divine significance of the lowly" and "illuminates his small corner of the world by teaching others of the dignity of the common life." To Carlyle, this quality made Burns "heroic." Harrison probably viewed both Burns and Dunbar in a like manner and considered work among "the lowly" to be "heroic"—much of his own life would be devoted to similar "heroic" work. Since he had done his "best" on his Dunbar piece, Harrison wrote in his diary, "the rest lies with God and the publishers." It appears that neither God nor the publishers did anything with it, however, and there is no indication that the article was ever published.[63]

After his Dunbar talk on March 1, 1906, Harrison continued to maintain an active presence at St. Mark's. He lectured three days later and then lectured again at the lyceum's Educational Day on April 1 along with the New York's first Black school principal and a future National Urban League founder and officer, Dr. William L. Bulkley. On April 12, he coordinated a debate on the protective tariff, and on September 13 and 20 he served as a lawyer along with the attorney and Democratic Party activist W. T. R. Richardson and the Colored Republican Club recording secretary and activist Arthur W. Handy at a mock trial on murder in the first degree.[64]

Over the next few years Harrison offered additional presentations at St. Mark's. In June 1908 he lectured on "Saint Francis of Assisi and the White Rose Home" and on "Negro Education and the Educated Negro." On November 19, 1908, he took the negative in a debate on whether voter qualifications should be regulated by the federal government and not by states. Cleveland G. Allen, John Dotha Jones, and George Young took the affirmative. Jones won first prize and Harrison second. After the debate Harrison noted that "many of the 'intellectuals'" were saying that he should have won first prize. He thought so, too, and he was "flattered by the conjoint voices of so many of 'the few.'" Nevertheless, he acknowledged that Jones, his friend and a future principal at Columbia Heights High School, Winston-Salem, North Carolina, "spoke very, very well altho neither his history nor his political science was very good." The following year, on December 16, 1909, Harrison spoke on John Brown before a large lyceum audience along with the Rev. Adam Clayton Powell Sr., the new minister of Abyssinian Baptist Church. Powell was already undertaking work that, over the next twenty-nine years, would develop Abyssinian into the largest Black congregation in the world and an important political base for New York City's first Black congressman, his son, the influential and long-serving Adam Clayton Powell Jr.[65]

St. Mark's was important in helping Harrison hone his critical skills. In his diary he described an October 17, 1907, St. Mark's forum at which "Professor" Allen W. Whaley, one of the better-known Black lecturers in the country, spoke on "The Negro in English Literature." Harrison described Whaley (an African Methodist Episcopal minister from Chelsea, Massachusetts, with whom he would later work in the Liberty Congress) as "both a faker and a great ignoramus" who "declared that Caesar's knees trembled before Candace, that Alexander burned the Alexandrian library to destroy the evidences of Ethiopian learning—and other things equally wonderful!" He was "an ass," and the Colored Republican Club activist and lyceum member Arthur Handy told him so during the discussion.[66]

Harrison observed that there had "never been such a terribly open arraignment and exposure of a faker in St. Marks's or any other lyceum." He was "glad," however, since it would "deter the others who may hear of it" and it would "simplify" his work, which he described as that "of getting at the poor ignorant masses and back of the ring of self-styled educated men." These so-called educated leaders he described as "stupid superficial fools who keep our people content with accepting magniloquent speech for actual knowledge, and are themselves too ignorant to be aware of their own ignorance."[67]

Figure 2.6. John Dotha Jones, c. 1924–1925. Philadelphia-born John Dotha Jones (1887–1927) was a Columbia University student active with St. Mark's Lyceum and the 135th St. Y, a future school principal, and a witness for Harrison's 1909 wedding. Harrison was eager to intellectually "drink delight of battle" with peers like Jones in the friendly give-and-take of lyceum debate. *Source:* Courtesy of Polly E. McLean.

St. Mark's also helped Harrison develop his political and organizational skills. On February 7, 1908, he attended the Lyceum's election night accompanied by "Mrs. Stewart" (probably Marie Jackson Stuart, a vocalist and long-time activist at St. Mark's), whom he described as "a fine woman to talk to, a fine chatter and a genial soul." Attendance was particularly slim, and in the election that followed, "Mrs. Stewart" won as recording secretary while Harrison lost the critic's position to the social worker Edith Leonard.[68]

Harrison apparently learned a little from his loss, and ten months later, on December 10, 1908, he was elected lyceum "critic" when he defeated John Dotha Jones while George W. Allen, a future activist with the National Association for the Advancement of Colored People, won the lyceum presidency over George Young. Harrison was the only winning candidate on his side of the ticket in a contest that he judged "the roughest, fiercest, most corrupt election" that he had ever seen at St. Mark's. The *Age* reported that the election was "entirely unsatisfactory" to lyceum members. Two days after the election, Harrison and Arthur Handy decided "to take concerted action" to nullify the election. According to the *Age*, the petition that ensued, led by the "prominent" lyceum members Handy and Harrison, declared "that the Lyceum's constitution was violated" by the use of old mailing lists and by allowing those absent for over three months to vote. The petition, which was signed and circulated by members, declared that "a great many who voted who had no right to vote" and it created "considerable stir in the Lyceum and church circles."[69]

The political rough-and-tumble continued, and the following year's election created another uproar. The handling of that election prompted George Young, a ten-year member and former president of the St. Mark's Lyceum, to write a protest letter to the *Age* explaining that for many years the lyceum had been "the glory of St. Mark's Church and the pride of New York" but, "its privileges have been abused and its purpose miscarried." Young, whose parents had been enslaved, was a self-educated bibliophile and bookseller about forty years old who worked at various times as a Pullman porter and postal employee and was active with the Ethical Culture Society. By 1921, Young's Book Exchange on West 135th Street would contain what was described as "the largest collection of books (8,000–10,000) by and about the negro race" that was "open to the public." Young's voice carried considerable weight, and he described the election improprieties as "disgraceful," adding that "many of the old members hung their heads in shame and left the room." The lyceum election, he declared, "was never intended to be swayed by political influence or to have commercial value," and "the noble ideals once set for the young have been thrown to the winds." While the young people of St. Mark's had formerly controlled the itinerary, that was no longer the case, and they were noticeably absent. Marie Jackson Stuart also wrote to the *Age* and said she was in "perfect sympathy" with the "timely, outspoken protest" contained in Young's letter, adding that "everything pertaining to the election was in absolute disregard of the constitution." She emphasized that the protesters sought to have St. Mark's, "the great beacon light in the great city," returned to its former high standing.[70]

Women like Jackson who were in and around St. Mark's helped nurture Harrison's support for women's suffrage. On April 1, 1909, the Woman's Suffrage League sponsored a pro-suffrage lyceum activity. On April 8, Frances Reynolds Keyser, the first president of the National Association of Colored Women's Clubs Empire State Federation, read a paper in favor of women's suffrage, and Marie Jackson (Stuart?) gave an oration on "Negro Citizenship." Harrison also spoke on women's suffrage at a Literary League event on December 8, 1910, at the Abyssinian Baptist Church. Irene L. Moorman, organizer of the Political Equality

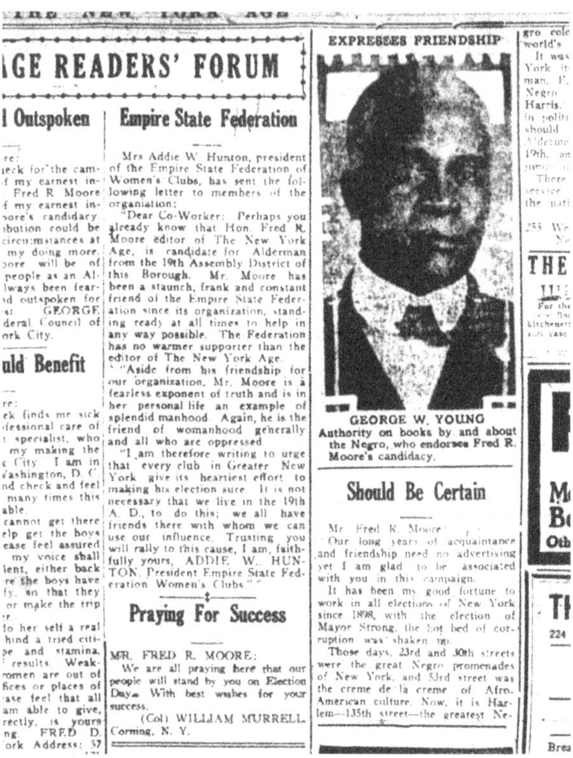

AGE READERS' FORUM

Empire State Federation

Mrs Addie W. Hunton, president of the Empire State Federation of Women's Clubs, has sent the following letter to members of the organiation:

"Dear Co-Worker: Perhaps you already know that Hon. Fred R. Moore editor of The New York Age, is candidate for Alderman from the 19th Assembly District of this Borough. Mr. Moore has been a staunch, frank and constant friend of the Empire State Federation since its organization, standing ready at all times to help in any way possible. The Federation has no warmer supporter than the editor of The New York Age.

"Aside from his friendship for our organization, Mr. Moore is a fearless exponent of truth and is in her personal life an example of splendid manhood. Again, he is the friend of womanhood generally and all who are oppressed.

"I am therefore writing to urge that every club in Greater New York give its heartiest effort to making his election sure. It is not necessary that we live in the 19th A. D., to do this; we all have friends there with whom we can use our influence. Trusting you will rally to this cause, I am, faithfully yours, ADDIE W. HUNTON, President Empire State Federation Women's Clubs."

Praying For Success

MR. FRED R. MOORE:

We are all praying here that our people will stand by you on Election Day. With best wishes for your success.

(Col) WILLIAM MURRELL.
Corning, N. Y.

EXPRESSES FRIENDSHIP

GEORGE W. YOUNG
Authority on books by and about the Negro, who endorses Fred R. Moore's candidacy.

Should Be Certain

Mr. Fred R. Moore:

Our long years of acquaintance and friendship need no advertising yet I am glad to be associated with you in this campaign.

It has been my good fortune to work in all elections of New York since 1898, with the election of Mayor Strong, the hot bed of corruption was shaken up.

Those days, 23rd and 30th streets were the great Negro promenades of New York, and 53rd street was the creme de la creme of Afro-American culture. Now, it is Harlem—135th street—the greatest Ne-

Figure 2.7. George Young, c. 1927. Virginia-born George Young (1870–1935), the son of formerly enslaved parents, was a self-educated bibliophile and bookseller who worked as a Pullman porter and postal employee and was active with Harrison at St. Mark's Lyceum. After Harrison's death, according to his daughter Aida, Young obtained a number of his books. Young later sold many books to the New York Public Library. *Source:* From the *New York Age*. Courtesy of Wilson Library, University of Minnesota, Minneapolis.

Association (and a future Harrison supporter and UNIA leader) presided, and Harriet May Mills, president of the Woman Suffrage League of New York State, spoke.[71]

When Harrison began work with the lyceums he was having great difficulty trying to make a living, and though he was continually involved in self-study and group activities, he looked to do more in the literary field. He had done some editorial work in 1904 as an associate editor for the *Unique Advertiser*, a pamphlet published "in the interests of the colored people" that was targeted at leading businessmen.[72]

But the lack of steady employment was a constant problem. In April 1906 John E. Bruce wrote back to him with regret to learn that he had "been out of employment so long." Bruce offered to help him with a typesetting job for eighteen dollars a week for a "white" newspaper in White Plains and to give him leeway in returning money for pamphlets that he had taken to sell on a commission basis of five cents per pamphlet. Soon thereafter Harrison did land a short-term editing job with New Rochelle's *Fair Play*, very possibly with Bruce's assistance.[73]

In his 1906 letter Bruce, one of the country's preeminent Black journalists, also mentioned having a quantity of poems by Black authors from 1900 to the present. He offered to collaborate with Harrison in a publishing venture and added, "I should be very glad to have the benefit of your wide learning and your advice in some matters which I am now thinking of putting in type to make some money. Perhaps we can combine, find a publisher and divide royalties." Apparently nothing came of this Bruce offer. A similar fate met a Harrison article written for the *New York Evening Post* in the summer of 1906 called "Santa Cruz—the Island of the Holy Cross." According to Harrison, "the Dane who was city editor returned it." Harrison didn't blame the "pore cuss," however, because the article "had told some unsavory truths about his people."[74]

Harrison's most important early literary pieces in his first decade in New York were two letters on literary criticism published on the front page of the *New York Times Saturday Review of Books* literary section. In the first letter, published on April 13, 1907, he explained that "I must demur to all sentimental considerations in the matter of literary criticism" as he excoriated the previous week's "critiques" as being "void of any sense." He then critically reviewed an article on progressive, intellectual women in ancient Greece and Rome by Hildegarde Hawthorne (granddaughter of Nathaniel Hawthorne), a piece on the English lyric poet and critic Algernon Charles Swinburne, a review of novelist Henry James's *American Scene*, and a sonnet to the American poet Edwin Markham. In the course of his review he judged the sonnet "a gem of pure ray" and compared it to a previous one by the Boston poet (and future recipient of the NAACP's Spingarn medal) William Stanley Braithwaite.[75]

In his letter Harrison judged that Hawthorne's piece threw no light on the work it reviewed and was "the merest buncombe," complete with a "schoolgirl's giggle" and "a boarding school rehash of two or three facts in Greek history." These comments provoked a series of responses in her defense, including one by Mary Hamlin Ashman, of Huntington, Long Island, who thought "it would be downright pusillanimous if some of us women did not take-up arms against Mr. Hubert Harrison for his altogether ungracious summary." Ashman argued that it was "the essence of femininity which Mr. Harrison does not understand, but which is defined by him only as the schoolgirl giggle." Then, in response to

Harrison's main criticism, she countered that a reviewer need not specifically describe the book being reviewed.[76]

Harrison responded to Ashman's letter with a second letter that appeared on April 27, his twenty-fourth birthday, and propounded his theory of literary criticism. The letter, according to *Times* reader "M.U.O." was "formidable" and led to a "flurry" of subsequent letters. Harrison described four different types of criticism ranging from simple impressionism to what he termed "creative criticism," which "creates new current of thought." Criticism, he explained, could be regarded as either science or art, but in either case "it has its laws and methods which must be followed if any good results are to be obtained." The first and lowest form of criticism was impressionism in which "the critic consults no general principle of the art, (or science,) but receives an impression." This subjective method was the "method of the man in the street," the admirer, the "essentially uncritical mind." Next was comparative criticism in which the critic compared two literary productions. Third was interpretive criticism, "in which the critic expounds the work of an author, gives that which is written between the lines, and helps the reader to understand more readily." Fourth and "highest of all" to Harrison was creative criticism, which had been defined by the English critic Matthew Arnold and "creates new currents of thought to act as points of departure." As an example of creative criticism he cited Thomas De Quincey's 1823 essay, "The Knocking at the Gate in 'Macbeth.'"[77]

With that prelude, Harrison observed that the *Times* often published criticisms of the first three types in reviews, letters, and notices. He asked, "Are we forbidden to judge them by the same standard which we elsewhere apply?" He didn't think so and claimed that "here, as elsewhere, charm of style is an inadequate substitute for criticism or reviewing."

He then described the characteristics of a competent book review. A good review needed to explain the author's purpose and judge whether it was attained. It also had to summarize the thesis or plot and explain "in what spirit the author's work is done—in short, it must tell what the book is." The purpose of such a review, he maintained, was to enable the casual reader to decide whether or not it is worthwhile to read the book.[78]

Harrison had challenged the analytical character, not the feminism of Ashman's letter. He concluded by bemoaning the fact that "in our day ignorance sits enthroned in high places." But, as he made clear, he would continue in the ranks of those who, "'stand aloof from all ideology and everything fanciful,' and dare to make known our belief that there is nothing essentially sacred or immune in feministic criticism." Over the years he would continue to apply similar standards to all works he reviewed in his style of "devastating candor" with "no personal malice."[79]

In 1907, after his letters on criticism were published, Harrison continued with literary commentary. In the *Times* Book Review Section of September 14, he responded to a *Times* editorial "On Writing English," a topic he considered especially timely since "in the whole range of our 'literature,' from Laura Jean Libby [a prolific author of dime novel romances] to Mr. Henry James," there was a "tendency to torture and mutilate the language." He urged restraint for writers and publishers but believed that financial considerations had greater weight than "benefit to literature" for the majority of publishers. A related problem was "the superficial character" of the "American 'literary' world," in which "the aim is not so much for value" as it is for "the extrinsic reward of cheap notoriety and the praise of those who are even less capable than the writers themselves." Harrison supported his position by arguing "that our non-literary writers . . . write better than our so-called literary people," and he cited positively William James, a psychologist; W. E. B. Du Bois, a sociologist; Christian Gauss, a literary critic; Josiah Royce, a philosopher; and Isaac Funk and Henry Charles Lea, historians. The explanation for this, he said, was that "history, sociology, psychology, and the other sciences cannot be mastered even 'for publication' without some intellectual ability—and 'literature' can."[80]

Harrison's interest in literary criticism continued to develop. In January 1908, while reading Oscar Wilde's *Intentions* and especially his "Critic as Artist," he judged that Wilde would have attained "an excellent reputation . . . as an interpretive and creative critic if he could only have taken himself seriously!" He considered "The Critic" to be a "masterly exposition of the critic's status" and contrasted it with "the hollow prose *and* cheap fleshiness and insincerity" in his "Pen, Pencil, and Poison" essay. In March, Harrison began an essay on the African American dialect poet James Edwin Campbell. After finishing the introduction and three and a half pages, he was proud of his effort, but, again, there is no indication that it was ever published.[81]

Harrison's efforts at making money from his writing were meeting with little success. Throughout the depression year of 1907 his economic difficulties continued, and they were vividly captured in December 1907 when he completed his twenty-three-page rewrite of his article on "Santa Cruz—the Island of the Holy Cross." Harrison wanted very much to sell it "to [a] newspaper or magazine!" In his diary he imploringly and rhetorically asked: "Who will give Xmas money? Who'll buy my wares?"[82] It was a question he could not answer. There appeared little economic future for a Black, night-school-educated literary critic and writer.

Poverty seemed to be an ever impinging constant, and Harrison faced serious economic difficulties throughout 1907 and into 1908. Nevertheless, even under such pressure, he was able to step back and comment philosophically about his condition. He recognized the powerful pressure poverty placed on people, yet he also realized that his own life would need to focus on much more than meeting the needs of daily existence. He elaborated in his March 7, 1908, diary entry:

> What a damned powerful modifier of a man's philosophy of life is poverty and the pressure of hunger! If ever I forget this as a starting-point for any scheme of things that I may construct I hope I'll go hungry for three days so that I remember it. It does seem strange that neither [Arthur] Schopenhauer nor even [Eduard von] Hartmann, the first great German pessimists, were ever under the pressure of it. I wonder just how much of it went to the making of [Friedrich] Nietzsche and Marc Stirner.
>
> The life of the philosopher and that of the fool are everywhere conditioned as Carlyle somewhere suggests by the same three factors: great need, great greed and little faculty. And the need is ever the most prominent. Thus spake Zarathustra.
>
> Will we ever arrive at any satisfactory solution of this problem of existence? I doubt it.
>
> I wonder what the majority of the people find to live for. They eat and sleep and rise again to procure the wherewithal to eat and sleep—just like so many oxen. If I had no more than they have to live for I wouldn't hesitate two hours to put an end to my life. The soulless brutes![83]

He may have been down economically, but Harrison was determined not to give up. The following month, on April 11, 1908, he finished an application letter to Henry M. Leipziger, supervisor of lectures of the New York City Board of Education. Though he would deliver one lecture for the board eight months later, it would take fifteen years and a different administrator before he secured regular board employment.[84]

Throughout his early years in New York, despite his financial difficulties, it was clear that money, or the lack of it, did not consume the autodidactic Harrison. His individual and community-based intellectual work did. He continued to read and write constantly; his letters to the *Times* had attracted considerable attention; he was doing some public speaking; and he was continuing to hone his skills in the lyceums. Somehow he would have to continue to develop and nurture these interests while tending to most basic matters of survival.

3

In Full-Touch with the
Life of My People
(1907–1909)

Harrison took a major step in addressing his financial difficulties on July 1, 1907, when, after having taken the Post Office Department entrance exam and passing with ease, he began his four-year postal career. He was a clerk, first grade, earning $600 per year for performing the job of separator. Simply securing postal employment was breaking difficult ground, and Harrison was one of only approximately 175 Black postal workers in all of New York City. His friend, John E. Bruce, a federal employee himself, knew the significance of the postal job and wrote to Harrison on October 16 congratulating him.[1]

Though postal employment was one of the choice jobs for African Americans in 1907 (its twelve-dollar-a-week salary was about twice that earned by 70 percent of Black men in the city), conditions in the Post Office were oppressive. Postal workers were subjected to President Roosevelt's "gag orders," which threatened dismissal for seeking legislative help or a raise. Twelve-hour workdays were common, as were workweeks of six or seven days. In addition noise, poor ventilation, dust, and abusive managers resulted in some 12 percent of the nation's postal clerks resigning in 1906 and 20 percent in 1907. The vacancies may have provided the opening for Harrison's employment, and the oppressive work conditions accelerated his development of a deeper class consciousness.[2]

While working long hours, Harrison continued his extensive reading, especially in the social sciences and humanities. Joel A. Rogers said that on his own he studied "all he could of sociology, science, psychology, literature, and the drama," and he was not consumed by his postal work. Rather, "the only outlet for his talent, ambition, sympathy, and deep sense of justice, seemed to lie in concentration on the problems affecting himself and his people."[3]

One important way in which Harrison began to address problems affecting "our people" was by convening a study circle with postal workers, which met at his apartment at 216 W. 134th Street. Included in the group were Percy Greene (a future teacher), Charles Burroughs (an actor and future theater director later active with the Krigwa Players), and two others—"Lee and Nelson." One of their projects was the formation of a committee "to reply to aspersions and misrepresentations of our people in the newspapers of New York City." Their meetings may have been held after late night shifts at work. Harrison noted in his diary how, after returning from work at 4:30 A.M. on September 23, he went out for a walk around the neighborhood and down to 123rd St. with Burroughs and Lee, who were "in hearty agreement with the plans for the Press Committee."[4]

The following month, in the wake of a major Cuban railroad strike, Harrison mailed a thirteen-page letter to a "Miss Serra" in Cuba detailing the Press Committee's genesis and asking her to join "the movement" as a Cuban representative and correspondent. He also mailed her the previous week's *Age*, New York's leading Black newspaper. Miss Serra may have been related to Rafael Serra y Montalvo, the Afro-Cuban activist and friend of Arthur Schomburg who had founded the social and political club Los Independientes in New York in 1888 and, in 1892 co-founded with Schomburg Las Dos Antillas organization, which worked for Cuban and Puerto Rican independence. Though the letter to Miss Serra has not been located, it may also have been related to the Independent Party of Color, which was founded in Cuba during 1907.[5]

The postal-worker study circle discussed race matters, books, and readings, including those related to a history project on the "Negro in America" with special emphasis on Reconstruction that Harrison was developing. His readings in this period reflect his interest in social change and included *The History of the Decline and Fall of the Roman Empire* by Edward Gibbon; *Twenty Years of Congress: From Lincoln to Garfield* by James G. Blaine (a key organizational leader of the Republican Party between Reconstruction and Populism and a well-known advocate of the separation of church and state); and *A Fool's Errand* (by the Radical Republican lawyer, judge, and novelist Albion Tourgée), which discussed "the *facts* of Reconstruction" and the early history of the Ku Klux Klan.[6]

Besides addressing societal problems, the study circle also brought Harrison intellectual and personal satisfaction. In his diary he described a conversation with a circle member who, he thought, had begun to admire his leadership. When he sensed that his friend's "heart had begun to overflow with a desire to help his people," Harrison "drove the nail hard home—and won him" to the Press Committee project. The friend even went further and "advocated a connection with the European and South American papers of importance, especially the anti-American ones." After that meeting Harrison commented in his diary, reflecting a bit of the egotism he acknowledged having, that "to lead men who are intensely individual is an exciting and interesting game (if skillfully played)!"[7]

It is not clear how long the postal study circle functioned, but Harrison also tried to start a literary club in early 1908 with Charles Burroughs and six or seven others. He felt the club would have "none of your airy, insubstantial, 'literary' chaff-producers," but would be "a genuine intellectual symposium." He wrote in his diary that he was eager to "drink delight of battle *with my peers*," to gather a group of equals, and to strengthen his mind through such contact. "For seven years" he had "longed to meet such men," and "except in the person of [John Dotha] Jones," the Columbia student active with St. Mark's (who would become the principal of a high school in North Carolina), he had "failed to find them till now."[8]

Harrison began to suffer eye problems while working long hours at the Post Office and staying up late to read and write. On November 25, 1907, he put his books down for a week because of eye pain that had started in February. He attributed his problems to "excessive reading by lamplight and the glare of the electric lights down at the Post Office," and he planned to go for an exam and glasses. He feared he had seriously hurt his eyes, and he was concerned because he had "much to do" over "the next twenty years" that would "require hard reading." A week later he still complained of the "very serious [eye] condition." Then, on December 8, he wrote: "I have been home ill; first with my eyes, then with a very bad cold, congestion of the lungs and the first, faint, discernible signs of lumbar pneumonia."[9]

The employment-aggravated eye problem (which did result in glasses) was one of several health problems Harrison would have over the years. He would also suffer from nerves and periodic depression, fight a continuous and not always successful struggle to stop smoking, and battle chronic appendicitis. In addition, according to J. A. Rogers, he suffered from vertigo.[10]

While working at the Post Office Harrison felt persecuted. On February 15, 1908, he went to see Charles W. Anderson, the collector of internal revenue for the Second District of New York, in order "to get his influence" in obtaining a transfer to nearby College Station in Harlem. The Ohio-born Anderson had been appointed to his post in 1905 by President Theodore Roosevelt, was a close associate of Booker T. Washington, and was the highest placed and most prominent Black Republican in New York. He assured Harrison "that he would do his best" and requested that he give him a letter on the matter. On February 17 Harrison finished writing the letter to Anderson and wrote a second one to Postmaster Edward Morgan in which he formally applied for the transfer. He thought the move would help to "put an end" to his "present persecution at the Post Office." (Whether they helped in this instance is not known, but both

Anderson and Morgan were later involved in Harrison's removal from the Post Office in 1911.)[11]

Harrison did not get the transfer, but over the next three years his postal record was exemplary and showed only one charge of lateness, for which no penalty was imposed. In July 1908 he received a salary increase to $800 per year and was promoted to clerk second grade; in 1909 he was promoted to the third rank at $900 per year; and in 1910 to clerk fourth grade at $1,000 per year.[12]

Though under pressure, Harrison did have the ability to put his personal persecution in a larger perspective. In 1911 he wrote a two-part exposé on the Post Office in which he described some of the more general pressures faced by clerks in the form of political tribute, patronage, discrimination, and antilabor practices. In particular, he described how political patronage worked. Employees were pressured to join political clubs, pay dues, and buy tickets for functions. Several times a year they would have to buy tickets that were sold by superintendents and their assistants against all official executive orders. By paying such tribute, Harrison explained, employees were able to keep in good standing in the club and were known as "protected" employees. No matter what these workers did in relation to rule infractions, "wise superintendents" would leave them alone. In November 1907, shortly after Harrison started in the post office, a clerk delivered a pro-Republican speech on the Lower East Side. The following week that clerk was given easy work, was exempted from studying distribution schemes, and was promoted to a "soft snap" job. In this way, "correct" political action was rewarded.[13]

Discrimination and wage violations were also common. Harrison explained, "if a clerk is a Jew, a negro, or a socialist, life can be made very hard." In addition, overtime work was not compensated, and at one station where he worked (Grand Central), employees even were forced to pay annually for iced water.[14]

How workers organized was a great concern. Harrison characterized the management policy toward labor organizations as a devious one of dividing and conquering. The promanagement union, the United National Association of Post Office Clerks (Local No. 1, which included supervisors), was encouraged, and the proworker union, the National Federation of Post Office Clerks (Local No. 10), was opposed by all means. Harrison described Local 1 as "an effete organization" that advocated "the identity of interest of postal clerks and the postal authorities" and was "run to suit the interests of the latter." In contrast, he described Local 10, an American Federation of Labor affiliated union founded in 1910 (with Black members from its inception), as "a self-respecting class-conscious organization" that could not be controlled by management and that existed to further interests of postal clerks. He noted that its national president, Oscar F. Nelson, was fired solely because of his organizational activities.[15]

In a later writing on the Post Office Harrison explained that United States postal employees "are as faithful and efficient a body of men and women as ever did work for the government." He discussed the amount of memorizing required for postal schemes and how clerks had to shake out sacks of mail containing "clouds of international dust," which, in many cases, resulted in "consumption." Yet, despite such work and risks, and despite a rising cost of living, their pay unjustly remained stationery for many years. From this and other writings and from his diary, it is clear that Harrison's postal work experience deepened his class consciousness.[16]

———

While working in the post office, Harrison continued to locate himself at the center of New York's Black community, which was shifting from Manhattan's West Side to Harlem. From his first apartment on West Sixty-second St. (in the old center), he had moved to West Eighty-seventh St., then, as the Black population moved northward, aided by the October 1904 completion of the Lenox Avenue Interboro Rapid Transit subway line, so did Harrison. In April 1907 he settled in Harlem, where he was to live, with one brief exception, for the remainder of his life. This move into Harlem coincided with the shift of the area of greatest Black residential concentration in New York. In 1907 Harrison lived at 7 West 134th St. in the midst of the twenty-four-block area between 132nd and 137th Streets and 5th and 8th Avenues that housed 20,000 Black people by 1911. Between 1907 and 1911 he also lived at 144 W. 133rd, 26-28 W. 135th, and 193, 216, 221, and 231 W. 134th, as well as 249 So. Seventh Ave., Mt. Vernon. The block on 134th Street between Lenox and Seventh Avenues, where he lived longest, was, by 1911, the most densely populated block in Harlem. Thus, from it's inception as the "Negro Mecca," Harrison was physically at the very center of the Harlem community.[17]

Harrison was at Harlem's center socially and intellectually as well. Despite the precariousness of his existence, his social life was intimately related to his intellectual interests, and he was an active participant in the vibrant community and intellectual life created by working-class Black New Yorkers. The lyceums and postal study groups were only a part of Harrison's expanding intellectual circles.

Sometimes, important get-togethers were held in people's homes. Particularly noteworthy in this respect was the Men's Sunday Club, a forum for self-trained historians that usually met at John E. Bruce's home, Sunny Slope Farm, in Yonkers, and discussed world issues and their relation to Black people. Frequent participants included Arthur Schomburg; the lay historian, polemicist, and former Pullman porter David Bryant Fulton (who often used the pseudonym "Jack Thorne"); the musician W. Wesley Weeks; and the expressionist painter, etcher, and Pullman porter William Ernest Braxton.[18]

Figure 3.1. The apartment building at 231 W. 134th St., New York, March 25, 1990. The Harrison family lived in this building from around 1911 into the 1920s. The block on 134th Street between Lenox and Seventh Avenues, where the Harrisons lived, was, by 1911, the most densely populated block in Harlem. From its inception as the "Negro Mecca," Harrison was physically and intellectually at the center of the Harlem community. *Source:* Courtesy of Jeffrey B. Perry.

In November 1907 Harrison spoke on "The Duties of the Educated Negro" at a club activity and saw the *Yonkers Standard,* a paper for which Bruce wrote, for the first time. He thought its editorials were "as well written as any in the *Times* the *Post* or the *Sun,*" deemed it "the most able Negro paper I have seen so far," and reaffirmed his commitment to write for it. Bruce wanted him to begin by writing an editorial in response to one in the *Times* of October 21, which argued that organizing the Black vote to break from the Republican Party was "Organizing Race Hatred," but Harrison noted in his diary that Bruce's editorial on the subject "was quite sufficient." He decided to write on Timothy Thomas Fortune's September 4 "extrusion from the editorship of the *Age*." Fortune, one of the most influential Black editors of the previous twenty years, had sold his interests in that paper because of problems he was having with alcoholism and poor health, and the paper quickly became more conservative under its new owner, the Booker T. Washington–affiliated and strongly pro-Republican Fred Randolph Moore.[19]

Another venue for dinner discussion was the home of Harrison's Virginia-born friend, Laura Forrester (who would later become the godmother of his first child). At an October 1907 dinner at Forrester's apartment, one of Harrison's friends, the Texas-born Charles Burroughs, introduced him to William B. Derrick, an AME Zion bishop from Brooklyn, and to his temporary secretary, Alexander Wayman Thomas, who taught at Wilberforce. Harrison described the sixty-four-year-old Derrick, born in Antigua, British West Indies, as "a man of full episcopal girth, with a face fat and pleasant, stately almost to pompousness, yet withal as genial and affable a man as one would like to meet." At the dinner Derrick spoke nonstop in response to Mr. Forrester's "disapproval" of a talk given ten days earlier by W. E. B. Du Bois, who had argued that the New York Board of Education discriminated against colored children. Burroughs felt that Du Bois was wrong, and Harrison said that he "detested" the New York *Age*, the city's pro-Washington weekly, but it had "caught" Du Bois on this issue. After hearing these critical comments Derrick assumed that Burroughs and Harrison "were opposed" to Du Bois and didn't realize that they were, as Harrison wrote, "Du Bois men" who favored "bold, aggressive agitation."[20]

Such "bold, aggressive agitation" marked Du Bois's criticism of the race leadership of Booker T. Washington. Washington had come to national prominence with a much publicized 1895 "Atlanta Compromise" speech, which called on African Americans to "cast down your buckets where you are," to forego political and civil liberties, and to demonstrate worthiness for civil rights by developing industrial skills and land ownership. In his 1903 publication, *Souls of Black Folk*, Du Bois, after paying his respects to Washington, openly challenged his leadership on the grounds that it had not achieved its stated goals and that since 1895 African Americans had, in fact, faced growing disfranchisement, the "legal creation of a distinct status of inferiority," and the "steady withdrawal of aid from institutions for the higher training of the Negro." Du Bois continued to challenge Washington, at times sparked by the work of the anti-Washington militant William Monroe Trotter of Boston, and in June 1905 he issued a call for "organized, determined and aggressive action on the part of men who believe in Negro freedom and growth." The resultant Niagara Movement, headed by Du

Bois (and, until 1907, Trotter), denounced the denial of civil liberties, the deprivation of suffrage, and the lack of equality and equal educational and economic
opportunities for African Americans. It was the most formidable challenge yet
presented to Washington's leadership.[21]

After his comments on Du Bois at Mrs. Forrester's, Derrick, an active Republican and a former principal owner of two newspapers, the *Globe* and the *West Indian Abroad*, detailed struggles that he and the civil rights activist, educator, and
Democratic Party politician T. McCants Stewart waged against segregation in
New York schools during the governorships of future presidents Grover Cleveland and Theodore Roosevelt. At one point Derrick affectionately put his arm
on Burroughs's shoulder and patted Harrison on the head and spoke to him of
the Barbados-born judge David Augustus Straker, who was the first Black person to write an American common-law textbook. Derrick hoped that Harrison
would emulate Straker and asked if he intended to study law. When Harrison
answered affirmatively, Derrick said he knew it. Burroughs then playfully asked
whether he saw it in the shape of Harrison's head. Burroughs and Harrison had
probably joked together before about the scientific studies then in vogue, which
purported to link craniological measurements to race. Harrison, who had a high
forehead, wryly commented in his diary that Derrick had "a remarkably low
forehead for a man of such undoubted power and ability."[22]

Harrison liked and was impressed by Thomas, who was educated at Lincoln
University and Boston University and had traveled in Europe. In his diary he
described him as "one of that younger generation of colored University men
of profound culture who are seeking, without any projection of their individual
selves, to ennoble the ideals of our young men and to send along some of the
spirit that is in themselves." Harrison told Thomas of work he was planning to do
with the YMCA, and Thomas was pleased with it's "purpose and the underlying
motive." When Thomas asked where he attended school, Harrison answered, "I
had educated and was educating myself."[23]

One of Harrison's more moving emotional experiences occurred in the wake
of the November 9, 1907, departure of his friend, Charles Burroughs, for Arkansas on a tour of half a dozen Black colleges in a solo rendition of Shakespeare's
Macbeth. Burroughs's departure opened the door for what Harrison described
as "one of the most enjoyable days of my life."[24]

On Sunday, November 10, Harrison went with Williana Jones to the Yonkers
home of John E. and Florence Bruce. The exceptionally bright Jones (whose
mother had been enslaved for sixteen years) was born in Petersburg, Virginia,
in 1882, was raised on Manhattan's West Side, and graduated from the Normal
College of the city of New York (later Hunter College) before becoming a public
school teacher. Harrison and Williana arrived at three and met the Bruces as
well as fellow Virgin Islander Dr. York Russell and others. A discussion ensued

CHARLES BURROUGHS
1872 – 1940

Figure 3.2. Charles Burroughs, undated. Charles Burroughs (1875?–1941?), was a postal worker and multitalented actor, director, and dramatic reader. He was one of Harrison's closest friends from about 1907 through 1909 and participated with him in a postal-worker study group, a press club, and later with the Liberty League. Burroughs married Harrison's first recorded love interest, Williana Jones, in 1909. *Source:* Courtesy of Carola Burroughs and Norris Burroughs.

"on the merits of certain forms of intellectual training for women," and Dr. Russell's mode of argument was, to Harrison, "both unkind and ungallant," evincing "not a whit of that culture which is supposed to come with education." Harrison entered the discussion "in a slight endeavor to hold the balance even and to soften the asperities of the arguments." Dr. Russell then got "rude even to the point of insulting," but Harrison, seemingly taking delight in the intellectual jostling, "'just smiled and smiled'—and smiling, slid from under," though Williana took the matter quite seriously. Harrison concluded that Russell, though he did have "some degree of learning—of acquaintance with fact," "like so many others" had "very little intelligence." In his diary Harrison commented that this showed "once again the dire effects of giving directly to men of unripe adaptabilities the *results*, instead of submitting them to the *processes*, of education." At that point, he entered in his diary a pledge to his "Mother Race" in Africa:

> Poor heart-sore and soul-starved Mother Race, who shall minister to thy deep desires, who shall bind up thy wounds and raise thee up again if these and such as these are to be thy prophets and thy priests? Oh Africa! when shall be the term of thy long degradation? Behold here, even now, I pledge thee, O my Mother, that I shall devote my years to thee, shall work for thy redemption even in the land of thine exile and set before mine eyes an ideal of service to thee inextricably blent with service for myself; shall love thee and be proud of thee and glory in thy power now lying dormant and shall strive to bring it to the light. Take my youth, my labors, my love, my life, my all and do thou when I shall have died for thee, take me to thy bosom, an untamed, untamable African.[25]

After dinner the group went to the local church for the "Men's Sunday Club" meeting at which Harrison spoke on "The Duties of the Educated Negro." He emphasized "the great need for men of genuine education" and "the necessity, on their part, for service, devotion, self-sacrifice and self-effacement." After that meeting Harrison and Williana returned to the Bruces' house and had a "most delightful time" talking to the Bruces and to Paul Henry Bray, the business manager of the Yonkers *Weekly Standard*, the paper for which "Bruce-Grit" wrote. They looked over Bruce's "curios," including his picture of Alexander Sergeyevich Pushkin (the Black man known as "the Father of Russian Literature") and African masks.[26]

When Harrison and Williana returned to her place, they got "into the pith of things—as usual—talking our hearts to each other." They discussed, as Harrison noted, "work and service (her idea of it and mine), our people and their needs and our special duties to them, and at last we settled on Burroughs." She wanted to know how Harrison came to like him, why he liked him, when he learned to like him, and more. Then, after Harrison told her what he thought of Burroughs, "she said with cowered eyes and deep emotion 'I am glad you like Mr. Burroughs, because he and I are engaged to be married.'" Harrison was crushed and in his diary he movingly described his feelings drawing some lines (at the end) from William Ernest Henley's "Invictus":

> In the deep silence of the evening a hush fell upon my heart as if while roaming in some deep forest-aisle I had suddenly come upon a sacred place, a shrine before which I fain would travel and offer reverence. So here they stand together in my heart—the man of the rising generation whom I most truly love and the woman for whom, as woman, I have felt the most regard. God

grant them true heart union and the blessing of perfect love. My happiness is in their happiness and my pleasure in their joy. And yet, a greater emphasis is given to my own inner loneliness. Shall I like him find love, or labor, as the fruitage of my life? Time will not answer now and no one can tell.

Since my boyhood days this question has risen up to face me: Why will I turn to Sorrow as my heritage? And ever my answer has been: I do not know. The infinite sorrow in the face of the Christ-man, deeper than unfathomable seas, the face of Carlyle, ridged with the furrows of travail and turmoil; the fire-chastened face of Dante that bearer of an immortal grief to the regions of underlying woe—these have always had a strange attraction for me. The things that sadden are more to me than the things that gladden and none on earth knows why. What is that life which I shall lead of which prefigurements—not to say—presentiments—hint darkly? I do not know.

> "Across the vale of wrath and tears
> Looms but the horror of the shade
> And yet the menace of the years
> Finds, and shall find me, unafraid."[27]

Though Harrison did not know what the future held, he was "unafraid." His reasons revealed his thoughts on the meaning of life and, drawing from Hebrews 1:1, he articulated a world-view that placed humanity at the center:

God the Unknown and Unknowable, "who at sundry times and in diverse manner spake in times past unto the prophets", will help to shape my ends to the service of those things that need me most, and whether the clouds darken over my pathway or the heavens smile thereon, it matters not. Here at the outset of the battle I defy alike success and failure. For man is more than life. There is assured, for those who think it.

> "Enough if something from our hand have power
> To live and move and *serve* the future hour."

there is assured for such an immortality more precious than that of their own individual existence. For every man who *does* is God and in his work he lives, as God, forever.[28]

Another important aspect of Harrison's community involvement was his work at the White Rose Home for Colored Working Girls at 217 East Eighty-sixth St., where he began to teach small classes in early 1908. The home was part of the White Rose Industrial Association, a pioneer African American social work

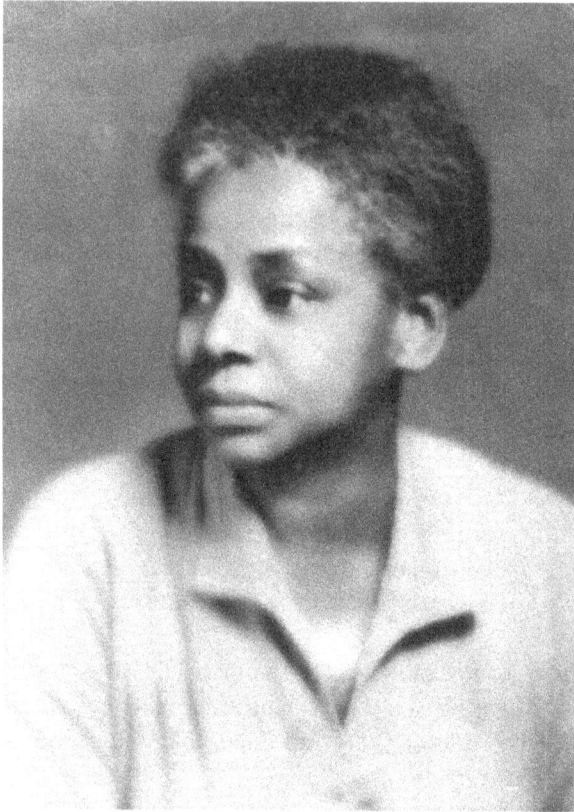

Figure 3.3. Williana Jones Burroughs, undated. Williana Jones Burroughs (1882–1945), a public school teacher and Harrison's first documented love interest, married his good friend, Charles Burroughs. She later became a member of the Socialist and Socialist Labor Parties before becoming a prominent Communist Party community and union activist and then a radio broadcaster in the Soviet Union during WWII. She worked politically with Harrison in the 1920s and, after his death, continued to praise his historical research and teaching. *Source:* Courtesy of Carola Burroughs and Norris Burroughs.

agency and "the only exclusively colored settlement in New York." Founded in 1897 by Mrs. Victoria Earle Matthews (who had been enslaved in her youth and then became one of the most prominent Black women in the country) the home focused on practical problems in housing, education, child care, and employment and catered to recently arrived females from the West Indies and the South and to children. Members paid a $1-a-year fee, received lodging and cooking privileges for $1.25 a week, and had access to a parlor for entertaining. Relief aid and job placement assistance were available and instruction was provided in domestic subjects, industrial skills, and "race history." The home also provided clubs and classes for youngsters, and by November 1911 it had reportedly sheltered over 10,000 women. A particularly important facility at the home was its library, which had a special section about Black people described as "one of the most unique special libraries in New York." Its collection included rare items such as a 1773 edition of the poems of Phillis Wheatley, an 1859 volume of the *Anglo-African Magazine* of New York with a detailed account of the Harper's Ferry battle and John Brown's trial, a first edition of abolitionist Lydia Maria Child's *Appeal in Favor of That Class of Americans Called Africans* (1833), and early abolition literature including the biography of the escaped slave "Linda."[29]

Aiding Mrs. Matthews as her principal assistant was the extremely talented activist and educator Frances Reynolds Keyser, an 1880 honors graduate (and the first Black graduate) of the Normal College of the City of New York (later Hunter College). Mrs. Keyser (who was widowed shortly after her marriage), was known for her dignity, manners, and breeding. She served as White Rose superintendent after Matthews's death in March 1907. While working at the White Rose Home, Keyser continued her full schedule of activities, serving on the board of the Young Woman's Christian Association, as a speaker at the Y and at church lyceums, and as president of the National Association of Colored Women's Clubs Empire State Federation. In 1909 and 1910 Keyser was also an important founding member of the National Association for the Advancement of Colored People and served on both its Executive Committee and its first Board of Directors. After leaving the home in 1912, she worked at the Daytona Educational and Industrial School for Negro Girls in Florida as principal assistant to Mary McLeod Bethune, who praised her "gentle virtues, her sweet benevolence, . . . and broad wisdom" and described her as a tireless worker whose "high intelligence bordered on genius."[30]

Mrs. Keyser was in her forties when Harrison met her on January 1, 1908, at the Emancipation-Proclamation Celebration of the YMCA. She was the person at the White Rose Home who most influenced him, and she soon became his very close friend and confidant and a person from whom he said he drew immense "spiritual values." This is not surprising since the remarkable Keyser played somewhat similar roles with Bethune and with the poet Paul Laurence Dunbar, who confided in her so much that he had submitted his *Lyrics of a Lowly Life* to her for criticism.[31]

Around 1908 Harrison started a race history class and a literary club at the White Rose Home. The latter was "formed for the girls" through Mrs. Keyser's initiative, and the objective was to have the young women develop the club, largely by their own activities, after being aided and directed at first by the White Rose ladies and Harrison, who "would act as a sort of advisory board." In addition to the class and the club, Harrison also delivered lectures and was

Figure 3.4. The White Rose Home Ladies, c. 1909. The White Rose Home for Colored Working Girls on East Eighty-sixth St. founded by Victoria Earle Matthews (1861–1907), a formerly enslaved, Georgia-born journalist and founder of the National Federation of Afro-American Women. The Home was a pioneer African American social work agency and "the only exclusively colored settlement in New York." In 1907 Frances Reynolds Keyser (center) became White Rose superintendent. In 1908 and 1909 Harrison delivered lectures on Reconstruction, started a race history class and a literary club, and took charge of the Boys Club at the Home. Harrison's work at the Home was done without pay and was part of his attempt to get "in full-touch with the *life* of my people" in order "to write their *history.*" *Source:* A.A. Moore, photographer. Courtesy of the Hubert H. Harrison Papers, Rare Book and Manuscript Library, Butler Library, Columbia University, New York.

in charge of the Home's Boys' Club. In his diary he described the kindergarten-aged youths he worked with as a "jolly little bunch" and, reflecting his own very human and playful manner, told of working on a ball of rags and odd bits of twine for them and bringing his "harmonica and a song-book or two" as they "talked, played, sang and enjoyed" themselves.[32]

In addition to his involvement with the White Rose Home, Harrison was also active with the Young Men's Christian Association at 252 W. Fifty-third Street near St. Benedict's Church. The "Colored Y," as it was known, was founded in 1900 through the efforts of Charles T. Walker and Mount Olivet Baptist Church and was the only Y in the city that catered to African Americans. It developed discussion groups, a Board of Education–sponsored Wednesday evening lecture series, young peoples' organizations, a literary society, a dramatics club, and a much-used library. By 1906 its membership exceeded five hundred, and its lectures over the next few years featured community leaders and, occasionally, socialists.[33]

The work that Harrison undertook at the Y (teaching and lecturing), like that at the White Rose Home, did not entail any salary; it was done to develop understanding for his writing and to make a social contribution. He paid particular attention to his students, and he entered a self-evaluation in his diary on October 12, 1907, which acknowledged that he did some good, but also noted how his efforts seemed to center on the use of a critical approach. In a revealing passage he explained:

In spite of my inherent selfishness—no better word—I find that I manage to do a good deal now and then in the interest of the other fellow—alias my people. I try to help along sometimes by the helping directly or by the inducing others to help when neither time nor labor is at my disposal, sometimes by giving sympathy and encouragement to promising young fellows, sometimes by praising Dunbar and Du Bois and [James Edwin] Campbell and getting people to read their works, by pointing out the good of Mr. [Booker T.] Washington, John E. Bruce and other serviceable men and getting others interested in learning about them, and sometimes—most of the time, I fear—by a contemptuous destructive criticism of those men and things which stand in the way of progress of my people.[34]

Freewheeling criticism, open debate, and organizational politics were part of the milieu of the young intellectuals with whom Harrison associated at the Y. One incident that he noted in his diary on January 29, 1908, is illuminating. A Mr. Lyle lectured on "The Man in Black," and, according to Harrison, he would "have good cause to remember the young black men of the Y.M.C.A" as they "flayed" him with hypothetical questions and elucidations and went at him "with a vengeance."[35]

Harrison's involvement with the Y continued through 1908. In November he spoke before the Y's Literary Society at a program of one-minute talks on the subject, "Does the Result of the Election Please Me?" Toward year end, he and John Dotha Jones were installed as judges of the society for 1909 along with Ferdinand Q. Morton (a future United Colored Democracy leader) as president and the South Carolina–born journalist Cleveland G. Allen as secretary.[36]

Harrison's most important Y talk of 1908 was on "Reconstruction in the South." It was delivered on December 9 under the auspices of the Y's popular Board of Education lecture series. The *Age* described him as "a brilliant young man" and "a deep student of the 'Reconstruction.'"[37]

Harrison was indeed "a deep student of the 'Reconstruction'"—but that study was part of a larger project he had marked out for himself. The plan was detailed in his diary of November 25, 1907, where he noted what he had not confided to anyone the specifics of his proposed work—"A History of the Negro in America," whose production "demands twenty years of labor." He envisioned years of patient research, examination of authorities and of the sources back of them, and then, after traversing the field and examining and exhausting all sources of information, he planned to "sit down to *make* my book." He explained his reasons for undertaking this project:

> I was led to embrace this partly by the surprisingly great ignorance on the part of American whites of what the Negro was and is in this country, and partly by the deplorable ignorance of themselves evinced by the great majority of Negroes here. Then again, American historians have treated us not too well. Prejudice plays as great a part in history as in life. Therefore to produce a work which will make it impossible for a white historian not to know—and dangerous to mis-represent the Negro historically made a strong appeal to me. Moreover I am not free from the desire to measure arms with the white man and to force him to see that he is not *facile princeps* [easily first or best] in everything—even at present. We can do some other things besides writing poetry and being otherwise emotional—as Du Bois is showing them. The Negro scholar is a fact of today. I also have the ambition to do something for myself as a black man and to do something for my Race as one of her children. She needs it. For all these reasons I have projected this work.[38]

Harrison felt that the "great lack of Negro scholarship" was "in the field of history," and there was no comparable competent authority such as Henry C. Lea on the Inquisition, James Ford Rhodes on Reconstruction—"(its white aspect)"—or Walter L. Fleming on Reconstruction in Alabama. While working on his project in September and October 1907, he actively searched for a text for beginners that would serve as "a skeleton to my teaching." He had heard the West Point graduate and army captain Charles Young speak on George Washington Williams's *History of the Negro Race in America*, the leading such history by an African American. Williams's two-volume work, first published in 1883, was well researched, though Harrison wrote in his diary that "I don't think much of it." He later realized that he had not yet seen the Williams work and had mistaken it for "a stupid little green book, [Edward A.] Johnson's *School History of the Negro Race in America*," first published in 1890. Johnson, a former school principal in Raleigh, N.C., was a successful attorney in New York City who, with the support of Harrison's Liberty League, would become the first African American member of the New York State Legislature (19th A.D.). After Harrison realized he had not seen the Williams book he determined that he was bound to get it if it was obtainable. Based on a reference to it in historian William A. Dunning's *Reconstruction, Political and Economic, 1865–77*, he reconsidered and judged it valuable.[39]

In his own writing Harrison desired "to go far beyond [such] previous" histories and he thought that his years of deep involvement in the community prepared him for the task. His November 25, 1907, diary entry explained:

> I do not intend to confine myself to proving that the race has progressed and is rising. That needs no such deep study. But a history of the American Negro that will bring a knowledge of psychology and sociology to the exposition of Negro history, that will be a storehouse of information yet no mere cyclopedia, that will attempt to bring to the history of the race something of a philosopher's insight the perception of laws running thru the mesh of deeds; all this my history must be. And thus my haunting of the YWCA, YMCA, the White Rose Home, disreputable clubs, streets of evil and sordid associations; my social work with the rest among the children of 62nd St. [where Harrison and his sister had lived], my attendance at revival meetings and prayer meetings which but for the psychological interest would disgust me—all this by putting me in full-touch with the *life* of my people will aid me in understanding them better than many another and fit me to write their *history*.[40]

This approach, this intimate involvement with the Black (overwhelmingly working class) community, this getting "in full-touch with the *life* of my people" in order to understand them better, was one of the outstanding strengths and distinctive features of Harrison as an intellectual.[41]

Harrison was aware that in doing his research much knowledge would come that he could not incorporate in the final work. This he planned to throw off in incidental volumes with the first to be on "The Negro and Reconstruction." Reconstruction, he noted, had "been treated both statically and dynamically, as a social process and a political one, as a process of adjustment and a phase of national development," but no one, to his knowledge, had regarded it "from the Negro's side" as "a process of racial development, one phase of the progressive adjustment of a people to the life of another people." This is what he proposed to do based on outlines he had drawn up in May that served as the basis for his class-work at the Y.[42]

Harrison desired to find time for his history project, wanted to free himself from problems at the Post Office, and wanted to support himself. One possible solution that he entertained was leaving New York for the Philippines. On January 29, 1908, he discussed taking the Philippines postal-service exam with a friend who had lived there. Harrison was worried, however, about the effects that such a relocation would have on his work. He felt that he could suspend personal and social ties "without the least regret for five years or so," but he hated to give up his Reconstruction history course at the White Rose Home and the series of lectures on Reconstruction he was scheduled to deliver beginning February 6. Despite the difficulties involved in relocating, Harrison saw much to be gained and felt that "five years with abundant leisure for study" would enable him to finish both a "text-book on Reconstruction and the more ambitious work on Reconstruction and the Negro." He also hoped to study law in the Philippines. Nothing ever came of these plans, and his lecture series went on as scheduled.[43]

On November 15, 1908, Harrison wrote to W. E. B. Du Bois and gave his friend Charles Burroughs his "Negro history note-book" to take to him "for an expression of opinion." Burroughs, a Spanish-American War veteran, had been a bright student of Du Bois at Wilberforce University around 1894. Eight days later Harrison received two books from Du Bois—*A Select Bibliography of the Negro American* (1908) and *Economic Co-Operation Among Negro Americans* (1907). He noted that the "bibliography in particular was much needed" and after glancing through the book on economic cooperation he found that like all of the Atlanta University sociological publications that Du Bois edited , it was "indispensable." In his diary he wished Du Bois good luck at an upcoming conference and in his work. Interestingly, in 1909 Du Bois received a July 12 letter from James R. L. Diggs, president of Virginia Seminary and College, which Du Bois interpreted as suggesting that he do "a set of histories of reconstruction from the Negro point of view," and in December 1909 he read a paper on "Reconstruction and Its Benefits" at a meeting of the American Historical Association in New York. Du Bois's thesis was critical of previous historical interpretations and similar to the view, articulated by Harrison, that Reconstruction should be treated "from the Negro's side." Du Bois's work, according to historian Eric Foner, "anticipated the findings of modern scholarship" and paved the way for later studies that challenged the white-supremacist version of Reconstruction.[44]

Harrison's interest in Black history would continue throughout his life, and he would earn praise for his efforts. Several months after his death, the New York City public school teacher Williana Jones Burroughs (Williana Jones married Charles Burroughs in 1909 [and then was vicitmized until 1925 by a law prohibiting married woman from teaching in the public schools]) praised his work for helping to counter the "attitude of self-depreciation" among Black people that "was deliberately fostered by the white ruling class." The well-known educator and civil rights activist William Pickens described him as "one of the fullest scholars and most effective teachers of history and literature that this country has produced."[45]

On a political level, Harrison's historical research fueled his growing opposition to the Republican Party. In March 1908, while continuing his Reconstruction study, he obtained a book that was to deeply affect his thinking. The book, *Letters and Addresses of Abraham Lincoln*, was edited by Mary Maclean, a socialist and a writer for the *New York Times*. Ms. Maclean later became a leading activist with the NAACP, managing editor of that organization's *Crisis* magazine, and one of the few close white friends of Du Bois until her untimely death in 1912. In her book Lincoln, the "Father of Emancipation" and standard bearer of the Republican Party, to which Blacks had been wedded since the Civil War, had his racial, and at times racist, views exposed.[46]

The Maclean book was timely. Though Harrison had arrived in New York wearing a Teddy Roosevelt badge, he had become disillusioned with the Republicans and President Roosevelt for their about-face on racial issues. Roosevelt, whom the *Age* had described in front page headlines as "The Black Man's Champion," had originally praised Black troops among the "Rough Riders." He now accused them of cowardice, spoke favorably of racist Southern traditions, and urged Black people to emphasize industrial education and ignore classical training. In his 1906 message to Congress he took up the argument that Harrison so opposed and charged that the cause of lynching was Black men assaulting white women. This matter outraged African Americans throughout the nation and even led the pro-Republican *Age* to declare that he had abandoned them.[47]

Most outrageous, however, was Roosevelt's conduct in the wake of the August 13, 1906, raid on Brownsville, Texas, by about a dozen men whom white witnesses alleged were Black. He immediately interceded and threatened all African American troops at nearby Fort Brown if the culprits were not identified. On November 5, the day after the 1906 congressional and state elections, with insufficient evidence, Roosevelt dishonorably discharged from the army and debarred from future enlistment or government employment all 167 men of three companies of Black troops of the Twenty-fifth Regiment. Those affected included six Medal of Honor winners and several people near retirement. The action was taken without courts-martial, deprived the men of future civil service employment, and outraged African Americans throughout the nation. According to historian August Meier, "No action of the President hurt and angered Negroes more than this one." It was not until sixty-six years later, on September 28, 1972, after congressional action, that the secretary of the army cleared the military records of the Black soldiers involved, all but one of whom had died.[48]

Roosevelt never altered his judgment regarding Brownsville; the African American community was united in its criticism; and, for the remainder of his life, Harrison never supported the Republicans. In criticizing them he would always cite Brownsville. Similar dissatisfaction was expressed by William Monroe

Trotter and Du Bois (who in 1908 backed Democratic presidential candidate William Jennings Bryan and in 1910 would back Democratic gubernatorial candidate Woodrow Wilson in New Jersey). Defections like those of Trotter, Du Bois, Bishop Alexander Walters, and Robert N. Wood signaled a break from traditional Black support for Republicans and reached a new high in 1912. In that year, during his presidential campaign, Wilson would win the support of the new Black leadership, including Walters and Wood's National Colored Democratic League and the National Independent Political League of Trotter and Reverend J. Milton Waldron. Harrison, however, did not reflexively turn to the Democrats. He first used his criticism of the Republicans as a consciousness-raising issue.[49]

One of Harrison's main contentions was that the Republicans were a harmful influence on Black leaders. Over time he increasingly became convinced, as he later explained, that the Republican Party was "the most corrupt influence among Negro Americans." He made this charge because the party consistently bought up "by jobs, appointments and gifts those Negroes who in politics should be the free and independent spokesmen of Negro Americans." Republicans subsidized these Black leaders, who often posed as independent radicals and were, in Harrison's words, "intellectual pimps," selling out the influence "of any movement, church or newspaper" with which they were connected. By capturing Black leaders in this way, Harrison felt that the Republican Party effectively sought Black votes "for nothing."[50]

In developing his overall criticism of the Republicans Harrison routinely cited the historical record and quoted Lincoln. The Maclean book was instrumental in developing his critique, and the underlining, markings, and comments he made in his personal copy are instructive. A prime example was a marked passage from Lincoln's August 27, 1858, Freeport, Illinois, debate for the U.S. Senate with Democrat Stephen A. Douglas, in which Lincoln explained that he was not opposed to the fugitive slave law, was not in favor of abolishing slavery in the nation's capitol, and did not desire to have Congress exercise the power of abolition. Among other Lincoln statements that Harrison marked for later use were:

> I am not, nor ever have been, in favor of bringing about in any way the social and political equality of the white and black races.
>
> I am not in favor of negro citizenship.
>
> I have no objection to its [the proposed Corwin Amendment prohibiting federal interference with slavery] being made express and irrevocable.
>
> My paramount object of this struggle is to save the Union, and is not either to save or destroy slavery. If I could save the Union without freeing any slave, I would do it.[51]

These quotes would be incorporated in a speech that Harrison prepared over the next few years and presented from 1911 until his death. The speech and related articles were all entitled "Lincoln and Liberty: Fact vs. Fiction." The talk emphasized that neither Lincoln nor the North sought to free slaves, that Lincoln denied protection to slaves who became soldiers, and that without these Black soldiers the North would not have won the war. Years later Harrison stated that he saw his lifelong aim as quite different from that of Lincoln. Whereas Lincoln's "paramount object" was to save the Union and not to free the slaves; Harrison countered that his purpose was to free the slaves, not to save the Union. In practice, Harrison's political view came to mean, with a slight play on words, that he consistently supported Black workers over and against the interests of any racist union—whether it was a labor union or the union of the United States.[52]

While continuing his Reconstruction study Harrison also took time for some deep personal reflection and self-evaluation. On his twenty-fifth birthday, April 27, 1908, he offered a self-assessment in his diary:

> To-day I am twenty-five years old. The reflexions to which this fact gives rise are so many that I hesitate to record any one of them. I don't think that I am any better than I was a year ago: in some things I am, perhaps, worse. But I have grown more both in knowledge and in intellect. And while it may be that my sympathies have shrunk, yet I have become more useful in some ways to other people. My Y.M.C.A. class is over until next Fall, but my work at the White Rose Home still goes on. In these two institutions I have managed, I think, to do some work which, if kept up, will be of real service in the end. I cannot always see the actual good and now and then my heart becomes sick with the thought that it is all bound to be of no use. Yet when my mind has re-established its balance I can see where my duty lies. After I, the thinker, have seen how the personal failure subserves the larger success and the individual service—unnoted and unrecompensed—secures the greater and more tangible general result, it is not for me, the worker, to see *how* my work will be of use. I must be content to do it, to hold the ground I've gained, certain that in the end *I shall* see. Considering these things in the light of my entry of October the 12th last [regarding his "inherent selfishness" and the "good" he still accomplished], I am of opinion that I may yet be of service.[53]

He felt his morals were "not much to speak of—with women especially" and recognized "a growing tendency (in three cases) to be as man proverbially is, i.e. to deceive in order to gain affection or, *re ipsa*, concession." But, he also found that his "attitude toward the girls and women" that he considered entitled to respect was unchanged and he would never dream of treating any of these women "in any way that does not comport with the highest respect." He would also never dream of trying to find out who is weak or who is strong, and he had "never made up to any woman whose actions, words or looks" had not led him "to infer that such was not entirely distasteful to her." As long as he kept alive his "love for Miss [Williana] Jones, Miss Conrad, and Miss Walker," his "respect for Miss Jones"—here "Mrs. Steward" crossed out—"and Miss Vergil," and his "reverence for Mrs. Keyser"—he felt he could not "sink too far into the mire." His friendships had increased in the past year, and of all those whom he admitted into the circle of friendship he rated Mrs. Keyser, the superintendent of the White Rose Home, *facile princeps* [easily first]. She was, "intellectual—and yet unassuming, tactful, kindly, meek as a martyr and as good as gold"—"What a woman!"[54]

Harrison judged that in the past year he had increased his "knowledge of the Negro American," but his reading was desultory and unorganized. He hoped that if he got his lectureship for the Board of Education he would do better. Though he had not yet acquired the faculty of sticking to one subject, he had "at least learnt to have one as a base." He also acknowledged "one great vice"—"the vice of borrowing money." It was "as a curse" and in order to get rid of it he wanted to "make more money—enough to have some always on hand."[55]

Still desirous of finding a means to carry out the study he planned, several weeks after his birthday Harrison finished and mailed a long, self-revealing letter to his close friend Mrs. Keyser. The May 20 letter, transcribed in his diary, explained his "conversion from Christianity" and the reasons for his "present inclination to Catholicism." His motives were many and various, and he enumerated them "in their orders of unfoldment" as "historical, intellectual (or logical), emotional (psychological) & utilitarian." He also suggested a possible reason for his present inclination—he thought he might be able to continue to pursue his intellectual interests if he could get, presumably for free, a Jesuit education. Harrison was looking for a way to sustain his twenty-year research project, and he was not averse to selling himself "for knowledge."[56]

Harrison began his letter to Mrs. Keyser by recounting in detail his break from orthodox and institutional Christianity, initiated in 1901. He noted that he was "so genuinely interested in the bases of religion" that he had "tried to keep in touch with it all along the line: Christian apologetics, ecclesiastics, history, higher criticism." He then offered his thoughts on Christianity in general, beginning with what he considered to be an unusual admission:

> I wish to admit here something that most Agnostics are unwilling to admit. I would pay a tribute to the power of that religion which was mine. It is only fair to confess that Reason alone has failed to satisfy all my needs. For there are

needs, not merely ethical, but spiritual, inspirational—what I would call personal dynamics; and these must also be filled. So I have often felt a hungering after the fleshpots of Egypt. I do not necessarily commit myself to [any belief in] immortality or any allied doctrine when I say that the *soul* yearns for the support of something. Scientifically, of course, I translate this as the power of inherited adaptabilities manifesting themselves in the sphere of psychology, even as it does in the sphere of biology [zoology]. And, rationally, I believe the scientific explanation to be the correct one. And yet—Shall we stunt the soul by refusing to develop it in any one direction while conceding the necessity for development in all other directions? Precisely because I am an Agnostic I object to this limitation. Now, if it can be shown that any given belief or set of beliefs can develop the spiritual side of man, why should we refuse the aid of the belief because its correspondence with fact can not be demonstrated?[57]

As to Catholicism, in particular, Harrison recounted how, not long after the historical impulse came to him, he sought to find out "the actual objective conditions under which Christianity originated." He had a "literary," "scientific," and "evolutionary" interest in these origins and began, as usual, to work back—from the Reformation. He was aided by translations and reprints from original sources by Columbia University professor James Harvey Robinson, and, although his own research efforts were comparatively superficial, he felt he was on the right road and "many beliefs and types of thought and feeling inexplicably bound up with the orderly development of Christianity but repudiated by the Protestants were made clear." Then, when he had got as far as the fourth and third centuries, he "really *saw*" and by "using the [ecumenical] council of Nicaea [A.D. 325] as a suspension point," he "swang alternately backward (as far as Irenaeus [c. 180 A.D.]) and forward (to the council of Antioch [341 A.D.])." One of his main conclusions was "that Catholicism was the representative type of Christianity; whatever was absurd in it (the three great doctrines of transubstantiation, papal infallibility and Mariolatry for example) was due to an absurdity inherent in the very texture of Christianity." Intellectually, as far as the Reformation went—"its main results were self-destructive" since the Protestant "right of private judgment—gave to all conclusions logically drawn from the Bible an equal validity in reason."[58]

Thus, as Harrison "found Protestantism more satisfactory as reason," he correspondingly "found it less satisfactory as Faith." While all this was done as an outsider, he was nevertheless convinced that if he "ever went back to orthodox Christianity it would be by way of Catholicism," and he didn't hesitate to say so. The basis of this preference was essentially "emotional." He preferred "the beauty and solemnity of its ritual," its "dignity," and the "antiquity and power of that vulnerable institution itself." Further, and quite importantly, as he got to

Figure 3.5. Frances Reynolds Keyser, undated. Georgia-born Frances Reynolds Keyser (1862–1932), an 1880 graduate of the Normal College of the City of New York (later Hunter College) and a prominent civil rights and women's rights activist, was White Rose Home superintendent from 1907 through 1912. Harrison trusted her so much that he detailed his break from religion to her in a lengthy May 1908 letter in which he expressed doubt that he would "ever be anything but an honest Agnostic" because, as he explained, "I prefer to go to the grave with my eyes open." *Source:* Courtesy of Bethune-Cookman Archives, Bethune Cookman University, Daytona Beach, Florida.

know more, he "found that Reason was not everything," and he "admired the sublime courage of the Church which boldly demands the subjection of Reason to faith." In contrast, Protestantism tried mainly "to hide from itself that the fundamental basis of theism is an assumption and constructs an elaborate chain of religious syllogisms to aid it." Catholicism, he explained, "hardly avows the Assumption" and "says 'Believe!' while Protestantism says 'Believe because—' Hence the difference."[59]

Harrison also admitted that both objective and subjective "utilitarian considerations" inclined him to Catholicism. He judged that he was "one of those natures that are the better for being curbed." Intellectually he tended to "range wherever I please"—and that had dangers. He sometimes thought "that to acknowledge some restraint would do me good." Overall, however, he thought that he had "a contribution to make to the world," and his desire was to "have that [be] as perfect as possible." For this reason he sought "to master the Latin language—to read it and write it as well as I do English." As a Catholic he "could obtain the great-advantage of a Jesuits training in Latin." He wondered, however, whether this was the evil temptation, "the cloven hoof?"—"Suppose I sell myself for knowledge, suppress a few negative convictions? Whose is the very small loss?" This was "the painful-part," which Harrison desired to discuss with Mrs. Keyser "face to face" rather "than on paper."[60]

In his letter Harrison felt that he had clearly elaborated the reasons why he had "thought seriously of becoming a Catholic." In total honesty, however, he admitted that he doubted whether he would "ever be anything but an honest Agnostic." As Harrison concluded his "chapter in the autobiography of opinion," he emphasized to Mrs. Keyser that the mere fact of his sharing such intimacies with her was "a compliment in the highest and truest sense of that word."[61]

———

While Harrison had a pensive side that was revealed in his diary entries and the letter to Mrs. Keyser, and while he had an intellectual and political side that gave direction to much of his social activity, he also had a very outgoing personal side, which, in sexual matters, was at times marked by a robust and (as Claude McKay called it) erotically "indiscriminate" sexualism. Harrison was very interested in sexual matters—he was not prudish; he developed a memorable erotica collection; he would lecture on sex and sexual topics; he claimed to have authored "Sex and Society" (which has not been located); he documented over ten passionate heterosexual relationships in his diary; he wrote extraordinarily passionate love letters to one 1922 lover; and he would write of having a wonderful time at a gay dance in Harlem. In his sexual relationships he could be conventional, but he could also challenge existing societal and racial mores. Some of the earliest documented instances of his sexual activities and thinking are found in diary entries from 1908 and 1909, and these writings contribute to a fuller picture of his personality.[62]

Throughout 1908 Harrison developed a series of relationships with different women. On several occasions his diary entries were encoded, a practice he often used when discussing affairs. In one such example, on March 3, 1908, Harrison wrote that he "Went out with Coksu Cppkg Ectobejcqls cpf urgpv c ngv qh oqpa—Dtamg." (This roughly translates as "Went out with Mrs. [Amiqs] Annie Carmichaels [Carmzchaojq] and spent a let of monoy—Broke [Bryke])." On April 29 he went to visit Miss Conrad before breakfast. He also "talked love with Lusie." On June 7 he went to see Charlotte Brown and then went to see a Miss Sandusky for the first time. While he was there, his friend Lee came in with a friend of his.[63]

Miss Sandusky soon roused Harrison's ire. On June 8 he learned from another friend that "for all her fair seeming," she was "a whited sepulcher whose inside is as foul as both vice and vulgarity can make it." Lee said that he had treated "her as if she were his sister," and Harrison sorrowed "for Lee and his friend." He observed that she had been "sweetheart-free with him on Sunday evening" and imagined that Lee's friend, Miss Sandusky, and Lee was a triangle similar to "Leo, Cora and me," and he considered it "a pity." He then wrote in a vengeful tone in his diary, that "she began by trying to deceive, she shall be deceived likewise. I only hope that the process will not be too expensive."[64]

The relations with Mrs. Carmichaels, who was presumably married, and with Miss Sandusky, who was probably white, suggest, as do other diary entries, that Harrison was willing to challenge existing mores. The fact that he commented on Miss Sandusky's motivations is not surprising in light of the fact that he was, in general, extremely bothered by what he perceived as racism in sexual relationships. In his diary of December 1, 1907, he indicated that he was "incensed by the doings of white men with colored women" on 135th St. and was so bothered that he wrote a letter, which he sent to the *Evening Post*, the *World*, and the *Tribune*. It was signed, with a satirical touch, "Hubert H. Harrison, Sec'y Eugenic Association." None of the papers published the letter. Other incidents that similarly bothered him included "the young white doctors at the Lincoln Hospital [on E. 149th St. in the Bronx] who debauch such of our girls as they can lead astray." In the case of the doctors, he judged that "shooting would be too good for the white brutes. They ought to be hung."[65]

While at different times in his life Harrison went out with several women at the same time, it was in the course of such dating that he settled on Irene Louise Horton, known affectionately as "Lin," who was a little over three years his senior. Lin was born on December 28, 1879, probably in Antigua, British West Indies. Her parents, Alex B. Horton and Euphiasia Evenson, were originally from Antigua and possibly also from Demerara. Irene's native tongue was English, although before she came to New York in 1908 she possibly spent time in Ponce, Puerto Rico, where her father may have been a minister.[66]

Harrison and Lin were dating seriously by October 1908, and his diary notes her name with the dates of October 13 and 19, November 23 and 27, and December 3, 1908. On the night of November 23, Harrison went to see Lin "and *saw* her" according to his diary entry. Again on December 12 he saw her. In December he wrote her "A Christmas 1908" love booklet, which suggested that his love for her was in full bloom. Then on January 17, 1909, he noted in his diary that the past week had been "a very full one, momentous and important too."

He had received a letter from Cora, "whom, during the past 2 months or more," he had "given up altogether in favor of 'Lin.'" Cora "intimated that she knew why" Harrison had "'deserted' her" and asked "for an interview." Harrison "relented," and they rode the elevated train together and discussed their "changed relations." He "agreed to take up the thread" where he "had dropped it," and they made additional plans to go out. When they went out on the 17th, according to Harrison's diary entry—"et animale duplicivertebrato vehabamur (quod [François] Rabelais) et qyuini coivimus, ter nocte, duo matutini (nos)" (which roughly translates as, "We were carried by the double-backed beast [i.e. two human beings joined as if one] and we had sex five times, three times during the night and twice in the morning." I reached home near 11 this morning")—he told her that he "would come back to her and that he had given up 'Lin.'" But, "after going over to see 'Lin,'" he wrote in his diary—that "such *desire* as I have runs toward her instead of toward Cora." Harrison planned to write to Cora and "tell her that my love for her has run dry and is played out."[67]

While all this was going on between Harrison, Cora, and Lin, he found himself "aiming for Mrs. La Touche," another married woman. She had asked him to go to church with her on January 17, and when he couldn't make it he promised to take her to the theater the following Tuesday. He thought she liked him and noted that "at any rate she shows it." Harrison described her as "a young wife, pretty, lively, sweet" and the "mother of two sons, one 17, whose sister she seems rather than mother." He reasoned that "—when such a saccharine morsel begins to call you a crazy boy, a foolish boy, a great boy, a dear boy—then look out! she is playing for your tour votre comraderie-de-lit, et je prense que je ne suis pas averse de cela, mois. Eh bien, ma chose jolie, je vous resterai votre plaisance et il reste a savoir quelle sequence il y servait." (Which roughly translates as, "She is playing for your hand, your company in bed, and I think that I am not averse to that myself. Oh, yes, my pretty thing, I will remain at your pleasure and it remains to be seen what hand is dealt.") He added that "no husband has a right to leave a young and lively wife ashore while he goes to sea for weeks at a time"—that was "surely the wisdom of a fool." Three weeks later he wrote in his diary—"The possum tonight for the first time." He went over to see Mrs. La Touche as he had done the day before. A week later, when he was ill, Mrs. La Touche sent one of her sons to see how he felt, and Harrison in turn "sent to ask her to come   tomorrow."[68]

In the same period of January 1909 in which Harrison was seeing Cora, Lin, and Mrs. La Touche, he also attended a January 30 party with some West Indian friends at the house of another friend, Sylvanie Murphy. The party was in honor of Miss Ward, a young Antiguan. According to Harrison, the young women danced wonderfully, especially a tall young Antiguan, Miss Mary Simmons, "whose sinuous, sensuous movements" moved him beyond his "usual self-restraint." Among his favorites, besides Miss Ward and Miss Simmons, was "Nora, *our* Nora, Lenora Larsen," a Virgin Islander. Harrison "didn't dance and didn't drink," but he "surprised" himself "as a love-maker." "Without going beyond the limits of decorum—at least, of West Indian decorum," he "made love to both Miss Ward and Miss Simmons," and "all thru the evening" he "was *facile princeps* [easily first] with these two, paying the most marked attention now to one, now to the other, and again to both at the same time." It was a "tangled skein": "Mary was facile and pliable" while "Miss Ward was also easy to catch but proved unmanageable in the holding." She even "displayed the first stormy indications of jealousy and in the end she sulked and was almost irreconcilable." Harrison was "not so sure" that he "reserved the balance of favor between them," but he planned to "go back to the house" to see Mary "and take up the thread of the argument with her." He "want[ed] her," too.[69]

He was also interested in "exactly what Nora thought." She had asked him to come "in such a winning way" that he consented. Harrison had written to her on January 16 "in a way that would almost imply that Nora had been the sole attraction" for him in that house for the past three weeks (or since he came upon her there and "learnt for the first time that she was . . . in America"). He also spoke with her once or twice and lent her his *Love Letters of a Violinist* (by Eric Mackay), which included some of his letters to the *New York Times* inside. He noted that she "seemed to disclose a personality with sensibilities refined far beyond those of her circle."[70]

A little over a week later Harrison met Mrs. R. H. Williams, who asked him to "come to see her." He followed this up with a letter. Then from February 15 through February 17, 1909, while he was very sick and in bed, he was visited by Cora on several occasions as well as by Mrs. La Touche's son.[71]

While Harrison was dating at least three women in early 1909, he wrote some numbers in his diary that suggested that he had impregnated someone around January 17 and that the child of such a pregnancy would be due around October 19. The person he had impregnated apparently was Lin when they went out together in January. As the pregnancy developed they decided to get married, and the ceremony was performed at St. David's Protestant Episcopal Church in the Bronx on April 17, 1909. John Dotha Jones and Williana Jones served as witnesses. Several years later Harrison wrote in his dairy that he "either drifted or . . . [was] driven" into marriage. Revealingly, in all of his remaining papers, correspondence, personal documents, and diary there is a noticeable lack of material indicating that he and Lin ever shared a driving, consuming, passionate love.[72]

On October 21, roughly nine months after the January 17 date he had noted in his diary, a first child, Frances Marion, was born to thirty-year-old Irene and twenty-six-year-old Hubert and delivered, possibly by a midwife, at 305 Jerome Avenue in the Bronx. The baby, like her father, was at first named differently—

Figure 3.6. Irene Louise Horton Harrison, c. 1909. Irene Louise Horton (1879–1962), known affectionately as "Lin," was probably born in Antigua, British West Indies. She began dating Hubert seriously in 1908 and they were married on April 17, 1909. Lin and Hubert had five children together, and Lin, in addition to taking on major responsibilities for raising the children, would take in work as a seamstress and take in boarders to help with family finances. At times, over the course of their eighteen-year marriage, Hubert lived apart from Lin and the children. *Source:* Courtesy of the Hubert H. Harrison Papers, Rare Book and Manuscript Library, Butler Library, Columbia University, New York.

in this case "Kathryn Marion." Years later, a dispute over the "date of birth of one or more" of his children, would cause problems with the U.S. Naturalization Service and delay Harrison's efforts to become a citizen. "Kathryn Marion," however, became "Frances Marion" some time after March 1910. She was quite possibly named after Frances Reynolds Keyser, who had so influenced her father. Over the next eleven years Frances Marion would be joined by three sisters and a brother. The financial burdens of this expanding family would impede

Figure 3.7. Frances Marion Harrison, 1910. On October 21, 1909, a first child, Frances Marion (named at first "Kathryn Marion") Harrison (1909–1931), was born to Irene and Hubert Harrison. Frances was very possibly named after Hubert's good friend Frances Reynolds Keyser. She was followed by sisters Alice Genevieve (1911–1987), Aida Mae (1912–2001), Ilva Henrietta (1914–1932), and brother William (1920–1984). *Source:* Courtesy of the Hubert H. Harrison Papers, Rare Book and Manuscript Library, Butler Library, Columbia University, New York.

many of Harrison's later pursuits. He, in turn,would constantly live in poverty and at times neglect family financial responsibilities in order to concentrate on intellectual and radical pursuits. For a working-class intellectual like Harrison, this conflict between family responsibilities and intellectual pursuits would affect his remaining years.[73]

Though married and with a family, Harrison's interest in other women would continue. On May 26, 1911, he wrote in his diary that "our second baby [Alice Genevieve Harrison] came on Monday morn (22nd) at 4:55. Here, perhaps, our married life begins afresh for us." Matters were not so simple. Two years later, on April 13, 1913, Harrison confided in his diary, after a quarrel with Lin, that he had been having trouble and planned to move out. He did not move at that time, but he did so later. Then, six days later, he wrote that the intense quarreling had been going on for three years and that it was the kind of thing that made him "hate" her. For the remainder of his life Harrison would move between expressions of caring for Lin and extramarital affairs, between periods of living together with her and periods of separation.[74]

———————

A very clear picture emerges from the self study, the early writings, the lyceums, the Y, the White Rose Home, the lectures, the forums and debates, the study circle and press club, the Reconstruction and race history classes, and the personal relations. All these assorted doings show that Hubert Harrison, a poor, working-class, Black Caribbean immigrant, had a vibrant, challenging, and stimulating intellectual life that was rooted in New York's Black community. Through his efforts at getting "in full-touch with the *life* of my people" and through the response of those people, Harrison's hunger for learning and his desire and ability to serve were nurtured. Though he had been given little to start, Hubert Harrison made much of what was available. His interest in learning and serving and his critical independence and break from religion soon led him in the direction of more radical approaches to social problems. His outspokenness on social issues would soon cost him his postal employment, severely hurt him and his growing family, and push him towards socialism.

CHAPTER

4

Secular Thought, Radical Critiques,
and Criticism of Booker T. Washington
(1905–1911)

Though married in a church and nurtured intellectually in church lyceums, Har-
rison's interests were becoming quite secular. He was an agnostic, and he was
attracted to science, evolutionary theory, and some of the more radical intellectual movements of his day, including freethought, Single Taxism, and socialism.
These movements were radical in the true sense of the word in that they aimed
to get at the root cause of the problems they sought to cure and they sought to
challenge and qualitatively change the status quo.

This secular and radical ideological bent increasingly distanced Harrison
from the two main political parties, Republican and Democratic, and from the
church, which, as he would explain, "exerts a more powerful influence than anything else in the realm of ideas" in the Black community. The Black church was
the principal autonomous institution in the African American community, and
besides serving a religious function, it also served as a social, educational, and
cultural center. Church leaders, especially ministers, were frequently spokes-
people for a community whose members were discriminated against in other
areas of society. In these matters of autonomy and influence the Black church in
the United States differed markedly from the church in the West Indies, where
ministers were often white.[1]

The freethought movement that attracted Harrison was based on adherence
to scientific methodology and opposition to thought "fettered by the dogmas and
principles of religion." Freethinkers relied on reason over supernatural authority.
They sought to examine both sides of issues and to encourage free inquiry, free
publicity of ideas, and free discussion of convictions. Though the freethought
movement was five hundred years old, it had grown rapidly in the nineteenth
century during the great debate between science and theology inspired by the

work on evolution of Charles Darwin and others. Its growth in post–Civil War America was often related to the growth in the labor and socialist movements.[2]

In the United States, organized freethought was a rationalist, antireligious movement with a strong base in New York and a weekly newspaper, the *Truth Seeker*, founded in 1873 by D. M. Bennett. From 1875, and for the next sixty-plus years, the Macdonald brothers were the paper's driving force. Eugene M. Macdonald edited the paper from 1883 through 1909, and, upon his death, his younger brother, George E. Macdonald, served as editor from 1909 to 1940. The *Truth Seeker*, whose masthead described it as "A Freethought and Agnostic Newspaper," held that its objective was "to educate the people out of religious superstition." It supported "Free Speech," "Free Press," and "Free Mails" and demanded taxation of church properties, discontinuance of military chaplains, complete separation of church and state, and ends to school prayers, blue laws, and courtroom oaths. Early-twentieth-century freethinkers supported science, denied the infallibility of the Bible, asserted the human origin of the Old and New Testaments, denied the existence of heaven and hell, upheld the theory of evolution as opposed to the biblical Genesis, and held that "morality and ethics—or man's relation to man" was "entirely independent of creed or religion." Most importantly, freethinkers were secular and held that ethical standards arose not from a Supreme Being but from human action toward other human beings. The period from 1875 to 1914 has been described "as the high-water mark of freethought as an influential movement in American society."[3]

Freethought attracted many prominent followers, and the *Truth Seeker* editor George E. Macdonald included in its historic lineup the suffragists Elizabeth Cady Stanton and Susan B. Anthony; the birth-control advocate Margaret Sanger; the popular orators Hugh O. Pentecost and Robert G. Ingersoll; the antislavery editor Horace Greeley; the abolitionist, Union Army colonel, and writer Thomas Wentworth Higginson; the attorney Clarence Darrow; the socialist Eugene V. Debs; and the authors Samuel L. Clemens (Mark Twain), Moncure D. Conway, Ernst Haeckel, and Herbert Spencer. Others influenced by freethought included the anarchists and labor activists Lucy Parsons and Emma Goldman; the future Communist Party leaders Louis Fraina and Charles E. Ruthenberg; the future socialist, labor, and civil rights activist A. Philip Randolph; and the poet and historian Carl Sandburg. Many Black leaders and writers of the early twentieth century In addition to Harrison and Randolph were influenced by freethought or atheism, including writers J. A. Rogers and George S. Schuyler; poets Claude McKay and Walter E. Hawkins; and journalist-activists Cyril V. Briggs, Hodge Kirnon, and Rothschild Francis. W. E. B. Du Bois, as indicated by his biographer David Levering Lewis, was "an agnostic and anticlerical."[4]

Harrison, according to the Harlem freethinker Hodge Kirnon, was easily "the first and foremost Negro in the cause of freethought." He was attracted by its critical approach, its focus on scientific as opposed to religious thought, and its understanding that humans were responsible for their actions. Similar thinking would soon draw him toward socialism, which made its own "Appeal to Reason," as indicated by the title of one of its leading publications. For years Harrison recommended books published by the Truth Seeker Company in New York and the Rationalist Press Association in London and his personal collection included books by Haeckel, Conway, and Ingersoll as well as books about Spencer and the deist Thomas Paine (author of the influential *Age of Reason*). He would also lecture before the Secular League on "Truth vs. Superstition: Some Fallacies of Freethought," indicating that in this area, like so many others, he maintained his independence of thought.[5]

Harrison's involvement with the freethought movement dates from at least 1903, when he participated in the Turner mass meeting. He is also reported to have participated with the Sunrise Club, one of the leading freethought-influenced organizations in New York, as early as 1905 and to have joined the club in 1908. The Sunrise Club, which held dinner meetings every other week with featured speakers, was organized in 1889 by Edwin C. Walker, who served as its secretary until his death in 1931. Walker was a proponent of "free love" and "free marriage," a contributor to the *Truth Seeker* magazine, and a writer on such other topics as anarchism, communism, and taxation of church properties. The club's aim was to "blend alert thought and sociability," while introducing people of all vocations, parties, creeds, nations, and races to one another. It encouraged wide ranges of opinion on all topics discussed, and among its many speakers over the years would be W. E. B. Du Bois, James F. Morton, the educator Kelly Miller, the anarchist Emma Goldman, the sociologist Lester Frank Ward, the author-editor V. F. Calverton, and Harrison.[6]

According to Joseph Rinn, president of the Metropolitan Psychical Research Society, Harrison assisted him at a Sunrise Club activity in January 1905. Rinn's MPRS had several hundred members interested in exposing fakers such as Mary S. Pepper of the First Spiritual Church of Brooklyn. Rinn prepared a circular challenging Pepper "to display" her "psychic powers" and declaring that he would perform feats of thought transference. More than one thousand people attended the activity, and two thousand were kept outside by police. Pepper did not appear, and Walker picked a committee of four, chaired by Harrison and including the Single Tax activist and writer James F. Morton, to assist Rinn. At the end of the night Rinn declared "that every test I gave here this evening is done fraudulently" and then explained the tricks and codes used in each instance. "From what we have seen tonight," said Harrison, "I feel we'll all leave here less cocky and sure of ourselves than when we came in."[7]

While his 1908 diary entry detailing his break from religion is the clearest indication of early freethought influence on Harrison, another indication was his

Figure 4.1. Edwin C. Walker, undated. New York–born Edwin C. Walker (1849–1931) founded the freethought-influenced Sunrise Club in 1889 and served as its secretary until 1931. The interracial club, which Harrison joined around 1908, held dinner meetings that encouraged the widest ranges of opinion on all topics. *Source:* From George E. Macdonald, *Fifty Years of Freethought: Being the Story of the "Truth Seeker," with the Natural History of Its Third Editor*, vol. 1. Courtesy of the Truth Seeker Company.

September 25, 1909, *New York Times* letter on "Moncure D. Conway and the Attitude of Virginians Toward Him." Conway was one of the most popular authors of the freethought movement, and Harrison's letter challenged a previous letter that held "that it never was impracticable for Conway, with his practical abolition views, to live in Virginia." Harrison reviewed how Conway petitioned "for a repeal of the law against teaching slaves to read" and was told "that no such petition could be read in the legislature of Virginia"; how his mother's house was visited by officious men "because she taught her slaves the catechism"; and how, when Virginia was "seriously considering the re-enslavement of her free Negroes," Secretary of State Henry Clay instructed the U.S. minister in London "to urge an agreement for the surrender of blacks who had fled to Canada,

Figure 4.2. James F. Morton, c. 1925. Massachusetts-born and Harvard-educated James F. Morton Jr. (1870–1941) was a newspaperman, attorney, lecturer, museum curator, and mineralogist active with the freethought and Single Tax movements, the Thomas Paine National Historical Association, the *Truth Seeker*, and the Modern School. He wrote *The Philosophy of the Single Tax* (n.d.) and *The Curse of Race Prejudice* (c. 1906). Harrison was active with Morton in many of these efforts and later explained that his own early reading moved from single tax literature, to economics, and "then turned to socialist literature." *Source:* From O. Ivan Lee, "Memorial for James F. Morton," *American Mineralogist* 27 (1942): 200–202. Courtesy of the Mineralogical Society of America, Chantilly, Virginia.

stating that Virginia and Kentucky were urgent in the matter." Such facts, as well as the long and deep opposition to free pubic schools in Virginia, indicated to Harrison that it was "impracticable" for Conway to remain in that state. Harrison emphasized that "American history owes much to the man [Conway] who wrote *The Life of Thomas Paine*."[8]

Related to Harrison's interest in freethought, his agnosticism, and his turn to science to address social problems was his interest in evolutionary theory. This interest, hinted at by his 1904 letter on chicken stealing, was expressed more directly in a revealing letter published in the May 29, 1909, *New York Times*. Harrison responded to a previous piece about the influence of the physician and botanist Erasmus Darwin on *The Origin of Species*, the 1859 book by his grandson Charles Darwin. He mentioned the work of the German poet and botanist Johann Wolfgang von Goethe and the French naturalists Etienne Geoffroy Saint-Hilaire; Georges Louis Leclerc, comte de Buffon; and Jean Baptiste Pierre Antoine de Monet de Lamarck, and discussed how their work was fiercely debated until Charles Darwin, after twenty-two years of research, "launched his book . . . and the whole fabric of scientific mythology based upon Genesis and a special creation collapsed at once."[9]

An insightful response to Harrison by S. Reswick, however, stated that Harrison's answer was "correct so far as it goes, but it only goes half way." He "missed . . . the main point that . . . Charles Darwin explained his origin of species by an altogether different theory from the rest: it is the 'origin of species by natural selection.'" All the other expounders of origin of species by evolution "had a different explanation for it—namely, development by use and heredity." Charles Darwin stood "alone except for his contemporary, A. R. Wallace, in the theory of origin of species by natural selection," and that is why he is "known all over the world as one of the greatest men of mankind."[10]

Harrison's letter clearly suggests that he was familiar with evolutionary theory. This familiarity very likely drew him further into the orb of socialist ideas since, as historian Mark Pittenger has explained, American socialists often grafted socialism onto evolutionary theories of nature and society, and Charles Darwin, Herbert Spencer, and Lester F. Ward were accepted by the socialist movement. Spencer, the originator of the phrase "survival of the fittest," enjoyed a great vogue among socialists, many of whom, though critical of his individualism, liked his agnosticism and his theory of society in flux. Ward's rationalist *Dynamic Sociology* favored a planned effort at social reconstruction, and, though he was not a socialist, he was also quite popular with many socialists. His writings would significantly influence future Black socialist leaders A. Philip Randolph and Chandler Owen.[11]

Familiarity with evolutionary theory not only paved the way for socialist theory, it also affected Harrison's developing understanding of "race." Socialist discussion of evolution, according to Pittenger, often showed "an uncritical deference to the authority of popular evolutionary racism" and, in so doing, "undercut the radical potential of American socialism." There were identifiable racist implications in the evolutionary schemas of Darwin, his principal defender Thomas Huxley, Spencer, and Ward. Though Harrison opposed white-supremacist arguments and later referred to Ward as a white man who exhibited "that traditional off-handed, easy contempt with which white men in America, deign to consider the colored population of 12 millions," no similar comments on Darwin, Huxley, or Spencer have been located. As late as 1921 Harrison considered Spencer's *First Principles* "the greatest" of the systematic surveys of knowledge and a work that makes one "think and think clearly." He also advised that Black people could "pick no more helpful guide" in general education efforts than Spencer, noting that "the Japanese found this out long ago, and we may all profit by their example."[12]

Harrison would later indicate a general awareness of the tendency for white-supremacist views to influence science. In 1926 he explained that since scientists are human and their "minds are colored by their social surroundings," it was "natural, therefore, that what we call science . . . should reflect the concepts and ideas which saturate the scientists." This was "especially . . . true of the sciences that deal with the subject of race: biology, psychology, sociology and anthropology—physical and social," in whose findings "the personal element plays a great part."[13]

A component of the theories of both Spencer and Ward was Lamarckianism—and the theory of the inheritance of acquired characteristics. The theory was associated with the late-eighteenth- and early-nineteenth-century French naturalist Jean Baptiste Pierre Antoine de Monet de Lamarck, who maintained that "all that has been acquired or altered in the organization of individuals during their life is preserved by generation and transmitted to new individuals which proceed from those which have undergone change." The historian Thomas G. Dyer claims that a "significant portion of American social scientists during the years 1890–1915 counted it as central to their understanding of race, culture, and evolution," and George W. Stocking Jr., adds that it was a "widespread popular scientific attitude."[14]

Despite criticisms of Lamarckianism from embryologist and Darwinian August Weismann, from anthropologist Franz Boas, and, later in the century, from many scientists and writers, the theories of evolution and of the transmission of acquired characteristics often went hand-in-hand for early-twentieth-century thinkers. One reason was that Lamarckianism seemed to bring hope to believers in evolution and offered an explanation of the agent of natural selection in an era before there was widespread familiarity with the genetic work of the Austrian Augustinian monk Gregor Mendel. Lamarckianism proposed that individual or social efforts, including use and disuse, led to adaptations, which could be passed on to offspring. In general, it suggested a more active approach to life than one might get from "random variation" and from (the often not clearly understood) "natural selection." To Lester Frank Ward, it was either accept Lamarckianism so humanity can "develop through its own exertions," or reject it, and be "completely at the . . . [hands] of the little known process of 'natural inheritance.'"[15]

In addition, Darwin's own words, which were probably read carefully by Harrison, left the door open for this linkage (and suggest a subtext to the Harrison and Reswick letters in the *Times*). In the conclusion to the *Origin of Species*, Darwin explains:

> I have now recapitulated the facts and considerations which have thoroly convinced me that species have been modified during a long course of descent. This has been effected chiefly through the natural selection of numerous successive, slight, favorable variations, aided in an important manner by the inherited effects of the use and disuse of parts, and in an unimportant manner, that is, in relation to adaptive structures, whether past or present, by the direct action of external conditions, and by variations which seem to us, in our ignorance, to arise spontaneously. It appears that I formerly underrated the frequency and value of these latter forms of variation, as leading to permanent modifications of structure independently of natural selection. But as my conclusions have lately been much misrepresented, and it has been stated that I attribute the modification of species exclusively to natural selection, I may be permitted to remark that in the first edition of this work, and subsequently, I placed in a most conspicuous position namely, at the close of the Introduction the following words: "I am convinced that natural selection has been the main, but not the exclusive, means of modification."[16]

Theories of evolution and of the transmission of acquired characteristics have implications for how one understands the concept "race" and how one conceptualizes the fight against white supremacy, and for these reasons they are important to understanding Harrison's developing thought. Basically, the theories raise questions as to whether "race" is a sociohistorical or biological category, or both; whether ideas, actions, and capabilities are transmitted socially or biologically or by some combination of the two; and whether efforts at social change should be directed primarily at social or biological factors. Simply put, if "race" and racism are sociohistorically derived, then racial oppression and racism can be subjected to eliminative social action and strategies for change can be directed at challenging white supremacy. If "race" is biologically determined or transmitted and racism is innate, then direct social action challenging white supremacy might have little effect and other strategies for change would have to be developed.[17]

Harrison primarily viewed the "shifting reality" of "race" as a sociohistorical category. In 1926 he explained, "The conception now prevailing that white people are superior and darker people inferior arose as the mental reflex of a social fact. That fact was the military and political dominations exercised by European whites over the darker people who as late as the fourteenth century had been superior to them." He added, the King James Version of the Bible "does not contain the word 'race' in our modern sense of a breed of people. . . . And that goes to show that as late as 1611 our modern idea of race had not yet arisen, or had not found expression in the English language."[18] Elsewhere he explained that the "Negro problem" was sociohistorically determined and that the source of white-supremacist views "is always sociologic rather than intellectual."[19] He was also emphatic that "race prejudice is not innate," that it was "diligently fostered by those who have something to gain," and that it was "acquired."[20]

Harrison also, however, supported Lamarckianism. This support was complex. Though he spoke of inheriting "our bodies and minds, our aptitudes and inclinations,"[21] he thought that the transmission of acquired characteristics occurred only in "some" cases. He did not view "races" as biologically immutable or as fixed categories in hierarchical order as did many late-nineteenth- and early-twentieth-century believers in Darwinian evolution. Rather, he viewed "races" as social and biological categories subject to influence and change from the social environment, which could, in some cases, be passed on biologically. These views were consistent with neo-Lamarckian thought, and, in private comments, he referred to himself as a "Lamarckian."[22] Overall, his approach had more of a social or environmental than a biological basis, although it did mix the two.[23]

This belief in some transmission of acquired characteristics would, at times, affect Harrison's subsequent thinking on "race" and the struggle against racial oppression.[24] To the degree that he viewed "race" as a social category and racism and "race consciousness" as socially derived, he considered racial oppression as something that could be eliminated by social action. To the degree that he understood "race" as biologically determined and race characteristics as biologically transmittable, there would be less reason to put effort into work among "white" workers and the class struggle. These matters would take on more importance as Harrison sought to develop struggle against class exploitation and racial oppression.[25]

———

Though Harrison was getting more involved with the freethought movement and reading widely in the evolutionary and social sciences, it was always done with an eye on the African American community. That community, as August Meier and Elliot Rudwick have described, faced conditions in the last years of the first decade of the twentieth century that were "the most oppressive" since the Civil War. Harrison was deeply concerned with this situation and with the efforts of Black leaders to challenge these conditions. In his scrapbooks he critically divided existing Black leadership into two broad categories—"The Subservients" and "The Protestants."[26]

Chief among Harrison's "subservients" was Booker T. Washington, the president of Tuskegee Institute in Alabama. Washington was the most powerful Black man in the United States, a position he had achieved by building an extensive patronage and pressure machine centered on money, jobs, and domination of sectors of the Black press. This "Tuskegee Machine" was made possible by virtue of the support he received from powerful whites, including former president Theodore Roosevelt and the financial giants John Wanamaker and Andrew Carnegie, and by the political influence related to his extreme loyalty to the Republican Party. Washington was the first such national Black leader chosen for African Americans, and he was chosen by whites. His loyalty to his white backers was at times extreme and he wrote in 1906, in reference to his relationship with President Theodore Roosevelt, that "I will oppose nothing that he wants done and will help forward all that he desires to have done." Washington advocated a policy of Black subordination in political and economic spheres—his core philosophy emphasized industrial over higher education for African Americans, thrift, Christian character, economic base building before demands for equal civic and political rights, and cooperation with Southern "white friends." He warned that "the agitation of questions of social equality is the extremist folly," advised that African Americans must begin "at the bottom of life" and "not at the top," and emphasized that "the Negro" was "not given to strikes or to lockouts." Harrison was critical of much of Washington's philosophy, which he referred to as "one of submission and acquiescence in political servitude."[27]

Although Harrison criticized Washington, there were other more prominent critics, led by William Monroe Trotter in Boston and W. E. B. Du Bois in Atlanta. In 1901 Trotter began publishing the most strident of the anti-Washington publications, the Boston *Guardian*, and in 1903 he unsuccessfully challenged Washington for control of the latter's Afro-American Council and took the lead in publicly heckling him in an incident widely publicized and referred to as the "Boston Riot." In a different manner, Du Bois, in his seminal 1903 publication, *The Souls of Black Folk*, more diplomatically took issue with Washington's program. In 1905 Du Bois and Trotter worked together to found the leading Black protest organization of the first decade of the twentieth century—the Niagara Movement, which advocated a program of full "manhood" rights, enforcement of the Constitution, an end to segregation, and real educational opportunities. Harrison considered its organ, *The Horizon*, "the most brilliant Negro periodical" of the era.[28]

As the Niagara Movement ebbed, the embryo of its successor protest organization—the National Association for the Advancement of Colored People—grew. The NAACP was officially launched as a permanent interracial organization of social reform on May 12, 1910. The NAACP grew out of the conflicting approaches of Washington and Du Bois, "Tuskegee" and "Niagara," and was developed out of a series of meetings that were held in response to the "race riot"/pogrom of August 14 and 15, 1908, in Abraham Lincoln's home town, Springfield, Illinois. The socialist William English Walling, an eventual NAACP founder, investigated the riot with his wife, Anna Strunsky Walling, and stressed that extreme Southern methods were on the verge of sweeping the North and that a "large and powerful body of citizens" was needed to come to the aid of Black people.[29]

Walling and Du Bois were two of the sixty prominent Blacks and whites who, on February 12, 1909, issued a "Call," written by Oswald Garrison Villard, to a conference in New York City to "Discuss Means for Securing Political and Civil Equality for the Negro." Other signatories included the journalist and lecturer Ida B. Wells-Barnett; the teacher and author Mary Church Terrell; the Washington, D.C., activist Rev. Francis James Grimke; the National Negro American Political League leader Dr. J. Milton Waldron; the African Methodist Episcopal Zion Church leader Bishop Alexander Walters; William Dean Howells; the social worker and settlement house leader Jane Addams; the journalist Lincoln Steffens; the Free Synagogue rabbi Dr. Stephen S. Wise; the publisher and editor of the New York *Evening Post* and *Nation*, Oswald Garrison Villard; and socialists such as Charles Edward Russell and Mary White Ovington. Plans were made to hold a series of conferences aimed at establishing an interracial organization to work toward "political and civil equality for Negroes." On May 31 and June 1, 1909, these plans were implemented as twenty leaders met at the United Charities Building in New York City, following an opening ceremony attended by 300 people.[30]

Harrison, although not in attendance, was apparently struck by many points in the discussion. Years later, he would entitle his first book *The Negro and the Nation*, which was the title of the presentation given by Dr. William A. Sinclair of Philadelphia and the subject of the pithy comments of Judge Wendell Phillips Stafford of the Supreme Court of the District of Columbia. Harrison was also probably influenced by Sinclair's observation that President William Howard Taft "bent his knee to the Baal of southern race hate," by his comments and those of AME Zion bishop Alexander Walters and William Monroe Trotter on the need for enforcement of the Fourteenth and Fifteenth Amendments on citizenship and voting rights; by Walters's reference to Reverend Quincy Ewing, an Episcopal clergyman from Louisiana; and by Trotter's proposal that lynching be made a federal crime (which was defeated by a vote of fifty-three to twenty-one). Each of these matters, detailed in the *Proceedings* of the conference, would be used by Harrison in later writings and oratory.[31]

Something else also attracted Harrison's attention. Years later he still recalled that at the meeting of the National Negro Committee in 1909, Celia Parker Wooley, a Unitarian minister of the Frederick Douglas Center in Chicago, noted that among Black people there was developing, though unrecorded and unreported, a race hatred against whites. According to Harrison, the New York *Evening Post* reported her comments, but "when the National Negro Committee (which later grew into the N.A.A.C.P.) came to print the proceedings of that conference, those words of Mrs. Celia Parker Wooley were elided from the records."[32]

When the NAACP was finally established in May 1910, it aimed to cooperate "with all agencies working for the uplift of Colored people." It planned to hold meetings; to publish pamphlets, articles, and an official organ, the *Crisis*; to redress cases of injustice; and to undertake studies of present conditions. Its early leadership included many leading white intellectuals and some dedicated socialists. Du Bois, the editor of the organization's publication, the *Crisis*, was the only African American among its six chief administrative functionaries.[33]

Though the NAACP offered a clear alternative to the leadership of Booker T. Washington, it still suffered from definite shortcomings in Harrison's mind. His objections, probably in embryo in 1910, centered on his appraisal that the NAACP limited itself to paper protests and that it was limited by white people's conceptions of how Black people should act. The Wooley matter was a graphic example. Harrison considered her comments on the developing race hatred of Blacks toward whites and the removal of those comments from the official record as clear indication "that some white people seem to think a certain public attitude toward white people to be fit and proper, and a certain other attitude— an attitude which white people would maintain if they were in the same situation—as unbecoming to black people." Thus, even in the NAACP, the race problem was "to be settled by the words, the mandates, the principles, the judgments and opinions coming from one side only—the white side." This posed serious problems "if these [white] minds at which you are aiming remain unaffected" and refused "to grant guarantees of life and liberty."[34]

Other criticism focused on the idea of the "Talented Tenth," which was developed by Du Bois. According to Du Bois, the Talented Tenth was the "educated and gifted" group whose members "must be made leaders of thought and missionaries of culture among their people" in order to lead African Americans forward. Harrison always emphasized education and self-development of the masses, the so-called common people. He also developed a different understanding of the Talented Tenth—an understanding that was probably in embryo by 1910. He increasingly equated the Talented Tenth concept with the concept of "Colored," as opposed to "Negro" leadership of the "Negro race." Harrison's opposition to such a leadership was because he did not think that such a Talented Tenth was in any way preordained to lead the "Negro race," nor did he think that it had provided the leadership needed by African Americans. Harrison rejected the white domination that unchallenged acceptance of such leadership implied. As he later explained in harsh and pointed language, for two centuries

African Americans had "been told by white Americans that we cannot and will not amount to anything except in so far as we first accept the bar sinister of their mixing with us." Thus, "always when white people had to select a leader for Negroes they would select some one who had in his veins the blood of the selector." Under slavery, according to Harrison, "it was those whom Denmark Vesey of Charleston described as 'house niggers' who got the master's cut-off clothes, the better scraps of food and culture which fell from the white man's table, who were looked upon as the Talented Tenth of the Negro race." Historically, "the opportunities of self-improvement, in so far as they lay within the hand of the white race, were accorded exclusively to this class of people who were the left-handed progeny of the white masters."[35]

Harrison's growing dissatisfaction with existing Black leadership and his desire to free Black thought from the shackles of the Booker T. Washington school soon led to a confrontation with Washington and his "Tuskegee Machine." This process began to unfold after Washington made some controversial statements in London in the fall of 1910. In response to Washington's comments, an "Appeal to England and Europe" was issued in pamphlet form by Du Bois and others with a listed address that was the same as the fledgling NAACP. This led to a major public controversy and greatly widened the gap between the Washington forces and the NAACP and others, including Harrison.[36]

The details of the controversy include a September *Age* report that Booker T. Washington was "Lionized in London" when he discussed "The Race Problem in America" in the London *Morning Post*. Washington was traveling in Europe, reportedly to study economic conditions, when he was quoted as saying that he "look[ed] forward to the future with hope and confidence" and that the situation in the South, "far from becoming more difficult or dangerous, becomes more and more reassuring." He also added that "the Southern States of the Union offer to the Negro a better chance than almost any other country in the world."[37]

"The Appeal" was a response to Washington's interview in the *Morning Post* and to comments on the status of the Negro that he made while speaking before the Anti-Slavery and Aborigines Protective Society in London that were quoted in the London *Times* of October 8. "The Appeal" charged that Washington skirted instances of wrongdoings, was unduly optimistic about race relations, and reportedly said that "there was wisdom, patience, forbearance, Christianity, and patriotism enough to enable each race to live side by side, working out its destiny with justice to the other." Du Bois wrote "The Appeal," and it was signed by thirty-two notable "Negro Americans" of "The National Negro Committee on Mr. [Booker T.] Washington" and issued as a pamphlet from 20 Vesey Street, the address of the NAACP in Oswald Garrison Villard's *Evening Post* Building, though the NAACP's address had been used without official permission.[38]

The "Appeal" argued that "if Mr. Booker T. Washington, or any other person, is giving the impression abroad that the Negro problem in America is in process of satisfactory solution, he is giving an impression which is not true." It went on to point out that Washington "has been for years compelled to tell not the whole truth, but the part of it which certain powerful interests in America wish to appear as the whole truth." After citing a host of discriminations and proscriptions in virtually every avenue of American life, "based solely on race and color," the "Appeal" called for "the moral support of England and Europe in this crusade for this recognition of manhood" waged by those fighting for equality. Though Harrison had criticisms of the NAACP, he clearly supported the political thrust of the "Appeal."[39]

The New York *Sun*, a major daily, published the "Appeal" on December 1, and this was followed by a *Sun* editorial on December 2 and a series of letters on the "Negro Problem." The editorial implied that the signatories were envious "exes" (former holders of prominent positions) jealous of Washington's position and advised these "uninvited spokesmen" that they were "not helping their cause" and that what was needed was "patience and perseverance," not "impotent lamentations." Responses included a rabidly racist one on December 5 signed by "D," who argued that "the white man will not, cannot, accord social equality, because he will not in a day or in a generation, in public or private, accept him [the African American] as an equal."[40]

It was in this setting that Harrison submitted his first letter to the *Sun*. It was written on December 7 and published on December 8, three days before he spoke on "The Status of Negro Leadership" at the Y. He had saved several clippings on Washington's European trip, and he felt that "Washington had lied in an article in *Die Zeit*, of Vienna, when he declared" that American whites "were absolutely fair and honest" in dealings with African Americans and that African American had nothing to complain about. The letter to the *Sun* argued for and was titled "Insistence Upon Its Real Grievances the Only Course for the Race." It criticized the *Sun* editorial and was a pointed attack on the leadership of Booker T. Washington. Harrison was now publicly and candidly criticizing America's most powerful Black leader—race leaders, like others, were not immune from his comments. In turn, Harrison would not be immune from the powerful influence of Booker T. Washington.[41]

The letter began by asking the *Sun* "whether it is assumed that the human nature of black men differs from that of white men?" because the paper had demonstrated "that patronizing attitude of the American mind toward the Negro intellect which is so unpleasant to self-respecting black people." It added, "While it is assumed that progressive Jews are more competent than outsiders to appraise the leaders of any Jewish propaganda, such as Zionism, it is everywhere assumed that outsiders are better able to do this for Negroes than progressive Negroes are to do it for themselves." Harrison then proceeded to present part of the case of the Black protesters "without any hysterical 'peevishness'" because he wished to show that their case was grounded on reason. In a direct response to both the racists and the Washington forces, he added that if Blacks had no right to think, there was no point for further discussion. In this sentiment he resembled what Du Bois, with perhaps a touch of haughtiness, later referred to as "the bumptious, irritated young black intelligentsia of the day [who] declared: 'I don't care a damn what Booker Washington thinks. This is what I think, and *I have a right to think.*'"[42]

As was his wont, Harrison examined the arguments of the position he wished to challenge and then countered them reasonably and factually. In this case he drew support from articles in his scrapbooks. He argued that Washington had declared to the world that all was well with African Americans and that this had been echoed in his "special mouthpiece the New York *Age*" at Thanksgiving when it declared that "the Negro" had more to be thankful for than any other group of Americans. Yet, Harrison pointed out, these pronouncements came "right on the heels of the Baltimore [residential segregation] legislation, the Oklahoma elections [in which a "grandfather clause" disfranchising two-thirds of the state's African Americans was passed], and the instructions of Texas to its Congressional representatives to work for the repeal of the last two amendments [the Fourteenth and the Fifteenth, granting citizenship to African Americans and the right to vote to African American males] to the Constitution." In contrast to Washington, the signers of the "Appeal" had declared that there were very real grievances crying for redress. To argue that the grievances did not exist would not do away with them. History had shown the way to right human wrongs: "first, by insisting that they were wrongs: and secondly, by fighting against them with tongue and pen and sword."[43]

Harrison also directly challenged Washington's philosophy. Washington argued that if Black people would cease harping on these grievances and acquire property and manual skill, the grievances, "the crux of the Negro problem," would decrease and disappear. Harrison replied with hard facts, not an "appeal to the philosophy of history or to anything that may even faintly savor of erudition" since "Washington and his satellites say that that is bad." He noted that in Virginia, North Carolina, and South Carolina, though Black people were 40 percent of the population they received only 14 percent of school funding, and he asked if it wasn't evident that Black children were being deprived of a fair chance in life? He didn't think that the reason this happened was because their fathers were so stupid as to allow it with their votes and he therefore criticized Washington for depicting "the agitation for the ballot as unwise."[44]

Next, Harrison challenged the notion that Washington's proposals for patience and thrift were the answer. He cited the situation in Baltimore, where African Americans had "shown industry and thrift," acquired wealth, and sought to buy better homes. Whites had then passed a city ordinance to segregate Black people by law. To Harrison, "the white people, through their city council," had made clear that "the right of Negroes to buy what they can pay for must be restricted in the interests of white people." Similarly, in Kansas City, Missouri, an African American who had saved $5,000 to put up for a piece of property had that property dynamited. Harrison concluded that though Washington said "that if the Negro will become a house owner he will get the good will and respect of his white neighbors," it seemed clear that he would also get "their envy and ill will."[45]

Harrison's most powerful argument, however, concerned an issue at the core of Booker T. Washington's program—industrial training in the absence of political rights. He cited the Georgia railroad strike of 1909. In that struggle, white laborers had organized to oppose "seniority rights" for Black workers in order to keep preferred jobs "lily-white," and the Brotherhood of Locomotive Firemen had urged the total elimination of Black firemen. That strike of white workers, reasoned Harrison, made clear "that any training which makes black men more efficient will bring them into keener competition with white men. . . . Their jobs will be taken away."[46]

After making his points, Harrison then defended his right, and that of the signers of the "Appeal," to criticize Washington and not be dismissed by the *Sun* as envious have-nots. He also criticized, as he would for the remainder of his life, the assumption that whites should choose Black leaders. As he continued his political development, one of his principal tenets would be that Black leaders should be chosen by the Black masses. In this case Harrison argued that though Mr. Washington was "a great leader," his leadership was "by the grace of the white people who elect colored people's leaders for them." This was something that Harrison would not support. Further, since Washington was as "likely to make mistakes as any other son of man," criticism of Washington from other African Americans, like criticism of any other person, need not be dismissed as mere envy.[47]

Two letters in defense of Washington and critical of the writers of the "Appeal" followed Harrison's. One, signed "L.A.W." and identified as being from "a colored man," argued that "there are a small number of negroes scattered through the country who have learned that almost the only way they can get their names in public print is either in a public speech or in newspaper articles opposing something that Mr. Washington had done or has not done." A second letter, from the Philadelphia-based attorney and Washington associate John C. Asbury, described the "Appeal" as "both illogical and unjust" and "made for the sole purpose of branding Dr. Booker T. Washington as one who 'misrepresents the truth.'"[48]

Harrison responded, and his second letter, in the December 19 *Sun*, argued that both "L.A.W." and J. C. Asbury evaded the question at issue—whether the "'real and crying grievances' exist?"—because if they did there was no point in abusing those who said so. He stated that the importance of the "Appeal" was "not its logic, but its truth," and the point was "not whether Europe can help, but whether Mr. Washington misrepresented the actual situation of the Negro in America to-day." Since that fact had not been denied, even by Washington's defenders, Harrison questioned the motives and manliness of those who so quickly criticized people demanding full democratic rights. He also declared that while "our American democracy is a sham," as "The Appeal to Europe" intended to point out, "large support is enthusiastically given to any school of opinion which will reconcile Negroes to the double standard of democracy." Harrison then boldly concluded with a direct attack on Washington's philosophy that called for an end to the "Tuskegee Machine":

> For a very long time such a school of Negro thought exercised such thralldom over the minds of black men that they have been afraid to make their dissent known. It has controlled political preferment, swayed the ignorant mass of ministers, controlled the Negro press and bludgeoned it into line by the help of the white press. This state of affairs must end sooner or later and I for one think it high time that the men who can think for themselves should speak out and not be afraid.[49]

In response to these two letters to the *Sun*, Washington's forces would soon retaliate forcefully against Harrison.

Before the retaliation was implemented, however, Harrison wrote a lengthy article that restated the positions in his two letters and articulated a more general critique of the racist press in the United States. The article appeared under the title "The Negro and the Newspapers," probably in early 1911, and began by commenting on a communication from the author J. Ellis Barker of London in an interview that appeared in the pro-Republican, pro–Booker T. Washington, New York *Age* of December 29, 1910. Barker claimed that people in Europe "do not understand the race problem, and we do not know the colored people," yet, before coming to the United States, he had developed a "prejudice against the colored people [that] was as great as that of any southern planter." This was caused by what he had been told in books and papers published in Europe, specifically that Blacks "were a race of barbarians and savages."[50]

Harrison responded that "the newspapers of this country have many crimes to answer for," and he cited examples of how the U.S. press fostered anti-Black views. He described how they featured "Negro" criminals in bold headlines (while "Negroes" of true substance, if covered at all, were "relegated to the agate type division") and how they "constantly appeal to the putrid passion of race hatred," creating "untold sorrow." Harrison concluded that newspapers' falsehoods had to be countered by "Truth"—but even this was no simple matter. "Truth" in the case of "Negroes" was more difficult to obtain since it needed "the widest publicity" and substantial prestige—and even "though Truth come[s] hot on the heels of Falsehood it could not quite undo its devil's work." Nevertheless, he stressed that, such effort "must be made."[51]

In his confidence in the ability of truth and reason Harrison was manifesting an attitude current in intellectual circles. Du Bois held a similar view and in this same period envisioned his "long-term remedy" as "Truth." Within a few years, however, both Harrison and Du Bois would undergo significant change, becoming far less sanguine about truth and reason and far more aware of economic and sociopolitical factors, of the relativity of moral values, and of the power of irrational thought and action.[52]

It was probably an increasing awareness of such forces, including the retaliatory forces of the Booker T. Washington machine, that led Harrison to proceed more cautiously when he next wrote to the *Sun*. This time he used a pseudonym (the first of many) and, with the playful touch that he would use in selecting such names, he wrote under the pen name of "E. T. Washington," an apparent takeoff on Booker T. Washington. His letter was in response to a letter of January 19, 1911, signed "T.A.O." and headlined "Negro Real Estate Sharpers: How They Prey Upon Their Race and Spoil Good White Neighborhoods." That letter decried Black real estate agents as "the worst enemies of the negroes of this city" because they attempt "to colonize the scum of the race in white neighborhoods." "T.A.O." advocated adding "a clause demanding that only negroes of proved respectability and character . . . be permitted to rent these apartments" to all leases. After this, the letter concluded, "there will be no negro invasion, present or remote, of localities heretofore exclusively white."[53]

That Black real estate sharpies did exist and that Harrison had reason to use a pseudonym there is no doubt. Philip A. Payton Jr., founder of the African American Realty Company, was notorious for renting property from "whites" and then rerenting to Blacks at prices 10 percent above the market price. In addition, among executive officers in Payton's company were three people who would play major roles in causing Harrison to lose his postal job: Fred Moore, publisher of the *Age*; Charles W. Anderson, the leading Black Republican in New York; and Emmett Scott, right-hand man to Booker T. Washington. All three were major parts of Washington's "Tuskegee Machine."[54]

Harrison's "E. T. Washington" reply, entitled "The Reverse of the Medal," appeared in the January 21 *Sun*. He openly criticized the real estate sharpies, yet, through the logic of his argument and a dose of irony, turned the racist assumption about "white neighborhoods" into a compelling argument for an end to both segregated housing and such neighborhoods. Harrison's letter assumed that "T.A.O." was white and gave him "credit for giving expression to the resentment felt by decent colored people at the heartless exploitation of their needs." He pointed out how, "as their wealth and influence increase," they would "increasingly insist upon the right of all American citizens to buy what their money can pay for."[55]

One reader of Harrison's 1910 letters to the *Sun* was Charles W. Anderson, the city's leading Black Republican politician, a close personal and political friend of both Booker T. Washington and the Republican-appointed New York City postmaster, Edward M. Morgan. In 1911 Anderson met with Washington, Emmett Scott (Washington's assistant), and Fred R. Moore, another strong Washington supporter and publisher of the *Age* in the paper's office. The three apparently decided on Harrison's removal from the Post Office. According to Harrison this was done because they could not "argue away the facts . . . presented in the *Sun*." They then initiated a campaign of harassment that ultimately led to his removal, and Charles W. Anderson was the man who engineered it.[56]

Harrison had transferred to the recently opened (1909) Grand Central Post Office to work in the paper section on February 8, 1911, and on April 18 he was bonded and received a 100 percent salary increase to $2,000 per year. Suddenly, on May 1, his salary increase was rescinded, and he was dropped back down to $1,000 annually. On July 1 he was "failed of promotion," and on September 1 he was charged with "leaving the floor of the work room before his tour of duty ended, and using insolent and disrespectful language to his superintendent." Harrison had never even been suspended, but there was something more at play here. The instigator was Washington's friend Charles W. Anderson, who on September 10 wrote a revealing letter to Washington:

> Do you remember Hubert H. Harrison? He is the man who wrote two nasty articles against you in the New York "Sun." He is a clerk in the Post office. The Postmaster is my personal friend, as you probably know. Harrison has had charges preferred against him and I think he is liable to be dismissed from the service. If not dismissed, he will get severe punishment. Can you see the hand? I think you can. Please destroy this, that it may not fall under another eye—unless it is Emmett's. I will attend to Harrison. If he escapes me he is a dandy.[57]

Harrison did not escape. He was denied a hearing and removed from the Post Office on September 23, 1911. This was done despite the fact that, as he later pointed out, he had no previous suspensions and "there was no proof of the charges." Further, Postmaster Morgan "knew" from Harrison's "written answers to the charges of various kinds" and from his service record that he was innocent. Nevertheless, though the father of two children, Harrison had lost his $1,000-a-year raise and then his $1,000-a-year job. Anderson took particular delight in the removal and again addressed a letter to Washington, sarcastically writing:

> I am sure that you will regret to learn that Mr. Hubert H. Harrison has been dismissed from his position as clerk in the New York Post Office. I am certain also that you will regret to hear that he is blaming me for his dismissal. As Postmaster Morgan is a *particular personal friend* of mine of long years standing, and as the charge against Mr. Harrison was considered (by Harrison) trivial that "brother" believes that some sinister influence was at work against him, and that influence was set in operation by me. Well, I can endure the charge with fortitude and good humor. Harrison had a dispute with the Superintendent of the Branch Post Office in which he was employed, and as he had had several of these disputes with this and other Superintendents before, I presume the Postmaster thought it high time to drop him and get a man who would talk less and work more. He is now stumping for the Socialist Party, and will probably have plenty of time in the future to learn that God is not good to those who do not behave themselves.[58]

Anderson was half-right. Harrison was stumping for the Socialist Party, but he did not gather any lesson about God's ways—for his antireligious, freethought activities also intensified.

The action of Washington's "Tuskegee Machine" was dastardly. On a personal level, its impact on Harrison and his family was devastating. After losing his postal employment Harrison often lived in deep poverty. Paying bills and feeding his family was extremely difficult. Over sixty years later his children still remarked on the financial difficulties and hard times they remembered from their childhood. The postal employment had paid a livable wage and offered some degree of security. Had he not been unjustly fired, it is reasonable to suspect that he and his family, which grew to seven, would have lived modestly but relatively well and that his family might have been decently provided for after his death. Instead, all seven family members would suffer.

The unjust firing not only had harsh personal and familial consequences, it also had important effects on Harrison's political work. At the time, the loss of the postal wage drove him in the direction of accepting work and pay from the Socialist Party. The nature of this new socialist work, as well as the pressure coming from the "Tuskegee Machine," temporarily pulled and pushed this young and talented potential leader away from the work he had been doing in

Figure 4.3. Booker T. Washington (seated) and his private secretary Emmett Scott (standing), c. 1906. Booker T. Washington (1856–1915) was born enslaved in 1856 and became the most powerful Black man in the United States, a position he achieved through ties to powerful whites and through an extensive patronage and pressure machine. Harrison was critical of much of Washington's philosophy, which he referred to as "one of submission and acquiescence in political servitude." After Harrison openly criticized Washington in two letters to the *New York Sun* in 1910, Washington, his loyal secretary Emmett J. Scott (1873–1957), and members of Washington's "Tuskegee Machine" took steps to have Harrison fired from his postal employment. The unjust firing had severe financial consequences on Harrison and his family. *Source:* Photo by Frances Benjamin Johnson. Reproduced from the collections of the Library of Congress.

the Black community. Over time, the firing had additional political impact. One of the major criticisms of Harrison concerned his handling of money. Several of his efforts would fail at critical times because of financial pressure. Often the amount of money needed was not great, though it was beyond Harrison's means. Had he retained his postal employment it is quite possible that subsequent political work—with the Socialists, with the Liberty League and *The Voice*, and with the International Colored Unity League—might have better addressed financial problems and had qualitatively different results.

While he was under increased pressure from the Booker T. Washington forces, Harrison began to attract attention in the freethought movement. When he spoke on "Tom Paine's Place in the Deistical Movement," at a freethought-sponsored Thomas Paine Commemoration Dinner in February 1911, he was depicted as "a Negro, who has the reputation of being the most scholarly representative of his race in America." A Reverend Marshall, who introduced him at that meeting, said that he had "an encyclopedic knowledge of literature."[59]

Harrison's lecture, printed in the *Truth Seeker* of February 11, argued for a democratization of knowledge and explained how Paine "popularized the arguments against Christianity and brought them down to the level of democracy," thereby quickening "the advance of freethought." He described how the deistical movement, the "broad movement of the human mind" from the seventeenth through the nineteenth centuries, "shattered the very foundations of superstition" and belief in a "traditional God, of Christian revelation," and how it led to the development of criticism—textual at first, then the scientific development of higher criticism, which grew in the nineteenth century into agnosticism and atheism. Harrison also discussed positive aspects in Paine's approach, including the commonsense criticism and numerical blunders in Chronicles and in the genealogy of Christ given in Matthew and Luke; historical criticism, such as the fact that the Pentateuch couldn't have been written by Moses since it included events after his death; and comparative and literary criticism such as that found in the second part of Paine's *Age of Reason*. Finally, in a glowing tribute, Harrison said that Paine initiated "a different method of dissent," one based in reason and brought "to the level of all," to "the level of democracy"—and in so doing he served as a forerunner of contemporary rationalists. He was also a forerunner of Harrison, who consistently sought to bring rational, democratic dissent to the masses.[60]

A few months after his talk on Paine, in July 1911, Harrison wrote a book review of *Half a Man: The Status of the Negro in New York*, by the civil rights activist and socialist Mary White Ovington. It appeared in the *Amsterdam News* of July 5, 1911, under the pseudonym "Hamlet." Harrison probably used the pseudonym because he was undergoing difficulties on the job over his *Sun* letters (and perhaps, like Hamlet, sensed that his problems were growing more serious). His postal salary increase was, in fact, rescinded on May 1, and he was denied a promotion in early July. Another reason for the use of the "Hamlet" pseudonym may have been because he felt the use of such a name, rather than his own, offered the best chance of getting the letter, critical of a white NAACP founder and leader, published in a Black weekly—in this case the two-year-old *Amsterdam News*.[61]

In his review, "Hamlet" said that *Half-a-Man* was "a scholarly compend of facts" but that it did not "accurately present the case of the Negro of New York" and did not contain any "new information for thoughtful colored people" since it was "too small in the first place, and too deferential in the next." He added that since statistics could not go very far and since "facts, like truth, are not so much to see as to see by," the book's emphasis on numerical analysis showed precisely "where the sociological method fails." He concluded that the work was "serviceable at just those points where she [Ovington] discards sociology—in the last three chapters."[62]

Shortly after his dismissal from the Post Office, Harrison wrote a front-page article, "Menace of Exemption," under his own name for the November 4, 1911, *Truth Seeker*. The article described how churches with property in New York City worth four to five hundred million dollars evaded payment of taxes. This time, he did not use a pseudonym, and this may have been because, having already lost his post office position, he no longer had that threat hanging over his head.[63]

The polemic and exposé argued for taxation of church property and against the idea that the United States was or should be a Christian nation that owed special privileges to the church. With his customary statistical rigor, Harrison cited Census Bureau figures for 1910 that showed that "not quite two-fifths of the population of the United States, were reported as church members," and he argued that the real number was much less because the Catholic Church persisted in reporting children, infants, and anyone baptized. It therefore made no sense to call this a Christian nation. In addition, since religious property was tax exempt, this meant that church property was supported by the taxes of many property holders who were not members of churches at all, a "monstrous injustice not only against three-fifths of the people but also against the secular property of the other two-fifths."[64]

Harrison asked, "How can the churches—especially the Christian church— reconcile this policy of public dishonesty with their professions of piety?" Advocates evidently assumed that church property should be tax exempt by virtue of "divine right." In taking on the divine-right argument Harrison was in his element, and he was ready to challenge an opposing view by quoting from the opposing camp. He explained that "neither the Bible nor the earlier fathers furnished any ground for such a belief, and the Christian Scriptures themselves contain an implied condemnation of the tax exemption theory." In the synoptic Gospels Jesus paid his taxes and laid down the principle governing such cases by offering the advice found in Matthew 22:21: "Render . . . unto Caesar the things that are Caesar's and unto God the things that are God's." This, he noted, was how "the first Christian paid his taxes."[65]

Harrison also offered a counter to the argument that the churches benefit society. He argued that between 1900 and 1909 the churches were flourishing and their property holdings tripled, yet "in that period the murder rate of the United States climbed rapidly from 21 per million of population to 59," making it "the largest murder rate in any civilized land." He considered the murder rate "one of the most elementary indications of a people's moral stability" and suggested that because church property value and the murder rate each trebled in the decade, the churches were not doing their job. Emphasizing that Jesus had proposed a secular test (explained in Matthew 7:16)—"by their fruits ye shall know them"—Harrison then, less than convincingly, suggested that "until the churches can reduce the murder rate they should be silent about benefiting the nation."[66]

Finally, Harrison offered a historical argument and pointed to the role that the church had played in the downfall of civilizations and nations from Rome to the more recent examples of France, Spain, and Portugal. Through "the extensive system of exemptions and privileges," he argued, "the church first secured a hold on the State and then strangled it." He concluded with a forceful call for taxation of church property:

> Since the exemption of church property from taxation is the very root of that power by which the church becomes a social and political menace; since we have the experience of the past and the present to show us the deplorable effects of this power in the national life of a people; since the churches themselves can advance no valid claim (even from their own Bible) to the tax-exemption of their property, and since the exemption of any but public property is unjust and dangerous on grounds of civil and political welfare—the churches ought to be compelled to pay their just portion of the burden of public expense.[67]

Harrison was posing clear and forceful challenges to the church, and in so doing he was distancing himself from the most powerful institution in the Black community. Thus, in 1911, as he began to move increasingly into radical, almost exclusively white intellectual circles, such as the freethought movement and the almost entirely white Socialist Party, Harrison moved further away from current and popular sentiment in the Black community. As he distanced himself from the Black church, he also limited his prospects as a mass leader of African Americans.[68]

In what would become a recurring theme, Harrison's intellectual pursuits, convictions, and forthrightness made him all too willing to challenge what he would later call "The Idols of the Tribe." Those idols, both (spiritual) gods and (human) leaders, often represented what people thought they wanted to see and hear, not necessarily what was best for them. The intellectual insights that led Harrison to challenge existing idols and existing currents of thought and that helped to prepare him for leadership at first distanced him from the community he would seek to lead. In one sense, his step forward, like every break from the past, was a deviation from the existing norm. It also, however, suggests more. His willingness to offer public criticism despite almost predictable political and personal consequences foreshadowed much of the road ahead. Harrison, the articulate and insightful critic and trailblazer, would never evidence sufficient internal organizational skills nor consolidate the organizational ties well enough to successfully lead a sustained mass movement or organizational effort. At the same time, he would manifest a certain heroic quality in his willingness to follow the course that he deemed best "and not the course mapped out for him by the multitude."[69]

By 1911, the indefatigable Harrison was ready to make his next major step forward. He had arrived as an immigrant eleven years before and had faced the problem of adjustment. Racial and class oppression as well as his colonial background shaped the place he found in society. His compassion for the oppressed and his critical and searching intellect moved him to challenge societally imposed barriers of race, class, and thought. Having served his apprenticeship in the church lyceums and the Y, where free and independent debate reigned and white-supremacist thought was challenged; having nurtured this independent spirit in the freethought movement, his study circles, and in his critical writings; more race and class conscious because of his life and work experiences and his reading; familiar with the most popular and leading intellectual thought of his era; scientific and modern in approach; rational and logical in thought; yet defiantly beholden to no ideology—Harrison would now merge this training with the more ideological activism of the Socialist Party of America.

Socialist Radical

5

Hope in Socialism (1911)

The Socialist Party that Hubert Harrison joined was founded in 1901 as a result of divisions and regroupings of various socialist organizations over the previous decade. The key merger was that between the Social Democratic Party of America, led by the American Railway Union organizer Eugene V. Debs and the Milwaukee newspaper editor Victor L. Berger, and a split-off faction from Daniel De Leon's Socialist Labor Party, headed by the New York labor attorney Morris Hillquit. In general, socialists believed that capitalism was an outmoded system; that it was the chief cause of both the rapidly intensifying economic inequality and the erosion of democracy in U.S. society; and that a socialist society was near and obtainable. Sympathy with socialism was considered an easy step for people to take, and the Socialist Party approached elections expecting a steady increase in their share of the vote. By the 1908 presidential election, the party had more than 40,000 members, and that year it polled more than 400,000 votes (3 percent of all votes cast).[1]

In its 1908 platform, the Socialist Party proclaimed itself "the party of the working class." The platform explained that political parties were the expression of economic class interests; it attacked monopolies and trusts, the high courts, and Congress; and it called for nationalization of industries, the eight-hour work day, a graduated income tax, women's suffrage, and public-works programs for the unemployed. The party's rational appeal, as described by Daniel Bell, offered that "in the nature of their social evolution," people "were becoming more rational," "were mastering nature and harnessing it," and, "in the course of events," they would "harness society and turn it to the common good rather than the profit of a few."[2]

Though the party was unified in its opposition to capitalism, it was not mono-
lithic, and its broad unifying appeal was accompanied by deep internal differences and debate. The major ideological difference was over whether socialism would come by evolution (through gradual political gains) or by ever more
militant strikes and revolution. The party's 1908 platform officially opposed reform work and declared that the "various 'reform' movements and parties . . .
are but the clumsy expression of widespread popular discontent." It noted that
these reform movements were "not based on an intelligent understanding of the
historical development of civilization" or "on the economic and political needs
of our time" and were "bound to perish." There was, however, strong internal
opposition in the party to this position from "constructive [evolutionary] socialists," who saw aspects of socialism in nationalization (such as in the Post Office)
and who saw socialism coming piecemeal, by reform and electoral gains. The
second pivotal issue was the trade union question. While all party leaders supported work with industrial (multicraft) unions, the debate was over whether
the party should work within the generally conservative trade-union movement,
headed by the 1.7-million-member American Federation of Labor, which focused
on craft unions and skilled trades (and did not challenge all-white unions or the
existence of segregated "'federal' Negro unions"). In 1901 the Socialist Party
had taken a position, reaffirmed in 1903, not to interfere in internal trade-union
questions, and since many AFL unions had racial exclusion policies, this issue
had particular bearing on how unions dealt with the "Negro" question.[3]

As the trade-union issue suggests, it is reasonable to question the Socialist
Party's appeal to African Americans. In fact, the SP had few Black members,
offered no special program, had a weak record on the "Negro" question, and
opposed reforms that were badly needed in the African American community.
It also had shortcomings as a functioning political party—it had very limited
political clout and was relatively powerless to implement change. In addition, as
the historian Philip S. Foner has described, "racism was well entrenched in the
Socialist party."[4]

The Socialist Party's record and lack of program reflect the fact that internally there actually were broad differences on the "Negro" question." While the
SP sought to overthrow the capitalist system, its attitude toward the role that
African Americans would play in the process was neither clear nor encouraging. Party theory and practice, according to Philip S. Foner, ran the gamut from
"outright racist advocacy of white supremacy," through the position that "the
Negro question was a class problem and nothing more," to the position that
"the Socialist party should conduct a consistent and persistent struggle against
racism." Victor L. Berger, who in 1910 would become the party's first elected
congressman, had argued as far back as 1902 that "negroes and mulattoes constitute a lower race." Ernest Untermann, a leading party theoretician, declared

Figure 5.1. Eugene V. Debs, speaking in New York, 1912. Indiana-born Eugene V. Debs (1855–1926), was a founding member of the Socialist Party of America (1900) and the Industrial Workers of the World (1905) and a five-time Socialist Party presidential candidate. Although Debs was considered one of the best Socialist Party members on the "Negro" question, he argued that the class struggle was "colorless," thought that African Americans' struggle was only part of the general labor struggle, and maintained that there was no need for "separate appeals" to reach African Americans. Harrison thought that Socialists should champion the cause of African Americans as a revolutionary doctrine; that they should affirm the duty of all socialists to oppose race prejudice; and that they should develop special appeals to and for African Americans. *Source:* Courtesy of Brown Brothers.

in a 1908 convention debate, "I am determined that my [white] race shall be supreme in this country and the world." Julius A. Wayland, editor of the weekly *Appeal to Reason* (which had a circulation of 500,000), was a strict segregationist who believed that Black people, like whites, preferred "to live in communities of their own." Even the influential five-time Socialist Party presidential candidate, Debs, long considered one of the best party members on the "Negro" question thought that African Americans, because of their experience in slavery, were not yet the equal of whites, that their struggle was only part of the general labor struggle, and that there was no need for "separate appeals" to reach them. He argued that the class struggle was "colorless," that the question of "social equality" was beyond party discussion, that there was no "negro problem apart from the general labor problem," and that to raise the race issue would run the risk of dividing the working class.[5]

The downplaying of struggle against white supremacy was increasingly manifested at Socialist Party conventions. At the first convention in 1901, a resolution passed, pushed by Black delegate William H. Costley, that in many ways evidenced the party at its best. That resolution recognized that "because of their long training in slavery," African Americans occupied "a peculiar position in the working class." It emphasized that capitalists sought to "foster and increase color prejudice and race hatred" among workers; stressed that Black people were betrayed by the "old political parties and educational and religious institutions"; identified the interests of all workers as the same; declared that "race prejudices spring from the ancient economic causes which still endure"; and solicited Black membership in the party while offering socialism as the solution for "the negro problem." The resolution, however, offered nothing special for African Americans and conspicuously failed to address any specific grievances such as lynching, segregation, or disfranchisement. An antilynching provision was vociferously opposed by leading party members before it was withdrawn on the grounds that it would lose votes in the South. The Costley resolution was little more than a paper document: it was never reaffirmed at a party convention, and it was so rarely published that hardly anyone knew of its existence. By 1903, Debs, the former head of an all-white union (which he had tried to integrate), called for its repeal because Blacks didn't need it and the party had "nothing special to offer the negro." At the 1904 convention, attempts to write a resolution similar to that of 1901 were rejected.[6]

Typical of the party's insensitivity to African American sentiment was its response to the 1906 Brownsville, Texas, affair, which so outraged the Black community. The party press produced no editorials on the subject, and party leadership actually defeated a motion to condemn President Roosevelt's handling of Brownsville. Right-wing party leaders objected to the motion as an "attempt to inject the negro question into the Socialist Party," while "left"-leaning members objected because the army was a capitalist tool with which socialists should not be involved. Other glaring instances of party insensitivity to the "Negro" question included: general neglect in the party press; failure of the party to change racist membership practices in the South; the party position of noninterference in the internal matters of AFL trade unions that left segregative and exclusionary policies unchallenged; the lack of strong opposition to lynching; and the widespread tendency in the party press of not capitalizing the letter "N" in "Negro."[7]

While the SP offered nothing special to African Americans, that was not its approach toward other groups—notably foreigners and women. In those cases the party was willing to make special appeals and allow special organizational forms. Harrison saw and noted the party's efforts in these areas and would later cite them as he struggled to draw more attention to the race problem.[8]

Party work among foreigners was in the midst of significant growth. In 1904 a Finnish Federation was formed, and this would be followed over the next eleven years by many other Foreign Language Federations, including Lettish, South Slav, Italian, Scandinavian, Hungarian, Bohemian, German, Polish, Jewish, Slavic, Ukrainian, Lithuanian, and Russian. These federations were affiliated with national and state offices in very loose fashion and were rarely in contact with party locals. They developed separate organizations and separate representatives and had considerable autonomy in their work and in making special appeals to their targeted groups. By 1917, given such an autonomous approach, roughly 33,000 out of a total of 80,000 party members were in Foreign Language Federations.[9]

Similar gains were also made in party work among women. At first the attitude of the majority of Socialist Party leaders toward equal rights for women was similar to their approach to the question of "Negro equality." The "Negro" question was "part of the general 'labor problem,'" and the "'woman question' was part of the 'labor question.'" Formally, however, as with the "Negro" question, there was not a single, coherent ideology on the woman question. The SP's parliamentary perspective, however, gave the issue of women's suffrage special importance. Thus, while the party's treatment of women, according to the historian Sally M. Miller, "often seemed less than equitable," the Socialists were the only major political party to allow women members and to support the goal of equal suffrage for women.[10]

The Socialist Party's progress on women's issues was strongly influenced by an independent women's movement. In 1901, party women formed the Woman's National Socialist League to teach socialist principles to women and to agitate for the party and its platform, which demanded "equal civil and political rights for men and women." Independent efforts, including women working outside of the party on political and broader social issues, helped to increase female party membership from 3 to 5 percent between 1904 and 1908. At the 1908 party convention, an all-female Woman's National Committee was established to focus on women's socialist activities and do electoral and suffrage work. After the 1908 convention, each party local was invited to organize women's branches or committees, which were in general linked to state-level committees and to urban central committees. As these women's groups grew, some were autonomous and others functioned under the auspices of party locals. In the process of developing this work, a parallel and distinct hierarchy within the party developed, and the key was the club structure. The all-women clubs were generally autonomous, and, though their officers were party members, they often developed their own strategies and programs. By 1910, there were 150 such clubs within the party locals. The work of these clubs, as well as the heightened struggle of women in the garment industry (from which the party recruited many new members), were major factors in the increase of women in the SP, and by 1913 women constituted 15 percent of party membership.[11]

It is likely that the intellectual character of Local New York of the Socialist Party had a certain appeal to Harrison. It was, according to the historian David A. Shannon, "the most articulate" center of socialism in the country, with "an unusual number of intellectuals" in its ranks. Included among its members were the NAACP founders William English Walling, Mary White Ovington, and Oswald Garrison Villard; the muckraker Charles Edward Russell; the publisher and historian Gustavus Myers; the painter John Sloan; the novelist Theodore Dreiser; the reformers Florence Kelley and Frances Perkins; and the attorneys Morris Hillquit and Louis B. Boudin. The local's intellectual appeal was bounded somewhat by the organizational leadership, which was generally evolutionary, conservative, nonviolent, and close to the AFL. The local was led by Morris Hillquit, who stressed immediate reforms and allied himself closely with trade unions.[12]

Though it had intellectual appeal, the party at first grew slowly in New York City and was relatively weak politically. Around 1908 its membership was probably over 99 percent white and composed largely of aging German immigrants in the skilled trades. The party's relative political weakness in New York City was reflected in elections—in New York State the party vote went from 12,000 in 1900 to 38,000 in 1908 while the city vote showed no growth; in 1909 the party candidate for mayor of New York City, Edward F. Cassidy, polled only 11,768 votes out of more than 600,000 cast.[13]

Local New York did, however, undergo a growth spurt, which was largely a function of the class struggle, particularly the general uprising of garment workers (spearheaded by women) in the November 1909 to February 1910 "Uprising of the Twenty Thousand." With this growth came a changing party makeup: between 1908 and 1912, SP recruits in Manhattan and the Bronx were 23 percent German, 13 percent Finnish, 3 percent Italian, 14 percent East European (non-Jewish), 39 percent East-European (Jewish), 8 percent Anglo-American, and 1% other (including Black). Even amid party growth in New York City, however, Black membership was strikingly low, and the few Black workers who joined were mostly from the West Indies.[14]

––––––––––

The actual date that Harrison joined the Socialist Party is not known. While it may have been as early as 1908 or 1909, it was more likely in 1911, after he lost his postal job. His decision to join the party, though extremely rare for a Black person, had a certain logic and rationality. Harrison was especially attracted by socialism's intellectual appeal and by the radical alternative it presented to the existing order. The historian Judith Stein, emphasizes that "Harrison was attracted to the Socialists' modern intellectual views. 'As a man of the 20th century,' he was, 'thoroughly disgusted' with the 'seventeenth century mode of translating ideas' displayed by leading black intellectuals." He was also likely attracted because of the possibility of remuneration for party work and for related public speaking.[15]

The party's rational, evolutionary emphasis undoubtedly interested him. He read books by or clipped newspaper articles on leading proponents of evolutionary theory, including Charles Darwin, Thomas Huxley, Herbert Spencer, and the German biologist Ernst Haeckel, and he read books by rationalists including Moncure D. Conway, the British critic of Christianity Walter R. Cassels, the Irish historian W. E. H. Lecky, the English freethinker Joseph McCabe, and the Scottish author and member of Parliament John M. Robertson. For the remainder of his life Harrison would recommend books by many of these authors, and he considered the autodidact, freethinking Robertson to be the "greatest all around scholar of present day England."[16]

In 1913 Harrison explained to a reporter for the *New Brunswick Times* how he came to socialism. He emphasized that his original attraction was intellectual. It came not from listening to speakers but through reading. He believed that in order to preserve his intellectual self-respect, any doctrine that represented the thinking of millions deserved to be studied on its merits. Curiously, he first read Single Tax literature and thought that it was socialism. Very possibly his readings included works by the Single Tax founder Henry George, the Single Tax–influenced journalist Timothy Thomas Fortune, and the Single Tax author-activist James F. Morton (who had reportedly participated in the 1905 activity at the Sunrise Club with Joseph Rinn and who would maintain a friendship with Harrison into the 1920s). Harrison moved from Single Tax material to economics (he particularly liked the works of the English economic historian James E. Thorold Rogers) and then turned to socialist literature. He had linked Single Taxism, reform Darwinism, historical criticism, and economic interpretations of history, and this not-uncommon linking was often made, according to the historian Eric F. Goldman, by those "who were angry at their America."[17]

The Socialist Party's theory and practice of class struggle likewise had their appeal. In terms of its theory, the SP was avowedly for the working class, and the Black masses were, as Harrison would emphasize, "more essentially proletarian than any other American group." Socialists, in contrast to the Republicans and Democrats, sought a radical change to U.S. society, dominated by the capitalist class. The SP was growing in influence, while existing Black organizations were having limited success in effecting societal change. The SP was also considered by many to be a viable alternative—it was a significant national party and part of a growing radical movement that posed a threat to capitalism. Around 1910 it entered a period of rapid growth—membership jumped from 58,000 to over

125,000 in two years, and in 1912 alone some 1,039 party members were elected to public office, including fifty-six mayors, eighteen state representatives, and two state senators. By that year, the party press boasted 8 foreign-language and 5 English-language dailies and 36 foreign-language and 262 English-language weeklies.[18]

Harrison's friend J. A. Rogers, who stayed with him and his family in the 1920s, offers more insight into Harrison's thinking. Rogers writes:

> He [Harrison] realized that the Negro's ill-treatment transcended color differences. . . . Color, he argued, was only the surface expression, and underneath it lay the world-old exploitation of man by his fellow-man, which manifested itself now under the guise of tribal and national relationship; now under religion; political belief; sex, color or anything else available.
>
> His study of modern science and sociology enabled him to see that the socialists had a clearer vision of this truth than either of the two great American political parties. Consistently, also, the Socialists were advocating the improvement of the economic lot of humanity, regardless of race or color. He thereupon joined the Socialists, who were few in number but very militant. This latter feature pleased him most.[19]

The Socialist Party's work with foreigners and women undoubtedly also appealed to Harrison. He was, according to party member Leonard Bright, "a great fighter for woman suffrage" and the "party was first to put in a plank for Equal Rights." In addition, evidence suggests that the party's special National Woman's Committee and its often autonomous women's clubs, as well as the autonomy and special appeals of the Foreign Language Federations, interested him. When he finally became a full-time party organizer in 1911, he would try to develop a somewhat similar "special approach" in organizing "Negroes" and in developing a Colored Socialist Club.[20]

Overall, it appears that socialism's intellectual appeal; its use of science, economics, and rational and evolutionary theory; its approach to women and foreigners; its potential for assisting Black progress; its analysis of the ongoing class struggle; its offering of an opportunity to make a better world for working people; and its militancy—as well as the potential for financial support and for personal recognition—made the party a viable option for Harrison. Clearly, it was not the party's position on the "Negro" question alone that drew him.

While his decision to join the party had a certain logic, his decision to work full-time for the party was almost forced upon Harrison economically. After he lost his postal job he found himself in need of work to support his family of four. Local New York offered such work, and he spent three very full years laboring for the Socialist Party cause.

Harrison became fully active with the Socialists in late 1911. At first he was doing freethought work, but he moved increasingly toward concentrated Socialist Party activity. His initial efforts were marked by abundant energy and a tremendous hope in the possibilities of socialism. Rogers noted that Harrison "showed so much zeal that he rose rapidly to be one the recognized leaders. His all-around knowledge; his grasp of economics; the logic of his thought; his fearlessness; his ability as a speaker; all brought increasing recognition to the party."[21]

In August 1911, shortly before Harrison was fired from the Post Office and engaged full-time by the Socialists, the SP in New York was shaken by instances of white supremacism in the national organization. Theresa Malkiel, a national organizer for the party, had gone on a speaking tour of the South. On August 21, the *Call*, New York City's two-year-old Socialist daily (circulation 15,000), published her report. It had a Memphis dateline and was entitled "'Socialists' Despise Negroes in the South: 'Comrades' Refuse to Allow Colored Men in Meeting Halls or Party." Malkiel explained that while on tour in Bald Knob, Arkansas, party members had refused to let her address a picnic of over 1,000 Black people who had invited her to speak to them on socialism. She also reported that the first Socialist local in Earl, Arkansas, had refused to allow any African Americans to join. This was similar to the situation in Mississippi, where 150 African Americans were party members at large (paying dues directly to the state secretary of the SP) and not allowed to be members of the appropriate local. Malkiel bemoaned the fact that the "Southern comrades" treat the "poor, poor darkies" "like dogs."[22]

Shortly after the Malkiel report, a letter to the editor appeared in the *Call*, apparently written by Harrison under the pseudonym "Nils Uhl." It was his first published writing for the Socialist Party, and he was still working in the Post Office, though under job pressure from the "Tuskegee machine." The style, phrasing, and irony are unmistakably Harrison's. The "Nils Uhl" letter began by responding to a previous letter about Malkiel's tour from "one who signs himself William Morris." "Uhl" referred to "William Morris" in quotes, suggesting that he assumed that the use of the name of the famous deceased socialist thinker and writer was merely a pseudonym. As for "Nils Uhl," he referred to himself as belonging to the Negro race, being a member of Branch 5 of the SP of Local New York, and having lectured to "the Yorkville Branch and to Branch 4." Since there was no "Nils Uhl" listed from Branch 5 in the minutes of the Convention of Local New York on November 26, 1911, and since the personal references seem to apply only to Harrison, it is assumed that he wrote the article signed "Nils Uhl." Other indications of Harrison's authorship include the similarity of the content to Harrison's *Sun* letters and "The Negro and the Newspapers"; the use of a pseudonym at a time when Harrison was using many; the use of phrases

that Harrison frequently employed ("Southernism or Socialism?" and "democratic . . . touchstone in the Negro problem)"; and the challenge to the use of the
small "n" in Negro, which was frequently made by Harrison, who never used the
small "n." That letter appeared in the issue of October 2, 1911, and it enunciated
various themes that Harrison would soon develop more fully.[23]

The "Uhl" letter focused on the theme of how "the newspapers of America deliberately manufacture sentiment against Negroes" and cited three main
ways. First, it examined the propensity to fabricate stories, a manifestation of
the "devilish ingenuity of American race prejudice." It described W. E. B. Du
Bois's experience at the Lyceum Club, the leading woman's club of London,
and how U.S. newspapers tried to imply that Du Bois wasn't allowed to speak
at the club because of threats of resignation by white members. "Uhl" included
Du Bois's disclaimer of that version of events. "Uhl's" second example was the
attempt to denote inferiority by refusing to capitalize the "n" in "Negro," and he
pointed out that "in the case of all other race groups the name by which they are
known is capitalized." His third example was the "policy to demean all Negroes"
by sensational treatment of crimes in which they were allegedly involved, particularly "the unmentionable crime [rape]." He cited the case of Thomas Williams of Asbury Park, N.J., unjustly accused of the murder of a ten-year-old girl.
He contrasted the sensational treatment surrounding his arrest with the lack of
flaming headlines that accompanied the subsequent arrest of the real culprit, in
this case, a German youth.[24]

"Uhl" then explained that the great source of such prejudice was the South,
although the "commercial conscience which shapes Northern sentiment into accord with Southern requirements" was spreading rapidly. What could be done?
The spread of such sentiment had to be stopped. Now, however, more was offered than the simple resort of telling the truth that Harrison had offered in
"The Negro and the Newspapers." For "Uhl," socialism was the answer to white
supremacy. Simultaneously, however, white supremacy was the challenge for socialism. The choice for America was simple: "Southernism or Socialism." "Uhl"
elaborated: "Some one must call a halt to the spread [of such Southern senti-
ment] and Socialism by its very nature is better able to do this than anything
else. For Socialism is the one gospel that cannot afford to indorse Southernism.
As soon as Socialism trims and temporizes it dies as Socialism, whatever else it
may be transmogrified into."[25]

Yet, African Americans, as Harrison well knew, were wary of socialism as of
all things that appeared to come from white America. "Uhl" stressed that "every
democratic movement in America" had found its "ultimate touchstone in the
Negro problem." Political democracy, education, trade unionism, and the civil
service had all "shivered at the touch of this Ithuriel's spear" (the spear that

exposed falsehood in Milton's *Paradise Lost*). Thus, explained "Uhl," "Negroes" still had "suspicion" of socialism. For them, like all workers in the South, "the adulterous union of Socialism and caste" was but a dream. "Uhl's" letter ended with the plea: "Let us wake them up."[26]

The *Call* dryly replied to "Nils Uhl's" letter. It denied that "the use of the word negro with a small n is for the purpose of derision" and it pointed out that 99 percent of the papers in the nation didn't capitalize it. Finally, the *Call* gave the falsely evenhanded argument that if the "n" in "negro" was capitalized, "it would be equally proper to capitalize the word white as it would be the word negro."[27]

Thus, in the "Nils Uhl" letter, Harrison's first socialist offering, we see both his enthusiasm for socialism as the answer to racism and a rebuff on the race question by socialist practitioners. Such a scenario was portentous. We also see him raise the question of the "touchstone" of democracy, the importance of not trimming or temporizing in the fight against white supremacy, and the centrality of the fight against white supremacy to America's future—themes that would be central to his future work.

It was Harrison's removal from the Post Office in September 1911 that freed his time for socialist activity. The loss of his job also freed him from the threat of being fired for public pronouncements. He acted quickly under this newfound freedom. He publicly identified as a Socialist, and he speedily built a reputation as an outstanding Socialist writer, speaker, and organizer, and as a specialist on "Negro" matters.

The first steps in this direction were made in October 1911. On October 12, less than a month after Harrison's removal from the Post Office, Samuel M. Romansky, recording secretary of Branch 5 of the Socialist Party of Local New York (headquartered at the Harlem Forum, 360 W. 125th St.), addressed a letter to Julius Gerber, the organizer of Local New York. Romansky asked Gerber to "take up without unnecessary delay" the matter of Wednesday night meetings at 134th St. and Lenox Ave. with Harrison as speaker. He noted that Branch 5 had the "largest segregation of negroes in the city in its territory" and emphasized the importance of such work. His request to Gerber stated:

> Comrade Hubert H. Harrison (colored) is a member of Branch 5. He exhibits a profound and practical familiarity with the history, the traits, the habits and inclinations of his race and is besides well-fitted to address an audience. He is a close friend of Professor Du Bois who recommends him highly as a man of intelligence and ability. Now Branch 5 proposes that Comrade Harrison be made a paid speaker and organizer for Local New York for special work in negro districts.[28]

Romansky emphasized that Branch 5 was "especially anxious" to utilize Harrison's services as quickly as possible. He explained that the branch realized "the lack of true facts, data and general information that prevails among socialists regarding the negro problem confronting the Socialist Party." The branch, therefore, asked that Local New York schedule a meeting for party members at which Harrison would speak on "how to reach the Negro vote."[29]

Local New York's Executive Committee, at its meeting on October 18, responded to Branch 5's request. Harrison was employed as a speaker for the remainder of the 1911 election campaign. He received eighteen dollars per week "to do special propaganda work among the colored people." A committee consisting of party members Caroline Dexter, Dr. S. Berlin, R. H. Asquith, and G. S. Gelder was elected to confer with him in order "to devise ways and means of doing effective agitation work among the colored race." The EC also referred to Local New York's Central Committee "the recommendation that Comrade Harrison be engaged as colored organizer." This was to be a more long-term assignment and to extend beyond the election campaign.[30]

Local New York's response was significant. The historian Philip S. Foner has noted that before 1911, "Local New York never once discussed the recruiting of Negroes, nor did it raise any specific demands of interest to blacks." Now, Harrison was recommended as the key figure in its efforts to reach African Americans, and he would be paid, at least during the election campaign, as a party functionary. Soon he would be hired as "colored organizer" on a permanent basis, and his articles on socialism and the "Negro Problem" would receive wide circulation in the party press.[31]

While Harrison was awaiting his commission to do organizing and while he was attracting the attention of Local New York leaders, he also kept busy undertaking other party work. In 1911 and 1912 he reportedly served as editor of the New York–based socialist literary monthly *The Masses* and worked under the general editorship of Piet Vlag, a Dutch restaurateur. By 1913, *The Masses*, under the revived editorship of Max Eastman and Floyd Dell, would become the leading radical literary publication in America.[32]

In this period Harrison also wrote his front-page, November 4, 1911, *Truth Seeker* article against church tax exemption ("The Menace of Exemption") and a two-part exposé on the Post Office, based on research and his own experience, which appeared in the *Call* of November 6 and 7. In the first postal article Harrison argued that the Post Office was "the one great example of the public ownership of a gigantic public business" and that it demonstrated the advantage of government ownership. These were common socialist positions.[33]

Harrison also described how the Post Office invited comparisons with privately controlled public industries such as railroads, coal mines, and lighting systems, which also should be nationalized. He emphasized that the argument for nationalization would be much stronger, however, if the Post Office was not run under a publicly proclaimed deficit, which made the argument for nationalization of other industry weaker. The postal deficit, he explained, was caused largely by bookkeeping procedures in which a fifth of the mail was carried free for various government departments. If this were corrected, and if the Post Office did not favor the railroads by paying them a higher rate for transportation than other large-volume shippers did, then the effectiveness of nationalization could be shown. Since the railroads were post roads and "parts of the public domain," he argued that they should actually pay less. In his concluding postal article Harrison discussed the oppressive work conditions and corruption and ended with a call for socialism, "a type of government necessarily owned by all the people," under whom "the post office would be at the service of all and its tremendous advantage would be distributed to all."[34]

These writings apparently impressed some party members. On December 17, 1911, Harrison was one of five comrades elected to investigate and report on the Socialist School Union, which was part of the effort of the Socialist Party to develop weekend schools for working-class children as part of a more formal alternative education. A dynamic leader in this effort was a modern languages professor at the University of Rochester, Kendrick Shedd, who described Harrison as "the most remarkable Negro I ever met."[35]

In late 1911 Harrison was paid by the Socialist Party to do party work among African Americans during the 1911 municipal election campaign. He immersed himself in this effort as he attempted to show, by specific actions, that African Americans could be reached with the socialist message. He was convinced that the traditional party allegiances of African Americans were breaking down and that their receptiveness to new doctrines was increasing. There was a basis for this position in the fact that some 20 to 40 percent of the northern Black vote had gone Democratic in the 1910 congressional elections. After those elections, the Black Socialist Thomas Sweeney wrote to the *Call* and quoted figures from the *Times* that indicated that an estimated 30,000 out of 45,000 Black voters had voted Democratic in New York State. Harrison believed that the African American vote was "the balance of power in the elections of six Northern States," including New York (the other states were New Jersey, Pennsylvania, Ohio, Illinois, and Indiana).[36]

He was also convinced "that the Negro vote can be got and that it is worth getting." How was this to be done? Harrison saw the answer in special work aimed at African Americans. He pointed out that "some comrades believe that 'Socialism is the same for all people—women, Finns, Negroes,'" but, and this was the key point, "the minds of all these are not the same and are not to be approached in the same way." Because "Negroes" had lived behind the color line, at a distance from many contemporary social movements, their minds were "somewhat more difficult of approach." Consequently, the task of bringing Negroes the socialist message was "a special work."[37]

Harrison put his views into practice in the election campaign and later explained in the pages of the *Call* exactly how the special work among "Negroes" was done. During the 1911 New York municipal election, Local New York distributed the pamphlet, *The Colored Man's Case as Socialism Sees It*, by the Reverend George W. Slater Jr., a Black Socialist minister from Chicago. To that pamphlet Harrison added a special argument for the campaign. Party members would take one of Slater's pamphlets and hold it so the title was visible and then approach an African American with it. Inevitably, "As soon as his eyes fell on the words 'Colored Men's Case,' his attention was arrested" and he would take it, read it, and listen to the Socialist street speaker. In addition, a general party pamphlet, by 1908 presidential candidate Debs, was then easily distributed. Thus, Harrison felt, in the territory of Branch 5 it had been demonstrated that "special literature had a special effectiveness."[38]

Similar results were obtained with a "special form of address." The simple "ABC arguments" were made, but they were crammed with facts "drawn from the Negro's own history and experience." Such a tactic also appealed to Euro-Americans and, rather than detracting from the general effectiveness of the speeches, often resulted in a situation in which from one-third to one-half of the audience consisted of whites "whose attention and interest were held just the same." In addition to this approach, one final effort, on the Tuesday before Election Day, capped the campaign—a two-hour program in pouring rain at which some 40 percent of the audience was white. Harrison was convinced that the overall effort demonstrated "the tremendous power of special addresses."[39]

In the *Call* article Harrison also explained why the "special equipment" of Black organizers was needed. He emphasized that one had to know "the psychology of the Negro," had to "know the people, their history, their manner of life, and modes of thinking and feeling." If this was not done, Black people would not be affected or impressed. It was especially important to make them "think—and feel," and arguments had to be addressed to the Black voter's "heart as well as to his head." Harrison thought this work could be better done by those "who are themselves Negroes [and] to whom these considerations come by second nature." Negroes, "intelligent and well versed in the principles of Socialism," could "drive home an argument with such effectiveness that white Socialists must despair of achieving." In discussing the question of Black Socialist Party organizers, Harrison noted that Debs had reported there were three Black national organizers. Harrison knew of Reverend George Washington Woodbey, a Christian Socialist minister from San Diego, California, considered his efforts "very effective," and felt there should be other national organizers. But, he emphasized, "there is no need to wait until we can get such colored national organizers"; the task should be taken up immediately by local and state organizations, particularly in New York, where the Black population numbered 100,000.[40]

This election campaign mention of Woodbey, like his mention of Slater, indicates that Harrison had some familiarity with his Black Socialist predecessors. The more prominent Black Socialists, including Woodbey, Slater, and Peter Humphreys of Cincinnati (who had joined the Workingmen's Party of the United States in 1876, one year after its founding, and then joined the Socialist Labor Party), had shared a similar range of experience. These activists had attempted to merge their Christian views with socialist theory, counseled against violence, and, despite encountering difficulties within socialist organizations, withheld their public criticism while party members. Harrison, aware and appreciative of his Black socialist ancestors, would, over the next few years, take a very different course.[41]

Harrison's work in the 1911 municipal election in New York was apparently effective. The Socialist Party vote increased by 6,000, and this figure included an increase in the Black vote. In New York County, where Harrison concentrated his work, the overall vote increased from 15,609 to 18,358. These results led party member John Burfriend to write a letter to the Local New York organizer Gerber in which Harrison's effort was lauded and related to "the increased interest in Socialism" among Black voters.[42]

On November 8, right after the 1911 elections, the Executive Committee of Local New York met in regular session. At that meeting the "Report of the Special Committee, elected to consider Ways and Means and work out a plan for the agitation and organization of the negroes of New York," proposed:

1. The immediate organization of a new branch consisting of colored members now belonging to existing branches to be transformed to the new branch.
2. That a permanent headquarters be established in the negro district or at least for the present, desk room be rented, also a place for weekly meetings.
3. That special literature be printed suitable for negroes.
4. That a permanent organizer be appointed for work among the negroes.[43]

The EC estimated expenses for this work at thirty-one dollars per week based on eighteen dollars for organizer's salary; three dollars for rent of desk room; four dollars for the meeting room; five dollars for literature; and one dollar for advertising. It also proposed that a special fund for "negro work" be opened in the party press and that every branch and foreign-language group be asked to contribute at least one dollar per week to the effort. Finally, the EC proposed that Harrison "be engaged to do such agitation work as is possible . . . such as holding one or two meetings a week in the section where most of the colored people reside for the purpose of establishing a nucleus of an organization among the colored people" and that the party "immediately issue a call to raise a special fund for the purpose outlined in the report of the Committee." The motion carried, but both the wording and the aim of the resolution would shortly cause considerable problems within the party since what was being suggested was "a branch"—the basic organizational unit of the party—for Blacks only.[44]

On November 22 these proposals were printed as the "Recommendations of the Committee on Propaganda Among Negroes." The phrase "colored members" was changed to "negro party members" in point 1, and all else remained the same. The recommendations were signed by S. Berlin, and the printed version said other signatories on the committee were G. S. Gelder, Caroline Dexter, R. H. Asquith, and H. H. Harrison. Whether or not Harrison actually signed is not clear since an existing copy of the document does not contain his signature. Four days later, at the convention of Local New York, the Credentials Committee recognized Harrison as a delegate from Branch No. 5, which consisted of the Nineteenth, Twenty-first, and Thirty-first Assembly Districts. He was elected to the Committee on Plans and Organizations, and the plan for work "among negroes" was approved. The November 28 *Call* then announced that the EC of Local New York had "at last taken definite steps toward extending Socialist propaganda work to the negroes." The plan, approved by the EC, was then forwarded to the CC, which decided to first issue an appeal for the necessary funds and, "in the meanwhile, to retain Harrison to do the preparatory work among the colored people."[45]

When Harrison first became a full-time Socialist Party organizer in late 1911, he did not limit himself to formal party activities; as always, he continued reading, writing, and self-study. In his "Papers" is a *"Res Facta"* (Things accomplished) covering the period from November 12, 1911, to March 23, 1912, which gives some idea of the breadth of his reading. For example, the week of November 12 to 19 he read *Lay of the Last Minstrel* by Sir Walter Scott; *The Social Revolution* by the Social Democratic Party of Germany's internationally influential theoretician Karl Kautsky; *Timon of Athens* and *A Winter's Tale* by William Shakespeare; and periodicals such as the leading Chicago literary journal, *The Dial*, and the NAACP's *Crisis* magazine. During the month of November, while continuing his study and reading, he also wrote eight major articles on "Negro" issues for the Socialist Party press—five that would appear in the daily New York *Call* and three that would appear in the monthly *International Socialist Review*. Hubert also found time to write letters soliciting lecture engagements and a teaching position. Over the next months he read books by other authors, including H. G. Wells, Rudyard Kipling, Mary White Ovington, Thomas Carlyle, and Herbert Spencer.[46]

During this period he also organized his self-study by work on his scrapbooks and through disciplined book collecting. Harrison started at least sixteen scrapbooks from 1910 through 1912, and almost all touched on "Negro Americans" and radicalism. The scrapbooks, besides being major research tools for talks and articles, were also a place where he would record his observations by writing alongside the clippings. Beginning in late 1911, he also sought to supplement his party income with money from lectures and from the sale of books at his talks. In the course of his book buying and selling, Harrison, a true bibliophile, began to amass a significant personal library. His usual practice with books he planned to keep was to put his name inside the book, indicate the date of receipt, and then mark up the text with asterisks, brackets, underlining, and written comments. Hubert's practice of selling literature at Socialist Party activities would draw some praise, but it would also later be cited as an offense when he was brought up on internal charges by another party member.[47]

Harrison's book dealing was probably inspired by George Young, his friend from St. Mark's, and Arthur Schomburg and John E. Bruce, his friends from St. Benedict's, and it probably began at about the same time in late 1911 that Schomburg and Bruce founded the Negro Society for Historical Research. The society grew out of the Men's Sunday Club and was a membership organization that sought "to instruct our people in Negro history and achievement" and to "inspire love and veneration" for the race's "men and women of mark." It aimed to institute "a circulating library, a bureau of race information, with a collection of all books, pamphlets, etc., by Negro authors and their friends, together with all data bearing upon race achievements in every form of endeavor." The NSHR was premised on the belief "that the race can be made stronger and more united if it can be made to know that it has done great things." The lay scholars Schomburg and Bruce were historical researchers of the first rank and devoted, race-proud gatherers of materials on the history of "the Negro Race." The seriousness with which they approached this work led them to be critical of the over-extended Harrison. Though the NSHR was an organization for which Harrison would later serve as secretary, he was not at first a major or regular contributor, and he evidently neglected or downplayed some activities in order to concentrate on work for the Socialist Party. Thus, in late 1911 when Schomburg was unable to complete a task on time, he wrote to his friend Bruce that he didn't want to "ask leave" lest it "looks as if I wanted to squirm duty like Harrison."[48]

Though Harrison may have been downplaying NSHR-type work, he was gaining more attention as a public speaker. His Abraham Lincoln lecture was fully developed, and he delivered it as "Lincoln and Liberty: Fact Versus Fiction" in late 1911 and again on February 11, 1912, before the Brooklyn Philosophic

Association in the Long Island Business College. On February 12 he spoke on "Lincoln the American" before the Workingmen's Circle in East Harlem. In late 1911 he also prepared a major talk on "Socialism and the Negro" for the December 31 Flatbush Free Forum, and this talk appeared in print in the July 1912 *International Socialist Review*.[49]

While the party discussion on "work among Negroes" continued, Harrison also served as secretary of a special Socialist Party meeting on an old-age-pension bill. The bill was a prime example of an evolutionary socialist demand and was put forward by the national party leader and congressmen Victor L. Berger of Wisconsin, a leading evolutionary socialist who had proposed other bills on government ownership of the radio industry, abolition of child labor, self-government for the District of Columbia, women's suffrage, nationalization of the railroad industry, abolition of the Senate, and public works for unemployed relief. Harrison reported to the *Call* on the November 19 special meeting of the EC of Local New York, which had passed an amendment asking the National Executive Committee to appoint a committee to redraft the old-age-pension bill. The special committee was to take into consideration objections voiced by party members, namely, the bill's appeal to nativism in its citizenship provision; its appeal to law and order in its felon-exclusion section; and its absence of provisions for government financing through a graduated income tax. While the SP was still deeply divided nationally over whether socialism would come by evolution through gradual reform and electoral gains or by militant strikes and revolution, Local New York, led by the party leader and theorist Morris Hillquit, was clearly in the evolutionary camp.[50]

Although Harrison's own stand on this issue is not recorded, there was one particular aspect of the debate that was important to his work. It was the question of whether such a bill could "be justified on sound Socialist principles." This issue involved two related questions: Was the bill aimed at amelioration of existing evils under capitalism and therefore a reformist effort that tended to stabilize the capitalist system? Was the bill purely propagandistic and not viewed as winnable under capitalism? The fact that in 1911 the Socialists in New York could endorse a reform bill that was not of pure socialist principle and was not at present winnable was not lost on Harrison. The same two issues were constantly raised about special work aimed at equal rights for African Americans. Harrison would cite socialist support for the old-age-pension bill as he pushed for Socialist Party support of demands for immediate redress of Black grievances. Before the end of the month, Harrison would write in the *Call* that reforms challenging white supremacy could point the way to revolutionary consequences, and he would declare that simple democracy for African Americans implied a revolution "startling to even think of."[51]

In the same November 28, 1911, issue of the *Call* that announced his appointment to work among African Americans, Harrison began the first article of a major five-part theoretical series on "The Negro and Socialism." The series was the first such effort at a comprehensive analysis by an African American in U.S. socialist history, and on many points it evidences a profound and still incisive understanding. In the series he elaborated on many of the points and examples made in the "Nils Uhl" letter. The lead article, "The Negro and Socialism: 1—the Negro Problem Stated," resembled another that he wrote in the period, "The Real Negro Problem," which was formally published six years later in his first book, *The Negro and the Nation*. In "The Negro and Socialism," Harrison took the position that the "Negro Problem" had a history in past social relationships and was at root a question of "social adjustment," of social control of relationships. He argued against a biological analysis of the race problem and maintained that race relationships have a history "much as the class struggle and the system of production have theirs."[52]

Harrison discussed the "materialist" basis to the problem, which he said was rooted in economics and social relations and was "not to be explained on the basis of the thinking or feeling of either party." He sought to interpret race relations "in terms of human relations and in the order in which human relations are established: (1) economic, (2) social, (3) political, and (4) civic." He placed primacy on economic causes because they contained "the real root of all race difficulties," and, he reasoned, "as long as white men can be taught to believe that the presence of black men threatens their means of existence, so long will their general attitude be one of enmity. So long as the fallacy of economic fear survives, so long will economic competition create race prejudice."[53]

The historic roots of the "Negro" problem, wrote Harrison, were "found in slavery" and the need to supply that system with laborers. He did not assume that "Negroes" were uniquely suited for slavery, and he challenged such a "racial" explanation by pointing out that Black people were not the first slaves in North America and that "under Spanish rule, the Indians of Florida and California had been enslaved, and under English rule white men, women and children from Ireland had been sold into American slavery as a result of [Oliver] Cromwell's Irish campaigns." He added that many English workers condemned to penal servitude received similar treatment.[54]

Under such a system, contradictions emerged. Black people were treated as chattels, but, "to the credit of our common human nature," steps had to be taken "to reconcile the public mind to the system of slavery." This reconciliation was accomplished by nurturing the belief "that the slaves were not really human" and "wherever the system was most profitable," that belief "was strongest." Such ideas seemed to take on a life of their own. Thus, in the early nineteenth century, slavery defenders argued "that the Negro was a beast," then "that he was a man of an inferior sort, consigned to slavery by God." After emancipation, when freed African Americans began to produce people of mark, it was said "that certain craniological peculiarities would prevent them from assimilating the learning and culture of Europe." More recently, "it was suddenly discovered that this is a white man's country."[55]

While aware of the role of racist ideology, Harrison developed an analysis that was, at its core, materialist. His understanding contrasted sharply with the view that the "Negro Problem" was simply a mental attitude that could be solved in the realm of ideas. To him, this "mental attitude" argument contained the real core of all racist theory—since it ultimately came down to the notion that racism is innate. He countered this position with an alternate one—that an economic analysis had to probe more deeply into the sociopolitical question of control of social relationships.[56]

Harrison argued that the "Negro problem" had been created by white Americans, who desired to fix and maintain the African American's status as inferior and the white man's status as superior. In identifying the locus of the problem in the white race, Harrison directly challenged the opinions expressed by influential Socialist Party writers that African Americans were a hindrance to social change and that the chief obstacles to class consciousness among Black people were their own deficiencies as a race. In the *International Socialist Review*, the party theoretician Algie M. Simons had argued that "the negro was but a helpless tool" whose "deficiency of education and incompetency" were "serious obstacles" to class consciousness, and Charles H. Vail maintained that "the negro" had "been more deceived than any branch of the working class." According to historian Ira Kipnis it was similarly held by many right-wing party members that "Negroes were inferior, depraved, degenerates." Harrison, by focusing on whites' role in the "Negro" problem, challenged such views—and pointed in another direction for the real problem.[57]

Harrison focused on the political implications of this analysis. He analyzed the speciousness of American democracy, the rationale for disfranchisement, and the value of a philosophy of submission. He argued that for those in power it was expedient to deny African Americans political rights since political freedom, if attained, would mean freedom "from industrial exploitation and contempt." In forceful and compelling language, he emphasized that "the Negro is the touchstone of the modern democratic idea," whose mere presence puts U.S. "democracy to the proof and reveals the falsity of it." The Declaration of Independence was a prime example—it "seemed a splendid truth. But the black man merely touched it and it became a splendid lie."[58]

Most significant, Harrison clearly saw the revolutionary implications of simple democracy for Black people in America. The power of this democracy was not lost on the enemy, identified as white capitalism. In a direct reference to the philosophy of Booker T. Washington, Harrison added "that the prevailing social philosophy among Negroes—that which white capitalism will pay to have them taught—is one of submission and acquiescence in political servitude." Harrison then explained the "general implications" of this philosophy, including the dehumanizing and anti-working-class effects of the betrayal of democracy. A key point he made was that "the broad denial of justice to colored men as exemplified in lynchings, segregation, public proscription and disfranchisement results in the vitiation of democratic faith." It also provides "the supplying power" for other deceitful practices. Thus, as the public mind accustoms itself to seeing such inhumanity, it becomes immunized to the injustice such as "the jailing of innocent labor leaders [probably a reference to the April 1911 jailing of John J. and James B. McNamara] and the murder of working girls in a fire trap factory" (a direct reference to the March 25, 1911, Triangle Shirtwaist factory fire in Greenwich Village, in which 146 workers died).[59]

In concluding his first article Harrison commented on the imperialist aspects of domestic racism. Still legally a colonial subject, he was particularly sensitive to both the missionary and "big stick" policies of the U.S. government. He accordingly described "the sending of American missionaries to Asia and to Africa," in light of domestic racial policies, as "so horribly humorous that it might well make the devil laugh."[60]

Harrison's second article, "Race Prejudice," appeared in the *Call* of December 4, 1911. He argued that racism had economic causes, that capitalists consciously fostered race prejudice, and that capitalists benefited and workers lost from racial discrimination. This position included aspects of the Socialist Party's neglected first convention resolution and some of the analyses of the left and center of the party, which, as historian Ira Kipnis explains, "laid the blame [for race prejudice] on deliberate incitement by capitalists who created Negro-white antagonisms the better to exploit both."[61]

As he made his argument, however, Harrison added new insights to the Socialist understanding of the race question. He pointed out that, at their core, all arguments defending race prejudice, including those of James K. Vardaman and the former minister Thomas Dixon, author of *Leopard's Spots* (1902) and *The Clansman* (1905) (and, later, the screenplay for *Birth of a Nation* [1915]), ultimately distill to the argument "that race prejudice is innate." Harrison suggested the fallacy in the "racism is innate" argument and cited three examples: white aristocrats who love to be surrounded by Black servants; white men's lack of revulsion from Black women; and the need for legislation to enact segregation. After citing these example, Harrison then declared that "the naked truth

[is] that there is nothing innate in race prejudice." Rather, it was "diligently fostered by those who have something to gain by it."[62]

The historian Theodore W. Allen suggests the importance of Harrison's point. Allen argues that to say that racism is innate implies that racism is "not subject to effective eliminative social action." In contrast, to say that racism arises from sociohistorical causes suggests that "it is susceptible of elimination by social action." Harrison, in the 1920s, would offer additional insight. The race problem, he would explain, "is not insoluble: no human social problem ever was. There is work to be done on it; and while it is primarily of the white man's making, the colored man must do most of the work."[63]

In "Race Prejudice," Harrison directly addressed the question of who gains from racism. He reasoned that if white workers are "protected to a certain extent by the courts, public opinion and the ballot" and African Americans are not, then "whenever they are thrown into economic competition the protected workers will take away the jobs of the other body of workers." He asked whether the workers, white or Black, really gained in such instances? Black workers clearly did not, for they were "a body of workers whose standard of living has been permanently lowered." As for the "protected," or privileged group of white workers? Their situation was also described as ruinous by Harrison. He explained that as the "protected" group demanded for itself "a larger share of its product in the form of higher wages or better conditions of labor and of life," the inevitable occurred. Its demands were met "with the cold fact that other wage slaves are doing as hard work or harder and doing it for less." If the "protected" group strikes, "the strike can always be broken by making use of that same body of workers whom the others have thus been breeding artificially as strikebreakers."[64]

Who gained, if not the workers? To Harrison, the answer was the capitalists; it was "in the interests of the capitalists of America to preserve the inferior economic status of the colored race, because they can always use it as a club for the other workers." By pitting the "white against black" workers, the capitalists kept the wage level "as low as possible." This not only created low wages but also fostered disunity in the working class. Thus, to Harrison, race prejudice was a "very useful tool" to "divide the workers."[65]

This division was aided by the press, particularly "the newspapers, owned by the capitalist class of the South." Those papers, "especially those larger Northern papers, like the *New York Times*, that are controlled by Southern capitalists" had "entered upon a campaign of deprecation, vilification, calumny and lies in an endeavor to use the ignorance and superstition of the workers against the workers." This was done by "playing up Negro crime," remaining silent about Black achievement, twisting press dispatches (notably in cases of alleged sexual assault), and by "deliberate lies." These northern papers sought "to make their readers think along one certain line and to make them think that everyone else thinks and feels in the same way." Thus, public opinion was "built up in favor of race prejudice." Further, since individual opinions were "mostly derived from the social atmosphere," it was "easy to see how people who grow up reading such newspapers, surrounded by others who are subjected to the same influence, get to believe that this carefully built up antipathy is innate."[66]

Harrison concluded "that there is no justification of American race prejudice on scientific, social, or ethical grounds." He closed by quoting from an article which "Comrade" H. G. Wells wrote for the *Independent* in February 1907. Wells, the well-known English novelist, historian, and writer of social commentary, declared that "there is no more evil thing in this present world than race prejudice; none at all"; it is "the worst single thing in life now."[67]

Harrison's third article addressed the evil of race prejudice and "The Duty of the Socialist Party" in combating it. He began this December 13 *Call* article aware that since socialism aimed to draw people to itself, it was "but natural to expect that within its limits there will be found various and divergent opinions." Such differences of opinion, he allowed, might "even extend to the fundamental postulates of Socialism," and, in the beginning, there would be some "calling themselves Socialists who do not quite understand what Socialism means." He then made particular reference to the January 24, 1911, letter to the editor of the *Call* from "A Southern Socialist" on "Racial Equality," which raised the bugaboo of "social equality." To Harrison, that letter and similar ones appearing in the Socialist Labor Party's *The Weekly People* suggested that "south of the 40th parallel [the historic division between Kansas and Nebraska, which also passes through Philadelphia and New Jersey] are some people who think that the Socialist movement can be made into a vehicle for the venom of their caste consciousness."[68]

It was necessary for the Socialist Party, argued Harrison, "to note the views of the professional Southerner—and to condemn them." The Socialist Party had to make clear that "if it is to be Southernism versus Socialism, we take our stand on Socialism"—and this stand had to be taken "with no intention of receding." The Socialist Party was "not a white man's party or a black man's party, but the party of the working class," and its "historic mission" was "to unite the workers of the world." That goal would never be accomplished as long as the party wavered on white supremacy.[69]

Harrison next discussed the bugaboo of "social equality"—and the related code words of "forced" racial intermarriage and "forced" racial socializing. Harrison noted that the question raised by parochial ("white") minds was always the same: "when they are asked in the name of democracy and decency to treat the black man as a man," they respond—"Shall I let him marry my daughter?" Such petty people were "always haunted with the specter of 'social equality,' which, like Banquo's ghost," drove them to distraction and never disappeared. The racist "social equality" fear tactic was aimed at whites to "dictate . . . that they shall not choose black friends," and that was "the whole sum and substance of this 'social equality' scare." For Harrison, there never could be "any such thing as 'social equality,' in this world"; the real issue was "social justice," which required "that society shall not dictate to a man what friends he shall choose."[70]

Harrison made clear that he did not expect that socialism would "at once remove race prejudice—unless it remove[d] ignorance at the same time." But, he did expect that it would "remove racial injustice and lighten the black man's burden," and that it would "take the white man from off the black man's back and leave him free for the first time to make of himself as much or as little as he chooses." Harrison expressed the belief, in late 1911, that he shared these expectations "with the overwhelming majority of Socialists North and South."[71]

Socialism existed "to put an end to the exploitation of one group by another, whether that group be social, economic or racial." That, said Harrison, was "the position of [Karl] Marx, [Frederick] Engels, [Karl] Kautsky and every great leader of the Socialist movement." It was "imbedded in the very fabric of the Socialist philosophy." To make such an affirmation was the general "present duty of the Socialist party."[72]

There was also a more particular, "a more practical duty" close at hand: "the duty of extending the message of Socialism to the Negroes of America, of teaching its tenets to them; of organizing them; of stimulating them with the splendid hope of . . . —the Brotherhood of Man." In the forthcoming battles, Harrison suggested, Black people might be of the highest value, but they needed to "first be enlisted, then organized."[73]

How was this work of bringing "the message of Socialism to the Negroes" to be done? Harrison addressed this question in his fourth theoretical piece in the *Call* of December 16, 1911. In the article entitled "How to Do It—And How Not" he offered concrete suggestions on how the Socialist Party could improve work among African Americans.[74]

He began by asking how one should treat strangers, and he answered succinctly: "treat them frankly as human beings." When he examined social practice in the Socialist Party, however, he was critical. He felt it necessary to "tender a word of advice to many members of the party." Too many, it seemed, uttered "such declarations as 'I have always been friendly with colored people'" or "'I have never felt any prejudice against Negroes.'" To Harrison, although possibly "well meant," this was "wholly unnecessary." His advice to white Socialists in their relations with Blacks was: "If your heart be in the right place, and this is assumed at the start, it will appear in your actions. No special kindness and no condescension is either needed or expected. Treat them simply as human beings, as if you had never looked at the color of their faces. It is wonderful but true that what people will be to you depends very largely upon what you are to them. So much for personal contact."[75]

Harrison offered that advice to white party members, but the problem that he wanted to focus on was "how the work of Socialism may be carried on among Negroes." It was here that he put forth the arguments for special work among African Americans. This was "the work [that] must be done if the party would not be derelict in its duty," and it "was not a question of charity." The real question was: "Does the Socialist party feel that it needs the Negroes as much as the Negro needs Socialism?" And the answer? If the party felt that it could "advance to the conquest of capitalism" with "one part of the proletariat" against it, it should say so. But Harrison hadn't the slightest doubt that the Socialist Party program "requires all the proletariat and we are all agreed on that."[76]

Harrison's concluding theoretical piece, "Summary and Conclusions," appeared in the *Call* of December 26. He reiterated his previously made points that Black people were brought here and placed at the bottom of society out of "economic necessity" and that "race prejudice developed . . . out of this fundamental fact of social relationship." Harrison then argued that "the ideas dominant at any stage of human culture do not descend out of the air. They are created and shaped by the basic conditions of society." This was a position similar to that taken by Karl Marx, who held that the "totality of the relations of production" is "the real foundation on which there arises a legal and political superstructure and to which there correspond definite forms of social consciousness." Harrison added, "Whenever large groups of men find profit in injustice to other men they will evolve a system of ethics to reconcile their minds to that injustice."[77]

In late 1911, however, Harrison saw a way out of capitalist oppression. His hope was socialism, and he felt that it offered salvation for the working class:

> If the overturning of the present system should elevate a new class into power; a class to which the Negro belongs; a class which has nothing to gain by the degradation of any portion of itself; that class will remove the economic reason for the degradation of the Negro. That is the promise of Socialism, the all-inclusive working-class movement. In the final triumph of that movement lies the only hope of salvation from this second slavery; of black men and of white.[78]

To achieve this victory, however, the Socialist Party had certain tasks. It had to espouse "the causes of all sections of down-trodden humanity," and "that duty it could not shirk." It was therefore necessary that "Socialist propaganda must be extended to the Negro people." It would also become, in Harrison's opinion, "more and more necessary for the party to take cognizance of certain definite acts of economic oppression—such as the suicidal policy of certain trades unions in excluding Negroes from membership—and to condemn them." This was a less than veiled criticism of the leadership of both the American Federation of Labor and much of the right wing of the Socialist Party, which supported the AFL. If any opposed this effort as inexpedient or impractical, Harrison had a counter—he brought up the debates on Berger's old-age-pension bill. He argued, "If it is expedient for us to present an old age pension bill that was not meant to be enacted into law, then surely there can be nothing against such a procedure on the ground of expediency."[79]

The tasks were thus before the party. To begin, it had to raise the necessary funds for "special work among Negroes" by having each branch and language group of the local contribute weekly and by having open subscriptions in the party press in which individual members may contribute. That was the preparatory work needed to obtain a headquarters. Then, when Blacks had joined the party in sufficiently large numbers, there would be no further need for a special fund. The work would be self-sustaining. Though Local New York had officially called for an all-Black branch, Harrison did not. In his *Call* article he suggested that "the colored Comrades" could "be drafted into those branches into whose territory they happen to live, thereby increasing both the finances and the working force of those branches." He was clearly not calling for all-Black branches.[80]

Finally, Harrison closed with some profound words of advice to the white comrades. He emphasized that "socialists in general need to learn a great many things from the Negro—not only of his racial psychology; but also of his history and of his present achievements in the various lines of human endeavor." Unfortunately, while Europeans knew little of Black people, "the white man of America knows a great deal that isn't so." Therefore, he advised the white comrades to "unlearn much before . . . [they] begin to learn."[81]

————

While Harrison was writing his groundbreaking theoretical series and the Socialist Party was preparing its "Appeal" to the members, an important discussion, involving some of the party's leading Black activists, was opened in the pages of the *Call*. It concerned the question of whether or not there should be an all-Black branch. The branch was the basic organizational unit of the party and a subdivision of a local (which comprised numerous branches).

As early as January 11, 1911, Thomas Potter, an active African American Socialist Party member had written to the paper calling for Black Socialist speakers to concentrate on work before Black church audiences (pointing out that "outside large cities their [African American's] social center is their churches"). In his letter, however, Potter had cautioned against "the advisability of forming negro branches."[82]

When the local proposed the establishment of an all-Black branch in November, new problems arose. On December 6, 1911, Reverend George Frazier Miller, rector of St. Augustine's Church in Brooklyn, a Niagara Movement founder in 1905, a Socialist Party member since 1906, and the man who had raised the question of socialism at the NAACP planning meeting in 1909, took issue with the *Call*'s November 28, 1911, article. That article, "To Push Agitation Among the Negroes," had spoken of the "plans for the immediate organization of a new branch consisting of colored members."[83]

Miller, a South Carolina–born African American, praised the plans to educate Blacks but was wary of segregation and its implications for both Blacks and whites. What particularly bothered him was the idea of a new branch consisting of colored members. He did not oppose the campaign "as an expedient of education" if its purpose was that "after Comrades are made from the ranks of the colored citizens," these "new-made Socialists join the locals of their respective assembly districts." But if the entire program was really a yielding to prejudice to soothe whites that "recoil from contamination," then "failure awaits this scheme," and "it is doomed like movements before it."[84]

Miller's intent was clear—he opposed segregation—but his wording was a bit confusing. In the Socialist Party in late 1911, Local New York consisted of ten "branches." The various assembly districts of New York were assigned to specific branches. For example, Branch 5, of which Harrison was a member, encompassed the Seventeenth Assembly and Aldermanic Districts in East Harlem, the Nineteenth A.D. in central-lower Harlem, the Twenty-first A.D. in central-upper Harlem, and the Thirty-first A.D. in the West Harlem–Morningside Heights area. Thus talk of "locals of their respective assembly districts," technically, made little sense. The previous party proposal had concerned an all-Black branch. Substantively, however, Miller's concern over the effects of an all-Black organizational unit had to be answered.[85]

Less than a week after Reverend Miller's letter, the "Appeal" of the Executive Committee of Local New York was printed in the *Call*. Its purpose was "to aid financially the work of Socialist propaganda among the negroes of the city." The "Appeal" acknowledged that the party had carried its propaganda "to the Polish, Hungarian, Slavic, Lithuanian and Finnish workers; to the organized and unorganized men and women." "But," it continued, "so far one section of the working class in America has not even been approached." This shortcoming would be addressed by Local New York's "perfected plans for the work among negroes." The plans centered on the "establishment of a headquarters in the negro district of New York [Harlem], where seven-tenths of the colored population live." Funds to meet estimated expenses of thirty dollars per week were also needed. It was "imperative" that this work begin immediately since the "Socialist party needs the negro as much as the negro needs Socialism," and, as the "Appeal"

Figure 5.2. George Frazier Miller, c. 1907. South Carolina–born George Frazier Miller (1864–1943), rector of St. Augustine's Episcopal Church in Brooklyn, was a founding member of the Niagara Movement in 1905, joined the Socialist Party in 1906, offered comments on party efforts to reach African Americans in 1911, and was a Socialist Party candidate for Congress in 1918. Miller was also active with the Liberty League and *The Voice* and praised Harrison's "wonderful grasp of history, theology, the social science, and literature." *Source:* Courtesy of the Special Collections Department, W. E. B. Du Bois Library, University of Massachusetts, Amherst.

added, because "now, more than at any time before, the Socialist party has a chance to gain the adherence of the negro." Since the Black vote carried the balance of power in six northern states, including New York, and since their interests had been betrayed by both Democrats and Republicans there was, for them, "'nowhere else to go.'"[86]

The "Appeal" then explained that the burden was on the Socialists. The party, which had "gone to all others," could not simply expect Blacks to come to it because they were both "ignorant of what Socialism means" and fully aware that "all other movements for democracy have broken down when they crossed the color line." Thus, the party's task in relation to the African American was to "enlighten his ignorance, remove his suspicion, and enlist his self-interest" on the party's side in the "great struggle of the working class." Funds were urgently requested to begin the "vigorous agitation" required.[87]

Fifteen days after the "Appeal" appeared in the *Call*, W. E. B. Du Bois, the most prominent African American member of the Socialist Party, one of the country's leading intellectuals, and editor of the NAACP's *Crisis* magazine, again raised questions about a separate organization for Blacks. Du Bois said he was "much interested in the efforts which the Socialists are making tentatively to interest colored people in the principles of their party." He would, however, "be very sorry to see the movement begin with a segregation of colored people in separate locals." This "would be transgressing the most fundamental of the principles underlying Socialism," and he urged the Executive Committee to oppose such action. He was in favor of "a Negro organizer" but felt that "his function should be to recruit members for the existing locals, and they should be distributed through those locals."[88]

Du Bois felt that in integrated locals, Blacks "would not only learn the principles of Socialism, but what is much more important, they and their white fellows would come to know each other as human beings." He emphasized that one of the main reasons that Blacks submitted "to segregation and separate institutions rather easily" was "because they wish to avoid insult and oppression." Since "there would not be, and is as yet no such barrier in the Socialist locals," Du Bois felt that "the argument that negroes want separate locals is absurd."[89]

Du Bois, a friend of Reverend Miller, appeared to have either spoken with him or to have been responding to his letter of December 6. In Du Bois's case, an incorrect and confusing point about "separate locals" was raised—a point similar to that made by Miller but different than that made by Local New York (which had spoken of a separate branch). On the larger issue, of an all-Black organizational unit, Du Bois raised a very important point. His view was that African Americans formed such organizations when forced to by prejudice and discrimination and, since there was theoretically no such prejudice in the Socialist Party, such an organizational form did not seem needed. Whereas Miller had expressed strong concern about the effects of segregation, particularly on whites, Du Bois was now expressing concern about its effects on Blacks.[90]

The party did not immediately respond to these criticisms. Two days after Du Bois's letter, a notice appeared in the *Call* announcing an agitational meeting to be held on December 29. The meeting was to be held by "The Colored Socialist Club" at the northeast corner of 134th Street and Lenox Avenue, with Harrison, Jean Jacques Coronel, and Louis J. Baum scheduled to speak. A "club" was different than either a branch or a local, which were the two basic organizational units of the party. The Colored Socialist Club would be a special project, and its participants would also belong to their neighborhood branches, which were part of the New York Local. The club's aim was to reach Blacks with the socialist message. Interestingly, Baum and Coronel may have been white, and the Colored Socialist Club was probably interracial.[91]

Two weeks after Du Bois's letter Harrison responded in the *Call*. He aimed to clear up the confusion. His letter was titled "No Segregation Intended" and it indicated that he probably had not signed the original "Recommendations of the Committee on Propaganda Among Negroes," which spoke of an all-Black branch. His signature does not appear on the existing copy. He further indicated that for some time he had been in favor of special organizing aimed at Black people to be accomplished through a separate organizational form [not identified as either a branch or a local] dedicated to reaching "Negroes where they concentrate."[92]

Harrison's response to Du Bois's letter stated that Du Bois's understanding that the party intended to establish separate locals "was based upon a misapprehension." He noted that, organizationally, "separate locals are an impossibility"—there was only one local in New York City, Local New York. It must be that Du Bois "meant separate branches." Harrison was explicit: "There is no intention to establish separate branches, or separate Socialist organizations for colored people."[93]

But since, as Du Bois had stated, "the treatment historically accorded to black people in America has bred in them distrust and suspicion to such an extent that they cannot be effectively approached by the average Socialist branch," a new means of reaching them was needed. It had to be "in part at least, by men of their own race and the work must be done where Negroes 'most do congregate.'" It was for this reason that "the Colored Socialist Club has been opened at 60 West 134th street." Harrison made clear that "when colored men or women become members of the Socialist party they join the branch in whose territory they live." Harrison was emphatic—"no segregation is intended." He added that "if it were," he "would be the most unlikely person to be selected for such work" and added that those "who know me well enough will realize this."[94]

Harrison's response seemed to answer both Miller and Du Bois. The original proposal of the "Special Committee, elected to consider Ways and Means and work out a plan for the agitation and organization of the negroes of New York," had proposed a separate "branch." The EC of Local New York, however, "after lengthy discussion," had agreed on "establishing a nucleus of an organization among the colored people." For Harrison, this nucleus of an organization was the Colored Socialist Club. The *Call* of November 28, 1911, had reported on the Special Committee's recommendations and not the final EC decision and had added to the confusion. The CSC would not replace the branch as the basic organizational unit. It would be a special project of those interested in devising special means of reaching "Negroes," and it would have Black organizers playing key roles.

Harrison pointed out that it was not an all-Black local or all-Black branch that was being considered. The party would maintain the principle of no segregation in its principal units of organization. Black people would continue to join branches. What was being proposed was a special club whose purpose was agitation and propaganda work to attract new recruits. Such recruits, who knew the racism of U.S. society, would best be reached by special efforts, which would be increasingly undertaken by Black activists. After the recruits became members, they would function in the integrated branches.

What is interesting is that Harrison, at this point, apparently more than Du Bois or Miller, was taking the lead in arguing for a special approach to reach African Americans. After they were reached with the ideas and program of socialism, he believed they would be able to function well in the official party organisms. In time he would change this position and argue that in the Socialist Party, as in U.S. society, white supremacy was so prevalent that a separate Black organization was needed. Harrison, however, would always argue for Black initiative in such autonomous organizational forms, and he would always oppose forced segregation of Black people. Five years later, when the federal government proposed segregated officer's training camps for training Black officers, a move backed by the chairman of the board of the NAACP, Joel E. Spingarn, and supported by Du Bois, Harrison would be one of the most forceful and articulate opponents of the effort.[95]

In 1912, however, Harrison, while functioning in an interracial organization, had undertaken a pioneering effort—striving for a degree of Black autonomy in agitational and propagandistic work aimed at the Black masses. In this, Harrison preceded a similar effort by Du Bois. Though Du Bois was critical of Harrison's effort in 1911 and 1912, by 1914, as editor of the NAACP's *Crisis* magazine, Du Bois would make a somewhat similar argument. While leadership of the NAACP remained in white hands, Du Bois called for Black autonomy in propaganda efforts aimed at the Black community. Further, beginning around 1934 and continuing into 1940 when he wrote his autobiography, *Dusk of Dawn*, Du Bois would argue for full Black organizational autonomy, a position that Harrison would reach by 1916.[96]

After Harrison's January letter, Socialist Party work continued. On January 13, 1912, a motion "that the Central Committee of the Socialist Party of Local New York appropriate $100 for Negro agitation" was defeated. Then, on January 20, the organizer Julius Gerber announced in the *Call* that the recently started fund had "already awakened interest and response" and $41.50 had been collected including $25 from the Finnish Branch." The plan—"the establishment of a permanent clubroom in the heart of the greatest negro population, an organizer who shall devote his entire time to the work of propaganda and the holding of meetings and circulation of suitable literature and advertising"—was being implemented. The *Call* predicted it would "undoubtedly arouse among the negroes a tremendous interest in our message." The local was already advertising widely and holding twice-weekly meetings on W. 134th Street, led by Harrison, whom the *Call* said was "an able speaker" and "an eager exponent of the plans to agitate among his own race."[97]

With Harrison as its secretary, the Colored Socialist Club showed signs of progress. Reports of activities among African Americans became more frequent. After four "very well attended meetings," he reported that "two of the colored converts" had gone out and distributed literature. The *Call* reported plans for a fifth lecture/meeting on "Unemployment" and for a January 27 literature distribution "in the negro sections of the 21st A.D.," in addition to the two regular monthly distributions of Branch 5. Since only two or three comrades had actually been involved in the literature-distribution work, party members and sympathizers living between 127th and 141st streets, west of Fifth Ave., who could spare a few hours were encouraged to volunteer for this work.[98]

On February 12 the *Call* announced that another $36.50 had been collected for "negro" work and it was reported that "interest and support is coming from widely separated localities." It was further reported that "the value and importance of the enterprise has become evident, even to those who are not directly connected with the local's activities, but are willing to lend their aid wherever such vitally necessary work is being carried on." Efforts to locate a permanent headquarters were underway. On February 24 Harrison addressed the CC of Local New York on "his estimate of the value of agitation and education of the colored people as conducted by Local New York."[99]

Thus, in mid-February 1912, Hubert Harrison, Local New York's leading Black organizer, exuded hope in socialism. He had put forth the first major analysis of the "Negro problem" by a Black Socialist in American history, and in this seminal series challenged many of the dominant positions in the party. His theoretical writings and internal party agitational work had led to the local's first special efforts at reaching African Americans. This had been accomplished in the face of white party members' long-standing inertia and despite the justified concern of two of the party's most prominent Black members. His work had not gone as far in the direction of autonomous clubs for an oppressed group as the Socialist Party had gone in the case of women, but, as with his theoretical work, it was the farthest the party had yet gone with Black people.

6

Socialist Writer and Speaker
(1912)

In late 1911 and early 1912, Hubert Harrison was Local New York's foremost Black speaker, its leading Black organizer and theoretician, and the head of the Colored Socialist Club. In the January 20, 1912, *Call* Julius Gerber, chairman of Local New York, stated that the future of the CSC held "great promise" and that Harrison was "an eager exponent of the plans to agitate among his own race."[1]

In such a setting Harrison had reason for optimism about the Socialist Party. This did not last long, however. Though he labored arduously in 1912, his efforts at special work among African Americans were rebuffed, in part because of white supremacism and in part because of reaction by party leaders to his movement left. By 1914 he would be utterly disenchanted with party leadership and practice at both the national and local levels. The core of his differences centered on the race question, but that question seemed to touch all others. The SP's policy toward "the Negro" was the touchstone. Socialist deficiencies on the race issue became manifest in other major questions the party addressed, including trade union work, "economic" vs. "political" demands, immigration, and "sabotage." Overall, Socialist Party failures on the "Negro Question" pointedly suggest why it failed in its quest for a working-class-led America.

As his efforts were thwarted by conservative party leaders, Harrison became increasingly attracted to the Industrial Workers of the World. The IWW was organized in June 1905 in Chicago by a diverse group of labor activists and socialists, including William D. "Big Bill" Haywood of the Western Federation of Miners; Eugene V. Debs of the Socialist Party; Daniel De Leon of the Socialist Labor Party; "Mother" Mary Jones, a legendary fighter for miners' and children's rights; and Algie M. Simons, editor of the *International Socialist Review*. The "Wobblies," as they were known, forthrightly called for "one big union," industrial (multicraft) unions instead of the racist and exclusionary craft unions of the American Federation of Labor, the organizing of unskilled and unorganized workers, racial equality, an end to segregation, and "direct action," which was understood as "any action taken by workers directly at the point of production with a view to bettering their conditions." While opposing racism, the Wobblies actively sought to recruit Chinese, Japanese, Filipino, Mexican, and African American workers, criticized the notion of a "yellow peril" and use of the offensive word "nigger," held integrated meetings, and organized twenty to twenty-five thousand Brotherhood of Timber Workers members, roughly evenly divided between Black and white, in the Deep South. Influenced by the syndicalist notion that capitalism would be overthrown by means of a general strike, they also disdained participation in electoral politics and, by 1914, officially endorsed "sabotage," which they defined as "excessive limitation of output" or "any obstruction of the regular conduct" of industry.[2]

Within the Socialist Party, although there was significant support for the IWW, the dominant political faction opposed the Wobblies. This faction was led nationally by Victor Berger and in New York State by Morris Hillquit. It favored working inside AFL unions and within the political arena via elections; it opposed direct action, militant strikes, and sabotage; and it offered nothing special on the race question in Hillquit's case, and rabid racism in Berger's. In such a setting, it was only a matter of time—and of more experience with Party leaders—before Harrison would clash with dominant party positions. The race question and support of the IWW were the two principal points of disagreement. The clash would develop over time and come in the context of his daily efforts to support a family, to agitate with pen and soapbox, and to struggle with ideas and party politics.[3]

In his series of articles from November and December 1911 in the *Call* and in his December 31 talk on "Socialism and the Negro" at the Flatbush Forum, Harrison clearly demonstrated that he was aligning with the left wing of the Socialist Party and moving towards the IWW. His December 26 *Call* article, in IWW-like fashion, emphasized that to reach "the Negro" the SP had to acknowledge "certain definite acts of economic oppression" and use party propaganda to expose "the suicidal policy of certain trades unions in excluding Negroes from membership and condemn them." Harrison's rationale for increased support of the IWW centered on the race question and on the IWW's opposition to race discrimination and segregation, its emphatic call to struggle against economic oppression (since African Americans were so preponderantly workers), its criticism of the racist practices of the AFL, and its support for the BTW. His public positions on these issues and his open support for the IWW challenged the reformist, pro-AFL, anti-IWW forces in the party and those leaders who, according to historian Sally M. Miller, were the consistent reinforcers of existing racist sentiment in the party.[4]

Harrison's movement left was demonstrated by his support for William D. "Big Bill" Haywood, the IWW founder and spokesperson for the left wing of the SP who was nominated for the party's National Executive Committee in November 1911. He ran on a platform that criticized the alleged neutrality of Socialist leaders regarding trade unions and pointedly attacked those party leaders who openly sided with corrupt AFL craft unions. Hillquit led in the attack on Haywood's candidacy, claiming that Haywood's lack of respect for the "property 'rights' of the profit takers" was "diametrically opposed to the accepted policy of Socialism," was "good anarchist doctrine," and would attract criminal types to the party.[5]

Haywood responded with a challenge to debate Hillquit. The debate on "What Shall the Attitude of the Socialist Party Be Toward the Economic Organization of the Workers?" was held at Cooper Union in New York City on January 12, 1912. At that meeting, Haywood called for SP support of the IWW and Hillquit called for an end to aid to the IWW and for work in the AFL, which he predicted "within five years" would "be socialistic." After the debate, according to Haywood, he spoke with Harrison who told him "that while Douglas had won the debate [a reference to the Abraham Lincoln–Stephen A. Douglas debates for an Illinois senate seat in 1858], Lincoln had carried the country [a reference to the 1860 presidential campaign]." This Haywood interpreted as meaning "that Hillquit had won the debate, but the workers of the nation were with me."[6]

In January and February 1912, while publicly expressing his left leanings, Harrison energetically went about his Colored Socialist Club work of organizing and speaking on behalf of the Socialist Party. However, less than two months after his published critique of AFL unions, and less than a month after his personal support of Haywood, Harrison found that support for his work by the leadership of Local New York was waning. After establishing the CSC, the local hadn't done anything to support the effort. In addition, Harrison also met with opposition from the police. He and Jean Jacques Coronel, organizer for Branch 5, were arrested in February for obstructing a sidewalk while attempting to address an audience at the corner of Lenox Ave. and 134th St. in Harlem.[7]

On February 22 Harrison wrote to the Central Committee of Local New York acknowledging that attendance at CSC functions had varied but pointing out that irregular attendance was not unusual for party functions and that attendance was not always a fair reflection of support. He claimed that in a little over two months there had been a "tremendous increase of Socialist sentiment among the Negroes of Harlem" and urged that it was now "imperative . . . that efforts be made to increase the attendance of the Colored Socialist Club." He also added that "the local had established the Club but has not done anything else" and that it "certainly" had "not done its full duties yet." After requesting an "outlay of about five dollars" to implement this work, he suggested that he attend the CC meeting of February 24 to discuss his proposals.[8]

These efforts were to no avail. Shortly after he wrote his letter, the EC of Local New York received a report from the Committee on Agitation Among Negroes, which cited the "depleted condition of the Party Treasury and the poor attendance of the meetings of the Colored Socialist Club" and recommended that the "present method of agitation among Negroes" should be ended. The report further recommended "that, rather than urge Negroes to come to meetings of the Socialist Party, speakers should be sent to Negro organizations to proselytize their members." An important reason given for this change was that "the idea of segregation of the Negroes into a separate club is likely to have a false impression to the intension [sic] of the Socialist Party." Such an argument was similar to those raised previously by Du Bois and Reverend Miller.[9]

Harrison's efforts had not overcome the inactivity and opposition of Socialist Party leaders. The Colored Socialist Club was not mentioned in the party press after the February EC meeting. On February 28, the *Call* did report that Harrison was scheduled to speak on "The Negro in American History," but he was listed as being from Branch 5, not from the CSC, which was never heard from again.[10]

The Socialist Party had answered the question of special organizational forms for "Negroes" by saying "No." The party's leading Black organizer in New York would not be working in a special Colored Socialist Club. He would only be a member of the branch in the area in which he lived. The work of socialist propaganda among Black people would be "neglected" between 1912 and 1917. When the SP would again undertake work in the African American community in 1917, it would be because of a major upsurge of Black race consciousness—a race consciousness for which Harrison, outside of the party, was the leading agitator.[11]

———————

In early 1912, however, with his efforts at special propaganda and organizing aimed at African Americans thwarted by Local New York, the indefatigable Harrison tried a new approach. He used three of the eight articles he had prepared in late 1911 in order to go over the head of Local New York leadership. His articles were presented to a nation-wide audience in the Chicago-based *International Socialist Review*, a significant national monthly with circulation between forty and fifty thousand, a political orientation described as "sharply towards the 'left,'" and a history of opening its pages to discussion of the "Negro Problem." The articles, "The Black Man's Burden" (in two parts) and "Socialism and the

Negro," posed a pointed challenge to Socialists preparing for the party convention in Indianapolis in May 1912. Very possibly, because of the challenge posed in the third article, its publication was delayed until July, after the convention ended.[12]

The first part of "The Black Man's Burden" stood Rudyard Kipling's internationally famous 1899 poem, "The White Man's Burden," on its head and simultaneously posed an alternate perspective to the position expressed by the Socialist Party leader Eugene V. Debs, who, in 1903, made reference to "the white burden bearer" in his article on "The Negro in the Class Struggle." Harrison pointed out that rather than the white man being faced with the "tremendous burden of regulating the affairs of men of all other colors, who . . . are backward and undeveloped," it was quite possible that "the shoe may be on the other foot" so far as the colored three-fourths of humanity was concerned. In contrast to Kipling's "white man's" view, Harrison proposed to put forth views, based on fact, from the "other side." He felt that these facts would "furnish such a damning indictment of the Negro's American over-lord as must open the eyes of the world."[13]

He then proceeded to arrange the facts he had marshaled in four areas: political, economic, educational, and social. Under political, he explained that there were over eight million African Americans disfranchised in sixteen southern states by fraud and force, Klan murder; the use of grandfather clauses, understanding tests, and the white primary system; and through such systematic exclusion that they were being told they "shall be political serfs." Under economic, he pointed out that political rights were the only sure protection of economic rights and, in a direct slap at Booker T. Washington, added that "every fool knows this," although "we have people who tell Negroes that they ought not to agitate for the ballot so long as they still have a chance to get work in the south." This position was specious, he argued, since there was real economic insecurity for Blacks in the South, exemplified by the peonage system, which "reduced many black men to . . . slavery unsanctioned by law." Harrison also cited examples from his scrapbooks, including the May 1909 Georgia Railroad strike during which white firemen challenged the seniority of Black firemen, went on strike, demanded that Black firemen be eliminated from the road, and "published a ukase to the people of the state proclaiming 'the white people of this state refuse to accept social equality.'" A second scrapbook example called attention to the white-supremacist position that opposed "Negro strike breakers" and cited how, in January 1912, delegates of the Painters', Plumbers', Masons', Carpenters', Steam Fitters', Plasterers', and Tinsmiths' Unions forced the Thompson and Starrett Construction Company, New York's second largest firm of contractors, to remove African American cold painters working on the Stern's department store annex. Black workers were not admitted to membership, and

The

Black Man's

Burden

BY

HUBERT H. HARRISON

PROVIDENCE, according to Mr. Kipling, has been pleased to place upon the white man's shoulders the tremendous burden of regulating the affairs of men of all other colors, who, for the purpose of his argument, are backward and undeveloped—"half devil and half child." When one considers that of the sixteen hundred million people living upon this earth, more than twelve hundred million are colored, this seems a truly staggering burden.

But it does not seem to have occurred to the proponents of this pleasant doctrine that the shoe may be upon the other foot so far as the other twelve hundred million are concerned. It is easy to maintain an *ex parte* argument, and as long as we do not ask the other side to state their case our own arguments will appear not only convincing but conclusive. But in the court of common sense this method is not generally allowed and a case is not considered closed until *both* parties have been heard from.

I have no doubt but that the colored peoples of the world will have a word or two to say in their own defense. In this article I propose to put the case of the black man in America, not by any elaborate arguments, but by the presentation of certain facts which will probably speak for themselves.

I am not speaking here of the evidences of negro advancement, nor even making a plea for justice. I wish merely to draw attention to certain pitiful facts. This is all that is necessary—at present. For I believe that those facts will furnish such a damning indictment of the negro's American over-lord as must open the eyes of the world. The sum total of these facts and of what they suggest constitute a portion of the black man's burden in America. Not all of it, to be sure, but quite enough to make one understand what the negro problem is. For the sake of clarity I shall arrange them in four groups: political, economic, educational and social. And first as to the political.

Political. I.

In a republic all the adult male natives are citizens. If in a given community some are citizens and others subjects, then your community is not a republic. It may call itself so. But that is another matter. Now, the essence of citizenship is the exercise of political rights; the right to a voice in government, to say what shall be done with your taxes, and the right to express your own needs. If you are denied these rights you are not a citizen. Well, in sixteen southern states there are over eight million negroes in this anomalous position. Of course, many good people contend that they may be unfit to exercise the right of

Figure 6.1. First page of *International Socialist Review* article by Hubert Harrison, May 1912. Hubert Harrison's article "The Black Man's Burden" in the April 1912 *International Socialist Review* was, in part, a response to Rudyard Kipling's internationally famous poem "The White Man's Burden" (1899). In contrast to Kipling's "white man's" view, Harrison proposed to put forth some views, based on fact, from the "other side." He felt that those facts would "furnish such a damning indictment . . . as must open the eyes of the world." *Source:* From *International Socialist Review.* Courtesy of Charles H. Kerr Company, Chicago.

the union delegates declared that "colored men would not be allowed to do this work," leading Harrison to comment sarcastically that these union men were "the same men who denounce Negro strike breakers."[14]

To Harrison, such racist occurrences were increasing, and this demonstrated that the livelihood of African Americans, without protection of the ballot, was "at the mere sufferance of the whites." In both the North and the South, the unwritten rule was (in a paraphrase reminiscent of the racial oppression described in the Dred Scott case) that "no black man shall hold a job that any white man wants." Harrison ended his first article by pointing out that it was a short step "from the denial of the right to work to the denial of the right to own," and he cited Hominy, Oklahoma, where, in late 1910, white night riders forced African Americans, including homeowners, out of town.[15]

In the second part of "The Black Man's Burden," Harrison took up educational facts, segregation, and lynching. He began by explaining that "in America, we subscribe to the dangerous doctrine that twelve million of the people should receive the minimum of education." He cited statistics from the South showing racial disparity in money spent on education and then criticized, though not by name, Booker T. Washington, by describing industrial education for Blacks as "labor-caste schools" and by challenging the assumption that "the Negro shall have a serf's equipment and no more." He also discussed how segregation laws were increasing nationwide and said that these were necessary for white Americans, who were "afraid that their inherent superiority may not . . . be so very evident" and, therefore, had "to enact it into law." Harrison cited "the first Ghetto legislation in an American nation" the previous year in Baltimore and the situation in Memphis, Tennessee, "where Negroes pay taxes for public parks in which they are not allowed to enter." In the United States such discrimination went even further, however, as the de facto law was "that Negroes shall not possess even their lives if any white persons should want them." Hence, "the institution called the lynching-bee." These were "the facts," and in light of them Harrison concluded that "the phrase, 'the white man's burden,' sounds like a horrid mockery."[16]

Harrison concluded his nationwide theoretical series in the July 1912 *International Socialist Review* with his seminal piece on "Socialism and the Negro," which was based on his pro-IWW speech of December 31 and delineated his core ideas on the subject. The printed version is noteworthy because it marked the first time the pro-IWW *ISR* printed the word "Negro" with a capital "N." This was consistent with Harrison's previous urging and was probably, in part, at his insistence. It also showed some progress, since in Harrison's two earlier articles in the *ISR*, the "N" was not capitalized.[17]

Harrison began with a description of the "Economic Status of the Negro" and anticipated by twenty-three years the point made by Du Bois, in *Black Re-*

construction, that the Black worker was "the ultimate exploited." As Harrison explained, "the ten million Negroes of America form a group that is more essentially proletarian than any other American group." Such an understanding implied that the just demands of the African American worker were demands thoroughly at one with the interests of the working class. Rather than viewing Black workers as a hindrance or retardant to the class struggle, as did other socialist theoreticians, including Algie M. Simons and Charles H. Vail, Harrison viewed them as a core component of proletarian struggle. It was the party members and periphery that Harrison sought to reach with this insight. Since the party mission was avowedly "to free the working class from exploitation," and since the African American was the "most ruthlessly exploited working class group in America, [then] the duty of the party to champion his cause" was "as clear as day." To Harrison this was "the crucial test of Socialism's sincerity," and in this, too, he anticipated Du Bois, who in a famous 1913 dictum stressed that the "Negro Problem . . . [is] the great test of the American Socialists."[18]

The implications of Harrison's analysis were profound. For the majority in the party, the key political debates concerned positions on revolutionary vs. evolutionary socialism and revolutionary unionism vs. AFL craft unionism. Harrison, in 1911 and 1912, proposed a new litmus test, a new "crucial test," for U.S. Socialists—"to champion" the cause of the "Negro." He thought this was the key to revolutionary strategy in the United States. For the rest of his life, he would seek "to champion" the cause of the "Negro" and to get others to do the same.[19]

In discussing "The Need of Socialist Propaganda" Harrison focused on the dangers inherent in the unofficial party practice of ignoring African Americans. He argued that if African Americans were not utilized by the Socialists they would be used to hinder the class struggle. These "ten million Americans, all proletarians, hanging on the ragged edge of the impending class conflict" had been left alone by the Socialists, he explained, and they could conceivably "become as great a menace to our advancing army as is the army of the unemployed, and for precisely the same reason: they can be used against us, as the craft unions have begun to find out." He cited the employment of Black workers at lower wages and the use of Black workers as "strikebreakers" when white workers went out on strike and argued that it was "imperative" for Socialists to enlist Black people in order to enlarge the movement and to "help to make us invincible." The reason this change was needed was the same one that was "impelling organized labor to adopt an all-inclusive policy; because the other policy results in the artificial breeding of scabs." Thus, both "common sense and enlightened self-interest" indicated it was time for Socialists to organize African Americans. He urged that be done quickly since American capitalists had "subsidized Negro leaders, Negro editors, preachers and politicians to build up

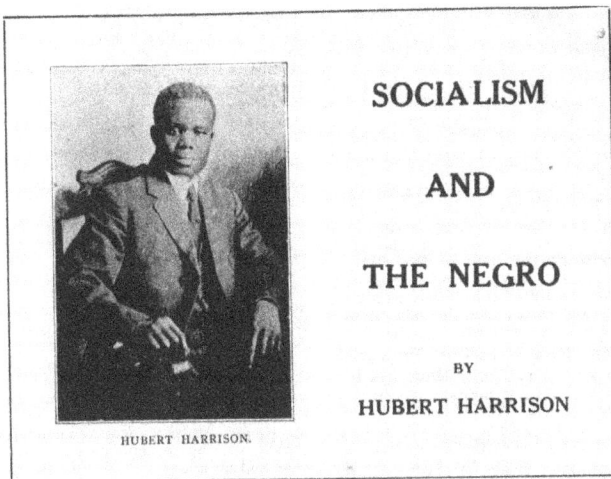

SOCIALISM

AND

THE NEGRO

BY

HUBERT HARRISON

HUBERT HARRISON.

1. ECONOMIC STATUS OF THE NEGRO

THE ten million Negroes of America form a group that is more essentially proletarian than any other American group. In the first place the ancestors of this group were brought here with the very definite understanding that they were to be ruthlessly exploited. And they were not allowed any choice in the matter. Since they were brought here as chattels their social status was fixed by that fact. In every case that we know of where a group has lived by exploiting another group, it has despised that group which it has put under subjection. And the degree of contempt has always been in direct proportion to the degree of exploitation.

Inasmuch, then, as the Negro was at one period the most thoroughly exploited of the American proletarian, he was the most thoroughly despised. That group which exploited and despised him, being the most powerful section of the ruling class, was able to diffuse its own necessary contempt of the Negro first among the other sections of the ruling class, and afterwards among all other classes of Americans. For the ruling class has always determined what the social ideals and moral ideas of society should be; and this explains how race prejudice was disseminated until all Americans are supposed to be saturated with it. Race prejudice, then, is the fruit of economic subjection and a fixed inferior economic status. It is the reflex of a social caste system. That caste system in America to-day is what we roughly refer to as the Race Problem, and it is thus seen that the Negro problem is essentially an economic problem with its roots in slavery past and present.

Notwithstanding the fact that it is usually kept out of public discussion, the bread-and-butter side of this problem is easily the most important. The Negro

65

Figure 6.2. First page of *International Socialist Review* article by Hubert Harrison, July 1912. Harrison's seminal article "Socialism and the Negro" in the July 1912 *International Socialist Review* marked the first time that the prominent national monthly printed "Negro" with a capital "N." Harrison's article described "the Negro" as "a group that is more essentially proletarian than any other American group" and urged, since "the Negro" was the "most ruthlessly exploited working class group in America, that the duty of the party to champion his cause" was "as clear as day." To Harrison this was "the crucial test of Socialism's sincerity." For the majority in the party the key political debates concerned positions on revolutionary vs. evolutionary socialism and revolutionary unionism vs. AFL craft unionism. Harrison proposed a new litmus test, a new "crucial test," for U.S. socialists—"to champion" the cause of the "Negro." He thought this was the key to revolutionary change strategy. *Source:* From *International Socialist Review.* Courtesy of Charles H. Kerr Company, Chicago.

in the breasts of black people those sentiments which will make them subservient to their will." To Harrison, chief among the subservient, as his scrapbooks indicate, was Booker T. Washington. Interestingly, Harrison's point about the potential "menace" anticipated similar analyses made seven and eight years later by those he would influence—the militant "New Negroes" and socialists A. Philip Randolph, Chandler Owen, and W. A. Domingo—and it was a point that attracted considerable attention after it was picked up by the Lusk Committee, New York State's Joint Legislative Committee to Investigate Seditious Activities.[20]

Harrison next examined how African Americans viewed socialism. He argued that it was imperative that members and leaders of the SP "first understand the Negro's attitude toward Socialism." While most Black Americans were "ignorant of what Socialism means," the fault was not theirs, for "behind the veil of the color line" not one "of the great world-movements for social betterment" had penetrated. Under slavery, it had been a crime to read, and after slavery, Black education was purposely and systematically kept to a minimum. In addition, they were justifiably suspicious of pronouncements from white people, particularly "any new gospel of freedom." Since statements declaring that "'all men are created equal,' meant only white men," Black people could "hardly be blamed."[21]

Despite this situation, a change in attitude toward the Republican Party that began with the 1906 Brownsville affair was underway. Many remembered Roosevelt's dishonorable discharge of the Black troops; how he, and his successor, William Howard Taft, pushed efforts against the soldiers to placate Southern white opinion; and how Taft "put in force the policy of pushing out the few near-Negro officeholders," all of which led the Black rank and file to increasingly see the Republican Party as "a great big sham." Though African Americans had been tied to the Republican Party, Harrison felt that by 1912, "that great political superstition" was "falling to pieces before the advance of intelligence among Negroes." They were beginning to realize "that they were sold out by the Republican party in 1876; that in the last twenty-five years lynchings have increased, disfranchisement has spread all over the south and 'jim-crow' cars run even into the national capital—with the continuing consent of a Republican congress, a Republican Supreme Court and Republican president."[22]

One indication that the betrayal was recognized was the defection to the Democrats of the Black political leaders James D. Carr, Ralph E. Langston, Bishop Alexander Walters, and Robert N. Wood of the National Colored Democratic League. "Colored democracy" was now "respectable," and it gave new meaning "to political heterodoxy." With a touch of biting irony, Harrison added that many Blacks had already gone over to the Democrats "because, as the *Amsterdam News* puts it, 'they had nowhere else to go.'" That last phrase was a takeoff on

Frederick Douglass's often cited words (from the 1872 Black worker convention in New Orleans) on why Blacks remained with the Republicans—"The Republican party is the deck, all else is the sea."[23]

While the bonds of African American political allegiance were clearly breaking down—in the 1910 congressional races, 20 to 40 percent of the Northern Black vote reportedly went Democratic—Harrison stressed that "the white world" knew "nothing" of these changes. The reason was that white men liked to choose their own "Negro leaders" and they chose those who said what they liked to hear. As examples, he cited the two leading Black newspapers in New York, which were "subsidized by the same political pirates who hold the title-deeds to the handful of hirelings holding office in the name of the Negro race." One, the *Age*, was "an organ of Mr. Washington," while the other, the *Amsterdam News*, pretended "to be independent," but in fact had to "be 'bought' on the installment plan." But, added Harrison, "Despite this 'conspiracy of silence' the Negroes are waking up; are beginning to think for themselves; to look with more favor on 'new doctrines.'" This, he reasoned, was the opportunity needed by the Socialists to reach African Americans.[24]

Harrison concluded his article by addressing "The Duty of the Socialist Party." He suggested that the party take up the "Negro Problem" at its upcoming national convention because the time was ripe "for taking a stand against the extensive disfranchisement." He cited instances of racism within the party, including the "recent dirty diatribes against the Negro [the reprinting of Kate Richards O'Hare's pro-segregation article "Nigger Equality"] in a Texas paper [*The Rebel*]" that was still on the national list of Socialist papers; the experiences of the party speaker Theresa Malkiel in Tennessee, "where she was prevented by certain people from addressing a meeting of Negroes on the subject of Socialism"; and "other exhibitions of the thing called southernism." He emphasized that the party had to address the question: "Southernism or Socialism—which? Is it to be the white half of the working class against the black half, or all of the working class? Can we hope to triumph over capitalism with one half of the working class against us?"[25]

Harrison had boldly placed his challenge before the national party leadership, and now he suggested what the response should be. He addressed the two large factions in the party, the political (evolutionary) and the industrial (revolutionary) Socialists, on their own terms. In each case, using the logic of their theoretical positions, he called for special emphasis on African Americans in the interests of the working class.

First he addressed the political socialists. Harrison agreed that the power of the voting proletariat could be expressed through the ballot and that with good political organization the workers could "secure control of the powers of government by electing members of the working class to office." Then, they could "secure legislation in the interests of the working class until such time as the workers may be able, by being in overwhelming control of the government, to 'alter or abolish it, and to institute a new government.'" He stressed, however, that in this work for "the abolition of capitalism, by legislation," the "Negro, who feels most fiercely the deep damnation of the capitalist system[,] can help."[26]

While recognizing the need for party work in electoral politics, Harrison also sought to reach the revolutionary socialists. He recognized that there were serious problems to be faced—the majority of African Americans, particularly in the South, were disfranchised. This fact led him to his ultimate conclusions on "The Negro and Industrial Socialism." He argued for IWW-style, point-of-production economic organizing, even in the South, and explained that "even the voteless proletarian can in a measure help toward the final abolition of the capitalist system." These workers, though absent the ballot, possess "labor power—which they can be taught to withhold," and they can organize themselves "at the point of production" and "work to shorten the hours of labor, to raise wages . . . [and] to enforce laws for the protection of labor." He noted that the Western Federation of Miners, an IWW union, had done this and had successfully won the eight-hour workday "without the aid of the legislatures or the courts." This approach required "a progressive control of the tools of production and a progressive expropriation of the capitalist class." In such work, African Americans could help. Thus far, many, under the influence of the capitalist philosophy of Booker T. Washington, remained unorganized industrially, but, "industrial unionism beckons to them and others." The program of the Socialist Party in the South, in Harrison's opinion, "could be based upon this fact."[27] Harrison had clearly put his strategy, his new "crucial test," for U.S. Socialists—"to champion" the cause of the "Negro"—before the party.

While Harrison was awaiting the national convention of the Socialist Party and how it would address the "Southernism or Socialism?" question, he became embroiled in a controversy with a Catholic priest, Father John L. Belford. Harrison was doing occasional reporting for the *Call*, and he decided to write an article about the vociferous right-winger, who had written a controversial piece for his church's publication, *The Nativity Mentor*, in March 1912. Harrison quoted Belford as saying that the power of socialists menaced the city, that the socialist "flaunts his red flag and openly preaches his doctrines," which attack religion, and that the socialist was "the mad dog of society," more dangerous than "cholera or smallpox," and "should be silenced, IF NEED BE BY A BULLET."[28]

These were fighting words, and Harrison responded with an article entitled "Murder as a Catholic Argument: An Interview with Father Belford" in the April 11 *Call*. He described the visit he made to Belford's sixteen-room, $110,000, rent-free, maid-serviced, tax-exempt house at Classon Ave. and Madison St. in Brooklyn. Harrison depicted the "large and somewhat flabby" Belford as one who exhibited "no ascetic enmity to the good things of the world." In order to engage him in frank discourse, Harrison told Belford that he was associated with the Church of St. Benedict the Moor and that he "was gathering materials from authoritative Catholic sources for a debate" in which he would argue that "Socialism is a detriment to society." Belford spoke freely, and his comments assured Harrison that he was "neither well read nor well informed." Belford maintained that Socialists "deny God altogether," "don't believe in marriage," and were a threat to American institutions and Christian civilization. He discussed the case of Francisco Ferrer (whom he mistakenly knew as "Ferro"), the Spanish educator and anarchist killed in Spain on October 13, 1909. Ferrer was the man for whom the Modern School, where Harrison would soon teach, was named, and Harrison was quite familiar with the true facts of his execution (including the involvement of church and state). Belford defended the killing and explained his position in words that Harrison was assured should "be taken literally"—"the government has a right to stop a man's mouth by putting him in prison, and if that does not stop him, it has the right to go further and kill him." Belford added that the "pestiferous [socialist] doctrines" should be driven "back to Europe, where they come from."[29]

Harrison's article in the *Call*, replete with Belford's quotations, was a scathing attack on the Catholic priest. Not surprisingly, Belford counterattacked with a letter in the Brooklyn *Daily Eagle* on April 12. Belford denied being interviewed by Harrison, though he admitted that "a Negro," who claimed to be a member of St. Benedict's, had requested information for a debate on socialism. Belford described Harrison's article as "thoroughly false," denied that his own statement about silencing words with a bullet should be taken "literally," and admitted that his choice of certain words was "unfortunate."[30]

The incident received considerable attention when the socialist press ran a large cartoon ("And When It Comes to Shin-Kicking") and letter from the editor ("The Nigger in the Belford Woodpile"). In addition, members of the Socialist Party from Belford's neighborhood claimed they felt threatened when they had to walk past his church and brought Belford up on charges. Then Harrison wrote a letter to the editor of the *Daily Eagle* that appeared on April 25 and called Belford's explanation "disingenuous." He added that his own "word is at least two degrees better . . . [than Belford's], because I am not a priest." He also commented "that yelling 'Negro' will not make this advocate of murder a safer moral guide for Brooklyn." This referred to the fact that Belford had injected the race question into the affair by making it a point to describe Harrison as a "negro" and by offering "immunity" when he only threatened to "kick the shins" of "negro" socialists, not greet them with a bullet as he proposed for other party members.[31]

The *Call* of May 6 published a letter in which W. A. Moss, secretary of the Eleventh and Seventeenth Assembly Districts of the SP's Local NY, included a challenge from Harrison to Belford to attend Harrison's lecture the next evening in Brooklyn on the subject of "Socialism and Anti-Socialism, Which?" Harrison challenged Belford "to come out into the open with your attacks on Socialism and Socialists, and not keep on in the cowardly fashion of attacking us from the pulpit and the pages of the *Nativity Mentor*." He also offered to give up wasting time and money on socialism if Belford could "prove to us that Socialism is unsound and no remedy for the existing evils of the present day such as poverty, prostitution, child labor, unemployment, long hours of labor, [and] murder in mines and factories."[32]

Harrison's talk on May 7 drew a full house, though Belford did not attend. After the talk, Moss wrote to the *Daily Eagle* describing the lecture. He wanted to show that Harrison's views were his own, not the official party position, because after the publicity of the Belford incident, the party was threatened with eviction by the owner of its headquarters building. In his letter, Moss supported the point Harrison made during his talk—that "capitalist newspapers are published to suppress news, not to issue news." In a discussion following the lecture, according to Moss, Harrison explained "that personally he was an atheist, because he had applied his scientific knowledge to religion and found it would not stand the test." Nevertheless, he proved with effective quotes from the party press that one could be a Roman Catholic and a socialist. In the discussion Harrison also reportedly said that he "would not defend any flag" since "the ideals which the flag were a token of were all that he was concerned about."[33]

————

As the Belford affair progressed, Harrison awaited a response to his *International Socialist Review* articles, and it soon became clear that they had fallen on deaf ears. The Socialist Party's National Convention met in Indianapolis from May 12 to 18, 1912, and essentially ignored the "Negro Problem." The only person who raised the issue was "Big Bill" Haywood, who argued that industrial unionism was the best way to organize disfranchised Southern Blacks. The convention, however, did not limit itself to mere indifference and neglect on the race issue. In the debate over Asian immigration, the Socialists, couched in the cloak of "science," expressed some of the most rabidly racist sentiments in U.S. leftist history and effectively gave Harrison the answer to his question, "Southernism or Socialism?" In this case, it was not only "Southernism" but "Westernism," too, for the racism in the party seemed to know no sectional bounds. Immigration was an issue of particular concern among "white" delegates from the western states, who spoke in fear of an influx of Japanese workers. Both the Majority Report and the Minority Report were approved, and each opposed Asian immigration. The Majority Report of the Committee on Immigration, energetically pushed by western delegates and signed by the party leaders Ernest Unter-

mann, J. Stit Wilson, and Robert Hunter, along with *Call* editor Joshua Wan-
hope, went even further and declared, in words Harrison would never forget:

> Race feeling is not so much a result of social as of biological evolution. It does
> not change essentially with changes of economic systems. It is deeper than
> any class feeling and will outlast the capitalist system. It persists even after
> race prejudice has been outgrown. . . . We may temper this race feeling by
> education, but we can never hope to extinguish it altogether.
>
> Class-consciousness must be learned, but race-consciousness is inborn
> and cannot be wholly unlearned.[34]

Here was the "racism is innate" argument that Harrison had dubbed the core of
all racist arguments, and it was proclaimed loudly by national leaders of the Socialist Party at their convention. If race feeling was innate, if race consciousness
superseded class consciousness, then the Socialist Party was implicitly saying
that corrective actions against racism would be minimal and of little importance
to a socialist agenda.

The significance of this convention for Harrison's future ideological development is clear. The majority resolution on immigration favored Asian exclusion as "legislation restricting the invasion of the white man's domain by other
races." In a similar debate at the 1908 convention, Victor Berger had argued
that socialism would be victorious only by keeping the United States a "white
man's country" and warning that if something were not done, it "would become
a black-and-yellow country within a few generations." Leading white socialists
were, in Harrison's words, putting the white "'race first' rather than 'class first.'"
Harrison later referred to these white Socialists as "the bourgeois opportunists
of the Socialist Party," and during the remainder of his life, both his theoretical
development and his race consciousness would be shaped by his efforts to respond to their position.[35]

In later writings, Harrison would cite passages from the 1912 convention's
majority report as he emphasized the necessity for African Americans to develop
race consciousness and to put "race first." He would call for race consciousness
as a protective reaction, as a means of defense, against the "white-race"-first
sentiments that permeated U.S. society and the labor and socialist movements.
As long as racist whites put "white race" interests first, he would argue, there
was a need for Black people to develop race consciousness and to similarly put
"race first."[36]

The overall relation between white supremacy and class consciousness in
the United States suggests an answer to one of the most important questions in
U.S. leftist history—which the German scholar Werner Sombart asked as early
as 1906—"Why is there no socialism in the United States?" Theodore W. Allen,

in an insightful essay entitled "'The Kernel and the Meaning . . . ,'" explains that at that time, "general historians, as well as labor and socialist specialists," were beginning to develop a "classical consensus," which fully matured by the second half of the century and sought to explain the relatively low level of class consciousness among American workers. That consensus, according to Allen, cited such factors as the early existence of the right to vote and other constitutional liberties, the heterogeneity of the working class, the existence of a free-land safety valve, the existence of higher wages and social mobility, and the historic precedence of trade unions over a labor party, which facilitated antisocialist, antilabor party policies of a corrupt "aristocracy of labor" within the working-class movement. Since each of these factors, as Allen points out, was historically shaped in a white-supremacist fashion, deeper meaning is given to Harrison's theoretical work. In contrast to the position of the leading party factions on the strategy to achieve socialism (evolutionary vs. revolutionary), and in contrast to the developing consensus on explaining the low level of class consciousness in the United States by leftist and labor historians, Hubert Harrison was suggesting that a primary reason for limited working-class consciousness and for the absence of socialism in the United States was white supremacy. Within a few years, he would more forcefully articulate that it was because "white" workers and socialists put race first before class. This is an extremely important and profound analysis. Over time, Harrison would respond by stressing that race consciousness among African Americans was necessary not only as a measure of self-defense but also as a means of challenging white supremacy, which was the principal roadblock to class consciousness among European American workers and the principal roadblock to socialism.[37]

At its 1912 national convention, the Socialist Party not only took its race-first position on the immigration question; it also took two other positions that would directly hinder its radical efforts. First, as historian Sally M. Miller has explained, activities of the women's sector were "abruptly terminated by an arbitrary decision by the party's executive committee." Here, too, the race question appears to be the touchstone—the demise of the Woman's Clubs had been preceded by, and was similar to, the demise of the Colored Socialist Club, the party's less popular effort at special work among African Americans.[38]

Second, the 1912 convention amended the party constitution to oppose "sabotage." The right-wing, evolutionary socialist leaders Victor Berger and William Ghent framed an infamous amendment to article II, section 6, of the party constitution, which called for expulsion of any member who "opposes political action or advocates crime, sabotage or other methods of violence as a weapon of the working class to aid in its emancipation." "Political action," heretofore vaguely defined, was now held to be "participation in elections for public office and practical legislation and administrative work along the lines of the Socialist party platform." After the amendment passed, the party was effectively split between the right-wing "politicals" and the pro-sabotage, pro-IWW left.[39]

The historian Ira Kipnis considers the Socialist Party to have been at "the zenith of its power, prestige, and influence" in 1912, but after the split at the convention it was seriously weakened. The split between right and left and the sabotage issue were certainly important reasons for an immediate decline in membership. But a deeper decline, reversed for a period by enthusiasm for revolution related to the Bolshevik revolution in Russia, took place over years, and other issues were also factors. These other issues included the loss of some members to the Progressives, a general tightening in the party after 1912, diminished women's activities, a split over positions on World War I, the growth of rival communist organizations by 1919, government repression, and, perhaps most important, as Harrison argued, the party's failure to deal effectively with white supremacism.[40]

The 1912 Socialist Party debate and the struggle that it reflected between evolutionary and revolutionary socialists had one other, more immediate consequence. As the historian Mari Jo Buhle has noted, the "internal party struggle" that culminated with "the proscription of the advocacy of sabotage in Party ranks had the effect of tightening Party discipline against all potentially dissident elements." Harrison was not only rebuffed on the race question; he was also in the minority ideologically in his support of the principles of revolutionary socialism. As an outspoken Black supporter of the left, he began to face organizational difficulties over the next few months from the Local New York leadership, a leadership that had done little on the race question and that played a prominent role in the party's right wing.[41]

On May 1, Harrison's relations with Local New York still appeared good. He was one of the party's featured English-language speakers before 50,000 people at their big May Day rally at Union Square. Twenty-three days later, he engaged in a debate on 103rd St. with Frank Urban[sky], a noted antisocialist speaker, on whether "Socialism is undesirable, impracticable, and unscientific." Later, when Harrison tried to hold a similar debate with the same Frank Urban, he would be brought up on internal party charges.[42]

Troubles surfaced at the end of May, after the national convention. Harrison offered his services as a paid party speaker for Local New York at three dollars per engagement, a fee that other speakers were paid and that he had previously received. At the time of his offer, the local was paying him only one dollar per engagement. His offer to Local New York was ignored, and Harrison accepted an offer with Local Kings County (Brooklyn). Then, on June 23, he wrote to the Central Committee of Local New York in response to a form mailed to party speakers, and he indicated that he was "anxious to do some campaigning" in his own local. He also pointed out that he was "a much better speaker" than he had been the year before and he emphasized that "justice to myself and my family" (which now numbered four, going on five—daughter Aida Mae was born on the Fourth of July, 1912) forbade his acceptance of the "very low terms ($1.00 a night)" that the local offered. He pointed out that "even speakers from New Jersey" were getting three dollars per day from Local New York, and he reasoned that "since I can render as efficient services on the stump I don't think that it would be fair to ask me to take less." Clearly, Local New York had moved far away from their previous position of special emphasis on organizing African Americans. Now, they were paying their leading Black orator less than other speakers.[43]

The situation was even more complex. Harrison was a member of Branch 5, and as far back as April 29, branch organizer Jean Jacques Coronel had submitted Harrison's name as a branch speaker. Local New York would now not even let Branch 5 schedule its own speakers. This lack of internal democracy led the Branch to protest this fact and to seek "autonomy" on the question.[44]

While these struggles went on and while awaiting the outcome of the party's national convention, Harrison served as a delegate from the local to the New York State convention in Auburn in late June. The convention was the largest in history, and Harrison was well received by the delegates. He reportedly "created a sensation" when he presented the minority report of the Committee on Organization.[45]

Nevertheless, on July 27, at a meeting of the Central Committee of Local New York, Harrison's request for three dollars per speaking engagement was referred to the Executive Committee. Two days later, the EC "decided not to increase the pay of Comrade Harrison." They further decided that "all speakers resident and members of Local New York, be paid $1.00 per meeting."[46]

The party tightening was beginning. The local's leading Black activist was complaining of inadequate and unfair treatment; an active branch complained it lacked autonomy; and in response to complaints from Harrison and Branch 5, measures taken against Harrison were applied more widely.

The party tightening occurred amid the historic 1912 presidential campaign, one of the most significant and hotly contested races in United States history. The election marked the first time since the Civil War that there was a legitimate three-way race for the presidency. The Republican incumbent, William Howard Taft, was running against a Progressive former president, Theodore Roosevelt; the Democrat governor of New Jersey, Woodrow Wilson; and a fourth candidate, the Socialist standard bearer, Eugene V. Debs. Unlike the three-way race during the Civil War period, when the Republicans stood out because of their stand on slavery, in the 1912 contest there was little significant difference between the three major parties other than that drummed up by politicians. Gabriel Kolko writes that "the specific utterances and programs of all three were identical on fundamentals, and party platforms reflected this common agreement." All were strongly pro-capital while nominally pro-reform, and none of them offered anything of note to African Americans.[47]

During the exciting 1912 election, Harrison campaigned vigorously for the Socialist presidential candidate, Debs. Though he was becoming increasingly dissatisfied with the positions of the Socialist Party and with party leadership, Harrison neither left the party, like Du Bois, nor supported the Democrats, like Du Bois, Trotter, and Bishop Alexander Walters. He still maintained a high regard for Debs, who somehow seemed to stand above the party's internal debate with his policy of not attending party conventions. On the race question, Debs still offered nothing special. He was, however, known to oppose discrimination openly, and he was generally considered one of the more sensitive Socialist Party leaders on the race question. For those reasons, for his anticapitalism, and because of his known sympathies for the IWW, he had Harrison's support.[48]

The *New York News* claimed that during 1912 Harrison was "the most trusted and valued speaker of the Socialist Party in the city" and "demands were sent to the Party for his services as speaker and debater all over the United States." After one of his talks at Wall Street in New York on September 13, the *New York Times* described him as "an eloquent and forceful negro speaker" who "shattered all records for distance in an address on Socialism in front of the Stock Exchange building." He reportedly "mounted the stand in front of the Socialists' banner at noon and started in with a description of life in the medieval ages." At first his voice reached the outermost limits of the crowd, but as the hours passed and his voice grew huskier, the circle of auditors drew closer. He went strong into the third hour and then talked himself into a hoarse whisper before ending. Shortly after the Wall Street talk, from September 16 through September 21, he was engaged as a speaker by the Central Committee of the Camden County (N.J.) Socialist Party. Then, upon his return to New York, he was one of more than forty soap-box orators on September 22 at the first series of speakers' meetings held by the Executive Committee of Local New York at the Cafe Monopol on Ninth St.[49]

Following these talks, on the last day of September, Harrison began an exhausting tour of New York State. He was scheduled for Poughkeepsie on September 30; Albany on October 1; Schenectady on the 2nd through the 4th; Utica on the 5th; Watertown on the 6th; Syracuse on the 7th and 8th; Rochester on the 9th; Buffalo on the 10th through the 12th; Auburn (the site of the SP's State Convention) on the 13th; Hornell on the 14th; Binghamton on the 15th; Newburgh on the 16th; and Yonkers on the 17th. His speech in Rochester on October 9 was part of a planned debate with the Reverend W. A. Byrd, a local Black preacher active with the Progressive Party. Though Byrd failed to appear, Harrison spoke on the virtues of socialism before an audience estimated at 3,000. He stressed that socialism was "not a matter of reform but a matter of revolution which . . . did not necessarily mean bloodshed." The University of Rochester professor Kendrick P. Shedd, a Socialist and the author of a pamphlet on "The Right to Free Speech," described Harrison as "an excellent logician" who "built up his argument point by point" and "owned" the audience. As he spoke, the crowd was reportedly so attentive that one could have heard a pin drop—except when it was periodically "convulsed with laughter." The October 12 *Buffalo Socialist* described Harrison as "the black Demosthenes" (after Greece's greatest orator) and as an "off-hand orator of remarkable ability" who was "sound in his reasoning relative to how the workers should organize on the industrial field."[50]

Harrison delivered a remarkable talk in Auburn on October 13 that received considerable coverage and offers an in-depth look at his anticapitalist oratory for the Socialist Party. The *Auburn Citizen* described him as "one of the most active workers for the cause of Socialism" and "one of the best speakers now stumping the country." In reviewing his talk, the *Citizen* added that his criticism "was not at all denunciatory" and that he had "endeavored in a clear way to illustrate the Socialist philosophy" by showing "that present discontent is not to be permanently remedied by reforms or patchwork amelioration, but only by absolute change as suggested by Socialism." Harrison compared the capitalist system to "an old suit, worn and outgrown, and unfit to meet the conditions of the future." He broke down the basic concepts of socialism into easily understood terms, explaining that "it is all a question [of] ownership of the three means of existence, food, shelter and clothing," and, in order to obtain these, "the laboring class must sell its commodity, labor, without receiving the fair share of the product it creates." He concluded predicting that the workers would receive their fair share in the future "when the means of existence are owned by the laboring class."[51]

The *Auburn Advertiser* lauded Harrison's effort and recounted his brief sketch of the growth of socialism in Belgium, England, and Germany, noting that he explained how socialism "is still in its infancy here [in the U.S.] and subject to infantile ills." In order to overcome these infantile tendencies, he saw education of the masses as the key, since socialism "grows with the growth of intelligence among the masses." One means of developing this intelligence, he emphasized, was by exposés. Harrison also offered insightful comments on the Progressive Party and Theodore Roosevelt. He stated that though the "Big Bull Moose"—Roosevelt—was "going through the country telling what he'll do for the people," he was "not the first Progressive . . . [Otto Edward Leopold von] Bismarck was . . . and he had more brains in his little toe than the Lobster Bay Bull Moose has in his whole anatomy." The reference to Bismarck—the leader in the Franco-Prussian War who became first chancellor of the German Empire and advocated German unification under Prussian (not Austrian) dominance—

was striking. Bismarck, like Roosevelt, had a patrician and military background and mass appeal, favored the acquisition of colonies and the building of empire, and sought to undercut social agitation through controlled reform and attacks on labor unions and socialists.[52]

In his Auburn talk Harrison also cited statistics that showed that in 1905 "the average annual wealth produced per capita" was $2,470 and the average wage was $437, or "for every $6 produced the producer got only one dollar, the other five having been filched from him." He described the plentiful supply of food in the country and criticized the fact that "in the midst of plenty people here in the United States die of starvation" and "countless numbers of men, women, and children are at the point of starvation during the entire course of their natural lives." That, he said, was "what the capitalist system does for us." To drive home the inhumanity of the system, Harrison cited several examples, including those of George Westinghouse's son's inheriting fifty million dollars "without ever doing a stroke of work" and seven wealthy women who gave an eight-thousand-dollar dinner in the Hotel Vanderbilt—"to seven dogs!"[53]

Finally, Harrison discussed how the strength of the socialist movement came from the working masses and how the workers had to remove the fetters of ignorance that hindered the growth of their class consciousness. He emphasized that before the Socialist Party came into being, Karl Marx "was urging the economic organization of the working classes" because the "working class united, and conscious of its proletariat aims, can, against the world, achieve anything." Though socialism was spreading in the United States, many remained ignorant because "the laboring class allows itself to be led by designing politicians" and because workers do not "try to grasp the economic anomalies which make them slaves of Capital." This "ignorance of the great economic truths" on which the socialist movement was based was what kept "the fetters on them." Harrison concluded his talk by pointing out that through the leadership of the IWW, as in the 1912 Brotherhood of Timber Workers strike in Louisiana, the "socialist light is dawning." It was dawning because, in the Timber Workers struggle, under IWW leadership, the white worker "found that . . . , it is to his interest to combine with the black."[54]

While Harrison's Auburn talk was geared toward a predominantly white audience, he also developed a core presentation for predominantly Black audiences in this campaign period. That speech, later published as "What Socialism Means to Us," began with historical background and explained that the struggle between North and South was one between contending groups of capitalists over how to exploit the laboring classes. In discussing race prejudice, he emphasized that the capitalist "creates and keeps alive these prejudices" because it "pays the capitalist to keep the workers divided." He attributed the growth of such prejudice to the fact that African Americans were put at the bottom of the economic ladder and that capitalists were able to get "white working people . . . to believe that their interests are different." The capitalists, according to Harrison, then used one portion of the working class to "club" the other. To counter this, Harrison advocated socialism, which stood "for the emancipation of the wage-slave" and sought to do away with the capitalist system. He believed that Black people who investigated socialism would "be convinced of two things: that Socialism is right, and that it is inevitable." He emphasized that any system "in which those who work have least while those who work them have most, is wrong." He concluded by calling for those who wished to join with other class-conscious, intelligent wage earners in ending this system to study socialism and work for its success, and he urged his listeners to "hear what they have to say" and "join hands with the Socialists."[55]

In this same period, as Harrison was agitating for Debs, the Socialist Party's national leadership further provoked his wrath. They "refused to route . . . Debs in the South" because, as Harrison later wrote, "the Grand Old Man let it be known that he would not remain silent on the race question while in the South." Party leaders "wanted the votes of the white South," and, he added, they "were willing to betray by silence the principle of inter-racial solidarity which they espoused on paper."[56]

Despite his increasing dissatisfaction with the party over the race question, it appears that, in 1912 as in 1911, Harrison's campaign efforts helped to increase the Socialist Party vote. Debs, though he came in fourth behind Wilson (41.8 percent), Roosevelt (27.4), and Taft (23.2), received 6 percent of the national vote, his highest total ever. The Socialist Party in New York State received 63,381 votes (4 percent of the total), which was up from 48,982 in 1910 and 38,451 in 1908. In New York City the SP vote increased to 33,000, some 11 percent of the citywide total, though in New York County (Manhattan), the vote went from 18,358 in 1911 to 18,128 in 1912. Since Harrison was a very active campaigner and popular speaker, and since he spent so much time upstate in the month before the election, it is likely that his efforts there helped increase that vote, while his absence from the city helps to explain the decrease in that count.[57]

As the 1912 election drew to a close, Harrison began to tutor privately in an attempt to provide for his family. In a November 7 advertisement in the *Call*, he offered private instruction in English grammar, composition, English and American literature, history (general, English, and American), Latin (first and second year), and civil-service arithmetic. A second advertisement offered instruction in the above subjects as well as in rhetoric and geography. His references included three prominent Socialists—the muckraker, NAACP founder, and candidate for governor of New York State, Charles Edward Russell; a "Committee for Agitation Among Negroes" member, Dr. S. Berlin; and the author and Sunrise Club member Moses Oppenheimer. Harrison's teaching was apparently innovative and compassionate, and many of his students were non-English-speaking immigrants. Years later, the journalist Floyd Calvin wrote that the Finns and Hungarians of New York remembered Harrison as "the man who devised a way of teaching them English without knowing a word of their language."[58]

Toward the close of the election campaign Harrison also wrote a wide-ranging philosophical book review that offered insightful criticism of rigid economic determinism and rigid materialist interpretations of history. In "The Materialistic Interpretation of Morals," in the November 3 *Call*, he reviewed *Puritanism* by Clarence Meilly, a book recently published by the socialist publishing house of Charles H. Kerr. He praised it as a scholarly book in which the socialist movement could take pride and as a "most comprehensive and concise study of morality, its content, origin and progress from the standpoint of pure materialism." Harrison showed both intellectual breadth and subtlety as he moved his socialist analysis beyond the fixed bounds of economic determinism. Of particular interest was his recitation of Meilly's explanation of the relation between the individual and the collective; of how as the "part played by each [individual] becomes now more largely the business of all . . . [then] even voluntary association implies a sacrifice of personal freedom." This implicitly challenged the "New Freedom" of Woodrow Wilson, which was premised on a type of individual freedom and the idea that the basic and "free" functioning of capitalism was in the best interest of the country. Harrison was arguing for collective control in the collective interest, a point more consistent with socialist theory. He also recognized the role of the individual, however, and he pointed out that Meilly described how the "application of the principle of association thus engenders a conflict between the interests and desires of the individual and the interests of the group as a whole." Some years later, Harrison would offer additional insights on the relation between the individual and the collective in terms of the Harlem community. In an article in the *Amsterdam News* he would write that it is "out of the development of a civic consciousness, of each citizen's organic relationship to the community and the community's responsibility for each citizen, that the Greater Harlem will arise."[59]

Harrison also discussed Meilly's coverage of the three "formal aids to communal or social conduct"—laws, morals, and manners. He described the class nature of the legal system and explained that the law was used "to crystallize into formal statement the dominance of the masters, and to adjust their private differences peacefully between themselves." This was an implicit rebuke of the other leading branch of Progressive Era thought, the "New Nationalism" of Theodore Roosevelt, which was premised on government regulation of a naturally competitive capitalist system and was largely a means of organizing a more efficient and effective capitalism. Harrison felt that the system did not need to be regulated so much as it needed to be overturned.[60]

Next, he examined the double-standard and the class basis of sexual relations. He detailed Meilly's description of the growth of sexual morality, the "transference of the line of descent from the mother's side to the father's," and the "tremendous importance which the hereditary principle gave to female chastity, especially under the feudal conditions of property." He noted how Meilly fixed "beyond any doubt the class purpose of this new ethic" and how "the chivalry and courtesy which developed as the social, spiritual and artistic reflex of feudalism 'were reserved for women of the proprietary class alone.'" In contrast, toward women of the working class, "the correct noble attitude was one of contemptuous brutality, coupled with a quite unregulated sexual license."[61]

Harrison also reviewed Meilly's treatment of religion and "the process by which the Christian Church was transformed into the most tremendous machine for the subjugation of the workers by the masters of the world's bread." He quoted Meilly that "never before or since" had "religion and morality discharged such important social functions" or had "any religion proven so utterly false to its pristine purpose and ideals." True, he added, those ideals were impossible dreams, but "that the gospel of the Nazarene carpenter should have become the chief sustaining power of a class system of exploitation" was "surely the greatest marvel" as well as "the supremest irony of history."[62]

In his review Harrison also challenged the man "considered by many to be the leading Marxist theoretician in America," Ernest Untermann. Untermann was one of the drafters of the 1912 Socialist Party majority platform on immigration and held extremely racist views, which he had expressed at the 1908 party convention. Harrison went at him hard and challenged "a certain wild thesis propounded by Untermann in his *World's Revolution*," that "institutional Christianity had its origin in a consciously conceived proletarian movement." He noted that Meilly seemed to accept this thesis. Harrison disputed it on historical grounds and explained how the proponents of this theory make their point of departure at the Council of Nicaea and hold that until then, "Christianity expressed a clearly conceived proletarian aim." But, as he noted, "the first history of the Christian Church was written about eight years before by Eusebius Pamphilus, bishop of Caesarea in Palestine," who had reviewed the Christian literature up to his own time; and "nowhere in all his writings can be found the possible elements of this proletarian consciousness or aim." Therefore, the proponents of this theory had no basis for their argument, and, to Harrison, "scientific studies of the origin of religion" furnished "more satisfactory explanations." His concluding advice was: "first prove your Jesus"—this was something, he added, that had "not yet been done."[63]

Next, Harrison challenged mechanical applications of historical-materialist analysis. He described "one more erroneous belief," namely, that "the reformation is to be fully explained on the sole ground of economic changes." His own examination of the historical evidence showed "that purely cultural causes played an important and impelling part in the movement known broadly as the Renaissance of which the Protestant Reformation was the final stage." He therefore argued that any "forced attempts to apply a doctrine as sound as the doctrine of historical materialism in certain details and under certain conditions where it does not apply can only serve to throw unmerited reproach upon that doctrine itself." Using notions on the role of the unconscious common to the Freudian view of psychology, Harrison challenged mechanical theorizing. He argued that the "underlying defect in such cases consists in assuming that men are, at every stage of social evolution, conscious of the . . . [ends] toward which their actions are shaping the human process." Harrison countered with an old saying: "Man proposes and God disposes," which he explained as meaning that "men, at any given stage, shape their actions, according to the material necessities of their situation—as they see them." He then advised that when utilizing "the materialistic interpretation to history," one must be "critic and historian" but one need not speculate and "assume the role of philosopher" because that was not "safe" historical scholarship.[64]

Harrison's review showed clearly that he had a deep and subtle understanding of Marxism. He was neither blindly dogmatic nor rigidly mechanical; he could draw on a wealth of knowledge from fields as disparate as historical criticism and modern psychology; and he was sensitive to the relation between the individual and the collective. The review also demonstrated that Harrison, who had openly criticized a leading party theoretician, was clearly an independent individual who could and would challenge party leaders.

The philosophical review did more, however. Bruce Dancis has pointed out that the Socialist Party of America "viewed the coming of socialism as inevitable, subject only to the inexorable working out of historical laws" and it "was never able to break out of the rigid economic determination that characterized most of the socialist parties of the Second International." Many socialists who emphasized political action believed that election gains would grow into a majority election victory. Others, who emphasized direct action, believed "that larger and more militant strikes would inevitably lead to the downfall of capitalism." Such economic determinism made the party inflexible to broader and more subtle political issues. One result was that the economic determinists would often pose their "class consciousness" against socialist feminist's "sex consciousness." Similarly, "class conscious" socialists, especially those who put the white race first, would frequently invoke interests of the "class" in downplaying special race demands of African Americans. Harrison, in his philosophical challenge to economic determinism, was probing yet other areas that reinforced white supremacy in the Socialist Party. He was implicitly arguing that the problems of racism and white supremacy, although clearly economic, had political, ideological, and psychological components that also had to be considered.[65]

————————

Throughout 1912 the appeal of the Wobblies grew stronger for Harrison, and he became increasingly involved in the debate within the Socialist Party over relations with the IWW. On November 24, he directly took up this issue in an Elizabeth, N.J., lecture on "Socialism—Political and Economic." In this talk, according to the *Issue*, a pro-IWW socialist newspaper, Harrison traced back to their foundations "the two great intellectual movements" represented in the Socialist Party: that which "lays the greater stress upon the political struggle" and "that which bears on the economic struggle." He showed that the powerful tendency toward "'industrial unionism,' 'syndicalism,' or direct action" was a "reaction against the old style craft unionism which had utterly failed to keep step with the march of industry" and mostly represented "the skilled and better paid workers." He spoke of an "increasing revulsion" on the part of many "toward the old trade unionism" and "toward the purely political and non-industrial Socialist propaganda." He also maintained that the Socialist Party was not addressing the issue squarely with its program, which centered on political (electoral) work, and he emphasized that the IWW was not opposed to Marxist fundamentals but simply differed from the Socialist Party in relation to methods.[66]

A week later, on December 1, Harrison again lectured in Elizabeth. The *Issue* described his speech on "Industrial Unionism" as "the most scientific explanation of this much discussed movement that has ever been delivered in this city." He based his talk on leading IWW authorities such as William Trautman and Austin Lewis and in so doing reportedly "showed the nature of industrial unionism of the most advanced type . . . syndicalism." Harrison discussed many key issues—sabotage, direct action, and the general strike—and gave "numerous instances of their application in various European strikes." The paper noted that "Comrade Harrison belongs to that wing of the party which believes that economic organization is the most important, and that the political movement in this country was unsound because not supported by a strong economic organization." His ability to defend that position was such that when the question and answer period followed his talk "some of the 'political' Socialists present tried to get through Comrade Harrison's armor," with little success. He apparently appealed to New Jersey listeners (who were most likely paying him more than the one dollar per talk Local New York had offered), and he was scheduled to speak in Passaic the following Sunday on "The Wreckage of Religion."[67]

Throughout 1912 there were constant themes in Harrison's political agitation. These included support for the IWW, support for industrial unionism and economic organizing, support for sabotage and direct action, challenges to organized religion, calls for special organizing efforts aimed at African Americans, and opposition to white supremacy. He was increasingly identified with the left wing of the party, and during the year he faced major rebuffs on the race question with the demise of the Colored Socialist Club and with the SP's white-race-first theoretical pronouncements. As he continually studied and agitated, he was repeatedly confronted with the white supremacism in the SP, and he moved further to the left. As he manifested more and more political independence and advocated his views openly, it became increasingly likely that he would face conflict within the ever-tightening structure of the Socialist Party.

7

Dissatisfaction with the Party
(1913–1914)

From late 1912 through 1914, Hubert Harrison agitated for the IWW brand of socialism as opposed to the more right-wing type advocated by most of the Socialist Party leadership. His left-wing sympathies were demonstrated in his speeches; in his defense of sabotage; and in his support of "Big Bill" Haywood, the Paterson, N.J., silk strikers, and arrested IWW activists. He was increasingly disenchanted with the party's position on the "Negro problem" and its generally conservative approach to the "economic" organization of workers. In addition, he was attracted to the IWW-style direct action, which he thought could be used (and fifty years later, in the form of sit-ins, marches, boycotts, freedom rides, strikes, etc., was used) to reach the discriminated against and often disfranchised Black masses.

These differences with party leadership became so manifest that twice in 1913 Harrison was brought up on internal charges, and in 1914 he was suspended by Local New York leadership. Harrison saw the suspension as related to ideological differences, to white supremacism, and to lack of freedom to dissent within the party. These experiences turned him away from the Socialists and toward independent activity, and then toward full-time work among African Americans in Harlem.

The crackdown on dissent in the Socialist party and the serious internal difficulties it spawned began in the wake of the 1912 convention, where article II, section 6 of the party constitution was amended to call for the expulsion of any member who advocated "sabotage." The amendment was upheld by 13,215 to 4,196 in an August referendum in which only 11 percent of the national membership participated. With the amendment in place and the right-wing leadership consolidating, party repression soon followed.[1]

On November 30, 1912, Julius Gerber, executive secretary of Local New York, brought charges against Frederick Sumner Boyd, an English intellectual, socialist, and *Call* reporter, for public criticisms he had made. Gerber specifically charged that Boyd (an IWW supporter) had called him "a liar" and said that he was "in conspiracy with the capitalists of New England to help bring [Joseph] Ettor and [Arturo] Giovannitti to the electric chair." (Ettor and Giovannitti were IWW leaders of the 1912 Lawrence, Massachusetts, textile strike charged with accessory to murder. They were later acquitted by jury.) Boyd denied both charges and at his hearing argued that "Gerber was guilty of lying" during the election campaign when he stated that the party was using all available speakers. At that time Boyd and his fellow party member and IWW supporter Alexander Scott were not being utilized. Boyd reportedly did not deny saying "that had Ettor and Giovannitti been sent to the electric chair, Gerber would have to be held responsible as much as any capitalist in New England."[2]

Boyd was found guilty on two of the charges, while two others were thrown out. On December 14, he was placed on three-month suspension by the Central Committee of Local New York. Then, a local referendum upheld his suspension 418 to 232, though Branch 5 (where Harrison and Boyd were members) voted against the suspension by 21 to 5. Two weeks after the suspension, Harrison, Boyd's friend and supporter, filled his spot as Branch delegate to the Central Committee. Nevertheless, despite Harrison's presence, on January 26, 1913, the CC denied Boyd's request for a retrial.[3]

In early December 1912, while Boyd was awaiting his hearing, "Big Bill" Haywood, a member of the Socialist Party National Executive Committee and an IWW spokesperson, again came to New York. The antisabotage *Call* published various prosabotage and pro-direct-action extracts said to be from his speeches, and based on these extracts the state committees of New York and New Jersey moved to recall Haywood from the NEC. At the December 14 meeting at which Boyd was found guilty, the CC passed a motion that Local New York prefer charges against Haywood along with an amendment that the local endorse the movement to recall him from the National Executive Committee and that members of the local be instructed to vote for the resolution-initiating referendum for the recall. The local eventually supported the referendum, 1174 to 273, though Branch 5 only voted 34 to 31 for the referendum.[4]

Despite the attacks on Boyd and Haywood, Harrison continued his party work. On January 11, 1913, he served as Branch 5's delegate to the Central Committee of Local New York and on January 26 he was elected to the Local Grievance Committee. He was also one of three people chosen to draft a resolution to be published in the socialist press in order to disprove the publication of a letter by the anarchist Hutchins Hapgood in the *Call*, and he was elected to a committee to look into the hotel workers' strike (in which there was concern that Black workers, who had been excluded from the union, would be used by management as "strikebreakers"). No record of his role on either committee has been located.[5]

Harrison's most public defense of Haywood in this period came as one of a group of thirty-seven prominent members of the Socialist Party who signed a "Resolution of Protest" that appeared in the *International Socialist Review* of February 1913. The "Resolution" quoted from various Haywood speeches and aimed to show that he "advocated class action on the political field" and "the necessity of class unionism on the economic field." It also argued that the campaign to recall him was "based upon alleged statements made by Comrade Haywood at public meetings, at which no authorized stenographic reports were taken." The "Resolution" described the attack on Haywood as an "unwise and unwarranted" action that tended "to create dissent and ill-will within the ranks of the Socialist Party," and it urged members throughout the nation to protest calls for Haywood's recall. Signatories, in addition to Harrison, included Margaret Sanger, Max Eastman, William English Walling, the future communist Rose Pastor Stokes, the party candidate for justice of the New York Supreme Court Louis B. Boudin, IWW author and organizer Frank Bohn, and journalist Walter Lippman, who, in the following year, would help found *The New Republic* magazine.[6]

Shortly after Harrison came out in support of Haywood, and after he spoke on "Industrial Unionism" in Queens, both men became involved in the major labor event of 1913, the Paterson, N.J., silk strike. That struggle took on general-strike proportions in February as it changed from a protest over a speedup and the resultant loss of jobs to a battle over workers' right to have their representatives recognized and to reduced hours with no loss in pay. The historian Steve Golin describes Paterson as a worker-controlled struggle for an industrial union, marked by the militancy of Italians, Jews, and women, in which an important bridge with radicals (including socialists, Wobblies, and intellectuals from New York) was built. The struggle drew national attention throughout 1913, including wide coverage of New Jersey rallies and of a famous June 7 Strike Pageant, in which workers and their families performed in New York City.[7]

The strike began on February 25 when more than 5,000 broad-silk weavers, mostly Jewish, walked out and marched to Turn Hall, the office of Local 152 of the IWW. They were joined over the next few days by dyers and unskilled Italian dyers' helpers. Mass meetings quickly replaced picketing as the principal activity of the strikers, and Monday through Saturday, from 10 A.M. to noon, ribbon weavers would gather at Helvetia Hall and dyers' helpers and broad-silk weavers at Turn Hall. On Sunday afternoon large meetings were held at sites like the house of the Botto family in nearby Haledon. These meetings were fueled by the fact that Police Chief John Bimson of Paterson had authorized the use of force and had had out-of-town speakers arrested. On the first day of the strike, the IWW agitators Elizabeth Gurley Flynn and Patrick Quinlan and the anarchist Carlo Tresca were arrested, and on February 28, the editor Alexander Scott of the Passaic County Socialists' *Weekly Issue* was arrested on charges of criminal libel and preaching hostility to the government. Scott had read aloud a newspaper article ridiculing Bimson's ignorance of constitutional rights. The arrest strategy backfired, however, and workers responded to the repression with increased organization and by spreading the strike. Outside support grew, and local militants controlled the general strike, which in March successfully spread to New York. As it spread, the repression continued—Haywood was arrested at the end of March and again in April he was along with Flynn, Tresca, and Quinlan.[8]

It was in such a setting (amid mass rallies and continued arrests) that Harrison, just short of his thirtieth birthday, came from New York to give the principal address at a mass meeting at Turn Hall on April 17. Flynn, the outstanding IWW organizer and agitator, was to have joined him, but she was detained at Helvetia Hall and arrived late. Harrison was described in the *Paterson Evening News* as one of the most controversial speakers in the five-month strike—partly because of the aggressively anticapitalist nature of his message and partly because he was a lone Black speaker before an all-white audience. African American men and women were noticeably lacking in the Paterson mills, where hiring practices effectively excluded Black people and focused on different European immigrant groups.[9]

On May 19 Harrison spoke again, along with Haywood, Quinlan, Boyd, and Flynn, at the Botto house. The *Evening News* described Harrison as "very bitter in his denunciations of the New York newspaper writers" and reported that he "commenced a tirade upon one of the writers in particular, and called him a— dirty dog." The antistrike *Evening News* wrote that he was "not in keeping with the I.W.W. line of speech making," that "his comparisons were very blasphemous and not fit for the audience to listen to or the papers to re-print," and that "the leaders would do well to leave Mr. Harrison in New York." Flynn, however, defended him, saying that "he tells plain facts and the bosses don't like them."[10]

By July 29 the strike was defeated, in large part because the mill owners were able to operate Pennsylvania annexes they had established. During the struggle, more than 25,000 silk workers were involved, 4,800 were arrested, and 1,300 were sent to jail. The defeat at Paterson soon became disaster, as the IWW came under attack from capitalists, socialists, anarchists, and AFL leaders. The resultant demoralization signified the end of IWW organizing in the eastern United States. The defeat also hurt the Socialist Party, which encouraged an internal struggle with its left wing and encouraged a destructive split with the IWW.[11]

In the course of the Paterson struggle there were two related events that particularly aroused Harrison's feelings. One was the arrest and jailing of Boyd,

Figure 7.1. Hubert Harrison, Elizabeth Gurley Flynn, and William D. "Big Bill" Haywood, c. 1913. In early 1913 Harrison was the leading Black Socialist in America and a strong supporter of the Industrial Workers of the World. IWW leaders Elizabeth Gurley Flynn (1890–1964) and William D. "Big Bill" Haywood (1869–1928) were two of America's most prominent labor agitators and radicals. All three spoke at that year's major labor struggle, the Paterson, N.J., strike of 25,000 silk workers during which 4,800 were arrested and 1,300 were sent to jail. This photo was probably taken when Harrison spoke to striking silk workers in Paterson, N.J. (April 17, 1913), or in Haledon, N.J. (May 19, 1913), or when he spoke in New York City at a mass protest meeting of the Paterson Defense Committee (February 4, 1914). The Paterson strike was defeated, and Harrison felt that Socialist Party's attacks on IWW activists came at "a critical stage" in the struggle when "every bit of financial and moral support" was needed. He soon left the Socialist Party. *Source:* Courtesy of the Communist Party of the United States Photographs Collection, Tamiment Library, New York University.

who was charged by local authorities with preaching sabotage to the public. On March 31 and April 1, at regularly scheduled mass meetings, Boyd spoke disrespectfully about the American flag and gave explicit instructions to workers on how to undertake acts of sabotage when they returned to the mills. He was defended by the IWW on the issue of free speech and because there was no law he had actually violated. After his arrest and the defeat of the strike, he was condemned, however, by New York Socialists.[12]

The second matter that aroused Harrison's concern occurred in June 1913 when, with the strike outcome still in doubt, the *Call* produced a stinging editorial challenging IWW statements that strikes were the revolution. This opened the door for similar attacks by the IWW's long-time opponent, President Samuel Gompers of the AFL, who argued that the IWW was bound to lose the strike because it conducted the struggle as if it were the revolution. The *Call* editorial stung most deeply since the paper had supported the strike and the attack came at "a critical stage" in the struggle when "every bit of financial and moral support" was needed. To the IWW publication *Solidarity*, the *Call* editorial was like a bullet fired "into the backs of the striking Paterson workers."[13]

While the Paterson workers were still maintaining their militant struggle, conditions within the Socialist Party began to change for Harrison. On June 2, the party member E. J. Dutton wrote to the CC and preferred charges "against Branch 5, and Hubert Harrison, the speaker, individually, for violation of the by-laws, or a well known established rule of the local, by taking up a collection at a street meeting of the said Branch held at 125th Street and Seventh Avenue on Saturday evening, May 31, 1913." On June 5, Executive Secretary Gerber wrote to the organizer of Branch 5, notifying him of the complaint and stating that "collections at street meetings [are] a violation of the rules of the Local." Gerber added that the Branch was requested not to take up collections at street meetings in the future except by special permission from the Central Committee. In July the EC decided that "there were no grounds for charges" against Harrison, who had written to them on January 6 requesting "some copies of the Local by-laws as soon as they are printed." There is no indication that such bylaws actually existed or that they were ever created. Nevertheless, in July the EC had Gerber again write to Branch 5 instructing the Branch not to hold collections without special CC permission.[14]

Though the charges against Harrison were dropped, the attacks continued. On August 25, at a regular meeting of the EC, it was reported that he would have to be replaced as a speaker since he had "resigned to take up work in Schenectady." (In fact, he was scheduled to go there for a series of lectures, but there was no indication that his engagement was to be long-term or that he had resigned.) Removal from the party speaker's list was a serious financial blow. More ominous, however, was the EC statement that "a number of complaints were received against Harrison concerning phases of his talks; but that nothing definite had been done in the matter." This probably referred to the Dutton charges as well as to the pro-IWW, prosabotage lectures.[15]

An additional item of future import appeared in the same EC minutes. The party member A. Golden reported that he had "given up the idea of debating with Urban" (the anti-Socialist orator, Frank Urban[sky]). Golden's report suggests that party policy on debates between members and nonmembers was left to the individual and not to the local. A short while later, when Harrison sought to debate Urban, the official policy would be presented as something quite different.[16]

Step by step, the leaders of Local New York of the Socialist Party were inten-sifying their attacks on Harrison and other left-wingers. Harrison's public ex-pression of support for Haywood and Boyd; his support for IWW principles; his direct opposition to the leadership-initiated recall of Haywood; and his overall dissatisfaction with party positions on the race issue continued to be his areas of major difference with these leaders.

––––––––

As Harrison's problems with the party worsened, he struggled to make a liv-ing by tutoring, teaching, and lecturing, and he underwent major difficulties at home. The outside struggles undoubtedly affected his life with Lin, who was caring for their three young daughters, Frances, Alice, and Aida. In 1913 these difficulties intensified, and he recorded a number of quarrels in his diary in April and July.[17]

Lin and Hubert's relationship continued to have its ups and downs, and with-in the year he would move out. Over the years he would move back and forth between living with his family and living apart from them. Throughout these years Lin would assume primary responsibility for caring for the children and, in addition, she would at various times do sewing work for hire at home and do-mestic work in others homes. Though he loved his children very much, Hubert consistently fell short in shouldering his family responsibilities.[18]

Money, or the lack of it, was an important aspect of Hubert and Lin's trou-bles. He was having great difficulty making a living, and the Socialist Party was opposed to his taking up collections at his lectures. Local New York was only paying one dollar per talk, and Executive Secretary Gerber emphasized the need to "get speakers able to present our principles in a way that will be a credit to the Party." In this setting, in February 1913, Hubert advertised in the leftist, foreign-language press for work as a tutor. His advertisement in the widely read Yiddish-language monthly *Zukunft*, and a similar one in the Ger-man-language weekly *Voerwärtz*, offered two private classes a week in English on subjects including beginner's English, grammar and composition, and ad-vanced English.[19]

Hubert received little money from tutoring, and it was principally as a speaker that he sought to make a living. His speaking schedule was as full as that of anyone in the party, and he was building his reputation as an outstanding orator. In the summer of 1913 he held seven separate lecture series sponsored, respectively, by Branches 1, 2, 4, 5, 7, 10, and 14 of Local New York. During June through August he averaged seven paid lectures a week and often gave as many as eight—six at night and two in the afternoon. These took place all over Manhattan, including at 181st St. and St. Nicholas Ave., 137th St. and Broadway, 133rd St. and Lenox Ave., 125th St. and 7th Ave., 116th St. and 5th Ave., 116th St.

and Lenox Ave., 110th St. and 5th Ave., 95th St. and Broadway, Carl Schurz Park east of 84th St., 39th St. and Broadway, 10th St. and 2nd Ave., Franklin Statue at the Junction of Park Row and Nassau St., Battery Park, and at the historic intersection of Broad and Wall Streets. The outdoor lectures were in many cases organized into series of talks. The schedule of six lectures offered for Branch 5 in June and July and Branch 4 in August and September included: "Socialism: What it is and why it is;" "The Socialist Indictment"; "The Nation's Wealth; who makes it, who gets it?"; "The Class Struggle and the Road to Power"; "Socialism and the City"; and "The Socialist Party."[20]

Harrison's talks were popular with rank-and-file members, and he was chosen as a representative to the Socialist Party's September 5 City Convention, where he was "the only Negro delegate" among the 200 people (185 men and 15 women) chosen. The convention attracted considerable attention not only for the nomination of Charles Edward Russell (who was twice the Socialist Party candidate for governor) for mayor but also for resolutions demanding women's suffrage, liberal Sunday laws, the right to strike for city workers, and public condemnation of the Paterson police for the February arrest of Alexander Scott.[21]

After the City Convention, Harrison traveled to Schenectady for one week, Buffalo for two weeks, and then to Connecticut for about three weeks in a state tour under the auspices of the Connecticut State Committee. Touring enabled him to earn money, and it also, as he explained in his diary, allowed him to "be away from home—and my wife—for some time." He viewed this as "a blessed relief," though he realized that he would "miss the children greatly" and would worry "about their falling out of the window" and other anxieties. He wondered how he would "manage to get along without them when I separate from their mother," and speculated that he could "get to see them several times a week," though this was "a dreary prospect to look forward to!" On September 10, while on the road, he wrote to Lin telling her that when he returned to New York he would "come home only to pack up and move out my things." He asked her, "in view of that fact, to look around for a suitable place for herself and the children" since he felt that after he was gone "it will be impossible to live there and pay the rent." He suggested she "make some arrangement with Mrs. Green," Frances's godmother, who had a place on Long Island.[22]

Harrison's speaking was controversial and often aroused the ire of capitalists, the press, party officials, and the police, and it often placed him in the middle of important free-speech fights. In 1912 he had been arrested with Jean Jacques Coronel for obstructing the sidewalk while speaking on 134th St. Undeterred, he continued to openly express his views. In late October 1913 his public speaking led to another arrest and ultimately to a free-speech victory in Rochester, N.Y.[23]

The two-state tour of upstate New York and Connecticut was well received from the beginning. In Buffalo the *Citizen Sun* described Harrison as "one of the best colored orators in the country." The *Buffalo Socialist* billed him as "the foremost colored Socialist orator in the Socialist movement" while the New Haven *Evening Register* described him as "one of the most brilliant socialist speakers" and a person who had "done great work for the cause among the colored people of the country."[24]

Harrison's Rochester talk on Saturday, October 25, at Main and North Water Streets, led Police Chief Joseph M. Quigley to issue orders that there would be no political street meetings on Sunday. Harrison, however, returned to the same corner the following day, accompanied by George Weber, the Socialist Party candidate for mayor. They spoke to a crowd of 1,000 to 1,500 on a street so crowded that it was practically closed to traffic. There were fifteen police in the crowd when Harrison was warned that the meeting was becoming too noisy. He reportedly responded: "If there is to be any 'moving on' or stop put to my talking I want to be arrested for it." He was arrested; Weber then mounted an automobile, spoke, and was also arrested. After Charles E. Wells, a college student and opponent of czarist practices, shouted that the police were using "Russian tactics," he, too, was arrested.[25]

Harrison and Weber were charged with "being a public nuisance by obstructing a public street," and the police at first refused to accept bail but later released all three on ten dollars bail each. When the case was called into court, the judge drew roars of laughter from the courtroom when he stated that Harrison and Weber had been arrested under section 1530 of the Penal Code and that he didn't "know what law was in regard to that." After the law was read the judge remarked that the charge wasn't brought under the proper city ordinance for obstructing the walk but under the Penal Code in a section that specified "interference with the comfort, liberty or happiness of a considerable number of persons." He did not think that law appropriate and ruled that since other political parties were making speeches from wagons it was only fair to let Harrison and the Socialist Party do the same. Both cases were dismissed, and Harrison and the people of Rochester had won a major free-speech victory.[26]

After these speaking trips Harrison returned to New York and began teaching, partly for income and partly because he enjoyed it. In 1913 he began a two-year period as instructor of English and economics at the Harlem School of Social Science at 360 W. 125th Street. The school was related to Branch 5 of the Socialist Party and was affiliated with the party's Rand School, which had been established in 1906 as the nation's first major workers school. His course on "Socialism and Elementary Economics" covered the economic revolution from feudalism to capitalism, the wage system and wage-working class, and the class struggle. Readings were drawn from Karl Kautsky's *The Class Struggle*, Paul LaFargue's *The Evolution of Property*, Mary E. Marcy's *Shop-Talks on Economics*, and Karl Marx's *Wage, Labor, and Capital*. According to J. A. Rogers, Harri son "applied the latest scientific theories to the position of the Negro and found much in Marx, [Henry Thomas] Buckle, Spencer, Nietzsche, Schopenhauer, Lenin, Bertrand Russell, Dewey and others, to support his own."[27]

———

As his reputation grew and his pro-IWW positions became better known, it was only a matter of time before some Socialist Party leaders took more serious concerted action against Harrison. A step in that direction occurred on October 6, 1913, when, at a regular meeting of the Executive Committee of Local New York, a request was received from Branch 3 to hold a debate on the question, "Is industrial action more important than political action?" Harrison was to speak for the affirmative and Adolph Benevy for the negative. Harrison had chosen to argue against the official party position, and Benevy, who was not a party member, was defending it.[28]

At the EC meeting a motion was passed not to grant the request because Benevy "cannot be allowed to represent the party's position" and because "Comrade Harrison as a member of the party cannot very well represent a position antagonistic to the party." Though Harrison's position in favor of industrial action was well known to the EC members, a second motion also passed at the meeting, that "Harrison be requested to state in writing his position as to the above question." The motion clearly had aims other than exposition. Since the same meeting received communication from the non-Socialist William Jennings Bryan, "declining invitation to debate with a prominent Socialist," the Socialist Party did not, pro forma, prohibit debates between Socialists and non-Socialists. Rather, it appeared that Harrison's public speaking and public pronouncements had created enough impact to upset the leadership of Local New York.[29]

That Harrison was upsetting Local New York leadership became more apparent in November 1913 when he again became involved in the sabotage issue. The split in the Socialist Party over sabotage at the 1912 convention haunted the labor movement. It was an issue over which Socialist support was clearly divided, and it came to the fore in the Frederick Sumner Boyd case, which opened the doors for capitalist attacks on both labor and the left. Harrison saw the importance of the sabotage issue and the Boyd case, and he concluded that the struggle for Boyd's freedom was a major political issue that should be addressed.[30]

The big pro-Boyd event in late 1913 was a November 30 meeting at the New Star Casino on East 107th Street called by the Paterson Defense Committee on the Right to Advocate Sabotage. Three days before the meeting, the *Call* published an article stating that Boyd had been arrested for advocating sabotage at Paterson and that New Jersey anarchist statutes prohibited inciting people to destroy property. The article reasoned that since there had been no charge of destruction of property, Boyd was prosecuted, convicted, and sentenced simply on the ground that he had uttered certain language, because "he exercised his right of free speech." The rally was to demonstrate that the workers would not stand for any persecutions of their fellows for taking part in the class war.[31]

More than five hundred people filled the hall and heard Harrison, the Socialist William English Walling, the IWW organizer Patrick Quinlan, the former Passaic *Issue* editor Alexander Scott, the IWW Lawrence strike leader Arturo Giovannitti, and Boyd address the crowd. Harrison's talk detailed the significance of the Boyd case and was cheered by both Socialists and Wobblies. He began by discussing the 1886 struggle for an eight-hour day and the arrest and murder of the Chicago Haymarket martyrs (Albert Parsons, August Spies, George Engel, Adolph Fischer, and Louis Lingg [who committed suicide the night before he was to be executed]). After this, he reviewed the recent West Coast case of John J. and James B. McNamara of the International Association of Bridge and Structural Iron Workers, AFL, who were accused of murder and dynamiting in the October 1, 1910, bombing of the *Los Angeles Times* building (where twenty-one people died) and the Llewelyn Iron Works, respectively. Harrison made clear his support for the defendants in each case as he declared that "we consider, whether right or wrong, every blow struck by labor against capital is a blow for labor." He pointed out the importance of the sabotage issue and of supporting Boyd, who, though out on bail, was the first person convicted for "advocating sabotage." "Sabotage," he added, "is feared by capitalists more than anything else" and "is our one great weapon." He ended with a defiant warning: "if Boyd goes to jail there is many a silk manufacturer in Paterson, that will know the reason why, and I think that thousands of dollars worth of silk will not be as good as expected."[32]

Harrison's talk was marked by its militancy and its direct appeal to the rank and file to challenge the laggard leadership of the AFL and the Socialist Party. He pointed out the contradictions between's the AFL's official position and its practice and noted that the AFL, "while it does not preach sabotage, does blow up bridges, for the Steel Trust!" Similarly, though the AFL opposed violence against capital, it hired thugs (with Socialist Party support) to violently beat up scabs in strikes. His message to the leaders of the Socialist Party was explicit and defiant: "No one asked the Socialist party to come into the strike. Let it stay out—if it dares." To the rank-and-file party members he emphasized, in words that captured the heart of his proletarian radicalism, "We Socialists must go to the workers to hear what we must do. The revolution is not coming from above, remember, but from below, working its way up from the depths."[33]

Though he agitated for Boyd's release Harrison saw the struggle in larger terms. He emphasized that the issue was not the capitalists' invasion of workers' rights because "we have none. We never had any." The struggle was "not to get rights, but to get might, and when we get that we will have right." When someone in the audience yelled "Vote," Harrison, fully worked up, responded that "only on election day is the vote of any use in a vital matter." He then closed his talk by reminding the crowd that "the workers have the power, and, using it could keep Boyd out of jail." The next day, Harrison sent a postcard to "Dear Comrade Gerber" at the Socialist Party headquarters, informing him, "I cannot and will not accept the nomination for Exec. Secretary. Please keep my name off." While this was most likely an instance of Harrison's biting sarcasm, it was sent at a time when Harrison's friend and political ally, Alexander Scott, was running against Gerber for executive secretary and Harrison would presumably not want anyone to use his name to draw votes from Scott.[34]

A response came quickly. At a regular meeting of the Central Committee on December 13, both Boyd and Scott were seated as delegates from the Twenty-first Assembly District, which covered part of Harlem and was Harrison's district. (The party's branches had been divided into their respective assembly districts—a move consistent with the aims of the "political" activists.) At the CC meeting, delegates from the German Branch of Yorkville on the Upper East Side of Manhattan reported that they had been instructed to move that the CC prefer charges against Boyd, Harrison, and Scott in connection with the November 30 New Star Casino meeting. The CC decided to investigate and report back to the next meeting.[35]

Sixteen days later the EC moved to place Caroline M. Dexter on the special committee appointed to investigate Boyd, Harrison, and Scott. At a January 5, 1914, meeting, the EC reported that it "finds it an inopportune time to proceed against Comrades Scott and Boyd at the present time (while their appeal is before the courts of New Jersey)." The EC also found that "it would not be advisable to proceed against Hubert H. Harrison alone." The EC recommendation that the matter against Scott, Boyd, and Harrison be dropped was approved only after several motions and amendments were lost. A specific motion that "the case against Harrison be given to Grievances Committee" was defeated, as were amendments to drop only the cases against Scott and Boyd for lack of evidence.[36]

While the various actions were being debated, Harrison wrote a January 19 letter to the *Call* that was not printed until February 5. He explained that on November 30 he spoke at the New Star Casino "to interest the workers of New York in behalf of Boyd and the other 'criminals' under sentence by the courts of New Jersey for the part which they took in the Paterson strike." Though portions of his speech were printed the next morning in the *Call* and other newspapers, he had not yet heard, nor seen in the *Call*, that a single statement in his speech "was in violation of any rule or by-law adopted by the Socialist party." Yet, he complained, "for six weeks the party's official representatives have gibbeted me, along with Alexander Scott and F. Sumner Boyd, as a person under suspicion." He argued for his right to a hearing and to know the charges against him and noted that "the party, in the case against us, has laid the foundation upon which any one who chooses [may assume our guilt]." Though the CC had discussed the question of whether to proceed against the three or not, in its minutes as printed in the *Call*, "it forgot to say for what." The CC then decided to refer the matter to the EC, which redelegated it to a committee of three, which then reported with the concurrence of the EC that "it was inadvisable to proceed further against Boyd and Scott, in view of the cases already pending against them" and that Harrison should be let off since it wouldn't be fair to proceed against him alone.[37]

To Harrison, if this didn't imply violation of "the laws of the party," or the commission of "some definite act calling for censure," then he didn't "know what it means." As a party member in good standing, he felt entitled to know his offense and to demand that of the party's representatives. Therefore, officially and publicly, he demanded that the party representatives tell him and his friends what they had done. If the party representatives did not do this, they would "seem guilty of a most contemptible form of persecution." As things stood, a cloud hung over their reputations, and Harrison wanted the matter cleared up. He had "taken the stump and the lecture platform for the party in four States"; had been elected by "comrades to represent them at two city conventions, and a State convention"; and he was "trusted to teach the principles of Socialism and economics in a Socialist school." Surely, he deserved "either a clear vindication" of his name "or a clear conviction." In "the open light of the day," he wanted his comrades "to see and know what manner of Socialist" he was. Therefore, he appealed "to the rank and file to watch this case—and draw their fair conclusions." He also pointed out how "bad" it looked that Scott (who "was a candidate for the office of executive secretary" of the party) and Boyd were both under sentence in New Jersey and under a cloud in the party. It was "obvious," he concluded, "that we must first do justice to the Comrades in our party before we can ask for any justice outside." As for his own treatment, he insisted "on getting justice here, or knowing the reason why."[38]

While the "gibbeting" persisted, Harrison continued his mass work. On January 10, 1914, he served as a representative of the Twenty-first A.D. at a meeting of the Unemployed Council of Local New York (SP). The meeting at the Labor Temple on West Eighty-fourth Street resolved to enlist speakers to approach labor organizations to support work for the unemployed and to participate in a large conference on unemployment. Unemployment was a growing problem that winter, and the Employment Bureau of the Society for Improving the Conditions of the Poor estimated that there were more than 300,000 unemployed men in the city. Within two months, groups of unemployed protesters, led by the anarchist and IWW-affiliated Columbia student Frank Tannenbaum and attendees of the Ferrer Association's Modern School, would march on city churches during services, and the Socialist Party would put out a call to locals to become active in unemployment work. By the spring, an IWW Unemployed Union of New York would be formed.[39]

Harrison also chaired and spoke at a mass protest meeting of the Paterson Defense Committee on February 4, in Manhattan. The subject was "Why Was Haywood Refused Cooper Union?"; the meeting centered on charges that the *Call* and Socialists "had willfully injured the Paterson strikers at the close of their long struggle last year with the silk interests." Other staunchly pro-IWW speakers included Haywood, Flynn, Tresca, Giovannitti, and Boyd. Though publicity for the event in the *Call* listed Harrison as a member of the Socialist Party, he distanced himself from the party as he read portions of his January 19 letter that had so strongly criticized the party. He said that he didn't know how long he would be allowed to remain in the party and indicated that some new "Radical Clubs" would be starting. The *Call* printed his letter the next day, probably pressured to do so by the fact that it had not yet run and yet Harrison had read it publicly.[40]

On February 14, Abraham De Young, recording secretary of Harrison's Twenty-first A.D. Branch, wrote to Gerber stating that a motion made by Morris Hillquit and adopted by the Branch at a February 10 meeting assigned him to secure the minutes of the EC and CC meetings on "the investigation of the charges preferred against Comrades Boyd, Harrison, and Scott." Gerber responded to De Young on February 18 and included the meeting excerpts as requested and even went so far as to provide wording of unpassed motions against Harrison, Boyd, and Scott. The letter had the appearance of being yet another part of a smear campaign since Gerber and Hillquit were both leaders of the anti-IWW forces.[41]

Harrison's experiences around Paterson, sabotage, and democracy were truly foreboding. After the Paterson defeat, the IWW witnessed an organizational tightening and internal repression that led to its demise in the east. The Paterson defeat set the stage for massive federal legislation against radicals from 1917 through 1919. In addition, as the historian William Preston Jr., points out, "the Socialists" became "the first group to create an index of permissible belief and action within the framework of discontent." This began with their antisabotage clause, which served as "the ideological forerunner of the criminal syndicalism laws and deportation statutes." It continued with their attacks on Harrison, Boyd, and Scott. The historian Philip S. Foner concludes that "the stand taken by the Right-wing Socialists at the 1912 convention" had "disastrous consequences for the entire radical movement in the United States." Harrison, who defended Boyd, Haywood, and sabotage, experienced first-hand the dangers that were ahead.[42]

Harrison was in noticeable opposition to the Socialist Party leaders. The IWW issue, Boyd, Scott, Haywood, and sabotage were major differences, but his dissatisfaction was greatest on the race issue. This was explained in a letter he wrote to the socialist monthly *New Review* in early 1914.

The *New Review* first appeared in January 1913, and its stated purpose was to "enable the Socialists of America to attain a better knowledge and clearer understanding of the theories and principles, history and methods of the International Socialist Movement." It consistently carried prosabotage articles, and by September 1913, the leadership of Local New York prohibited its sale or distribution by branches at meetings. The New Review Publishing Association considered such actions "high-handed and usurpatory" and noted that members of the board were also members of the party who felt they had a right to distribute their views, even if they included "criticisms of Party principles and tactics."[43]

The *New Review* paid particular attention to the race question. In its January 4, 1913, inaugural issue, W. E. B. Du Bois wrote "A Field for Socialists," in which he maintained, echoing Harrison in the *International Socialist Review*, that "there is a group of ten million persons in the United States [African Americans] toward whom Socialists would better turn serious attention." In the February 1, 1913, issue he declared, again echoing Harrison's July 1912 *ISR* article, that "the Negro problem is the great test of the American Socialist." In the September 1913 *New Review*, NAACP founder Mary White Ovington authored "The Status of the Negro in the United States" and commented that "in some Southern states [Socialists] . . . have, at times, shown a race prejudice unexcelled by the most virulent Democrats."[44]

Ovington's article elicited a controversial response from Ida M. Raymond, state secretary of the Socialist Party of Mississippi, which was published as "A Southern Socialist on the Negro Question." Raymond responded to Ovington and said that she opposed Blacks and whites meeting together and she opposed integrated locals of the Socialist Party because such integration would "do more to retard" efforts at educating both races "than any other thing that can be done." Raymond maintained that the "Negroes" of the South were without education and "worse than the 'Uncle Tom' of slavery days," adding that if "Negroes" were given rights currently denied them by state constitutions, they would resurrect those "awful days" of "Negro domination" seen after the Civil War, which necessitated the rise of the Ku Klux Klan in order "to take matters in their own hands and save their women, their homes, and their country."[45]

Harrison wrote a response to the editors of *New Review* that offered serious criticisms of the Socialist Party. The editors chose not to publish the reply, and it was published only years later by the *Negro World* when Harrison was a contributing editor. The letter began by asking whether Raymond opposed Ovington's advocacy of having whites and Blacks meet on equal terms "'at this present time'" or "whether she would be in favor of it at any future time?" To Harrison it was clear that Raymond had "imbibed the Southern attitude from her Southern environment, and it vitiates even her notion of history." He then challenged her historical understanding by pointing out that "the constitutional right to vote was given to Negroes in 1868, while the Ku Klux Klan began its terrorism in the winter of 1865, long before the vote was given to Negroes in the South." He pointedly criticized the Southern Socialists for being "'Southerners' first and 'Socialists' after" and, to drive this point home, cited "the shattered remains of the Granger and Populist movements," which had similarly started out in a positive direction and faltered.[46]

Harrison left little doubt that his personal leanings were toward the IWW and not the Socialist Party because of the IWW's more advanced stand on the race question. He emphasized that the IWW "has no scruples about affirming the full import of its revolutionary doctrine at all times and places—even in the South," and he cited how the IWW opposed race prejudice, with success, in Louisiana, as it organized 18,000 white and 14,000 Black timber workers in "mixed locals." He then concluded, "I wonder now, whether any Socialist, Southern or other, could blame me for throwing in my lot with the I.W.W."[47]

The letter to the *New Review* was meant to be an open statement of Harrison's growing dissatisfaction with the Socialist Party, but it was not published. His similar public expression of dissatisfaction regarding Local New York was printed only after he read it openly at the February 4 meeting. He was repeatedly challenging party leaders, and they, in turn, were attempting to silence him. He was doing what his most prominent Black Socialist predecessors had not done, challenging the party from within its ranks.

Harrison's pro-IWW and anti–Socialist Party agitation was effective and would no longer be tolerated by party leaders. For action to be taken against him, however, an incident was needed. That incident was found—the "Urban Affair." Frank Urban(sky) was a popular antisocialist speaker in lower Manhattan. As far back as June 28, 1913, the party member Fred Gaa suggested to the CC that the local send some of its best representatives to his meetings to combat his arguments.[48]

On February 27, 1914, the Third and Tenth Assembly District Branches of Local New York, headquartered on East Tenth Street, made plans to hold a debate between Harrison and Urban. The activity, under their auspices, would be on April 2 at the Labor Temple on East Eighty-fourth St. Two hundred tickets were sold (particularly to Urban's followers), expenses were incurred, and the event was advertised in the *Call*. Precedent for such a debate had been set by Branch 4, which had previously advertised in the *Call* and held a similar debate between a party member and Urban. That debate had not been censored by either the EC or the CC.[49]

In this case, however, the EC vowed to block the debate. The decision was reached on March 23, and the following day a letter was sent to Joseph W. Pomarlen, organizer of the Tenth A.D. Branch, informing him of its resolution and directing him to remind the Third and Tenth A.D. Branches of the rule "forbidding Branches to arrange debates with non-party members, without the approval of the Executive Committee." The letter stated that the EC had not approved the proposed debate with Urban, ordered the Branch to discontinue all arrangements, and requested that Pomarlen call a special meeting for Branch members and notify the EC, which desired to send a delegate to explain its decision.[50]

A committee claiming to be from the EC came to the meeting of the Third and Tenth A.D. on March 25 and formally announced that the EC had passed a motion to call off the debate. At that same meeting the members of the Third and Tenth A.D. decided to hold the debate despite the EC order. Then, on March 31, only two days before the scheduled debate, a letter was sent to Harrison from Anna M. Sloan, the acting executive secretary of the Socialist Party of New York County, informing him that the EC had asked her to notify him "not to debate with Urban on Thursday, April 2."[51]

Harrison was quite upset by this. It followed the previous incidents: the demise of the Colored Socialist Club; the 1912 convention debate on immigration; the party's general stand on the race question; the sabotage issue; the Paterson strike; Boyd, Scott, and Haywood; the persecution and smearing of his reputation; being asked to put his views on trade unions on paper; and being sent speaker forms to fill out while being denied the same pay as other speakers. Harrison responded to Sloan's letter, in a handwritten rejoinder at the bottom of the original. His pointed response read: "Please tell the Executive Committee to go chase itself." He then placed his signature after that single sentence response, and added—"& By the way, if my color has anything to do with it this time I should thank you to let me know." Clearly, Harrison felt that racism in the Socialist Party was manifest not only in SP theory but in the practice of leading SP officials.[52]

Underneath Harrison's handwritten response, in the copy of the letter on file with the Socialist Party Papers, is yet another handwritten remark. This comment, presumably by Sloan, reads: "Central Com[mittee]: Pref[er] charges for the contempt he has shown the Ex[ecutive] Com[mittee]." Whether the note was written before or after the next CC meeting is unclear, but both Harrison and the members of the Third and Tenth A.D. soon came under further attack.[53]

On April 11, at the next regular meeting of the CC, a "communication" from Harrison on the Urban debate (most likely his short rejoinder) was read. It was then moved that the Acting Executive Secretary prefer charges against him "on account (1) of the contempt shown to [the] order of the Executive Committee and (2) for disobeying the order." The vote carried by a margin of thirty-one for and six against. On the same day, the CC accepted a recommendation of the EC to dissolve the Third and Tenth A.D. and elected a committee to do so, apparently for not calling off the Harrison-Urban debate.[54]

Members of the Third and Tenth A.D. responded. At a joint meeting on April 16, 1914, they passed a resolution that deemed such methods as those of the Central Committee to be "underhanded, undignified, unfair and militating against the principles and best interest of the Socialist party." They cited article XIV, section 13, of the constitution of the SP of New York County, which held that "no Branch shall be dissolved while there are seven dissenting members." That same day, Acting Executive Secretary Sloan wrote to Local NY stating that she had preferred charges against Harrison pursuant to the motion, and Dr. S. Berlin, secretary of the Grievance Committee, wrote to Harrison notifying him "to appear before the Grievance Committee of Local New York, as instructed by the Central Committee." Harrison was informed that his hearing would be at a meeting on April 23, at party headquarters, and that he should bring his witnesses and evidence. Berlin added that if he failed to appear he would lose the case by default. On April 17 formal letters went out to members of the Third and Tenth A.D. notifying them that the A.D.'s were dissolved and the Branch no longer existed.[55]

On April 21, Harrison responded to Berlin and the Grievance Committee. He pointed out that he taught courses every Wednesday at 9:30 P.M. and that since he had only just received Berlin's letter he was unable to advise the school of any schedule change. He therefore asked for "a slight extension of time" before his hearing. His case was postponed until May 6.[56]

Branch 3 appealed the CC decision to dissolve the Third and Tenth A.D. to the State Committee of the Socialist Party of New York on May 5. The appeal provided background to the case and argued for maintaining the Branch. Its rationale included previous agreements, finances, and the danger of putting "ammunition in the hands of our anti-Socialist opponents" that would redound "to the discredit of the Socialist Party." The appeal also cited the SP's National Platform, which "explicitly" set forth as "cardinal principles of the Socialist Party . . . freedom of speech; freedom of press; freedom of assemblage." It pointed out that the National Executive Committee "encourages, rather than discourages debates between Socialists and renegades from our ranks" and that it had never objected to such debates previously. Finally, the appeal claimed that the CC action was unconstitutional for two reasons: First, it argued that a Branch with seven dissenting members couldn't be dissolved. This was especially important since the Third and Tenth A.D. had unanimously voted "not to be dissolved." Second, it argued that there had been no hearing, that the CC had no constitutional right to dissolve a Branch, and that individual party members could not be automatically suspended "without any charges having been brought."[57]

Harrison's trial was on May 6, and the notes of Dr. S. Berlin, the secretary of the Grievance Committee, are the only record. Berlin reported that Harrison "objected" to Comrade Stark as a member of the Grievance Committee because Stark had said at a meeting of the Third and Tenth A.D., "We will kick him out of the Party in a few weeks." Harrison argued that he earned his living lecturing and that he would have lost five dollars if the debate were canceled and that the "executive Com. can not prescribe" to a member of the Socialist Party how one could make one's "bread and butter," though it could exercise control regarding the branch that held the debate. He maintained that he "did not speak about the principles of the S.P." As for the contempt toward the EC issue, Berlin reported that Harrison said the reason that he treated the EC contemptuously was because the committee "was 'picking' at him all the time." The Grievance Committee voted three to one for Harrison's suspension of "three months" (the one dissenting vote favored a six-month probation). On May 18, Julius Gerber, executive secretary of Local New York, wrote to Harrison notifying him that he had been found "guilty of disobeying the order not to debate with Frank Urban" and that he was suspended for three months.[58]

The desire of Hubert Harrison, the leading Black organizer, orator, and theoretician of the Socialist Party, to carry on special work aimed at African Americans, to agitate for revolutionary socialism and industrial unionism, to earn the same fees as other speakers, and to be free to debate and speak publicly had touched some very sensitive nerves in the Socialist Party. It took time for the responses to consolidate, but when they did the party leadership was firm. The message by 1914 was clear—there would be no special agitation or organizational forms for African Americans, there was tightened control over Harrison's speaking, there were major restrictions placed on his principal means of making a living, and he was suspended from the party. As the historian Winston James concludes, "American socialism did not keep faith with Hubert Harrison, Harrison kept faith with socialism."[59]

Though aimed at Harrison, the party's responses had broadly deleterious effects. The party denied not only his own right to speak but the right of individual Socialist Party members to schedule their own debates. Not only were left-wing views opposed, their proponents were driven from the party. Not only were special efforts for reaching African Americans thwarted, efforts at autonomous activities by branches were also stymied. Most importantly, not only was Harrison attacked, his strategically important message on the centrality of the struggle against white supremacy and the revolutionary potential of true democracy and equality for African Americans would not be heard again in party publications or on party speaking platforms.

Despite his differences with the Socialists, however, Harrison, as was his style, did not let his years of activity go for naught. What he learned, both positive and negative, was put into his later work. Also, as with other organizations he worked with, he was able to maintain a principled working relationship with Socialists years after leaving that organization. He even rejoined the Socialist Party for a short while in 1918, only to leave it again later that year.

In 1914, however, Hubert Harrison looked outside the Socialist Party to reach a different audience and to make his living.

8

Toward Independence
(1914–1915)

*Harrison made his ideological break with the Socialist Party over race, class, or-*ganizational, and strategic issues. Charges were brought against him by the Executive Committee of Local New York in April 1914, he was suspended in May, and the suspension was upheld in June. In his diary he wrote that he "dropped out in the spring of 1914." Though he was periodically identified as a Socialist for years afterward and though he would rejoin and then resign from the party in 1918, the ideological break, followed by the suspension, marked a major turning point. He felt he was on the verge of setting out on his own course for the first time in his life.[1]

In part he was still being pushed by external forces. The Socialists, like the "Tuskegee Machine" and the Post Office, would tolerate only so much outspoken independence, and for the second time in three years Harrison lost his principal means of livelihood for expressing his views. Previously, his postal firing pushed him toward the Socialists, and now his party suspension pushed him toward independent radical activity. Like his postal firing, it also negatively affected his family life.

When the Socialist Party reduced his fees and limited his speaking engagements, Harrison's financial situation became precarious. His main source of income had been from lecturing and from the sale of books related to his lectures. His financial situation was further complicated by the fact that the winter of 1913–14 was bitterly cold and snowy and the economy witnessed the most severe economic depression since 1907–08, the winter that had previously been so hard on him. Unemployment ran in the millions nationwide, and hundreds of thousands were out of work in New York City.[2]

By June 1914, as the sole support of three daughters and a wife who was pregnant with a fourth child (daughter Ilva Henrietta, was born on August 25, 1914), Harrison's situation was almost desperate. He, Lin, and the family lived at 231 W. 134th St. in a six room "railroad flat" (with indoor bath and room for a boarder) that had been obtained when he had his postal job. That summer his relations with Lin reached a breaking point, in part because of the increasing economic pressures and in part because of his strenuous political schedule, and in part because of his "double standard" regarding sex roles.[3]

In his diary on June 15 Hubert wrote, "My domestic affliction [wife Lin] is on the warpath again . . . This is her gem 'Oh Gawd! Either take him [Hubert] out of the world where I know that he isn't . . . or take them (i.e. the children).'" Hubert explained that "during the last three months she has repeatedly expressed in the most brutal way her desire to have the children die, *or to kill them*, or, in a not so open way, to kill me." This diary entry details further events of that day: Lin slapped Hubert "after she had been indulging in the filthiest talk" about his "whores and bitches" and then thrust her face into his. He laughed; she struck; he laid hands on her; she hit his hands; he slapped her face; she seized his penis; he dragged her into a room and threw her on the bed; she became frightened; he and she dressed for the street; he finished first and kissed the three girls and went out; she implied she was going out and the children "would be locked in the house"; and he told her that if she did that he would "see to it that she got her just desserts." After that incident Hubert wrote: "Think I shall move tomorrow. Then I can study and think and write—and perhaps, there will be time yet to do a man's work in the world."[4]

Harrison's double standard—studying, thinking, and writing equaling a man's work and care for the children a woman's work—was clearly negatively affecting his family. If the double standard extended into sexual relations, which it did at times (although there is no clear evidence of any ongoing affairs at this time), its negative impact could easily become unbearable for Lin. This was likely the case when the family was under intense financial pressure and she was six and a half months pregnant and burdened with the care of the three young girls. Nevertheless, despite the burdens on Lin, Harrison (desirous of doing his intellectual work and quite possibly desiring other women) moved the next day to the Beatrice at 35 W. 131st St. His family remained behind on 134th St.[5]

On June 27, after moving away from his family, Harrison joined the Grand United Order of Odd Fellows and San Manuel Lodge (No. 1794). The Odd Fellows was the largest Black fraternal organization in the country, with 300,000 male members and 4,000 lodges. His friend, James Glasgow, had encouraged him to join, and though he hoped "to make good," Harrison seldom attended meetings and did nothing with the group for eighteen months.[6]

In 1914, as his family problems were worsening, Harrison set out to organize his own lecture schedules. Starting in April he held outdoor lectures at 181st St. and St. Nicholas Avenue. During the summer, he spoke on science, evolution, and literature; against religious superstitions; and in support of women's suffrage and "birth control." The IWW publication *Sabotage* announced that on July 20 he would speak at the Lenox Casino Hall at Lenox Avenue and 116th Street on the "Materialistic Interpretation of Morality," with "special reference to sabotage and free love." Later that night he would speak at 351 East Eighty-first Street on "Charles Dickens the Novelist of the Common People."[7]

While delivering his lectures Harrison again sought to earn money teaching. Around August 1914 he ran two advertisements in the Black weekly *New York News* entitled "A Splendid Offer to Young Men of Ambition." He was billed as one "who for the last three years has been teaching exclusively among white people in a private capacity as an instructor in English and economics at the Harlem School of Social Science" and was "now free to devote some time to pupils of his own race." He offered a class in civil service instruction, which would enable those who enrolled to pass the post office examinations in November.[8]

In this period Harrison also did some pioneer lecturing on birth control. Socialists and freethinkers were prominent in the birth-control movement, and its founder, Margaret Sanger, had been a member of Harrison's Branch 5. Before 1914, according to W. E. B. Du Bois, there had been little formal work on birth control done in the Black community and "practically none by Negroes." Du Bois attributed this to a significant lack of information and "a good many misapprehensions." Harrison, however, made efforts to counter this lack of information, and his open support for birth control was undertaken at some risk. While he agitated in favor of birth control, he was, as his later writings indicated, also aware of white-supremacist aspects of the issue. In 1920 he would publicly express his opposition to the practices of "the white doctors [who] in their hospitals from the South to Harlem" performed "operations on colored women—unbeknown to them—to be sure that they would not be breeders of men."[9]

As Harrison made his living lecturing on street corners and selling books, his themes were influenced by his socialist and freethought views; his antireligious positions; his support of women's suffrage and birth control; and his class and race consciousness. In New York City in 1914 such a combination of ideas, coming from a Black man, was bound to meet with opposition from both police and thugs. Threats were made on several occasions "to force him to stop speaking," and at his outdoor talks he was at times forced to defend himself physically from mobs. Harrison was a staunch proponent of free speech who put his beliefs into practice, however, and, according to J. A. Rogers, he repeatedly "fought back courageously, never hesitating to speak no matter how great the hostility of his opponents."[10]

On June 26 his noontime lecture at Madison Square (Broadway and Twenty-third St. at Madison Avenue) was interrupted when the police arrested him for "holding a religious meeting without a permit." His lecture was of a historical and critical nature and probably included sales of Thomas Paine's *Age of Reason*, which Harrison referred to as the "Fifth Gospel," that of "St. Thomas." According to one freethought account, the talk aroused opposition from Catholic and Protestant antagonists who couldn't match his "superior readiness and erudition." The complaint was filed by a man named Seager, who objected to Harrison speaking on religion without a license. Though Seager was more aroused by the blasphemous language of those who opposed Harrison, none of the opposing troublemakers was arrested despite their conduct. The policeman who made the arrest claimed that he was not bothered by Harrison's lack of license or by the content of his discourse but that his reason for making the arrest was concern over a possible riot because of the large crowd.[11]

Magistrate Joseph E. Corrigan ruled in Harrison's favor, as he would do in several similar cases. He pointed out the statutory distinction between holding services, which required a license, and speaking on religion, which did not. Corrigan stated that he would not tolerate discrimination against a speaker for his views, but a speaker's interference with traffic would provide grounds for police action. He then released Harrison and warned him that he would deal sharply with him if he persisted in the future in defying the police and holding meetings tending to cause disturbances.[12]

Harrison appreciated the just treatment he received from Corrigan, and three years later, when the magistrate ran as an independent candidate for district attorney, *The Voice* reprinted a letter Harrison wrote to him on March 19, 1915. In that letter Harrison explained that since it was common to be outspokenly critical when a public servant did something wrong it was only fair "that when they do what is conspicuously right, we should be no less outspoken in our praise." The letter acknowledged "the fine courtesy and judicial fairness" that Harrison received at Corrigan's hands and recounted several clashes with "bigoted citizens" and three or four appearances before the judge on free-speech issues. In each case Corrigan's final word had been "Discharged!" Harrison expressed his "sincere appreciation" in light of the fact that Corrigan's own religion was twice involved and since "being a Negro is a constant source of prejudice (judicial and other) in America."[13]

Though he had won a minor legal victory, Harrison was soon tested by extra-legal methods. When he spoke uptown at 181st St. and St. Nicholas Avenue, the *Truth Seeker* asked that formal charges be brought against Captain O'Brien of the police department for abetting disturbances at his talks by forcing listeners into the street and attempting to provoke disturbances as a pretext for breaking up meetings and arresting speakers. In particular it cited the trick of assign-

ing only one policeman to a meeting, having him make a fake arrest on one of
Harrison's assistants, and then, while the policeman was away, allowing rowdies
to upset the talk.[14]

Seemingly complicit police behavior was involved in a serious physical confrontation with an uptown mob on August 11, 1914. According to the *Truth
Seeker*, at about 10:30 P.M., after a talk that included a bitter attack on the church
in general and on the Catholic Church in particular, a group of about fifty rowdies
waited until the crowd dispersed and then went after Harrison with "murderous
intention." As he entered the underground passage leading to the subway and
walked in front of the ticket booth, the mob rushed him and began to beat him.
Harrison had been warned of danger and was ready, having "provided himself
with a leg of the table from which he spoke, as means of defense in case of assault." As he was attacked by the group, the ringleader, William McElroy, struck
at him with an iron bar. Harrison parried the blow and struck back, sending
McElroy to the ground and then to the hospital while his cohorts dispersed.[15]

Harrison had thwarted the potentially lethal, extra-legal fist, but he was soon
subjected to the hand of the law. Police reserves suddenly appeared and arrested him, but none of his assailants. He was taken to the 177th St. station
house and locked up on a charge of felonious assault and placed under $500
bond. Since he had nowhere near the required bail, he was forced, after a brief
hearing, to stay in jail for three days until he went before Magistrate Campbell
at the 57th St. court. Campbell had only recently placed a very severe sentence
on another radical, Bouck White, and had no apparent sympathy for Harrison's
views. Again, however, Harrison, who argued self-defense, won acquittal.[16]

Throughout his ordeal Harrison received no help from the Socialist Party,
though he was nominally a member. The *Call* entirely ignored the case. The
support he did receive came from freethinkers, anarchists, and various radical
groups like the Harlem Educational Alliance, for which Harrison had spoken,
and it was to such radicals that he now turned.[17]

By August his outdoor lectures were regularly scheduled for 125th St. and
Seventh Ave., 181st St. and St. Nicholas Ave., 163rd St. and Prospect Ave. in the
Bronx, 37th St. and Broadway, and Madison Square (between 23rd and 26th
Sts. and Broadway and Madison Aves.). This last spot is where a young Henry
Miller "learned standing at the foot of his soapbox." Half a century later Miller
still remembered his "quondam idol, Hubert Harrison," speaking there with joy
and playfulness as he interacted with and drew sustenance from his crowd of
listeners:

> There was no one in those days . . . who could hold a candle to Hubert Har-
> rison. With a few well-directed words he had the ability to demolish any op-
> ponent. He did it neatly and smoothly too, "with kid gloves," so to speak. I de-

scribed the wonderful way he smiled, his easy assurance, the great sculptured head which he carried on his shoulders like a lion. I wondered aloud if he had not come from royal blood, if he had not been the descendant of some great African monarch. Yes, he was a man who electrified one by his mere presence. Besides him the other speakers, the white ones, looked like pygmies, not only physically but culturally, spiritually. Some of them, like the ones who were paid to foment trouble, carried on like epileptics, always wrapped in the Stars and Stripes, to be sure. Hubert Harrison, on the other hand, no matter what the provocation, always retained his self-possession, his dignity. He had a way of placing the back of his hand on his hip, his trunk tilted, his ears cocked to catch every last word the questioner, or the heckler put to him. Well he knew how to bide his time! When the tumult had subsided there would come that broad smile of his, a broad, good-natured grin, and he would answer his man—always fair and square, always full on, like a broadside. Soon everyone would be laughing, everyone but the poor imbecile who had dared to put the question.[18]

As Harrison continued to speak throughout the city his popularity grew. The *Truth Seeker* reported on August 8 that "the people hear him gladly" and on numerous occasions his two-and-a-half hour talks drew fifteen hundred people "without exhausting the[ir] interest." He was described as "scholarly, versatile, humorous, and instant in reply" and his talks treated subjects as diverse as history, literature, politics, and religion. The talks on religion, regularly included "digressions into polemics and textual criticism of the Bible" and Harrison stressed the "historical and evolutional point of view." The *Truth Seeker* attributed a "new freedom for street propagation" in New York City (where open-air meetings without a permit had been prohibited prior to April 1914) to the efforts of Harrison and the anarchists, who were similarly involved in these free speech fights. Historian Theodore G. Vincent claims that "the man most responsible for building the tradition [of Black street oratory] was Hubert H. Harrison."[19]

Inspired by the success, Harrison concentrated on a new plan for lecture centers in New York. In the August 22 issue of the *Truth Seeker* he recounted the successful efforts of lecturer Hugh O. Pentecost, one of the orators who had attracted him to freethought. Pentecost, until his death in 1907, had gone from minister to agnostic to atheist to anarchist in pursuit of truth, and his lectures attracted large audiences because he had both daring and integrity and was willing, as Harrison said, to change "the old garb of truth for a newer one." Since his death, no one had picked up the torch, and Harrison assessed that the times were ripe for again doing such work. He noted that the radicals of New York were scattered in various organizations and movements including socialists, anarchists, eugenists, single taxers, and atheists and that since they were generally separated from one another because of the needs of their organizations, they did not have access to "the awakening breath of the larger liberalism," which was needed to waft "through the dogmatic corridors of their separate creeds."[20]

Harrison thought that his outdoor lectures over the previous four months had demonstrated the need for a forum in which people could meet on equal terms. Many of his listeners had expressed the desire to have such lectures established as a permanent feature of radical life in New York, and it was in response to this demand that he decided to establish three such forums in Manhattan—in Washington Heights, on West 125th St., and on the Lower East Side—all predominantly white areas. In Washington Heights, when he broached the subject of a more formal lecture program, a businessman told him that he and his friends had already discussed the matter and were trying to get a large hall where Harrison could give indoor talks in winter and spring. They were eager to start such a forum and to solicit pledges to meet initial expenses. In Harlem the same thing was done by hundreds who gathered on West 125th street to listen to his lectures there. Some young ladies volunteered to sell literature at his talks, and two supporters, Professor Joseph Nathan and Abraham De Young, offered to provide music.[21]

The forums were envisioned as a series of lecture courses on popular science, history, drama, politics, sociology, economics, and religion. Lectures in any given series were to be every two weeks with alternate dates used for popular lectures on various topics. There would be an admission fee of fifteen cents, but no additional collections would be made. Literature for each subject would be sold, as well as radical and freethought periodicals such as *The Truth Seeker*, the *New Review*, the *Single Tax Review*, the *Menace*, and the *Melting Pot*. Harrison realized that such a forum "with a man of African descent as lecturer" would "be unique in the history of New York," but he thought that shouldn't matter much to "any genuine radical." Further, as he pointed out, "that fact of itself may be an added attraction."[22]

With plans for his lectures in place, September 27, 1914, marked a major turning point in Harrison's life. He was living apart from his family at 140 W. 136th Street, and on that day, according to his diary, he formally started his own "Radical Forum" and took control of his life. On September 28 he wrote one of his most personally revealing diary entries:

> Yesterday I took one of the momentous steps of my career. Perhaps I might more accurately say that I began my career yesterday when I delivered the first lecture at the Radical Forum under my own auspices. *La carriere ouvert au talents* ["careers open to talent"—an equality of opportunity concept associated with the French Revolution]. Heretofore every step in my progress since I came to this country has been forced upon me. From the early days

when I began to appear in debate upon the floor of St. Benedict's Lyceum to my "teachership" of English and Economics in Branch Five's School (1913–1914)—my entrance into the Postal Service and into the Socialist Party; as editor of *St. Mark's Mirror* and of the New Rochelle *Fair Play*, as elevator-man, hall-boy, porter; at the Sunrise Club or the [freethought-influenced] Harlem Liberal Alliance—in all these situations (even into marriage) I have either drifted or been driven. This I owe to the promptings of a friend, and that to the enfoldment of circumstance which left me no other course.

But the new work upon which I embarked yesterday was constructed of my own conscious ambition and marks the first shapings of my own destiny. Here I essay to climb the first modest rung of the ladder of fame.[23]

He then described the Radical Forum, which was to be "a forum for free spirits" where people "sick of the insincerities of cults and creeds" could gather. It would include lectures on Sunday afternoons on popular science, sociology, economics, history, religion, literature, and drama, and it would be "comprised of white people, most of whom are proud to be known as my followers and supporters." He knew of no precisely similar situation in the history of the country, though he was familiar with a Black man in North Carolina in the early nineteenth century who taught the sons of white aristocrats at a private academy; a Black professor, George Boyer Vashon, who, later in the nineteenth century, taught at New York Central College; and one or two Black ministers who permanently presided over white congregations. In Harrison's case, however, "the compulsion of religion, [or] the initial compulsion of parents or the state" was lacking. The people attending these lectures were enlightened adults, while the instructor had "no college diplomas nor academic degrees to dazzle them with." Instead, as he wrote in his diary, "my three years of work, indoors and out, first for the Socialist Party and occasionally for other radical groups, then later (during the last five months) for myself, has impressed them with the idea that I have a knowledge of certain things and that I have the ability to set forth these things in such a way as to benefit them." He concluded, "If I 'make good' there is honor, fame and a competence in store for me. Ergo, I must bend to the task and I must 'make good.'"[24]

During the remainder of 1914 Harrison delivered lectures for the Radical Forum six days a week at the New Harlem Casino (formerly the Lenox Casino) at Lenox Avenue and 110th St. and throughout the city. He opened with a lecture on "Modern Materialism," followed by a talk on "Jesus Christ and the Working Man: A Challenge to the Christian Socialists." Ensuing lectures focused on "The Natural History of Religion" and included such topics as: "The Nature of Religion," "The Class Struggle: A Criticism and Confession," "The Roots of Religion: A Study in Primitive Psychology," "Sex, Sinners, and Society," "The Worship

Figure 8.1. Hubert Harrison, 1914. In the winter of 1914–15 Harrison founded the Radical Forum; lectured indoors and out on birth control, religion, and the racial aspects of the war; and was involved in numerous free speech fights. His work brought him in closer contact with the freethought publication *Truth Seeker*. Freethought was based on adherence to scientific methodology and opposition to thought "fettered by the dogmas and principles of religion." Freethinkers relied on reason over supernatural authority, and they sought to examine both sides of issues and to encourage free inquiry, free publicity of ideas, and free discussion of convictions. They also supported science, denied the infallibility of the Bible, asserted the human origin of the Old and New Testaments, denied the existence of heaven and hell, and upheld the theory of evolution as opposed to the biblical Genesis. *Source:* From the *Truth Seeker*. Courtesy of the Truth Seeker Company.

of Death," "Romanism and the Republic," "How God Grew: The Evolution of the Idea of God," "Evolution: Social and Organic," "The Manufacture of Gods," George Bernard Shaw's new play *Androcles and the Lion*, "The Materialistic Interpretation of Morals," "The Origin of the Priesthood," and "A Defense of Atheism."[25]

Harrison's opening lecture on "Modern Materialism" prompted an interesting letter to the editor of the *New York Globe*, from John T. Carroll, a white Southerner, who heard the talk and was compelled to "a change of conviction on . . . the subject of the Negro in America and especially in New York." Carroll explained that whites "so often regard the whole [Negro] race as inferior to ourselves that it comes as a shock to see any one of them on a plane of intellectual parity with us," but he had experienced such a shock while "in a large and respectable looking white audience listening to Harrison." At first he was "angry," but, at the end of the lecture he "discovered with amazement" that he "had been interested, charmed, and instructed." He went back three more times to hear Harrison lecture on anthropology, economics, and religion and felt thankful to New York "for widening my mental horizon." Overall, Carroll was amazed that such an audience of white people turned out every Sunday afternoon "to listen to a man who is not merely colored but black." He added, "they seem to glory in it, as I have almost come to do myself."[26]

The Radical Forum lecture series also put Harrison in contact with old friends and with new circles of people, and it provided opportunities for him to meet and form personal relationships with other women. On Sunday, October 11, a friend who had been out of the country, Susie Grandison, attended his talk on "The War in Europe and the Socialists." He "prevailed on her" to stay till the end, and then they went to a little restaurant on West 132nd St. near Lenox Avenue where they had dinner in a private room and "celebrated her homecoming." He added in his diary, "*Victoria ad finem, post multos annos!* [victory at last, after many years!]."[27]

On Tuesday, October 13, he went to see Mrs. R. Tardos, a Hungarian lady, after telephoning to let her know of his "intent." Mrs. Tardos, probably thirty-seven year old Rella Tardos of 510 W. 146th St., told him how she came to know him three years earlier through his street lectures for the Socialist Party on 181st Street and St. Nicholas Avenue. Her husband had brought her to a talk, and though she "did not wish" to "stand so near a Negro," she was "enthralled by the lecture" and became one of his "most enthusiastic admirers." Mrs. Tardos let him know that she loved him for his October 11 lecture on "The War in Europe and the Socialists." On December 9, Hubert went back to see her and found her alone. They "spent a most enjoyable afternoon and for the first time made marvelous love." (He wrote in his diary, "*Et pro primo tempore nos id faciunt A'sehercle! Sed sine ullo dubitatione, haec est feminia, mirabilis, delectanda, profectata! Haec erat caelestia gloria!* [and for the first time we for that reason made hot damn. Beginning over and over and going on trips all the time. But without any doubt this is a woman, amazing, delightful really. This was a heavenly glory!].")[28]

In January 1915, the Radical Forum for "Harlem Socialists and Their Radical Friends" moved from the New Harlem Casino to a new home at the old Branch 5 Socialist Party headquarters on W. 125th St. Harrison gave the inaugural address on "Rudyard Kipling and the Reaction in Literature." He was scheduled to speak Sundays on "Literature or the Drama from a Socialist Point of View" in a series that included a featured talk on the socialist writer "Jack London—and the Literature of the Revolution."[29]

The audience at Harrison's Radical Forum was primarily white: "liberals, radicals and others." Radicals of all stripes were paying increasing attention to the European conflict, which pitted the Central European powers headed by Germany against Russia, France, and England. One of the principal causes of the war was the intense European economic interest in Africa. This "scramble for Africa" in search of raw materials and outlets for capital was led by monopolistic finance-capital organizations, backed by their respective European nations, and it led to European control of 90 percent of the continent. The Great War resulted, by Harrison's later estimates, in 13 million war dead, 6 million dead from disease, and more than 20 million other civilian deaths.[30]

As the war raged, Harrison's lectures, such as "The War in Europe and the Socialists," were increasingly influenced by what he termed an "international consciousness." Harrison, a former colonial subject, was a thoroughgoing internationalist who believed that before "the negroes of the Western World can play any effective part they must acquaint themselves with what is taking place in the larger world whose millions are in motion." He made it a point to stay abreast of, and to encourage others to stay abreast of, world developments—and he did this with a very perceptive eye.[31]

He later explained that as far back as 1915 he had pointed out in his lectures "that the racial aspect of the war in Europe was easily the most important," despite the fact that no American paper, not even William Randolph Hearst's rabidly racist *New York Evening Journal*, presented that side of the matter. Harrison stressed this "point of priority" because in 1920, T. Lothrop Stoddard's *Rising Tide of Color: Against White-World Supremacy*, though written from a very different perspective (it played on white-supremacist fears of a Black upsurge), became, according to Harrison, "the most widely talked-of book of the year." In an article published several years later on "The White War and the Colored World," Harrison delineated some of the ideas expressed in his talks delivered to white audiences during 1915 and 1916.[32]

A paramount point in his talks was the fact that twelve hundred of the seventeen hundred million people of the world were "colored—black and brown and yellow" and they were at peace until the white minority determined otherwise. The war was a conflict among the various nations that made up "the white race," and the stakes were "the lands and destinies of this colored majority in Asia, Africa, and the islands of the sea." The white nations at war sought to decide who should control the lands of Africa and Asia and who would be "dictators of the lives and destinies of their colored inhabitants." Though the white race had a material superiority, it was because it had "the guns, soldiers, the money and resources"—the word "armed," not the word "civilized," best explained it. Such "superiority" was flawed, however, since fratricidal strife was "burning up, eating up, consuming and destroying" its base.[33]

In his talks Harrison also put forth a moving plea or prediction on behalf of the "black race" and the colored peoples of the world. He explained that "the majority races cannot be eternally coerced into accepting the sovereignty of the white race." They were "willing to live in a world which is the equal possession of all peoples—white, black, brown and yellow," if the white race was willing to live at peace, but "if it insists that freedom, democracy, and equality are to exist only for white men, then, there will be such bloodshed later as this world has never seen." Since there was "no certainty that in such a conflict the white race will come out on top," it was not only "the destinies of the world, but the destinies of the white race" that were at stake.[34]

Harrison focused on the racial aspects of the war, but he understood the conflict in its larger economic and political context. Several years later he explained that it was "capitalist imperialism which mercilessly exploits the darker races for its own purposes." He described imperialism as "the most dangerous phase of developed capitalism" and emphasized that it was what led to "conflict of races and nations." In one of his most pointed statements on the cause of modern war Harrison wrote:

It is the same economic motive that has been back of every modern war since the merchant and trading classes secured control of the powers of the modern state. This is the natural and inevitable effect of the capitalist system. . . . For that system is based upon the wage relationship between those who own and those who operate the gigantic forces of land and machinery. Under this system no capitalist employs a worker for two dollars a day unless that worker creates more than two dollars' worth of wealth for him. Only out of this surplus can profits come. If ten million workers should thus create one hundred million dollars' worth of wealth each day and get twenty five or fifty million in wages, it is obvious that they can expend only what they have received, and that, therefore, every nation whose industrial system is organized on a capitalist basis must produce a mass of surplus products over and above, not the need, but the purchasing power of the nation's producers. Before these products can return to their owners as profits they must be sold somewhere. Hence the need for foreign markets, for fields of exploitation and "spheres of influence" in "undeveloped" countries whose virgin resources are exploited in their turn after the capitalist fashion. But, since every industrial nation is seeking the same outlet for its products, clashes are inevitable and in these clashes beaks and claws—armies and navies—must come into play. Hence beaks and claws must be provided beforehand against the day of conflict, and hence the exploitation of white men in Europe and America becomes the reason for the

exploitation of black and brown and yellow men in Africa and Asia. And, therefore, it is hypocritical and absurd to pretend that the capitalist nations can ever
intend to abolish wars.[35]

This analysis of the racial and political-economic significance of the war reflected Harrison's critical independence. It was not the official view of the socialists, who, both domestically and internationally, were divided on the war.
Domestically, most Socialist Party members opposed the war, although a significant minority, including many prominent theorists, would support the war
effort and call for defeat of Germany. Internationally, most of the leading socialist parties were prowar and would advocate "Defense of the Fatherland," while
a minority, including V. I. Lenin, the Russian Bolsheviks, and the "Zimmerwald
Left," challenged that position with their opposition to "the Imperialist War."[36]
Harrison's views were also a step ahead of those in the African American
community, which in general did not at first exhibit any great enthusiasm about
the European war. Initially, at least, many African Americans considered it a
"white man's war," and it was often heard that "the Germans ain't done nothing to me and I ain't doin' nothing to them." African American interest in the
war, according to historians Arthur E. Barbeau and Florette Henri, "grew slowly
from the neutral stance of 1914" to one of stronger sympathy with the Allies by
1917. After the United States entered the war in April 1917, many Black leaders
would be eager to prove their patriotism and loyalty. Harrison's opposition to the
war, its agony, and bloodshed, and his highlighting of its racial and economic
significance contrasted with the views of many older Black leaders. Differences
on the war would increasingly become a dividing line between the "New Negro"
political leadership, which Harrison came to represent, and the older generation
of race leaders.[37]
It was this older generation of race leaders, along with a general conservatism among African Americans, that Harrison saw as major problems to be addressed by any new Black leadership. He examined the root cause of what he
called the "conservatism" of the American Negro in an article that appeared
in the September 12, 1914, *Truth Seeker*. The article, "The Negro a Conservative: Christianity Still Enslaves the Minds of Those Whose Bodies It Long Held
Bound," clearly showed the influence of rationalist atheism on his thinking since
he attributed the root cause of conservatism among African Americans to the
ideological hold of Christianity. The article also suggests how central he felt the
break from religion was to his own radicalization. He wrote:

It would be a difficult task to name one line of intellectual endeavor among
white men in America, in which the American Negro has not taken his part.
Yet it is a striking fact that the racial attitude has been dominantly conserva-

tive. Radicalism does not yet register to any noticeable extent the contributions of our race in this country. In theological criticism, religious dissent, social and political heresies such as Single Tax, Socialism, Anarchism—in most of the movements arising from the reconstruction made necessary by the great body of that new knowledge which the last two centuries gave us—the Negro in America has taken no part. And today our sociologists and economists still restrict themselves to the compilation of tables of statistics in proof of Negro progress. Our scholars are still expressing the intellectual viewpoints of the eighteenth century.[38]

How did he account for this? It was because "Christian America created the color line; and all the great currents of critical opinion . . . found this great barrier impassible." It imposed definite barriers to intellectual efforts and anyone behind it had "to think perpetually" of it. There were clearly other factors at play, such as the paltry fifty-eight cents spent annually on educating Black children in Southern counties, the fact that the prominent Black leader Booker T. Washington "decries 'higher' education," and the invidious role of the press, but Harrison focused on the Christian Church. He described how it cloaked the beginnings of slavery, opposed the abolitionists, and made sure that religion taught to slaves stressed "the servile virtues of subservience and content." Pointing out that in the Black community the Black church "exerts a more powerful influence than anything else in the sphere of ideas," he emphatically added, "show me a population that is deeply religious, and I will show you a servile population, content with whips and chains, contumely and the gibbet, content to eat the bread of sorrow and drink the waters of affliction."[39]

Harrison lamented Black speakers "vaunting the fact" that during the Civil War, "there was no Negro uprising to make their masters pay for the systematic raping of Negro women and the inhuman cruelties perpetrated on Negro men." How was this to be explained? The answer was that "their spirits had been completely crushed by the system of slavery" and the "most effective instrument" in this process was "the Christianity of their masters." To support his argument, he cited *The Conflict of Colour*, B. L. Putnam Weale's 1910 book, which explained how white people were aware of the subjugating aspect of Christianity and used it "for their own ends."[40]

Under current leadership, Harrison did not envision significant change coming soon. He explained that "so long as our 'leaders' are dependent on the favor of our masses for their livelihood, just so long will they express the thought of the masses." This theme was one he would refer to later and had to do with the subject of a book manuscript he was working on ("The Idols of the Tribe"), which focused on the interrelation between the education level of the masses and the role played by leaders. The never completed manuscript was to be a "study of the sociological foundations of modern civilized thinking: common, scientific, and philosophical." Its first chapter was completed on March 2 and amended on May 1, 1915, but, according to Harrison's correspondence, no more than a ragged skeleton was done through November 13, 1920. The work focused on the power of mass psychology and "the tremendous weight of the social proscription which it is possible to bring to bear upon those who dare defy the idols of our tribe." This group pressure was, to Harrison, a necessary "social imperative" or motivating force of the oppressed, and he later described it as a law of social pressure that "any population as marked as the Negro," in its formative stages, tended to "stick together" in response to "pressure from outside." It was therefore true, he said, that "those who live by the people must needs be careful of the people's gods."[41]

Despite his criticisms of the church, Harrison did try to challenge white supremacy in church ranks. Shortly after writing his *Truth Seeker* article, on October 8, 1914, he attended the thirtieth annual Conference of Church Workers Among Colored People at St. Philips Protestant Episcopal Church in Harlem. He was impressed by the Rev. George Chalmers Richmond, the white rector of St. John's Church, Philadelphia, who delivered "one of the finest talks" he had ever heard and explained how "the power of the church is in the hands of rich and powerful men who elect their representatives to the Board of Bishops." After the regular meeting, Rev. George Frazier Miller, Harrison's friend from the Socialist Party, and Rev. George Marshall Plaskett, of the Epiphany Mission in Orange, N.J., invited Harrison to attend a caucus meeting "of colored Episcopal clergymen to decide upon ways and means for pushing the propaganda, for the creation of Negro bishops, among the Episcopal clergy." Miller, asked him to speak, and he did, "creating a very favorable impression" among those present.[42]

Shortly after writing "The Negro a Conservative" and attending the conference, Harrison attended the October 13, 1914, commemoration of the fifth anniversary of the death of Francisco Ferrer at the Forward Building (home of New York's leading Jewish daily) at 175 East Broadway on Manhattan's Lower East Side. Leonard Abbott, the president of the Ferrer Association, the Thomas Paine National Historical Association, and the Free Speech League, former Socialist, associate editor of *Current Literature*, driving force of the Harlem Liberal Alliance, and an instructor at the Ferrer Modern School, had written to him asking him to speak. At the meeting Abbott presided, and Harrison and anarchists Alexander Berkman and Harry Kelly spoke. Harrison wryly commented in his diary that Berkman paid him "the compliment" of making his plea "for more extensive knowledge" the basis of a Berkman attack. Kelly, a charter member of the Ferrer Association, then responded, championing Harrison's view of the

Figure 8.2. Francisco Ferrer, undated. In 1914 and 1915, Harrison taught comparative religion at the Ferrer Association's Modern School on East 107th St. in East Harlem. The school was founded in 1910 as an outgrowth of protests of the October 1909 murder of the Spanish anarchist and educator Francisco Ferrer y Guardia (1859–1909), who had helped to establish the Escuela Moderna in Barcelona in 1901 and similar schools throughout Spain. The schools encouraged self-expression, individual freedom, social change, and practical knowledge and reinforced brotherhood, cooperation, support for the poor and oppressed, anticapitalism, antimilitarism, and antistatism. The "modern education" at the New York Modern School involved "a shift from emphasis on instruction to emphasis on the process of learning, from teaching by rote and memorization to teaching by example and experience, from education as preparation for life to education as life itself." *Source:* From the *Truth Seeker.* Courtesy of the Truth Seeker Company.

matter while harmonizing it with Berkman's and with that of another noted anarchist, Dr. Ben Reitman of Chicago.[43]

Abbott, Kelly, and Reitman were all involved with the Ferrer Modern School, which had been founded in 1910 and had moved to 62 East 107th St. in East Harlem in 1912. The school was an outgrowth of protests of the October 13,

1909, murder by church and state of the Spanish anarchist and educator Francisco Ferrer y Guardia, who had helped to establish the Escuela Moderna in Barcelona in 1901 and similar schools throughout Spain afterward. The schools encouraged self-expression, individual freedom, social change, and practical knowledge, and they reinforced brotherhood, cooperation, support for the poor and oppressed, anticapitalism, antimilitarism, and antistatism.[44]

The Ferrer Modern School in New York attempted to apply the principle of freedom in education and to challenge the habits and culture reinforced by the educational system, which helped to maintain the existing social order. The Modern School leader Harry Kelly described a "modern education" as one involving "a shift from emphasis on instruction to emphasis on the process of learning, from teaching by rote and memorization to teaching by example and experience, from education as preparation for life to education as life itself." Noted luminaries on the school's faculty over the years included the anarchists Emma Goldman, Hutchins Hapgood, and Berkman; the anarchist and freethought editor-activist Abbott; the Single Tax and freethought writer-activist James F. Morton; the artists Robert Henri, George Bellows, and John Sloan; the IWW labor agitator Elizabeth Gurley Flynn; the NAACP leader William English Walling; the muckrakers Lincoln Steffens and Upton Sinclair; the philosopher Will Durant, and the attorney Clarence Darrow. The historian Paul Avrich emphasizes that the Ferrer Modern School was "an important focus of cultural and social ferment" at a time when "many of the seminal ideas of twentieth-century politics and art were being developed." Avrich adds that "anarchism, socialism, syndicalism, revolution, birth control, free love, Cubism, futurism, Freudianism, feminism, the New Woman, the New Theater, direct action, the general strike" were all "intensely discussed" at the Modern School.[45]

Harrison worked at the school as an adjunct professor of comparative religion from late 1914 through 1915. In 1914 he lectured to Saturday-night adult classes on the natural history of religion, and from February 18 through April 1, 1915, he taught comparative religion. The outline for the comparative course included lectures on the religions of China and India; Islam; paganism and Christianity; religion and the proletariat; and religion and culture. He also lectured on religion and science and in his classes, according to J. A. Rogers, expounded "modern socialistic ideals and tendencies."[46]

In 1914 and 1915, Harrison, inspired by his "international consciousness," cognizant of the racial and economic significance of the war, impressed by freethought and anarchist-influenced educational theories, and sensing the social tendencies of his age, began to articulate his vision of the new African American leadership that was needed. It would be a leadership modern and scientific in thinking and teaching, one that would be intimately connected with the community and would focus on addressing the education of the masses—it would

Figure 8.3. Leonard Abbott, c. 1905. Leonard Abbott (1878–1953), a pacifist, rationalist, humanist, an-archist, and proponent of sexual freedom, was a founder of the Socialist Party–affiliated Rand School, president of the Free Speech League, president of the Thomas Paine National Historical Association (for whom Harrison spoke in 1911), president of the Ferrer Association, and instructor at the Ferrer Modern School. In 1914 and 1915 Abbott, like Harrison, was a former member of the Socialist Party teaching at the Modern School. In this period Harrison lectured on freethought, sexual freedom, birth control, literature, and the racial aspects of the war. *Source:* Photograph by William M. Van der Weyde. Courtesy of the Van der Weyde Archives, Thomas Paine National Historical Association.

"be based, not on the ignorance of the masses, but upon their intelligence." He saw "little hope of change" under current Black leaders whose scholastic de-velopment consisted of "superficial acquaintance with 'letters' and a flair for the cryptic phrase." He thought, according to A. Philip Randolph, that the wider "knowledge of the Negro was too limited" to directly "develop a vanguard in the field of revolutionary social change." That, added Randolph, was the reason he "talked about Herbert Spencer, *Origin of the Species*, things of that sort, and . . . sold books on the streets . . . such as Ward's *Dynamic Sociology* and all of the various scientific forms of literature."[47]

Harrison wanted to reach the African American masses with a liberating pedagogy. In "The Negro a Conservative" he called for a new race leadership, abreast of modern and scientific thought, to "shake off the trammels of such time-serving leaders as Mr. Washington, and attain the level of that 'higher education' against which he solidly sets his face." The ideas on education of the masses, which Harrison thought would be integral to developing new leadership, were articulated in his writings over the next few years and were likely present, at least in embryo, in 1915.[48]

His conception of the education needed by the African American masses was significantly influenced by the rationalist, freethought, anarchist, and socialist theories to which he had been exposed, and in this they differed from the views of both Booker T. Washington and W. E. B. Du Bois, the nation's most prominent Black leaders and commentators on education. Particularly notable were Harrison's calls for integral education, for emphasis on the process of learning, for teaching by example and experience, and for education as life itself—all of which were part of the freethought, anarchist, educational tradition of the Modern School. Harrison also emphasized an education of the masses as opposed to Du Bois's emphasis on "the higher education of a Talented Tenth who through their knowledge and modern culture could guide the American Negro into a higher civilization." The new intellectual leadership, Harrison explained, would have to "come down from the Sinais and give it [education] to the common people."[49]

To Harrison, the real "essence" of the intra-race debate over education was not "the easy distinction between 'lower' and 'higher' education," but rather that between "'the knowledge of things' versus 'the knowledge of words.'" Harrison urged the learning of "modern science, modern languages and modern thought." He emphasized that science was "organized observation" and that it needed to be popularized. Black people needed to develop knowledge of "nitrates and engineering, of chemistry and agriculture, of history, science, and business," and he encouraged Black colleges to "establish modern courses in Hausa and Arabic," the "living languages of our brothers in Africa," as well as courses "in Negro history and the culture of West African peoples."[50]

One of Harrison's main emphases was on the need for constant reading, self-study, and the formation of independent opinions by individuals. People needed to "Read!," to "get the reading habit," to "read, reason and think on all sides of all questions," to spend "spare time not so much in training the feet to dance, as in training the head to think." He stressed that "Negroes must take to reading, study and development of intelligence as we have never done before," patterning "ourselves after the Japanese who have gone to school in Europe but have never used Europe's education to make them apes of Europe's culture." He encouraged young people to prepare for leadership by getting training "not only in school and in college, but in books and newspapers, in market-places, institutions, and movements" and not to think one knew until one had "listened to ten others who know differently" and "survived the shock."[51]

Harrison considered such modern educational work a necessary revolutionary endeavor. He later described how, in "the dark days of Russia, when the iron heel of czarist despotism was heaviest on the necks of the people, those who wished to rule decreed that the people should remain ignorant." In response, "Leo Tolstoi and the other intelligentsia began to carry knowledge to the masses." Then, as "knowledge spread, enthusiasm was backed by brains, and the developing Russian revolution began to be sure of itself.'" It was an example that he thought people should learn from.[52]

By early 1915 Hubert Harrison had moved away from the Socialist Party and toward independent lecturing. His first steps had been with white radicals, but he was paying attention to world events, developing his ideas on what type of education African Americans needed, probing the psychology of the Black community, and seeking to determine how to reach Black people with radical ideas. However, by attacking the church, the most powerful institution in the Black community, he was not fully heeding his own advice to "Beware the Idols of the Tribe." He was a perceptive critic and a person of vision. But it was a difficult path, and his efforts, with little organizational support behind them, were largely individual. Nevertheless, with his skills and limitations and with some new promptings, Harrison would soon move away from his white audiences toward concentrated work with African Americans in Harlem.

The "New Negro Movement"

9

Focus on Harlem

The Birth of the "New Negro Movement"

(1915–1917)

*Between 1915 and 1917 Harrison's indoor and outdoor lectures increasingly fo-*cused on the racial aspects of the war. He was encouraged to speak more in Harlem, and he wrote several important theater reviews that helped him to further analyze the "psychology of the Negro."[1] By late 1916 and early 1917 his new focus was clear, and his militant, race conscious lectures at The "Temple of Truth" would signal the dawn of a new era—the birth of "The New Negro Manhood Movement," better known as the "New Negro Movement." It would be a race conscious, internationalist, mass-based movement for "political equality, social justice, civic opportunity, and economic power" geared toward "the Negro common people" and urging defense of self, family, and "race" in the face of lynching and white supremacy.[2]

When his Harlem Casino lecture series ended in late February 1915, Harrison offered his explanation of the racial significance of the war to white audiences at the Brownsville (Brooklyn) Radical Forum in three lectures on the European conflict. One talk focused on the immediate causes of the war and on Heinrich Gotthard von Treitschc, the outspoken advocate of Anglo-Saxon superiority, from the University of Berlin. Harrison followed these presentations with three of his more popular lectures: "Lincoln and Liberty," "Sex, Sinners, and Society," and "Education out of School," the last probably being an elaboration of his views on education coupled with encouragement of self-education efforts. His talk on self-education was apparently well received because the next year, when he was scheduled to speak on the subject, the *Monatlisches Zeitung Turn-Verein Vorwarts* of Brooklyn raved, "No speaker in the country is better qualified to treat this topic and the lecturer's personality and style bespeak a very enjoyable and instructive evening."[3]

The Harlem Casino lecture series was renewed from March to May 1915 and opened with "Who Put the Bomb in St. Patrick's Cathedral? With a Word of Warning to Millionaires and the Public." Billed as an "Inside Lecture," the talk likely described the entrapment by an undercover police agent of Frank Abarno and Carmine Carbone, two young members active with the Ferrer Modern School, who were charged with placing bombs at St. Patrick's Cathedral and the Church of St. Alphonsus on October 13, 1914, the fifth anniversary of the execution of Francisco Ferrer. The bombs caused minor damage and the men were sentenced to six to twelve years in prison. Subsequent Harrison talks in the series included "Advertising Fakes in the Big Stores," "Our Patriotic Prudes: Sex Control and the Price They Pay for It," "The Social Significance of Billy Sunday" (the frenetic fundamentalist who was America's leading evangelist and whom Harrison considered a great deceiver), and "Starve America First—the Reason for the Hard Times and How to Prevent Them." The "Starve America First" theme was likely a satirical takeoff on capitalist greed and on "America First," the title of President Woodrow Wilson's April 1915 speech calling for American neutrality in the European conflict. It was also probably related to the "starve the war and feed America" slogan urged by antiwar and anti-involvement socialists after the war started and in their subsequent August 14, 1916, manifesto.[4]

In advertisements for the Harlem Casino series, Harrison was billed as "America's foremost Negro lecturer." This was high praise since the lecturer held a unique place in American society as both educator and entertainer and was often an immensely popular figure in the community. Harrison considered the well equipped lecturer to be "a public teacher and benefactor," and by all accounts he excelled in this role. He was class and race conscious; he was skilled in language and pronunciation; he used satire, irony, and humor; he had vast knowledge and an excellent memory and was capable of quick recall and fast associations; and, when appropriate, he was extremely interactive with his audience. It was an extraordinarily effective mix of skills and talents.[5]

Lester A. Walton, an editor for the *New York Age* and a feature writer for the *New York World*, described the "well read" Harrison as "in a class by himself as a street speaker," particularly in his ability to "talk interestingly on many subjects." Walton pointed out that "long before soap-box orators were heard in North Harlem, Harrison was talking to large crowds made up of white persons on the east side and in other sections of Manhattan" and he "always was able to gather about him a large number of hearers whenever he spoke in Harlem." He usually "discussed some important phase of the race question" and "invariably ended by telling of some valuable books or pamphlets which he offered for sale." A. Philip Randolph, who was greatly influenced by Harrison in his youth, similarly remembered him as the first and "most successful" of the Harlem street speakers, "quite articulate," "a good logician, quite analytical," with "a very fine mind . . . that reached in all areas of human knowledge." Claude McKay reminisced on how he "spoke precisely and clearly, with fine intelligence and masses of facts" and with a "sense of humor [that] was ebony hard."[6]

J. A. Rogers described how "crowds flocked to hear him" and "auditors would stand hours at a time shifting from foot to foot, entranced" as he presented "the most abstract matter in a clear and lively fashion." At his talks Harrison "sold literature," and Rogers reported that he was so "able . . . in this respect that on one occasion he disposed of one hundred copies of a book on sociology at a dollar each, within an hour, on Lenox Avenue in Harlem." This "was all the more remarkable," noted Rogers, "in view of the fact that the purchasers were Negroes, who as a group, are very little inclined to buy books."[7]

The *New York News* concurred with these views and emphasized the importance of Harrison's outdoor talks. The *News* suggested that part of the appeal of outdoor lectures was that they were "virile and unconventional," while indoor talks were often "platitudinous, artificial and lack[ing in] courage." A speaker "burdened with the weight of a church, a school, a lyceum or some other institution" was often "afraid to say some of the things which Harrison said boldly on the street-corner." While "indoor talks" were "generally limited, muzzled, tongue-tied," Harrison's talks were "unchained, free, even daring." The *News* compared him to Socrates and called attention to his contact with the masses as it concluded, "Perhaps, like Socrates, we must pursue truth on the street-corners and in the highways, and seek the Beautiful and the good in the mob among the outcasts."[8]

Harrison's oratorical abilities were recognized throughout the Harlem community, and around the time that the Harlem Casino lecture series ended Gertrude Cohen, a librarian at the 135th St. Public Library, suggested that he concentrate his efforts on work in the Black community. This idea received support from James Weldon Johnson, an editorial writer for Fred R. Moore's *Age*, the city's leading Black weekly, which was strongly pro-Republican and secretly, since 1907, under the control of Booker T. Washington. Despite Washington's influence, Johnson, a former U.S. consul in Venezuela and Nicaragua, maintained some independence in his column, as evidenced by the May 6, 1915, editorial he sent to Harrison (a long-time Washington critic).[9]

Johnson's editorial suggested establishing "An Open Air Lecture Course" in Harlem upon subjects of interest to the Black community. This would serve as "a university extension carried to the farthest point" and could attract people on the street who wouldn't go to a lecture but who would listen if a lecture was brought to them. Johnson added that there were "a great many things that the colored people of . . . [New] York should be taught and told, things they do not hear . . . [either in] school or in church," and he recommended "one colored speaker [Harrison]," who, if he could be secured, "would give a series of lectures that would be more than equivalent to a year of college, and of incalculable benefit to the community." Johnson concluded by calling on the public-spirited race leaders of Manhattan to do something of great practical value at a relatively small cost—to take the necessary steps to establish such a lecture course.[10]

On May 12 Harrison responded to Johnson, thanked him for sending a copy of the editorial, and explained that John T. Clark of the Urban League was working out the details of a similar idea. "Unfortunately," wrote Harrison, Clark's plan only considered "the establishment of certain relations between Negro customers and Negro tradesmen and business men," while Johnson's idea covered "a wider field and would really develop into an institution capable of rendering a great social service."[11]

During that late spring of 1915, Harrison visited often at the offices of the Urban League to talk with Clark, a graduate of Ohio State University who was the head of the league's housing bureau and a young man he personally liked. In his diary Harrison detailed how Clark broached the proposition of "speaking on the streets in the Negro neighborhood on behalf of the Negro business men in a propaganda designed to induce Negro purchasers to patronize Negro businessmen." Clark then brought a group of business leaders together, but unfortunately the meeting "was a failure, due partly to the obstructionist tactics of [the United Colored Democracy leaders] W. T. R. Richardson and D. E. Tobias, and mainly to the autocratic Booker Washington methods and tactlessness of the chairman, Mr. Fred R. Moore, [the Republican] editor of the *New York Age*." Clark also held out to Harrison "the ultimate hope of the editorship of a magazine, which the Urban League would eventually found, a publication somewhat like the *Southern Workman* [of the Hampton Institute]." That publication would appear eight years later as *Opportunity*, with Charles S. Johnson, who held a Ph.D. from the University of Chicago, as its editor and with funding from the Carnegie Corporation. As of his June 3, 1915, diary entry, however, Harrison had "not spoken a word to anyone" on this matter.[12]

Though the various plans were being discussed, Harrison was again lecturing on the streets on popular science, biology and philosophy. On June 2 he had "a fair measure of success," selling Herbert Spencer's *First Principles* at fifty cents and *Famous Speeches* of Robert G. Ingersoll, "The Great Infidel," at twenty-five cents, though the weather presented real difficulties. It was so cold in New York that people were wearing overcoats, and over the previous two weeks it had been so "distressingly chilly" that it seemed to Harrison "as if the Great Ice Age were returning." Harrison's financial difficulties, further aggravated by the weather, undoubtedly affected his family situation. Two weeks later, when he brought the money from one of his meetings into the kitchen and called in Lin to tell her of his plans "to begin giving her all the money" so as to "keep tab on myself financially," he was strongly rejected. In his diary he wrote: "The lady met me with insults and rebuffs and began a quarrel on her own hook. Another attempt killed." His handling of money and his lack of attention to family financial matters remained serious problems.[13]

Under increased financial pressure, Harrison soon decided to move in the direction suggested by Cohen and Johnson. He did not, however, receive financial support from wealthy Harlem race leaders, though an additional push came from the realtor John M. Royall of the United Civic League. Royall had founded the Negro Civic League, later renamed the United Civic League, on September 2, 1913, for the purpose of conducting a civic, industrial, political, and educational campaign among members of the race. The UCL charged monthly and annual dues and attracted many of Harlem's wealthiest residents. From the beginning it sought to run Black candidates for office, and in 1913, while he was a member of Booker T. Washington's National Negro Business League, Royall ran for alderman in Harlem's Thirty-first District. He won the Progressive primary, lost the Republican primary, and lost in the final as a Civic League candidate, though he reportedly won 85 percent of the Black vote. Despite that loss, the UCL was able to grow because of the general disarray in both major parties' work among African Americans and because of its own mass appeal, which was heightened by the use of outdoor lectures and meetings at the Palace Casino on Sunday afternoons.[14]

On June 3, 1915, Royall invited Harrison to his office for a long talk. In his diary Harrison noted that during the last election campaign he "ran his own ticket (Independent Progressive) and polled 2200 votes forcing the three political parties to recognize political manhood in the Negro." Royall narrated the history of the UCL and provided insight into the development of his own ideas on Black civic advancement. He explained that he started out as a supporter of Booker T. Washington but was led by a consideration of the financial forces backing Washington's program to recast his estimate of the man and his theories. Harrison was very impressed and wrote in his diary that "Royall has a firmer and finer grip on the financial, economic and political factors of the Negro situation, and of their inter-relations than any other Negro American with whom I have spoken. He has a splendid mind and I feel sure that, if he lives, it will be heard from with considerable effect."[15]

In the course of their meeting Harrison and Royall discussed the National League on Urban Conditions Among Negroes (later the National Urban League), founded in 1911 by prominent Blacks and whites, and its connection with Booker T. Washington. The Urban League had been described by Harrison as a "scab organization" during the Waiters' Strike of 1912, when he saw "that its policy was to corral young Negroes of ability and harness them to the wagon of its social-uplift program in such a way as to keep them in the straight road of conservatism." He judged that "the League was successful in this endeavor based on a study of the personalities of George Edmund Haynes, their Negro director, and Eugene Kinckle Jones, the assistant-director." Harrison described Haynes's sociological method (his doctorate was in economics) as "one whose finest flowering consists solely in the gathering of dead statistics, a proceeding conducive to static views of life rather than to dynamic ones, and fruitful in the production of intellectual bell-wethers." Royall had reached similar conclusions on the goals of the league, "although his grip upon the process and methods was more detailed and extensive, filling in the gaps between the local branch of the League and Mr. Washington and his and their financial supporters." Harrison was impressed that Royall also seemed to know "something of the interlocking directorates device in social and philanthropic work."[16]

Based on their meeting, Harrison judged that Royal wanted to "insure" his "detachment from the Urban League group" and "insure" his "attachment to . . . the United Civic League." Harrison was "not averse" to this since there was "no attachment" to the Urban League other than his personal liking for Clark. He wrote in his diary that he planned "to move slowly and with caution, making myself a pawn in no man's game, however I may approve of him." Two weeks earlier, in mid-May, he had asked Clark to present his application for membership in the Urban League, and a week later Assistant Chief Executive Eugene Kinckle Jones had sent him a slip independently asking him to join the league. Royall also sent him a request to join his Civic League. In his diary of June 3 Harrison indicated that he planned to "join both, inasmuch as each declares that its work is not in necessary opposition to the other." No record has been located indicating that he ever joined either organization.[17]

Despite the Urban League's interest, nothing came of the editorship or the lecture course. One very possible reason was Booker T. Washington. The *Age* reported that Washington spoke at four meetings in New York and Brooklyn under National Urban League auspices on May 16, and it is quite possible that Washington, long a subject of Harrison's criticism and the man behind his dismissal from the Post Office, may also have been involved in blocking plans for the open-air lecture series or editorial work with the Urban League.[18]

Though there may have been some intrigue regarding work for the NUL, and though he was cautious toward both the NUL and the UCL, one thing is clear—by the middle of 1915 Hubert Harrison, a year removed from the Socialist Party, was on the verge of moving away from work as a lecturer and teacher among white people. He had decided, as he later, explained "to give myself exclusively to work among my own people." An important step, which reflected that decision, occurred on June 22, 1915, when he signed a "Declaration of Intention" to become a United States citizen.[19]

This decision to cast his lot in the United States would play a major role in Harrison's future political development. He had no plans to return to the Caribbean (as would fellow activist and boyhood friend D. Hamilton Jackson, when he came to the States) or to emigrate to Africa (as had fellow Virgin Island intellectual Edward Wilmot Blyden)—his struggle would be in the United States. He believed, as he would explain in 1919 when commenting on the U.S. government's refusal to grant passports to the African American activist William Monroe Trotter and the businesswoman Madame C. J. Walker in their attempt to attend the Paris Peace Congress, that "the fight is here, and here you will be compelled to face it."[20]

One of the matters mentioned by Clark—inducing "Negro purchasers to patronize Negro businessmen"—prompted subsequent comment by Harrison. Several years later he described, in an article entitled "Patronize Your Own," how these campaigns were put into effect in Harlem in the period around 1915. He explained that the slogan "patronize your own" flowed from a more important doctrine, which he described as the "Race First" idea, and that Black businessmen in Harlem used the "Race First" concept although they never really supported it. Instead, they opted for the secondary principle of "patronize your own," which was "subject to the risk of being exploited dishonestly—particularly by business men." These businessmen seemed to forget that "'do unto others as you would have them do unto you'" was "a part of the honest application of this doctrine," and many seemed "to want other black people to pay them for being black," while they offered "high prices, dirty places, and imperfect service." In contrast, Harrison commended the "New Negro business man" in whose stores "the application of prices, courtesy and selling efficiency are maintained." This, he emphasized, was genuine race-first business practice, and he predicted that if it was pursued widely, it would lead to "a full and flowing tide of Negro business enterprises gladly and loyally supported by the mass of Negro purchasers to their mutual benefit."[21]

As a negative example of a "Patronize Your Own" campaign, Harrison cited brown-skinned dolls. He explained that at the turn of the century the Black child's only choice was "between a white Caucasian doll and the 'nigger doll,'" which, at the lower levels were equally priced. These were followed in turn by the "picturesque poupee," known also as the "'Negro doll,' the 'colored doll' and the 'brown-skinned doll,'" which were sold by white stores at almost prohibitive prices. This pricing made it "three times as easy for the Negro child to idolize a white doll as to idolize one with the features of its own race." However, as race-first principles began to be expressed, there were Black businessmen who saw a chance to exploit the situation "by appealing to a principle for whose support . . . they had never paid a cent." Factories producing brown-skinned dolls sprang up, and most merely received the dolls from white factories and then either stuffed them with saw dust, excelsior, or another filling, or simply changed their wrapper. The businessmen charged three to five dollars for dolls that should have sold for seventy-five cents to a dollar and a quarter, and the result was that 90 percent of the Black children in Harlem were "forced to play with white dolls, because rapacious scoundrels" capitalized on "the principle of 'patronize your own' in a one-sided way." If, on the other hand, they had lowered the prices, they could have had wonderful success. Their actions played into the hands of the sellers of white dolls and made it more likely that Black children used white dolls. They thus both limited their market and restricted the "development of a larger racial ideal."[22]

By the summer of 1915, because of a huge influx of Southern migrants and West Indian immigrants, the Harlem community in which Harrison was increasingly focusing his efforts numbered upward of fifty thousand.[23] As he considered the offers of Clark and Royall and the suggestions of Cohen and Johnson, Harrison set himself the immediate task of analyzing "if Negro society [was] in any sense distinct from American society"—a task very similar to what historian Nathan I. Huggins has identified as the recurring "task of Negro intellectuals . . . to delineate Negro character and personality in the American context."[24] Harrison had previously analyzed economic, political, social, and educational aspects of "Negro" existence, read the history, and frequented community haunts. He now attempted to analyze the psychology of the "Negro" and his entrance to this subject was through the frontier of art. He would apply his finely honed critical skills to the stage in order to gain a perspective on the psychology of "race relations" in the United States.[25]

Harrison planned and began writing a book on "Negro Society and the Negro Stage," of which two or three chapters were written, though the main essay was not published until 1917. He felt the chapters might be of some value to the race "as a partial explanation of its own social mind," and in writing it for publication he intended "to create the impression that it had been written by a white man," for which he felt he didn't "owe any one an apology." His reasons were ones that he would cite again over the years. First, he believed that his subject matter, coming from a Black man, would be too controversial for many race leaders, most of whom were of lighter complexion and most of whom, he felt, practiced a intra-race color discrimination. In his outdoor talks, as later reported in the March 1918 *New Negro*, Harrison was repeatedly sarcastic "when referring to our 'cullud' editors" who "self-applied the term 'colored' to their 'section' of the Negro race and secretly as well as openly 'despised' their Negro ancestors." A probable second reason that Harrison gave the impression that his article was written by someone white was that he believed many "Negro" leaders were so dependent on white leadership that they would not accept contributions from undiscovered Blacks but only from whites or white-discovered Blacks. This belief would later lead him to advise J. A. Rogers to pretend that he was white in order to get his first book published.[26]

When Harrison began writing, though he had studied the broader society rigorously, he "knew practically nothing of Negro actors in the legitimate drama." This was not surprising since Black actors had previously been forced from the "white stage" and, as Huggins points out, there had been "no truly Negro ethnic theater." The book Harrison planned was "a study of the Negro vaudevillian and the social conditions lying back of his art." At the time of his initial writings, comedy and vaudeville dominated the Black theater, and the future big three of New York's Black stage—the Anita Bush Stock Company, the Lafayette Stock Company, and Ridgely Torrence's Negro Players—were still in embryo.[27]

Harrison began by using his training in both criticism and Marxist theory to define some broad concepts. First, he suggested that a critic (Matthew Arnold) who had earlier defined literature as "a criticism of life," had provided a "matchless" description "of the real function of literature." He added that this was true of any art, and he defined art as "one kind of human activity, the end of which is pleasure." He then argued that "art erects a mirror of the social soul" and explained that

> since what is pleasure depends upon the kind of mind to which it is presented, and the kind of mind is determined by social inheritance and surrounding social conditions, it is inevitable that, in drawing its available materials from these, every art must reflect that in some way. Furthermore, every artist *selects* his materials from the mass available and, in so doing, registers his individual preferences, the sum of which constitutes the taste or culture of his time; and by means of this the mind of a period or a people is revealed. Thus, whether we are noting the things selected or those rejected, every art erects a mirror of the social soul, and whatever allowances must be made for the known laws of its refraction, that mirror will reflect only what it receives. That is why it is possible to reconstruct and interpret the life of any period from its literary and artistic remains.[28]

Harrison maintained that drama deserved serious attention from social historians and sociologists because it presented the mental and spiritual characteristics of a people and reflected the special modifications produced by changing times and special circumstances. In drama, he explained, art is both "a record of individual expression and of social expression"; the author and the age are equally on view. By presenting "the art of the Negro actor," the social background of the art, and the interrelations between the two, he hoped to glimpse "the Negro's soul" as well the character of the Negro playgoer. Harrison paid special attention to the central role of the playgoer, whose response to the performance reacted back upon both the actor and the playwright, and he emphasized that it was the playgoer who "determines to a measurable extent the form and substance of the Negro drama." He concluded, since drama was "a mirror of social situations," the distinctiveness of Black drama would demonstrate the distinctness of "Negro society." The Black community was the community he sought to reach; he felt it was distinctive; and he now wanted to capture the essence of that distinctness.[29]

After delineating his theoretical approach, Harrison examined the African American actor. He pointed out that when one spoke of "the Negro actor in America," one had to exclude "the Negro tragedian and the actor in the 'legitimate' drama," since social pressures had forced this type to disappear. There were no more great actors like the nineteenth-century Shakespearian tragedian Ira Aldridge, playing roles like Othello before large audiences (though the talent was there in actors such as Charles Burroughs). The reason that there were no more great Black actors in America was because there existed "a body of opinion which insists that the Negro must be kept 'in his place,'" a place "collectively lower than that of the rest of the American people . . . in church, in school, in government, and public places."[30]

Harrison concluded his first essay by emphasizing that the "conditions prevailing before the floodlights reflect[ed] themselves behind them." Thus, as long as "we take a people as inferiors, as the butt of our jokes," we will not "allow representatives of the same people to stand where they can be the recipients of our serious admiration and applause unmodified by a due consciousness of our superiority." Since Black people were barred from the best hotels and otherwise segregated, they would continue to be barred from the best places on the stage also. It was different, noted Harrison, for the comic actor. In America, the comedian "ministers to our enjoyment in an inferior capacity—as mountebank." That was why "Negro comedians" could be accepted, "but not Negro actors in the legitimate drama." Harrison later explained that "if Negroes were [considered] people then it would be proper that Negro actors should get accustomed to seeing Negroes as drawing room guests, doctors, detectives, governors, financiers, etc. in the glow of the floodlights." But, "if folks can't be considered as people unless they are unlike Negroes, then, of course, our actors should never look like Negroes." This was the case on the stage, he noted, "except in the mockery of musical comedy."[31]

Harrison's views on the theater were essential to his developing radical perspective on race. So, too, were his developing thoughts on "the mulatto," which were articulated between 1915 and 1917. In his second 1915 article on "Negro Society and the Negro Stage" he probed more deeply into the psyche of Black America and in the process developed two themes: that the "Negro Theater" reflected conditions in existing society and that there was a distinct "Negro culture," which was marked by color prejudice by light-skinned African Americans toward those of darker color. Harrison focused on color prejudice within the

African American community as distinguished from race prejudice by whites against Black people.[32]

He began by citing the example of the initial failure (later turned to success after modifications were made) of entertainers Bob Cole and J. Rosamond Johnson and their "high class" singing, piano playing, and dialogue. Cole had left New York for over four years after his successful "low comedy" (appealing to white audiences) hit *A Trip to Coontown* and in the interim had drifted away from the "'coon' ideal" and the "polite" (to white audiences) act. Harrison quoted the *Age* that "the average white theatergoer . . . [was] not disposed to enthuse to any extent over the work of a performer of ebony hue unless he resorts to low comedy and comes up (down?) to the playgoer's idea of how a colored performer should dress, talk, and act."[33]

In contrast, argued Harrison, the "unparalleled and long-continued success of [Bert] Williams and [George] Walker, America's peerless comedians, was due largely to the fact that they have never disputed the claims of that social convention which has decided how Negroes shall appear upon the stage." The reason:

> The status of the Negro actor is determined by the status of his own social group and, in turn, determines the relation which he shall maintain to his public, be that public black or white. It decrees that in playing before white audiences he must appear only in Negro roles, and must strive at his peril to present their conception of what a Negro is or should be.
>
> So only can he be sure of securing their support and that measure of success upon which his economic welfare depends.[34]

"But," added Harrison, "this basic fact has another consequence which serves to determine the whole scope of the Negro drama." Since the Black playgoers were creatures of their times and conditions, their very notions of self and group were built upon models derived from the larger world—thus, the dialectical relationship between the Black artist and the Black audience. To Harrison, the Black actor and the Black playwright, in order to survive financially, selected those aspects of life and manners that their audiences would accept. The Black actor before a Black audience had a choice to either "play to that conception of life and its stage-presentation which they have derived from white people," or to "play to their higher ideals and the real lives they live." The first choice was "neither a high nor a serious one," and the second choice offered little hope of support, "at any rate not just at present."[35]

Given this situation, there were definite contributions made by the Black actor and the Black playwright. "Negro vaudevillians" were a case in point. They played before both white and Black audiences and, whether they played to the one view or the other, they could not avoid making their art the vehicle of social criticism. Harrison saw such criticism to be of "tremendous significance" since it elicited and reflected "the actual flow of the common life." Thus even "passing quips and seemingly idle jests," the "light pre-occupations of the comic spirit," were "the certain index of social situations." It was especially in these that the artistic value of Black playwrights and comedians were manifested. Both consciously and unconsciously, they presented aspects of "Negro life in its social and moral aspects which the writer of Negro books dares not touch."[36]

As a prime example, Harrison cited the comedian "String Beans" (Butler May), who often sang a humorous little song which went, "'the ... is brown-skin.'" "String Beans" forced the phrase on the audience at the end of every second line. This repetitive emphasis showed, argued Harrison, "that the dramatic and comic value of the refrain" was "solely in the fact" that color was "the great social obsession among our Negroes." Thus, with other things equal, "one's social value in this group is in direct ratio to one's lightness—a fact with many implications as to the Negro character and the forces which moulded it."[37]

This was a point of departure as Harrison moved to what he considered the real essence of his argument—color prejudice within the race. As he explained, it was common to hear Black speakers lecturing white audiences on the evil effects of "color prejudice," all the while ignoring the fact that "there is no such thing as color prejudice in America—except among 'colored people.'" On the Black stage there were "chromatically select circles" where very Black women were particularly discriminated against. In Black society one would hear references to "good" color and "good" hair—"good" in this sense stood for similarity to white people's. Such phrases, he added, ran the gamut from "tantalizin' browns" to "high yallers." Harrison described hearing people talk "of 'high' color, referring disparagingly to others as 'black niggers,' and 'loads of coal.'" He pointed out that "the slang term 'nigger' is heard more frequently among Negroes themselves than among white people; and in love, courtship, marriage and their social life generally, lightness of color is perhaps the greatest desideratum." All this, Harrison argued, reinforced the fact that "the craze for color runs all through Negro society in the United States."[38]

"Negro society," he maintained, was "a mulatto society" in which "darker men and women are always made to feel in ever so many ways that they, as inferiors, are not a welcome part of the upper crust." The mulatto "thinks himself superior to the black or brown person," and this results in a "silent ostracism of the blacks, which can be made very galling," though it "finds no frank expression in words, and is hidden with especial care from the white outsider." This "social separatism" displayed its "most striking organized form in the churches," such as St. Philip's in New York and Francis James Grimké's Fifteenth Street

Presbyterian Church in Washington, D.C. (in which a dark person immediately sensed "the impalpable forces of social ostracism indicating one is 'in the wrong church'"). This awareness of the color prejudice of "colored churches" was probably an added factor in Harrison's forceful antichurch positions and in his belief that Christianity and race prejudice went hand in hand.[39]

Harrison felt that this color prejudice was only slightly mitigated by the influx of darker West Indians into the United States. The dark complexion in African American society was, however, viewed as a stain. He was not categorical in his criticism, however, and he added that there were many "mulattoes" who were leaders "in writing and speaking against the caste-proscriptions from which their race suffers at the hands of white people."[40]

Harrison also examined a curious social product of this color prejudice— the large numbers of advertisements in the Black press for "'anti-kinks,' skin-bleaches, blond face-powders and other devices for straightening the hair and lightening the complexion." These were all indications, he argued, of "Negroes" who were not "pleased with the visible marks of their racial ancestry." He recounted how the New York *Evening Mail*, a white paper, had remonstrated with Fred Moore's *Age* over the number of such advertisements that paper carried. Moore, a business associate of Booker T. Washington, replied that Black people used these things to make themselves lighter in order to get work because white people preferred to employ light-skinned Blacks. Harrison viewed Moore's defense as both a rationalization and something that was simply "not true." It was, to Harrison, not the economic pressure for employment but the color prejudice within the race that was the explanation.[41]

The radical, race- and class-conscious intellectual Hodge Kirnon offered insight into the significance of Harrison's theoretical work on art, society, and intra-race color discrimination. Kirnon explained that "unlike many of his contemporaries," Harrison "understood that there is an inextricable relationship between the arts and philosophy," the first "being the medium . . . through which life mirrors itself" and the second, "the instrument for its exploration." His "discursive and discerning mind made it possible for him to appreciate and evaluate the drama, music and other forms of human expression" as both "the strivings of the mind in search of truth" and "as manifestations of the social characteristics of the age." Because of this, adds Kirnon, Harrison was "always able to catch glimpses of truth and of new ideas and to interpret them in both their ideological and practical aspects."[10]

The theater reviews not only demonstrated Harrison's increased attention to Harlem's Black community; they also demonstrated how he learned from the community. In the fall of 1915, he took another step in the direction of that community—he authored a weekly column, entitled "Our Civic Corner," in the *New*

York News. The *News* was a Black weekly edited and published since 1913 by its founder, Kansas-born and Harvard-educated George W. Harris, a Republican Party politician and a Harlem alderman from 1920 to 1924.[43]

Harrison had a long-standing interest in Black journalism and for years he had focused the majority of his scrapbooks on "Negro" subject matters. Since 1912 he had been regularly reading and clipping the *African Times and Orient Review*, the London-based magazine published by Dusé Mohamed Ali. The *ATOR* sought to be a "Pan-Oriental Pan-African journal" that would express "the aims, desires, and intentions of the Black, Brown, and Yellow races." Harrison also regularly read the *Age* and the *Amsterdam News*, New York's two leading Black weeklies. With such familiarity with the Black press, he now had a brief opportunity to put his journalistic skills to use.[44]

His September 2, 1915, *New York News* column opened with a slogan, which he would use in *The Voice* and which would later be picked up by the Universal Negro Improvement Association in its early years. The slogan, the source of which was not identified by Harrison (or later by the UNIA), was based on the final stanza of the British poet George Linnaeus Banks's "What I Live For" and read:

> For the wrong that needs resistance;
> For the cause that lacks assistance;
> For the future in the distance;
> And the good that we can do.[45]

The column urged a new measure of self-reliance. When asked whether Black people should sell their votes at election time, Harrison wrote, "we always do—every one of us. The only question worth discussing is, What should we sell them for?" He advised "selling our votes for the highest we can get—such as more schools and playgrounds, lower rents, higher wages, better treatment at the hands of policemen, court attendants and judges and a larger measure of American manhood." In order to begin to achieve this "manhood," Black people would have to "get together" in terms of money, organization, and "push." Above all, he advised, Black people "must depend upon ourselves and not upon white people." The philosophy of self-reliance that he urged was a marked contrast from that of New York's two leading civil rights organizations, the NAACP and the National League on Urban Conditions, whose work was premised on the idea of interracial cooperation. Harrison suggested that "white" support, allegedly necessary in financial and organizational efforts, was in fact, more a fetter than an aid.[46]

Once again evincing his playful side as he discussed broader social issues, Harrison's column included a satiric piece that poked fun at those who put on airs with titles, and it had some pithy social commentary about the Health Department and high rents. It also offered public comment to Samuel A. Duncan, a friend from Harrison's lyceum days and an editor of the *New York News*, who, within two years, would temporarily replace Marcus Garvey as head of the Universal Negro Improvement Association. Harrison remarked on the fact that Duncan's wife had bypassed a Black-owned store in order to shop in a white-owned store in which she was rudely treated. He suggested that she would have been better off shopping in the Black store.[47]

Finally, Harrison's September 2 column carried interesting commentary on the women of Harlem organizing block clubs or committees "to bring the social service of our womanhood to bear upon the civic problems affecting their homes, streets and neighborhoods." He noted as problems in need of work: health, public sanitation, police and fire protection, short weights and measures, pure food, and public recreations. The column then closed with some lines from Paul Laurence Dunbar's poem "Right's Security," which emphasized the important role that the individual and minorities can play in social progress.[48]

Harrison's next column, on September 9, opened with another poem (drawn from Josiah Gilbert Holland's "Wanted"), which touched the theme of manhood and womanhood also. The column again discussed the block clubs and recommended that they combine their efforts with those of John M. Royall's United Civic League. He cited for particular praise the efforts of Club No. 2 on W. 136th St., led by community activists Mrs. David Martin, Mrs. E. H. Tolliver, and Mrs. Lelia Robinson. He suggested that those with police problems, an important concern in the community and an issue that he would continually address, follow the example of Block Club No. 1 on 134th St. between 5th and Lenox Avenues and write to him care of the *New York News*.[49]

The September 9 column also discussed the question of Black library staffers for the 135th St. Public Library. It reprinted a letter in which the writer doubted "whether you would find an Irish library staff in a Jewish neighborhood, or vice versa." The writer added, "a librarian taken from the people who use the library most is apt to be more responsive to the special needs of that neighborhood in regards to books and other equipment and service." The letter then explained how necessary this was for Harlem, noting that Harrison himself had "vainly compiled lists of colored peoples' books to be printed and hung up in the local library as a guide to the local reading public." Unfortunately the head librarian never saw fit to consult Black reading needs, and the number of books on racial matters was "outrageously inadequate." The letter called on Harrison and others of his standing "to lead an agitation for a colored librarian and library staff in the 135th street library." Five years later, Catherine B. Allen would be the first African American appointed to the library staff, in significant part because of the work and agitation of Harrison and others.[50]

Finally in the September 9 column, Harrison took some shots at Black people "who put on false airs assuming titles they had not earned." Since he himself would later at times employ the title "Dr." as he sought work as a lecturer, his comments are of particular interest. He reasoned that "many ministers append the letters D.D. to their names" standing for "'Doctor of Divinity,' a title which, among civilized people, is conferred by the faculty of a university—not a college." Thus, any "D.D." that was "given by a congregation, or a con-college, or assumed, as so many of our ministers assume it, is a fake, fraud and flim-flam." He asked: "'Madame,' 'Professor,' 'D.D.'—why do we use them so lavishly? Simply because we feel our own insignificance." If the individual "amounted to anything," Harrison stressed, "he or she would not need the assistance of a faked or foolish title to get people to notice them." Further, since the practice was a silly one, the best way to stop it, he argued, was "to poke fun at those who indulge in it" and "to ridicule those who make our race look ridiculous."[51]

In addition to his newspaper journalism during the fall and early winter of 1915 Harrison also lectured indoors in Harlem. In the early fall he spoke on Wednesday nights at PS 89 on 135th St., where two-thirds of his students were white, and, starting on November 7, he presented a lecture series at the Harlem Casino. It was in these and other talks that he gave from 1914 through 1916 that he developed the embryo of his race-conscious message.[52]

Harrison recognized that conditions throughout the world were changing and that the war was quickening the development of race consciousness. He later explained that as the Great War expanded, it helped "to liberate many ideas undreamt of by those who rushed humanity into that bath of blood." "Democracy" was the prime example. Though it "was widely advertised," mainly as "a convenient camouflage behind which competing imperialists masked their sordid aims," and though those who proclaimed new democratic demands most loudly never had any intention of extending them, the call soon came back to "plague the inventors." While the "cant of democracy" was intended as "as dust in the eyes of the white voters" and "bait for the clever statesmen," the oppressed millions took democracy "at its face value—which is—Equality" and demanded that it "be made safe for them."[53]

Thus, while the white world played with democratic slogans, it simultaneously and ruthlessly ruled the overwhelming majority of the world—"Black, Brown and Yellow" peoples—for whom democracy was never meant to apply. The resultant double standard was evident: when whites insisted upon the right to control their ancestral lands, it was variously described as "'democracy' and 'self-determination'" and when Blacks, Hindus, and Egyptians sought control of their lands, it was called "impudence." Harrison emphasized that this failure to extend democracy was "the main root" cause of the "great unrest" that developed throughout the world and that in the United States this situation affected the mental attitude of those African Americans who developed new ideas of self and race, new conceptions of their powers and destiny, and "race-consciousness."[54]

As Harrison elaborated this analysis of the racial significance of the war in his talks, he made two bold predictions. First, on the international level, he forecast that the European conflict for colonial possessions would awaken racial and national consciousness in the nonwhite areas of the world and that white Europe would sow the seeds of its own destruction in the war for imperial control. Second, on the domestic level, he forecast the "sweeping tide of racial consciousness" that ultimately found expression in "Negro newspapers and magazines . . . called radical." He warned that there would be repercussions from a war fought for racial supremacy in which the masses were told the fight was over democratic ideals.[55]

In elaborating on the domestic advertising of "democracy" Harrison used the analogy of the National Biscuit Company's "Uneeda Biscuit" advertising campaign. The biscuits were developed in 1898 by National Biscuit's A. W. Green, who took a flaky soda cracker, hired the N. W. Ayer and Son advertising agency, adopted a trade name with exclusive "trademark and trade right," and registered the cracker in 1900 with the U.S. Patent Office as "Uneeda Biscuit." With its new marketing techniques and advertising program, Uneeda Biscuit developed sales of over ten million packages a month by 1902 and towered over all competitors, whose total cracker sales were only forty thousand.[56]

Uneeda Biscuit was a concrete example, which people understood, and Harrison used it to drive home his point. He explained—"When you advertise U-need-a Biscuit incessantly," "people will want it." Similarly, when you "advertise democracy incessantly the people to whom you trumpet forth its deliciousness are likely to believe you, take you at your word, and, later on, demand that you make good and furnish them with the article for which you yourself have created the appetite."[57]

The Uneeda Biscuit analogy is suggestive of how, during wartime, Harrison agitated for democracy and equality. As he explained several years later, "While the war lasted those of us who saw unpalatable truths were compelled to do one of two things: either tell the truth as we saw it and go to jail, or camouflage that truth that we had to tell." In his case, he said, he "told the truth for the most part, in so far as it related to our own race relations; but, in a few cases camouflage was safer and more effective. That camouflage, however, was never of that truckling quality which was accepted by the average American editor to such a nauseating degree." Harrison emphasized, "I was well aware that Woodrow Wilson's protestations of democracy were lying protestations, consciously and deliberately designed to deceive. . . . I chose to pretend that

Woodrow Wilson meant what he said, because by so doing I safely held up to contempt and ridicule the undemocratic practices of his administration and the actions of his white countrymen in regard to the Negro."[58]

Beyond his general comments on the war, Harrison also delved into concrete analysis of specific international situations. One matter that aroused his concern was Haiti. On July 28, 1915, the United States sent three hundred and thirty marines into Haiti in what was originally purported to be a short-term measure to counter any efforts by Germany to establish submarine bases that would threaten Panama Canal shipping. The invasion, according to historian Hans Schmidt, was "a logical extension of America's quest for empire." In this case the occupation lasted until August 1934 and led to what Harrison later described as "unlicenced butchery and horror" upon both "Hayti [where some 15,000 people reportedly died] and Santo Domingo."[59]

Following the invasion, around August 19, 1915, Harrison prepared some notes for a historical talk on Toussaint-Louverture and the revolution in Haiti. Though no copy of the talk remains, his notes indicate that he discussed the international slave trade, which he claimed absorbed 100,000 people per year by 1778 (not including the 15,000 corpses thrown overboard each year) and included 20,000 slaves sent to Haiti. He paid particular attention to the "Condition of Mulattoes," some of whom were rich proprietors and all of whom were a "sort of public property" subject to public humiliation "(like Negroes of [the] South)." Harrison added (in an analysis that predated by over twenty years a similar one developed by C. L. R. James in the *The Black Jacobins: Toussaint L'Ouverture and the San Domingo Revolution*) that such discriminatory treatment helped to explain the "consequent revolutionary character" of mulattoes in Haiti during the revolution. In discussing Toussaint-Louverture, Harrison emphasized how he read and imbibed the prediction of the Abbé G. T. F. Raynal that "a courageous chief" was wanted to lead the "vexed, oppressed, and tormented." The talk then outlined key elements of Toussaint-Louverture's life, and it discussed the influence of the American and French Revolutions and the doctrine of the rights of man on the "petits-blancs, mulattoes & Negroes" and on the Haitian Revolution.[60]

While Harrison was delivering his increasingly race-conscious talks, he also wrote a supportive letter, dated October 4, 1915, to Cyril V. Briggs, editor of the *Colored American Review*. The Nevis-born Briggs, who later founded the race- and class-conscious African Blood Brotherhood and became a prominent member of the Communist Party, started the probusiness publication on October 1, 1915, with "no white men on its staff and no white [financial] backers." The first issue explained that it aimed to "enlighten the struggling colored business man"; to promote "every honest and worthy Negro business man or firm, and also the white business men and firms that employ colored help"; and to criticize "all Negro business men and firms . . . who allow themselves to be used as the tools of dishonest white business men and firms, in depriving the race not only of their honest savings, but impeding our progress as a whole." Harrison wrote that he publicly supported the magazine's ideas and the publication was "great stuff"—"just what we have needed for years!" He added that "every person who respects himself and the race to which he belongs will give you 'God speed.'"[61]

In the December issue, edited by Lovett Fort-Whiteman (another future prominent Black Communist; he would also lead the communist-led American Negro Labor Congress), Harrison was listed as a contributing editor. He was scheduled to present "the opinions of leading Negroes" on Booker T. Washington, who had died on November 14, 1915. When the article on Washington eventually appeared in January 1916, however, Harrison was not listed as its compiler. Harrison did, however, contribute his poem "The Black Man's Burden (A Reply to Rudyard Kipling)." It was his response to Kipling's famous 1899 poem "The White Man's Burden," and it was written under the pseudonym "Gunga Din," the name of the young Indian water bearer in Kipling's similarly famous 1892 poem of that name. Harrison's poem offered a pointed response to Kipling from the perspective of one on the other side of the "color line." It read in part:

> Take up the Black Man's Burden
>   Send forth the worst ye breed,
> And bind our sons in shackles
>   To serve your selfish greed
> To wait in heavy harness
>   Be-deviled and beguiled
> Until the Fates remove you
>   From a world you have defiled.
> (2)
> Take up the Black Man's burden—
>   Your lies may still abide
> To veil the threat of terror
>   And check your racial pride;
> Your cannon, church and courthouse
>   May still our sons constrain
> To seek the white man's profit
>   And work the white man's grain
> (3)
> Take up the Black Man's burden—
>   Reach out and hog the earth,
> And leave your workers hungry
>   In the country of their birth

Then when your goal is nearest,
  The end to which you fought,
Watch others' trained efficiency
  Bring all your hope to naught.

. . . .

(6)
Take up the Black Man's burden—
  Ye cannot stoop to less.
Will not your fraud of freedom
  Still cloak your greediness?
But, by the gods ye worship,
  And by the deeds ye do,
These silent, sullen peoples
  Shall weight your gods and you.
(7)
Take up the Black Man's burden—
  Until the tale is told,
Until the balances of hate
  Bear down the beam of gold
And while ye wait remember
  That Justice, though delayed,
Will hold you as your debtor, till
  The Black Man's debt is paid.[62]

————

In the latter part of 1915 there were also several political and social developments and activities that drew Harrison's attention. In October and early November he began, for the first time, to apply the race-first principle of to the
electoral arena while delivering open-air lectures on Wall Street among wealthy
campaign contributors. In his talks he described a new mood among Black voters, warned that the Black vote would no longer be easily marshaled by the established parties, and advised that the "colored editors who said that they could
control the Negro vote were simply telling lies." From that time on, he noted, it
became more difficult for the old-style political "leaders" to get money for their
campaigns.[63]

    Around December 1915, after eighteen months of inactivity, Harrison began
to participate actively with the fraternal order of Odd Fellows. He was appointed
recording secretary to the Vice-Grand Dragon, served on four committees, including the sick committee, and suggested the formation of a legal committee.
He subsequently was elected executive secretary on March 24, 1916, started on

his way through the chairs, and was elected Vice-Grand of his lodge on June 23, 1916.[64]

In late 1915 there was also an incident that spurred Harrison to seek to assume more leadership in the Black community. The incident was a talk by Kelly Miller of Howard University at the Sunrise Club in New York. Miller, a professor of mathematics and sociology and a nationally prominent Black intellectual, "shocked" Harrison with his "ignorance of modern science and modern thought." Harrison described Miller's biology as "of the brand of Pliny who lived about eighteen hundred years ago" and added that he made it appear that "Darwin and Spencer and Jacques Loeb [one of America's most well known scientists] had never existed nor written." In his diary Harrison described Miller's "ignorance of the A.B.C.'s of astronomy and geology" as "pitiful." Some years later, in a review of Miller's book *The Everlasting Stain*, he again portrayed him as "innocent of learning" and said his book didn't "illuminate the racial discussion with a single idea or a solitary item of knowledge."[65]

After hearing Miller's talk, Harrison was convinced that Miller, like many other Black leaders, did not have enough political perspective, understanding of the psychology of the Black masses, or familiarity with contemporary scientific thought to lead African Americans forward. It was a criticism he would repeatedly offer of other Black leaders who failed to provide independent, modern, non-white-dominated ideas and leadership to African Americans. In early 1922, while noting the difficulty that Claude McKay and J. A. Rogers had in being "discovered" by such leaders, Harrison commented: "The truth is that many of our 'brightest' minds have not yet developed any intellect of their own." They could give a brilliant exposition on George Bernard Shaw, Paul Laurence Dunbar, or the Prix Goncourt–winning novelist René Maran only if the subject had "previously been explained for them." Harrison felt that leaders like Du Bois, James Weldon Johnson, Chandler Owen, A. Philip Randolph, Shaw University's Benjamin Brawley, and Miller, when forced to form their own opinions, were "stuck"—the required "quality of independent judgment that is certain of itself and sure of its ground" was lacking in such leaders, who regularly substituted "'education' (which can be poured into a person)" for "intellect, which is one's own." In contrast, he would positively cite philosopher-educator-author Alain Leroy Locke, the Howard University research scientist Ernest Everett Just, and Hodge Kirnon as examples of people who "can think for themselves in the face of a new fact." By 1910, however, Harrison's dissatisfaction with the old-style leaders would spur his own plans to exert the leadership that he felt was needed.[66]

In March 1916, as he continued to concentrate his activities on the Harlem Black community, Harrison began what would be his first published theater criticism. His previous efforts on "Negro Society and the Negro Stage" had helped to focus his thoughts, but they were not published until 1917. His new work shed light on the contemporary stage, the cultural level of the African American community, and the role of art in society. It also created a stir as it exposed the subservience to advertisers of a major New York Black weekly, the *Amsterdam News*.[67]

Harrison's review, "Leaves Torn from the Diary of a Critic—the Race in Drama," was sold to the *Amsterdam News* and appeared in July 1916. As was his style, "praise and blame were honestly distributed." He traced the evolution of the Anita Bush Stock Company into the Lafayette Stock Company, recounted Bush's idea "to present colored actors in the legitimate 'drama,'" and noted how this innovation "took." He praised the outstanding work of the original company of Bush, Carlotta Freeman, Dooley Wilson, Andrew Bishop, and Charles Gilpin (all of whom had significant acting careers), and, though "they had their defects," he emphasized that "to them belongs all the credit of courageous pioneers." In contrast, he criticized the Lincoln Theater plays written by Billie Burke, a white promoter, as "beneath contempt in structure, plot, and dialog." He cited examples of white, aristocratic young ladies of the pre–Civil War South speaking 1915 Bowery slang and "lurid" Indian plays in which "every other remark was punctuated by gunplay or knife flourish."[68]

His opinions of the actors and actresses were drawn from his diary and had a certain "outspoken quality" and "lack of form." In reviewing his notes from March 30, he commented that he had been to the Lafayette Theatre twice that week to see the Lafayette Stock Company perform *Within the Law*. He concluded that, "taken all in all, the Lafayette Stock Company is the greatest aggregation of colored actors that ever trod the boards." In particular he praised Gilpin as "an actor every inch, an actor who played every part assigned with the same brilliancy of conception and superb finish of execution," and whose "genius . . . shone forth conspicuously from the very first," despite the "handicap" of the plays.[69]

In discussing the Lincoln Stock Company, which replaced the Lafayette Players at the Lincoln, Harrison praised their stage manager for excellent selection of actors for proper roles and for accomplished training and drilling of the performers. He also evaluated the performances of three "fairly good actors"—Clarence Muse, his wife, Ophelia Muse, and Charles H. Olden—as well as the "less praiseworthy effort" offered by Miss Mattie Wilkes. After further even-handed comments on Cleo Desmond, Mrs. Charles H. Anderson, and J. Frances Mores, he again praised Gilpin, whose performance as Police Inspector Burke was described as "peerless." Harrison observed: "It doesn't seem to matter what part he plays. One comes to expect perfection of him as one does the sun." Interestingly, in 1924 Gilpin, who by that time had earned major acclaim in the title role of Eugene O'Neill's *The Emperor Jones*, authorized Harrison to serve as his agent.[70]

Figure 9.1. Charles Gilpin, c. 1920–1930. In 1915 and 1916 Harrison wrote a number of theater reviews, which developed the theme that the "Negro Theater" revealed the "social mind . . . of the Negro." His decision to concentrate on race-conscious work in the Black community was made through the frontier of art. He paid particular attention to the pioneering work of the Anita Bush Stock Company and the Lafayette Stock Company, which he described as "the greatest aggregation of colored actors that ever trod the boards." He described Charles Gilpin (1878–1930), who performed with both companies, as "an actor every inch, an actor who played every part assigned with the same brilliancy of conception and superb finish of execution," and whose "genius . . . shone forth conspicuously from the very first." Harrison later wrote a review of Gilpin in *The Emperor Jones* that was highly praised by playwright Eugene O'Neill, and Harrison also served as an agent for Gilpin. *Source:* Courtesy of the Library of Congress.

Harrison also described two controversies that arose after he completed his review. First, when he spoke with another drama critic up the street who was "indiscriminately 'boosting' rotten plays and bad ac[t]ing 'somewhere in Harlem,'" the critic rationalized his subservience by saying that though the plays he praised were childish and silly, the "colored people of Harlem could not appreciate anything better." Harrison opposed this view pointedly and argued that "the 'standing room only' after two o'clock at the [1,250- to 2,000-seat] Lafayette proves that our section of New York now knows what is good, and can also insist on getting it."[71]

A second controversy arose when, because of his criticisms, the proprietors of the Lincoln Theater withdrew all advertising from the *Amsterdam News*. For over a week the paper's editor made constant visits to the Lincoln seeking to regain the advertising. Harrison was appalled by this and felt that it was necessary to "tell the Negro people that a theater which made its living from them was practically denying them the right to form and express any opinion of its work except a servile, flattering one." His advice wasn't followed by the *Amsterdam News*, however, and the Lincoln advertisement was restored. One year later Harrison noted that not a word of adverse comment had appeared in the paper since his original criticism. This startling lesson would point him toward an entirely different and independent advertising policy when he eventually started his own newspaper in 1917. (Interestingly, it also appears that the *Amsterdam News* did not publish another Harrison article or review for seven full years.)[72]

Consistent with his developing political philosophy, Harrison began to propound a new thesis for Black political leadership in his indoor and outdoor lectures in the summer of 1916. His views were, in part, sparked by the Easter Rebellion, the short-lived and militant effort for Irish national self-determination that, before its defeat, proclaimed an Irish Republic during the week of April 24 through 29, 1916. Harrison's thesis was "that the Negro people of America would never amount to anything much politically until they should see fit to imitate the Irish of Britain and to organize themselves into a political party of their own whose leaders, on the basis of this large collective vote, could 'hold up' Republicans, Democrats, Socialists or any other political group of American whites." He insisted that "since Negroes in America (like Irishmen in Ireland) were defenseless," and since "lynchings and pogroms were indulged in because they cost the aggressors nothing," a "stout and costly defense" by the Black prospective victims of such terror would be the most effective means of reducing "white" attacks.[73]

Related to this political perspective, around June or July of 1916 Harrison prepared to launch a militant, race-conscious "Negro paper" of his own. The

Figures 9.2 and 9.3 (opposite page). In 1916, two young men, A. Philip Randolph (1889–1979) and Chandler Owen (1889–1967), were attentively following all of Harrison's talks at 135th Street and Lenox Avenue. Following Harrison's lead, they soon became outstanding radical orators. After dabbling with the Republicans and then the Democrats, they turned to work with the Socialist Party. Within a little over a year they would become class-first Socialists and be considered the most prominent Black Socialists in the country. Years later, Randolph still recognized Harrison's important influence and referred to him as the "Father of Harlem Radicalism."

Figure 9.2. A. Philip Randolph, c. 1918. *Source:* Courtesy of the Schomburg Center for Research in Black Culture, New York Public Library, Astor, Lenox, and Tilden Foundations.

Figure 9.3. Chandler Owen, 1918. *Source:* Courtesy of the Schomburg Center for Research in Black Culture, New York Public Library, Astor, Lenox, and Tilden Foundations.

paper was to agitate for intellectual and political independence, a new political direction, and the necessity of a stand on racial self-defense. He gave his plan to two young men who had been following his lectures, A. Philip Randolph and Chandler Owen. Though the two attended all his talks at 135th Street and Lenox Avenue, they were also attending talks at the Socialist Party's Rand School of Social Science, and neither they nor he acted on the plan until Harrison revived and implemented it in June 1917.[74]

That summer, Randolph and Owen took a different course; they formed the Independent Political Council. The IPC did not at first agitate for socialism among Harlem's African Americans but rather, according to Harrison, dabbled with the Republicans. Then, as late as June to August 1917, Owen and Randolph made weekly visits to Charles F. Murphy, boss of the powerful Tammany political machine since 1902, in an attempt to get on the Tammany (Democratic) payroll. Within a little over a year they would be the most prominent Black Socialists in the country—ardent "class-first" Socialists (whose periodical, *The Messenger*, unlike Harrison and publications he edited, would never criticize racism within the ranks of the Socialist Party). Harrison later suggested that Socialist money was the key to the "scientific radicalism" of Owen and Randolph. "The Gold Dust Twins," as he called them, became "radicals overnight" after being provided funds from the Socialists.[75]

Harrison's 1916 newspaper plan was built around race-first priorties, internationalism, political independence, mass appeal, and good editing, and it had five prongs: "news policy, editorial policy, financial support, plan of campaign, and advertising policy." It sought to provide current knowledge of international events through well digested news summaries and analysis and to interpret events in light of the "Negro's" own interests. The class-first perspective of the socialists was to be replaced with the race-first concept, and the paper was to be dedicated to "the Plain people of Negro ancestry"—"the Negro common people"—who, as "the real Negro journalism in Africa believes . . . are worthy of the best in intellect, talents, and service." The publication would strive for the "elevation of Negro manhood and Negro culture to, at least, an equal standing with any other manhood or culture."[76]

Harrison felt there was a great opportunity for a newspaper "whose editor was not compelled to hold his hand out behind for money in political campaigns, nor in front for an appointment." With a little money, he explained, "a paper could be established, independent in tones and spirit, with a bias against unreasoning affection in politics," that would combine "courtesy with courage" and "high thinking with plain speaking." He was convinced that African Americans would support "a paper which in all things maintains the principle of 'Africa First!'" ("in its racial rather than geographical sense"). This well-conceived plan "slumbered" for eleven months, however, until June 18, 1917, when Harrison resurrected it and used it as a basis for *The Voice*—the first newspaper of the "New Negro Movement"—which made its debut on July 4, 1917.[77]

With his plans for a newspaper temporarily shelved, in late 1916 Harrison's criticisms of both Republicans and Democrats increased as he pursued his policy of political independence. He was thoroughly dissatisfied with President Woodrow Wilson, whom he considered "a sayer of great things whose deeds bore no consistent relation to his words." Based on the record, he predicted that Wilson would "go out of office the most thoroughly discredited President since Andrew Johnson."[78]

Wilson's record was indeed deplorable on the race question. Though he had promised "absolutely fair dealing" with African Americans, his policies were detrimental in almost every respect. He cut back federal appointments and yielded to the opposition of such racist Southern congressional leaders as James K. Vardaman, Hoke Smith, and Ben Tillman; supported showings of the racist film *The Birth of a Nation* for himself, his cabinet, Congress, and the Supreme Court; ordered the occupation of Haiti by the U.S. Marines; maintained that segregation was in African Americans' interest; permitted civil service employment to require photographs, a policy used to bar African Americans; stood by silently as segregation was formalized in the departments of the Post Office, Treasury, and Interior, the Bureau of Engraving and Printing, and the navy; and did nothing as almost two dozen segregatory legislative attempts, including exclusion of Black immigrants, segregation of streetcars, and a ban on interracial marriages in the District of Columbia, were introduced in the House and Senate.[79]

Harrison thought that his dissatisfaction with Wilson kept clear of the "temporary aberration" of "Negro radicals like Randolph and Owen and liberals like Du Bois," who were "praising him and urging his re-election to the presidency in 1916." Du Bois later claimed that he had changed his attitude on Wilson and opted for the Republican, Charles Evans Hughes. But, Harrison, unlike Du Bois, did not feel compelled to choose the lesser evil, and he did not turn to the Republican presidential candidate; nor did he support Wilson. Instead, Harrison favored allowing both parties to work to earn Black support.[80]

Much of Harrison's effort aimed to break clear of the argument for the "lesser evil" that was the basis of Du Bois's decision in 1916 as it had been in 1912. In 1912 Wilson had promised "fair justice" to African Americans in his letter to Bishop Alexander Walters, and that led Du Bois to support Wilson and to resign from the Socialist Party after his "attitude in the political campaign ... [was] called in question." In 1916 Du Bois claimed that dissatisfaction with Wilson turned his support to the Republicans. Harrison, however, never lost sight of the vacillation and lack of clarity that he felt was demonstrated by Du Bois and other leaders, and this led him to repeatedly stress the need for a new Black leadership.[81]

Harrison's call for genuine political independence was supported by his practice. In 1916, he openly aided Ferdinand Q. Morton, leader of the United Colored Democracy, when Morton was in trouble on a Harlem street corner. The UCD, the segregated, citywide Black democratic political machine founded in 1898, was actively trying to increase its membership from the fewer than 1,000 it had in 1915 when Morton took over the leadership. Morton's task was difficult because of African American ties to the Republican Party. As recently as the turn of the century, Harrison later explained, "those Negroes who joined the Democratic Party were regarded by their fellows much as white Americans [came to] regard pacifists and pro-Germans in War time—and they were treated accordingly." When Morton faced the "angry Harlem street-crowd," Harrison successfully appealed "for fair play and a hearing on a platform from which they [the UCD] had been driven the night before." This was a clear indication of his political independence and courage since the Democratic Party was considered a "white man's party" in New York, since Harrison opposed democratic President Wilson, and since Black opposition to Wilson and the Democrats ran so high that Wilson's Harlem headquarters were wrecked on election night. Harrison's task was made somewhat easier by the fact that the Black Democrats were also starting to criticize Wilson.[82]

During the 1916 election period and into early 1917, Harrison continued to live apart from his family, though he visited the children frequently. Relations with Lin were particularly strained as he moved several times and developed relationships with other women. He nevertheless took special delight in his children's activities and on June 15 recorded some in his diary, including clever sayings and deductive reasoning from six-year old Frances and observations by five-year old Alice and four-year old Aida. In this, as in the few other diary entries concerning his children, a sense of his loving concern and joy in their activities emerges. On July 5, he noted that Frances finished her first year in school, having gone thru three half-grades (1a, 1b, and 2a) and, had he not been living apart from Lin (at 148 W. 131 St.), and "had the conditions at home been better I should have had her in 3a, at least—perhaps in 4a." That night he also mentioned that Ella, who was not otherwise identified, came to see him and for the fist time they made love, which he described as "Deliciosa!"[83]

Economic difficulties continued to beset Harrison, and on December 22, 1916, he moved to a Mrs. Dempsey's at 222 W. 134th St., and then on January 21, 1917, he moved to a Mrs. Bass's at 65 W. 132nd St. Both addresses were in the neighborhood of his family's Harlem apartment. When a female friend, Ayesha, gave him a locket to pawn to enable him to get his first pair of eyeglasses on Saturday, February 17, he noted in his diary that he "hadn't been to the house where my wife lives since Sunday—which was my first visit for a week." When he did go, his "heart was wrung" when he met a Mrs. De Knight, who told him "with the tears streaming down her face in what destitute circumstances the children were." It seemed that Lin had been seriously sick for two weeks. Hubert left what money he had after speaking with Mrs. Forrester and with Frances, who had a bad cough. He planned to go back the next day and roll up his sleeves and do what he could "to straighten things out." A little over two months later, on April 24, he wrote that he had moved again, to 649 Lenox Ave. (again in his family's neighborhood) but was taking meals at home.[84]

Though his family situation was extremely troubling, Harrison, as always, was determined to pursue his intellectual and political work. His 1916 plans for a race-first paper had not been implemented, so "America's Foremost Negro Lecturer" set about creating the conditions that could nurture such an effort. What was particularly new was his conception of, and approach to, race unity. As he later explained, many who sought race unity were unclear of what they actually meant—was it to be "unity of thought and ideas," "unity of organization," "unity of purpose," or "unity of action?" For Harrison unity of thought was neither desirable nor possible except in the graveyard, and unity of organization was exceedingly difficult and unlikely. Unity of purpose was, however, a real possibility, and the fault with previous efforts was that the uniters (such as Washington and Du Bois) had "generally gone at the problem from the wrong end." As he explained, "they have begun at the top when they should have begun at the bottom." "To attempt to unite the 'intellectuals' at the top" was "not the same thing as uniting the Negro masses," who were the key to racial solidarity.[85]

Interestingly, in his 1940 autobiography, *Dusk of Dawn*, Du Bois reached a similar conclusion. As Du Bois explained, Booker T. Washington had proposed "a flight of class from mass in wealth with the idea of escaping the masses or ruling the masses through power placed by white capitalists." Du Bois added that he, in turn, had opted for "flight of class from mass through the development of a Talented Tenth; but the power of this aristocracy of talent was to lie in its knowledge and talent and not in its wealth." The problem with this, he wrote, was that it, too, "left controls to wealth," a problem that he admitted he never foresaw. By 1940 Du Bois concluded that "the mass and class must unite for the world's salvation." This was the position—the unity of the leadership class with the masses—that Harrison arrived at in 1916.[86]

During the winter of 1916–17, Harrison moved his outdoor lectures indoors and held regular weekly talks at Lafayette Hall, renamed by him the "Temple of Truth." These talks were his effort at developing race unity from the bottom up, at reaching "the Negro common people." By December 1916, the free lectures on Sundays at eight P.M. were firmly established. Eleven years later he described "Harlem's First and Foremost Forum" as the one that he organized in 1916. At that time the forum was founded, he said, "Harlem Negroes gathered to discuss only two topics: Religion and politics," but "this Forum not only discussed sociology, economics, the drama, literature, history and science—it preached the propaganda of RACE when no one else had courage or initiative enough to do so. It was the earliest promoter of the study of Negro history in Harlem and many hundreds and thousands of Harlemites drew their earliest inspiration from it."[87]

His talks increasingly focused on political leadership and centered on his understanding of the role of the masses. He was interested in developing "a New leadership," which was to be "based not upon the ignorance of the masses, but their intelligence." The old leadership was able to maintain itself "partly because the masses were ignorant," he said, but, as African Americans became more educated and literate and gained more access to educational facilities, there would be a basis for challenging the old leadership.[88]

It was with such aims clearly in mind that Harrison presented his December 10 talk on "Infidelity Among Our Ministers." He sought to challenge the leadership position of the clergy, a leadership that he felt was rooted, in part, in the masses' ignorance of historical criticism and modern science. The iconoclastic Harrison argued that the Bible was not the word of God, that Moses didn't write its first five books, that the Apostles didn't write the Gospels, and that these views were known and "advocated by the most prominent Christian Ministers," including the Archbishop of Canterbury and Henry Ward Beecher. It was likely a lively presentation since Beecher, a Congregationalist clergyman, was a well known abolitionist and public speaker who believed in evolution and rejected the resurrection and whose adultery trial was one of the most famous trials of the nineteenth century.[89]

His December 17 lecture was entitled "Where Did Man Come From?" and handouts emphasized that crowds at his talks were made up of "White and Colored" men and women. The handouts were printed by the Black-owned Cosmo-Advocate Publishing Company, possessor of Harlem's first multigraph machine, whose officers included three Barbados-born activists, Orlando M. Thompson, Isaac Newton Braithwaite, and Richard B. Moore. In 1917 they would print Harrison's first book. Thompson and Braithwaite would subsequently become leaders in the Garvey movement, and Moore would become a prominent Black socialist and then communist.[90]

Harrison's December 24 talk, "When the Negro Wakes: A Lecture of 'The Manhood Movement' Among the Negro People of America," drew a large crowd and stands as the birthday of the "New Negro Manhood Movement." The crowd size made it clear that a larger hall was needed. The lecture discussed "the Social and Political Strivings of the Negro-Americans," the meaning of the last election, and "the failure of some of our foremost leaders." Harrison added entertainment to the program and included operatic singer Pauline Dempsey, composer-pianist DeKoven Thompson, and two good friends—vocalist and

Figure 9.4. Richard B. Moore, 1919. Barbados-born Richard B. Moore (1893–1978) followed Harrison's talks and became an outstanding Socialist then Communist orator and activist. In 1916 and 1917 he worked with the Cosmo-Advocate Printing Company, which printed Harrison's handouts for his first Liberty League rally and printed Harrison's first book, *The Negro and the Nation*. Moore was led into book collecting by Harrison in 1918 and then later owned an important Harlem bookstore. In later years he remained a prominent Caribbean militant in Harlem and actively worked to keep Harrison's memory alive. *Source:* Courtesy of Joyce Moore Turner.

actress Abbie Mitchell from the Lafayette Stock Company and organist and musical director Melville Charlton. A week later, on December 31, Harrison lectured before the Paterson Philosophical Society at eight P.M. on "Shall the Negro Become the Dominating Race?"[91]

Harrison's probing lecture on Negro psychology—"The Art of the Theater and How to Understand It: With Especial Reference to the Lafayette Stock Company," had been scheduled for December 24 and was rescheduled for January 7 at the Temple of Truth. It was a more developed version of his views on the Black theater and included evaluations of current actors and actresses in an attempt to meet the pressing need for "helpful and enlightening criticism." He began

Figure 9.5. Melville Charlton, undated. The musician Melville Charlton (1880–1973) was a close personal and political friend of Harrison. He was the first African American to pass the academic examination of the American Guild of Organists and served as organist at the Union Theological Seminary, at the Jewish Temple of Covenant, and at St. Philip's Episcopal Church on 134th St. in Harlem. He performed at Harrison's Temple of Truth in 1916, at the founding meeting of the Liberty League in 1917, and at various Harrison-led activities throughout the 1920s. *Source:* Courtesy of the Hubert H. Harrison Papers, Rare Book and Manuscript Library, Butler Library, Columbia University, New York.

by explaining that the function of the critic was not to find fault but to interpret and explain so that listeners were able "to perceive for themselves" whether the subject "is either good or bad—and why." The critic's duty was to help the observer see and understand what the art in general and the production in particular aimed to do and whether the goal was accomplished. Good criticism, he explained, would help theatergoers "to form reasoned judgments of their own" and gain an intelligent understanding of what they saw and heard.[92]

After discussing the function of the critic, Harrison turned to the theme of "The Stage [as] a Mirror of Social Life" and emphasized "the part which the people play" in shaping the contemporary stage. He explained the role of the author who builds a play from the facts which the playgoers of the time consider "interesting, valuable, or reasonable." The drama thus drew its material from social situations as understood in its day, whether the subject matter was contemporary or historic, like the treatment that the Irish playwright and Fabian socialist George Bernard Shaw gave Jesus and the Christian church in *Androcles and the Lion*.[93]

Harrison's social interpretation of the theater emphasized that drama was a social product and its "social character" could be expressed either through the point of view of the audience, or of the author. The preferences and aversions of theatergoers "express[ed] the social forces (intellectual, artistic and moral) . . . in society," and the dramatist had to keep an eye on them to build a play. In so doing, the dramatist reflected the audience. The drama was thus "a presented picture of human beings in their social relations," and the writer's selection of a subject reflected "the nature and conditions of any society," which, in turn, were reflected in the drama.[94]

These talks were intellectual, but they could also inspire a deep racial pride. On January 14, 1917, Harrison spoke at the Temple of Truth on "The Social Leadership of the Mulatto." He expounded the thesis that "there is no color-prejudice in America except among colored people," prompting John E. Bruce, in a review, to comment that "those who know Mr. Hubert Harrison will not accuse him of being a moral or physical coward. He isn't." According to Bruce, Harrison explained how the stage, which supported a so-called Negro drama, was used to emphasize "the erroneous idea that the Colored element, not the black race, is the superior of the black race." He also described how so many of the stage actors were "so fair as to be almost undistinguishable from white people." Then, after criticizing the "Colored" practices of complexion bleaching and hair straightening so as not to be "mistaken for Negroes," Harrison described how "these 'Colored' people balk at the term 'Negro,' regarding it as offensive and insulting when applied to them as a class," yet they don't balk at the money which "Negroes" pay to see them perform.[95]

Harrison also explored the mulatto's obsession "with the idea that his color, his hair and his infusion of 'white blood'" were things "to be proud of" and made one "far superior to the black." He cited "the silly attempts" of mulattoes in Washington, D.C.; Charleston, S.C.; Cleveland, Ohio; and the West Indies "to organize 'Lily White' societies of 'Colored' people with the hope of popularizing the idea that the near white Negro is different." He also criticized the color prejudice practiced in some "Colored" churches and cemeteries and again emphasized that "there is more color prejudice among Negroes against Negroes than exists among white people against Negroes." Harrison also sarcastically added that "these 'Colored' people, who hate to be called Negroes, . . . are to-day the self-appointed spokesmen of the Negro, when not appointed by white men to be our Moses."[96]

Harrison later explained that he objected "to the high wall of caste, based on the ground of color" that light-skinned Black people erected and that so many "black Negroes have heretofore worshipped." He considered it a "degrading view" to think "that a man who is but half a Negro is twice as worthy of their respect and support as one who is entirely Black." He did not approve of the selection of race leaders because of the lightness of their skin, and he was firmly of the opinion that as long as Black people continued to "acquiesce in the selection of leaders on the grounds of their unlikeliness to our racial type," just so long would the race face the argument "that white blood is necessary to make a Negro worth while." Such "'colored' men," when "addressing the whites on behalf of some privilege which they wished to share with them, would be in words, as black as the ace of spades," yet, "when it came to mixing with 'their kind,' they were professional lily-whites." Harrison argued against such color preferences, which he viewed as detrimental to the interests of the African American masses.[97]

The Temple of Truth lectures continued. On January 21, 1917, Harrison spoke on "The War in Europe and What It Means to the Darker Races" and included a reading of his powerful poem, "The Black Man's Burden." He followed this with talks on every Sunday in February on "The Play and What it Means," "Lincoln and Liberty: Fact Versus Fiction," "The Actors and What They Do," and "The Lafayette Stock Company, or The Theatre in Our Midst." In this period he also began a Monday-night class on drama at his apartment at 65 W. 132nd streets on February 5, and he delivered a talk on "Historical Materialism" for the New York Secular Society at the Harlem Masonic Hall, 310 Lenox Avenue at 126th Street.[98]

The February lectures were followed by "Six Lectures on Sex" on Sunday nights at the Temple of Truth from March 17 through April 22. The topics included: "The Sexual Appeal of Spiritualism and Some Other Religions," which set out to explain "why women who have no husbands flock to Spiritualist and Revival Meetings"; "Marriage Versus Free Love," which pointed out "the difference between what we like to say and what we like to do"; "Is Birth-Control Hurtful of Helpful?" which included "what every woman should know"; "Why Men Leave Home," which included a discussion of "whether we are monogamous by nature"; "The Origin of Our Sex Ideals," which discussed the history of civilization and religion; and "The Society for the Suppression of Vice: The Value and Meaning of its Work," which discussed Anthony Comstock's organization. Sex and matters sexual were of particular interest to Harrison; Richard Bruce Nugent, who knew Harrison in the 1920s, notes in his book *Gay Rebel of the Harlem Renaissance*, that Harrison's "superlative collection of erotica literature" was "second to none in New York."[99]

By early 1917, in response to the racial oppression, glaring racial inequality, and white supremacy of U.S. society as well as the "white-first" attitude of the organized labor movement and the Socialist Party, Harrison had developed a race-conscious, race-first message. That core message, which became more pronounced during the sacrifices and social upheaval of the First World War, would remain his political staple for the rest of his life. As he explained it, the war, "by virtue of its great advertising campaign for democracy and the promises ... held out to subject peoples ... fertilized" the "Race Consciousness of the Negro people." It chiseled "the channels of race-consciousness deeper among American Negroes than any previous external circumstances," and it nurtured that which bloomed in the hearts of "the Negro masses"—"racialism, race-consciousness, racial solidarity." Harrison's call to race consciousness would become the center of his strategic perspective, and it was basically a call to African Americans to recognize the racial oppression they faced and to use that awareness to unite, organize, and respond as a group.[100]

This was necessary, he concluded, because "white American labor" and "white people" were "pronouncedly anti-Negro." Until that situation changed, Harrison advocated an active policy. Later, in the *Negro World*, he explained his dissatisfaction with strategies that sought "to secure certain results by affecting the minds of white people" when, in fact, African Americans had "no control" over those minds and had "absolutely no answer to the question, 'What steps do you propose to take if those minds at which you are aiming remain unaffected?'" As an alternate strategy he advocated "the mobilizing of the Negro's political power, pocket book power and intellectual power," which were "within the Negro's control," in order "to do for the Negro the things which the Negro needs to have done." This would be accomplished "without depending upon or waiting for the co-operative action of white people." Though interracial cooperation, whenever it came, would be "a boon" that "no Negro, intelligent or unintelligent" would "despise," he emphasized, that Black people could not "afford to predicate the progress of the Negro upon such co-operative action" because such action "may not come."[101]

At first, in the early stages from perhaps 1915 through around 1920, Harrison advocated the propagandistic doctrine of race first. He considered it "propaganda" and described it as "a response to the Class First of the Socialists" and to the "America First" put forth by Woodrow Wilson. Harrison emphasized to the Socialists: "We say Race First, because you have all along insisted on [white] Race First and class after when you didn't need our help."[102]

J. A. Rogers explained that since white American Socialists "habitually thought 'White First,'" Harrison's slogan "became 'Race First'—in opposition to his earlier socialistic one of 'Class First.'" Though he still considered himself a socialist at this time—he simply refused to put "either Socialism or . . . [the Socialist] party above the call of his race." As the war progressed, if Blacks functioned "in terms of 'America First,' or 'Class First,' they would be neglecting their own interests—at least until the time that the Whites—socialist-minded and otherwise—underwent a real change of heart." Hence, explained Rogers, Harrison argued "in self-defense, Negroes must think 'Negro First.'"[103]

When first developed, Harrison's "race-first" call seemed to be a reflexive response to both the "white-race-first" of the Socialist Party and the labor move-ment and to the inadequacy of the Socialists' "class-first" call in the face of class *and* racial oppression. Over time, Harrison replaced his call for "race first" with a call to develop "race consciousness." Though the phrases were at times inter-changeable, the call to race consciousness suggested a broader and deeper ap-peal, more compatible with class consciousness, more temporal and not rigidly deterministic. It is this message that his children remembered Harrison deliver-ing. There was, however, overlap in his use of the slogans, and nowhere did he clearly compare and differentiate the two concepts.[104]

In his writings Harrison would explain that race consciousness was needed as a self-defense measure under existing societal conditions and that it was a necessary corrective to white supremacy. It was also a strategic component in the struggle for a racially just and socialist society. Thus, where "the feeling of racial superiority" among the white population was pronounced, there was necessarily produced "in the mind of the masses of the black, brown and yellow peoples" what is termed in psychology "a protective reaction." This protective reaction was "race consciousness," and, like loyalty, it was "neither an evil nor a good." The "good or evil of it" depended "upon the uses to which it is put." As long as the outer situation remained the same, reasoned Harrison: "we must evoke race-consciousness to furnish a background for our aspirations, readers for our writers, a clientele for our artists and professional people, and ideals for our future."[105]

Race consciousness took various forms. Harrison cited opposition to "Jim Crow," objection to "educational starvation," "racial independence in business," opposition to mimicking "whites," rejection of "our conservative leaders," and "reaching out into new fields of endeavor" as manifestations. The slogan did not mean that Blacks "hate white people," he noted, but it did mean "that in sheer self-defense, we too must put race very high on our list of necessities." If such effort hadn't been made all along, there would have been no "'Negro progress' to boast about" as proof of equal human potential. Black churches, newspapers, life-insurance companies, banks, fraternities, colleges and political appointees all indicated Black race consciousness.[106]

Organizing efforts among working people offer a clear example of what Har-rison's race conscious message entailed. Essentially, it was an active policy that did not wait for "white" labor to act in its own class interest by struggling against white supremacy. Harrison pointed out that "the Black worker was opposed by the general run of white working men, who kept him out of their unions for the most part and yet called him 'scab' for getting their jobs at the only time when those jobs were available to him." Though he called on Black workers to support "the program of the advanced labor movement in this country," he also advocated that African American workers—when confronted by racist unions—"form your own unions." By 1921 he would urge the use of "every effort to line up all Colored workers in unions composed of Colored workers only." These unions could then "co-operate in every possible way with the white unions," when "allowed that right." He considered this policy not "the best," but "the most helpful."[107]

The strategic importance of this race-conscious message in terms of labor would be revealed in 1920, in a review of labor leader William Z. Foster's *The Great Steel Strike*. Foster, arguably the preeminent militant labor leader of that era, a former member of both the Socialist Party and the IWW and a future prominent leader of the Communist Party, wrote that Black workers expressed "open hostility" to organized labor, "allowed themselves to be used freely as strikebreakers," often took a "keen delight in stealing the white men's jobs," and in general made "a wretched showing" during the strike. He argued that "the best negro leaders must join wholeheartedly in destroying the pernicious anti-union policies so deeply rooted among their people." Harrison, who held no brief for "white men's jobs," countered that it was a principal duty of whites to oppose white supremacy and that until that was done there would be little prospect for real joint effort:

> It is up to the white unions and the American Federation of Labor and the great railroad brotherhoods themselves and not up to the Negro leaders to change this deep seated aversion which American Negroes have for white American labor. It is conceded on all sides that the white organized labor movement has been and still is pronouncedly anti-Negro. And as long as that remains true, just so long will self-respecting Negro leaders abstain from urging the laboring masses of their race to join forces with the stupid and short-sighted labor oligarchy which refuses to join forces with them.[108]

In 1921 Harrison offered more on the importance to his strategic perspective of both race consciousness by African Americans and white opposition to racism. After clarifying that the principal enemy of the darker peoples of the world was "capitalist imperialism" and its "economic motive," he explained that "structures of racial self-protection" were "defensive structures" that arose in response to white "racial solidarity." He emphasized that it was particularly the task of white revolutionists to "show their sincerity by first breaking down the exclusion walls of white working men before they ask us to demolish our own defensive structures of racial self-protection." The reason was that Black race consciousness "arose as a consequence of the former, and the cause should be removed before the consequence can fairly be expected to disappear." He emphasized that those "who will meet us on our common ground will find that we recognize a common enemy in the present world order and are willing to advance to attack it in our joint behalf."[109]

For Harrison, the key to the class question and to class unity was the breaking down of white racial solidarity and the system of racial oppression. Harrison, who was a generally consistent class radical, concluded that U.S. progressives would have to go through race to get to class. Most particularly, as long as white supremacy remained, challenges would have to be made against it in order to sharpen genuine class struggle.

The particular significance of Harrison's call for race consciousness should not be overlooked. The historian Nathan Huggins in his perceptive *Harlem Renaissance* has argued that race consciousness "most likely leads to provincialism," that it can be tied to an identity crisis and to race guilt, and that it is often reflected in a hatred of whites. In Harrison's case, however, we see something quite different. Rather than a provincial, he was a genuinely well educated (though self-educated) and critically independent intellectual. He had traveled some, he kept abreast of domestic and international events, and he was well versed in modern and scientific thought, history, politics, literature, and the arts. He was not undergoing an identity crisis or expressing race guilt; rather, he quite rationally and in a well thought out fashion was attempting to point a way forward. His analysis was based on his study of society as well as his understanding of the role that subjective elements play in determining human actions.[110]

Rather than moving from a "white hate" analysis, Harrison, an internationalist and a true educator, was approaching the Black masses with a call for self- and group awareness. Quite simply, after considerable practical experience and intellectual analysis, he had concluded that as long as the United States remained a white-supremacist society, a needed and necessary corrective, in the interest of all, was for African Americans to develop race consciousness. In the United States, where a system of racial oppression was central to capitalist rule, in order to wage effective class struggle, the people would have to struggle against the supremacy of "the white race."

With his understanding of the need for Black people to develop race consciousness clear, Harrison, by early 1917, was ready to implement his plans for a new organization and newspaper. The organization would be the Liberty League, and the paper, *The Voice*. They would begin in the summer of 1917.

10

Founding the
Liberty League and *The Voice*
(April–September 1917)

In November 1916 Woodrow Wilson was elected to his second term as president of the United States on the slogan "He Kept Us Out of War." Five months later, on April 2, 1917, without strong popular support, he went before a joint session of Congress and formally requested a declaration of war against Germany while proclaiming that "the world must be made safe for democracy." On April 4, the U.S. Senate passed the war resolution 82 to 6; on April 6 the House adopted it 373 to 50; and Wilson formally declared war on the German imperial government.[1]

As patriotic fervor swept the country, glaring examples of racial oppression—discrimination, disfranchisement, and lynching—continued to mar the land, and specific new grievances emerged. Black draftees were forced to travel separately to training camps, where they were then segregated; plans were developed for segregated camps for Black officers; and, despite the government's professed efforts at recruitment, Black military volunteers were repeatedly denied enlistment. In the month following the war declaration, attention continued to focus on lynching, especially after the horrific burning at the stake of Black woodchopper Ell Persons in a public lynching in Memphis on May 22. In New York's San Juan Hill section, a group of whites attacked a Black man on May 26, and more than 2,000 combatants were involved in an ensuing "race riot," in which a Black man was killed by a policeman. This was followed by additional "race riots" in the San Juan Hill area on June 18 and July 3. To African Americans and others, such racial injustice flew in the face of the government's patriotic exhortations and calls for democracy.[2]

As the war effort unfolded it brought important changes to U.S. society, including new employment, travel, social, and political opportunities. Labor and loyalty were needed, and the dominant classes were forced to respond to demands from the general population. The mobilization and entrance into the war, according to historian Judith Stein, quickly "enhanced the power of the masses." Harlem, in particular, was transformed. Its population grew from almost 50,000 to 73,000 between 1914 and 1920, and it changed from a predominantly white, semirural, middle-class community into "the Negro metropolis." The exodus of whites and influx of Blacks created a large and concentrated Black community primed for political agitation. Political demands "summarily rejected in prewar years" now became "negotiable." The stage was set for the full blown emergence of the "New Negro Movement" in Harlem in the summer of 1917.[3]

Harrison became the principal leader in shaping this new race consciousness. His major steps in this direction occurred in the summer of 1917, when he founded the Liberty League of Negro Americans and began publishing *The Voice*, which were, respectively, the first organization and the first newspaper of the New Negro Movement. As he explained, from the Liberty League came "the mighty structures of racial propaganda" that eventually led to the Garvey movement. *The Voice* was "the first Negro journal of the new dispensation, and, for some time, the only one." It lasted, on and off, until March 1919 and effectively left its mark on the Harlem masses and on a generation of radical "New Negroes." "Unlike the Negroes of the 'old conservative crowd'" who were ever-willing to compromise the interests of the race for "a miserable pittance and some sympathy from his former master," these "New Negroes," explained Harrison, were "Negro first, Negro last, and Negro always." They demanded "no special privileges"; they wanted "equal justice before the law and equal opportunity"; and they were against the war, politically independent, and internationalist.[4]

Radical public events took off with a rally, which Harrison initiated, on June 12, 1917, at Harlem's Bethel African Methodist Episcopal Church, at 52-60 W. 132nd Street off Lenox Avenue. Financial resources for the 8 P.M. event were limited, no preliminary advertising was done in the press, and the public was only notified through word-of-mouth and through one handout, which invited all who believe in "Negro Manhood" and "Negro Womanhood" and who love "Your Country" and "Your Race" to attend a "Mass Meeting of Colored Citizens." The meeting's aim was to "Stop Lynching and Disfranchisement in the Land Which We Love and Make the South 'Safe For Democracy.'" Music was to be provided by bandmaster E. E. Thompson, and speakers would include Harrison, the young activist Chandler Owen, Dr. Adam Clayton Powell Sr., the pastor of the Abyssinian Baptist Church, and other prominent ministers and laymen.[5]

Bethel A.M.E. Church had a history of activism, particularly since the period of 1907 through 1912 when it was headed by the Socialist minister Reverdy C. Ransom. The fact that Harrison, the long-time freethought agitator, scheduled his first organizational mass meeting at a church was probably dictated by space

needs, but it also reflected his independence, his ability to work in different set-
tings, and an awareness that the Black church was the primary arena for political activity in the Black community. It may also have been directly related to the
fact that the Rev. A. R. Cooper, Bethel's minister, had only arrived from work in
Albany, N.Y., the previous month.[6]

Harrison was ably prepared for the role he assumed. He was a popular
speaker and an exceptional writer; he had organizational experience with the
Socialists and other radicals; and he had been delivering his indoor and outdoor
lectures, which increasingly focused on the Harlem's Black community and
the racial significance of the war. His popularity had grown with his "Temple of
Truth" lectures, and he had acquired recognizable influence. As the *New Negro*
magazine later explained, Harrison had "nursed, cradled, and championed" the
"infant spirit of the New Negro"—he now "chiseled the path which 'the new
crowd'" would follow.[7]

The Bethel meeting was officially called by the Liberty League of Negro-
Americans, organized under Harrison's leadership. It represented, according
to Harrison, a "breaking away from the orthodox respectable leaders" and was
"characterized everywhere as 'the young Negro movement.'" Members were
"'Negro-Americans, loyal to their country in every respect, and obedient to her
laws.'" The League's stated purpose was to take steps to uproot the twin evils
of lynching and disfranchisement and to petition the government for a redress
of grievances. It would "carry on educational and propaganda work among Negroes" and "exercise political pressure wherever possible" in order to "abate
lynching." The League claimed to offer "the most startling program of any organization of Negroes in the country," and it demanded democracy at home for
"Negro-Americans" before they could be expected to enthuse over democracy
in Europe.[8]

At the Bethel meeting the church was packed with 2,000 people. The audience rose in support during Harrison's introduction when he demanded "that
Congress make lynching a Federal crime and take the Negro's life under national protection." Resolutions were passed calling the government's attention
to the continued violation of the Thirteenth, Fourteenth, and Fifteenth Amendments (outlawing slavery, establishing national citizenship and equal protection,
and guaranteeing the right to vote); to the existence of mob law from Florida
to New York; and to demands that lynching be made a federal crime. Lynching
was clearly the main subject, and particular attention was paid to the burning of
Ell Persons.[9]

In his Bethel talk Harrison reasoned that since lynching was murder it violated both federal and state laws and it was therefore appropriate that African
Americans take steps "to maintain the majesty of the law." His call for retaliatory self-defense urged African Americans to "put down the law-breakers by

The Actors and What They Do.

4. Sunday, Feb. 25th,

The Lafayette Stock Company, or
The Theatre In Our Midst.

For further details, see Mr. Harrison's articles in The Amsterdam News
on "The Art of The Theatre." Remember how much the actors and their

1917

STOP LYNCHING

AND

DISFRANCHISEMENT

IN

THE LAND WHICH WE LOVE

AND MAKE

THE SOUTH
"SAFE FOR DEMOCRACY"

A Mass Meeting

OF COLORED CITIZENS

WILL BE HELD AT

BETHEL CHURCH, 52-60 West 132nd Street
On TUESDAY, JUNE 12th, at 8 P. M.

UNDER THE AUSPICES OF

THE LIBERTY LEAGUE of Negro-Americans

To take steps to uproot these two evils and "to petition the government for
a redress of grievances."

IF YOU BELIEVE IN NEGRO MANHOOD
IF YOU BELIEVE IN NEGRO WOMANHOOD
IF YOU LOVE YOUR COUNTRY
IF YOU LOVE YOUR RACE

COME!

The meeting will be addressed by

MR. HUBERT H. HARRISON
MR. CHANDLER OWENS
REV. DR. CLAYTON POWELL
other prominent ministers and laymen
BANDMASTER THOMPSON
Regiment will furnish music worthy of the occasion.

N. Y.

organizing all over the South to defend their own lives whenever their right to live was invaded by mobs which the local authorities were too weak or unwilling to suppress." The League was not afraid openly to take the position that lynching would never be stopped until it became a costly business for the white people who undertook it. This was clearly a step further than the NAACP was prepared to go.[10]

Other speakers at Bethel included Reverend Cooper; a young Cornell University–educated lawyer, James C. Thomas Jr., who, later in the year, would run unsuccessfully for Alderman in Manhattan's Twenty-sixth District; and Marcus Garvey, a relatively unknown former printer from Jamaica who had spent some time in Costa Rica, England, and touring the United States. Resolutions were adopted and a petition to Congress prepared and circulated.[11]

Meeting attendees also agreed to send a telegram to the Jewish people of Russia congratulating them upon their acquisition of "full political and civil rights" and expressing the desire that the United States would soon follow Russia's democratic example. The reference to full political rights undoubtedly referred to the fact that Russian Jews—who had been subjected to pogroms, excluded from public service, and prohibited from acquiring rural land—were now celebrating new rights under the Provisional Revolutionary Government. A recent March 6, 1917, PRG proclamation had officially called for the abolition of all social, religious, and national restrictions.[12]

As the Bethel meeting progressed, two hundred dollars were raised to extend the Liberty League's work nationwide and to establish its official organ, *The Voice*, as the "medium of expression for the new demands and aspirations of the 'New Negro.'" In the elections that were held, Harrison was chosen president; Edgar Grey, a Sierra Leone–born former postal worker, secretary; and James Harris, treasurer. Another mass meeting was also scheduled for Carnegie Hall, and it was announced that similar meetings were scheduled in Boston at the same time.[13]

Figure 10.1. "Stop Lynching and Disfranchisement in the Land Which We Love and Make the South 'Safe For Democracy,'" handout, c. June 12, 1917. On June 12, 1917, a rally at Harlem's Bethel African Methodist Episcopal Church on W. 132nd Street off Lenox Avenue drew 2,000 people to the founding meeting of Harrison's "Liberty League," the first organization of the "New Negro Movement." The audience rose in support as Harrison demanded "that Congress make lynching a Federal crime"; urged support of resolutions calling for enforcement of the Thirteenth, Fourteenth, and Fifteenth Amendments (outlawing slavery, establishing national citizenship and equal protection, and guaranteeing the right to vote); encouraged retaliatory self-defense in the face of mob attack; and called for democracy for "Negro-Americans." *Source:* Courtesy of the Hubert H. Harrison Papers, Rare Book and Manuscript Library, Butler Library, Columbia University, New York.

After the meeting Harrison sped to Boston on an overnight train to attend a meeting headed by William Monroe Trotter, the editor of the *Guardian* and a long-time fighter against racial injustice. In May, in absentia, Harrison had been elected by ministers in Boston to the position of chairman of the Board of Managers of a proposed Colored National Liberty Congress. At the June 13 meeting, attended by delegates from every section of the country, Harrison urged African Americans to "rise against the government, just as the Irish against England," unless they get their rights. The conference closed with a public meeting in Faneuil Hall, the "Cradle of Liberty," at which Harrison described the New York activity. The New York and Boston organizations agreed to link up, and Harrison was elected chairman ("Grand National Organizer") of a national committee of arrangements that was to issue a call to "race patriotic citizens" and "to every Negro organization in the country" to organize Liberty and Equal Rights Committees and send delegates to "a great race-congress" in Washington, D.C., in September or October. The Liberty Congress aimed to put demands before the U.S. Congress, but, because of difficulties, it was not held until June 1918.[14]

The "Resolutions" adopted by 2,000 people at the June 12 Bethel meeting were an example of the defiant demands of militant "New Negroes," and they were to be spread around the globe in order that, when the world was made safe for democracy, Black people would "not be forgotten." The document's preamble was internationalist, placed developments in the context of the war, called for democracy at home for "Negro-Americans," and focused on civil rights, lynching, segregation, and disfranchisement. The "Preamble" began:

> *We believe that this world war will and must result in a larger measure of democracy for the peoples engaged therein—whatever may be the secret ambitions of their several rulers.*
>
> *We therefore ask, that when the war shall be ended and the council of peace shall meet to secure to every people the right to rule their own ancestral lands free from the domination of tyrants, domestic and foreign, the similar rights of the 250,000,000 Negroes of Africa be conceded. Not to concede them this is to lay the foundation for more wars in the future and to saddle the new democracies with the burden of a militarism greater than that under which the world now groans.*
>
> Secondly, we, as Negro-Americans who have poured out our blood freely in every war of the Republic, and upheld her flag with undivided loyalty, demand that since we have shared to the full measure of manhood in bearing the burdens of democracy we should also share in the rights and privileges of that democracy.
>
> And we believe that the present time, when the hearts of ninety millions of our white fellow-citizens are aflame with the passionate ardor of democracy which has carried them into the greatest war of the age with the sole purpose

of suppressing autocracy in Europe, is the best time to appeal to them to give to twelve millions of us the elementary rights of democracy at home.

For democracy, like charity, begins at home, and we find it hard to endure without murmur and with the acquiescence of our government the awful evils of lynching, which is a denial of the right to life; of segregation, Jim Crowism and peonage, which are a denial of the right to liberty; and disfranchisement, which is a denial of justice and democracy.[15]

The existence of the cited evils in the United States was contrasted with recent international developments, which "helped to make good the democratic assertions" by "countries of the old world." Three international examples were mentioned. First, "Imperial Russia, formerly the most tyrannous government in Europe," had been "transformed [since the February Revolution] into Republican Russia" as "millions of political serfs" were "lifted to the level of citizenship rights." The other two examples concerned England, which had offered "the meed of political manhood to the hitherto oppressed Irish and the down-trodden Hindu." These examples laid the basis for the resolutions of the Liberty League, which were concisely put forth:

That we, the Negro people of the first republic of the New World, ask all true friends of democracy in this country to help us to win these same precious rights for ourselves and our children;

That we invite the government's attention to the great danger which threatens democracy through the continued violation of the 13th, 14th and 15th amendments, which is a denial of justice and the existence of mob-law for Negroes from Florida to New York;

That we intend to protest and to agitate by every legal means until we win these rights from the hands of our government and induce it to protect democracy from these dangers, and square the deeds of our nations with its declarations;

That we create adequate instruments for securing these ends and make our voice heard and heeded in the councils of our country, and

That copies of these resolutions be forwarded to the Congress of the United States and to such other public bodies as shall seem proper to us.[16]

The demand for enforcement of the Fourteenth Amendment is instructive. The amendment was originally ratified in 1868 to provide citizenship rights; protection of life, liberty, and property; and equal protection under the law for African Americans. It was established to challenge white supremacy by protecting the African American masses. The amendment, however, was historically not used in this way but instead as a principal weapon in the service of big business and white supremacy. Ernest Kaiser explains that an analysis of Supreme Court decisions demonstrates that the Court "killed the Fourteenth Amendment as a bulwark against Negro discrimination and segregation but used this Amendment constantly and consistently to protect industrial capital." A 1912 study by Charles Wallace Collins argued that in the period from 1868 to 1911, out of 604 decisions involving the amendment, only 28 affected African Americans' rights and, of these, 22 were decided negatively. It was not African Americans but accumulated and organized capital that looked to the Fourteenth Amendment for protection from state activity. This was the application of the amendment that Harrison and the Liberty League aimed to reverse, and their demand for enforcement of the Fourteenth Amendment and for equal rights challenged an important intersection of ruling-class and white-supremacist interests.[17]

The Liberty League's petition to the House of Representatives was circulated at the June 12 meeting and then sent to Congress on July 4, 1917. It sought "redress of the specific grievances and flagrant violations" of U.S. law and called attention to "the discrepancy . . . between the public profession of government that we are lavishing our resources of men and money in this war in order to make the world safe for democracy, and the just as public performances of lynching-bees, Jim Crowism and disfranchisement in which our common country abounds." The petition demanded that "the nation shall justify to the world her assertions of democracy by setting free the millions of Negroes in the South from political and civil slavery through the enactment of laws which will either take the Negroes under the direct protection of the U.S. Congress by making lynching a Federal crime, or (by legislative mandate) compelling of several States which now deprive the Negroes of their right to self-government, to give them the suffrage as Russia has done for her Jews."[18]

The significance of this demand for federal antilynching legislation should not be underestimated. In 1917, according to historian Robert L. Zangrando, the NAACP, the nation's leading civil rights organization, "actually declined to make an open push for" federal antilynching legislation on the grounds that the proposed legislation was "not constitutional." For several years, in response to lynching and mob violence, its approach had been "on site investigations, efforts at prosecution [under state law], fund-raising, protest meetings, news releases, and a campaign to win passage of appropriate civil rights legislation." NAACP failure to wholeheartedly support the antilynching legislation reflected the fact that it "was reaching for southern support and still pulling its punches on the matter of federal statute." For the time being, "exposé" remained its "chief weapon." Thus, the Liberty's League's call for federal antilynching legislation was, as Harrison claimed, a "startling" initiative.[19]

Harrison later explained how the Liberty League grew out of recognition of "the need for a more radical policy than that of the N.A.A.C.P." He felt that the

NAACP made "a joke of itself" by professing "to think that lynching and other evils which beset the Negro in the South" could "be abolished by simple publicity." He argued instead for armed self-defense and for active steps to mobilize those resources "within the Negro's control" to seek to implement "the things which the Negro needs to have done."[20]

Harrison personally drew up the "Declaration of Principles" of the Liberty League, which was first published in the September 1 issue of *The Clarion*, a newspaper put out by League members. It pledged support "to the program of the manhood movement for Negroes" and "to the elevation of our race as to at least equal standing with any other race." To achieve those goals it put forth its international perspective; focused domestically on lynching, segregation, equal rights, and developing a political voice; and then called attention to its special duty to Africa and Africans worldwide.[21]

The "Declaration" began, as did so much of Harrison's political analysis, from an international perspective. It explained:

> The Liberty League of Negro-Americans was born of the great World War into which Europe entered in 1914 and the United States in 1917.
>
> Whatever the compelling causes of this conflict may have been, the participants on that side which our country has embraced are all declaring at the present time that they are fighting "to make the world safe for democracy" [and] out of this welter of war will come democracy—the right of every people to rule their own ancestral lands, free from the domination of tyrants, domestic and foreign. And this result will be attained no matter what the will of the rulers and spokesmen on either side may be. Already the Russian people, the Irish and the Hindu have seized the moment to strike for the realizing of those ideals which their respective governments professed.

In such an "era of revolutionary ferment all over the world," it reasoned, "Negro-Americans" must "voice our demands for equal justice, protection and opportunity at this time."[22]

To Harrison, international consciousness was a major difference between the "New Negro" and "Old Negro" leadership. He later described how these "first, faint stirrings of an international consciousness" developed. In the past, he explained, "one of the classic slogans of 'the old Negro' in these United States was: 'This is the only country we know anything about.'" This was said "boastfully, as if our colossal ignorance of the vast world were some thing to be proud of." That older generation of leaders knew nothing of "'Jim Crow' cars in Nigeria, a pass-system in South Africa or parks in Shang'hai [such as Huangpu Park] with such notices as 'Chinese and dogs not allowed.'" The solutions they advanced "for the Negro problem" were "tinged with the insular notion that it stood in peculiar isolation from all the other political, economic and racial problems of the world." The "Swadesha movement in India, the West African National Congress movement, the Egyptian Nationalist movement and the Senussi movement in North Africa" were "unknown to them." Then, during the war, this all began to change. Black troops came to know that "there were white men in the world to whom a dark face was not an invitation to be mean and nasty," and they met "other colored people from Senegal, Cochin-China, Cape Colony, India and Egypt." They learned "the essential similarity of their sufferings and sentiments in the shadow of that Color Line . . . [that ran] from Boston to Benares and from Tulsa to Tientsin." This was a "new Crusade" and, as in the earlier one, "the multiplication of contacts was the mother of culture" and "the very cause for which they believed that they were fighting evoked questions and speculations which reached out far beyond the parochial limits to which their 'leaders' had accustomed them."[23]

The "Declaration" then moved from the international perspective to the domestic situation and proclaimed:

> The Negro people of America feel that this is the right time to make a bold bid for some of that democracy for which their government has gone to war. They insist that the constant recurrence of horrible lynchings, where perpetrators go unpunished, and the status of disfranchisement for ten millions of Negroes living in the Southern Section of this land, can not be reconciled with any idea of liberty or democracy. And the Liberty League came into existence to voice not merely their protest, but the demand that this nation of which they are a part shall first abolish the twin evils of lynching and disfranchisement at home before it can expect the world to take seriously its professions of democracy.

It maintained that the first right of all is to their lives and this was being "denied us by mobs of our white fellow-citizens all over this land, with the continuing consent of the national government which has never taken a single step to discourage and put down lynching; and with the active connivance of state and county authorities in the south where the greater portion of our people live." Accordingly, it demanded and pledged to work for "the enactment by the U.S. Congress of such legislation as will make lynching a Federal Crime, and thus take the Negroes of America under national protection, pending the granting to them of universal adult suffrage."[24]

Harrison used the example of federal prohibition of alcoholic beverages in order to argue for federal lynching legislation. On August 1, 1917, the Senate would approve a Prohibition resolution and on December 18 it would be proposed as the Eighteenth Amendment to the U.S. Constitution by resolution of Congress. The "Declaration" stressed that the nation "makes illicit whiskey distilling a federal offense" and "invades the domain of state to put down the illicit distilling of whiskey" because it "wants the enforcement of the revenue laws" and "will not trust such cases to the local prejudices of a local court and jury." It then reasoned that since "the lives of its Negro subjects are worth more to the government than the revenues saved by the putting down of moonshiners," and since the "national government can override the state government for the raising of revenues," then "it can and should override them for the protection of life." The directness of Harrison's challenge was clear. The white South, the home of lynching and of the defense of states' rights, was also home to strong Prohibition sentiment. The logic of the Prohibition argument (federal intervention) directly challenged the logic of the white South argument (states' rights), which was used to oppose antilynching legislation.[25]

The Liberty League "Declaration" next called for "an effort to have all parts of the constitution equally enforced, as the first step toward the securing of absolutely equal political rights." If the national government refused to "protect its Negro people from murderous mob-violence," then the League was prepared to "call upon our people to defend themselves against murder with the weapons of murder." There was no mistaking this call for armed self-defense. Harrison, a long-time proponent of direct action, recognized that Southern Blacks decreased lynching by the direct action of migrating north. He would later describe how Black migration "struck a body blow at the most powerful interests in the South" and "compelled them to exert their influence against lynching." The ultimate form of direct action, however, was armed self-defense—and Harrison militantly argued that with Black life no longer cheap, "the cure follows from the nature of the cause."[26]

The "Declaration" went on to raise the radical demand for a political voice. It did so by using President Wilson's words of April 2 on the essence of democracy being "the right of those who submit to authority to have a voice in their own government." Harrison later explained that "I chose to pretend that Woodrow Wilson meant what he said, because by so doing I safely held up to contempt and ridicule the undemocratic practices of his administration and the actions of his white countrymen in regard to the Negro."[27]

In order to exercise a "political voice," the "Declaration" explained, the Liberty League was "organized to secure the ballot for every adult Negro man or woman who owe allegiance to our flag and who obey our country's laws." Attention was called to the continued violation of the Fourteenth and Fifteenth Amendments "with the consent of the national government." It declared that such violation "constituted the gravest menace to stability of that government." In its effort to obtain equal enforcement of the constitution, the "Declaration" demonstrated its political independence by urging that "the Negroes of the North, who have the ballot . . . disclaim allegiance to any and all political parties," "organize their votes independently," and "by swinging them in their own interest . . . play the same part which the Irish Home Rule party played in British politics." It stressed: "We must be loyal to our race first in everything."[28]

The "Declaration" also pointed out that the Liberty League had "an international as well as a national duty" and emphasized its responsibility to the "seventeen hundred millions" who are "colored—black and brown and yellow" and who seek to live "free from the domination of a [white] minority." The League was "ready to affiliate itself with similar organizations of the darker races in other lands; to sympathize with their just aims and afford them such aid as may be within its power." In particular, it emphasized "a special sympathy" for "the 250 millions of our brethren in Africa" and pledged to "work for the ultimate realization of democracy in Africa—for the right of these darker millions to rule their own ancestral lands—even as the people of Europe—free from the domination of foreign tyrants."[29]

The Liberty League, in June 1917, also adopted a tricolor flag. Because of the "Negro's" "dual relationship to our own and other peoples," explained Harrison, "[we] adopted as our emblem the three colors, black brown and yellow, in perpendicular stripes." These colors were chosen, because the "black, brown and yellow, [were] symbolic of the three colors of the Negro race in America." They were also, he suggested, symbolic of people of color worldwide. It was from this black, brown, and yellow tricolor that Marcus Garvey would later, according to Harrison, draw the idea for the red, black, and green tricolor racial flag which the UNIA would popularize, and which later would become identified as Black Liberation colors.[30]

At the big June 12 rally at Bethel Church that inaugurated the Liberty League, it is doubtful, as has been passed down, that Marcus Garvey "swept the whole meeting" or that "no one could match him [and he] caused all of Harrison's followers and the meeting to rally around him." Harrison was at that time unrivaled as Harlem's greatest orator; Garvey had no such reputation, nor past performance. It was Harrison's organization, not Garvey's organization, that grew in the wake of that meeting. Further, the early accounts of the rally either did not mention Garvey or barely mentioned him; it was only some years later, as he grew to mythic proportions, that the notion of Garvey sweeping the meeting was elaborated.[31]

Descriptions of Garvey's role at the Bethel Church rally actually changed considerably over the years. In *The Voice*'s initial July 4 coverage, as well as in a later reprint of the coverage in the September 19, 1917, *Voice*, no mention was made of Garvey. In September 1917 the *Jamaica Times*, quoting from the *Brooklyn Advocate*, simply mentioned that Garvey was one of the speakers at the event. Over three years later, in additions placed in a reprint of the July 4,

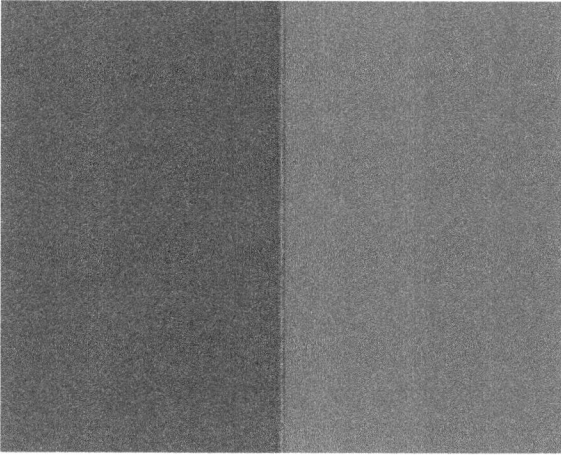

Figure 10.2. Tricolor flag of the Liberty League. Harrison explained in June 1917 that because of the "Negro's" "dual relationship to our own and other peoples" the Liberty League "adopted as our emblem the three colors, black brown and yellow" because they were "symbolic of the three colors of the Negro race in America." They were also, he suggested, symbolic of people of color worldwide. It was from this tricolor flag that Marcus Garvey would later, according to Harrison, draw the idea for the tricolor flag that his organization, the Universal Negro Improvement Association, would popularize. Garvey's red, black, and green—not Harrison's black, brown, and yellow—would become identified as Black Liberation colors. *Source:* Courtesy of Tomie Arai and Jeffrey B. Perry.

1917, article, which appeared in Harrison's second book (*When Africa Awakes*), Garvey's appearance was mentioned. This was done after Garvey was extremely well known; after Harrison had indicated his support for Garvey's movement in debate with the Black Socialists A. Philip Randolph and Chandler Owen; while Harrison was functioning as principal editor of the *Negro World*, the official organ of Garvey's UNIA; and, as Harrison's new book, a testimony to his work and a source of potential income, became available for sale. In the reprint of the original article, "The Liberty League of Negro-Americans," Harrison added that "Mr. Marcus Garvey, president of the Jamaica Improvement Association, was next introduced by Mr. Harrison [at the June 12 meeting]." This was Garvey's first introduction to a major Harlem crowd, and, according to the reprint, he "spoke in enthusiastic approval of the new movement and pledged it his hearty support." Garvey was so impressed he reportedly joined Harrison's Liberty League.[32]

In 1930, James Weldon Johnson (whose literary work had by that time been subjected to one of Harrison's pointed literary reviews) described the Bethel meeting as "Harlem's first real sight of Garvey." Johnson added that Garvey's "magnetic personality, torrential eloquence, and intuitive knowledge of crowd psychology were all brought into play" and "he swept the audience along with him." His speech was "an endorsement of the new movement and a pledge of his hearty support." Garvey, however, "was not of the kidney to support anybody's movement." He had seen the United States and Harlem and "doubtless been the keenest observer at the Liberty League organization meeting," and, according to Johnson, "it may be that it was then that he decided upon New York as the centre for his activities." An account by Charles Willis Simmons said that when Garvey spoke at Bethel Church his speech "was not for such a [Liberty] league, but for the Universal Negro Improvement Association and its programs." Based on the various accounts as well as previous and subsequent events, what is likely is that while Garvey's June 12 comments may have focused both on the Liberty League and on his own organization, his plans and energies would focus, as Simmons and Johnson suggest, on building his organization, not Harrison's Liberty League.[33]

The version of Garvey's meteoric rise to race leadership is very questionable. The Jamaica-born Garvey had come to the United States in March 1916 in order to raise funds to set up an industrial school in Jamaica along the lines of Booker T. Washington's Tuskegee Institute, which he admired. Garvey, according to Robert A. Hill, had "a static view of political abstinence," and his organization put forward fraternal benefit, race pride, mutual improvement, and cultural self-improvement as an alternative to local political action. While in Jamaica Garvey had gone so far as to state that "the society [UNIA] is non-political," and he had asked his supporters "to eschew politics as a means of social improvement." With such a program and such a past, Garvey, at first, did not fare very well in the United States. He had, in his own words, "made up his mind to return to Jamaica in the spring of 1917, when he became associated with [his old boyhood friend] Mr. W. A. Domingo and Mr. Hubert Harrison." Domingo served as assistant secretary of the Liberty League and introduced Garvey to Harrison. Though Garvey had plans to leave, he had, according to Harrison, "discovered a method of living without working." Harrison and others provided food and shelter for Garvey. Then Harrison supplied Garvey a major speaking platform on June 12, and Garvey joined Harrison's Liberty League.[34]

The notion that Garvey won followers from Harrison because of superior oratorical skills—that "Garvey swept the whole meeting" and that "no one could match him [and that he] caused all of Harrison's followers and the meeting to rally around him"—is, based on the record, not convincing. The journalist Lester A. Walton, in a review of street speaking in Harlem, described Harrison as "in a class by himself as a street speaker." In the summer of 1917 Harrison was already an oratory prize winner and a renowned public speaker. He was at the

Figure 10.3. Marcus Garvey's wedding photograph, Christmas 1919. Hubert Harrison introduced Marcus Garvey (1887–1940) to the audience at the Liberty League's first meeting (June 12, 1917) and Garvey joined Harrison's organization. A relatively unknown former printer from Jamaica, Garvey had previously planned to return to Jamaica but, inspired by Harrison's oratory, decided to stay in the United States. By September or October 1917, some members of the Liberty League began moving towards Garvey's organization, the Universal Negro Improvement Association. Former Liberty League members would play major roles in Garvey's UNIA, *Negro World*, and Black Star Line, and they would be instrumental in developing the Garvey movement into the largest race-radical movement in U.S. history. Harrison would later become the unofficial managing editor of Garvey's *Negro World*, and, despite differences with Garvey, he was a principal radical influence on the Garvey movement. *Source:* Courtesy of the Schomburg Center for Research in Black Culture, New York Public Library, Astor, Lenox, and Tilden Foundations.

height of his race-conscious, political oratory, and he was unquestionably the leading figure in the radical "New Negro movement."[35] Garvey's oratory, on the other hand, had not been all that impressive. He did not place among the winners in the one recorded elocution contest that he entered, and he had also fallen or been laughed-off the stage in his first New York public speaking engagement—winding up prostrate on the floor. Significantly, in September 1917, when *The Clarion* was supporting both Harrison's Liberty League and Garvey's UNIA, it described Harrison as "the Race's most prominent agitator."[36]

Harrison later explained what was actually going on. In his diary of May 24, 1920, he wrote, "When we had organized the Liberty League Garvey used to attend our meetings" and "at the same time he began to organize a branch of the Jamaica Improvement Association, which finally blossomed out into the U.N.I.A. and A.C.L." "Everything that I did he copied," "yet I was generous enough to introduce him to my audiences in New York at the Bethel meeting on the night of May [June] 12th 1917 and also at my lecture-forum in Lafayette Hall, as also in Brooklyn later." Sometimes Harrison would close his meeting in Lafayette Hall "earlier than usual" and ask his audience "to go down to give him a crowd." Yet, later, "when Garvey had gone up in the world and the U.N.I.A. was 'going strong' never a reciprocal courtesy was forthcoming from him." Harrison, knowing full well that his work that "had failed had laid the foundation for his [Garvey's] success," refrained from burdening Garvey's movement with his presence. Edgar Grey, secretary of the Liberty League and later general secretary of the UNIA, subsequently said, according to Harrison, "that he again and again asked Garvey to call me [Harrison] in and utilize my abilities in counsel and service; but he would always refuse with the groundless excuse that 'Harrison has his own propaganda', and that he was 'dangerous.'"[37]

On Thursday, June 14, Harrison spoke at another Liberty League meeting run under the auspices of the *Brooklyn Advocate* at a Fleet Street Church in Brooklyn. In addition to Harrison, who was described as "an orator and lecturer of note," other speakers included the Rev. George Frazier Miller, Chandler Owen, Marcus Garvey, the Elks leader George Wibecan, and "other prominent ministers and laymen." The meeting specifically protested "against the atrocious crimes and disfranchisement heaped upon our brothers and sisters in the southland" and aimed to provide them an environment truly "safe for democracy."[38]

While the June 12 meeting at Bethel Church formally founded the Liberty League and raised money for its newspaper, and while there were other meetings shortly thereafter, it was the July 4, 1917, rally at the Metropolitan Baptist Church on 138th Street between Lenox and Seventh Avenues, which drew national attention to the organization and saw the first edition of *The Voice: A Newspaper for the New Negro*. The rally was planned to celebrate "Liberty's Birthday, July 4th," to protest against lynching and disfranchisement, and to get out "The Liberty Issue" of *The Voice*, "The Negro Paper with a Back-Bone." Scheduled speakers included Harrison, the civil rights leader William Monroe Trotter of Boston, and the socialist reverend George Frazier Miller, rector of St. Augustine's Church in Brooklyn. Scheduled entertainers included Harrison's longtime-friend, organist Melville Charlton; another friend, the actress and singer Abbie Mitchell from the Lafayette Theatre Company; and pianist Luckey Roberts, master of the style known as "Harlem stride."[39]

The July 4 meeting came in the wake of race riots on July 1 through 3 in East St. Louis, Illinois, the most severe race riots since the Springfield, Illinois, riot (almost a decade earlier that had led to the formation of the NAACP. East St. Louis was one of the major industrial sites on the Mississippi River, and its African American population had doubled to almost 13,000 between 1910 and 1917. Due to oppressive conditions in the South and war-related production needs, East St. Louis became a destination site of the "Great Migration" north. The city's African American population increased by some 2,400 in 1916 and 1917 alone. Local Democrats attributed the increase to Republicans who, they said, were importing Black workers to be used as voters and potential strikebreakers.[40]

Two series of "race riots" erupted in this racially inflamed situation. In the first, from May 27 to 30, one African American was killed and hundreds were forced to flee. In the second, the bloody riots of July 1 to 3, the Illinois National Guard was called out. Reports on the number of African Americans killed ranged from 39 to 250; property damage was at least $373,000; and 244 buildings were totally or partially destroyed. The author Edward Robb Ellis claims that in the heinous assault Black women were actually scalped and four Black children slaughtered.[41]

These riots were widely attributed to "white" labor's opposition to Black workers coming into the labor market, and they were directly precipitated by a car of white "joy riders" who fired guns into the Black section of the city. Officials of organized labor served as prominent apologists for "white" labor's role in the rioting. Samuel Gompers, president of the American Federation of Labor, placed principal blame for the riots on "the excessive and abnormal number of negroes" in East St. Louis, while W. S. Carter, president of the Brotherhood of Locomotive Firemen and Enginemen, maintained that "the purpose of the railroads in importing Negro labor *is to destroy the influence of white men's labor organizations.*" The House of Representatives subsequently established a committee to investigate the riots. It found that the local police and Illinois National Guard had inadequate riot training, were inept and indifferent, and, in specific instances, supported the white mobs.[42]

The East St. Louis riots were a racist pogrom in which white mobs savagely slaughtered and burned Black people (often in their own homes) in acts of indescribable savagery, and as the country focused attention on the horrific acts in that Illinois city, the Liberty League held its July 4 meeting in the largest church in Harlem. This was also the day after a "race riot" in the San Juan Hill section of Manhattan (the third in six weeks) in which 2,000 people fought after a reserve policemen arrested a uniformed Black soldier standing on a street corner who allegedly refused to move fast enough. The *Times* reported that at the July 4 Liberty League rally a thousand Black men and women were present and

Figure 10.4. East St. Louis Race Riot, July 2, 1917. The African American community of East St. Louis, Illinois, was subjected to two series of "race riots" from May 27 to May 30 and July 1 through 3, 1917. They were the most severe race riots since the Springfield, Illinois, riot, which had led to the formation of the NAACP. Estimates of the number of African Americans killed ranged from thirty-nine to two-hundred-fifty. The riots were widely attributed to "white" labor's opposition to Black workers coming into the labor market, and officials of organized labor served as prominent apologists for "white" labor's role in the rioting. Samuel Gompers, president of the American Federation of Labor, placed principal blame for the riots on "the excessive and abnormal number of negroes" in East St. Louis, while W. S. Carter, president of the Brotherhood of Locomotive Firemen and Enginemen, maintained that "the purpose of the railroads in importing Negro labor *is to destroy the influence of white men's labor organizations.*" In the wake of the East St. Louis riots, Harrison's Liberty League called a major July 4 meeting at which *The Voice* appeared for the first time and Harrison advised Black people who feared mob violence to take direct action and "supply themselves with rifles and fight if necessary, to defend their lives and property." The call for armed self-defense and the desire to have a political voice heard marked the new spirit of the Harrison-led "New Negro Movement." In a number of editorials, Harrison would also challenge the white-race-first policies of such labor leaders. A House of Representatives investigation of the East St. Louis riots found that the local police and Illinois National Guard had inadequate riot training, were inept and indifferent, and, in specific instances, supported the white mobs. In this photo, the militia stand by while the white mob attacks a Black victim (lower right) in front of the street car. *Source:* Courtesy of the Special Collections Department, W. E. B. Du Bois Library, University of Massachusetts, Amherst.

enthusiastically cheered the speakers who were "all Negroes." Every speaker was reported to have denounced the East St. Louis rioters as ruthless murderers, and each condemned the authorities for not preventing the atrocities and for not providing protection.[43]

Edgar M. Grey, secretary of the Liberty League, chaired the July 4 meeting. He informed the audience that the League had sent its message to Congress and appealed for a thorough and impartial investigation of East St. Louis, Black lynchings, and the treatment of Black people throughout the land. Harrison spoke next and reportedly said that "they are saying a great deal about democracy in Washington now," but, "while they are talking about fighting for freedom and the Stars and Stripes, here at home the white apply the torch to the black men's homes, and bullets, clubs and stones to their bodies."[44]

As president of the League, Harrison advised Black people who feared mob violence in the South and elsewhere to take direct action and "supply themselves with rifles and fight if necessary, to defend their lives and property." According to the *Times* he received great applause when he declared that "the time had come for the Negroes [to] do what white men who were threatened did, look out for themselves, and kill rather than submit to be killed." He was quoted as saying, "We intend to fight if we must . . . for the things dearest to us, for our hearths and homes," and he encouraged Black people everywhere who did not enjoy the protection of the law "to arm for their own defense, to hide their arms, and to learn how to use them." He also called for a collection of money to buy rifles for those who could not obtain them, emphasizing that "Negroes in New York cannot afford to lie down in the face of this" because "East St. Louis touches us too nearly." As he later put it, " 'An eye for an eye, a tooth for a tooth,' and sometimes two eyes or a half dozen teeth for one is the aim of the New Negro." Harrison stressed that it was imperative to "demand justice" and to "make our voices heard."[45]

This call for armed self-defense and the desire to have the political voice of the militant "New Negro" heard informed all of Harrison's activities in 1917. He had already, on several occasions, made clear his belief in the need to fight back in defense of lives and community—an attitude that the historian Robert A. Hill describes as "the touchstone of the new black militancy." Harrison had called for retaliatory violence at the Bethel rally, and he did so again on June 13 in Boston. To Hill, Harrison's Boston call was "especially noteworthy" because it "was *uttered* before the outrages committed against blacks in the East St. Louis riot."[46]

The emphasis on a political voice ran across the masthead of *The Voice*, which quoted Woodrow Wilson's April 2 speech to the joint session of Congress: "We will fight for all the things we have held nearest our hearts—for democracy—for the right of those who submit to authority to have a voice in their own government." Several years later, Marcus Garvey, who learned from Harrison, emphasized that the "new spirit of the new Negro . . . does not seek industrial opportunity; it seeks a political voice, and the world is amazed, the world is astounded that the Negro should desire a political voice, because after the voice comes a political place, and . . . we are not only asking but we are going to demand—we are going to fight for and die for that place." According to Robert A. Hill, this demand for a political voice marked the new spirit of the "New Negro" and keyed the later radicalism of Garvey's UNIA.[47]

It was Harrison, however, who was first among the militant "New Negroes" to focus on this central demand—and his paper, *The Voice*, was the prime example. It "really crystallized the radicalism of the Negro in New York and its environs," wrote Hodge Kirnon. *The Voice*, as Hill points out, was "the radical forerunner" of the periodicals that would express the developing political and intellectual ferment in the era of World War I. It was followed in November 1917 by the *Messenger* of A. Philip Randolph and Chandler Owen and in August 1918 by the *Negro World* of Marcus Garvey and the *Crusader* of Cyril Briggs. These four publications, led by *The Voice*, manifested "the principal articulation of the New Negro mood."[48]

The first issue of the Liberty League's "political voice"—*The Voice: A Newspaper for the New Negro*—appeared at the Wednesday, July 4, rally and sold for a penny. It reviewed the "tremendous success" of the June 12 meeting and featured a Harrison editorial on "The East St. Louis Horror." It also offered an in-depth description of the aims, editorial objectives, and news policy of the paper and contained a reprint from the June 1917 *Crisis* of an article by Sir Harry M. Johnston (first published in the London *Sphere*) that described how European desires for African riches were a principal cause of the war. In addition, the first issue contained advertisements for Socialist Party meetings and activities.[49]

The editorial on "The East St. Louis Horror" argued that although the nation was at war to make the world "safe for democracy," until the nation was made safe for African Americans, they would refuse to believe in the country's democratic assertions. Harrison stressed that "New Negroes" would not echo "patriotic protestations of the boot-licking leaders whose pockets and positions testify to the power of the white man's gold" and, despite what Black people might be forced by law to say publicly, "the resentment in their hearts will not down." Then he described the core feeling of the new militancy developing in the wake of East St. Louis:

> *Unbeknown to the white people of this land a temper is being developed among Negroes with which the American people will have to reckon.*

At the present moment it takes this form: If white men are to kill unoffending Negroes, Negroes must kill white men in defense of their lives and property. This is the lesson of the East St. Louis massacre.

He emphasized that Black people "must protect themselves" and that "the United States Supreme Court concedes them this right."[50]

Harrison encouraged both financial and physical retaliatory self-defense. He urged African Americans in East St. Louis and other cities where race riots occurred to draw their money from the local banks and place it either in banks in other cities or in a postal savings bank. He also was encouraged by reports coming out of East St. Louis, which, though suppressed by most news media, gave evidence that Black people there had organized and fought back under Black leadership. This fact, he predicted, would help to quickly increase the membership of the Liberty League, which had organized precisely "to take practical steps to help our people all over the land in the protection of their lives and liberties."[51]

With such a fiery editorial, *The Voice* sold extremely well. Mrs. Irena Moorman-Blackston, the community activist who had a subway-entrance newsstand at the southeast corner of 135th St. and Lenox Avenue, reported that she sold 750 copies of the paper in one day, "more than she has sold of any Negro paper in a week." Harrison held some copies out of newsstands to be sent to Europe, Africa, and to contemporaries in other U.S. cities. Other than those, the entire first issue of 3,000 copies was sold out early, even though the paper's staff wasn't able to get it to all the Harlem newsstands and despite the fact that newsdealers and others were "clamoring for more."[52]

Harrison considered "the most astonishing feature of the first issue" to be "the large number of white people who read *The Voice*." Moorman-Blackston reported that seventy-six white people had bought the paper up to Friday afternoon, whereas the regular demand for all other "'colored' papers" by white people was only five or six. In addition, many white friends called at the office to take subscriptions and give assistance in many ways. They folded papers, solicited subscriptions and advertisements, and offered to write articles and contribute cartoons. One reporter, from a large metropolitan daily, brought twenty-five subscriptions in two days. Another white supporter, a linotyper, offered to come in on Monday nights to read and revise galleys. While white support was encouraging, Black readers "simply outdid themselves" by selling subscriptions, soliciting advertisements, and circulating *The Voice*. Foreign-born Black people "lined up behind the native-born to do their bit," and they were similarly "'tickled to death' about the paper and its program."[53]

While there were whites who eagerly supported Harrison's effort, at least one noted "radical" and activist for Black advancement did not. Mary White

Ovington, a leading Socialist Party member, a founder of the NAACP, and at that time the chairperson of the NAACP's New York Branch, wrote to Harrison that she didn't "see any reason for another organization, or another paper" and suggested that if he "printed straight socialism it might be different." Harrison considered Ovington to be "a fairly good representative of the class of 'good white friends of the colored people'" and considered her letter both "bossy and dictatorial." He would soon provide her a scathing response in print.[54]

Others also noticed *The Voice*. The competing *New York News* wished it "success" while noting that Harrison's opinion on drama "always carries weight." More forebodingly, *The Voice* also drew notice from the New York City Police and the Military Intelligence Branch of the War Department. C. L. Hay, of Military Intelligence in New York, wrote to his superiors in Washington after Inspector Ryan of the Sixth Inspection District of the New York City Police informed him of the paper.[55]

In the July 10 issue Harrison described to readers "How *The Voice* Took." He explained that it consistently "maintained the principle 'Africa First' ['in its racial, rather than geographical sense']." The "Africa First" slogan also appeared on Liberty League of Negro-Americans membership cards and on pledge cards to support organization and the paper. Based on this race-first principle, *The Voice* implemented a five-pronged policy—news, editorial, financial support, plan of campaign, and advertising—which Harrison described.[56]

Under the new news policy, instead of receiving money for printing news, as was the practice with other papers, *The Voice* was willing to pay, either by sending its trained reporters to get it or by subscribing to a news syndicate. It aimed to make friends of newsgatherers and proposed that for the first year the person bringing the news must be a subscriber. The paper would "be free to investigate such news before presenting it" and to decide the relative importance of all news articles. Unlike other papers *The Voice* decided that "when Mr. John Smith weds Miss Mary Jones, that isn't news" and any "offer to pay money for its presentation" would "not make *The Voice* print it."[57]

Harrison also described component parts of a good newspaper—it should have a record of events, it should discuss what is being thought in the world and what the editors themselves think, and it should also analyze institutions and ideas and their impact. The "gripping, vital, interesting happenings of the church lodge or street" were news, while "the trivial personal items" were not. As examples of bad news he cited papers that clip from the columns of the white papers although they have a whole week in which to assemble their news; front pages "full of Negro crime"; and advertising matter for which someone has paid. By August 14, after implementing this news policy for six weeks, Harrison judged that there was "more news in the four pages of *The Voice*" than "in any three of our contemporaries in the city" and it was no longer true that the *Chi-*

cago Defender carried the most news in the Black press on New York. In order to consistently develop good news *The Voice* announced that it would seek to train six to twelve bright young men and women.[58]

On matters of language and editing Harrison's scrapbooks proved useful. For years he had been pasting in them examples of slipshod journalism from the Black press. In an article entitled "Lessons in Language" in the July 10 issue of *The Voice* he reprinted examples of such bad journalism "culled from the columns of our 'Colored' contemporaries." He explained that "the slipshod silly English which appears in some Negro papers would disgrace a child of fourteen" and helped "to earn the white man's contempt." He cautioned, however, against the other extreme, "the bombastic, big-worded, 'high-falutin,' sentences of the so-called 'literary' Johnnie," which were not "journalistic" and which wouldn't do in a newspaper. As examples of good journalist technique he cited the efforts of John E. Bruce and James Weldon Johnson. Harrison was convinced that good journalistic skills could be taught.[59]

In terms of editing, there was little doubt that *The Voice* was excellently prepared. Its pages were professionally done. Harrison claimed that "no such paper has been seen among Negroes since T. Thomas Fortune edited the earlier *Age*." Under Fortune's editorship from 1887 to 1907, the *Age* had been America's leading Black newspaper and was well known for its forceful editorials on equality.[60]

After reading the first issue of *The Voice*, veteran journalist John E. Bruce congratulated the editor on "snappy columns," "neat typographical appearance," an "able editorial page," and "its worthy and tantalizing news." Two weeks later Bruce joined the Liberty League and sent Harrison a letter of introduction to give to John Wesley Cromwell in Washington, D.C. Cromwell was a prominent intellectual and historian who had founded the Bethel Literary and Historical Society and was secretary of the American Negro Academy. Bruce sent the introduction to help *The Voice* become "a national organ" and to help its editor get to know "men of national repute all over the country."[61]

Despite such support, Harrison's principled advertising policy encountered some difficulty. As he explained, *The Voice* opposed "those disgusting and degrading Anti-Kink and Whiten-Up ads." Businessmen were encouraged to advertise in the paper not as "an act of charity," but rather, as "a good stroke of business" since *The Voice* claimed to offer "more solid publicity" for the money than could be obtained elsewhere in Harlem. The "Big Negroes," the realtors Philip A. Payton Jr. and John M. Royall and the undertaker Howard Adolph Howell, were singled out as businessmen who should advertise. Friends of the paper were encouraged to "enforce the necessity of advertising in *The Voice* on every business man with whom you spend your money" and to patronize those that so advertised. The paper didn't say "don't patronize the others," but it did say, "let them wait, if they let your VOICE wait." It also made clear that advertisements were needed in order to meet plans of going from four to eight pages by mid-August, and to twelve pages by the end of the first year. Despite these efforts, however, the "Big Negroes" withheld their help.[62]

After the first issue of *The Voice* sold out 3,000 copies, the second issue on July 10 sold 5,000 copies. The paper was a weekly, appearing on Tuesdays, and plans were made to increase its circulation to 10,000 in one or two weeks. These plans were apparently met, and by August 7 sales reportedly reached 11,000 copies. The significance of these numbers should not be underestimated.[63]

Though accurate readership statistics are difficult to obtain it is possible to get a broad picture of *The Voice*'s impact. In 1917 the Black population in Harlem, because of a major influx of Southern migrants and Caribbean immigrants, was approximately 60,000. In New York City, including Brooklyn, the Black population was about 120,000. Based on existing statistics, perhaps half of the African American population (30,000 in Harlem and 60,000 citywide) was adult and perhaps 90 percent to 95 percent of these were literate. Thus the target Black readership in Harlem and New York might have been 28,000 and 56,000 respectively. In a major 1922 study, *The Negro Press in the United States*, Frederick G. Detweiler estimated that, principally because of hand-to-hand distribution, readership of the Black press was approximately five times that of circulation. Further, it appears that *Voice* circulation was predominantly among Black readers, unlike the forthcoming "class-conscious" *Messenger* of A. Philip Randolph and Chandler Owen, which, according to Owen, had a readership that was two-thirds white. Thus with readership estimated at five times circulation and with easily half or more of its readers Black people, the "race conscious" *Voice* may have approached a readership of 55,000, and a Black readership of more than 30,000. Even if this figure is high, given the number of adult Black readers in the city, it appears that *The Voice* swept the New York Black community with its "race-conscious" message.[64]

Further, if the figure is accurate, the circulation of 11,000 after four weeks compared favorably with that of New York's leading Black weekly, the *Age*, which had a reported circulation in 1910 of 14,000. It also compared favorably with the circulation of other well established Black papers like the *Chicago Whip*, which, as late as 1922 (after the heightened racial awareness of the summer of 1919), had a circulation of 8,000, and the Baltimore *Afro-American*, which reached a regional (East Coast and Southern) circulation of approximately 20,000 by 1922. Only nationwide Black papers circulation, such as the *Chicago Defender*, which jumped from 10,000 in 1916 to nearly 100,000 by 1918, and the *Pittsburgh Courier*, far outdistanced *The Voice* circulation figures.[65]

It was obvious to Harrison that "the people want[ed] the paper" and were "working to push it as they have never pushed any paper, white or 'colored.'"

Mrs. Eslanda Cardoza Goode of 7 West 131st Street organized a group of "society girls" known as "The Voice Volunteers." (Mrs. Goode was the mother of Miss Eslanda Cardoza Goode, the future Mrs. Paul Robeson, who may have been one of the volunteers.) They were "to sell the paper on the streets; to solicit subscriptions, and go to the churches on Sunday" in order to distribute the paper as the crowds came out.[66]

Harrison felt that rapid growth of the paper would be possible since he was in a slightly different position than most Black editors who had to be totally supported by their papers. He claimed that he had "two independent professions"—public lecturing and private teaching—from which he could "at any time derive an income for his expenses." Accordingly, he felt he was not under the pressure others faced, and he felt sure that he "wouldn't miss his meals nor any other customary pleasure." He seriously misjudged time, however. Over the next thirteen weeks he learned many things, including "that one cannot do much lecturing or teaching and at the same time edit successfully a paper such as *The Voice*." He was forced to totally give up teaching and to limit his lectures only to those for the Harlem People's Forum on Sunday nights at the Palace Casino. Money that he made by lecturing was put back into *The Voice*.[67]

Unfortunately, putting out *The Voice* called for more money and, according to Harrison, the paper was already "paying the highest war prices for printing." Nevertheless, the "Common People" supported the paper "beautifully—with their personal help, their pennies and their loans," made at street meetings and indoor talks. A major problem, however, was that "the 'Big Negroes' withheld their help—even in the matter of advertisements." Though circulation and the number of advertisements went up, they didn't increase rapidly enough to justify the paper's further expansion. *The Voice* "would not truckle and it would not cringe before the Exalted Ones," and it "continued to place its dependence upon the Negro masses." When things were going badly, R. B. Minor, a prominent Virginia-born African American businessman in Harlem, arranged for a carnival at Manhattan Casino to raise funds for *The Voice* and the Liberty League. Although the carnival was well attended, its expenses approached $500 and wiped out almost all profit. These economic difficulties necessitated a hasty reorganization and the formation and incorporation of a company. At that point it became clear to Harrison that an independent Black paper "had to be financially independent of its advertisers." For *The Voice* to obtain this "margin of manhood" he judged that sales income should cover and surpass weekly operating expenses.[68]

The paper's price became an important issue. Other Black papers with national circulation sold for five cents. This was true of the twelve-page *Chicago Defender*, the eight-page *Boston Guardian*, *Richmond Planet*, *Philadelphia Tribune*, and *Indianapolis Recorder*, as well as the four-page *Cleveland Gazette* and *Houston Observer*. It was pointed out that, except for Trotter's *Boston Guardian*, all these papers carried "those disgusting and degrading Anti-Kink and Whiten-Up ads which make every self-respecting Negro ashamed to open them in public places where white people may see." Harrison decided that if Black people would buy those other papers for five cents, they would pay the same price for *The Voice*. In order not to cringe for big advertisements the paper would try to survive with a circulation of ten thousand at five cents per copy. With its "manhood margin assured," *The Voice* wouldn't have "to bite its tongue, to 'sell out' to white politicians, nor to hold back from 'showing up' the highly placed Judases who are selling the race and its future for a mass of pottage." Thus, "owing to the high price of manhood," *The Voice* was forced to go up to five cents after thirteen weeks. By October 18, 1917, however, it was back down to two cents. In November 1917, after the New York municipal elections, *The Voice* would eventually halt publication, not to appear again until July 1918.[69]

In July 1917, however, *The Voice* was definitely reaching a mass audience and sweeping Harlem with its race-conscious message. As summer wore on and moved into fall, the Liberty League and *The Voice* played an ever more important role in reshaping Harlem politics. Harrison's July 4 editorial on East St. Louis drew strong criticism from the *Age*, the largest and most influential Black weekly in the city. In the *New York Tribune*, the editor of the *Age*, Fred Randolph Moore, a staunch Republican and former associate of Booker T. Washington, declared that: "the representative Negro does not approve of radical socialistic outbursts, such as calling upon the Negroes to defend themselves against the whites." Then, in its own editorial, the *Age* insisted that "no man, or woman," who "publicly advises a resort to violence" is "a friend to the race."[70]

Harrison responded that although *The Voice* sought no quarrel with the *Age*, it was "forced to dissent from this cringing, obsequious view which it champions." Harrison pointedly added that the "group which once held that view went to pieces when Dr. Washington died." He also noted that "*white* papers" repeatedly gave examples showing that Black people in East St. Louis "not only counselled self-defense, but actually practiced it," yet the *Age* was "the only *Negro* paper in New York City which excluded these items from its news columns." He reasoned that if the newspaper reports were accurate, "then *The Voice* told the simple truth when it spoke of the new temper which was being developed 'unbeknown to the white people of this land.'" Harrison suggested that *The Voice* "was a better friend to the white people by letting them know this, than *The Age* was by trying to lie about it."[71]

The real difference between the *Age* and *The Voice*, he explained, revolved around the answers to two questions: did Black people have "a right to defend themselves against whites?"; and, should they? To make sure that matters were crystal clear, he added: "this, of course, means violence." *The Voice*'s answer was "Yes!" and the *Age*'s was "No!" To settle the dispute Harrison argued that "every law-book and statute-book, every court in the civilized world and in the United States" maintained "that every *human* being has the legal as well as moral right to kill those who attack and try to kill him."[72]

He then probed more deeply the issue of self-defense. He pointed out how the *Amsterdam News* in its coverage of "the massacre" showed that "whenever the white mobs found a group of Negroes organized and armed, *they turned back*." The *Age* had tried to totally avoid the issue. Comparing the two responses, Harrison concluded: "When murder is cheap murder is indulged in recklessly; when it is likely to be costly it is not so readily indulged in." He stressed that whatever the *Age* said, the fact was that "Negroes will fight back as they are already fighting back" and they would "be more highly regarded—as are the Irish—because of fighting back."[73]

There was one additional major activity in that first week in July related to East St. Louis. At a Carnegie Hall meeting to discuss democratic Russia on Friday July 6, right after East St. Louis, former president Roosevelt denounced the white murderers while the American Federation of Labor president, Samuel Gompers, on the same platform, defended them. Gompers blamed East St. Louis on the importation of "Negro" laborers. Roosevelt then crossed the stage and shook his fist at Gompers, saying, "I am not willing that a meeting called to commemorate the birth of democracy in Russia shall even seem to have expressed or to have accepted apologies for the brutal infamies imposed on colored people. . . . Let there be the fullest investigation into these murders."[74]

Roosevelt's response drew praise from Harrison and was widely applauded in the Black community. On July 7 Harrison sent a Western Union telegram to Roosevelt saying that "*The Voice* congratulates you Colonel and your manly American stand for the rights of all Americans at Carnegie Hall[;] bully for you we Negroes will remember." It was signed by Harrison as editor of the *Voice*, but the address was incorrectly listed as 225 Seventh Avenue instead of 2305 Seventh Avenue. Similar telegrams were sent by other African American leaders, including W. E. B. Du Bois, Charles W. Anderson, the activist minister William Bolden, and George W. Harris, editor of the *New York News*. On July 11 Roosevelt sent Harrison a thank-you telegram, which was apparently never received because of the incorrect address.[75]

Gompers's attitude prompted another Harrison editorial, entitled "The Negro and the Labor Unions," in which Harrison took to task the "white" AFL labor leadership and elaborated his views on trade unions. He noted in response to East St. Louis that the president of the Brotherhood of Locomotive Firemen, W. S. Carter, expressed concern for "white men's labor organizations." Harrison's response was to stress the need for Black people to "return the compliment" and similarly "put Race before Class." He pointed out that though there were in fact two types of unionism, the exclusionary and often segregatory, craft-based unionism of the AFL, and the all-inclusive, industrial or multicraft unionism of the IWW, "the Negro has been taught to think that all unionism was like the unionism of the American Federation of Labor." Because of this ignorance of the other unionism, the Black worker's "attitude toward organized labor has been that of the scab." But, as Harrison pointed out, "for this no member of the A.F. of L. can blame the Negro" since "the policy of that organization toward the Negro has been damnable."[76]

Even some bosses had a better record in race relations than the AFL. Harrison pointed out that "the big capitalists who pay low wages (from the son of Abraham Lincoln [Robert Todd Lincoln] in the Pullman Co. [where he was president] to Julius Rosenwald [president] of the Sears Roebuck Co.) have been rather friendly to the Negro." Rosenwald, in particular, gave millions to Colored Young Men's and Young Women's Christian Associations and to the Rosenwald Rural Schoolhouse Building Fund. Thus there was ample reason to understand why "the Negro people are anti-union." Harrison, referring to the AFL, explained how "Labor unions were created by white working men" in order "that they might bring the pressure of many to bear upon the greedy employer and make him give higher wages and better living conditions to the laborer." But, when these laborers became "so greedy" that they excluded "the majority of working people, by high dues and initiation fees," they no longer represented the interests of the working class.[77]

To Harrison, such unions stood "in the way of this class's advancement—*and they must go.*" These unions would have to leave the way clear for the "20th century type of unionism," which held that to "leave a single worker out is to leave something for the boss to use against us." Therefore what was required was to "organize in One Big Union of *all* the working-class"; this was "the I.W.W. type of unionism." Harrison, in his continued support for industrial unionism, was a leader in the Black community and he was far in advance of many Black leaders who opposed trade unions. Chandler Owen and A. Philip Randolph, who followed Harrison's lead, called attention to the fact that the "old line Negro political fossils" knew "nothing of the Labor Movement," did "not believe in labor unions at all," and had "never taken any active steps to encourage such organization."[78]

In his editorial Harrison examined the AFL's contrasting stance toward African Americans and how it claimed partial responsibility for the East St. Louis outrage. This AFL position was "playing with fire," warned Harrison, and the "American Negro may join hands with the American capitalist and scab them out of existence." To make matters totally clear, he added, "the editor of *The Voice* calls upon Negroes to do this." The AFL had been tolerated "just about long enough." He called on Black workers to "form your own unions ... and make a truce with your capitalist enemy until you get rid of this traitor to the cause of labor. . . . Then get rid of the A.F. of L." He urged: "Join hands with the capitalists and scab them [the AFL] out of existence—not in the name of scabbery, but in the name of a real organization of labor."[79]

Harrison did not consider the organizing of all-Black unions to be an antilabor position. He emphasized that he had been a member of a party that "stood for the rights of labor and the principle of Industrial Unionism" and that he understood the labor conditions of the country and desired to see the working class victorious. "But," he wrote, as editor of *The Voice*, "his first duty, here as everywhere, is to the Negro race." Harrison refused "to put ahead of his race's rights a collection of diddering jackasses which can publicly palliate such atrocities as that of East St. Louis and publicly assume, as Gompers did, responsibility for it." Several years later, he explained that the Liberty League supported "the program of the advanced labor movement in this country" and was trying to organize Black workers into all-Black unions that would cooperate with the "white unions" when "allowed that right." He clearly preferred "to see workers of all colors and creeds in one union." But, since "the white worker of America" did "not yet realize the need for lining the colored worker alongside of him and treating him as his social equal," the Black laborer was forced to fight "independently of the white trade union movement."[80]

In 1926, in the context of the Lafayette Theatre strike in Harlem, Harrison again commented on trade union work, Gompers, and East St. Louis. He put forth the position "that, unlike Abraham Lincoln," his "prime object was not to save the union, but 'to free the slaves.'" His "long previous acquaintance with the American Federation of Labor," he explained, "did not predispose him to be friendly to its unions." Their policy "seemed so constructed that, whereas the white worker could consider his fight for bread to be directed solely against the capitalist, the black worker was opposed by the general run of white working men, who kept him out of their unions for the most part and yet called him 'scab' for getting their jobs at the only time when those jobs were available to him." Harrison claimed that his attitude on this was "maintained consistently since 1917, when Samuel Gompers assumed at Carnegie Hall, in the face of Colonel Roosevelt, responsibility for the East St. Louis riots on the ground of an alleged necessity for the white unionists to defend their jobs by murder against the Negro workers whom they had shut out of their unions—as Negroes."[81]

After the great success of the first issue Harrison's task was to get out *The Voice* regularly. The next issue included a letter from John E. Bruce about a new and relatively unknown poet, the freethinker and railway mail worker Walter Everette Hawkins (who would later edit *The Messenger*'s poet's corner), as well as editorials on the start of *The Voice*, its advertising policy, and its writing style. That second issue also contained an article on a police attack on an epileptic African American, which was the first of a series of articles on police brutality that the paper would run. Police brutality was a major concern in the Black community during the 1914 to 1918 administration of Mayor John Purroy Mitchel, and the *Voice* regularly ran articles exposing brutal and discriminatory treatment as well as articles on the glaring discrimination in both police and fire department hiring.[82]

The July 17 issue of *The Voice* reportedly sold out 10,000 copies. The paper was taking Harlem by storm and challenging the city's other Black weeklies— the *Age*, the *New York News*, and the *Amsterdam News*. A highlight of that third issue was Harrison's lead editorial on "Arms and the Man," which took both the *Age* and the *Amsterdam News* to task for wavering on *The Voice*'s call for armed self-defense in the face of "white" race riots. An agitational article in that third issue told how John Henry Woodson, a Black fireman, was publicly denied a merited medal for bravery. Other Black papers, most notably the *Age*, had accepted unverified information from city sources that Woodson had received a medal. *The Voice* exposed that story as "one of the greatest hoaxes of the age," staged by "white papers—and the 'colored' ones copying them." It stressed the lesson that "our 'colored' contemporaries would do well hereafter to go out and cover their own news and not be content to transcribe the release notices of the department or the white newspapers." In a later issue *The Voice* reprinted a letter from Fire Commissioner Robert Adamson confirming that Fireman Woodson was given a class 3 award, which did not carry a medal with it. This led Harrison to conclude that coverage such as that on Woodson's "medal" was a prime example of how Black voters were being "sold like sheep by the ministers, editors and politicians to the present city administration."[83]

The fourth issue of *The Voice* also reportedly sold 10,000 copies, and in it, Harrison, who was far from personally prudish, addressed the sexual suggestiveness of plays at the Lincoln and Lafayette Theaters. His article elicited a very supportive letter from John E. Bruce, who wrote that the critique was "admirably phrased" and that the "salacious" plays had "a deleterious effect on our young." Bruce added that "Black men have not fallen so low in the scale of morals as the American *White Slaver*."[84]

The fourth issue (July 31), also contained a fiery editorial entitled "A Call to Action." It argued that the "brutality of certain white policemen was never so clearly and scathingly set forth as it was done by Magistrate [Joseph] Corrigan last Monday when he flayed policeman 669 of the 135th St. station." The "drunken brute had viciously and criminally assaulted a Negro who had protested against the dirty language which he had been using to Negro women," and *The Voice* demanded that he be removed from Harlem and called on Blacks to "remember that the policeman's number is 669."[85]

Harrison used the police brutality issue to challenge prominent Black leaders. "What are the 'big Negroes' of Harlem going to do" about such police brutality? he asked. He referred specifically to the leading Black Republican Charles W. Anderson, the realtors Philip Payton and John M. Royall, the actor Bert Williams, the beauty products businesswoman MMe. C. J. Walker, and "people of their standing." Feeling that something had to be done, he offered "to meet them more than half way" and urged these leaders to organize a "Vigilance Committee" to meet with the mayor and police commissioner to demand that culpable "policemen and detectives" were "made to pay the double penalty of dismissal and criminal prosecution." If they didn't do this, he feared that matters would "go along the way of war in Harlem." The reason was that "the average Negro" was "developing hatred in [the] heart against such officers of the law as '669,'" and if this continued, "'direct action'" might "be resorted to in self-defense." (The following year such a vigilance committee would meet with the police and, in addition to Harrison, its members would include James Weldon Johnson, John B. Nail, George W. Harris, Rev. Adam Clayton Powell Sr., Father Plunkett of St. Mark's Church [on 138th Street], the activist William Bridges, John Royall, Bert Williams, and others.)[86]

Harrison also offered some plain words to the police commissioner: "give us more black policemen in our district and you will have less trouble in keeping order." At the time of his writing, Harlem's 135th Street precinct had only two Black policemen, and the entire city only one or two more. Harrison emphasized that "when policeman [Robert] Holmes tells a Negro crowd to 'move on,' they move" and "when he goes to arrest a Negro he can, if he chooses, leave his pistol and club at headquarters." Black people listened to Black policemen because they did not think that they were "indulging in racial arrogance and spite at their expense." He concluded: "We want more Negroes on the force and we look forward eventually to a Negro police captain sitting at the desk in West 135th St. . . . And if we don't get them, we will make some one suffer politically in ways that they don't suspect."[87]

Since 1916 Harrison had continually raised demands for Black police officers and firefighters, and the *New York Times* described him as "the first to advocate Negro policemen for Harlem." This demand for Black police officers (particularly at a time when there were no more than four in the city) distinguished his race-conscious radicalism from the class radicalism of the Black Socialist Chandler Owen. Harrison explained that more Black policemen were wanted because "with white policemen we are forced to take a chance and their conduct depends entirely on the goodwill of the Police Commissioner. With Negro policemen (in spite of Mr. Owen's argument) [probably the argument that all police were 'tools of the capitalist class'] the chance of police brutality to Negro citizens is reduced."[88]

As July wore on and Harlem simmered politically and thermally (the temperature on July 27 was reportedly the hottest on that date in twenty-five years),

Harrison continued to agitate for independent political action and for race-first activity. One of the major activities was the Saturday, July 28, Silent Protest Parade, in which ten to fifteen thousand African Americans marched down Fifth Avenue from Fifty-sixth Street to Twenty-third Street and Madison Square amid muffled drums and an estimated 20,000 Black viewers. The protest, which had been planned for several months by an NAACP-influenced ad hoc committee, came after two days of race rioting in Chester, Pennsylvania, in which three Black people were killed, four others shot, and sixty arrested. Protesters demanded an end to lynching and called for democracy at home—the two principal demands of the Liberty League. A circular, explaining "Why We March," noted that "the growing consciousness and solidarity of race, coupled with sorrow and discrimination, have made us one." This Silent Protest Parade was the largest demonstration of African Americans in New York City history, and it set the stage for a mass meeting the next day at the Palace Casino at 135th St. and Madison Avenue.[89]

At the Palace Casino meeting on Sunday, July 29, a Citizen's Committee was scheduled to report to Harlem's Black voters on how it had been turned down by the local Republican Party when it sought to have its Black candidates run on the party slate. As part of the buildup for this meeting Harrison published an editorial entitled "The Drift in Politics" in which he declared that "the Negroes of America—those of them who think—are suspicious of everything that comes from the white people of America." He also advised that any Black politician who wanted the support of Black voters would have to give "more than piecrust promises" because the "drift in politics" was toward the new independent, race-first demands of the "New Negro." He called for genuine political representation and wrote:

> We demand what the Irish and the Jewish voter get: nominations on the party's ticket in our own districts. And if we don't get this we will smash the party that refuses to give it.
>
> For we are not Republicans, Democrats or Socialists any longer. We are Negroes first. And we are no longer begging for sops. We demand, not "recognition," but representation, and we are out to throw our votes to *any* party which gives us this, and withhold them from any party which refuses to give it. . . .
>
> Rebuffs will make for manhood—if we are men—and will drive us to play in American politics the same role which the Irish party played in British politics. That is the new trend in Negro politics, and we must not let any party forget it.

In articulating this position, Harrison emerged as a leader in the "campaign for Black district leadership" in Harlem as "New Negroes" began to seek the independent political voice that he called for.[90]

The Palace Casino meeting showed the bold political face of the "New Negro." The meeting was called by the United Civic League. John M. Royall chaired, while Harrison, Minister Reverdy C. Ransom, Asa Philip Randolph, Mrs. Marie C. Lawton, and Mrs. B. H. Lewis all spoke. Four people were named as nominees for elective office: James C. Thomas Jr., an attorney and activist with the Liberty League and candidate for the Twenty-sixth Aldermanic District; Edward Austin Johnson, an attorney and historian and candidate for the Nineteenth Assembly District; George W. Harris, the *New York News* publisher; and Charles W. Anderson, New York City's leading Black Republican politician and the honorary president of the Republican Club of the City of New York. In addition to the nominations, resolutions were passed calling for the establishment of a public bathhouse in the Black community and warning against "unscrupulous labor leaders who seek to enrich themselves through the threat of paralysis of the industries of this country." The meeting also pledged aid to new Black arrivals in the city and planned a follow-up meeting for September 28.[91]

It was the speeches, however, and Harrison's in particular, that drew most attention. Before a crowd of 3,000, he openly attacked former President Theodore Roosevelt. Less than four weeks earlier he had praised Roosevelt for denouncing AFL president Gompers at Carnegie Hall. On July 29, however, Harrison responded to a statement made by a previous speaker that Roosevelt's "denunciation of the East St. Louis killings had 'hurled Brownsville deeper than the bottom of the sea.'" The reference to Brownsville was to the outrage the Black community felt over Roosevelt's action as president in dishonorably discharging the Black troops a decade earlier. Harrison publicly countered: "Roosevelt's act in Carnegie Hall may have buried Brownsville," but, "that is the trouble with us Negroes. We remember a little thing like a pat on the head, but we forget deep injuries." In direct reference to Roosevelt's inaction on the lynching question Harrison added: "When Roosevelt's action would have had the backing of political position, he did absolutely nothing for us. If, when he was President, he had insisted upon Federal law against lynching, I would be for him." Harrison then went further in his effort to arouse race consciousness. "We know," he said, "that white people will love us just as long as they can use us, and that they cannot be trusted any longer." "What we want," he explained, "is not their love, but their respect." He concluded, "Before allegiance to the flag itself comes our allegiance to the Negro race."[92]

Harrison's comments at the July 29 meeting apparently made some leaders squirm and the next night over 200 African Americans met at the UCL building to voice "a vigorous protest against" Harrison's statements. Royall informed the crowd that a letter had been sent to Theodore Roosevelt explaining that the meeting "had shown no antagonism to him" and "cheered heartily" every time he was mentioned." Royall added that "a wrong impression had gone abroad

respecting the exact meaning of Mr. Harrison's remarks" and he assured Roosevelt that he was held in high esteem by the colored race, despite some dissatisfaction with his position on Brownsville. The July 30th UCL meeting closed
with nominees for the Board of Alderman and for the Assembly and with demands for a squad of firemen and a squad of colored police to be assigned "in
the Negro district." These demands were similar to those made by Harrison,
who was not at the meeting. Harrison did respond, however, with an editorial,
"Peanuts and Politics," in *The Voice* of August 14. In the editorial he predicted
that without a change of course the efforts at leadership by these Black political
aspirants would remain fruitless.[93]

By early August 1917 Harlem was energized with militant, race-conscious
political activity, and Harrison, *The Voice*, and the Liberty League were in the
vanguard. Harrison is known as the "father of Harlem radicalism" because of his
radical writing, oratory, and ideas and because of the shaping influence he had
on militant movements, on radicals and "common people," and on the race-conscious and class-conscious leaders who were making Harlem a radical center of
Black activity and thought. A listing of those who followed his lead reads like a
virtual who's who of Harlem's militant leaders over the next decade.[94]

Among those significantly influenced by the Liberty League and *The Voice*
were the socialist-leaning radicals Richard B. Moore, Cyril V. Briggs, Wilfred A.
Domingo, Chandler Owen and Asa Philip Randolph. Randolph and Owen were
always present when Harrison gave his outdoor lectures, and they began to lecture on corners themselves. Alan W. Whaley occasionally spoke at meetings
with Harrison and was a leading organizer, along with Harrison, of the 1918
Liberty Congress. Samuel Duncan, Harrison's friend from his Lyceum days and
from the *New York News*, also followed his lead and was quite possibly a member of the Liberty League before he became president of the UNIA. Marcus
Garvey had been persuaded by Harrison's work to stay in New York and he, like
the others, joined the Liberty League and followed Harrison. Briggs, the journalist and future Communist Party member, estimated that total membership
in the Liberty League was never more than a few hundred. Nevertheless, the
individuals involved were to play major roles in reshaping the politics of Harlem
and would effectively challenge the white-supremacist notion that Blacks could
not successfully organize without whites.[95]

According to the *Call*, Liberty League membership was "mostly young men
and women" and "numbered in the hundreds."[96] No membership lists are
known to exist, but a list (culled from various sources) of those activists who
either worked with Harrison's Liberty League (1917 to 1921) or were associated
with *The Voice* (1917 to 1919) or the Liberty League–affiliated *Clarion* (1917),
includes the following:

Isaac B. Allen: Political activist, Liberty League member (?)

Henry B. Alston: *Voice* stockholder

Charles H. Anderson: Dancemaster, Liberty League member (?)

Mr. Armstrong: Liberty League Quartet member

Albert Banfield: *Voice* stockholder

John Batson: *Voice* stockholder

August Valentine Bernier: Publisher and journalist, Liberty League member

Lawton D. Birch: *Voice* stockholder

Edward O. Boddie: Treasurer of *The Voice*

Mr. Bolden: Liberty League Quartet member

Cyril Valentine Briggs: Journalist, with Liberty League

John Edward Bruce: Author and correspondent, *Voice* director and correspondent, Liberty League member

Charles Burroughs: Actor, lecturer for the Board of Education, *Voice* director

James Cornelius Canegata: Organizer of the Pullman Porter's Union, *Voice* director

James D. Carr: Democratic Party leader in New York State, assistant corporation counsel for *The Voice*

Melville Charlton: Organist, musician for Liberty League activities

Rev. Dr. A. R. Cooper: Speaker for Liberty League

M. I. Daniel: *Voice* stockholder

Wilfred Adolphus Domingo: Journalist, assistant secretary of the Liberty League

W. Clayton Dowdy: Activist in the Elevator and Switch-Board Operator's Union, *Voice* director

Mr. Elkins: Liberty League Quartet member

Gertrude Miller Faide: Activist, writer for *The Clarion*

Charles H. Florney: Treasurer of *The Voice*

Lovett Fort-Whiteman: Activist, collaborating editor of *The Clarion*

John A. Fountain: *Voice* stockholder

R. Benjamin Fray: Liberty League member (?)

Marcus Garvey: Liberty League member

James A. Glasgow: *Voice* stockholder

Mrs. Eslanda Cardoza Goode: Organizer of "*The Voice* Volunteers," Liberty League Member (?)

George H. Green: Speaker for the Liberty League

Edgar Mussington Grey: Journalist, secretary of the Liberty League, writer for *The Voice*

James Harris: Treasurer of the Liberty League

Hubert Henry Harrison: President of the Liberty League, editor and publisher of *The Voice*

Cornelius A. Hughes: Prominent Democratic Party political leader, *Voice* director

Anselmo R. Jackson: Journalist, columnist for *The Voice*, Liberty League member

J. H. Johnson: *Voice* stockholder

W. D. Jones: *Voice* stockholder

Arthur E. King: Liberty League member

Charles T. Magill: Liberty League member

Rev. Dr. George Frazier Miller: Rector of St. Augustine's Church Brooklyn, *Voice* director, speaker for the Liberty League

R. B. Minor: Liberty League member (?), *Voice* stockholder

Abbie Mitchell: Actress, singer, performer at Liberty League activities

Irena Moorman-Blackston: Newsdealer, Liberty League member, seller of *The Voice*

George H. Nelson: *Voice* stockholder

Andrew C. Pedro: *Voice* stockholder

Rufus L. Perry, Esq.: "Foremost Negro lawyer of the State," founder of the Afro-American Democratic Association, *Voice* director

Daniel E. Petersen: Liberty League vice president

Miss Julia Peterson: *Voice* stockholder

Rev. Adam Clayton Powell Sr. : Speaker for the Liberty League

Alexander Rahming: Journalist, speaker for the Liberty League

William H. Randolph: *Voice* stockholder

Emil M. Rasmussen: Liberty League member

Dr. E. Elliot Rawlins: Physician, speaker for the Liberty League

Andreamentania Paul Razafinkeriefo: Poet, poetry for *The Voice*

Arthur Hilton Reid: Treasurer of the Liberty League

C[harles] Luckeyeth "Luckey" Roberts: Pianist, entertainer at Liberty League activities

Mrs. A. C. Schuster: *Voice* stockholder

Auto Scott: Secretary of the Liberty League

Charles Christopher Seifert: Bibliophile, historian, Liberty League speaker

Mr. Slater: Liberty League Quartet member

Mrs. Bernia L. Smith: of the Indol Corporation, *Voice* Director

Joseph Smith: *Voice* stockholder

Arthur Sye: *Voice* stockholder

James C. Thomas Jr. : Attorney, aldermanic candidate, speaker for *The Voice* and Liberty League

Julius A. Thomas: Active in the Alpha P.C. Club, *Voice* director and secretary

E. Thompson: Bandmaster, musician at Liberty League activities

Orlando Montrose Thompson: Publisher, "*Voice* Stockholder"

Charles E. Toney: *Voice* stockholder and attorney
William Monroe Trotter: Speaker for the Liberty League
A'lelia Walker: Heiress, speaker for the Liberty League
Madame C. J. Walker: Businesswoman, Liberty League member (?)
Sinclair Wilberforce: *Voice* writer
Dr. Reverend William: Liberty League member[97]

Overall, *The Voice* and Liberty League activists were a diverse group—from Pullman porter to attorney, Democratic Party leader to Socialist, Caribbean-born or Africa-born to native-born. The group was outstanding for the caliber of people involved—many had superior organizational skills, as evidenced by both past and subsequent activities. It was Harrison and his Liberty League and *Voice* that united in Harlem, for the first time, such a leadership group in such a radical, race-conscious effort.

In this setting of heightened political activity it was almost inevitable that there would be opportunists jumping on the bandwagon. It was in this context that Harrison received a portentous "Personal" letter from John E. Bruce, written after Bruce attended a Liberty League meeting on August 2, 1917. It read:

> I listened with pain to the yawking of your recalcitrants last night and I was greatly pleased with the way you handled matters. You are laying a bigger foundation than you perhaps realize in the formation of the Liberty League and your handicap at the very inception of the scheme is lack of co-workers with large vision—unselfish and patriotic leaders who have faith in your leadership. But you will win [in] spite of these butterheaded fellows who have been driven into the limelight by your oratory and work for racial betterment. They would never have been heard of had you not evolved the scheme which is at once the most sane and practical that have been put forward in the past fifty years. Your plan to go before Congress with the race grievances is *the plan*. Weed out the handkerchief heads from your privy council and surround yourself with new loyal and true who will hold up your hand and help to make you what nature has destined you to be a courageous leader of your people from the ranks where all real leaders should come from. keep cool.[98]

This letter, marking Harrison as the potential race leader "from the ranks," was also foreboding. It suggested that people uniting around him were not to be trusted and might be the cause of future problems. Differences did soon surface in the Liberty League, and they centered on Harrison's radical position on the racial aspects of the war, his militant call for loyalty to race before flag at home, his stand for political independence, and disputes over how the money for *The Voice* and Liberty League should be handled. Within a short time, W. A.

Domingo, Charles Christopher Seifert, Alexander Rahming, August V. Bernier, Gertrude Miller-Faide, Irene Moorman-Blackston, and Edgar M. Grey would all leave to work with Marcus Garvey.[99]

Harrison continued to advocate "Race First" and the campaign was having an effect. In the August 7 *Voice* readers were again urged to "patronize the places that advertise in THE VOICE and let the others wait." The "Theatrical Notes" column in that issue reviewed how the previous week's *Voice* had made some remarks that took the Lincoln Theater to task for the amount of sexual sug- gestiveness in the jokes of certain actors and how it "pointed out the anomaly of having many white acts and only one Negro act on the bill of a Negro play- house." After that column, the Lincoln sent someone to *The Voice* to complain that it wasn't covering the theater like the other "colored" papers did. Harrison concluded that *The Voice*'s opinion "right now counts for more with the theater than the opinion of any other Negro newspaper." The fact that this was accom- plished after only five weeks was attributed to "being independent and fearless and outspoken" and not "cringing for ads."[100]

The Voice was doing extraordinarily well. On August 11, 1917, it came out with the "First Extra Edition" in Harlem newspaper history. The August 14 issue reported that sales were up to 11,000 and included the first publication of Harri- son's important article "The White War and the Colored World." The article was based on his talks of 1914 through 1916, and it emphasized how the fratricidal strife in Europe over the division of the nonwhite world was a self-destructive battle in which the white race would suffer. Despite the paper's success, big advertisers were lacking. The August 14 issue again wondered on the where- abouts of advertisers Philip A. Payton, John M. Royall, Howard Adolph Howell, and others. The "Peanuts and Politics" editorial in that issue then put forth a call for a changed leadership course.[101]

August 1917 also witnessed the appearance of a two-page "Propaganda Circu- lar," *The Clarion*, which represented an alternate effort by other Liberty League members. Harrison was not mentioned as being on its staff, although his name was used in its advertising. The printer and publisher was Liberty League mem- ber August V. Bernier, who, in two years, would combine efforts with Harrison in the *New Negro*, which Harrison would edit and he would publish.[102]

The second two-page circular issue of *The Clarion*, on August 15, stated that the constitution of the Liberty League was to be presented for consideration at the regular meeting on Sunday, August 19. Bernier declared passage of the League constitution to be "of the greatest importance." The paper also indicated that League meetings were held on Sunday afternoons in rooms at the Lafay- ette Building (131st St. and Lenox Avenue) at 3 P.M. and they were followed by Harrison lectures at 8 P.M. During August Harrison also held open-air meet- ings at "Liberty's Corner" (134th Street and Lenox Ave). Officers of the Liberty

League, in mid-August 1917, were listed as: Harrison, president; Daniel E. Petersen, vice president; Auto Scott, secretary; W. A. Domingo, assistant secretary; and Trinidad-born Arthur Reid (who would later be active with the UNIA, the African Blood Brotherhood, and the Communist Party), treasurer. League speakers included George H. Green, Alexander Rahming, and the Barbados-born bibliophile Charles C. Seifert.[103]

The second issue of *The Clarion* announced plans for an upcoming three-in-one carnival to benefit Harrison's three main projects—the Liberty League, *The Voice*, and the Harlem People's Forum. The carnival was scheduled for September 4 at the Manhattan Casino at 155th St. and 8th Avenue. It was to be chaired by Dr. E. Elliot Rawlins, a physician, and would include short talks by Harrison and by the hair-products millionaire Mme. C. J. Walker. Entertainment was to be provided by Miss Daisy Tapley, the Martin Mason Trio, the Liberty League Quartet, and the Honey Bunch orchestra under the direction of William A. Riker. The popular dancemaster Charles H. Anderson was to be the floor manager, and businessman R. B. Minor, chairman of the Carnival Committee.[104]

In addition to mentioning other Liberty League activities, *The Clarion* included a portentous article that noted, "Mr. Marcus Garvey's meeting last Sunday afternoon [August 12] at Lafayette Hall was a big success; almost everyone joined the organization." Garvey had scheduled his meeting at 3 P.M., the same time as the Liberty League meeting. According to Liberty League member J. Domminick Simmons, Garvey had approached Mr. Bright, the caretaker of Lafayette Hall, and purposely tried to schedule his meetings to conflict with Harrison's. Garvey would soon move these meetings to the Palace Casino and continue to purposely schedule them to conflict with the meetings of Harrison's Liberty League.[105]

The sixteen-page third issue of *The Clarion*, published by Bernier on September 1, listed Lovett Fort-Whiteman as collaborator and declared, "Our platform is that of the Liberty League and is fully expressed in the *Declaration of Principles* [of the Liberty League] printed on page 3." It stated that Harrison, the "president of the Liberty League of Negro Americans, and the Race's most prominent agitator," was "arousing all Harlem, and bestirring our conservative Negro leaders to madness." The issue also included articles by Gertrude Miller-Faide and W. A. Domingo, poems by Bernier and Rahming, and letters from Bishop T. Frederick Selkridge and from "A Proud New Negro" (which discussed Harrison's "soap box" oratory and preference for using the name "Negro" over "colored").[106]

In an editorial entitled "The Future of the Negro," Bernier's *Clarion* stated that the Liberty League "has embraced in its platforms some of the most progressive principles of the day; standing out for universal suffrage for both men and women, it is waging a strong campaign that our women may have the ballot, and that the millions of our brothers in the South may again have the right to vote for better conditions for their Posterity." Bernier added that the League "also believes that the so-called race problem can and will be solved by ourselves as soon as we realize the value of Business and its great effective powers among the other races of the world." His editorial concluded that "independent commercial development" was "one of the sure ways by which we may advance successfully even to the point of placing ourselves on a footing with other races and nations."[107]

While that editorial hinted at developing entrepreneurial aspirations of some within the New Negro Movement, even more revealing was the *Clarion* editorial, "Our Foreword," which explained that "we have united our efforts with the labors of the Liberty League of Negro-Americans as also with that of the Universal Negro Improvement Association [Garvey's organization]. From both organizations our efforts have received hearty approval, and under whose auspices we are working to attain the desired end." This was followed by a brief piece that mentioned that Garvey, founder and president of the Jamaica Division of the UNIA, spoke at a meeting of the New York branch presided over by President Rahming at Lafayette Hall at 3:30 P.M. on Sunday, September 25 and that "many new members were added to the roll which is steadily growing." Of additional interest was a prominent reprint from Shakespeare's anthology of poems, "The Passionate Pilgrim," with the parenthetical note, perhaps directed at Harrison, "An egoistic Editor, might find a moral here."[108]

In August 1917, in the midst of such heightened activity, Harrison completed his first book, *The Negro and the Nation*. It contained reprints of articles from 1910 through 1914 and was published by the Cosmo-Advocate Publishing Company, headed by Orlando M. Thompson, a future vice president of the Black Star Line. Harrison was at a highpoint in popularity, and the book's "Introductory" described how the World War had quickened the development of race consciousness.[109]

The book was described as "a Product of the People and for the People" by *The Clarion*. That appraisal hints at the relationship that existed between Harrison and his Black constituency. It was a relationship in which Harrison, in his courageous and often pioneering efforts, was encouraged, emboldened, and sustained over the years by support coming from the Black community in which he was so deeply rooted. It was also a relationship in which Harrison's efforts, in turn, enlightened and pointed the way forward for that awakening community. Years later Harrison's children still remarked on how well known, loved, and respected their father was as he walked around the streets of Harlem. Harrison and the community developed through an intimate relationship with each other, a relationship in which a strong race- and class-conscious individual strengthened and, in turn, was strengthened by, the growing strength and consciousness of a racially oppressed and overwhelmingly working-class community.[110]

One particular Harrison strong point was his ability to look at his own efforts objectively. His comments about *The Negro and the Nation* written three years later demonstrate this. In 1920 correspondence with the author T. Lothrop Stoddard he explained that the book's articles were somewhat dated when the book was published and they would have been more timely three or four years earlier. He also judged that the book would have benefited from editing since the presentation of materials showed little design or plan. It appears, based on his comments, that in publishing *The Negro and the Nation* Harrison was trying to provide some radical, race-conscious material for people to read. He may also have been attempting to ride the crest of awakening race consciousness toward some remuneration for his work.[111]

In his preface to *The Negro and the Nation* Harrison indicated that he planned, in the near future, to write a book "on the New Negro" that would "set forth the aims and ideals of the new Manhood Movement among American Negroes which has grown out of the international crusade 'for democracy.'" He eventually did complete that book—his 1920 Porro Press publication, *When Africa Awakes: The "Inside Story" of the Stirrings and Strivings of the New Negro in the Western World*, which again used Africa, in the racial, not geographical, sense. That book, too, was a collection of essays put together with limited overall plan. When Stoddard wrote to Harrison in 1920 that this second book contained "a good deal of repetition" (a criticism also appropriate for his first book) and offered some editing suggestions, Harrison indicated that he hated to rewrite and reedit his articles. He responded with a confession: "I fear that I am too lazy to go over the thing again. Having done it once, I am through. . . . after having read my own stuff six or eight times, I am so thoroughly sick at looking at one of the pages that I almost hope I will never see it again except as marketable commodity."[112]

Despite its editorial limitations, Harrison desired to have *The Negro and the Nation* circulated as widely as possible "among Negroes and white people." It was published in a run of 5,000 at the popular price of twenty-five cents. The book was well received domestically, and it appears that virtually all copies were sold or otherwise distributed. Internationally, the revolutionary government that emerged in Russia also recognized its importance. When Claude McKay traveled to the Soviet Union in 1922 and 1923, he was commissioned by the State Publishing Department of Moscow to write a book on "The Negro Question." One of the books provided to him for the project by his Comintern (Communist International) hosts was Harrison's *The Negro and the Nation*. Though McKay completed his work in 1923, it was not translated into English until it was printed in the United States as *The Negroes in America* in 1979.[113]

On August 17, 1917, the Cosmo-Advocate Publishing Company, which published *The Negro and the Nation*, also agreed to print *The Voice* at 2305 Seventh Avenue. The contract called for the weekly printing of "not less than 10,000 copies." It is possible that Harrison used his bargaining power in arranging *The Voice* contract to facilitate publication of his book, or vice versa.[114]

With his book in circulation, Harrison continued to edit *The Voice* in a militant, race-conscious fashion. In the August 28 issue he wrote another fiery editorial on a race riot. This time it was the August 23 riot in Houston, Texas. The Houston riot was directly related to the increase in lynchings nationwide and to East St. Louis. Seasoned regular troops of the United States Army's Twenty-fourth Infantry, Third Battalion, were stationed at Houston while they were used in the building of nearby Camp Logan. The soldiers, Black men from North and South, faced tightened Jim Crow regulations, which they resisted. They refused to be limited to Jim Crow sections of theaters and streetcars, to drink from separate water barrels in camp, and to be denied the dignity their service and their military status should have commanded. The city of Houston responded through its police force, and the soldiers were repeatedly insulted, beaten, and arrested.[115]

On August 23, a month after the battalion arrived, a Black soldier intervened as a white policeman was beating a Black woman, and the soldier was beaten and arrested. When Corporal Charles Baltimore went to inquire, he, too, was beaten and arrested, and rumor quickly spread that he was killed by the police. Pitched battles then ensued between the Black soldiers and white police and armed white civilians. Two Black soldiers and seventeen whites, including five policemen were killed. For so defending themselves the men of the Twenty-fourth regiment were disarmed and immediately arrested. Sixty-four were subjected to the largest courts-martial in American military history—lasting twenty-two days and including 169 prosecution and 27 defense witnesses, filling 2,100 typed pages, and resulting in thirteen soldiers being sentenced to death, forty-two receiving life sentences, four receiving long prison terms, and five acquitted.[116]

The trial of these soldiers lasted through November 1917, and, on the morning of December 11, before their sentences were publicly announced, thirteen of the men (who sang a hymn on the way to the gallows) were summarily and secretly hanged. The army then tried an additional fifty-five soldiers in two more courts-martial, and sixteen more were sentenced to hang (six did) and twelve to life in prison. The African American community was outraged since the December 11 hangings were in private, before the public knew, and before the president or the secretary of war had reviewed and given approval to the decision. Pressure from the African American community eventually saved ten of those sentenced to death, whose sentences were commuted to life. While the Houston soldiers were charged, racist "white" Southern sentiment against the stationing of Black troops in the South reached new highs.[117]

In his editorial "Houston vs. Waco," Harrison explained that Houston and Waco were both in Texas, and both had killings. On May 15, 1916, at Waco, 15,000 white people had expressed enjoyment as a mentally retarded Black adolescent, Jesse Washington, had his eyes gouged out and his body horribly mutilated in a public square before being burned to death in an iron cage in the presence of a crowd that reportedly included thousands of women and children and the mayor and other city officials. The case attracted major attention after the NAACP's *Crisis* magazine mailed 42,000 copies of a special eight-page supplement on the murder to subscribers around the country. A year after Waco came Houston, and Harrison discussed the connection between the two events. At Houston, he wrote, "whites were the sufferers and Negroes the perpetrators." Killings at both places were illegal, he argued, but "every fool knows that the spirit of lawlessness, mob-violence and race hatred which found expression in the first was the thing which called forth the second." He than offered an important conclusion—Black soldiers, he wrote, would "always be a menace to any state which lynches Negro civilians."[118]

In late August Harrison again addressed problems of leadership. His militant, race-conscious paper, widely popular among the Black masses, was not getting the support of the established Harlem leaders or of the white Socialists. In addition, there was disagreement within the Liberty League leadership. In the August 28 *Voice* he wrote "Politics and Personality," an editorial that further revealed his views on the relation between the individual and the collective, the importance of confronting issues, and the role of criticism in an organization. The editorial, probably written in partial response to reactions to his comments at the July 29 mass meeting, recommended that "politics and personal friendship must be kept separate," that dissenting opinions could be tolerated in work for similar goals, and that criticism could be an asset. He noted that there were some "little men" who did not understand "the personal conditions of politics" and who, if opposed politically, went on to "make a personal matter of it." These men think that if you do not constantly hold their political views then you must either not speak or become their "personal enemies." To Harrison, this was true of most Black leaders since these were "the conditions under which Negro politicians live and move and have their being—in state and church and lodge room."[119]

He realized that his own development, from the days of his apprenticeship—at St. Benedict's and St. Mark's lyceums, where "the fiercest opposition in debate, could not take from the cordiality of personal friendship"—was quite different. It was that attitude he sought to bring to public life as he stated that whether it was John Royall, Charles Anderson, Asa Philip Randolph, or any other personal friends or acquaintances, he would insist "on the right to differ from them, to criticize their policies and to dissent from any part of their program" that he believed wrong. This would be done "openly and publicly, without beating the devil around the stump." He would later stress the need for "courage, fortitude, [and] heroism" in Black leaders and the need "to guard against the same faults in our own leaders" that "we condemn in white leaders"—including "lack of knowledge" and "swaggering pretentiousness."[120]

Harrison used this general introduction to move into the issue of the upcoming local elections and to stress the need for true political independence. *The Voice*, besides reporting on the traditional Black Republicans, would cover the Socialists, staunchly advocate independent Black candidates, and, for the first time in the history of Harlem weeklies, provide a front-page interview with a Black Harlem Democrat—Ferdinand Q. Morton, the head of the United Colored Democracy. Harrison saw the upcoming local election campaign in New York as a *Voice* "try-out" for "the real contest to come," the November elections. The community would be able to judge the paper and evaluate it in comparison with its competitors. Harrison warned that any papers "that attempt to keep up the old game of 'selling-out' will be driven to the journalistic bone-yard . . . by the common people who stand behind us." He expressed confidence that *The Voice*'s example would help "put an end to our 'colored' newspapers peddling their support at campaign time."[121]

Shortly after the "Politics and Personality" piece, in September 1917, Harrison wrote one of his more forceful editorials, "The New Policies for the New Negro." It was a persuasive call to move from appointed to elected representation. He explained that the current period in which new democratic issues had "brought forth new ideas of freedom, politics, industry and society" was "essentially [a] new turning point in the path of human progress" and the "new Negro" was "just as responsive to these new impulses as other people." In the past, Harrison explained, it had been easy to have Black people follow in the footsteps of others, and "mere mention of the name Lincoln or the Republican party" was sufficient to secure allegiance "to that party which had seen him stripped of all political power and civil rights" without any significant protest. Matters were different now, and the "new Negro" was "no longer begging or asking," but "demanding elective representation" as "a right" that he would enforce.[122]

Such a demand "bewildered" the "old political leaders" whose "old idea of Negro leadership by virtue of the white man's selection ha[d] collapsed." This old idea had been the established practice, in both parties and at the national and local levels, while Booker T. Washington was alive. Essentially, in exchange for either votes or community quiescence, white-appointed Black leaders would receive some money and some political appointments. In New York, the Republican Party maintained a segregated political club system, while the Democratic Party had (since 1898) a segregated citywide organization—the United Colored

Democracy. Under this setup, the Black party leader was, according to Marsha Hurst Hiller, "directly accountable only to the white Party leader at the top," not to Black voters. "Usually," explained Hiller, "the Black leader who acted as the chief buffering agent was hand picked by the white politicians," and this "assured them not only that the new man would be loyal, but that he would be satisfied with advances in his own political influence without demanding general advances of political influence or material well-being for the race." The effect of this political arrangement was clearly against the interests of the Black masses. Now, however, as Harrison made clear, "the new Negro" political leader would have to "be chosen by his fellows—by those whose strivings he is supposed to represent."[123]

Harrison explained that anyone who aspired "to lead the Negro race" had to "set squarely before his face the idea of 'Race First.'" This was because Black people were realizing that "our first duty is to ourselves" and were "intent upon being Negroes before they are Christians, Englishmen or Republicans." Harrison forecast that in the Western world, Black people, with no power in government or in politics would have to "follow the path of the Swadesha movement of India and the Sinn Fein movement of Ireland," two movements whose names meant "ourselves first." He concluded his editorial by predicting that "*The new Negro race in America will not achieve political self-respect until it is in a position to organize itself as a politically independent party and follow the example of the Irish Home Rulers*."[124]

On September 4 Harrison used his *Voice* editorial, "Why Is a Negro?" to probe more deeply into the subject of racial awareness. For a long time he had advocated the use of the term "Negro" as a form of positive racial self-assertion and opposed the term "Colored," which was often preferred by lighter-skinned people. In his editorial he responded to an argument, made by some, against use of the word "Negro" with a capital "N." He challenged the argument they offered—that "Negroes will be lynched, segregated and snubbed because they call themselves Negroes and capitalize it." Harrison argued that what should be stopped was "not the calling but the *being* 'niggers.'" He reasoned that "when we respect ourselves more and act up to the full measure of manhood—any manhood,—we will not only make ourselves respected but our name also." Harrison suggested that Black leaders "use their influence to make Negroes stop calling one another 'niggers,'" adding that if this were done, maybe even "the white men would follow their example."[125]

Harrison did believe that the excitement over the choice of a racial name was legitimate, and he emphasized that readers would know why when *The Voice* published its upcoming articles on "Negro Society and the Negro Stage" (which appeared in the issues of September 19 and October 3). In those articles, Harrison challenged the specious claim "advanced, explicitly and implicitly, by

Negroids of mixed blood [who called themselves 'colored'] to be considered the natural leaders of Negro activities on the ground of some alleged 'superiority' inherent in their white blood," and he challenged the alleged superiority of the "mulatto" and the color prejudice existing within the African American community.[126]

Some barbs were aimed directly at George W. Harris, publisher of the Black weekly *New York News*, who was having problems with the preaching of "Race First" for "'Negro' Americans." Harrison reviewed Harris's article on "The Negro's Part in the Discovery and Exploration of America" in the July 1906 issue of J. Max Barber's *The Voice of the Negro* and noted that Harris used the word "Negro," and no other words, as "a designation of the race (to which he very nearly belongs)" some fifty-nine times. Harrison then asked Harris to explain what had happened in the ensuing eleven years to change his mind on the subject. Finally, Harrison concluded his argument by pointing out that terms such as Protestant, Whig, and Christian were at first terms of opprobrium. Yet those so called responded by making themselves "great and respected." Because of this the names were now "among the proudest in the records of humanity." The task ahead was clear, he thought. "Negroes" should "stop selling ourselves and our race to the white man," should "stop bending the knee and bowing the head to every insult and contumely," and should "stop growing a wish bone where our backbone ought to be." By so doing, he predicted, "the name Negro, by which we call ourselves (except when we are ashamed)," would be respected.[127]

Harrison's race-conscious themes influenced every piece in *The Voice*. Even short filler boxes promoted racial awareness. A September 4 "News and Views" question box raised pointed questions over a Black man being removed from the State Artillery; over Jewish store owners on Lenox Avenue refusing to rent stores to Black businessmen; and over the young men at the newly established, segregated, Black officers' training camp in Des Moines, Iowa, being "requested to sign blanks pledging themselves to accept appointment as Sergeants rather than Lieutenants." The September 4 issue also included a little piece sure to provoke a reaction from "New Negroes." It was a letter from Rev. W. M. Spearman of Union City, Georgia, to the editor of the *Atlanta Constitution*. Spearman made such statements as "the southern white people . . . are and always have been" the Negro's "'best friend'" and "for the last fifty years they have helped educate us, and now they have brought us sunshine. They have taught us all that we know." Harrison, didn't even comment, he simply entitled the piece: "Why They Call Us 'Niggers.'"[128]

Harrison did not blindly promote racial pride because he was concerned about the use to which it could be put. Thus while he continued to agitate for race consciousness, he also continued to criticize Black realtors who charged excessively high rents. In the September 4 issue he offered a satirical piece on high rents entitled "Real Estate News from Siam." The article was printed under the pseudonym "Yung Cheng" ("Yung-chen" was the name of the emperor who in 1729 prohibited the sale and smoking of opium in China). It was claimed that "Yung Cheng" was the paper's Cambodian Correspondent from French Indo-China. "Yung Cheng" claimed that Chinese minority landlords were skinning rents just like the majority landlords. The article urged the minority people not to be so quick to move into houses vacated by the majority in order to keep the rents down, and it ended: "Send us some news from America when you write and let us know whether you have any problems like ours in your country."[129]

The Liberty League and *The Voice*, the first organization and the first newspaper of the "New Negro" movement had created a powerful and unprecedented impact. By the late summer and early autumn of 1917, Harrison was exerting major influence over a developing generation of militants and "common people" with his race-conscious and radical mass appeal, and he was pointing the way toward new organizational forms and political activity. However, as John Bruce had forewarned, the Liberty League and *The Voice* were soon subject to internal difficulties.

CHAPTER

11

Race-Conscious Activism
and Organizational Difficulties
(August–December 1917)

During the late summer and early autumn of 1917, as The Voice *put out its mili-*
tant, race-conscious message, it nurtured the "New Negro movement," influenced a growing number of radicals and "common people," and addressed local,
national, and international issues. Problems emerged, however, with both the
Liberty League and *The Voice*, some activists moved toward other organizations,
and by mid-November the paper temporarily stopped publication. Harrison excelled as an educator, agitator, and race-conscious propagandist, but he was falling short in tending to organizational needs.

Money was a major problem. One issue was the question of the newspaper's
base of support. The problem was simple. To finance a newspaper money was
needed. Where would that money come from? Related problems concerned how
the money would be spent and who would control the spending.

Specifically, in the case of *The Voice*, as a race-conscious, "Race First," paper,
support from whites was not relied upon. As a class-conscious paper, advertisements from wealthy donors were generally not forthcoming. On principle, Harrison refused what he considered to be demeaning advertisements for beauty
products that "whitened." Because of the paper's firm position of political independence, it lacked consistent support from the established political parties and
political machines. The main source of income came from the low-paid Black
masses, whose resources were limited.

In the Black community a major market was developing, a market that would
reach a nationwide circulation for Black newspapers of approximately one million by 1922. This potential market was partially limited by illiteracy, which hovered around 22 percent for Black people nationwide, though in New York City
it was less of a problem—Black illiteracy was only about 5 percent in the city. In

New York, however, there was competition from three major weeklies—the *Age*, the *Amsterdam News*, and the *New York News*. Marcus Garvey would later solve similar financial problems, in part, by developing a host of related financial efforts, including the Black Star Line and the Liberian Construction Fund, which were geared toward Black consumers and supporters.[1]

The issue of political independence was particularly important. William H. Ferris, who later served as associate editor of the *Negro World*, explained that Black America at first "produced more educated men than we had a professional class to support them" and under such circumstances "colored editors had to fall back on politicians to run their papers because there were few color[e]d men advertising in their papers." This was especially true in New York City, where papers such as the *Age* and *New York News* were long associated with the Republican Party. In contrast to such past practice, Harrison's *Voice* clearly showed too much political independence for Republicans, Democrats, and Socialists in New York in 1917.[2]

Besides the broader question of the base of financial support, there were also very specific money-related problems that arose. First, two of *The Voice*'s pro-Republican competitors took action against it. Economic pressure was put on the printer of *The Voice*, William H. Willis of the Beehive Printing Company, by the *Age* and the *New York News*. Harrison suggested that Emmett Scott, the former principal assistant of Booker T. Washington and a person intimately involved in Harrion's firing from the Post Office, may have used his close political and financial relationship with the *Age* to get that paper to pressure Willis. Both the *Age* and the *News* had larger circulations than *The Voice*, and they forced Willis, who owned the printing facility in the basement of 2305 Seventh Avenue where the three papers were printed, to print their papers first. Printing of *The Voice* was put back one day each week, and Harrison was forced to announce that the paper would come out on Wednesdays instead of Tuesdays.[3]

As a means to counter this economic pressure, Harrison announced that there would be a Sunday edition of *The Voice* beginning on September 16. The Sunday edition was to be a "Family Paper," with departments for women and children and with columns on sports, travel, drama, and humor. It would also include biographies of distinguished Black people from Africa, America, and the West Indies, historical sketches, and many illustrations. *The Voice* would be the "first bi-weekly Negro paper in the United States—perhaps in the world," and it would sell for five cents.[4]

These plans led to two other specific money-related problems: who would control *The Voice*'s funds and how these funds would be used. Anselmo Jackson, a Frederiksted, St. Croix–born, Harlem-based, writer for *The Voice*, later reported that a dispute arose over the control of funds. He suggested that Harrison wanted to control the funds and others in the organization opposed this in favor of control by the organization. Richard B. Moore, a board member of the Cosmo-Advocate Publishing Company, similarly reported that dissension arose over *The Voice*'s ownership. According to Moore, Harrison claimed ownership while several members of the Liberty League said it should be owned by the organization.[5]

Harrison's handling of money also aroused concern. Jackson indicated that Harrison did not spend the money of the Liberty League and of *The Voice* wisely and that he overspent. In the September 19, 1917, *Voice*, Harrison described how "large bodies move more slowly than small ones," and *The Voice*'s board of directors "less rapidly than" the "editor alone did." The board felt that movement at this slower pace was "laying a more sincere foundation," and the *Sunday Voice* was put off, presumably for at least another month. Actually, it never came out. It appears that when faced with the general pressure from the lack of regular advertising from both wealthy Harlemites and the established political parties, and with the specific pressure from the competing newspapers, Harrison's response was to fight back by seeking to expand operations and to try to have the paper come out more frequently. This was opposed by other board members as impractical. Harrison's overspending was probably related, at least in part, to his desire to expand rather than contract in the face of competitive pressure.[6]

Such a scenario is supported by other evidence. Throughout his life Harrison was both a fighter and a poor handler of money, though he had no personal desire to amass wealth. Sixty-five years after *The Voice* was founded, his children still remarked on his underestimation of the importance of money and his inability to handle money matters adequately. He was an intellectual who loved learning and teaching. His thoughts were often far removed from day-in, day-out financial matters. Further, he never received remuneration from employment equal to the skill and energy he contributed and, therefore, did not have money of his own with which to cover losses.[7]

Another problem area involving money was the question of its source. Harrison reported in July 1918 that a major dispute arose in December 1917 over his refusal to accept $10,000 from a white patron. He did this in order to maintain *The Voice* as a Black-controlled paper. Harrison would allegedly refuse a similar offer, several years later, from the Communist Party in order to maintain political independence. In this his approach differed from that of Booker T. Washington, who received large sums from wealthy white financiers and industrialists. It differed from that of W. E. B. Du Bois, who received considerable money from white liberals and socialists, and from that of the Black socialists A. Philip Randolph and Chandler Owen (whom Harrison referred to as "the Gold Dust Twins" and "the Subsidized Sixth) and of the soon-to-be communist, Cyril V. Briggs, all of whom reportedly received significant financial backing from their white socialist or communist supporters.[8]

From September 1917 onward *The Voice* was in serious financial trouble. In the issue of September 12 Harrison announced that the paper was up for sale and urged readers to take part in its ownership. *The Voice* would be incorporated for $25,000, with 2,500 shares at $10 each. Officers were Harrison, president; the postal worker Julius A. Thomas, secretary; and Edward O. Boddie, treasurer. The first sales, totaling about $150, were made on Sunday, September 9, at the Palace Casino. Additional pledges totaling $1,360 were made by a group of twenty-two people, including Boddie, Thomas, Harrison's boyhood friend James A. Glasgow, the attorney Charles E. Toney, the printer Orlando M. Thompson, the businessman R. B. Minor, and Harrison (who put up $150).[9]

Harrison emphasized that the paper could be ten times better and that Black people had "been waiting for years for a paper which they could open in street cars and other public places without feeling ashamed." *The Voice*, he wrote, would not carry "the 'Kink-No-More,' 'Kongolene Knocks Kinks,' 'Oxonized Ox Marrow,' "Raddrizator Hair Straightening Outfits,' and the big black person turned into a white person in two ticks, which disgrace so many of our 'colored' journals." As he explained to readers, "If the policy of racial self-respect is what the Negro people want in a paper of their own," then it was up to them to show it by buying the stock of *The Voice*.[10]

Harrison intended to continue providing Black people the race paper he felt was wanted and needed, but his efforts soon faced additional, internal, problems. The September 19 issue of *The Voice* carried a large advertisement announcing a mass meeting for members and friends of the Liberty League to be held at the Palace Casino on Sunday, September 23, for the purpose of completing the organization of the League, ratifying the election of officers, adopting the constitution, discussing "the Problem of 'Negro Soldiers vs. Negro Citizens,'" and considering the resignation of the organization's president. In the same issue Harrison indicated there was a split in the Liberty League between himself and those, including August V. Bernier, who had put out *The Clarion*. Harrison disavowed any connection with *The Clarion* and warned readers about being stung for advertisements in that paper, which was using his name under false pretenses.[11]

It appears that this break was somewhat formalized with the appearance of the October 13, 1917, issue of the Bernier-edited *New Negro* newspaper magazine (identified as vol. 1, no. 4, and formerly *The Clarion*). Other staffers included Gertrude Miller-Faide as managing editor, Wilheminia Morton-Williams (an elocutionist, basketball coach, and motorcycle driver) as sports editor, Frank Billups as advertising manager, Beatrice Ione-Wade (an elocutionist from Brooklyn) as traveling agent, Florence Ryerson as an advertising agent, and Irena Moorman-Blackston, Arthur Reid, Emil M. Rasmussen, W. A. Domingo, and Alexander Rahming as contributing editors. The prominent involvement of women in this "official organ of the New Negro Manhood (and womanhood, of course) movement" was also reflected in the establishment of the "New Negro Willing Working Women's Club." Moorman-Blackston was identified as president of the UNIA Woman's Division and Miller-Faide as associate secretary and stenographer of the UNIA. The issue discussed an October 7 talk at a UNIA activity by Mary Church Terrell of Washington, D.C., and the fact that Marcus Garvey addressed the crowd and introduced the officers of the New York Branch of the UNIA, including Rahming, its president, and Blackston, Miller-Faide, Charles S. Seifert, John E. Bruce, Bishop T. Frederick Selkridge, Mrs. Sims, J. H. Porter, E. D. Smith, Ethel Oughton Clarke, and James Harris. A December 15, 1917, *New Negro* was again edited by Bernier, with Miller-Faide as managing editor, Pope Billups as advertising manager, and Domingo, Rahming, William H. Scott and Andrea Razafkeriefo as contributing editors. Many of these people were, or had been, Liberty League members.[12]

It was in this period around September through December 1917 that significant members of the Liberty League appear to have begun to gravitate away from that organization and toward Marcus Garvey, who was holding meetings that at times conflicted with Harrison's. According to Domingo, Garvey got his UNIA organized "with some of the dissidents of Hubert Harrison's organization, the Liberty League."[13] As indicated in *The Clarion* and *The New Negro*, people who attended Harrison's talks and Liberty League meetings also attended Garvey's talks. For many, the appeal of the meetings—"the call to racial self-help and racial self-sufficiency"—was probably quite similar.[14]

Garvey did not simply sweep away Harrison's followers in 1917. Between late 1917 and 1920, the torch of race leadership did pass from Harrison to Garvey, but it did not happen at once. It is certainly arguable that Harrison remained the more prominent race leader, at least through the summer of 1918, when he chaired the Liberty Congress in Washington, D.C.[15]

Garvey's early efforts had sputtered noticeably. When he arrived in New York he sought to follow the course of Booker T. Washington, but this course had limited mass appeal in World War I–era New York. Similarly, Garvey's extremely "non-political" approach did not win him a great following in the new, increasingly politicized climate in which more militant, race-conscious "ground had been prepared" by "outspoken voices" such as Harrison's. Harrison was at the top of his form as a street speaker, and he was the leading radical "New Negro" at a highpoint of the "New Negro movement." Any explanation for the shift from Harrison to Garvey has to look beyond a notion of Garvey's oratory completely sweeping audiences from Harrison in the summer of 1917.[16]

Certain individual characteristics of the two men are particularly important in assessing their leadership roles. Harrison was an intellectual who, in general, discouraged admiration and flattery. He was direct and unsparing in his criticism, spent little effort acquiring worldly possessions other than books, and favored exacting and scientific truth over exaggeration. His appeal was primarily intellectual. He was not oriented toward material measures of a person's worth; he was decidedly radical in his opposition to the capitalist system and imperialism; and his critical style was not one that either cajoled followers or fed their egos. In addition, Harrison had wide-ranging interests—intellectual, social, and political—and he was not consumed with organizational matters. Harrison was also a freethinking agnostic/atheist, and he was openly critical of the role played by Christianity and the church.[17]

Garvey, in contrast, as Robert A. Hill explains, judged material possessions as a measure of one's worth. He supported capitalism and desired empire. This was very much acceptable in World War I America, in which capitalist and entrepreneurial ideology held sway. Garvey was also a self-aggrandizer without peer and a man who, through pomp and titles, was willing to feed the self-images of many followers. He was a master of the emotional appeal. Garvey would do, on a large scale, what Harrison desired to do—stir the hearts of the African American masses. He would prove to be capable of winning and holding, at least for a time, large groups of followers. He also had little time for anything that was not directly connected with his organizational efforts, and he was able to incorporate religion and religious leaders in his movement.[18]

The political differences between Harrison and Garvey were particularly important. First, there was the different approach toward capitalism and imperialism, both of which Harrison opposed. There was also the prescient warning of John E. Bruce that though Harrison was the man to lead African Americans forward, many of those around him were careerists and opportunists, not half his equal—people who could not be trusted and who had no backbone, "handkerchief heads" who lacked his "large vision." The issue of the political direction of the Liberty League and *The Voice* and the question of finances seemed to bring Bruce's warning to life.[19]

The individuals who went from Harrison's circle to Garvey's suggest that political reasons accelerated the move from the Liberty League. First and, according to J. Domminick Simmons, most important, were Harrison's lectures. His militant stands on the racial and imperialist implications of the war and on domestic matters distanced him from some of his followers. Harrison later pointed out in the *New Negro* magazine that when *The Voice* appeared it "was the first and only paper to say fight back in the face of mob attack." This bold position in wartime America was certainly not one for the weak-willed. Harrison's radical political direction was a more difficult path to tread in the prowar atmosphere of 1917. His militant political stance was a principal reason that some of his followers went toward Garvey, who had no such troublesome image in wartime and had previously asked his supporters to stay out of politics. Garvey, according to

Richard B. Moore, was "not as aggressive then as he later became," and he was soon able to organize "with some of the dissidents of Hubert Harrison's Liberty League."[20]

Those with more traditional political ambitions likely felt threatened by Harrison's militance and more at home with Garvey, who was politically safer. (According to Richard B. Moore, other radicals "did not consider Garvey a radical.") Further, political parties were traditionally a source of funding for Black newspapers and organizations, and Harrison's independence from the established political parties made it extremely unlikely that his paper and organization would draw such money. With Garvey's UNIA there was a chance to turn the organization toward political funding, particularly if organizational control could be obtained. Harrison had already shown that, despite internal opposition, he would maintain control of the Liberty League and *The Voice*. With Garvey's organization there was a chance to seize control and an actual seizure of control by the "politicals" did take place.[21]

The group interested in traditional political activity that moved toward Garvey included Samuel A. Duncan, the attorney Louis A. Leavelle, and Barbados-born Isaac Allen, a former longshoreman. Duncan would run in Harlem's Nineteenth Assembly District in 1921 as an Independent Republican and be disqualified. Leavelle had been a Progressive nominee for the Twenty-first Assembly district in Harlem in 1914 and would run again in 1922. In 1924 he would become a Democratic nominee for Congress from the Third Congressional District in the Bronx. Isaac Allen would run in 1924 as an Independent Republican for a seat in the Twenty-seventh Aldermanic District in Harlem and be disqualified. With these politicals so influential in the UNIA, it is not surprising that a split soon ensued in that organization. Garvey claimed it was because these three led an effort to turn the UNIA into a political club and to support political candidates. For a while they were successful in their efforts to control the UNIA. By November 27, 1917, Allen was listed as the president of the UNIA, Duncan as third vice president, and the former Liberty League activists Charles C. Seifert, John Bruce, and Irena Moorman-Blackston were, respectively, the second vice president, chairman of the advisory board, and president of the ladies division of the UNIA. By January 20, 1918, Duncan was the president; Moorman-Blackston, first vice-president; Leavelle, sergeant-at-arms; Seifert, chaplain; and Bruce, chairman of the advisory board. Garvey had resigned. Then, he claims, he was "forced into court," and he "had to somewhat beat up Duncan in detaching him from the presidency of the newly formed division of New York." The use of the courts and the use of physical intimidation were responses that Garvey would call on again in the future.[22]

Others who left the Liberty League or its periphery to go with Garvey were those with entrepreneurial aspirations, including W. A. Domingo (who developed a West Indian import business), the former postal worker Edgar Grey, and Charles Seifert. According to J. Domminick Simmons, among the first to go were Domingo, Seifert, Grey, Alexander Rahming, and the business-oriented August V. Bernier. Others who went toward Garvey early included Irena Moorman-Blackston, Anselmo Jackson, and John Edward Bruce. The Liberty League treasurer Arthur Reid and the *Voice* publisher Orlando M. Thompson also began to work for Garvey. Domingo, in particular, distanced himself from Harrison. Grey suggested something more. He said that it was Domingo who turned Garvey away from Harrison's direction. Domingo, a businessman as well as a journalist, also influenced Garvey in an entrepreneurial direction, according to Grey. If Grey is correct, it was Liberty League members who at first pulled Garvey from Harrison, and not the opposite.[23]

While some with entrepreneurial and political aspirations moved toward Garvey, it is clear that he did not simply sweep all of those around Harrison into his orbit. The former Liberty League member John E. Bruce is a good example. Bruce's name appeared as a UNIA officer and on UNIA stationery in November 1917, yet he was likely very critical of Garvey at that time. In January 1918 he was publicly quoted as appraising Garvey extremely unfavorably and in an open letter to the *New Negro* asked Garvey, "Who are you anyhow and what is your game?" Then, around June 1918 he described Garvey as a man who "has about as much influence with the 400,000,000 [Garvey's number] people of Africa who are to be consolidated under his leadership into one great, powerful and influential Negro nationality, as the Statue of Liberty." Bruce added that "Garvey is fooling only the unthinking among the people of the Negro race in this city."[24]

In this period Bruce and Moorman-Blackston still seemed to follow Harrison's lead, suggesting that movement toward Garvey was not clear, decisive, or sweeping. Bruce began to more strongly support Garvey in October 1919, after a very significant "Two Negro Radicalisms" article by Harrison endorsed Garvey over the socialist-leaning radicals. Then, after Harrison became principal editor of the *Negro World* in early 1920, Bruce became a journalist for the paper. Moorman-Blackston went with Garvey in late 1917, yet though she was active with the UNIA, she continued to support Harrison for years. In 1918 she paid his passage to Washington, D.C., for the Liberty Congress, and as late as 1921 she was an active Liberty League member.[25]

Individuals from the Liberty League quickly assumed major roles with Garvey. The October 13 *New Negro* indicated that Liberty League activists were now working with the UNIA and Alexander Rahming was president of the New York Branch, with Irene Moorman-Blackston, Charles S. Seifert, Gertrude Miller-Faide, and John E. Bruce listed as officers.[26] By late 1918 Garvey would publish the first issue of the two-page *Negro World*, and its first editor would be the former assistant secretary of the Liberty League, W. A. Domingo. The former

Figure 11.1. W. A. Domingo, undated. Jamaica-born Wilfred Adolphus Domingo (1889–1968) served as assistant secretary of the Liberty League. He had first introduced Marcus Garvey (whom he knew in Jamaica) to Harrison and he then later switched from Harrison's Liberty League to Garvey's movement, where he served as first editor of the *Negro World.* Domingo, a socialist, was one of the first Liberty League members to move towards Garvey, and the Liberty League secretary Edgar M. Grey suggested that it was Domingo who turned Garvey away from Harrison's direction. *Source:* Courtesy of Joyce Moore Turner.

Voice writer Anselmo Jackson served as a *Negro World* reporter. By 1919, Edgar Grey. a former secretary of the Liberty League, was business manager of the *Negro World* as well as general secretary of the UNIA, assistant secretary of the Black Star Line, and secretary of the New York local, the organization's largest. As 1919 wore on—flamed by major race riots—the UNIA, with Grey as a principal organizer, and the *Negro World*, with Domingo as editor, began to grow. *Negro World* circulation soon hovered around 10,000, the same figure attained by Harrison's *Voice* in 1917. On July 26, 1919, the *Negro World* would run a fiery editorial entitled "Race First" that echoed sentiments from Harrison's lecturers and writings and identified him as the coiner of "Negro First."[27]

The influence of Harrison, Domingo, Grey, and other Liberty League members on Garvey reveals an important fact. In the period around 1917 the relation between Garvey and other Liberty League members was a two-way street. It was not simply that Garvey pulled members away from the Liberty League. He was also deeply influenced by them. In fact, in these early stages, the preponderance of influence seemed to be going from Liberty League members to Garvey.[28]

Garvey's experiences in the United States—with white supremacism, with the race consciousness of African Americans, and with activists like Harrison— began to reshape his views. The Liberty League, *The Voice*, and the activists around the two played particularly important roles in Garvey's decision to stay in the United States and in his developing ideas and organization. After Domingo introduced Garvey to Harrison, Garvey decided to stay in New York. The Liberty League member Seifert, according to Harrison, developed the idea for the Garvey movement's Black Star Line shipping enterprise. Harrison unequivocally stated that the Black Star Line was "an idea which Garvey took bodily from Seifert, one of the original members of the Liberty League." Domingo, the Liberty League's assistant secretary, also aided Garvey in parliamentary procedures during 1917 and 1918.[29]

It is clear that the core people who served as key progressive leaders of the Garvey movement over the next few years came from Harrison's Liberty League and *Voice*. A simple listing of some of the leadership people who moved from *The Voice*–Liberty League orbit to work with the UNIA–BSL–*Negro World* includes:

Isaac Allen: President of the UNIA, second vice president of the Black Star Line

John E. Bruce: Regular columnist and contributing editor for the *Negro World*, chairman of the advisory board of the UNIA

W. A. Domingo: First editor of the *Negro World*

Gertrude Miller-Faide: Associate secretary and stenographer of the New York Branch of the UNIA

Marcus Garvey: Potentate, president, and international organizer of the UNIA, editor of the *Negro World*, president of the Black Star Line

Edgar M.Grey: Advertising and business manager of the *Negro World*, general secretary of the UNIA, secretary of the New York Local of the UNIA, director and assistant secretary of the Black Star Line

Hubert Henry Harrison: Editor and columnist for the *Negro World*

Anselmo Jackson: Writer for the *Negro World*

Irena Moorman-Blackston: President, Ladies Division, of the UNIA, first vice president of the UNIA

Dr. E. Eliott Rawlins: Writer of "Health Talk" column for *Negro World*

Andy Razaf: Poet for *The Voice* and for *Negro World*

Arthur Reid: Black Star Line stock salesman

Charles Christopher Seifert: the originator of the idea for the Black Star Line, chaplain and second vice president of the UNIA

Orlando M. Thompson: Vice president of the Black Star Line[30]

In addition, Alex Rahming and August Bernier helped form the early UNIA in New York. Also, Harrison's long-time acquaintance, fellow *New York News* columnist Samuel A. Duncan, who became the third vice president of the UNIA and briefly seized control of the organization as president, was probably also a Liberty League member (though not identifiable as such).[31]

It was not simply the core organizational leadership that Garvey drew from Harrison. Perhaps most significant was Harrison's influence on Garvey's developing radicalism. Garvey, as a thinker, had a recognizable eclectic quality. Robert A. Hill points to the significance that diverse sources, including S. A. G. Cox, Dusé Mohamed Ali, Booker T. Washington, and the Irish liberation struggle had on Garvey. Judging by the comments of contemporaries, however, particularly those seemingly in position to know, Harrison, his *Voice*, and his Liberty League exerted a signal influence on Garvey's radical development.[32]

There is ample testimony to this fact. Anselmo Jackson, a writer for both Harrison's *Voice* and Garvey's *Negro World*, writes that beginning in 1916,

> outdoors and indoors, Hubert Harrison was preaching an advanced type of radicalism with a view to impressing race consciousness and effecting racial solidarity among Negroes. The followers of Harrison, responding to his demand that a New Negro Manhood movement among Negroes be organized, formed the Liberty League fo[r] Negro-Americans, a short while prior to Garvey. . . . The . . . atmosphere was charged with Harrison's propaganda; men and women of color thruout the United States and the West Indies donated their dollars and pledged their support to Harrison as they became members of the Liberty League.
>
> Garvey publicly eulogized Harrison, joined the Liberty League and took a keen interest in its affairs. . . . Harrison rendered memorable educational and constructive community service to the Negroes of Harlem. It may be truly said that he was the forerunner of Garvey and contributed largely to the success of the latter by preparing the minds of Negroes through his lectures, thereby molding and developing a new temper among Negroes which undoubtedly made the task of the Jamaican much easier than it otherwise would have been. In justice to both and with equal truth, it may be declared that the success of Garvey was built on the ruins of Harrison's failure.[33]

Harrison's influence was also recognized by others. William H. Ferris, the assistant *Negro World* editor and assistant president general of the UNIA, maintained that Garvey "rapidly crystallized" Harrison's ideas.[34] Garvey's boyhood associate, and the first editor of the *Negro World*, W. A. Domingo, said that "Garvey came at the psychological moment. There had been the East St. Louis riot, he visited the scene and then came back here. However, before him there was Hubert Harrison. He was a brilliant man, a great intellectual, a Socialist and highly respected. Garvey like the rest of us followed Hubert Harrison."[35] J. A. Rogers, a frequent contributor to the *Negro World*, explained that "one of the men who was very much influenced by Harrison was Marcus Garvey." Rogers added that "Garvey's emphasis on racialism was due in no small measure to Harrison's lectures on Negro history and his utterances on racial pride, which animated and fortified Garvey's views." Rogers emphasized that "the Garvey Movement" was "fructified by the spirit and teaching of Harrison."[36]

In the fall of 1917, despite the fact that there was movement underway between the Liberty League and the UNIA, Harrison and the Liberty League took a most active role in the New York municipal elections. Those elections featured a four-way mayoral contest that was among the most hotly contested in the history of the city. William Bennett was the Republican nominee. John Purroy Mitchel, the incumbent, was a Republican who had lost the primary and ran as a Fusion candidate (an alliance of defecting Republicans and anti-Tammany Democrats) with the backing of the former Republican presidents Teddy Roosevelt and William Howard Taft and the former New York Governor and 1916 Republican Party presidential candidate, Charles Evans Hughes. The Brooklyn judge John Hylan, the Democrat, was a low-profile Tammany candidate who was also backed by William Randolph Hearst, while Morris Hillquit was the Socialist Party contender. In addition to a host of Socialists contesting other offices, there were also two Black candidates who had fought their way to nominations in the primaries—the attorney Edward A. Johnson, for assemblyman in the Nineteenth Assembly District, and the attorney James C. Thomas Jr., for alderman in the Twenty-sixth Aldermanic District. The Nineteenth A.D. in which Johnson ran was from one-third to one-half Black. The Twenty-sixth Ald. D. in which Thomas ran had been gerrymandered and included parts of the Nineteenth, Twentieth, Twenty-first, and Twenty-second Assembly Districts and was about one-third Black. In addition to the specific races, the 1917 ballot was to decide on the question of women's suffrage. Harrison, *The Voice*, and the Liberty League took dead aim on the 1917 election campaign.[37]

In *The Voice* of October 18 Harrison presented an overview of the upcoming election. He noted that the Twenty-first Assembly District, covering Washington Heights and upper Harlem, was almost half Black, and the Nineteenth A.D., in lower Harlem, was about one-third Black. Though Harlem was still predominantly white, he emphasized that in the coming election "the Negro vote will be worth more than it ever was worth before." The reason was that all the parties were willing "to pay a higher price for it than they have ever paid" and it was the first time in New York City's history that the Black vote could be "the pivotal the deciding element."[38]

He was partly right. In large part because of migration from the South and arrivals from the Caribbean, Harlem in 1917 had approximately 60,000 Black people, about one-fifth of whom were West Indians. In this "New Negro Mecca" in the North, where Black men had the vote, African Americans were moving to a position where they could clearly influence (and soon determine) election results. This was a significant change that was reshaping Black political strategy and leadership.[39]

Another significant change was related to the death of Booker T. Washington on November 14, 1915. In the aftermath of his death, the old Tuskegee political machinery was breaking up, and new avenues for political action were opening. The Washington option of a client-patron relationship to white politicians and the Du Bois option of uniting the intellectuals at the top and moving in favor of whoever made the most symbolic gesture toward fair treatment (as in the 1912 and 1916 elections) were no longer the only alternatives. Harrison was advocating a new strategy: the uniting not of those at the top but of those "at the bottom"—the "Negro masses." With the Black vote, at least in certain aldermanic and assembly district elections where Black voters held the balance of power, there was now the possibility for Black pressure groups and Black self-assertion to influence and shape such elections. In Harlem, according to Michael Louis Goldstein, "the migration of substantial numbers of Blacks" into the Nineteenth and Twenty-first Assembly Districts "provided an opportunity for independent Black leaders to mobilize mass support for a new racial modus vivendi." As the objective conditions changed, the twofold task of subjectively awakening racial consciousness and of developing organizational means to voice political demands became pressing.[40]

Whether or not Black voters in Harlem in 1917 would see the decisive potential of their vote and act accordingly was a question. What they would seek for their vote and what demands they would make were other questions. In the October 18 *Voice* Harrison analyzed the various parties to see what they offered.

First he examined the Republican Party and its mayoral candidate, Bennett. To Harrison, it was not clear what the party was fighting for. Bennett had won the primary by beating former mayor Mitchel, who was backed by Roosevelt, Taft, Hughes, and "the organized plunderbund of Wall Street." Mitchel refused to accept the decision of the Republican primary, split the Republican vote in half, and made the party's dependence on Black voters greater. It was now "up to the Negro voters to demand a higher price" for their votes. Unfortunately, however, "'colored' Republican leaders" had not pressed such a demand as they were mired "in the sloth of stupid 'allegiance.'" The "New Negro candidates," Johnson and Thomas Jr., however, were not beholden to white leaders in the party since "they had to fight them tooth and nail—and beat them"—to get their nominations. Further, Harrison pointed out that there was no guarantee that party leaders, "who deliberately gerrymandered the Negro district to make the election of a Negro highly improbable," would be trustworthy on any count. He presciently added that there was, therefore, ample reason to distrust most of these Republican leaders, particularly men like Mitchel.[41]

In relation to the Republicans the tactic that Harrison advocated was to demand and receive concessions—before the election. He said that Black leaders should have "gone down to City Hall—not like [*Age* editor and staunch Republican] Fred Moore, a lick-spittle leader of nothing but himself—to promise to fight like h—— for Mitchel; but to have the city administration pass at once the bill for a big bathhouse in Harlem." They should also have demanded and received before the election "twenty Negro policemen appointed in Harlem and the condign punishment of those white policemen and detectives who have 'beaten up' Negro citizens," Black appointments to the Fire Department in Harlem, and a medal for Fireman Woodson. Because the leaders had failed to do this, it was unlikely that the Black community would get any more from Mitchel's wing of the Republican "party of plutocracy" than had been previously obtained, which, as Harrison wryly noted, was only "raidings, clubbings, shootings, insults and neglect." These comments referred to the fact that Mitchel, after his election victory in 1913, restored the practice of police use of clubs (often against African Americans), which his predecessor, Mayor William J. Gaynor, who tried to reform the police force, had abandoned. Harrison also did not lose sight of the fact that Mitchel, the "reform" Fusion candidate, had been linked, since 1913, with the much abhorred policies of the Democratic Wilson administration. From the Bennett wing, nothing was obtainable before the election, "except a little cash," because that wing had "nothing to give." Postelection gains were a matter of speculation. Since Bennett was not likely to win, his only value, according to Harrison, would consist "in splitting the Republican vote and helping to insure Mitchel's well-deserved defeat."[42]

Regarding the Democrats and their candidate, Judge John Hylan, Harrison noted that Tammany Hall had "dealt more decently by Negroes than Negroes have by Tammany Hall." Everyone was told that Tammany Hall was corrupt, he added, but "too many fakers" had "made their political fortunes by fooling the people into believing that when they swat Tammany Hall their troubles will be over." In fact, Tammany remained a political power, and the reason for this, Harrison reasoned, was that it was "no more vicious than the voters of New York are." Unfortunately, Black voters in New York had not shown "enough horse-sense to make an honest deal with Tammany Hall," and, therefore, they had no reason to expect anything from it. If Hylan were elected it might be possible to "get a better deal" from the city Democrats than was ever obtained from the Republicans, but this was "only a hope."[43]

Finally, Harrison discussed the Socialist Party—"clean and straight and standing out of the muck of mere politics, with the sunlight on its face, fronting the dawn of a better day." Harrison, the propagandist, in discussing the SP candidate Hillquit, chose not to mention his own Socialist experiences and declared that from the man and the party "no oppressive act toward the Negro has ever come." He noted that three years earlier, "a Negro was on its City Central Committee, helping to manage the affairs of tens of thousands of white Socialists—without any Negro voters behind him as the price of this high office." In this 1917 election the SP was offering the Black voters "nothing special," other than "what it offers to all downtrodden workers: Justice, liberty and absolute equality—not only in words, but in deeds," and this was what Mitchel, Bennett, and Hylan feared. To Harrison a Socialist Party victory would mean an "absolute cessation of police brutality and the conscienceless evictions by conscienceless landlords; would mean bathhouses and playgrounds; municipal markets to cut down the high cost of living, municipal ownership of ice and milk." These were not simply issues foisted upon the public at election time, he added; these were the issues of the Socialists over the years. Now, for the first time, Socialists had an opportunity to win. Even Tammany, the New York *World*, and other papers, conceded this.[44]

Harrison urged that *Voice* readers vote for the Black candidates Thomas and Johnson and for the Socialists. He also advised that, in this election, "talk of 'throwing away your vote' is sheer humbug." Finally, he stressed, as he had in 1912, that it was "better to vote for that which you want, and not get it, than to vote for what you don't want—and get it."[45]

Although he officially endorsed Hillquit, the Socialist candidate, Harrison was indeed politically independent, and the October 18 issue of *The Voice* contained a front-page interview with the attorney Ferdinand Q. Morton, the Harvard-educated leader of the United Colored Democracy. Harrison explained in "A Square Deal to All" that *The Voice* was the only Black newspaper that gave space to Democratic political doings, including the primaries, and he thought such coverage proved "that *The Voice* is neither a Republican, Democratic nor Fusion paper, but, as it proudly proclaims, a newspaper for the New Negro." Its policy was to publish news "about any political organization" and to "sell our advertising space to all of them." Its editorial opinion, however, was "not for sale to any of them," and the paper would form its own political opinion, "under our own hats and not under the cheques which we get for our advertising space."[46]

Harrison also offered a very candid analysis of "The Negro Candidates," which began by asking whether they were really interested in winning. The election was only three weeks away, yet neither Johnson nor Thomas had provided *The Voice* with any campaign literature. *The Voice* had heard and feared that "there may be a deal on to trade votes and freeze them out," but it was "prepared to ask the Negro voters of Harlem to fight for Thomas and Johnson, and to split whatever ticket they voted so as to include them, as the Negro Democrats are going to do." This could not be done if the candidates remained mute. Harrison made clear that *The Voice* was "not interested in the success of the Republican party—as some of their 'non-partisan' sponsors of the United Civic League are," but, in the candidates "as Negroes." He advised that "if they make the fight as Negroes they will get every Negro vote that we can influence—Democratic, Republican, Socialist, and Mitchelite"; if "they make the fight as Republicans, they will deserve only Republican votes." The choice was left up to them. He was clear on the Black candidates' purpose, however, and later explained that it was "to furnish a focusing-point around which the ballots of Negro voters may be concentrated for the realization of racial demands for justice and equality of opportunity and treatment." Such candidates could take "the Negro voter out of the ranks of the Republican, Democratic, and Socialist parties" and enable "their leaders to trade the votes of their followers, openly and above-board, for those things for which masses of men largely exchange their votes."[47]

Harrison's work during the 1917 election season included opposition to the war. He delivered a lecture for a United Civic League Forum on "Why Should the Negro Go to War?" He also offered favorable comments in the September 19 *Voice* on the antiwar pamphlet *Terms of Peace and the Darker Races* by A. Philip Randolph and Chandler Owen and on John E. Bruce's *A Defence of the Colored Soldiers Who Fought in the War of the Rebellion.*[48]

Harrison's review of *Terms of Peace and the Darker Races* offered encouragement, not animus, toward Randolph and Owen, whom he described as "two brilliant young leaders of the Independent Political Council." He described their pamphlet as "unique" and pointed out that it was rare to find "Negro leaders who are radical—on the subject of their race"—and who also have well founded positions on other issues. "Frequently," such leaders knew "so little of anything else" and had "no radical attitude, no opinions worth while on anything else." In the case of "comrades-in-arms" Randolph and Owen, however, Harrison felt they evidenced worthwhile knowledge and opinions on world politics, history, economics, and "the twisted tricky course of war-time diplomacy and lying." Their stance was "bold—perhaps too bold for safety's sake"—but, he added, in "these days of cowardly compromise and shifting surrender we cannot find it in our heart to condemn the opposite qualities." Harrison also noted that the pamphlet supported President Wilson's demand for "peace without victory" and the demands of the darker races for their lands (over which the war was being waged). He emphasized that *Terms of Peace* should be read by both Blacks and whites throughout the civilized world.[49]

The IPC was an organization of Black Socialists that Randolph and Owen had recently formed. In a later article, when he was far more critical of them, Harrison explained how Owen and Randolph sought both Republican and Democratic backing and how they "dickered with the Democrats up to within a month of 'flopping'" to the Socialists "because they 'couldn't make it' elsewhere." Owen reportedly made weekly visits to Tammany chief Charles Frances Murphy from June to August 1917, seeking to be put on the Democratic Party payroll, and Murphy sent him to Ferdinand Q. Morton, head of the United Colored Democracy, who refused to provide him the backing he sought. Then, according to Harrison, finding Republican and Democratic "doors closed" to his "itching palms," Owen "rang the Socialist bell."[50]

Shortly after the influential Harrison's review, Owen and Randolph, representing the "Independent Political League of Harlem," made an appearance on October 10 before the Executive Committee of the Socialist Party of Local New York and said that they were "anxious" to do work for the SP during the campaign. A committee met with them and apparently accepted the plan. Owen and Randolph declared that the IPC's "primary, sole and immediate aim" was "to fight for a progressive, clean and honest government" and to use the ballot (the "mightiest weapon of the ages") to obtain "a just political status for the colored people in particular."[51]

The election campaign began to heat up on October 16 at a meeting called by the IPC on 135th Street at which Harrison made scathing attacks on President Wilson and former presidents Roosevelt and Taft. Before a crowd of 1,200, he openly criticized the last three presidents for their records on the race question. He called Roosevelt "the arch-hypocrite" and pointed out that he was "quick to say we are out to make the world safe for democracy, but he had nothing to say when the rights of five or six million Negroes were taken away from them." Harrison claimed that the "first President to 'Jim Crow' the Negroes was fathead Taft," and, regarding the current president, he explained, "I love Wilson as much as I love—well, it would be treason to say it." Allowing his propagandist zeal to predominate, he then predicted that Hillquit would be elected Mayor of New York. The crowd cheered "Hillquit, Hillquit. We want Hillquit!" and "Hillquit and Socialism!" Harrison also praised the *Call* for opposing what he termed "wartime jackass patriotism." As he closed, Harrison said: "They call Mitchel our fighting Mayor . . . but who the hell did he ever fight? Who ever heard of Mitchel being where bullets were flying thick? When it comes to a showdown, we are [N]egroes first, last and all the time, and to hell with—." His comments, according to the *Globe*, were "drowned out in wild cheering."[52]

Five days later, at the October 21 meeting of the EC of the Socialist Party of Local New York, Harrison appeared and asked that the EC give him an advertisement for *The Voice*. The motion on this matter was referred to the City Campaign Committee and apparently approved. At that meeting it was also reported that a committee previously appointed to do "special propaganda in the negro section of New York" reported that preparation for a giant meeting at the Palace Casino on October 29 was very successful and that "25,000 leaflets giving the reasons why negroes should vote the Socialist ticket" were ready and that another leaflet was being printed.[53]

That same week, according to the *Chicago Defender*, several Republican Party speakers "received a severe shock" when they were chased out of Harlem. "Putting up a bitter fight against the Republicans" were a group of editors led by "Harrison, Randolph and Owens." It was increasingly feared that the Republican Harlem vote "will shift to the Socialist party."[54]

Amid the heightened activism engendered by the political campaign, Harrison attended a mass meeting under the auspices of the Colored Liberty Conference at the Palace Casino on Sunday afternoon, October 28. Its purpose was to select delegates for the National Liberty Conference scheduled to be held in Washington, D.C., in December. Allen W. Whaley, former pastor of the Chelsea, Massachusetts, People's African Methodist Episcopal Church, presided, and Harrison spoke along with Dr. York Russell, Rabbi Stephen Wise; the Hungary-born social reformer and supporter of Black causes; and the Rev. W. S. Holder, the minister of the Harlem Congregational Church, who was active with the National Equal Rights League.[55]

The big election campaign activity of 1917, however, was the meeting on the night of Monday, October 29, at the Palace Casino, and it was to include talks by Fusion mayoral candidate Mitchel and Republican Party idol Roosevelt. *The Voice* described the meeting as "a huge success, but not for Fusion," despite the fact that all of Fusion's big guns—Roosevelt, Mitchel, and Taft—were the advertised speakers. Roosevelt and the others came up "to stem the tide of anti-Mitchel sentiment" that was sweeping Harlem. It was, however, too late—as Harrison had predicted two years earlier in his open-air lectures on Wall Street.[56]

The meeting was packed "with Negroes who seemed bent on being Negroes first." When William A. Prendergast, the Regular Republican and Fusion candidate for comptroller, tried to speak, he was met with shouts of "'SHUT UP!' 'SIT DOWN!' 'GET OUT!'" This was clearly "a new and unexpected mood—for Negroes and the experience was sobering" as each succeeding speaker faced the same response. When Mayor Mitchel attempted to speak he was hissed and booed throughout the hall. Clearly rattled, he denounced the audience. This didn't stop the boos, and he had to sit down, "his face purple with indignation." Former president Roosevelt spoke next, and the audience briefly paid attention while he chose not to mention Mitchel's name once. Instead, he stressed that the choice was only that between the Fusion candidate and the Democrat and that he was there to ask them to "vote the Fusion ticket." It was at that point that the heckling of Roosevelt began, and he appeared "considerably peeved" as cries from all over the hall were heard for "'HILLQUIT! HILLQUIT! HILLQUIT!'" Roosevelt's inability to explain why he backed Mitchel, whose administration was noted for the police force clubbing Black people, elicited further hissing and cries of "Why didn't you take a stand on Brownsville?"[57]

It was about this time that James C. Thomas Jr., the Black candidate for alderman, entered the hall. Thomas and Johnson, the UCL candidates, had both been successful in Republican primaries and were running on the Republican Party ticket. The hall rocked as Thomas, a former Cornell track star, moved down the aisle and the 3,000 in attendance rose to their feet, waived their hats, and their cheers shook the hall. They wanted Thomas—"Nobody but Thomas." Roosevelt was defeated; he sat down briefly and then left with the Fusion candidates as the two Black candidates, who were originally to be used as showpieces by the Mitchel forces, had the meeting to themselves. While all this was going on, John M. Royall, head of the United Civic League, looked troubled, reportedly because he had endorsed the Fusion ticket. Harrison described the night as "a terrible setback for Royall in Harlem."[58]

Outside the casino one Fusion backer, Sol Johnson, declared that the trouble "was all the doing of 'those d—— West Indians.'" Fred R. Moore, editor of the *Age*, who had been on the platform with Roosevelt and Mitchel, denounced the "Socialistic agitators" and reportedly also "denounced [Chandler] Owen from the platform as a 'damned nigger.'" Harrison added that there were rumors that Moore's support of the Republicans was tied to money changing hands. Neither the antisocialist nor anti–West Indian prejudice went very far. Harrison later explained how the anti–West Indian prejudice "had worn so thin by 1917 that in the political campaign of that year West Indian and American Negroes were pulling together like two horses in a team, working for the election of James C. Thomas, Jr., to the Aldermanic Board and for the principals of elective representation which has since been accepted by all political parties in Negro Harlem." He also emphasized that it was "the Liberty League under whose banner the West Indian and American Negroes first cooperated on anything like a large scale."[59]

The socialist presence was a final important feature of the evening that Harrison mentioned. There were meetings held by both Democrats and Socialists in the hall and on the street corner. The Socialists' 25,000 leaflets offered reasons that Black people should vote the Socialist ticket, and their many able speakers addressed and captured the overflow crowd as well as the remains of the Thomas and Johnson audience.[60]

In light of this strong and militant demonstration Harrison observed that Black voters were "sick and tired of being fed on pap." They desired more, and, not getting it, their temperature was on the rise, and Harlem would soon be "too hot to hold the Negro preachers and real-estate sharps" who had been "making their thirty pieces of silver by selling out their race's rights." He warned that the Black community would no longer "smile and look nice" while being "crucified upon a cross of gold." In sum, Harrison declared the meeting of October 29 "a glorious night for manhood and race loyalty in Harlem."[61]

Several years later in "An Open Letter to the Socialist Party of New York City" published in the *Negro World*, Harrison described events surrounding that meeting and how, before it, he and others had warned the white Republican leaders that Blacks were becoming anti-Republican and their mood would probably not change until Republicans "changed their party's attitude toward the Negro masses." The "white politicians did not think it necessary to come and find out for themselves," and they ignored such warnings "because the Negroes whom they had selected to interpret Negro sentiment for them," people like *Age* editor Fred R. Moore, "the selected index," still "confidently assured them that there had been no change of sentiment on the part of the Negro people."[62]

In effect, wrote Harrison, the white party bosses "were lied to by those whose bread and butter depended on such lying," and as the election drew near it was already too late. Assurances regarding the secured Black vote were extended at the meeting to Roosevelt and Mitchel, and "most of the Negro ministers had received for their support sums ranging from two to six hundred dollars." Journalist Cleveland G. Allen, in his *Harlem Home News* column in January 1918, gave credence to Harrison's charges by reporting on a so-called Fusion "Slush Fund" that included Reverends George Henry Sims, W. W. Brown, Adam Clayton Powell Sr., Henry Arthur Booker, and L. H. Twishy as alleged recipients of Fusion money. The "real truth," Harrison wrote (and Allen echoed), was that the Black masses were "seething with hostility," but the Republican leaders realized this too late. This all became clear at the October 29 meeting when Mitchel and Roosevelt "were hissed off the platform" and at other campaign events when Mitchel's outdoor speakers were unable to speak on Harlem street corners.[63]

In a larger sense, what the Republican leaders had done was what he had warned against—they had a "selected Negro spokesman" on whose word they chose "to rely for information as to the tone and temper of Negro political sentiment." The white Republicans assumed that those Blacks with whom they were in contact somehow monopolized the intellect and virtue of the Black race. It was obvious that they were wrong. This "faulty method of the white Republican politicians" and their persistence in hand-picking Black leaders could no longer work. The reason, according to Harrison, was that African Americans were increasingly intent on choosing their own leaders.[64]

The Black community was learning in wartime, wrote Harrison, "that while white people spoke of patriotism, religion, democracy and other . . . themes, they remained loyal to one concept above all others, and that was the concept of race"—it was "'race first' for whites." From such understanding "was born the new Negro ideal of 'race first'" for Negroes—the concept that started to shape Black electoral activity in New York. To Harrison, this race-first sentiment was "bred by the attitude of white men here and everywhere else where white rules black."[65]

The October 31, 1917, issue of *The Voice* was the preelection, issue and it included paid political advertisements from candidates of all political persuasions. Among the advertisers were Sheriff Al Smith (the future four-time governor of New York and Democratic presidential candidate) for president for the Board of Alderman; Sampson Friedlander, candidate for judge of the 7th District, Municipal Court; William A. Prendergast, Regular Republican and Fusion candidate for comptroller; John Hylan, Democratic candidate for mayor; Morris Hillquit, Socialist Party candidate for mayor (along with the entire Socialist ticket); Edward Swann, Democratic candidate for district attorney; Joseph E. Corrigan, non-partisan candidate for district attorney; and Edward M. Morgan (who as postmaster was responsible for firing Harrison), the Republican and Fusion candidate for county clerk of New York County. *The Voice* explained that its policy was to take virtually any political advertisements, while simultaneously maintaining its right to openly criticize any advertiser. Harrison explained that the political advertisements in the paper did not express *The Voice*'s point of view: they were made by the advertisers, and some were true and some were not.[66]

In one editorial Harrison discussed the advertisement of former postmaster Edward M. Morgan, the Republican-Fusion candidate for county clerk. From his advertisement, wrote Harrison, "one would suppose that the '400 colored men employed as clerks and carriers in the Post Office' during Morgan's administration were employed by him as a favor to Negroes." This simply wasn't true, and had Morgan been "the worst Negro-hater in America there was no way in which he could have prevented their appointment under the civil service rules." Harrison then mentioned Morgan's role in his removal from the Postal Service in conspiracy with Booker T. Washington, Emmett Scott, and Fred R. Moore and how Morgan had refused even to give him a hearing in his own defense, yet now "he comes with these unblushing lies about his record as post-master to honey-fugle Negroes into electing him as a county clerk." Harrison concluded with the sincere hope that Morgan wouldn't get elected. A defeat would give him the time needed to meditate on the value in "giving a square deal to every man." Harrison had used Morgan's advertisement to go into a scorching critique of his candidacy: it was surely an advertising policy that would scare most potential advertisers.[67]

Another man involved in Harrison's postal removal, Charles W. Anderson, New York's leading Black Republican, was also the subject of a preelection *Voice* editorial by Harrison. *The Messenger* had taken Anderson to task as "a peculiar Republican" who "advised Negroes to vote for all Democrats in the recent primaries," even though Black candidates ran as Republicans. *The Messenger* asked whether Anderson was "a Democratic Republican or a Republican Democrat?" and suggested that the question "would make a splendid editorial for THE VOICE." *The Voice* took up the challenge and asked, "Where does Mr. Anderson stand in Negro politics?" *The Voice* had already printed charges from a "Mr. Doyle" that "Anderson and [J. Frank] Wheaton, both Negroes, secretly instigated him to run against young [James C.] Thomas [Jr.], a Negro, in order to effect the defeat of Thomas." Despite *The Voice*'s queries asking Anderson to answer this charge, he hadn't responded, and the paper was "compelled to announce" that, "as a Negro political leader," Anderson was "totally discredited—not only in the eyes of the Negro race at large." Understanding that Anderson had "trained with the late Booker T. Washington and Emmett Scott, and learned his political ethics from that school of thought," *The Voice* was not at all surprised at "his loyalty to white men at the price of underhanded treachery to Negroes," who were striving "for racial justice within the ranks of the Republican party."[68]

There were, however, several lessons to learn from this. First, Harrison instructed "that the old type of Negro barnacle on the bottom of the Republican ship" could "not be trusted to stand for 'Negro first,' last, or anywhere." Second, it was now clear that Black political leaders could not be trusted "until and unless, we elect them to office ourselves." Only then would the Black community's "grip on them be firmer than the grip of the white ward-heelers whose dirty work they now do." *The Voice* strongly suggested that this last point would be lost unless Black members of the Republican Party at the next County Committee meeting had "the manhood to speak 'right out in meeting' and tell them to their teeth that Charles W. Anderson can no longer act as their political leader because they are ashamed of him." Unless this was done, Blacks would consider such politicians to be complicit in Anderson's shame. After such a stinging denunciation, the ever-courteous Harrison apologized for being forced to say what he had said and added that his personal relations with Mr. Anderson remained "as cordial as we could wish." Harrison was clear, however, that "personal relations should carry no weight when the welfare of our race is in the balance." Courtesy was extended as far as "humanly possible," but "the fact that no other Negro paper has had the courage or the manhood to say an editorial word about it [Anderson's betrayal]," made the exposé necessary. Again, *The Voice* had used an advertisement to go into a strong critique of the advertiser.[69]

During the 1917 election campaign period Harrison also spoke on women's issues and on the upcoming Race Congress as part of a series of talks held throughout Harlem "to arouse the colored people relative to their economic and industrial rights." The Congress, though planned for December, was not held until the following June. On November 4 Harrison was scheduled to lecture for the Harlem People's Forum at Lafayette Hall on "Our Women." Other speakers that day included William Pickens of Morgan College in Maryland and Mrs. Eslanda Cardoza Goode of the "new group of suffrage workers." At a September 28 meeting of the suffrage workers, chaired by Mrs. Goode, Harrison and Allen W. Whaley spoke on the Race Congress. Two days later an "immense gathering" heard Harrison and Mrs. Goode (who spoke on "The New Negro Woman") at a Liberty League meeting on "Liberty Corner," 134th St. and Lenox Avenue."[70]

Harrison also wrote an editorial on "Woman Suffrage" for *The Voice* of October 31. Extending "race first" into yet another area, he explained that he had "always stood for the principle of Woman Suffrage" and that he stood for it now, but, "above the claims of suffrage he puts the claims of his race." Accordingly, "since the white woman suffragists of New York City" were "willing to flout the Negro women of New York," Harrison lined up "behind the women of his race" and opposed suffrage for women "until the white women have been properly chastened."[71]

Harrison was attempting to support Black women in the face of white-supremacist appeals being made by suffragists. According to historian Aileen S. Kraditor, the ongoing campaign by individual states for a women's suffrage amendment to the Constitution had, particularly since 1916, "found the desirability of white supremacy and the federal amendment to be perfectly compatible." Most suffrage supporters accepted both aims and "were perfectly content to secure the vote without enfranchising any Negroes." Throughout the amendment campaign, "suffragists North and South repeatedly resorted to the two principal arguments involving the Negro: that white women ought not to be the political inferiors of Negro men and that woman suffrage would insure or at least not threaten white supremacy in the South." Nancy F. Cott adds that "the suffrage movement since the late nineteenth century had caved in to the racism of surrounding society, sacrificing democratic principle of the dignity of black people if it seemed advantageous to white women's obtaining the vote." In response to such practice, *The Voice* asked Blacks "not to vote for Woman Suffrage on the sixth of November" in order to give the white suffragists "time to think it over so that they may learn what the Hebrew prophet meant when he asked each man 'to do justly, to show mercy, and to walk humbly with thy God.'"[72]

Harrison's position was similar to one advocated by Mrs. Goode, the Negro Women's Campaign Committee, and, later, the educator and civil rights activist Nannie Burroughs. Goode's "new group of suffrage workers of Harlem" urged the Negro men of Harlem "to vote against the Woman Suffrage amendment." The Negro Women's Campaign Committee urged "colored men to withhold their vote with regard to the amendment calling for Woman Suffrage until the Woman's Suffrage party declared itself on the status of colored women." Burroughs advised "Negro men and women . . . to kill woman suffrage because it is willing to throw us overboard in order to get white women into the ship."[73]

Harrison explained that he was aware his position was "not sound logic." But, he responded, "life is larger than logic," and when Black people push demands for justice the answer is "that granting of them is not 'practically expedient.'" Therefore, he argued, Blacks should enter "politics on the same basis" and be "willing to defer the 'principal' until our 'interest' has been conceded." Others who spoke in support of the Negro Women's Campaign Committee's effort included Reverend Charles Martin, John E. Bruce, and the attorney A. B. Carey. After the election, in which the women's suffrage amendment was passed, a Women's Political and Economic Association was formed, with Mrs. M. Sharpson Young as president. The association's stated purpose was to give lessons "relative to the use of the ballot."[74]

The pre-election October 31 issue of *The Voice* had other articles by Harrison as well as poems by Andrea P. Razaf[in]keriefo ("Prayer of the Lowly" and "Friend Jones") and Walter Everette Hawkins and a reprint of Harrison's poem, "An Ode to the Dead." Harrison offered a new column, "In the Crow's Nest," by "Gunga Din" (a pseudonym he had first used in 1915). He also had an insert entitled "A Course in Languages," which made fun of Theodore Roosevelt's tendency to meddle in everything. In it Harrison used a passage from the English playwright and librettist William Schwenck Gilbert's "The Yarn of the 'Nancy Bell'" that he would later use to describe Marcus Garvey:

> Oh, I am a cook and a captain bold,
> And the mate of the *Nancy* brig;
> And a bo'sun tight and a midshipmite,
> And the crew of the captain's gig.[75]

The October 31 *Voice* included a letter from a student to the editor on the "Gary System and How It Works." In Gary, Indiana, a city with a rapidly increasing Black population and a history of school segregation, an educational plan was developed for an experimental vocational system of elementary education. The plan included racially segregated schools, racially segregated classes in integrated schools, and Black teachers for Black students. In New York there was support for a similar effort known also as the "Rockefeller Plan." A leading proponent was the Board of Education member Abraham Flexner, an influential Mitchel supporter and assistant secretary of the Rockefeller-financed "General

Education Board." The unpopular "Gary" plan was opposed by the Socialist Party, by the Democratic candidate, Hylan, as well as by Harrison and *The Voice*. The student's letter to *The Voice* protested the new "long-hour" schedule as a hindrance to out-of-school study and work.[76]

The preelection issue of *The Voice* had three additional items of note. One advertisement mentioned that the Harlem People's Forum had transferred its meeting from the Palace Casino to Lafayette Hall at 164 West 131st Street. A letter to *The Voice*, written by Milton Lehrman on October 18, stated that Harrison's "editorial on 'The Coming Election' has put a thrill through me" and showed that he was "far, far from being cut-off from the working class movement." Lehrman confessed to "some fear," before reading *The Voice*, that the editor was "no longer the Harrison I used to know, honest in your ideas; as much devoted to the downtrodden white as to the colored brethren of your race." His fears were assuaged, however, as he read *The Voice*, which he considered "one of the best edited papers of the city."[77]

Finally, a letter from A. P. Razafinkeriefo, dated October 22, described the writer's letting "out a war whoop" and being "so overjoyed" upon reading *The Voice*. "Raz," an outstanding, militant, race-conscious poet (and the future lyricist for Fats Waller) who would be published widely throughout the "New Negro" press, praised Harrison's "excellent lecture" at the Forum the previous night. The talk was "well reasoned with satire," a trait he described as "second nature" to Harrison. "Raz," with apparent satire of his own, then added his hope that Harrison would "in the near future, lecture on 'Saving Money,' and 'Respecting Our Own Race'—especially our women. Both of these virtues are sadly lacking amongst our people and until we learn to do these two things we will be (and should be) doomed to the white man's tyranny."[78]

Since it was later said that two of the reasons for difficulties within the Liberty League involved Harrison's handling of money and his sexual appetite, Raz's letter merits comment. Anselmo Jackson and Richard B. Moore both attributed Harrison's difficulties in the Liberty League to his handling of money. Their remarks, plus the remembrances of Harrison's children on the subject as well as comments in Harrison's diary, papers, and books give credence to the money thesis. Money problems did undoubtedly affect the Liberty League and *The Voice*. Rather than dishonesty or embezzlement, however, it appears that Harrison did not give proper priority to the handling of money and didn't handle money well. Also, since he constantly functioned at or near a basic subsistence level and since he did not have personal or family funds to fall back on, all money problems were easily magnified.[79]

Harrison's sex life was the subject of a U.S. War Department Military Intelligence Division report in 1921. That report, which was on most accounts highly inaccurate, said the reason why "the very intelligent and highly edu-

Figure 11.2. Andrea Razaf[in]keriefo, undated. Madagascar-born Andrea Razaf[in]keriefo (1895–1973), known as Andy Razaf and called "Raz," was the leading poet of the "New Negro Movement" and, later, an extremely popular lyricist. He wrote poems for the Harrison-edited *Voice* (1917 and 1918) and *New Negro* (1919), was a member of the *Crusader* staff (1919), and was a frequent contributor to the *Negro World* (from 1920 on). In the 1920s and 1930s he wrote popular songs with his cousin, the jazz composer Fats Waller, and he teamed with the pianist-composer Eubie Blake. "Raz" wrote poems about Harrison and about *The Voice* in 1918 and about Harrison after his death in 1927. *Source:* Courtesy of the Hubert H. Harrison Papers, Rare Book and Manuscript Library, Butler Library, Columbia University, New York.

cated" Harrison failed "in nearly all his undertakings" was his "abnormal sexualism." These MID reports contain racist attitudes similar to those from the Bureau of Investigation (which in 1935 became the Federal Bureau of Investigation) in their assessment of the sexual activity of African American leaders. The historian David J. Garrow advises "a healthy skepticism toward what one does find in the [FBI] files," and this should also apply to the MID files.[80]

Claude McKay later described Harrison as "erotically indiscriminate"; historian Winston James refers to him as a "philanderer"; and Harrison's diary indicates more than ten affairs, including one which occurred right around the time, November 1917, that *The Voice* ceased publication. The diary disguises the woman's name, but it indicates that what he describes as their "love" started four or five years earlier (perhaps around the time of the birth or conception of Hubert and Lin's most recent child). By mid-January 1918, after several months of occasional indulgences, it was "rapidly ripening," and they were "wrapped up entirely in each other." It was a passionate affair in which, as he writes, "the merest touch of their hands or bodies sent the intensest thrills through them" and "sexual indulgence" became for both "a delirium of delight." According to Hubert, they "wanted to keep each other!" The woman desired a child and Hubert took what he considered the "Man like" course. He "tried to dissuade her, urging considerations both social and economic." Reason was consumed by passion, however, and in an effort to have "a boy to bear the family name and qualities," he agreed to do as she asked. Their efforts at creating a child and linking "forever" their love "by a third life" were ultimately thwarted when his lover became sick and aborted. There is no indication the affair lasted beyond this period. What effect, if any, it had on the Liberty League is not clear, although the timing of the relationship, the closing of *The Voice*, and Razaf's letter suggest that the relationship could have been a factor.[81]

As election results were tabulated, *The Voice* of November 7 carried a scorching Harrison editorial entitled "Our Professional Friends." Harrison set his sights on "the business known as 'being the Negro's friend,'" which, he explained, "was first invented by politicians, but was taken up later by 'good' men, six-per-cent philanthropists, millionaire believers in 'industrial education,' benevolent newspapers like the *Evening Post*, and a host of smaller fry of the 'superior race.'" He described how the border state politician Henry Clay of Kentucky, the organizer of the American Colonization Society, was the "first great 'friend' of the Negro." But, Frederick Douglass, William Still, James McCune Smith, Martin R. Delany, and other "wide-awake Negroes" demonstrated that the society's "real purpose was to get rid of free Negroes" so that their freedom was not an inducement to slaves to run away and their accomplishments an example to whites of real Black capabilities. Harrison then cited more recent instances of such "friendship," including white friends who constantly advised that Blacks should "go slow." The recurring message was that if Black people "would only follow the counsels of 'the good white people' who really had their interests at heart, instead of following their own counsels (as the Irish and the Jews do), all would yet be well."[82]

Harrison felt that too many Black people had "a wish-bone where their backbone ought to have been" and that they aided this "white" effort. The prime example was "Mitchel's man," Fred R. Moore, the editor of the *Age*, who in July had complained about *The Voice's* indiscreet utterances. Harrison made clear, as he had in July, that *The Voice* would not be silenced.[83]

He also responded to a letter that the Socialist Party member and NAACP leader Mary White Ovington sent to him after she saw an early issue of *The Voice*. Ovington saw no "reason for another organization, or another paper" unless it "printed straight socialism." Harrison wrote on August 3 that though he hoped he could help her to see, he didn't think her blindness on this point mattered much since the paper was already selling 10,000 copies per issue. In his reply he noted that he included his membership dues and was once again a member of the Socialist Party organization that printed "'Straight Socialism'— whatever that is." He also invited Ovington to *The Voice's* upcoming carnival and said that he sent his membership fee to the Socialist Party secretary to let Ovington see the difference between his spirit and hers. Citing these examples, he argued that such "'good white people' must really forgive us for insisting that we are not children" and that "while we want all the friends we can get, we need no benevolent dictators." To Harrison, it was clear that Blacks, not whites, "must shape Negro policies." If whites cared to "help," based on this understanding, their assistance would be appreciated.[84]

He then explained how whites, even in the South, were feeling the "Manhood" demands of the "New Negro." Of particular interest was the support for these militant demands coming from the Southern white papers that feared the developing exodus north of Black laborers. He noted that the columnist H. L. Mencken and others agreed and argued that the South should accede to just Black demands. Harrison reasoned that those who had paraded "as our professional friends" should similarly support "this manhood movement," but, "the movement seems to have left them in the rear." Thus, while African Americans demanded full rights, these "friends" were "angry at us for going further than they think 'nice.'"[85]

Harrison then took dead aim at the NAACP and its leaders, who, he charged, had asked "in the November *Crisis*, that we [Negroes] put a collective power-of-attorney into their hands and leave it to them to shape our national destiny." Led by Chairman Joel E. Spingarn, the NAACP had urged Negroes "to compromise our manhood by begging eagerly for 'Jim Crow' training camps." Harrison was referring to the segregated Fort Des Moines (Iowa) Training Camp for Colored Officers that had opened on June 18, 1917, with 1,250 officer candidates under the direction of white general, Charles C. Ballou. In April, when war was declared, there were fourteen officer's training camps in operation and Secretary of War Newton D. Baker had publicly assured that there would be no discrimination. White-supremacist sentiment, however, opposed both integrated camps and the establishment of all-Black camps, particularly in the South. To Harrison this was another case, "during the throes of war," in which "white people remained loyal to one concept above all others, and that was the concept of race"—"it was 'race first' with them" and so it had to be "race first" for Blacks also.[86]

Harrison's next target was the "spirit of 'benevolent despotism' and 'moral trusteeship' on the part of the Negro's good white friends." Joel E. Spingarn took the lead (along with James Weldon Johnson and W. E. B. Du Bois) and on behalf of the NAACP proposed the separate camp for Blacks "at the very moment," according to Harrison, "when the government, badgered by the chorus of purely Negro criticism, was about to throw open to them [Negroes] the training camps in which white men in the north were being made into officers." Harrison later wrote that "the government was just getting ready to open the camps to Negroes when some of our stupid old women in trousers piped up for a Jim Crow training camp. We got it." The comment (marred, in part, by the male-supremacist choice of words) pointed to a major point of difference between the "New Negroes" and the "old" crowd.[87]

Harrison's charges had basis in fact. Spingarn had been a prominent supporter of the "preparedness movement," had played a leading role in the Home Defense Committee, and had been recommended for a commission in the army by both Franklin D. Roosevelt, his neighbor in Dutchess County, N.Y., and the assistant secretary of the Navy, and by former president Theodore Roosevelt. After reporting to officer-training camp in May 1917, Spingarn was one of only three out of 2,500 candidates to be immediately promoted to major. He quickly engineered a deal with General Leonard Wood, the former commander of the Eastern Department and newly appointed head of the Southeastern Military Department, to establish a camp for Black officers if two hundred suitable applicants were found. Three hundred and fifty Black men, mostly from Howard University and the Hampton Institute, quickly applied, and on May 19, at Spingarn's urging, the War Department approved the plan. In June qualified candidates reported to Fort Des Moines, Iowa, and by October the camp had produced 629 officers of the total of 1,200 that would ultimately be commissioned.[88]

Charles Flint Kellogg, historian of the NAACP, points out that the "Negro press as a whole bitterly condemned" Spingarn's proposal. Because of actions like these, Harrison began to refer to the NAACP as the "National Association for the Acceptance of Color Proscription" and the "National Association for the Advancement of Certain People." Because of the leading role of whites like Spingarn in obtaining the camps, Harrison maintained that "the brighter minds among Negroes of today hate them [such 'white' friends] with a ['savagery' crossed out] hatred comparable only to the way in which a similar class of Negroes hated the white supporters of ['Booker Washington' crossed out] the Am[erican] Colonization Society."[89]

The issue of the segregated officer-training camps is instructive. Du Bois at first opposed the segregated camps as an "insult" to all African Americans, but, "strong, sober second thought" led him to change his position and to argue that "we face a condition, not a theory." There was, to Du Bois, "not the slightest chance" of African Americans being admitted to white camps, and he viewed the choice as simply one between either segregated camps or "no colored officers."[90]

Du Bois's diagnosis of a "condition not a theory" suggests another difference with Harrison. Racial oppression, as both would agree, was an objective and manifold fact, not simply a bad idea that would be overcome by morally superior theory. What Harrison emphasized, however, was that though Black people continued to be racially oppressed, there were changing objective conditions and political pressure and power could be exerted successfully. What was needed was to raise the group's racial consciousness and to consolidate race power behind clear aims and goals. This is the direction that Harrison was moving.

The historian Nathan Huggins has explained how Du Bois's ultimate support for the camps reflected the limited political power he represented. Du Bois, according to Huggins, believed in "civilization" and "democracy" and wanted to remain loyal to the United States. Harrison represented the new organization of race-conscious power. Harrison believed that "civilization" was a code word for armed might, and, while he wanted true democracy, he believed that "as long as the Color Line exists, all the perfumed protestations of Democracy on the part of the white race" were "simply downright lying" and that the cant of "democracy" was being used as a sham and cover for "sordid imperialist aims." Harrison, born in St. Croix, challenged the notion of loyalty to "America First" with a new concept, that of "Race First," or loyalty to race before loyalty to a white-supremacist country.[91]

The Liberty League challenged the NAACP's policies and leadership, just as Du Bois's Niagara Movement and the NAACP had challenged the policies and leadership of Booker T. Washington. Harrison recognized that the NAACP had "done much good work for Negroes—splendid work—in fighting lynching and segregation" and that as Negroes "we owe it more gratitude and good will than we owe the entire Republican party for the last sixty years of its existence." But this did not mean that African Americans should "abdicate our right to shape more radical policies for ourselves." It was the realization of the need for a policy more radical than that of the NAACP "that called into being the Liberty League of Negro Americans." Lynching was a prime example. Harrison felt that the NAACP was wedded to letter writing and could "never rise above the level of appeals" when what was really needed was a more militant policy of direct action and armed self-defense. The camps issue and the attitude toward the war were other major areas of difference.[92]

In his article on "Our Professional 'Friends,'" Harrison also raised the lynching matter as he criticized another long-time "friend of the Negro," Oswald Garrison Villard, the grandson of the famed abolitionist William Lloyd Garrison. The pacifist Villard was another NAACP founder, its former chairman, and its current treasurer, and he owned *The Nation* and the New York *Evening Post*, which "was known far and wide as 'a friend to Negroes.'" Harrison referred to Villard and his associates somewhat disparagingly as "the Vesey St. liberals" after the 20 Vesey Street address of the *Evening Post* building (which also provided the first office space for the NAACP). According to Harrison, the *Post*'s friendship had "given way to indifference and worse." Whereas in the old days when every lynching received editorial condemnation from the *Post*, now the three great lynchings of 1917 that preceded the East St. Louis riots found absolutely no editorial condemnation from the paper. Yet as soon as Black soldiers in Houston, "goaded to retaliation by gross indignities," did some shooting of their own, the *Evening Post*, which hadn't condemned the lynchers, "joined the chorus of those who were screaming for 'punishment' and death." The *Post*'s editorial of August 25, which held that "no provocation could justify the crimes committed by mutinous Negro soldiers at Houston, Texas," and that "no condemnation of their conduct can be too severe," was cited.[93]

Harrison also explained how *The Voice* could not forget that while the *Post*'s editor sought "a diplomatic appointment (like some other editors)" during the first year of Woodrow Wilson's first administration, the *Post* "pretended to believe that the President didn't know of the segregation practiced in the government departments." The NAACP had similarly "pretended to the same effect," added Harrison, in reference to the period between July and September 1913 when the *Crisis*, like Villard, failed to criticize the segregation policies of the Wilson administration. Thus, after witnessing such "frightful friendliness," *The Voice* concluded "that the time has come when we should insist on being our own best friends." Harrison recognized that mistakes would be made, but he felt that Blacks "ought to be allowed to make our own mistakes—as other people are allowed to do." If friendship meant "compulsory compromise foisted on us by kindly white people, or by cultured Negroes whose ideal is the imitation of the urbane acquiescence of these white friends," then, advised Harrison, "we had better learn to look a gift horse in the mouth."[94]

As the 1917 election came to a close Harrison provided *Voice* readers an in-depth analysis of their significance. The final election results showed that in the mayoralty contest the Democrat Hylan won with 313,956 votes. He defeated the incumbent Fusion candidate Mitchel, who had 155,497 votes, the Socialist Hillquit with 145,322 votes (22 percent of the total), and the Republican Bennett, who only polled about 45,000 votes. While awaiting the final official figures, Harrison predicted that they would demonstrate "concrete evidences of treachery on the part of the local Republican organization and a certain person [Charles W. Anderson]."[95]

Harrison first analyzed the Socialist vote, which had increased by nearly 400 percent and resulted in the election of eight aldermen, ten assemblymen, and a municipal judge. He considered this "cause for rejoicing," and though Hillquit was defeated for mayor, he felt that "the party of the Common People" had "opened the doors of our state and city governments, and stepped inside." Of particular importance was the fact that one-fourth of the Black vote in Harlem went to Hillquit. The Democrat Hylan had polled the most Black votes, but Hillquit surpassed the incumbent Mitchel among Black voters. An overly optimistic Harrison predicted that the Socialist vote among Blacks would likely to go "to 50 per cent at the next election" and that "fear of losing the Negro vote" would cause both Republicans and Democrats "to bestir themselves more in the Negro's behalf in the future than any certainty of allegiance could make them do in the past."[96]

Beyond the Socialist vote, which increased from 33,000 (11 percent of the total in 1912) to 143,000 (22 percent of the total in 1917), Harrison thought that "the second great, out-standing result" of the election was the enfranchisement of women. Though *The Voice* had opposed women's suffrage "in the latter part of the campaign," it had done so, "not on principle, but as a protest against the cowardly race prejudice of the white women of the Woman Suffrage Party." Now, however, women's suffrage was a reality. It had been strongly supported by Hillquit and the Socialists, and Harrison considered it "undoubtedly, a great step in the direction of democracy at home." As of January 1, African American women would have the vote, and Harrison doubted that they would "be as easy meat for the politicians (of both sexes) as our Negro men have been." With women now having the vote, Harrison felt safe to "confidently predict" playgrounds, baths, and clean streets in Harlem within a year and a half. He also expected that politicians charging high rents as landlords would soon learn that such practices "will bar them from political preferment in the future."[97]

Next he analyzed the election of Edward Austin Johnson, the first Black assemblyman in New York State history. Johnson had won his Assembly seat by 300 votes in a three-way race and had polled some 88 percent of the votes cast in predominantly Black election districts in the Nineteenth Assembly District. The third candidate, from the Fusion ticket, drew enough white voters from the Democratic nominee to enable Johnson to win. Harrison saw this as "the opening wedge of real political equality for the Negroes of New York." The tasks were now to assure that there would always be a Black representative in Albany and "to keep an eye on the white politicians who would gerrymander our districts so as to make it harder for a member of our race to get elected to office."[98]

Harrison, the propagandist, saw Johnson's election as the "death knell of the barnacle type of Republican leader," and he thought that Charles W. Anderson, in particular, was "dead for keeps." No longer would "a Negro political leader be hand-picked for us by our white masters"; no more would they maintain themselves in power "by being dumb on the great demands" of African Americans; and no more would leadership simply mean "doing the dirty work of ward heelers and saloonkeepers" or "dining one's way into popularity." From this point forward, predicted Harrison, "the Negro leader in politics will be responsible first to the race that made him what he is." This seemed to be the case on Monday, November 12, when Harrison was one of a host of speakers at a mass meeting at the Palace Casino in celebration of Johnson's victory. The meeting was chaired by Louis F. Baldwin, and among the speakers were the future candidates for political office Isaac B. Allen, Chandler Owen, A. Philip Randolph, William Bridges, and Louis A. Leavelle.[99]

James C. Thomas Jr., the aldermanic candidate in the Twenty-sixth District had been defeated 2,866 to 2,500 by Democrat Frank Mullen in a strongly contested election. Thomas polled 76 percent of the vote in predominantly Black election districts and publicly declared that he was cheated. He cited voting irregularities and noted that despite "the squirming statements of Mr. Royall's Civic League, it remains true that Edward A. Johnson was openly 'knifed' in the voting below 130th Street"—that is, in the white section of Harlem—where "white Republicans stood at several polling places and told those going to vote that Johnson was a Negro and that they shouldn't vote for him." For such actions two men had already been arrested. Thomas, who ran in a district with 5,000 Black voters, claimed that he was in the lead on election night, was tricked out of the count, and that his opponent had run a strictly racial campaign, encouraging whites not to vote for a Black candidate. Since Johnson's three-way campaign was run "on strictly party lines," Harrison asked, "what was to be expected in the case of Thomas, whose campaign was not 'on strictly party lines?'" He referred to the fact that in Thomas's two-way contest, many white Republicans voted "white" (i.e., for the white Democratic candidate) rather than Republican. Harrison said that the task was now for Blacks to "make that defeat as costly as possible to those responsible for it."[100]

Overall, the 1917 election was of historic importance. Voters supported women's suffrage, the Socialists made a strong showing, and the African American masses played a more important role than ever before in city politics. From that date forward in every New York City election, African Americans would win elective office. Despite these gains, however, efforts would soon be made to steer the increasingly race-conscious Harlem community toward more traditional politics.[101]

After the November election, Harrison received a supportive letter from William Monroe Trotter, who, after reading the November 7 *Voice*, congratulated him for his "manly, independent stand." Trotter added that "such racial manliness and independence is the greatest need of the Colored American people today and you are a worthy and needed advocate and leader in this cause of intrinsic equality." He believed that as an individual "and as a leader" Harrison deserved "endorsement," particularly because of his efforts at uniting with "other Colored American organized movements," and he thought that Harrison's support of the Colored National Liberty Congress demonstrated that he was "wise and unselfishly interested in the cause of equality of rights for your race." Trotter also mentioned that Harrison was admired by two friends and supporters, Reverend George Frazier Miller and Professor Allen W. Whaley, and he advised that it was now important for him to "be reasonable, determined and undiscourageable" in his "work of leadership and organization." In expressing agreement with Harrison's stance toward white help, Trotter reaffirmed Harrison's position that "while we want all the friends we can get we need no benevolent dictators. It is we, not they, who must shape Negro policies." Trotter then closed with a "Confidential" postscript telling Harrison that he wanted "to enlarge the Liberty Congress arrangements by including the Liberty [League] program," and he asked Harrison to assist in getting additional support, mentioning Owen and Randolph by name.[102]

The November 14 issue of *The Voice* appeared shortly after the November municipal elections and was the last issue of 1917. Publication was suspended and did not resume until July 1, 1918, when a second run of about nine months began. Harrison's fiery speeches and editorials had caused a stir, but the paper ran out of money because of the competitive pressure from the *Age* and the *New York News*, the lack of adequate financial backing, and the organizational difficulties within the Liberty League. Harrison did attempt a fundraiser, the First December Dance of the Harlem People's Forum, on December 6 at the Palace Casino. It was a joint activity to benefit the Liberty League and *The Voice*, but though well attended, profits were small. After the dance, on December 10, the Race Publishing Company was incorporated by Harrison, Julius A. Thomas, W. Clayton Dowdy, Charles T. Magill, and the actor Charles Burroughs. The amount of capital stock was to be $25,000 based on 2,500 shares at $10 each. When *The Voice* resumed publication it was owned by the Race Publishing Company, and the new ownership, responding to the economic pressure, moved the printing downtown, out of 2305 Seventh Avenue.[103]

The all-Black Race Publishing Company would pledge to "run and own the paper," and Harrison informed *Voice* readers that a white man in Harlem had offered to put up $10,000 in December 1917 "to own it in partnership with the Editor" and the offer was rejected. Instead, "every friend of freedom" who believed in the paper's "policy and spirit" and believed that it couldn't "be bought off" was urged to support it financially by buying stock shares. Such a mass-based funding policy was qualitatively different from that which had shaped Booker

T. Washington's Tuskegee machine, the NAACP (and its *Crisis* magazine), the Urban League, and the Republican and Democratic Parties' Negro affiliates. In addition, explained Harrison, editorial policy would be "shaped" by the stockholders, who could help make it "the greatest Negro paper in America." *The Voice's* board of directors included the attorney and lay historian Rufus L. Perry; the Socialist Rev. Dr. George Frazier Miller of St. Augustine's Church, Brooklyn; the businesswoman Bernia L. Smith, of the Indol Corporation; and the journalist John E. Bruce, another Harrison friend from the Lyceum days. Readers were told that under able business management, investments in the paper would be "earning money every week."[104]

After only a few months, *The Voice* had left an indelible mark as the pioneer publication of the "New Negro" movement. It was, according to historian Robert A. Hill, "the radical forerunner" of a host of New Negro publications that soon emerged, including the *Messenger* of A. Philip Randolph and Chandler Owen (November 1917), the *Negro World* of Marcus Garvey (August 1918), and the *Crusader* of Cyril Briggs (also August 1918). Such publications, explained Hodge Kirnon, exerted "a tremendous influence in inspiring the people with the highest racial ideals and aspirations" and inculcated "into every Negro a sense of race pride and determination" that was "without parallel in the history of the race." Kirnon emphasized that Harrison's *Voice* "really crystallized the radicalism of the Negro in New York and its environs."[105]

After *The Voice* ceased publication in November 1917, Harrison turned to public speaking. His Harlem People's Forum lecture series, which began in December, included talks on: "Socialism: What It Is and Why It Is"; "Has Man an Immortal Soul?"; "Negro History and Its Place in Education"; "Does Religion Make Men Good?"; "What Is Conscience Worth?"; "Lincoln and Liberty: Fact Versus Fiction"; and "Paul Laurence Dunbar, His Poetry and Life." The big event in December, however, was a debate between Harrison and Chandler Owen on December 23, at the Palace Casino. Billed as "The Greatest Debate in Years," Harrison was to take the affirmative and Owen the negative on the subject: "Resolved: That the doctrine, 'Negroes First,' is sound, logical or DEFENSIBLE." In the publicity for the event, however, Owen (who handled the publicity) changed the billing in the socialist *Call* of December 22 to that of a debate on the question "Is the Doctrine of 'NEGROES FIRST' a Logical and Sound Socialistic Position?"[106]

Owen's handling of the publicity led Harrison to write a very critical letter to the editor of the *Call* on January 7, 1918. Harrison began by reminding *Call* readers that many knew him "as a student and teacher of Socialism, its principles and ideals" and, while he may have made "human mistakes and been occasionally wrong, like others," he had never "given anyone reason for thinking that I could be so big a fool as to maintain that the doctrine of 'Negro First' was 'a logical and sound Socialistic position,' as was stated in the advertising which Mr. Chandler Owen inserted in *The Call* of December 22."[107]

Harrison explained that the "debate was strictly on the merits of a line of propaganda for Negroes which asks 'that they should put concern for their own racial interests ahead of concern for the interests of a nation which goes 3,000 miles to fight for democracy in Europe while ignoring the demand of 12,000,000 Negroes for democracy at home.'" He recognized that the propaganda could be "faulty, illogical or utterly wrong; but it certainly has never been advanced as any part of Socialist doctrine." To Harrison, Owen's advertising was "downright dishonest," and Harrison claimed he only found out about it thirty minutes before the debate. He immediately remonstrated with Owen who responded that he had put out such publicity "only to get the Socialists interested enough to attend the debate," an explanation that Harrison promptly indicated was totally unsatisfactory.[108]

At the beginning of his speech Harrison addressed the advertisements issue and made it clear that the debate was, as he and Owen had previously agreed, "along lines of its own and never as any part of Socialism." He further noted that although Owen had put out all the advertising as per their agreement, "in that large part of it intended for Negro eyes he said not a word about Socialism." Harrison emphasized that he opposed "duplicity of the sort that tends to alienate my friends, or, at least, to make them think me unsound in my view of Socialist principles." In his letter to the *Call* Harrison enclosed his notes from the talk—to show how "thoroughly misleading" the advertising was.[109]

Other Harrison comments suggest more on the direction of the debate. He later wrote that the "Callow Colored Socialists" (Owen and Randolph), were "ignorant alike of History and Literature" and they "asserted that there was no such thing as Negro history or Negro Lit: one of their editors even denied that there was such a thing as *Negro Music*." Further, according to Harrison, "the 'radical' Owen fiercely maintained [in 1917] 'that the doctrine of race first was an indefensible doctrine,'" while Harrison maintained that it was "the source of the salvation of the race." Both Owen and Randolph, added Harrison in 1920, had run "true to form ever since."[110]

Randolph and Owen were "class-first" socialists, yet, according to J. A. Rogers, even they were "profoundly influenced" by Harrison. In November 1917 they organized the Messenger Publishing Company, and in December they organized "a club for the purpose of introducing socialism among the colored people" of Harlem. Interestingly, the "class-first" Socialists organized what they later described as "the first Socialist Branch among Negroes." It was almost a retake of Harrison's effort with the Colored Socialist Club, six years earlier. But conditions were objectively different because of the northern migration and more favorable wartime employment possibilities. They were also subjectively different because of the awakened race consciousness and new militance in the community.[111]

By 1917 conditions had changed markedly since those faced by Harrison in 1912 when there was no comparably significant autonomous African American movement in New York City. Now, such a movement existed, and Harrison led it. This created a climate in which Socialists were able to make gains. In the year 1917 the Socialist Party was reportedly able to recruit one hundred Black members in New York City, "all" of whom were described as "professionals and small businessmen." While the Socialists claimed credit for these membership gains, Harrison felt this was improper and incorrect—they "took credit for an upsurge [that was] due to race." Even that growth was limited, however, since Randolph and Owen continued to downplay the race question. By 1925 Randolph would explain that the *Messenger's* "editorial policy has been changed" and "we have eliminated all definite Socialist propaganda." He explained, "We eliminated socialist propaganda because we found that it alienated the very group we wanted to reach—the Negro workers." The change was "based upon the belief that it is more important that Negro workers be organized into trade unions than that they vote the Socialist ticket or that they be organized only as Socialist workers."[112]

It should be emphasized that Harrison did not express objections to the socialist theory of Karl Marx. Rather, his differences were with the white-supremacist theory and practice and the lack of understanding of the need for Black race consciousness that were displayed by those who professed to be proponents of socialism in the United States. In March 1920, while editing the race-conscious *Negro World*, Harrison explained that he still considered himself "a Socialist," but because of the Socialist Party's white supremacy and because he did not consider himself "a fool," he refused "to put either Socialism" or the Socialist Party "above the call of his race." Two months later he would argue that the Socialist Party message could still be brought to Black people and he would advise Socialists that if they sent anyone (Black or white) up to Harlem "to put the case of Karl Marx, freed from admixture of rancor and hatred of the Negro's own defensive racial propaganda," they "may find that it will have as good a chance of gaining adherents as any other political creed." But, he added, "until you [Socialists] change your tactics or make your exponents change theirs your case among us will be helpless indeed."[113]

As 1917 ended, Hubert Harrison continued to agitate for race-conscious activity by the Black masses. He had already left an important legacy. His class and race agitation, articles, and oratory had influenced the Harlem masses and a group of upcoming radicals. Forums in Harlem, started by Harrison, were by 1918 being held by Marcus Garvey and the Universal Negro Improvement Association, by A. Philip Randolph and Chandler Owen and the "Colored" Socialists, by the United Civic League, and by the Women's Political and Economic Association. Radical publications (like the *Messenger*, the *Negro World*, and the *Crusader*) and radical organizations (like Garvey's UNIA, Cyril Briggs's African Blood Brotherhood, and Randolph and Owen's Messenger Group), were, or would soon be, following the lead of *The Voice* and Liberty League.[114]

Harrison had laid the ideological and organizational groundwork for the race radicalism of Garvey and the class radicalism of Randolph and Owen. These radicalisms would emerge full blown by 1920. He had also delineated the core ideas on the importance of race-conscious activity, and, by 1934, even Du Bois would declare that "it is the race conscious . . . cooperating together . . . [in] institutions and movements who will eventually emancipate the colored race."[115]

12

The Liberty Congress and
the Resurrection of *The Voice*
(January–July 1918)

In the early part of 1918, while his organizational efforts were slowed and his newspaper suspended, Harrison was particularly concerned about the war and heightened racism and repression at home. He paid special attention to the increase in lynchings of African Americans (from thirty-six in 1917 to at least sixty in 1918), to continued segregation and disfranchisement, and to incidents like those he recorded in his scrapbooks on the wholesale dismissal of Black postal clerks in Charleston, South Carolina, and the firing at of fifty Black female civil servants (who were then replaced by white women not required to take the Civil Service Exam) at the Bureau of Engraving in Washington, D.C.[1]

Harrison also paid attention to the new legal attacks on the general population. The Sedition Act of May 16, 1918, amended the June 15, 1917, Espionage Act and called for a $5,000 fine, up to twelve years imprisonment, or both, for those who "willfully utter, print, write, or publish any disloyal, profane, scurrilous, or abusive language" about the U.S. government or in support of an enemy country. Prosecutions under this legislation totaled 988 from June 15, 1917, to July 1, 1918.[2]

In this setting he chose a course of action that included public opposition to white-supremacist practices and the war's white-supremacist aims, involvement in labor organizing, and renewed membership in the Socialist Party. He was not heavily engaged in organizational work, however, and financial hardships, family problems, and draft difficulties related to the May 18, 1917, Conscription Act assumed more prominence in his daily life.

Though he struggled to make a living, Harrison's diary entries make clear that his four children were never far from his thoughts and he was concerned about providing money for them and Lin. His marriage, however, was undergoing an especially difficult period—he lived apart from Lin, and he was apparently sexually involved with another woman. To make a living he continued to lecture and sell books and, in the first week of March 1918, he began giving outdoor talks at Madison Square and at 135th Street. Selling books at such talks was a difficult ways to earn a living, however, and he was summoned to court by "an Irish policeman" and charged with selling books without a license. That case was dismissed. Three weeks later he began an indoor lecture series with a talk on "Education and the Negro." A diary entry from March 30, 1918, gives indication of his skill as an orator and bookseller, his family concerns, and his proximity to abject poverty:

> Today I began the day's work with a dollar and twenty cents. I bought six copies of [Herbert] Spencer's *Education* at 18 cents and sold them at 50c in Madison Square in a 15 minutes talk. Then, with the income I bought 15 more copies and sold them (and received money for others) at 134th St. & Lenox Ave. I finished the day's work with $12.50. Bought a chicken (96c) and some flowers for the kids and gave their mother some money.[3]

While facing such financial difficulties in early 1918, Harrison sought to rejoin the Socialist Party (it is not clear what happened regarding the membership payment he said he was sending in November 1917). The party stood for the working class, and it was the major organized force in opposition to U.S. involvement in the war. In addition, Socialists were making new overtures to African Americans similar to those Harrison had previously sought. On February 27, 1918, A. Philip Randolph went before the Executive Committee of the Socialist Party of Local New York and said there were a number of "Negroes" eager to join the party and to do work in the "Negro section" of the Nineteenth Assembly District. He requested that the Local contribute toward the establishing of such a branch. It was fully six years since Harrison's effort with the Colored Socialist Club, and the EC now voted to support Randolph's proposal on "Negro activity" for two months with fifteen dollars per month. Since Harrison was looking for a way to make a living and the party had paid him a livable wage in the past, it was reasonable to think it might find a way to help his financial situation again.[4]

While the possibility of financial assistance existed, Harrison considered his decision to return to the Socialist Party a political matter. In his diary he explained that he liked the party's first stance on the war, presumably the one that grew out of a meeting of March 10–11, 1917, of the National Executive Committee in Chicago and was adopted at a Special Convention in St. Louis in April, only days after Wilson's war declaration. At St. Louis the party reaffirmed "allegiance to the principle of internationalism and working class solidarity the world-over," proclaimed "its unalterable opposition to the war," and declared that "modern wars as a rule have been caused by the commercial and financial rivalry of capitalist interests" and "they obscure the struggles of the workers for life, liberty, and justice." This was consistent with Harrison's view that the war was a product of capitalist imperialism and that it was an attempt to counter domestic efforts at social change.[5]

Harrison was readmitted to the Socialist Party on March 27, and his stay this time was short. In all probability his Socialist connections and party membership, coupled with Liberty League contacts, helped him to land jobs as a labor-union organizer with both the Pullman workers and the hotel workers. The party membership may have also helped him later to obtain a party advertisement for *The Voice* when it began publication again in July. There is little indication that he did any other party work in this period. He submitted his final resignation to the Socialists on September 16, 1918, and in his diary he attributed his decision to resign to "the dirty deal which Randolph & [Chandler] Owen had made with [Julius] Gerber, the Party's Secretary." He was probably referring to the Socialist Party's plan to run Randolph and Owen for candidates in New York's Nineteenth and Twenty-first Assembly districts, respectively, in a move that directly interfered with the chances of two electable Black candidates.[6]

This SP election move pitted the two Black Socialists against two Black Republicans with good chances for victory, Edward Austin Johnson in the Nineteenth and John C. Hawkins in the Twenty-first. This was the first time that New York City Republicans had ever officially backed Black candidates in these Harlem Assembly Districts. In the Nineteenth AD, Randolph drew 8 percent of the vote (1,129 votes) and attorney Johnson lost to the Democrat Martin J. Healy by 8.7 percent (1,220 votes). In the Twenty-first AD, Owen polled 4.5 percent (563 votes) and seriously threatened the victory of Hawkins, which he achieved with only 51.6 percent of the vote.[7]

To Harrison, the Gerber-Randolph-Owen deal showed "that the party was still hopelessly in the control of petty-bourgeois reactionaries," and he therefore "dropped out for ever." In his letter to the Executive Committee Harrison explained that his resignation was not tendered "as a prelude to any public attacks upon my former comrades" and stated that "I shall hold myself free, on grounds of private friendship as well as of public policy, to work for the election of the Rev. Geo. Frazier Miller to Congress as a member of your party." Miller was running as a Socialist, and although he was running against another African American with socialist leanings, the Rev. Reverdy C. Ransom, support of Miller did not threaten to snatch victory from Ransom, who was running as an independent. Harrison's opposition to Randolph and Owen was not the same as the "anti-Bolshevist" stance of the *Age*. It was also distinguished from the support given to Owen and Randolph over Johnson and Hawkins by Cyril Briggs, editor of the *Crusader*. The first position rejected a socialist perspective, and the second position tended to undermine potentially victorious race efforts in the Nineteenth and Twenty-first Assembly Districts. Harrison, who supported the socialist Miller as well as Johnson and Hawkins, took a stand that called for class solidarity and the need to break the white monopoly on holding office.[8]

In early 1918, amid his continuing financial problems, Harrison looked toward labor-union-related work as a possible source of income. The wartime migration of Black workers north and persistent Black demands for equality intensified pressure on both the government and the American Federation of Labor. The federal government's War Labor Board, established on April 8, recognized the right of workers to organize into labor unions and the AFL president, Samuel Gompers, proclaimed federation support for organizing Black workers and hiring Black organizers at the AFL's June convention. Despite this proclamation, the reality was that the AFL did little to organize Black workers.[9]

Harrison started his union work between the April government action and the June Gompers statement. He served as an organizer for the International Federation of the Workers in the Hotel, Restaurant, Club, and Catering Industry, a "white" organization of about 65,000 members that was seeking to recruit Black workers. His organizing work concentrated on Atlantic City, Philadelphia, and Washington, D.C.—cities in which Blacks did almost all the cooking. In his diary he recorded his effort on May 23, when he spoke at a nine P.M. general membership meeting in the union's Philadelphia headquarters, and then again at one A.M. in an unsuccessful attempt to attract night workers. The union work paid thirty-five dollars a week plus expenses, and this represented a marked improvement in his finances. It also offered some mobility and, in late June, this enabled him to go to Washington and play a leading role at the Liberty Congress.[10]

Just before attending the Liberty Congress, on June 20, Harrison spoke before 300 Pullman porters at one of their first local organizational meetings at the Civic League Hall, 184 W. 135th Street in New York. Other speakers included William Collins, general organizer of the AFL; Counselor Cornelius W. McDougald; the Rev. George Frazier Miller; and two labor unionists and Liberty League activists, Charles H. Florney and James C. Canegata. Some 218 workers joined the union that night. Despite such efforts, the AFL leadership did not show serious interest in organizing Black workers or supporting Black organizers at that time.[11]

While financial and personal matters consumed much of Harrison's time and energy, he found that his political views and citizenship status put him in a precarious position. After the United States entered the war it became dangerous to speak out against the government. Harrison's position was particularly insecure because his citizenship status was unclear. Although the United States had purchased the Virgin Islands, Harrison "didn't know" if he "was a citizen, half-citizen or alien" because he was "not quite clear as to certain meanings of the treaty by which St. Croix was acquired by the U.S.A. in 1916–1917." His confusion was well founded since the 1917 treaty purported to give Crucians "a choice of becoming 'citizens *in* the United States,'" but not *of* the United States. This ambiguous wording, according to historian William Boyer, "deceived them [Crucians] into believing they were being accorded American citizenship when in fact the United States intended to deny them that status." Overall, Harrison's murky citizenship status and opposition to the war meant that if he was deemed an alien, although he would be allowed to enlist in the military, he might be deported. If he was deemed a citizen he was potentially subject to be drafted into military service and he might encounter the severe persecution faced by other radical critics (as later exemplified by the ten-year prison term that would be meted out to the Socialist Party leader Eugene V. Debs in September 1918).[12]

Harrison was concerned about being drafted. On March 27, 1918, he went to see Charles W. Anderson, the Negro Republican leader he had previously criticized in *The Voice* and the man who had helped to engineer his removal from the Post Office. The seemingly always well placed Anderson was chairman of the Selective Service Exemption Board, no. 139, at 127th St. and Lenox Ave. in Harlem. Harrison wanted to find out "whether it was possible to enter an officers' training camp and to prepare for ultimate service in the Army in the event that the war comes over here"—this was apparently the only condition under which he desired to serve. Anderson informed him that there were plans underway to organize the military services of older and more intelligent than average Black draftees, and he advised him to write to Emmett J. Scott (another old nemesis), who had been appointed special assistant (for "Negro Propaganda") to Secretary of War Newton D. Baker, in order to find out whether and how his services could be used.[13]

Immediately after writing the letter Harrison had a change of heart. It was spurred by the March 27, 1918, *Evening Sun*, which carried a "malignant article" from "its 'cracker' correspondent in France" where, as Harrison noted, Black soldiers from the United States were "offering their lives for this nation." These soldiers, whom the U.S. military command had not released to fight, had been "lent" to the French, who finally gave them marching orders. As Harrison described in his diary, the *Sun* article "cleared the air for me":

> Until the white men of this country can put patriotism ahead of race I shall not. So long as they will treat us as "niggers" rather than as fellow citizens will those of us who respect themselves keep from fighting for a damned "Jim-Crow" democracy whose tangled threads of hypocrisy, cant and cruelty will weave their dangerous web across the nation's path to self-respect.[14]

Though March 27 was the day that Harrison reaffirmed his "race-first" response to the remainder of the war, the letter to Emmett Scott was already sent. Scott never replied, and it was not until 1922 that Harrison "discovered that despite my being above the draft age, and being exempt anyway as the only support of a family of 5 [6], I had been put in the *First Class*." He observed, "Such was the malignancy of the Scott-[George E.] Haynes gang!" Haynes, whom Harrison had dealt with at the Urban League, had assumed the position of special assistant to the secretary of labor and headed the Division of Negro Economics of the Department of Labor. Harrison wanted the heads of both Scott and Haynes, and when he got the chance a year later he would work to have them dumped from leadership positions. He later claimed in his diary that he was instrumental in having Haynes removed as head of the Urban League.[15]

Harrison registered for the draft on September 12, 1918, probably in response to changes in the law that extended age limits of draftees to eighteen and forty-five and required registration by that date. His assumption of dirty dealings concerning his draft status appears to have merit. There were, in addition, other factors at play. The period was one of extralegal tactics, most notably illegal roundups or "slacker raids" conducted by the Justice Department, local police, sailors, soldiers, and "patriots" of the American Protective League. It is likely that Harrison was prompted to register by the September 3 through 6 "slacker raids" in which more than 50,000 men were apprehended, many by bayonets, and forced to show their Selective Service papers. On September 3 and 4 alone, some 21,402 people from Manhattan, Brooklyn, and the Bronx were apprehended and detained by vigilante forces. Another factor suggesting "dirty dealings" was the generalized disparate treatment faced by African Americans, who were over 50 percent more likely than whites to be classified as eligible Class 1 (some 51.65 percent of Blacks and only 32.53 percent of whites were so classified).[16]

After registering, the thirty-five-year-old Harrison returned his draft questionnaire on September 28. He listed his address as 2441 Seventh Avenue, c/o Tippett, a further indication that he was not living with his family. Most important, on the questionnaire he claimed exemption on three grounds:

(1) Class 3L: The necessary assistant or associate manager of an industrial enterprise—in this case the (by then) resurrected *Voice* at 2295 Seventh Ave.
(2) Class 4A: A man whose wife and children are mainly dependent on his labor for support
(3) Class 4D: A necessary sole managing, controlling, or directing head of necessary industrial enterprise

Though each of the claimed exemptions could be challenged, it was not on such basis that he was declared eligible. Rather, he was given a 1A status (single without dependent relatives), allegedly because he gave no answer to the questions relating to citizenship. Since the status of Virgin Islanders was unclear, for this to be the basis of his 1A status did smell of foul play. Possibly, it was, as he suspected, the work of the Scott-Haynes gang, perhaps with Charles W. Anderson again playing the role of hatchet man. Fortunately for Harrison, his 1A registration status was not mailed until November 12, 1918, the day after the armistice was declared.[17]

While his draft status hung over his head, Harrison's March 27 diary entry showed he would not downplay his race-conscious opposition to white supremacy. In this area he was still the pivotal figure on the Harlem scene. Even though *The Voice* was no longer publishing, Harrison still influenced those former Liberty League members who were involved with the *New Negro*, owned by August Valentine Bernier and published by the Clarion Publishing Company. By March 1918 the *New Negro* staff included Beatrice Ione-Wade, John Edward Bruce, Alexander Rahming, Andrea P. Razafinkeriefo, and William H. Scott, and that month's issue positively discussed Harrison's "soap box oratory."[18]

In this period Harrison continued to pay attention to international matters. He consistently took the position that Africans of the diaspora had much to learn from Africa and Africans. "LEARN WHAT THEY HAVE TO TEACH US (for they have much to teach us)," he later advised, and in early 1918 he continued to delve deeper into African studies and African history. He recorded in his diary a March 1918 discussion in his rented room at 2237 Seventh Ave. with the bibliophile Arthur Schomburg and a young Liberian waiter who was in the country studying. After talking until one in the morning on books relating to Black studies and African affairs, Harrison wrote that Schomburg had "read more widely on Negro History than any man whom I have met" and had a private library that was "the best public or private collection of books on the Negro that there is in the United States."[19]

This interest in Africa also led Harrison to further his readings on Islam, a subject that he would study for the remainder of his life. He found Edward Wilmot Blyden's *West Africa Before Europe* to be "a very inspiring book" and decided to write to the Sheik-ul-Islam of England in order "to get in touch with organized Mohammedanism in the United States and to learn the Arabic Language." In this period he also read the Koran, as well as books as diverse as David Livingstone's *Missionary Travels and Researches In South Africa* and George. W. Ellis's *Negro Culture in West Africa* (a personal favorite that he later gave to all his children). While studying Islam, Harrison also continued his philosophical probing of religion by reading Walter R. Cassels's *Supernatural Religion*, Moncure D. Conway's *Life of Thomas Paine*, and Mark Twain's *What Is Man?*[20]

While his interest in Africa and African peoples continued to grow, Harrison's major activity in the summer of 1918 concerned the June National Liberty Congress, which had been planned for over a year and had grown, in particular, out of his work and that of William Monroe Trotter in Massachusetts. The congress was to be the major wartime national meeting of militant Black leaders. In a wider sense, however, it was, as Harrison explained, "the result of the words which the Negro American hears and the things which he sees" and "the disparity and the differences between both." Harrison had previously been elected chairman of the Board of Managers and chosen as grand national organizer of the congress.[21]

The official April 1918 "Call" for the congress specified that it would be held from June 21 through 29 at the John Wesley A.M. E. Zion Church in Washington. All "Colored" churches, businesses, and civic, literary, and fraternal organizations and societies were requested to send delegates, and the congress aimed "to press the just claim of the Colored American citizens . . . to share in the world democracy for which they are subject to fight" and "to take positive measures to secure from the Government guarantee of the abolition of disfranchisement and of all caste discrimination, civil and political." The Liberty Congress was to be an all-Black affair, and it would lay before the U.S. Congress "methods by which President Wilson and the Government may best carry out his great war slogan—'To make the world safe for Democracy, to make the world a fit place to live in.'" It also hoped "to make Democracy safe for the world." A formidable national committee was listed, which included the Rev. Adam Clayton Powell Sr., of New York, president; Allen W. Whaley of Massachusetts, national organizer; Marion F. Sydes of Rhode Island, recording secretary; Rev. D. S. Klugh of the People's Baptist Church in Boston, treasurer; Harrison, chairman of the board; Mrs. Sarah J. Allen of Massachusetts, corresponding secretary; and William Monroe Trotter, executive secretary. By June 1 Harrison was also listed as secretary.[22]

As word of the Liberty Congress spread in April, May, and June, major steps were taken by the Military Intelligence Branch of the Army to block and undermine it, to counteract "the erosion of black loyalty," and to woo more conservative editors. The principal architect of this counter-effort was Joel E. Spingarn, the independently wealthy chairman of the board of directors of the NAACP, who was a particularly close friend and a former financial supporter of W. E. B. Du Bois. Du Bois would later write, "I do not think that any other white man ever touched me emotionally so closely as Joel Spingarn." Politically, Spingarn was strongly behind the U.S. war effort, and he had been placed, with the help of Emmett Scott, with Military Intelligence on May 27, 1918. His work was in MI-4 or "negative intelligence," the counterintelligence and antiradical branch of military intelligence specializing in surveillance and the "stopping of enemy propaganda" in the United States. Basically, according to historian Roy Talbert, that meant "spying on American radicals." In particular, Spingarn was to carry out intelligence activities on left-wing radical groups and African American "subversive" tendencies. Spingarn was, according to Mark Ellis, a nationally prominent "civil rights activist in the most reactionary agency of an antiradical administration," and though he recognized that African American's "grievances were real," he had "misgivings about them being aired during the war" and "believed an important objective of MIB work on race should be that of molding black opinion."[23]

Spingarn sought to involve Du Bois in his plans. Shortly after he joined the army he learned from the assistant U.S. attorney in New York that the NAACP's *Crisis* was being monitored for possible violations of the 1917 Espionage Act. To counter the MIB's anti-NAACP reports and to protect himself, Spingarn, over the signature of the MIB director, Colonel Marlborough Churchill, warned NAACP legal adviser Charles H. Studin (the law partner of Spingarn's brother, Arthur, who was chairman of the NAACP's legal committee) that the government would "not tolerate . . . utterances likely to foment disaffection and destroy the morale of our people for the winning of the war." Studin was advised to "make a special effort to eliminate all matter that may render the paper liable to suppression in the future." Studin promised to comply.[24]

Joel Spingarn and Du Bois met in Washington, D.C., on June 4 and discussed the possibility of creating a new agency to enlighten the government on racial matters and to promote Black loyalty. Spingarn provided Du Bois with a copy of some proposed antilynching legislation. Du Bois, like Spingarn, believed that full Black participation in the war effort would further the cause of civil rights and saw the MI "Negro Subversion" program as "constructive." At that time, Du Bois, as the editor, reportedly "promised to change the tone" of *The Crisis*, to make it "an organ of patriotic propaganda hereafter," and "to submit all matter" to a "designated person in advance of publication." He also agreed to apply for a commission as captain in the MIB, as suggested by Spingarn.[25]

As Spingarn was maneuvering with Du Bois, Captain Fred W. Moore, a Boston-based intelligence officer, was working on William Monroe Trotter. On June 5 Moore wrote to Colonel Churchill that he had, as requested by his superiors, interviewed Trotter regarding the Liberty Congress. Moore claimed to have explained "the dangerous possibilities in all possible lights" and to have "urged him . . . to secure a postponement of the Convention." Trotter did not back down, however, and would not postpone the Liberty Congress.[26]

Spingarn took steps to implement other plans. On June 5, through Emmett Scott, he wrote to George Creel of the Committee on Public Information and requested a conference "at an early date" of approximately twenty Negro editors and a dozen or so others influential among Negro people. The conference was to be held in Washington from June 19 through 21; that is, it would end the day of the informal start of the Liberty Congress. Spingarn's Colored Editors' Conference would be held with full government backing and financial support. Roy Talbert Jr., a specialist on "Negative Intelligence," matter-of-factly refers to this conference as "the Military Intelligence's Black Conference." It was set up to steal the Liberty Congress's thunder and to undermine the its impact.[27]

Next, at Spingarn's suggestion, a special wartime antilynching bill was submitted to the Republican congressman Leonidas C. Dyer of Missouri, a known lynching opponent. Since antilynching legislation was a centerpiece of the agenda of Harrison, Trotter, and the Liberty Congress, Spingarn's effort had the appearance of attempting to steal a march on them. In fact, however, Spingarn was advocating antilynching legislation only as a wartime measure (pursuant to Article I of the Constitution granting Congress the right "to declare war, to raise and support armies, [and] make all laws which shall be necessary and proper for carrying into execution the foregoing powers"), not as consistent with the Fourteenth Amendment, as Harrison was proposing. The Spingarn proposal would be applicable only in wartime and would have been irrelevant after November 1918. Even so, the bill was a marked advance over previous NAACP positions. Though it was part of Spingarn's overall effort to undermine the more militant Liberty Congress, at the same time it showed that the pending congress and the heightened level of racial protest were shaping national events.[28]

While the Liberty Congress planned to petition Congress to make lynching a federal crime, neither the federal government, the NAACP, nor Spingarn was prepared to go that far. In February 1918 the Justice Department had advised President Wilson that there was no constitutional basis for federal antilynching laws and that lynching incidents were not connected with the war in any such way to justify the action of the federal government under the war power. From 1918 to 1922 the NAACP, despite educational and agitational work against lynching, stopped short of calling for federal antilynching legislation. One major reason was its long-standing effort to gain Southern support. Its president and principal legal adviser, Moorfield Storey, repeatedly raised constitutionality issues regarding such federal antilynching legislation. In these arguments he conceded considerable ground to the states' rights arguments of the South.[29]

Overall, Spingarn's ideas and methods in the area of "Negro Subversion," were, according to Ellis, "hastily improvised, unfocused, and overambitious." The reason is clear. Spingarn was hastily trying to undermine (Trotter's *Guardian* said "to thwart") the impending Liberty Congress, which represented autonomous, militant, race-conscious, Black protest and was scheduled to formally begin on June 24.[30]

Not only was Spingarn trying desperately to block the Liberty Congress and promote the Editors' Conference; he was on a larger scale attempting, as

Figure 12.1. Joel Elias Spingarn, 1918. Joel E. Spingarn (1875–1939), a former Columbia University professor of comparative literature, was the chairman of the Board of Directors of the NAACP; creator of the Spingarn Medal, awarded annually by the NAACP for outstanding achievement by a Black American; and a close friend of W. E. B. Du Bois. Spingarn, seen here in military uniform, had supported the "preparedness movement" and "segregated officers' training camps" before becoming a major in the Military Intelligence Branch of the Army, which monitored the radical and African American communities during World War I. In 1918 Spingarn played a major role in seeking to undermine the autonomous protest of the Liberty Congress, led by Hubert Harrison and William Monroe Trotter, and in drawing Du Bois into that effort. *Source:* Courtesy of the Library of Congress.

Harrison later charged, to plot the course of the struggle for Black Americans. On June 13 Spingarn wrote to Moore that he was "arranging a confidential conference of the colored race" to discuss "the present status of the American negroes." He explained that at the conference "a general policy and program for future work will be formed," and he told Moore that it was "highly undesirable before the policies to be adopted by this conference are put in operation that any convention airing the grievances of the colored people should be held at Washington or elsewhere." He added, "Mr. Trotter should be informed that in the opinion of the military authorities his convention or conference should be postponed for four or five months."[31]

Moore so informed Trotter, but the government authorities had underestimated the breadth and depth of Black dissatisfaction and the commitment of the militant leaders. On June 15 Robert R. Moton, who had succeeded Booker T. Washington as president of the Tuskegee Institute and was a very moderate leader, wrote a revealing letter to President Wilson. Moton complained: "There is more genuine restlessness and perhaps disaffection, on the part of the colored people than I have ever before known."[32]

It is clear that the articulated grievances were real. This was a principal reason that the Spingarn-initiated government action backfired and spurred more resentment. Spingarn had presumed to tell the Black leaders of the Liberty Congress that they should not meet, since it was not the time to present their grievances. It was not simply the convening of the congress that was involved; the whole matter of autonomous Black protest and the problem of "whites" attempting to control Black activity were at issue. This became clearer at the Editors' Conference.[33]

The Editors' Conference of June 19 through 21 went pretty much according to plan. Emmett Scott followed Spingarn's suggestion and persuaded George Creel to hold the Conference in Washington. Scott's aim was that "Negro public opinion should be led along helpful lines, rather than along lines that make for discontent and unrest." The conference attracted forty-seven more moderate Black leaders, including thirty-one from the press. There were no women in attendance, labor was not represented, and the South was underrepresented. Among those in attendance were editors of leading Black newspapers, including John H. Murphy, Baltimore *Afro-American*; George W. Harris, *New York News*; Edward A. Warren, New York *Amsterdam News*; Robert L. Vann, *Pittsburgh Courier*; Fred R. Moore, *New York Age*; Benjamin Davis, *Atlanta Independent*; and Robert S. Abbott, *Chicago Defender*. Du Bois, of *The Crisis*, attended, as did Charles W. Anderson, Kelly Miller, and Robert R. Moton (president of the Tuskegee Institute). Prominent speakers included the secretary of war, Newton D. Baker; the CPI chairman, Creel; the assistant secretary of the navy (and future governor of New York and president of the United States), Franklin D. Roosevelt; Major Joel E. Spingarn of MIB; and his brother, Captain Arthur Barnett Spingarn of the Medical Reserve Corps and also of the NAACP.[34]

Two documents emerged from the conference. One was "A Bill of Particulars on Which It Is Suggested That Action Might Be Taken," which was to be submitted privately to bureau heads in Washington. The second was an "Address to the Committee on Public Information," written by Du Bois and signed by all forty-seven conferees, which was forwarded by Creel to President Wilson. The "Address" reaffirmed loyalty and promised to do all that was possible to maintain Black support "at the highest pitch." It also, however, stated in words that Harrison would later cite: "we believe today that justifiable grievances of the colored people are producing not disloyalty, but an amount of unrest and bitterness which even the best efforts of the leaders may not be able always to guide."[35]

An *Official Bulletin* of the conference that extracted from the adopted resolutions and was basically Du Bois's draft, sanitized by Scott and Spingarn, was issued on June 29. Among the passages omitted from the June 21 address when it was reprinted in the August *Crisis* were the most important—those dealing specifically with the "justifiable grievances" of Black Americans, which said: "First and foremost among these grievances is *lynching*"; "Federal intervention to suppress lynching is imperative"; Congress should pass legislation that "will enable the federal Government to go to the limit of the Constitution, under its war powers, to stamp out this custom"; and action should be taken against discrimination in services and travel.[36]

The Editors' Conference had been called with government support and much fanfare, and it purposefully aimed to undermine the Liberty Congress. Talbert concluded that the MIB's Colonel Churchill, "saw the editors' conference as a counter measure to . . . [the] radical Colored Liberty Congress." It kept discussion of African American grievances a subdued and private matter and publicly came out in support of President Wilson's war effort. Trotter's *Boston Guardian* argued similarly and blamed Scott and Spingarn. James Weldon Johnson concurred, observing that "the Negro has been counselled to refrain 'at this time' from pressing his claim to the full rights of American citizenship." He added, however, that "we are not heeding such counsel."[37]

Chief among those not heeding such counsel was Harrison, who, while extremely critical of Scott and Spingarn, placed principal blame on Du Bois for this betrayal. Harrison would explain in his article "The Descent of Dr. Du Bois" that his suspicions had first been aroused by the government investigation of *The Crisis*, after which the magazine stopped publication of material critical of the government. The government's approach, wrote Harrison, was "tantamount to a declaration that protests against lynching, segregation and disfranchisement were outlawed by the government." He added that after a softer government approach was implemented, in the form of the calling of the Editors' Conference, his suspicion was further aroused—it all appeared to have been done for a purpose. These Harrison criticisms, however, did not appear till after the Liberty Congress. In late June that was the first order of business for both Trotter and Harrison.[38]

The Liberty Congress began with organizational planning from June 21 to 23, and this was followed by the actual congress—a grueling six days and five nights from June 24 to the 29, with three sessions held daily from Monday through Friday and two on Saturday. The morning and afternoon sessions were for delegates only, and the evening sessions were open to the public. The congress was attended by 115 delegates, including five women, from thirty-three

Figure 12.2. William Monroe Trotter, 1907. William Monroe Trotter (1872–1934) was a prominent Black protest leader of the older generation, a critic of Booker T. Washington, and a founder, along with W. E. B. Du Bois and others, of the Niagara Movement. Trotter supported Harrison's organizational efforts and the Liberty League program and worked with Harrison to build the Liberty Congress in 1918. He staunchly refused government efforts to persuade him to cancel or postpone the June 1918 Liberty Congress, and he consistently agitated, as did Harrison, for federal antilynching legislation and enforcement of the Thirteenth, Fourteenth, and Fifteenth Amendments. *Source:* Courtesy of the Special Collections Department, W. E. B. Du Bois Library, University of Massachusetts, Amherst.

states and the District of Columbia. They came from ten southern states and as far away as Oklahoma. Congress officers included: Harrison, chairman or president, Trotter, chairman of the board; W. H. Twine, Oklahoma; W. E. Hester, Tennessee; and Allen W. Whaley, Massachusetts, vice-chairmen; Professor J. W. Bell, Kentucky; Mrs. M. Cravath Simpson, Massachusetts, assistant secretary; Dr. S. H. Harrison, Oklahoma, corresponding secretary; Hon. Isaac B. Allen, N.Y., assistant corresponding secretary; Rev. W. C. Brown, Washington, D.C., treasurer; Rev. A. C. Garner, Washington, D.C. chaplain; and W. M. Shields, Washington, D.C. and Edward C. Calvin, N.Y., sergeants at arms. Among others in attendance were the Rev. Matthew A. N. Shaw of Boston, Maurice W. Spencer, Washington, D.C., Rev. M. F. Sydes, Rhode Island, the attorney William Ashbie

Hawkins, Maryland; C. S. Morris, N.Y.; J. Finley Wilson, editor of the *Eagle*, Washington, D.C.; J. Milton Waldron, Washington, D.C.; Ms. Irena Moorman-Blackston, N.Y.; Rev. C. H. Stephan, Maryland; Rev. H. D. Martin, Georgia; Rev. C. M. Tanner, pastor of the Metropolitan A.M.E. Church; and Dr. P. A. Stephens, Tennessee. Harrison claimed that "on the whole, this was the most notable gathering of Negro-Americans in a generation—and most of the delegates felt this." Unlike the delegates to the Editors' Conference, whose expenses were paid by the federal government, virtually all of these delegates paid their own way. Because of this, Harrison thought it was "clear even to 'crackers' that they were not moved by any 'irrelevant personal grievances,'" because people "make such sacrifices only under the pressure of great necessity."[39]

Harrison summed up the general theme of the Liberty Congress in one of his speeches as "Protest-protest." During the public sessions of the congress the church was filled every night in what he told the audience was "a Vision of the Future, of a Race, responding to a great Occasion, throbbing with the Hope of Democracy; breaking the bonds of subservience forged by our lick-spittle leaders, and reaching forth to lay your hands on the reasonable Rights which are yours by virtue of the sacrifices you have made." Harrison had "no doubt," as he wrote in his diary, "that the administration's 'white men's niggers' and their masters" were "worried about the size and quality of the protest we are making."[40]

Harrison played a central role during the entire congress. He arrived in Washington around six P.M. on Saturday, June 22, and though he was nominally there as an organizer of the hotel and restaurant workers, his trip was actually paid for by Irena Moorman-Blackston. He immediately threw himself into the maelstrom of informal activities and then, on June 24, reported to the John Wesley A.M.E. Zion Church, the largest Black church in the city, where the sessions were held. Some delegates "were bent upon interminable wrangling and disputation," and Harrison noted that "it was only by the most skillful combination of tact and repression that they were constrained to do practical work." He was requested to chair the meeting of the preliminary body, and, after presiding for an hour, "to the chagrin of Monroe Trotter," he was unanimously elected president of the congress. He commented in his diary, "If I were given much to megalomania my head would have grown as big as the church."[41]

Monday, the first day, consisted largely of details and formation of committees. The principal committees were Resolutions, Lynching, Segregation, and those to confer with the Speaker of the House of Representatives (which included Trotter, Harrison, and Isaac B. Allen) and president of the Senate. The recommendations of the main committees were to be embodied in a petition to Congress. Harrison, as chair, got down to business the very first day and on Monday night, ordered an all-night session of all committees, an action that

Figure 12.3. Hubert Harrison and delegates at the Liberty Congress, Washington, D.C., June 24–29, 1918. Hubert Harrison, second from right, was at the pinnacle of race leadership as he and William Monroe Trotter (third from right and next to Harrison) cochaired the major national protest meeting of African Americans during World War I, the Liberty Congress. The meeting of 115 delegates from 35 states was held in Washington, D.C., in June 1918. It opposed segregation and discrimination, sought enforcement of the Thirteenth, Fourteenth, and Fifteenth Amendments, petitioned Congress for federal antilynching legislation (which the NAACP did not advocate at that time), and demanded true "democracy" for the "colored millions" worldwide. The Liberty Congress was a precursor to the March on Washington Movement during World War II (led by A. Philip Randolph) and the March on Washington for Jobs and Freedom during the Vietnam War (led by Randolph and Martin Luther King Jr.). *Source:* Courtesy of the Hubert H. Harrison Papers, Rare Book and Manuscript Library, Butler Library, Columbia University, New York.

resulted in what he described as "greater efficiency of the entire Congress." On Monday night Harrison addressed the packed audience and, as described in his diary, took "Washington by storm."[42]

On Tuesday, upon instructions from the Liberty Congress, a committee comprising Harrison, Trotter, and Sandiford of Washington, D.C., went to meet with leaders of the U.S. Congress. According to Harrison, they "waited upon the President of the Senate (whom we didn't see) and upon the Speaker of the House of Representatives, [James B.] Champ Clark [Dem., Mo.], who accorded us a kindly and genial reception." They went to request that a joint session of both houses of Congress consider the grievances of twelve million African Americans and the "demand for democracy at home." In his diary Harrison indicated that he and others "thought the request for a joint session silly, in as much as this is done only when the President addresses Congress and when war is declared. But we went as we were bid." "Champ" Clark, "for all his genial kindliness, couldn't see his way to a joint session," and Harrison reported this to the Tuesday afternoon session "of *our* Congress."[43]

Also on Tuesday, Robert N. Owens and Trotter had an audience at the War Department with Judge Advocate General Col. Mayes and were told that the War Department would insist on equal transportation for white and Black soldiers. In addition, they saw General Kane, the adjutant general, and discussed General Charles C. Ballou's infamous Bulletin Number 35, which held that Black soldiers should take no action, "no matter how legally correct, that will provoke race animosity" in whites. Kane indicated that the order, which was widely detested by African Americans, was not approved and that he would correct any injustices within his jurisdiction. Tuesday night the Liberty Congress heard addresses by Rev. Sydes and Hawkins and, according to Harrison, "two brilliant and eloquent speakers"—Charles Morris Jr. ("The Boy Orator" who was "just 19 years old, but thoughtful and capable beyond his years") and Professor Bell.[44]

By Wednesday virtually all work was complete. That night, a mammoth audience heard Martin P. Madden, Republican representative from Chicago; Allen Whaley of Boston, "Trotter's assistant and alter ego," who delivered what Harrison claimed was "the best speech that I had ever heard from his lips"; and Jamaica-born Dr. M. A. N. Shaw of Boston, whose speech Harrison had "never heard surpassed" for "the happy welding of critical thought and forceful presentation." Harrison claimed he "could have listened all night" to Shaw who ended at 11:55 P.M., late for a Washington crowd that regularly went home by 10:30.[45]

As the clock approached midnight Harrison was introduced by Chairman Spencer and "begged the audience" to hear him the next night. They responded "No way!" and "there were cries from all over the church for 'Harrison! Harrison!'" When Spencer asked those who insisted on hearing Harrison that night to stand, about four-fifths of the audience did so. Harrison then spoke for about forty minutes on "Negro Democracy," explaining "that as a Priest of democracy, he would preach a sermon from a single text." He began by emphasizing: "*We shall fight for the things we hold nearest our hearts; for democracy, for the right of all those who submit to authority having a voice in their own government.*" He continued on explaining that "the Congress of liberty-loving Negroes had the express approval of the President of the United States who had uttered these words in his speech to the War Congress affirming the war aims of the eighty-eight million whites, and twelve million Negroes, making up the people of the United States of America."[46]

Harrison described how "the white man tries to make it appear that he doubts our loyalty, but he is a liar"—"he knows we are loyal," and this is evidenced when "they take our brothers and lynch them and then expect us to go to war as loyal citizens." He discussed how they "say that the Federal Government cannot protect us here, but they can go over to Serbia, a small place scarcely on the map and re-establish government." He next explained that "a good many 'flannel mouthed' agitators among conservatives" were "talking German intrigue" and "when Negroes demand justice" these conservatives "shout GERMANISM" in order "to establish in the minds of the Negroes, the proposition that justice for Negroes is only conceivable as a German idea." "Such people," he added, "whether they are simply stupid or cunningly disloyal—are no friends of the people or Government of the United States." In fact, he argued, since "German money is being spent all over the south among the cracker element," and since lynchings reduced manpower and "destroy[ed] the morale of the twelve million loyal American Negroes," it "could therefore be of benefit only to the Kaiser and his Huns."[47]

Harrison next explained that the white men who run the country had finally learned that their "lackeys" and stool pigeons could no longer be trusted as "exponents of Negro sentiment." He quoted the words of Moton, who told Secretary of War Baker: "I want to say to the white people that I have done my best and they have now got to do something. If they don't, I hope they wouldn't hold me responsible for the result." To Harrison, "this was a typical confession of the old leaders, the confession that they were truly powerless to guide the masses any longer by lies, trickery, and subservience." He then challenged the United States to win the war by giving its best effort, which required "the change of twelve million Negroes from the status of 'nigger' into that of man." On completing his speech Harrison received a mammoth ovation, larger even than that on Monday night.[48]

One important development related to the Liberty Congress involved surveillance by the Bureau of Investigation. On Wednesday night, June 26, Harrison was scheduled to speak at non-congress activities on "Workers in War Time and Why They Should Combine" and on "the White and Colored Workers of Washington, D.C." The first talk was scheduled for eight-thirty P.M. at the headquarters building of the Workers in the Hotel and Restaurant Industry, the organization for which he was nominally doing work in Washington. In literature for the event he was listed as editor of *The Voice*, organizer of the hotel and restaurant workers, and chairman of the Colored Liberty League. According to the Bureau of Investigation agent Joseph G. C. Corcoran, the eight-thirty meeting was moved. (Harrison was next scheduled to speak on "Workers in War Time and Why They Should Combine" on June 30, before the Women Wage Earners' Association.)[49]

Corcoran's surveillance is one of the earliest instances of the Bureau of Investigation's monitoring of a Black radical. Corcoran had received instructions from his superiors to locate a meeting of "colored folks" at which Harrison, the subject of his investigation, was to speak, "as well as two white men alleged to be propagandists, in whose company the subject has been seen all during the days." That meeting was supposed to be under the auspices of the John Wesley A.M.E. Zion Church. Corcoran first went to the Labor Hall at 1008 Pennsylvania and learned that people had been there earlier "but due to the stormy weather," they had transferred the meeting to the church at Fourteenth and Q Sts. It appears that the union organizing meeting may have been steered into the larger public meeting of the Liberty Congress. During his ensuing monitoring of Harrison and the Liberty Congress, Corcoran would use the services of special officer C. E. Addison, a "colored plain clothes man [from the] second colored precinct" and Dr. Arthur Ulysses Craig, "a high class [undercover] colored informant" who was a high school teacher and a former instructor at Tuskegee and employee of the Educational Division of the Food Administration.[50]

On Friday another large Liberty Congress audience heard Trotter read the "Petition to the House of Representatives," which had been submitted to Representative Frederick Huntington Gillett (Rep., Mass.) who entered it into the *Congressional Record* on June 28. The "Petition" demanded that lynching be made a federal crime and was approved unanimously and signed by eighty-one delegates from twenty-one states (including ten Southern states) and the District of Columbia. It was circulated on behalf of 12,000,000 "colored Americans . . . desiring liberty and the rights of democracy." It protested against racial proscriptions in three-fourths of the states and the national capital, in public carriers in one-third of the states, in interstate travel, in government military and naval schools, in officer schools in the navy, in the executive department of the federal government, and in elections and representation "both indirectly by congressional representation based on disfranchisement and directly through intimidation, trickery, or State statutes and constitutions." It also denounced the denial of protection by the police and courts and (white-supremacist) "robbery, ravishing, mob violence, murder, and massacre." In seeking redress it sought application of "the mandatory powers of the thirteenth, fourteenth, and fifteenth" Amendments of the Constitution, "to the end that there shall be no involuntary servitude, no denial of the equal protection of law, no denial of the exercise of suffrage because of race, color, or previous condition." The "Petition" also demanded legislation "extending the protection of the Federal Government to all citizens . . . by enacting that mob murders shall be a crime against the Federal Government, subject to the jurisdiction of the Federal courts."[51]

The Liberty Congress gained national attention by petitioning Congress for federal legislation against lynching. Through its militant wartime demands, wrote Harrison, it also called the attention of the people of the United States "to the danger into which democracy is put by disfranchisement, discrimination, and lynching." That this was a valid premise, he argued, was even demonstrated by the Editors' Conference, which, despite efforts to lead it along what Scott termed "helpful lines," spoke of the "justifiable grievances of the colored people" that were "producing not disloyalty, but an amount of unrest and bitterness which even the best efforts of the leaders may not be able always to guide."[52]

After the close of the Liberty Congress, Harrison began very publicly to address the subject of Black leadership. He was particularly troubled by the role that Du Bois had played. His concern was particularly aroused when Du Bois wrote what was probably the most controversial editorial of his life, "Close Ranks," in the July 1918 issue of *The Crisis*. Only two paragraphs long, its last two sentences were aimed at African Americans and read: "Let us, while this war lasts, forget our special grievances and close ranks shoulder to shoulder with our own white fellow citizens and allied nations that are fighting for democracy. We make no ordinary sacrifice, but we make it gladly and willingly with our eyes lifted to the hills."[53]

Clearly accommodationist in spirit, the editorial was written at Joel Spingarn's urging as Du Bois sought a commission as captain in Military Intelligence, the agency of the U.S. General Staff that monitored and intimidated both Blacks and radicals. The editorial was a key part of the government effort to undermine the militant and autonomous Liberty Congress. It was also a significant departure from the position taken by the NAACP as recently as its May 1917 national conference, at which it proclaimed, "Absolute loyalty in arms and civil duties need not for a moment lead us to abate our just complaints."[54]

Though Du Bois denied that there was any relation between the editorial and the commission, Harrison took him to task over this. Harrison charged that "it was learned that Du Bois was being preened for a berth in the War Department as a captain (adjutant) to Major Spingarn," and this suggested that the government had "tampered with" Du Bois's "racial resolution." His motives quickly became a subject of intense debate in the Black community. As Harrison correctly predicted, the controversy severely tarnished Du Bois's position as an "influential person among Negroes" and as an uncompromising opponent of race discrimination. Partly because of this editorial, Du Bois, over the next forty years, would refer to his activity around the period of the Great War with what Ellis describes as, "a mixture of shame and bitterness."[55]

Harrison was correct in linking the editorial to Du Bois's quest for the captaincy. Before the publication of the editorial, while Du Bois was in Washington for the Editors' Conference, Colonel Marlborough Churchill, director of Military Intelligence, arranged for him to take a physical examination at the Army Medical School. Though Du Bois failed the physical, that fact did not appear to be a major obstacle, and Joel Spingarn sent details of Du Bois's career to Military Intelligence. On June 24, as the Liberty Congress opened, Du Bois applied for the commission in Military Intelligence. That same week his editorial in *The Crisis* (dated July) appeared and, according to Ellis, "the timing and the tenor of the 'Close Ranks' editorial were vital to the decision of the War Department to offer Du Bois a commission."[56]

On June 26, while being interviewed by Secretary of War Newton Baker, Emmett Scott, who had been briefed in advance by Spingarn, elaborated on the success of the Editors' Conference and the "fine attitude" displayed by Du Bois. He also showed Baker the "Close Ranks" editorial and produced a prepared letter addressed to Col. Churchill that apparently approved Du Bois's "designation." Baker signed the letter, and Churchill described the editorial as "very satisfactory."[57]

Then, around July 1, Du Bois informed the directors of the NAACP that he was willing to accept the military commission if offered. He indicated that he would like the NAACP to supplement any potential military pay to maintain his salary of $3,500 per year. Word quickly spread that he was seeking a commission. When the NAACP board met on July 8 it rejected his proposal, claiming that it was "imperative" to have a full-time editor for *The Crisis*. In addition, according to David Levering Lewis, Du Bois's "Close Ranks" editorial "evoked bitter reproach from . . . much of the African-American press."[58]

Ultimately, Du Bois was denied the commission, in large part because of Harrison, who, on the prompting of Major Walter Howard Loving of Military Intelligence, wrote a scorching critique of Du Bois that was published in the July 25, 1918, issue of a resurrected *Voice* as "The Descent of Dr. Du Bois."[59]

Major Loving was, for a time, the only Black officer in Military Intelligence, and he specialized in race relations. He had retired from the Philippine constabulary and, in the summer of 1918, sought a recommission into the army and was awaiting a response when it suddenly appeared that Du Bois, with no military experience but the highest academic credentials, would get a commission and supersede him. Because Loving was "aware of the kind of barrage Harrison could deliver," and because he viewed him "as one of those 'radicals' qualified to furnish such," Loving asked Harrison for a "summary" of the debate ranging among Blacks over Du Bois's commission. By having Harrison elaborate "radical" opinion on the Du Bois editorial for MIB, Loving was able to undermine any claim that Du Bois should get a captaincy based on his deep understanding of the developing views of African Americans. Harrison's account indicated that Du Bois was distrusted in the Black community and implied he would be of little value to military intelligence. Loving then incorporated Harrison's analysis in a report to his boss, Col. Churchill, a week before it was published in the July 25 issue of *The Voice*. The summary was of personal value to Loving because it cast grave doubt on Du Bois and ridiculed "Close Ranks" for suggesting that Blacks should "consent to be lynched—'during the war'—and submit tamely and with commendable weakness to being Jim-crowed and disfranchised." Harrison claimed that *The Voice* reprinted the letter as an editorial "without changing a single word" and that Loving told him that the editorial "was one of the main principal causes of the government's change of mind regarding the Du Bois captaincy."[60]

Harrison's response to Du Bois marked him as a spearhead of the opposition to "Close Ranks" and as a spokesperson for the militant "New Negro Movement." William Monroe Trotter soon issued a similar critique, and in a short time so did the *Negro World*. The series of events surrounding and including the Liberty Congress and the Editors' Conference led in the eyes of Harrison and others to the decline of Du Bois as the preeminent race leader in the post–Booker T. Washington era—and Harrison was the leading proponent of this view. Harrison then used these developments to offer suggestive comments on autonomous Black leadership and the response of both the government and the white left to such leadership.[61]

Harrison opened his *Voice* editorial by citing "a recent bulletin of the War Department" that described how "'justifiable grievances' were producing and had produced 'not disloyalty, but an amount of unrest and bitterness which even the best efforts of their leaders may not be able always to guide.'" He emphasized that this was "the simple truth" and said the "essence of the present situation" was the fact "that the people whom our white masters have 'recognized' as our leaders (without taking the trouble to consult us) and those who, by our own selection, had actually attained to leadership among us are being revaluated and, in most cases, rejected." The "most striking instance from the latter class" was Du Bois, and his case was "the more significant because his former services to his race" were "undoubtedly of a high and courageous sort."[62]

In a sense Harrison was responding to Du Bois as Du Bois had responded to Booker T. Washington fifteen years earlier in *The Souls of Black Folk*. At that time Du Bois criticized Washington's leadership and pointed the way for the next generation of struggle. Similarly, Harrison now attempted to criticize Du Bois (whose leadership "ascendancy was a fact" by 1916 according to his biographer David Levering Lewis) and to point the way forward for a generation of struggle.[63]

In particular, Harrison attacked the clause, "forget our special grievances," by which Du Bois "first palpably sinned." He pointed out that Du Bois knew better than virtually anyone the "special grievances" of "lynching, segregation, and disfranchisement," grievances that even the War Department termed "justifiable." Du Bois also knew that "the Negroes of America cannot preserve either their lives, their manhood or their vote (which is their political lives and liberties) with these things in existence." Accordingly, Du Bois's exhortation was "the deepest cut of all." Further, because Du Bois "was one of the most prominent of those editors 'who were called '" to the Editors' Conference, he was held largely responsible for the course of counsel that stressed the "servile virtues of acquiescence and subservience." With his "racial resolution" so "tampered with," Du Bois had "failed," and his leadership days were, for Harrison, a thing of the "past."[64]

Harrison also explained the nature of the concern in the African American community:

> "But," it may be asked, "why should not all these words be taken as a mere slip of the pen or a venial error in logic?" Why all this hubbub? It is because the so-called leaders of the first-mentioned class [those whom "white masters have 'recognized' as our leaders"] have already established an unsavory reputation by advocating this same surrender of life, liberty and manhood, masking their cowardice behind the pillars of war-time sacrifice? Du Bois's statement, then, is believed to mark his entrance into that class, and is accepted as a "surrender" of the principles which brought him into prominence—and which alone kept him there.
>
> Later, when it was learned that Du Bois was being preened for a berth in the War Department as a captain-assistant (adjutant) to Major Spingarn, the words used by him in the editorial acquired a darker and more sinister significance. The two things fitted too well together as motive and self-interest.

Harrison compared Du Bois to "a knight in the middle ages who had had his armor stripped from him" and considered him "ruin[ed] . . . as an influential person among Negroes at this time, . . . whether he becomes a captain or remains an editor." To Harrison, Du Bois's editorial indicated "the moral downfall of another great leader."[65]

Harrison rightly surmised that Du Bois was responsible for the Editors' Conference resolutions, which seemed to him to extol "servile virtues of acquiescence and subservience." In sum, wrote Harrison, the sequence of events between Spingarn's military appointment in May, the investigation of *The Crisis* for alleged seditious activities, the June Editors' Conference, the July "Close Ranks" editorial, and the offer of the commission, seemed (even to NAACP supporters)

> to afford proof of that which was only a suspicion before, viz., that the racial resolution of the leaders had been tampered with and that Du Bois had been

Figure 12.4. W. E. B. Du Bois, 1918. For most of the first two decades of the twentieth century, William Edward Burghardt Du Bois (1868–1963) was the nation's most prominent Black protest leader. In his early years in New York Harrison considered himself a "Du Bois man," but over time differences began to emerge as Harrison advocated a Colored Socialist Club and as Harrison stressed the need for a militant, race-conscious emphasis on the Black masses in contrast to Du Bois's emphasis on the "Talented Tenth of the Negro Race." Between May and July 1918 Du Bois became involved in plans developed by Joel E. Spingarn, sought a captaincy in the Military Intelligence Branch, and urged African Americans to forget "special grievances" and "Close Ranks" behind Woodrow Wilson's war effort. Harrison's exposé, "The Descent of Dr. Du Bois," was a principal reason that Du Bois was denied the captaincy he sought in MIB, and it marked a significant break between the "New Negroes" led by Harrison and the older leadership. *Source:* Courtesy of the Library of Congress. Photo by Cornelius M. Batttey, 1918.

privy to something of the sort. The connection between the successive acts of the drama (May, June, July) was too clear to admit of any interpretation other than that of deliberate cold-blooded, purposive planning. And the connection with Spingarn seemed to suggest that personal friendships and public faith were not good team-mates.

Harrison considered Du Bois to be tarnished as an influential Negro leader, and he concluded: "For the sake of the larger usefulness of Dr. Du Bois we hope he will be able to show that he can remain as editor of the *Crisis*; but we fear that it will require a good deal of explaining. For, our leaders, like Caesar's wife, must be above suspicion."[66]

Harrison was not simply critical of Du Bois. He also offered a positive counterproposal. Assuming that Du Bois's reason for the sentiments of "Close Ranks" was to win the war, Harrison reasoned "that America can not use the Negro people to any good effect unless they have life, liberty, and manhood assured and guaranteed to them. Therefore, instead of the war for democracy making these things less necessary, it makes them more so." Accordingly, the way forward was toward full democratic rights and justice for African Americans, not downplaying these demands.[67]

In 1920, reviewing this "Close Ranks" situation, Harrison also commented on Joel Spingarn's role. He noted that "a strikingly new element" in the leadership problem was raised—the question of "outside interference." He asked, "Should the leading of our group in any sense be the product of our group's consciousness or of a consciousness originating from outside that group?" His answer was that Black leadership should come from within the group and it should bring Black grievances to the fore. In reference to the scenario of events around the Liberty Congress, he added:

The time has long passed when white people, however benevolent, could safely and successfully, limit the range and determine the scope and pattern of the Negro people's aspirations—as Dr. Spingarn tried to do in 1918 when as a major in the Intelligence Dept. of the Army he presumed to tell the promoters of the First National Race Congress that they must not convene that gathering as that was no time for Negroes to present their grievances, their objections to a continuance of lynching, disfranchisement and the ghetto. . . . And it was because Dr. W. E. B. Du Bois followed the lead of such white sponsors in the subservient and acquiescent tone of the wartime editorials in *The Crisis* and wanted to secure a position as semi-civilian captain under Major Spingarn to carry on in that spirit of such a policy that he stumbled and fell from the pinnacle of racial leadership, a point to which all the strenuous pulling and handling of his white friends has never been able to lift him since.[68]

Harrison, who repeatedly saw the "future in the distance," explained that "the test of vision in a leader is the ability to foresee the immediate future, the necessary consequences of a course of conduct and the dependable sentiments of those whom he assumes to lead." "In all these things," he judged, "Du Bois has failed," and a subsequent attack Du Bois made on Emmett Scott and "his belated discovery of [Woodrow] Wilsonian hypocrisy" were not enough to "enable him to climb back into the saddle of race leadership." He had "rendered good service" in his day, "but "that day is past" and his "personal primacy . . . has departed, never to return. Other times, other men; other men, other manners." Harrison added, "The Negro leaders of the future . . . will be expected to go straight all the time; to stand by us in war as well as in peace; not to blow hot and cold with the same mouth, but 'to stand four-square to *all* the winds that blow.'" He concluded, "While it is as easy as eggs for a leader to fall off the fence, it is devilishly difficult to boost him up again."[69]

Overall, the Liberty Congress showed the difference between Harrison's bold New Negro leadership and that of the older generation of leaders (Trotter was obviously somewhat unique among the older generation of leaders). A key difference, as James Weldon Johnson indicated, was that the militants were not heeding the advice to refrain from protest during wartime. The Liberty Congress effort also demonstrated, quite clearly, how "white friends" like Spingarn sought to mitigate the militant demands of the leaders of the African American struggle.[70]

On Friday, July 26, President Woodrow Wilson issued a mild statement on "Mob Action," which came from the Committee on Public Information. It criticized "the mob spirit which has recently here and there very frequently shown its head amongst us" and noted that "there have been many lynchings and every one of them has been a blow at the heart of ordered law and humane justice." Wilson's statement was clearly a response to the moderate Editors' Conference and the militant Liberty Congress. The militants considered it to be too little and too late.[71]

Following Wilson's mild statement, the War Department decided that the wartime antilynching bill, the key to Spingarn's agenda, was irrelevant. It also decided against Spingarn's proposed advisory committee to the General Staff, which was to be headed by Du Bois and was to carry out "counter-espionage" activities among Black Americans. Colonel Churchill announced that Military Intelligence would limit work on racial matters to the morale of black troops. Du Bois's application for the special advisory position was officially rejected, in part for medical reasons, but primarily, according to Churchill, because "any attempts on the part of the Military Intelligence Branch to solve the question of negro subversion among the civil population would duplicate the efforts of agencies already charged with the solution of the same problem." On July

30, Churchill stated that the special propaganda program for blacks was to be abandoned.[72]

According to Du Bois, the official reason that he was denied the captaincy was because it would "lead beyond the proper limits of military activities." Du Bois felt, however, that the real reasons were suspicion of Spingarn in the War Department, opposition from other African Americans, and the influence of white Southerners. Emmett Scott, who as Assistant secretary of war was in a position to know, suggested that Du Bois was denied the position because Black opposition to Du Bois was growing and his nomination was tending to divide rather than unify Blacks in wartime America. Scott and Arthur Spingarn attributed the denial to the furor around "Close Ranks." Joel Spingarn essentially agreed, though he held the NAACP particularly responsible for refusing to meet Du Bois's request for supplemental income and for exposing the matter to the public. Joel Spingarn resigned as NAACP chairman, reportedly being "wholly out of sympathy with the attitude of some of the directors on various problems." The contention of both Loving and Harrison that the Harrison editorial "was one of the main principal causes of the government's change of mind regarding the Du Bois captaincy" appears quite true.[73]

————

In early July 1918, within a week of his return to Harlem from Washington, a reenergized Harrison announced in a leaflet that *The Voice* was "Coming Out to Stay!" He invited all who were striving for justice in wartime and working for democracy at home to attend a mass meeting on Thursday evening, July 4, at Bethel AME Church on W. 132nd St., where the first issue of the second year of the paper would be available. The attorney James D. Carr and the Democratic Party activist Cornelius Hughes were scheduled to speak; the attorney Charles E. Toney would bring the finance books and answer questions; and the corporation counsel Rufus Perry would bring stock certificates, the stock book, the transfer book, and the seal. Harrison planned to directly address rumors about previous financial mismanagement of *The Voice*, including what happened with the money. He would also make first-time disclosures of "sensational correspondence" with Emmett J. Scott, the former aide to Booker T. Washington and current special assistant secretary of war for Negro affairs. The correspondence would tell "The Whole Story of the Paper," suggesting that Scott was behind the difficulties with *The Voice*. (It is very possible that Scott had used his close relationship with the powerful *New York Age* to get that paper to pressure William H. Willis of Beehive Printing to change its weekly printing schedule so as to undermine Harrison's militant *Voice*.)[74]

The resurrected *Voice*, whose front page banner described it as "A Newspaper for the New Negro," contained four pages of race-conscious domestic and international news, editorials, letters, chatty and satirical pieces, and poetry. It sold for two cents and was scheduled to come out on Thursdays. The front page of the July 11 issue featured a poem by the leading poet of the New Negro movement, Andy Razaf (Andrea Razaf[in]keriefo), urging all who opposed racial injustice to read and support the paper:

THE VOICE

A sheet no enemy can buy,
That will not cringe, that will not lie,
That will not stoop to advertise,
In words that hurt our wary eyes.
A sheet that we can open wide
On car or street with joy and pride,
For it is clean and neat and strong
And stands for everything—but Wrong!

Yea Negro, let your heart rejoice
For in this sheet you have a Voice
That will speak out and dare all laws;
The greatest champion of your cause.

Let all of ye who claim to stand
For racial justice in the land,
Hold up this sheet which is your fort,
By giving it your full support![75]

Harrison, who was now recognized as a prominent national leader, soon announced plans to establish *The Voice* as a national organ of Black protest. After the July 25 issue (containing the Du Bois editorial) sold out quickly he told readers of additional plans to expand the paper and to establish a branch in Washington, D.C. From there he planned to take his message into the South—the home of 80 to 90 percent of the African American population and the center of racist reaction, legal segregation, disfranchisement, and lynching. The magnitude of the Black population and the intensity of the oppression in the South gave his plan an audacious logic.[76]

Harrison had a vision. Whether he would have the organizational support and the following to meaningfully implement his plan was not clear.

————

What was clear, however, was that by the summer of 1918 Harlem had become the "symbol of Black America" and St. Croix–born Hubert Harrison, who had moved there in its earliest days as a "Negro Mecca" and lived on its most densely populated block, was the leading voice of Harlem radicalism. Though only thirty-five years old, he was widely recognized as a brilliant orator, writer, thinker, and activist. He had challenged the powers of capitalism and white supremacy, had been the leading Black activist and theoretician in the Socialist Party, had founded the New Negro Movement, and was now a major Black protest leader in wartime America. As the nation's leading proponent of Black race conscious-ness he stressed that as long as white labor and the white left put the "white race first," Black people needed to organize in a race-conscious, mass-based way to carry on struggle against white supremacy and for just demands. As the most class-conscious of the race radicals and the most race-conscious of the class radicals, he had influenced a generation of developing activists and "common people" and laid out broad parameters that would shape and influence much Black radical discourse for the remainder of the century.

Harrison had already left an enduring legacy, a legacy that was memorialized that year in another poem written by the unofficial poet laureate of the "New Negro Movement," Andy Razaf:

HUBERT H. HARRISON

Speaker, editor and sage,
Thou who wrote a brighter page
In the Negro's book of thought—
What a change thy work hath wrought!
Men with timid intellect,
Who would never circumspect,
Woke to think and did rejoice
At the thunder of thy "Voice."
Men with longing in their breasts
Struggled with a new unrest;
Scornful ones who ne'er would heed
Paused to listen and to read.
Men, made cowards by despair,
With a laugh came forth to dare
For thy manly tongue and pen
Made them bold, proclaimed them Men![77]

The legacy of Hubert Harrison—the "Voice" of Harlem radicalism—extends beyond Razaf's words and his immediate era, however. As his friend Arthur Schomburg explained, Harrison "was ahead of his time."[78]

Nowhere is this more the case than in the realm of some of his most basic yet radical ideas on social change and on democracy. Hubert Harrison understood white supremacy to be central to capitalist rule in the United States. He emphasized that those desiring significant social change would have to struggle against it to succeed, and he emphasized that Black people should develop race consciousness as both a measure of self-defense and as a key strategic component in that struggle. He understood that African Americans are "the touchstone of the modern democratic idea," that "while the color line exists," the "cant of democracy" is "intended as dust in the eyes of white voters" and used in wartime to mask sordid imperialist aims, and, perhaps most important, he understood that true democracy and equality for African Americans implies "a revolution . . . startling even to think of."[79]

Appendix

Harrison on His Character

In March 1926, in volume 2 of his copy of David Duncan, *Life and Letters of Herbert Spencer* (New York: Appleton, 1908), 246–273, Harrison offered a glimpse at a self-portrait. He writes (on p. 246), "Having myself been born on April 27th [Spencer's birthday] I was curious to note the traits in which my character as I know it resembles that of Herbert Spencer. I have ventured to check the similarities with a cross #—and leave the verification of the assumed similarity to my friends." The passages he denoted with the # were clearly marked and delineated. The exact words he marked follow (with their page numbers in parentheses):

His disregard of authority, human or divine, was disregard of *personal* authority only, and was accompanied by whole-hearty fealty to principles.

(247)

. . . strongly condemned language which appeared irreverent.

(250)

. . . no host could have been more solicitous for the comfort of his guests than he was.

(256)

Even such notoriety as could not fail to be associated with his name was distasteful, leaving him to go out of his way to avoid the manifestations of it, and causing regret, and sometimes offence, to those who wished to show their regard for him.

(257)

. . . he was far from kind to his disciples and admirers, and very disconcerting to those who had contrived to gain a sight or a word for them.

(258)

. . . he certainly did not conceal, as most of us do, what he had of that quality [egotism]; but a truly vain and self-regarding man would surely not have discouraged admiration and flattery as he did.

(258)

. . . was not in the habit of toning down the terms of a refusal: his reply being usually more blunt than suave. He thought more of making refusal plain than of how it would be taken. . . .

(259)

"I always felt so strongly my inability to say anything adequate in the way of consolation that I am habitually debarred from attempting it."

(260)

He often referred to what he called his constitutional idleness, seeming to be rather proud of it than otherwise. . . . But, even in that sense, the man who could gather together and assimilate the wealth of facts to be found in his books cannot have been so wanting in industry as some of his remarks would make it appear.

(261)

If there was any defect of verbal memory it was compensated for by the readiness to grasp logical relations, as well as the natural relations of things. His defective memory for words and arbitrary relations, had, in his own opinion, much to do with the development of his mind, favouring as it did internal building up as much as it retarded external building up.

(261)

But argumentative and disputatious as he was, he never argued for victory. Always there was a principle to be contended for.

(262)

Whenever doubt was hinted as to the sufficiency of his grounds for making them, he was always ready to pour out a string of examples that seem to have been, if not in his theatre of consciousness when he spoke, at all events in an antechamber of it, whence they could be summoned at will.

(264)

. . . few writers have so seldom left their readers in doubt.

(264)

Unlike . . . [those] who wrote and re-wrote their compositions, he made comparatively few changes in his manuscript.

(265)

[He was an essentially methodical man] . . . with his papers of all kinds. These were all classified and put away in certain receptacles according to a definite plan, so that when required they could be found without any bother. When the time came for using any particular group of materials for the work in hand, that group would be subjected to a sub-classification, and so on, until the materials for a particular section were assembled together.

(266)

He had few indoor relaxations. . . . whist . . . [was] played occasionally, but he was not good at [it] . . . , nor did he like playing for money.

(268)

"Life is not for learning, nor is life for working; but learning and working are for life."

(268)

From worldly ambition, the desire to amass wealth—to "get on" in the ordinary sense—he was singularly free. *He often spoke as if he had a mission.*

(269)

His sincerity, truthfulness and honesty, impressed all who knew him. "He was absolutely sincere himself."

(269)

Of course he was an inveterate critic. He says so himself.

(273)

Abbreviations

GP   *The Marcus Garvey and Universal Negro Improvement Association Papers*. Robert A. Hill, ed., Berkeley: University of California Press, 12 vols. projected, vols. 1–7 and vol. 9, 1983–1995, vol. 10, 2006.

HD   Hubert Harrison Diary (in Hubert Harrison Papers)

HH   Hubert Harrison

HP   Hubert Harrison Papers, Rare Book and Manuscript Library, Columbia University, New York.

HR   *A Hubert Harrison Reader*. Jeffrey B. Perry, ed. and intro. Middletown, Conn.: Wesleyan University Press, 2001.

WGMC   J. A. Rogers. *World's Great Men of Color*. Ed., intro., commentary, and new bibliographical notes by John Henrik Clarke. 2 vols. 1946–1947; New York: Collier Books, 1972.

Notes

Introduction

Note on figure 0.1: Harrison is buried alongside the remains of the otherwise un-identified Daniel Joseph, who was probably related to two of Harrison's friends, Casper Holstein and Arturo Alfonso Schomburg. The St. Croix–born Holstein, a Joseph family member, was a prominent activist on behalf of Virgin Island causes, a philanthropist to Black cultural and community causes, Harlem's numbers king-pin, and the person who paid Harrison's burial expenses. Schomburg, the son of Mary Joseph of St. Croix, was a renowned bibliophile who worked with Harrison at St. Benedict's Lyceum, on the Negro Society for Historical Research, and on the founding committee of the 135th St. Public Library's Department of "Negro Litera-ture and History," which grew into the internationally famous Schomburg Center for Research in Black Culture in Harlem. At Harrison's funeral Schomburg, with his profound sense of history, presciently eulogized that the influential and popular Har-rison "was ahead of his time."

1. *WGMC*, 2:432–33. Earlier versions of this introduction appeared in Jeffrey B. Perry, "An Introduction to Hubert Harrison, 'The Father of Harlem Radicalism,'" *Souls* 2, no. 1 (Winter 2000): 38–54; *HR*, 1–30; and Jeffrey B. Perry, "Hubert Har-rison: Race Consciousness and Socialism," *Socialism and Democracy* 17, no. 2 (Sum-mer–Fall, 2003): 103–30.

2. Henry Miller, *The Rosy Crucifixion, Book Two: Plexus* (1963; New York: Grove Press, 1965), 560–61.

3. William Pickens, "Hubert Harrison: Philosopher of Harlem," *Amsterdam News*, February 7, 1923, 12 (hereafter *AN*).

4. *An American Century: The Recollections of Bertha W. Howe, 1866–1966*, recorded, ed., and with a biographical intro. by Oakley C. Johnson (New York: A.I.M.S. Humanities Press, 1966), 80–81.

5. Eugene O'Neill to HH, June 9, 1921, HP.

6. Edwin R. Lewinson, *Black Politics in New York City* (New York: Twayne Publishers, 1974), 194; and Nathan I. Huggins, *Harlem Renaissance* (New York: Oxford University Press, 1971), 13.

7. Hodge Kirnon, "Hubert Harrison: An Appreciation," *Negro World*, December 31, 1927 (hereafter *NW*).

8. Joyce Moore Turner, *Caribbean Crusaders and the Harlem Renaissance*, with the assistance of W. Burghardt Turner, intro. by Franklin W. Knight (Urbana; University of Illinois Press, 2005), 58.

9. Mary Adams (pseudonym for Williana Jones Burroughs), "Record of Revolt in Negro Workers Past," *Daily Worker*, May 1, 1928.

10. W. A. Domingo, interview by Theodore Draper, January 18, 1958, New York, Theodore Draper Papers, Robert W. Woodruff Library for Advanced Studies, Emory University, preliminary listing as Box 20, Folder 7, "Negro Question for Vol. 1 (cont.)," Notes re: W. A. Domingo, 2.

11. "Lament Dream of Dr. Hubert Harrison: Eulogized by Several Who Knew His Life and Work," *AN*, December 28, 1927, 1.

12. David Levering Lewis to author, August 13, 2001; Eric Arnesen, "Jeffrey B. Perry, ed., *A Hubert Harrison Reader*," *African American Review* 37, no. 1 (March 2003): 160–61, esp. 160; Henry Louis Gates Jr., to author, December 12, 1996; Gerald C. Horne, BRC-Discuss, General Internet Discussion Group of the Black Radical Congress, June 1, 2001; and Winston James, *Holding Aloft the Banner of Ethiopia: Caribbean Radicalism in Early-Twentieth-Century America* (New York: Verso, 1998), 123.

13. On the "need of a [Harrison] biography" see Philip S. Foner, *American Socialism and Black Americans: From the Age of Jackson to World War II* (Westport, Conn.: Greenwood Press, 1977), 397 n. 17. See also Lewis to author, August 13, 2001. Google searches show Du Bois and Washington receiving well over a thousand times as many results as Harrison. A Google search on July 28, 2007, returned 755 results for "Hubert Harrison," 730,00 for "Marcus Garvey," 1,380,000 for "Booker T. Washington," 38,200 for 'William Monroe Trotter," 658,000 for "W.E.B. Du Bois," and 542,000 for "W.E.B. DuBois" (an incorrect though common alternate spelling of his last name). Google Scholar returned 105 results for "Hubert Harrison," 4,180 for "Marcus Garvey," 7,570 for "Booker T. Washington," 508 for "William Monroe Trotter," 9,040 for "W.E.B. Du Bois" and 7,100 for "W.E.B. DuBois." On many of Harrison's views becoming "the stock-in-trade" of the Black left in the twentieth century, see Winston James, "Notes on the Ideology and Travails of Afro-America's Socialist Pioneers, 1877–1930," *Souls* 1, no. 4 (Fall 1999): 45–63, esp. 54. On Harrison's important role in Black intellectual thought see, for example, Corey D. B. Walker, "Rethinking Race and Nation for a New African American Intellectual History," *Black*

Renaissance 4, nos. 2/3 (Summer 2002): 173–86. Harrison's glowing tribute to "the common people" is found in HH, "The Common People," *Boston Chronicle*, May 17, 1924, in *HR*, 404–5.

14. "Hubert Henry [Harrison]," July 7, 1883, in "Baptisms Solemnized During the Years March 3, 1883–October 21, 1899," St. John's Episcopal Church, Christiansted, St. Croix.

15. HH, ["Response to Clarana, II"], *NW*, April 30, 1921, 5, HP; Rayford W. Logan, *The Betrayal of the Negro: From Rutherford B. Hayes to Woodrow Wilson*, new enlarged ed., originally published as *The Negro in American Thought and Life: The Nadir, 1877–1901* (1954; New York: The Macmillan Company, 1970), 11, 62; and Daniel Bell, "The Background and Development of Marxian Socialism in the United States," in *Socialism and American Life*, ed. Donald Drew Egbert and Stow Persons, 2 vols. (Princeton, N.J.: Princeton University Press, 1952), 1:213–405, esp. 268.

16. Race consciousness and class consciousness refer, respectively, to awareness of generalized racial oppression and class exploitation and of the need for the oppressed and exploited, on the basis of such understanding, to organize, unify, and struggle to overcome such oppression and exploitation.

17. Turner, *Caribbean Crusaders*, 19; and Richard B. Moore, "Africa Conscious Harlem," *Freedomways* 3, no. 3 (Summer 1963): 315–34, esp. 320. See also, for example, Robin D. G. Kelley, "But a Local Phase of a World Problem: Black History's Global Vision, 1883–1950," *Journal of American History* 86, no. 3 (December 1999): 1045–77, which points out (1056) that Harrison's *When Africa Awakes* was "one of the most profound and widely read texts linking black concerns with international politics." On democracy, see for example, HH, "The Negro and Socialism: 1—The Negro Problem Stated," *New York Call*, November 28, 1911, 6, in *HR*, 52–55, esp. 54; and HH, "Our Larger Duty," *New Negro*, August 1919, p. 5, in *HR*, 99–101, esp. 100.

18. *WGMC*, 2:437, discusses some of these themes, which are developed more fully throughout this work. Ira Kipnis, *The American Socialist Movement, 1897–1912* (1952; reprint, New York: Monthly Review Press, 1972), 335, states that "the Socialist party reached the zenith of its power, prestige and influence between 1910 and 1912." On the Garvey movement, see Randall K. Burkett, *Black Redemption: Churchmen Speak for the Garvey Movement* (Philadelphia: Temple University Press, 1978), 3.

19. Moore, "Africa Conscious Harlem," 320. On the shift, see Cary D. Wintz, *Black Culture and the Harlem Renaissance* (Houston: Rice University Press, 1988), 1, 22.

20. Jervis Anderson, *A. Philip Randolph: A Biographical Portrait* (New York: Harcourt Brace Jovanovich, 1973), 79–80; and Roi Ottley and William J. Weatherby, eds., *The Negro in New York: An Informal Social History* (New York: New York Public Library, 1967), 223.

21. See, for example, HH, "Prejudice Growing Less and Co-Operation More, Says Student of Question," *Pittsburgh Courier*, January 29, 1927, sec. 2, p. 7 (hereafter *PC*), in *HR*, 250–53, esp. 252. On his approach to work with African peoples, see *HR*, 119–22, 210–12. On his influence on Black radical thought, see, for example, Jeffrey

Babcock Perry, "Hubert Henry Harrison, 'The Father of Harlem Radicalism': The Early Years—1883 Though the Founding of the Liberty League and *The Voice* in 1917" (Ph.D. diss., Columbia University, 1986), viii and 707; and James, *Holding Aloft the Banner*, 123, 129 (which also discusses his influence on Caribbean radicalism).

22. *WGMC*, 2:432; HH, "No Negro Literary Renaissance," *PC*, March 12, 1927, sec. 2, p. 1, in *HR* 351–55, esp. 353; and HH, "Cabaret School of Negro Literature and Art," c. March 1927, HP, in *HR*, 355–57, esp. 355. The languages were English, Danish, Latin, French, German, and Arabic. Jean Blackwell Hutson, "African Materials in the Schomburg Collection of Negro Literature and History," *Africana Studies Bulletin* 3, no. 2 (May, 1960): 1–4, discusses Harrison's book donations to the library and Sarah A. Anderson, "'The Place to Go': The 135th Street Branch Library and the Harlem Renaissance," *The Library Quarterly* 73, no. 4 (Oct. 2003), 383–421, esp. 383, discusses his weekly talks to promote the library.

23. On the need to have "eyes wide open" see HD, March 23, 1924, and May 20, 1908.

24. HH to the editor, *New York Sun*, December 8 and 19, 1910, both p. 8; Charles W. Anderson to Booker T. Washington, September 10 and October 30, 1911, in Louis R. Harlan and Raymond W. Smock, eds., *The Booker T. Washington Papers*, 13 vols. (Urbana: University of Illinois Press, 1972–1984), 11:300–301, 351.

25. HH, "Socialism and the Negro," *International Socialist Review* 13 (July 1912): 65–68, in *HR*, 71–76, esp. 72–73; W. E. B. Du Bois, "Socialism and the Negro Problem," *New Review* 1, no. 5 (February 1, 1913): 138–141, esp. 140; and HH, "Race First Versus Class First," *NW*, March 26, 1920, in *HR*, 107–9, esp. 109. See also HH, *The Negro and the Nation* (New York: Cosmo-Advocate Publishing, 1917).

26. On Harrison's pioneering role, see HH to the editor, "New York Lecture Centers," *Truth Seeker*, August 22, 1914, 539; HD, September 28, 1914; Lester A. Walton, "Street Speaker Heralds Spring in Harlem," *New York World*, March 23, 1928, p. 17; and Theodore G. Vincent, *Black Power and the Garvey Movement* (San Francisco: Ramparts Press, 1972), 137. For the descriptive quotes see: *WGMC*, 2:433; Claude McKay, *A Long Way From Home: An Autobiography*, intro. St. Clair Drake (1937; New York: Harcourt Brace & World, 1970), 41; Wendell Wray, "The Reminiscences of A. Philip Randolph," interview, July 25, 1972, Oral History Project, Butler Library, Columbia University, New York, 154; A. Philip Randolph to Mrs. Hubert Harrison, December 21, 1927, HP; and Miller, *Rosy Crucifixion*, 560–61. Unfortunately, no recordings of Harrison speaking have been located.

27. On the theater, see HH, "Negro Society and the Negro Stage," part 1, September 19, 1917, HP, in *HR*, 370–73, esp. 371–72. In 1916 Harrison began speaking of a "New Negro Manhood Movement." By 1917 he spoke also of a "New Negro Womanhood Movement" and a "New Negro Movement," and over the years "New Negro Movement" predominated. See, for example, "When the Negro Wakes, A Lecture of 'The Manhood Movement' Among the Negro People of America by Hubert Henry Harrison . . . Dec. 24, 1916," handout, HP-Scrapbook 34. On Harrison's leading role

see [HH], "The Liberty League of Negro-Americans: How it Came to Be," *Voice*, July 4, 1917, in *HR*, 86–88. Virgin Islands–born Frank R. Crosswaith, special organizer of the Sleeping Car Porters and prominent Socialist, wrote: "The story of the New Negro's fascinating fight for a man's place in our time, is the story of Hubert H. Harrison" (Frank R. Crosswaith to Mrs. [Irene Louise (Lin)] Harrison, December 20, 1927, HP).

28. HH, "Program and Principles of the International Colored Unity League," *The Voice of the Negro* 1, no. 1 (April 1927): 4–6, in *HR*, 399–402, esp. 400. Locke served as special editor for the March 1925 *Survey Graphic* (subtitled *Harlem: Mecca of the New Negro*), which included articles, stories, and poems by prominent Black writers. Eight months later he brought out *The New Negro*, an anthology that included, in revised form, many of the pieces from *Survey Graphic* and called attention to the "new race consciousness" and "internationalism"; to the fact that the "rank and file" were "leading" and the "leaders" following; and to the fact that the "New Negro" was "an augury of a new democracy in American culture." See Henry Louis Gates Jr. and Nellie Y. McKay, gen. eds., *Norton Anthology of African American Literature* (New York: W. W. Norton, 1997), 960–70, esp. 960, 964–65, and 969; and Alain Locke, *The New Negro* (1925; New York: Atheneum, 1980). Locke's work, however, tended to transform the militancy associated with the more political "New Negro Movement" into what Henry Louis Gates Jr., refers to as an "apolitical movement of the arts." See Henry Louis Gates Jr., "The Trope of the New Negro and the Reconstruction of the Image of the Black," *Representations* 24 (Fall 1998): 129–55, esp. 147. Nathan Irvin Huggins, *Voices from the Harlem Renaissance* (New York: Oxford University Press, 1974), 8, writes that "the 'New Negro' was actually a creature of the pre-war years . . . [and its] radicalism was more sharply political in the early years of the war than it was to be in the 1920s."

29. HH, "Liberty League of Negro Americans," 87.

30. HH, "Our Professional Friends," *Voice*, November 7, 1917, HP, in *HR*, 143–47, esp. 146; and [HH], "Shillady Resigns," *NW*, June 19, 1920, 2, in *HR*, 177–178, esp. 178.

31. See HH, *The Negro and the Nation* (New York: Cosmo-Advocate Publishing, 1917), 3; HH, "Politics and Personality," *Voice*, August 28, 1917, HP; HH, "Prejudice Growing Less and Co-Operation More," 252; and [HH], "What It Stands For," *Voice*, September 19, 1917, HP, reprint of [Liberty League,] "Declaration of Principles," *Clarion*, September 1, 1917, in *HR*, 89–92, and HH, "The Liberty League of Negro-Americans," 87, on the program.

32. HH, "Marcus Garvey at the Bar of United States Justice," *Associated Negro Press*, c. July 1923, HP, in *HR*, 194–99, esp. 197; and HH, "Two Negro Radicalisms," *New Negro* 4, no. 2 (October 1919): 4–5, HP, in *HR*, 102–5. On Harrison's movement laying the basis for the Garvey movement, see Anselmo Jackson, "An Analysis of the Black Star Line," *Emancipator*, March 27, 1920, 2; and William H. Ferris, "The Spectacular Career of Garvey," *AN*, February 11, 1925, part 2, sec. 2, p. 9.

33. For the Randolph quotation, see Anderson, *A. Philip Randolph*, 21. The March on Washington Movement led to President Franklin Delano Roosevelt's signing of Executive Order 8802 on June 25, 1941, which stated that it would be the "policy of the United States that there shall be no discrimination in the employment of workers in defense industries or Government because of race, creed, color, or national origin," and called for the establishment of a Fair Employment Practices Committee. After Order 8802, the African American presence in war industries increased from 3 to 8 percent. The 1963 march led to the 1964 Civil Rights Act, which forbade discrimination in public accommodations and employment. Executive Order 8802 of June 25, 1941 is available at http://www.eeoc.gov/abouteeoc/35th/thelaw/eo-8802.html. See also Herbert Garfinkel, *When Negroes March: The March on Washington Movement in the Organizational Politics for FEPC* (1959; New York: Athenaeum, 1969), 56–57, 60–61, 117–21, and 127–31; James Gilbert Cassedy, "African Americans and the American Labor Movement," *Prologue* 29, no. 2 (Summer 1997): 113–20, esp. 119; and Paula E. Pfeffer, *A. Philip Randolph, Pioneer of the Civil Rights Movement* (Baton Rouge: Louisiana State University Press, 1990), 269–71.

34. See HH, "The Descent of Dr. Du Bois," *The Voice*, July 25, 1918, in *HR*, 170–73; and HH, "When the Blind Lead," *NW*, c. February 1920, in *HR*, 173–74. Du Bois apparently never forgot Harrison's criticism—he never once mentioned him in the pages of *The Crisis* and seemingly went out of his way to avoid doing so. See Hodge Kirnon, "Kirnon Flays Monthly Magazines," letter to the editor, *New York News*, February 28, 1928, HP; Irma Watkins-Owens, *Blood Relations: Caribbean Immigrants and the Harlem Community, 1900–1930* (Bloomington: Indiana University Press, 1996), 97; and HH, "No Negro Literary Renaissance."

35. On the *Negro World* see HH, "Connections with the Garvey Movement," HD, March 17 and 18, 1920, in *HR*, 182–88; *GP*, 2:571–78, 582. See also Hubert H. Harrison, *When Africa Awakes: The "Inside Story" of the Stirrings and Strivings of the New Negro in the Western World* (New York, 1920).

36. On the criticisms of Garvey see [HH], [Notes on Marcus Garvey], HD, n.d. and March 23, 1924, and *HR*, 182–200. On the struggle being in the United States, see "Dr. Harris(on) Candidate for Congress on Socialist [Single Tax] Ticket," c. June 7, 1924, HP; "Wants State for Negroes: Unity League Launches a National Movement for Political, Economic and Spiritual Co-operation; Dr. Hubert Harrison Touring U.S. In Its Interest," *Boston Chronicle*, June 21, 1924, HP; and "Negroes Plan New American State: International Colored Unity League Organizing Branches to Further Project," *Christian Science Monitor*, June 7, 1924, 5B, HP.

37. [HH], "Shillady Resigns," 178; and, on the ICUL platform, HH, "Program and Principles of the International Colored Unity League." See also "Dr. Harris(on) Candidate for Congress"; Joseph G. Tucker, "Special Report of Radical Activities in the Greater New York District for Period Week Ending July 26, 1924," File 61-23-297, Federal Bureau of Investigation, United States Department of Justice, Washington,

D.C.; and "Wants Exclusive Negro Territory in U.S.," *New York World*, August 3, 1924, HP.

38. Previously, Harrison had articulated two other subsequent Communist Party positions—that it was a principal duty of white workers and radicals to challenge white supremacy and that "the cause of the Negro" was "revolutionary." A fourth Communist position—that the "Negro" question was sociohistorical rather than biological—was regularly maintained by Harrison, though he also, at times, emphasized biological factors.

39. "Public Gets New View on Race History: Noted Lecturer Opens Unity League Forum," *Chicago Defender*, June 18, 1927, 4.

40. See HH, "The Right Way to Unity," *Boston Chronicle*, May 10, 1924, in *HR*, 402–4, esp. 403; and HH, "The Common People."

41. W. Burghardt Turner and Joyce Moore Turner, eds., *Richard B. Moore, Caribbean Militant in Harlem: Collected Writings 1920–1972* (Bloomington: University of Indiana Press, 1988), 216. Harlem "symbolized the central experience of American blacks in the early twentieth century—the urbanization of black America" (Wintz, *Black Culture*, 3).

42. *WGMC*, 2:433, 435, 437. See also Wray, "Reminiscences of Randolph," 154; "Lament Dream"; "Harlem Community Church Renamed in Honor of the Late Hubert Harrison," *New York Age*, May 12, 1928; and "Hubert Harrison's Portrait in Library," *AN*, September 10, 1930.

43. Tony Martin, *Race First: The Ideological and Organizational Struggle of Marcus Garvey and the Universal Negro Improvement Association* (Westport, Conn.: Greenwood Press, 1976), 360.

44. See Harrison's comments on himself in his copy of David Duncan, *Life and Letters of Herbert Spencer*, 2 vols. (New York: D. Appleton, 1908), 2:246, 273, and in the appendix. HH to Jaime C. Gil, April 19, 1921, HP; HH, "Bridging the Gulf of Color," c. April 22, 1922, HP, in *HR*, 273–77, esp. 276; and HH, "To the Young Men of My Race," *Voice*, January 1919, in *HR*, 175–77, esp. 176. Baal, a god of the Canaanites often represented by a calf, was considered a false god by the Israelites. See Hosea 13:1.

45. *WGMC*, 2:439.

46. HH, "The Negro a Conservative," *Truth Seeker* 41, no. 37 (September 12, 1914), in *HR*, 42–46, esp. 45.

47. Kirnon, "Kirnon Flays Monthly Magazines." Journalist Edgar M. Grey added, "big Negro newspapers and business houses, schools and other organizations who had positions allowed themselves to be so hateful that they would not hire him [Harrison]"; Edgar M. Grey, "Why Great Negroes Die Young," *New York News*, December 31, 1927, 21, HP.

48. Comparisons to Socrates are found in Cleveland G. Allen to Irene Harrison, December 18, 1927, HP; Oscar Benson, "Literary Genius of Hubert Harrison," *New York News*, December 24, 1927; McKay, *Long Way From Home*, 41–42; Anderson,

A. Philip Randolph, 79; and John G. Jackson, *Hubert Henry Harrison: The Black Socrates*, ([Austin, Tex.]: American Atheist Press, 1987).

49. *WGMC*, 2:432; and "Hubert H. Harrison!" *PC*, December 31, 1927, sec. 2, p. 8. See also Portia P. James, "As Far as Thought Can Reach: Hubert Harrison and the New Negro Movement," unpublished ms., 1989, possession of author; and the final chapter ("As Far As Thought Can Reach: A.D. 31,920") in [George] Bernard Shaw, *Back to Methuselah: A Metabiological Pentateuch*, rev. ed., with postscript (1921; New York: Oxford University Press, 1947), 189–245. A. Philip Randolph, in Wray, "Reminiscences of Randolph," 154, adds, "Harrison . . . was poor. He had no clothes of any consequence."

50. HH, "The Brown Man Leads the Way: A Review of *The New World of Islam* by Lothrop Stoddard [concluding Part]," *NW*, November 5, 1921, 5, in *HR*, 315–19, quotation at 317. See also chapter 4.

51. Edgar M. Grey, a *New York News* columnist and former UNIA leader, said that "Harrison was the most complicated character, the most brilliant writer, and possessed the mightiest intellect that has sprung from our group." See "Lament Dream." Rogers, *WGMC*, 2:438, adds that "Harrison's life-long enemy, like that of most scholars was poverty." Though his "enthralling oratory should have paid him well, yet, like so many scholars, he was so thoroughly wrapped up in his work, that this aspect of the situation quite escaped him. Whatever money he had usually drifted to him as food to a polyp attached to the piles of piers." See also Bill Fletcher Jr., "Radicals Known and Unknown," *Monthly Review* 53, no. 7 (December 2001): 57–59, at http://www.monthlyreview.org/1201fletcher.htm.

52. Rogers, *WGMC*, 2:432–33, described Harrison as the Black leader with the sanest and most effective program. Rogers's comments bring to mind an observation by George W. Stocking Jr., in *Victorian Anthropology* (New York: Free Press, 1987). 112, that "standing outside the normal process by which intellectual traditions are transmitted, the autodidact may embody the spirit of his age in an unusually direct way." See also Mark Ellis, "J. Edgar Hoover and the 'Red Summer' of 1919," *Journal of American Studies* 28, no. 1 (April 1994): 59, which points out that J. Edgar Hoover of the Bureau of Investigation, who headed government surveillance of radicals, maintained that any "radical black organization for constitutional rights . . . endangered the American social order."

53. Theodore [W.] Allen, "The Most Vulnerable Point," n.p., October 1972, 4, possession of author, writes that "the principal aspect of United States capitalist society is not merely bourgeois domination, but bourgeois white-supremacist domination." He discusses the origin of the system of racial oppression and its centrality to class rule in the United States in Theodore W. Allen, *The Invention of the White Race*, 2 vols., 1: *Racial Oppression and Social Control*, and 2: *The Origin of Racial Oppression in Anglo-America* (New York: Verso, 1994, 1997), 1:32–35, 133–35, 143–50, 2:221–22, and 239–59.

54. Benson, "Literary Genius of Hubert Harrison."

1. Crucian Roots (1883–1900)

1. HD, December 8, 1907, HP, uses "Santa Cruz." Jeannette Allis Bastian, *Owning Memory: How a Caribbean Community Lost Its Archives and Found Its History* (Westport, Conn.: Libraries Unlimited, 2003), 10, discusses how historical records have been "virtually inaccessible to Virgin Islanders." The past difficulty in obtaining documentation on Harrison's early years is indicated in Jorgen H. Anderson, archivist, Landarskivet, the Archives of Sealand, Lolland-Falster, and Bornholm, Copenhagen, Denmark, to author, January 14, 1985, possession of author, and was reinforced by this author in research trips to St. Croix (1985 and 1992) and Copenhagen (1989). George F. Tyson to author, February 19, 2008, possession of author, discusses how the St. Croix African Roots Project (SCARP), administered by the Virgin Islands Social History Associates (George F. Tyson, Svend E. Holsoe, Poul E. Olsen, and Roland Roebuck) is addressing this problem through the creation of a St. Croix Population Database, which, when completed by the end of 2008, will contain nearly two million biographical entries transcribed from the rich body of archival documentation compiled during the period of Danish rule (1734–1917). Also see George Tyson, "African Roots," summarized by Robin Swank, secretary, *St. John Historical Society Newsletter* 9, no. 1 (August 2007), at http://www.stjohnhistoricalsociety.org/Articles/AfricanRoots.htm. I am deeply grateful to the historian George F. Tyson for most generously sharing and discussing his research findings on Harrison and St. Croix, which are primarily drawn from the SCARP material.

2. Harrison became a citizen through naturalization on September 26, 1922 (HD, September 26, 1922). Shortly before that date, using the pseudonym "A St. Croix Creole," he wrote a letter to the editor of the New York *Evening Post* explaining that "Virgin Islanders occupy a most anomalous position. In consequence of the dodging tactics of the State Department the 20,000 of them living in New York City are neither citizens nor aliens. They cannot vote and they cannot get naturalized because they have no 'allegiance' to forswear. Their status is a standing disgrace to democracy and ought to be speedily changed. But there has been no discussion of the fact before the American people." See "A St. Croix Creole" [HH], letter to the editor, *New York Evening Post*, May 15, 1922, in *HR*, 240–41. For a discussion of the elliptical arguments used by U.S. government officials to argue that the 1917 treaty of cession granted "citizenship in the United States" to Virgin Islanders not wishing to remain Danish subjects, but not "citizenship of the United States," and that they were therefore "entitled to the protection of the government, but have not the civil and political status of the United States," see William W. Boyer, *America's Virgin Islands: A History of Human Rights and Wrongs* (Durham, N.C.: Carolina Academic Press, 1983), 136–37. Isaac Dookhan, "The Search for Identity: The Political Aspirations and Frustrations of Virgin Islanders Under the United States Administration, 1917–1927," *Journal of Caribbean History* 12 (1979): 1–34, esp. 3, points out that the sales treaty did not intend to confer U.S. citizen-

ship on the mass of Black Virgin Islanders but only on those who previously had Danish citizenship.

3. From 1893 until WWI, deportation was an administrative act, not a punishment for crime. Since it was noncriminal, the Bill of Rights did not apply, and merely being classified as an alien made one subject to arrest and deportation. See William Preston Jr., *Aliens and Dissenters: Federal Suppression of Radicals, 1903–1933* (1963; New York: Harper and Row, 1966), 11–13.

4. Erik J. Lawaetz, *St. Croix: 500 Years, Pre-Columbus to 1990* (Herning, Denmark: Poul Kristensen, 1991), 431; Pearl Varlack and Norwell Harrigan, *The Virgins: A Descriptive and Historical Profile* (St. Thomas: The Caribbean Research Institute College of the Virgin Islands, 1977), 5–10; and Tyson to author, February, 19, 2008.

5. Arnold Highfield, *St. Croix, 1493: An Encounter of Two Worlds* (St. Thomas: Virgin Islands Humanities Council, 1995), ix, 4, 9–54, esp. 20, 29; Tyson to author, February 19, 2008; Florence Lewisohn, *St. Croix Under Seven Flags* (Hollywood, Fla.: The Dukane Press, 1970), 1–19; Isaac Dookhan, *A History of the Virgin Islands of the United States*, intro. Richard B. Sheridan (St. Thomas: Caribbean Universities Press, 1974), 15–30; and *GP*, 7:183n. 1.

6. Tyson to author, February 19, 2008; Highfield, *St Croix, 1493*, 63–69; and Lewisohn, *St. Croix*, 1–6.

7. Tyson to author, February 19, 2008; and Highfield, *St. Croix, 1493*, xii, 76, 91, 131, 133.

8. Highfield, *St. Croix, 1493*, 133–35, 138–39; Tyson to author, February 19, 2008; Boyer, *America's Virgin Islands*, 6; and Lewisohn, *St. Croix*, 26, 41, 46, 73–74.

9. Tyson to author, February 19, 2008; Boyer, *America's Virgin Islands*, 9–11; and Lewisohn, *St. Croix*, 74–80.

10. Tyson to author, February 19, 2008. In George F. Tyson and Arnold R. Highfield, eds., *The Danish West Indian Slave Trade: Virgin Islands Perspectives* (St. Croix: Virgin Islands Humanities Council, 1994) see the following articles—George F. Tyson, "Introduction," v–viii, esp. v; Colin Palmer, "The Atlantic Slave Trade," 1–10, esp. 7; Arnold R. Highfield, "The Danish Atlantic and West Indian Slave Trade," 11–32, esp. 11, 21–22, 27; Svend E. Holsoe, "The Origin, Transport, Introduction, and Distribution of Africans on St. Croix: An Overview," 33–46, esp. 33–34, 37; and Sandra E. Greene, "From Whence They Came: A Note on the Influence of West African Ethnic and Gender Relations on the Organizational Character of the 1733 St. John Slave Rebellion," 47–67, esp. 48. See also Svend E. Green-Pedesen, "The Scope and Structure of the Danish Negro Slave Trade," in *Bondmen and Freedmen in the Danish West Indies*, ed. George F. Tyson (Christiansted: Virgin Islands Humanities Council, 1996), 18–53, esp. 19, 35; Dookhan, *History*, 120–39; Neville A. T. Hall, *Slave Society in the Danish West Indies: St. Thomas, St. John, and St. Croix*, ed. B. W. Higman (Baltimore, Md.: Johns Hopkins University Press, 1992), 56–59 and 71 (on Oldendorp); Eva Lawaetz, *Free Coloured in St. Croix, 1744–1816* (Christiansted: Eva Lawaetz, 1979), 1, 47; Boyer, *America's Virgin Islands*, 13–18; and E. J. Lawaetz,

St. Croix, 121. James A. Rawley, *The Transatlantic Slave Trade: A History* (New York: Norton, 1981), 100, states that between 1733, when Denmark acquired St. Croix, and 1802, the last year of the legal trade, "Denmark exported an estimated 50,350 slaves from Africa."

11. Malik Sekou, "Political and Economic Aspects of Emancipation," in *Emancipation in the U.S. Virgin Islands: 150 Years of Freedom, 1848-1948*, ed. Arnold R. Highfield (Christiansted: The Virgin Islands Humanities Council, 1999), 26–35, esp. 32; Boyer, *America's Virgin Islands*, 19–29; N. Hall, *Slave Society*, 56–59; and Dookhan, *History*, 145, 154–58.

12. Tyson to author, February 19, 2008; N. Hall, *Slave Society*, 125–37; Boyer, *America's Virgin Islands*, 22, 24, 29–31; and Dookhan, *History*, 161–80.

13. Peter Hoxcer Jensen, *From Serfdom to Fireburn and Strike: A History of Black Labor in the Danish West Indies, 1848–1916* (Christiansted: Antilles Press, 1998), 133.

14. Hall is quoted in B. W. Higman, "Danish West Indian Slavery in Comparative Perspective: An Appreciation of Neville Hall's Contribution to the Historiography," in *Bondmen and Freedmen in the Danish West Indies*, ed. George F. Tyson (Christiansted: Virgin Islands Humanities Council, 1996), 1–17, esp. 11. See also Jensen, *From Serfdom to Fireburn*, 98; Sekou, "Political and Economic Aspects of Emancipation," 34; George F. Tyson, "A Selection of Historical Documents relating to Emancipation in the Danish West Indies," in *Emancipation in the U.S. Virgin Islands: 150 Years of Freedom, 1848-1948*, ed. Arnold R. Highfield (Christiansted: The Virgin Islands Humanities Council, 1999), 37–74, esp. 39. On "Buddhoe," see George F. Tyson, "John Gottliff: The Man Behind Buddhoe," *St. John Historical Society Newsletter* 8, no. 1 (June 2006): http://www.stjohnhistoricalsociety.org/Articles/JohnGottliff.htm?limited=1; George F. Tyson and Svend Holsoe, "Timeline of the Emancipation of the Danish West Indies," *St. John Historical Society Newsletter* 8, no. 1 (June 2006): http://www.stjohnhistoricalsociety.org/Articles/Emancipation-Timeline.htm; George F. Tyson to author, February 10, 2008, possession of author, citing John Gottliff's baptism on March 19, 1820, in the Holy Trinity Lutheran Church Register (Mission) of 1805 and 1831, St. Croix censuses of 1841 and 1846, and Record Group 55 of the National Archives; Aesha Duval, "Legends Abound on Buddhoe's Role in 1848 Uprising and Emancipation," *Virgin Islands Daily News*, February 15, 2005; Bastian, *Owning Memory*, 45–51; Arthur A. Schomburg, "History of the Emancipation of the Virgin Islands," *Negro World*, April 29, 1922, 3 (hereafter *NW*); Boyer, *America's Virgin Islands*, 55–57; and N. Hall, *Slave Society*, 215, 226–27. It is likely that Harrison knew of "Buddhoe, who was a legend among the Crucians." Arthur Schomburg, whose mother was from St. Croix, recalled: "When I was a boy I remember hearing from the lips of an old Negro man, friendly and paternal, the story of the horrors practiced by the slave owners. He told with precise details the incidents that led to and surrounded the early life of the Negro, Buddhoe." Cited in Winston James, *Holding Aloft the Banner of Ethiopia: Caribbean Radicalism in Early*

Twentieth Century America (New York: Verso, 1998), 201–2, 333n. 26. Lewisohn, *St. Croix*, 255, describes English sailors in Christiansted Harbor supporting the 1848 struggle by putting water casks stamped with the word "Liberty" on them on shore for the insurgents. In 1917 Harrison founded the Liberty League.

15. George F. Tyson, "'Our Side': Caribbean Immigrant Labourers and the Transition to Free Labour on St. Croix, 1849–1879," in *Small Islands, Large Questions: Society, Culture and Resistance in the Post-Emancipation Caribbean*, ed. Karen Fog Olwig (London: Frank Cass, 1995), 135–160, esp. 135–37, 140, 143–45; Jensen, *From Serfdom to Fireburn*, 98, 102, 155, 166, 186-89, 232, 234; and Norwell Harrigan and Pearl I. Varlack, "The U.S. Virgin Islands and the Black Experience," *Journal of Black Studies* 7, no. 4 (June 1977): 392. Statistics and information on Barbadians in the 1878 struggle and in the 1880 and 1890 censuses are also provided in George F. Tyson to author, February 12, possession of author, and Tyson to author, February 19, 2008.

16. Tyson, "'Our Side,'" esp. 145, 148–51, 153, 155–56; Jensen, *From Serfdom to Fireburn*, 132–44, quotation at 133. Boyer, *America's Virgin Islands*, 60, 67–71; Dookhan, *History*, 224–32; Lewisohn, *St. Croix*, 322–24, 328; U.S. Department of Commerce, Bureau of the Census, *Census of the Virgin Islands of the United States, November 1, 1917* (Washington, D.C.: Government Printing Office, 1918), 94, 117; *New York Herald*, November 28, 1878, 1; E. J. Lawaetz, *St. Croix*, 196–204; and Clifton E. Marsh, "A Socio-Historical Analysis of the Labor Revolt of 1878 in the Danish West Indies," *Phylon* 42, no. 4 (1981): 335–45. Statistics and information on Barbadians in the 1878 struggle and in the 1880 and 1890 St. Croix censuses are also provided in George F. Tyson, February 12, 2008.

17. See U.S. Department of Commerce, *Census, 1917*, 11–27, 37, 117, 124; and Jensen, *From Serfdom to Fireburn*, 234–35. Gloria Joseph, interview by author, Judith's Fancy, St. Croix, June 16, 1985, emphasized capitalist greed. Harrison, "The Virgin Islands: A Colonial Problem," October 31, 1923, in *HR*, 243, cites a "love of freedom" as an inspiration for fellow Virgin Islander Denmark Vesey, who, in 1822, "organized a slave revolt in Charleston, South Carolina which all but succeeded." On December 29, 1900, the U.S. State Department announced that negotiations for purchase of the Danish West Indies (DWI) were completed and congressional approval (which did not come for seventeen years) was needed. A treaty with Denmark for purchase of the DWI was signed by the U.S. Senate on June 24, 1902, but the Danish Rigsdag rejected it. The United States grew concerned with military control of the Caribbean after construction of the Panama Canal, large-scale American investment of capital in Cuba, and warnings of German activities in the region as WWI progressed. According to Peter M. Bergman, *The Chronological History of The Negro in America* (New York: Harper and Row, 1969), 380, in August 1916, as the United States was arranging the purchase, the American minister, responding to the Danish foreign minister, stated that Americans were "so well acquainted with the true character of the Negroes that they could make them more content than the Europeans." A December 14, 1916, Danish plebiscite favored the sale to the

United States. The treaty for the $25 million purchase was ratified in January 1917; the formal transfer occurred on March 31. U.S. marines then occupied the islands and Congress imposed a military government that lasted until 1931. See "Extracts from the Official Report of the . . . Danish West Indies . . . September 20, 1916," File 811 s:00/37, RG 59, National Archives, Washington, D.C.; and Hans Schmidt, *The United States Occupation of Haiti* (New Brunswick, N.J.: Rutgers University Press, 1971), 56–57.

18. HH, "'Subject' Vs. 'Citizen,'" *NW*, January 22, 1921, HP-Scrapbook B (hereafter HP-Sc). See also Isaac Dookhan, "Changing Patterns of Local Reaction to the United States Acquisition of the Virgin Islands, 1865–1917," *Caribbean Studies* 15, no. 1 (April 1975): 50–72, esp. 53; Darwin D. Creque, *The U.S. Virgins and the Eastern Caribbean* (Philadelphia: Whitmore, 1968), 97; and D. C. Canegata, *St. Croix at the Twentieth Century: A Chapter in Its History* (New York: Carlton Press, 1968), 131. Gardner L. Harding, "Virgin Islands Electoral Plan Restricts Franchise to 2 P.C.," *Christian Science Monitor*, December 5, 1923, 13, gives a figure of 424 voters out of a population of 26,000. Harrison always realized that U.S. democracy was not all it could be. See also HH, "Hubert Harrison Answers Malliet," *Pittsburgh Courier*, October 22, 1927, sec. 1, p. 3 (hereafter *PC*).

19. Valdemar A. Hill Sr., *Rise to Recognition: An Account of Virgin Islanders from Slavery to Self-Government* (St. Thomas: Valdemar A. Hill Sr., 1971), 47.

20. Lewisohn, *St. Croix*, 275, 302–3, 309, 328, 332; and Dookhan, "Changing Patterns," 53. See also Dookhan, *History*, 231; Casper Holstein, "Crackerism and Judicial Oppression Invade St. Croix," *NW*, June 3, 1922, 2; Holstein, "The Virgin Islands," 344–45; Boyer, *America's Virgin Islands*, 71; and Jensen, *From Serfdom to Fireburn*, 17 and 213.

21. N. Hall, *Slave Society*, 111. See also Neville Hall, "Slaves Use of 'Free' Time in the Danish Virgin Islands in the Late Eighteenth and Early Nineteenth Century," *Journal of Caribbean History* 13 (1980): 21–43, esp. 22, 29; E. J. Lawaetz, *St. Croix*, 89–90, 118–22; HH, "The Virgin Islands," 243; Joseph, interview; HD, December 8 and 10, 1907, and November 1, 1923; and Lewisohn, *St. Croix*, 137.

22. HH, "The Virgin Islands," 243. See also N. Hall, *Slave Society*, 114.

23. HH, "The Virgin Islands," 243–44. The Virgin Island journalist Geraldo Guirty, in *Sixtonian: Vignettes 'bout "Amalia"* (New York: Vantage Press, 1991), 16, explains that "generally the people lived a mere existence," and though "jobs were not plentiful, nobody really starved or was homeless" because people "knew each other and gave everyday assistance."

24. Gordon K. Lewis, *The Virgin Islands: A Caribbean Lilliput* (Evanston, Ill.: Northwestern University Press, 1972), 60–61; quotations from *Report of the Educational Survey of the Virgin Islands*, authorized by the secretary of the navy and conducted under the auspices of the Hampton and Tuskegee Institutes (Hampton, Va., 1929), 42–43; and HH, "The Virgin Islands," 244. See also Edward A. O'Neill, *Rape of the Virgin Islands* (New York: Praeger, 1972), 36; and Lewisohn, *St. Croix*, 302.

25. J. A. Rogers, "The West Indies: Their Political, Social, and Economic Condition," *Messenger*, September 1922, 484, challenged "the impression that there is no color line" in Caribbean societies. That "proud boast," he explained, was "very superficial, and far from correct." There was a "color line"—it was just drawn differently than in the United States. James, *Holding Aloft the Banner*, 109–10, adds that "black people in the Caribbean were generally kept down," though this was not done with "the *relatively* crude kick-'em-in-the-teeth discipline of Jim Crow, nor by the terror of lynch ropes and the pyres of the Ku Klux Klan," but by a more subtle process. On the historical development of the "white race" and on the "mulatto" buffer social control role see Theodore W. Allen, *The Invention of the White Race* 2 vols. (New York: Verso, 1994 and 1997), vol. 1: *Racial Oppression and Social Control*, 12–14, 23–24, esp. 11, and vol. 2: *The Origin of Racial Oppression in Anglo-America*, 13 and 223–59, esp. 238.

26. U.S. Department of Commerce, *Census, 1917*, 94, 117, 120; Paul Blanshard, *Democracy and Empire in the Caribbean: A Contemporary Review* (New York: Macmillan, 1947), 51; and Jensen, *From Serfdom to Fireburn*, 219.

27. Theodore William Allen, "Summary of the Argument of *The Invention of the White Race*," *Cultural Logic* 1, no. 2 (Spring 1998), 2 parts, part 1, par. 8 and part 2, par. 102, available at http://clogic.eserver.org/1-2/allen.html; Eric Williams, "Race Relations in Puerto Rico and the Virgin Islands," *Foreign Affairs* 23, no. 2 (January, 1945), 308–317, esp. 310; Boyer, *America's Virgin Islands*, 22; and N. Hall, *Slave Society*, 24, 154–161, esp. 160. Also see Allen, *Invention*, 1:19; David Lowenthal, "Race and Color in the West Indies," in *Color and Race*, ed. John Hope Franklin (Boston: Beacon Press, 1968), 302–48, esp. 303, 307, 310, 315; David Lowenthal, *West Indian Societies* (New York: Oxford University Press, 1972), 45–62; Ira De A. Reid, *The Negro Immigrant: His Background, Characteristics, and Social Adjustment, 1899–1937* (1939; reprint, New York: AMS Press, 1970), 38, 54–55, 111; U.S. Department of Commerce, *Census, 1917*, 37, 45, 94; Creque, *U.S. Virgins*, 49; Lewisohn, *St. Croix*, 234, 266; E. J. Lawaetz, *St. Croix*, 284–86; Dookhan, *History*, 144–46; Harrigan and Varlack, "U.S. Virgin Islands," 389–96, esp. 395, which discusses good behavior and standing; and Charles Edwin Taylor, *Leaflets from the Danish West Indies: Descriptive of the Social, Political, and Commercial Condition of These Islands* (1888; reprint, Westport, Conn.: Negro Universities Press, 1970), 146. Tony Martin, *Race First: The Ideological and Organizational Struggle of Marcus Garvey and the Universal Negro Improvement Association* (Westport, Conn.: Greenwood Press, 1976), 29, discusses the "need [of] the support of the buffer mulatto element" in the islands. For additional population percentages, see Allen, *Invention*, 2:246–47; and Sekou, "Political and Economic Aspects of Emancipation," 32–33.

28. Jonathan Scott and Greg Meyerson, "An Interview with Theodore W. Allen," *Cultural Logic* 1, no. 2 (Spring 1998), available at http://clogic.eserver.org/1-2/allen%20interview.html, discusses the "normal social distinctions characteristic of class systems." Theodore W. Allen, *Invention*, 1:113, describes "the contrast in the systems of bourgeois social control [as]—national oppression in the West Indies,

racial oppression in the United States." See also Allen, "Summary of the Argument," part 2, esp. par. 118.

29. T. W. Allen, *Invention*, 2:251, and Theodore W. Allen, *Class Struggle and the Origin of Racial Slavery: The Invention of the White Race*, ed. and intro. Jeffrey B. Perry (1974; reprint, Stony Brook, N.Y.: Center for Study of Working Class Life, State University of New York, Stony Brook, 2006), 1–3, 13–17. J[oel]. A. Rogers, *WGMC*, 1:16, states that: "the white colonists of America, thanks chiefly to continued and fairly large immigration, did not need the mulatto to help them keep the blacks in check and thus did not elevate him . . . but generally lumped blacks and mulattoes together. South of the Rio Grande, however . . . the whites there erected the mulattoes into a caste above the blacks." Monroe N. Work, "Problems of Adjustment of Race and Class in the South," *Social Forces*, 15, no. 1 (October, 1937): 108–17, esp. 109–10, discusses how "social controls were devised for serving and promoting the interests, economic, political, and social, of the planter class"; how in the United States this "internal control" was strengthened by "emphasizing white solidarity"; and how, as "the economic interests of the poorer whites were subordinated . . . their class consciousness remained undeveloped while at the same time their ideas of racial superiority attained a high degree of development."

30. N. Hall, *Slave Society*, 6, 13; Albert A. Campbell, *St. Thomas Negroes: A Study of Personality and Culture*, Psychological Monographs no. 55, ed. John F. Dashnell, (Evanston, Ill.: American Psychological Association, 1943), 18; and Higman, "Danish West Indian Slavery in Comparative Perspective," 7–10. See also U.S. Department of Commerce, *Census, 1917*, 37, 45, 94; Michael Craton, review of "Slave Society in the Danish West Indies St. Thomas, St. John, and St. Croix," by Neville A. T. Hall, *Journal of Caribbean History* 27, no. 2 (1993): 206–9, esp. 207; Lewisohn, *St. Croix*, 234; and James, *Holding Aloft*, 110, 184–85.

31. Gwendolyn Midlo Hall, *Social Control in Slave Plantation Societies: A Comparison of St. Domingue and Cuba* (Baltimore, Md.: Johns Hopkins University Press, 1971), 153; and Claude McKay, "A Negro Poet and His Poems," *Pearson's Magazine*, September 1918, 275. See also HH, "The Virgin Islands," 241, 246–47; *GP*, 1:xxxviii; Harrigan and Varlack, "U.S. Virgin Islands," 395–96; Reid, *Negro Immigrant* 54–55; Creque, *U.S. Virgins*, 75; Lewis, *The Virgin Islands*, 51, 54; James P. Pitts, "Editor's Introduction" to "Working Papers in the Study of Race Consciousness, Part I," *Journal of Black Studies* 5, no. 3 (March 1975): 227–32, esp. 228–29; and James, *Holding Aloft*, 3, 5, 110, 185. Eric Williams, "Race Relations," 311–12, writes that in the Virgin Islands "legal discrimination . . . is unknown. . . . Lynchings are unheard of."

32. N. Hall, *Slave Society*, 33; Tyson to author, February 19, 2008; Tyson, *Bondmen and Freedmen*, 11; E. J. Lawaetz, *St. Croix*, 118, 284–86; Boyer, *America's Virgin Islands*, 38–44; Joseph, interview; and N. A. T. Hall, "Anna Heegard—Enigma," *Caribbean Quarterly* 22 (June–September 1976): 67.

33. U.S. Department of Commerce, *Census, 1917*, 77, 94, 117, 120, 128, 130. In St. Croix "Negroes" and "colored" constituted 50 percent of the farm owners and 95 per-

cent of the population. In selected "Black Belt" counties in the U.S. South, according to James S. Allen, "Negroes" (including colored) constituted 17 percent of the farm owners and 57.7 percent of the population. The ratio of farm ownership to population in St. Croix was 1.786 times that in the selected Black Belt counties—almost 80 percent higher. See James S. Allen [Sol Auerbach], *The Negro Question in the United States* (New York: International Publishers, 1936), 212, 218; and Monroe N. Work, *Negro Year Book, 1921–1922* (Tuskegee, Ala.: The Negro Year Book Publishing Company, 1922), 324.

34. Inge N. Ovesen, trans., *The Central Management of the Colonies: Introduction to Vejledende Arkivregistratar XX* (Copenhagen: Koloniernes Certralbestyrelse, 1979), 2. See also Lowenthal, "Race and Color," 303, 307, 310, 315; James, *Holding Aloft*, 108–9; Carl N. Degler, *Neither Black Nor White: Slavery and Race Relations in Brazil and the United States* (New York: Macmillan, 1971), 5; and Franklin W. Knight, "Introduction," in *Richard B. Moore, Caribbean Militant in Harlem: Collected Writings, 1920–1972*, ed. W. Burghardt Turner and Joyce Moore Turner (Bloomington: University of Indiana Press, 1988), 7.

35. HH, "Prejudice Growing Less and Co-Operation More, Says Student of Question," *PC*, January 29, 1927, sec. 2, p. 7, in *HR*, 250–53, esp. 252; and HH, "Negro Culture and the Negro College," *New Negro* 4, no. 1 (September 1919): 4–5, in *HR*, 120–22, esp. 121. See also Lewisohn, *St. Croix*, 235, 338; Guirty, *Sixtonian*, 76; and Boyer, *America's Virgin Islands*, 44–46, 55–56. On education in St. Croix in this period see Jensen, *From Serfdom to Fireburn*, 213–19, esp. 215 on the May 7, 1884 ordinance, Concerning Schools and Education in St. Croix.

36. Lewis, *The Virgin Islands*, 54; and HH, "The Virgin Islands," 247. See also Scott Nearing and Joseph Freeman, *Dollar Diplomacy: A Study in American Imperialism* (1925; New York: Monthly Review Press, 1969), 215; "Where Color Doesn't Count" (c. 1902) in D. C. Canegata, *St. Croix at the Twentieth Century: A Chapter in Its History* (New York: Carlton Press, 1968), 28–30; Lewisohn, *St. Croix*, 349–50; Harrigan and Varlack, "U.S. Virgins Islands," 395; and Jack D. Foner, *Blacks and the Military in American History: A New Perspective* (New York: Praeger, 1974), 103–6, 124. For a different view on race relations in St. Croix, see Roy Simon Bryce-Laporte, "Black Immigrants: The Experience on Invisibility and Inequality," *Journal of Black Studies* 3, no. 1 (September 1972): 29–57, esp. 39–43.

37. HH, "The Virgin Islands," 247. For somewhat similar views from Marcus Garvey, see *GP*, 1:4, 43, 179–83; from W. E. B. Du Bois, see *GP*, 1:183; and from St. Thomas native Adolph Sixto, see his *Time and I, or Looking Forward* (n.p., n.d.), 25–26, quoted in Dookhan, "Changing Patterns," 54.

38. HH, "The Virgin Islands," 249. On Virgin Islanders' reactions to the U.S. navy see Lewis, *The Virgin Islands*, 51–56; Boyer, *America's Virgin Islands*, 117; Dookhan, *History*, ix; "Virgin Islanders Denounce Autocratic Administration in Their Home," *NW*, March 29, 1919, 4; "Virgin Islanders at Monster Mass Meeting Protest Naval Rule in St. Croix," *NW*, June 17, 1922, 3; and "Virgin Isles Societies Hold Mass Meeting, *NW*, May 10, 1924, 2.

39. "Hubert Henry [Harrison]," July 7, 1883, in "Baptisms Solemnized During the Years March 3, 1883–October 21, 1899," St. John's Episcopal Church, Christiansted, St. Croix (hereafter SJEC). George Tyson, "Hubert Henry Harrison Family History," c. February 10, 2008, possession of author; George F. Tyson, telecom with author, February 10, 2008; and George F. Tyson to author, February 21, 2008, possession of author. In this and ensuing paragraphs on Harrison's family in St. Croix George F. Tyson, using the SCARP database, provided invaluable assistance.

40. U.S. Department of Commerce, Bureau of the Census, "Fourteenth Census of the United States: 1920—Population," New York City, Enumeration District 932, sheet 1, line 87; Tyson, "Hubert Henry Harrison Family History"; Lewisohn, *St. Croix*, 240, 274; Tyson to author, February 12, 2008, points out that Cecilia's last name was not a common one on St. Croix before 1860, but it was a common surname among Bajans who came to St. Croix over the next two decades; and Tyson to author, February 21, 2008. Cecilia's Bajan roots are also indicated in "Dr. Harrison's Rise as Orator Is Like Fiction: Educator, Writer and Speaker Now Ranks with Best in His Line," *Chicago Defender*, January 19, 1924, part 2, p. 1; "Hubert Harrison Dies," *Amsterdam News*, December 21, 1927, 1 (hereafter *AN*); Richard B. Moore, "Harrison, Hubert Henry," in *Dictionary of American Negro Biography*, ed. Rayford W. Logan and Michael R. Winston (New York: W. W. Norton, 1982), 292; and U.S. Department of Commerce, *Census, 1917*, 61, 64–65. On the Barbadian immigrants also see Jensen, *From Serfdom to Fireburn*, 166, 186-89.

41. Tyson, "Hubert Henry Harrison Family History," citing St. Croix censuses of 1880 and 1890 and St. John's Anglican Church Marriage Book of 1867–1901; and Tyson to author, February 21, 2008, possession of author, which cites "Christine Cauling" in Register of Deaths in Christiansted Jurisdiction, National Archive, Record Group 55, Entry 397 (NARA Microfilm Reel M1884, Roll 20, Sec. 1), and Christiansted Probate Court Register of Reported Deaths, 1888–1920, St. Croix Recorder of Deeds Office, and speculates that Cecilia ("Christine") was buried in the cemetery at Aldershvile, which abutted Orange Grove and was owned by the Catholic Church. When Cecilia [Haines] Collins died on January 31, 1899, she was listed as fifty years old in death record of "Cecilia Collins," January 31, 1899, "Register for Burials Performed During the Year 1883–1899," SJEC.

42. Baptism Record of "Emily Frances," June 5, 1875, "St. John's Baptism Book, 1875–1883," SJEC; Tyson, "Hubert Henry Harrison Family History," which also cites death record of "Cecilia Collins"; and Tyson to author, February 21, 2008.

43. Tyson, "Hubert Henry Harrison Family History," citing "St. John's Baptism Book, 1807–1075", IID, inside front cover; Aida Harrison Richardson, interview by author, New York City, October 10, 1991; Aida Harrison Richardson and William Harrison, interview by author, New York City, August 4, 1983; "Aunt Mamie" [Mary C. Francis], interview by William Harrison, February 1, 1951, "William Harrison Notebook," HP; Affidavit of Mary C. Francis, March 31, 1920, HP; "Mary Frances [Mary Francis]," U.S. Census, 1910, Manhattan Ward 22, New York, Roll T624-1048,

p. 4B, Enumeration District 1376, Image 389; "Celebrated Harlem Mass Leader Dies After Operation," *New York News*, December 24, 1927; and "Dr. Harrison's Rise as Orator Is Like Fiction." Mary's 1893 arrival is listed in United States of America, Bureau of the Census, *Thirteenth Census of the United States, 1910*, Washington, D.C.: National Archives and Records Administration, 1910, T 624_996; p. 12A, Enumeration District 1412.

44. Tyson, "Hubert Henry Harrison Family History," citing "St. John's Baptism Book, 1867-1875"; HD, inside front cover (which does not list this Cecilia as being a living sister); and Aida Harrison Richardson, interview by author, New York City, October 10, 1991, which indicated no knowledge of this relative.

45. Baptism Record of "Emily Frances," June 5, 1875; Tyson, "Hubert Henry Harrison Family History," citing "St. John's Book, 1875–1883," the "1901 [St. Croix] Census," the "St. John Church Baptism Book of 1883–1889," and the "St. John Marriage Book of 1902–1918"; and HD, inside front cover, which lists a sister named Emma who, according to information given to Harrison's daughter, Aida, later became Emma Simmons. Tyson also indicates that on August 19, 1906, Emily Perry, age thirty, employed on estate Clifton Hill, married Nathan Allen, a laborer and that James Parris, a laborer, at Mt. Pleasant, was listed as Carmelita's father.

46. Tyson, "Hubert Henry Harrison Family History," which cites the St. John Church Baptism Books of 1865–1882 and 1875–1883, the Holy Cross Baptism Book 1865–1882, "1880 [St. Croix] Census," "1890 [St. Croix] Census," and the "1901 [St. Croix] Census," which indicates that Alexander Conton, age twenty-five, a laborer, was living with his half brother James Conton, age twenty-one, a laborer at Strand St. 34 C in Christiansted. James was born January 1, 1880, and baptized February 2. His parents were Elisa Petersen and Alexander Conton (born 1860), who, according to George F. Tyson, "most certainly also fathered Cecilia's Alexander Conton." Alexander Conton also appears in the "1911 [St. Croix] Census," the "St. John Church Marriage Book, 1902–1918," and the "St. John Anglican Church Book of 1899-1929."

47. Baptism Record of "David Elias," August 4, 1881, "Baptisms, 1875–1883," SJEC, 160. In his diary, where other family members were listed, Hubert made absolutely no mention of David Elias, born two years before him. See HD, inside front cover. Also see Lewisohn, *St. Croix*, 335.

48. Marriage record of "Robert Collins and Elizabeth Haines," in "Marriages, 1867–1901," no. 555, December 22, 1889, SJEC; George F. Tyson to author, February 13, 2008, possession of author; Tyson, "Hubert Henry Harrison Family History," citing the "1890 [St. Croix] Census," a list of "Immigrants 1881–1884" in U.S. National Archives, Record Group 55, Box 329 and the Danish National Archives, Rigsarkivet, VILA, 3.81.585, also notes a Robert Collins, age twenty-five, who arrived in St. Croix from Barbados aboard the schooner *Mermaid* on August 26, 1869, and began work at Estate Grange in Queens Quarter. This, too, may be Harrison's stepfather. See also Tyson to author, February 21, 2008, which cites Christiansted Cemetery Burials 1888–1892, 1895–1902 NARA/RG55/Box 302 (NARA Microfilm M1884, Roll 21;

Register of Deaths in Christiansted Jurisdiction, National Archive, Record Group 55, Entry 397 (NARA Microfilm Reel M1884, Roll 20, Sec. 1); and Christiansted Probate Court Register of Reported Deaths, 1888–1920, St. Croix Recorder of Deeds Office,

49. Moore, "Harrison, Hubert" 292–93, esp. 292. Hubert Harrison cites William A. Harrison as his father in "Marriage Certificate for Hubert Henry Harrison and Irene L. Horton," St. David's Protestant Episcopal Church, Bronx, N.Y., April 17, 1909, HP. When this work began, three of Harrison's children were alive, daughters Aida and Alice and son William. William died on February 22, 1984; Alice died on September 10, 1987; and Aida died on June 28, 2001. Hubert's other daughters, Frances Marion and Ilva, died on December 18, 1932, and August 7, 1933, respectively. His wife, Irene Louise Horton Harrison, died on May 28, 1962, and his sister, Mary C. Francis, died in 1954 or 1955 (Aida Harrison Richardson, telecons with author, August 17, 1985, October 10, 1991, and June 30, 1998). Aida Harrison Richardson and William Harrison stated that they had no information concerning the circumstances of their father's birth, nor information on his father, other than their belief that William was named after his grandfather (A. Richardson and William Harrison, interview, August 4, 1983). Hubert's father was listed as Adolphus in State of New York, Department of Health of the City of New York, Bureau of Records, Standard Certificate of Death, "Hubert Harrison," register no. 28066, Bellevue Hospital, December 17, 1927. June A. V. Linqvist, whose great-aunt was Irene Louise Horton Harrison (Hubert's wife), helped to locate Harrison's children. Ms. Linqvist was a librarian at the Von Scholten Collection of the Enid M. Baa Library, in Charlotte Amalie, St. Thomas (June A. V. Lindqvist to author, March 5, April 8, and May 15, 1983).

50. Tyson, to author, February 18, 2008, possession of author, citing the 1857 [St. Croix] census.

51. Tyson, to author, February 18, 2008, citing the 1870 [St. Croix] census; and Lord God of Sabaoth Lutheran Church Book, 1871–1899. In the 1880 census, Madalene Cornelius and Wilford Harrison were living together in Christiansted, at Hill St. 38, with her son, Samuel Issac, age twelve.

52. Tyson, to author, February 18, 2008, citing 1870, 1880, 1890, 1901, and 1911 [St. Croix] censuses, and Lord God of Sabaoth Lutheran Church Book 1871–1899. See also Tyson to author, February 21, 2008, which cites Christiansted Cemetery Burials 1888–1892, 1895–1902, and Christiansted Probate Court Register of Reported Deaths, 1888–1920, St. Croix Recorder of Deeds Office, 185.

53. Tyson, to author, February 18, 2008, citing Estate Rattan inventories of 1815, 1817, 1819, and 1820, Estate Rattan Vaccination List of 1824. The St. Croix census of 1841 shows Philis, 28, Anglican, a member of the Big Gang, with zero living children on Estate Rattan, the census of 1846 records Philis, thirty-three, Anglican, Big Gang, with two children on Estate Rattan, but there are no children named Adolphus or Wilford on the estate. The 1850 census, lists Philis, thirty-six, Anglican, unmarried living at Estate Rattan (Adolphus and Wilford are not listed among the children at Estate Rattan), and the 1855 census indicates Adolphus Harrison, eleven, Moravian,

is living on Estate Rattan with Phillis, forty-one, Anglican, unmarried, and Wilford, eight, Lutheran.

54. Tyson, to author, February 18, 2008, citing Lord God of Sabaoth Lutheran Mission Church Register 1845–1860, the 1850, 1855, 1857, 1860, 1890, and 1901 St. Croix censuses, and the Estate Rattan Vaccination List of 1824.

55. Tyson, to author, February 18, 2008, citing Holy Trinity Roman Catholic Church Book 1788–1844, the Estate Salt River Vaccination List of 1834, and the 1841, 1846, and 1855 St. Croix censuses. Tyson adds that Ned appears as Neddy, age three, in 1834 (there is no Edmond on that list); as Ned, nineteen, Roman Catholic, unmarried, Big Gang, living on Estate Salt River in 1841; and as Ned, age twenty-five, Roman Catholic, unmarried, Big Gang, living on Estate Salt River in 1846. In 1855 Ned was still living on Estate Salt River, in the same household as his brother, Henry, and mother, Brigit.

56. Tyson, to author, February 18, 2008, citing NARA, Record Group 55, Register of Deaths [Center District] 1865–1872, Microfilm 1884/Roll19/Section 1.

57. "1890 [St. Croix] Census," and "1901 [St. Croix] Census," Dookhan, "Changing Patterns," 60; "Dr. Harrison's Rise as Orator Is Like Fiction"; and U.S. Department of Commerce, *Census, 1917*, 56. On the parceling-out, see Boyer, *America's Virgin Islands*, 73; Dookhan, *History*, 233–34; Jensen, *From Serfdom to Fireburn*, 54; and Canegata, *St. Croix*, 156–58. Oswald Schjang, longtime recorder of deeds in Christiansted, confirmed information on estate size and confiscation during a telephone conversation with author, St. John and Fredericksted, St. Croix, June 15, 1985.

58. "Hubert Harrison Dies," 1; "Celebrated Harlem Mass Leader Dies After Operation"; and "1880 [St. Croix] Census." While drivers did take sexual advantage of women working under them, Wilfred (who could, in theory, have been Hubert's father) was married and living with Mary Harrison, age twenty-eight, a Moravian, and they both, along with Elizabeth James, had witnessed Alexander Conton's baptism. On the inside cover of his diary, Harrison also lists a foster sister, Letitia Shaw, about whom no information has been located.

59. Rogers, *WGMC*, 2:433; HH, "Bridging the Gulf of Color," c. April 1922, in *HR*, 273–77, esp. 277; and N. Hall, *Slave Society*, 18–19. The figures on English speakers are from 1917 but likely reflect the percentage on St. Croix when Harrison was born. See U.S. Department of Commerce, *Census, 1917*, 18, 41, 73–74. G. James Fleming, professor emeritus of Political Science at Morgan State University and a native Virgin Islander who knew Harrison in the 1920s, says that "many Virgin Islanders of past years could speak Danish fluently" (G. James Fleming to author, September 29, 1983, possession of author.). Further indication of Harrison's familiarity with Danish is "Booker Washington hos Kong Frederik," in [?], October 5, 1910, HP-Sc 1.

60. "Hubert Harrison Dies," 1. Harrison was attracted by Spencer's intellectual achievements, in part, perhaps, because Spencer, like Harrison, never attended college. See HH, "Education Out of School," *Boston Chronicle*, February 23, 1924, HP, in *HR*, 125–26, and see the appendix.

61. James, *Holding Aloft the Banner of Ethiopia*, 117–19, esp. 117–18.

62. "Aunt Mamie," interview; William E. Schmidt, "High School Days Now Would Tickle Tom Brown," *New York Times*, November 2, 1992, (hereafter *NYT*).

63. In the 1840s, the Danish colonial government implemented an "Edict of Free Compulsory Education for Slave Children" and compulsory education persisted after emancipation. See Lewisohn, *St. Croix*, 235; Guirty, *Sixtonian*, 76; and Hill, *Rise*, 53.

64. On Harrison's education see Joseph J. Boris, *Who's Who in Colored America: A Biographical Dictionary of Notable Living Persons of Negro Descent in America* (New York, 1927), 86; "Hubert Harrison Dies," 1; "A St. Croix Creole" [HH] to the editor, in *HR*, 240–41; Oscar Benson, "Literary Genius of Hubert Harrison," *New York News*, December 24, 1927; and "Aunt Mamie," interview. On education in St. Croix see Eva Lawaetz, "A Capsule History of St. Croix," 46; Boyer, *America's Virgin Islands*, 122; and E. J. Lawaetz, *St. Croix*, 205–6.

65. "Dr. Harrison's Rise as Orator Is Like Fiction," states that Harrison attended school for some time in St. Thomas. In HP-Sc 29, 141, Harrison wrote that he was "in St. Thomas in 1892." On March 11, 1892, a major celebration was held on St. Thomas and "every available boat from St. Croix was filled with Crucians who went over for the event." See Lewisohn, *St. Croix*, 339. On the labor protest see Hill, *Rise*, 65.

66. Daniel David Hamilton Jackson (b. September 23, 1884–1946) was selected as St. Croix's representative to go before the king of Denmark and the Danish parliament in 1915, and that year he put out the first issue of the *Herald*, a voice of the laboring and poor people. He then headed the January 1916 "general strike," which led to the first labor union in the Virgin Islands. In 1922 he won the first of many elections as an island legislator, and in 1931 he was elected judge of the Police Court of Christiansted. Karen C. Thurland, interview by author, June 15, 1985, Christiansted, St. Croix; Karen C. Thurland, "Black Moses [D. Hamilton Jackson]," *Virgin Islands Education Review* 1, no. 12 (November 1984): 2, 3, 21; Jensen, *From Serfdom to Fireburn*, 152–58; and C. E. Rappollee, Despatching Secretary, to Henry M. Hough, Governor, St. Thomas, Virgin Islands of the United States, "Report on activities of one D. Hamilton Jackson," February 10, 1923, RG 59, 811S.00/37, National Archives, Washington, D.C. In April 1921 Jackson wrote to Harrison and asked him to "to go out to the West Indies and lecture on the racial phases of the labor problem, as an introduction to the people of St. Croix." He wanted Harrison to associate permanently with him and his work. At that time Harrison was not a U.S. citizen. When they met again in New York in August 1921 Jackson again asked Harrison to return "to Santa Cruz" during the winter "for a three-months trial as a lecturer and field secretary of his labor union movement." Harrison did not go (and the reason why is not known). He did, however, provide Jackson with outline notes on the Liberty League, which he was resurrecting. See HD, April 13 and August 12, 1921.

67. In HH, "The Virgin Islands," *HR*, 244, Harrison commented that when the United States eventually did purchase the islands it was because of "the rise and potency" of the island's wartime "labor-movement as expressed mainly in the St. Croix

424 1. Crucian Roots

Labor Union which determined the planter-element in the islands to revive and support the movement for the transfer of the Virgin Islands to the United States." Elsewhere he wrote that "it was the success of this cooperative labor movement [led by Jackson] which, more than anything else, disposed the Danes to sell the islands, in order that resident whites could control their black labor problem in approved American fashion." See "A St. Croix Creole" [HH] to the editor, in *HR*, 240–41. For background on the decisive impact of Black labor unrest on Denmark's decision to sell the Virgin Islands, see Gregory R. La Motta, "Virgin Islanders and the Transfer," in *The Danish Presence and Legacy in the Virgin Islands*, ed. Svend E. Holsoe and John H. McCollum (Frederiksted: St. Croix Landmarks Society, 1993), 103–14; and Poul E. Olsen, "The View from Government House: Governor L. C. Helweg-Larsen and the Administration of the Danish West Indies 1888-1917," in *The Danish Presence and Legacy in the Virgin Islands*, ed. Svend E. Holsoe and John H. McCollum (Frederiksted: St. Croix Landmarks Society, 1993), 89–98.

68. Thurland, "Black Moses," 2, 3, 21; "A St. Croix Creole" [HH] to the editor, in *HR*, 240–41; Lewisohn, *St. Croix*, 359–60; E. J. Lawaetz, *St. Croix*, 210–14; and Guirty, *Sixtonian*, 70–74.

69. "A St. Croix Creole" [HH] to the editor, in *HR*, 240–41. Information on Wilford Jackson is based on Thurland, interview; Evelyn Richardson, interview by author, Frederiksted, St. Croix, June 14, 1985; Hill, *Rise*, 60; and Rappollee to Hough, February 10, 1923.

70. Communion Card of Hubert Henry Harrison [fragment], March 18, 1896, SJEC, HP; "Aunt Mamie," interview; N. Hall, *Slave Society*, 206; Tyson, telecom with author, February 10, 2008; and HH, "The Negro a Conservative: Christianity Still Enslaves the Mind of Those Whose Bodies It Has Long Held, Bound," *Truth Seeker* 41 (September 12, 1914): 583, in *HR*, 42–46.

71. "Dr. Harrison's Rise as Orator Is Like Fiction."

72. [HH] "To My Mother" (n.d., "about 1901"), handwritten, HP; death record of "Cecilia Collins," January 31, 1899, SJEC; "Aunt Mamie," interview; "Hubert Harrison Dies," 1; and HD, cover page.

73. "Aunt Mamie," interview; and Maldwyn Allen Jones, *American Immigration* (Chicago: University of Chicago Pres, 1960), 276–77. Harrison was listed on his naturalization papers as "white," which may indicate an error or may indicate a belief, by Harrison or someone processing the form, that a Black Crucian seeking naturalization might encounter additional difficulties, since "they have no 'allegiance' to forswear." (HH, "Petition for Naturalization Filed June 22, 1922, and approved September 26, 1922, Records of Naturalization, U.S. Department of Labor, Immigration and Naturalization Service, U.S. District Court, S.D., N.Y., 172 Docket No. 42659 and "A St. Croix Creole" [HH] to the editor, in *HR*, 240–41). The naturalization process was technically open to persons of African nativity or descent through 16 Stat. 256, which was passed on July 14, 1870. See Joel Buchwald, *Index to Naturalization Petitions*

of the United States District Court for the Eastern District of New York, 1865–1957: Records of District Courts of the United States Record Group 21 (Washington, D.C.: National Archives Trust Fund Board, National Archives and Record Administration, 1991), 3. On women who paved the way for other family members, see Louis J. Parascandola, ed., *"Look for Me All Around You": Anglophone Caribbean Immigrants in the Harlem Renaissance* (Detroit: Wayne State University Press, 2005), 9.

74. *HR*, 251. On the weather and economic conditions, see E. J. Lawaetz, *St. Croix*, 207, 330, 333, 432, 434–35, 437, 442; and W. Burghardt Turner and Joyce Moore Turner, eds., *Richard B. Moore, Caribbean Militant in Harlem: Collected Writings, 1920–1972* (Bloomington: University of Indiana Press, 1988), 4. On the possibility that he traveled in 1899, see "Peter Jackson Dying," *Journal*, 1899 [New York?], HP-Sc 1, 366. This clipping suggests that Harrison may have traveled abroad earlier than 1900. The clipping, however, may also be from 1900 or 1901 (since Jackson actually died on July 13, 1901, in Roma, Queensland, Australia, after several years of illness). See Tom Langley, *The Life of Peter Jackson: Champion of Australia* (Leicester, U.K.: Lance Harvey, 1974), 77. A possible, but unlikely, brief first stay in New York in 1899 is suggested by "H. H. Harrison, Colored Orator to Speak Here," *New Brunswick (N.J.) Times*, August 29, 1913, which says that "Mr. Harrison came here from the West Indies about 14 years ago." On Rogers's acceptance of the 1900 arrival date see Rogers, *WGMC*, 2:433. It should be noted that Rogers witnessed Harrison's 1922 "Petition for Naturalization" and, at times, lived with Harrison's family (HH, "Petition for Naturalization"; and A. Richardson and Harrison, interview).

75. "Dr. Harrison's Rise as Orator Is Like Fiction"; "A St. Croix Creole" [HH] to the editor, in *HR*, 240–41; J. Domminick Simmons, interview by William Harrison, [New York], February 23, 1951, in William Harrison Notebook (on Glasgow); and Thurland, interview (on Jackson). On Harrison's education also see "Hubert Harrison Dies," 1; and Benson, "Literary Genius of Hubert Harrison." On the schools and teachers see Eva Lawaetz, "A Capsule History of St. Croix," 46; E. J. Lawaetz, *St. Croix*, 204; and U.S. Department of Commerce, *Census, 1917*, 96.

76. The "deepened his interest" quotation is from "Hubert Harrison Dies," 1, and is similar to one in "Dr. Harrison's Rise as Orator Is Like Fiction." An editor's introduction in the *Pittsburgh Courier*, January 29, 1927, sec. 2, p. 7, mentions the countries. Benson, "Literary Genius of Hubert Harrison," and Rogers, *WGMC*, 2:433, also discuss the "Wanderjahre." William Harrison thought that his father may have been a seaman (A. Richardson and Harrison, interview).

77. Norman J. Brouwer, curator of ships and marine historian, South Street Seaport Museum Library, New York, telephone conversation followed by an interview by author, July 10, 1997, New York City, confirmed the starting age for cabin boys and said such work was indeed possible for Harrison. Claude McKay wrote that Harrison's claim that he had lived in Denmark and Japan was false. See Claude McKay, *A Long Way from Home: An Autobiography*, intro. St. Clair Drake (1937; New York:

Harcourt Brace & World, 1970), 41–42, 67; and Wayne F. Cooper, *Claude McKay: Rebel Sojourner in the Harlem Renaissance: A Biography* (Baton Rouge: Louisiana State University Press, 1987), 107–10.

78. "Peter Jackson Dying"; *WGMC*, 2:554; Langley, *Life of Peter Jackson*, 77; and Edna Rust and Art Rust Jr., *Art Rust's Illustrated History of the Black Athlete* (Garden City, N.Y.: Doubleday, 1985), 136–37, on Fleisher's assessment.

79. "Dr. Harrison's Rise as Orator Is Like Fiction." and HH, "Petition for Naturalization" use the 1900 date. Information from the September 19, 1900, *Danish West-Indian* was provided in George F. Tyson to author, February 21, 2008, and the *Madiana* departure and arrival times can be found in *New York Times*, September 22, 1900, 16. Reid, *Negro Immigrant*, 235, 240, discusses the immigration figures, and "Aunt Mamie," interview, discusses her work. The *Roraima* was a 340-foot iron haul steamship that transported cargo and passengers. A trip from St. Croix to New York took about five days in 1900, and the ship's next scheduled sailing, after the September 21 arrival date cited by Harrison, was on September 25 for Bermuda. The *Roraima* sank in the harbor at St. Pierre, Martinique, in the devastating volcano eruption of May 8, 1902, which killed more than 29,000 people (Brouwer, telephone conversation and interview; *Lloyd's Register of Shipping, 1900–1901*, Steamers, 492; Lewisohn, *St. Croix*, 339; and *NYT*, September 23, 1900). The *Madiana* was wrecked on a coral reef near Hamilton, Bermuda on February 10, 1903. See "All Passengers on the Madiana Saved," *Boston Globe*, February 11, 1903, 1; and "Madiana Passengers Brought Back Here," *New York Times*, February 17, 1903, 16. The possibility exists that Harrison arrived in the United States as a stowaway. Passenger lists for the Port of New York for 1899 through 1903 on file at the New York Public Library were checked, and Harrison's name was not found.

80. "Aunt Mamie," interview, discusses his arrival. Gilbert Osofsky, *Harlem: The Making of a Ghetto, Negro New York, 1890–1930*, 2nd. ed. (1963; New York: Harper and Row, 1971), 12, discusses the San Juan Hill area. E. J. Lawaetz, *St. Croix*, 207, discusses Roosevelt's support for the purchase. Richard B. Sherman, *The Republican Party and Black America from McKinley to Hoover, 1896–1933* (Charlottesville: University of Virginia Press, 1973), 23–24, points out that Roosevelt actually viewed African Americans as inferior to "whites" and fit for industrial work and that he disparaged their performance in the Spanish-American War (57). On Brownsville, see Anne J. Lane, *The Brownsville Affair: National Crisis and Black Reaction* (Port Washington, N.Y.: National University Publications, Kennikat Press, 1971), 6–7, 12–24, 69–130, 164; and "Soldiers Discharged," *New York Age*, November 8, 1906, 1.

81. U.S. Department of Commerce, *Census, 1917*, 41 discusses the population decrease. Regarding New York, Eugene Kinckle Jones, "Negro Migration in New York State," *Opportunity* 4, no. 37 (January 1926): 8, later pointed out that "the cosmopolitanism of the city attracts the Negro" and that its "heterogeneity" generated "an atmosphere of freedom and democracy." Boyer, *America's Virgin Islands*, 165, says twenty thousand Virgin Islanders lived in Harlem by 1930, a number almost equal to

the island population. On Blyden, see Hollis R. Lynch, *Edward Wilmot Blyden: Pan Negro Patriot, 1832–1912* (1967; New York: Oxford University Press, 1970), 4; and Rogers, *WGMC*, 2:518–20. Harrison had two obituaries of Blyden in his scrapbooks: "Liberia's Great Man Dead," *New York Evening Post*, February 8, 1912, HP-Sc 1; and "Dr. Blyden Dead," *New York Age*, February 15, 1912, HP-Sc 1. Years later, Harrison listed works by Blyden in his recommended reading lists. See HH, "A Few Books," *Boston Chronicle*, March 1, 1924, HP; and [HH], "Our Little Library," *New Negro*, n.s., 4, no. 2 (October 1919): 16. In 1915 Harrison obtained Edward Wilmot Blyden, *African Life and Customs* (London, 1905), HP.

82. HH, The Virgin Islands," in *HR*, 244; and HH, "Prejudice Growing Less," *PC*, 251. Earlier he defined the character of the early immigrants as that of "the adventurous middle class including students, doctors, and lawyers" and the later immigration as "a peasant movement, predominantly . . . related to the downfall of the sugar industry." See [HH], "The West Indian in the United States," [notes for a lecture], March 30, 1924, 1, HP. Harrison lists as examples of the first group York Russell, Dr. Tunnell, Rev. Everard W. Daniel, Arthur Schomburg, and Bert Williams.

83. Hill, *Rise*, 54.

84. The general characteristics of the West Indian immigrant are drawn from Reid, *Negro Immigrant*, 77–92, which also discusses the particular reaction of West Indians to U.S. racism (111–12) and the boldness of the move from one's homeland (221). G. James Fleming, to author, September 4, 1983, emphasizes that Harrison "was self-educated as many West Indians were during his generation." Winston James discusses how, in general, "Caribbean migrants were not only more literate than Afro-Americans, they were more literate than white Americans, whether foreign-born or native." He also discusses their "extraordinary love of books, education, and the written word," a "similar attachment to the spoken word," and other characteristics. See James, *Holding Aloft*, 50–91, 258–59, quotations at 78. Frank Hercules, *American Society and Black Revolution* (New York: Harcourt Brace Jovanovich, 1972), 27–28, states, "The boldness of the black West Indian was the result of their relative freedom from the terror, psychological no less than physical, to which the black Americans were subjected by white power. The black West Indians experienced the terror when they arrived in America and it was the very unfamiliarity of the experience that shocked and stung them."

85. Rogers, *WGMC*, 2:439. In J. A. Rogers, *As Nature Leads* (n.p., 1919), 129–35, Rogers describes "handicaps" or "effects of color prejudice."

2. Self-Education, Early Writings, and the Lyceums (1900–1907)

1. HH, "Declaration of Intention [to Naturalize]," No. 114310, June 22, 1915, Records of Naturalization, U.S. Department of Labor, Naturalization Service, U.S.

District Court, S.D., N.Y., 172 Docket No. 42659, on height and weight; J. A. Rogers, *WGMC*, 2:437, on Harrison's head; HD, October 13, 1907, HP, on the joking; Richard B. Moore, "Harrison, Hubert Henry," in Rayford W. Logan and Michael R. Winston, eds., *Dictionary of American Negro Biography* (New York: W. W. Norton, 1982), 292–93, esp. 293 on facial features; and Claude McKay, *A Long Way From Home: An Autobiography*, intro. St. Clair Drake (1937; New York: Harcourt Brace & World, 1970), 41.

2. James Weldon Johnson, *Black Manhattan* (1930; New York: Atheneum, 1977), 127; J. G. Speed, "The Negro in New York," *Harper's Weekly*, December 22, 1900, in Allan Schoener, ed., *Harlem on My Mind: Cultural Capital of Black America, 1900–1968* (New York: Random House, 1968), 19–21, 20. See also Gilbert Osofsky, *Harlem: The Making of a Ghetto, Negro New York, 1890–1930* (1963; New York: Harper and Row, 1971), 46–52, esp. 48.

3. Marsha Hurst Hiller, "Race Politics in New York City, 1890–1930" (Ph.D. diss., Columbia University, 1972), 74; Seth M. Scheiner, *Negro Mecca: A History of the Negro in New York, 1865–1920* (New York: New York University Press, 1965), 24–32, 193, 221–22; and Osofsky, *Harlem*, 159–62.

4. The description of the area is based on Scheiner, *Negro Mecca*, 19, 27 ("worst"), 32; Florette Henri, *Black Migration: Movement North, 1900–1920* (Garden City, N.Y.: Anchor Press/Doubleday, 1975), 88; and M. C. Brooks, "The San Juan Hill Charge," *New York Evening Post*, February 19, 1911, letter, HP-Scrapbook, 1:364 (hereafter HP-Sc).

5. Charles Lionel Franklin, *The Negro Labor Unionist of New York* (New York: Columbia University Press, 1936), 71; and Henri, *Black Migration*, 138, 141.

6. HH, "Prejudice Growing Less and Co-Operation More, Says Student of Question," *Pittsburgh Courier*, January 29, 1927, sec. 2, p. 7 (hereafter *PC*), in *HR*, 250–53.

7. Educational opportunities are discussed in Scheiner, *Negro Mecca*, 59, 176, 179; Osofsky, *Harlem*, 36; and W. E. B. Du Bois, "Blessed Discrimination," *Crisis* 5 (February 1913), in Daniel Walden, ed. and intro., *W. E. B. Du Bois: The Crisis Writings* (Greenwich, Conn.: Fawcett, 1972), 92–95, esp. 92.

8. "Aunt Mamie," interview by William Harrison, February 1, 1951, William Harrison Notebook, HP; *WGMC*, 2:611; Joseph J. Boris, *Who's Who in Colored America: A Biographical Dictionary of Notable Living Persons of Negro Descent in America* (New York: Who's Who in Colored America, 1927), 86; and "Garvey Aid and Author Passes Away," *Chicago Defender*, December 24, 1927, sec. 1, p. 2 (hereafter *CD*).

9. "Speaker's Medal to Negro Student: The Board of Education Finds a Genius in a West Indian Night Pupil," *New York World*, April 5, 1903, sec. 1, p. 10; and "Evening School Prizes Awarded," New York *Commercial Advertiser*, April 1, 1903, p. 17. The school may have been PS 67 at 120 W. Forty-sixth Street.

10. Carr's comments appear in "Speaker's Medal," 10; Oscar Benson, "Literary Genius of Hubert Harrison," *New York News*, December 24, 1927 (hereafter *NYN*);

and "Who Is Hubert Harrison?" handout card, c. November 1920, HP. See also *New York Age*, February 10, 1910, 2 (hereafter *NYA*).

11. HD, April 27, 1908. On the residences, see "Speaker's Medal," 10; HH to the editor, "A Negro on Chicken Stealing," *New York Times*, December 11, 1904, 6 (hereafter *NYT*); and "Aunt Mamie," interview.

12. "Celebrated Harlem Mass Leader Dies," *NYN*, December 24, 1927. For the statistics, see Francis Blascoer, *Colored School Children in New York* (1915; New York: Negro Universities Press, 1970), 111. HD, February 9, 1909, indicates that Harrison visited DeWitt Clinton Evening High School to see his old Latin teacher, Mr. White, who requested that he give a short talk to the class. Joan Hubbard, records secretary, Martin Luther King, Jr. H. S., New York, to author, February 12, 1993, writes that the New York City Board of Education was not able to locate records on Harrison and that many such records were missing.

13. HD, June 7 and November 23, 1908. In the *New York News* in 1915 Harrison specifically criticized those who put on such "false airs." In his case it appears that economic survival, not psychological self-aggrandizement, was the motivating factor. When he used the "Dr." title in 1919 he had four children and no regular source of income. See HH, "Our Civic Corner," September 2 and 9, 1915, *NYN*, HP; "Dr. Hubert Harrison" [to talk on "Negro History and Negro Education"], *Richmond Planet*, April 30, 1919, HP-Sc 34 (which claims that he had a "Ph.D. from the University of Copenhagen"); HH, "With Our Contributing Editor," *Negro World*, December 24, 1921, 10; and "Celebrated Harlem Mass Leader Dies."

14. Rogers, *WGMC*, 2:433; and HD, May 23, 1908. Winston James, "Explaining Afro-Caribbean Social Mobility in the United States: Beyond the Sowell Thesis," *Comparative Studies in Society and History* 44, no. 2 (April 2002): 218–62, esp. 241–44 (on Caribbean immigrants). John E. Bruce to HH, April 20, 1906, HP and HD, May 20, 1908 (unemployed period). On the autodidacts, including Herbert Spencer, Toussaint-Louverture, Abraham Lincoln, Frederick Douglass, and the historian Henry Thomas Buckle, see HH, "Education Out of School," *Boston Chronicle*, February 23, 1924, HP, in *HR*, 125–26. For Harrison's critical views on education and educators see HH, "The Negro a Conservative: Christianity Still Enslaves the Minds of Those Whose Bodies It Has Long Held Bound," *Truth Seeker* 41, no. 37 (September 12, 1914): 583, in *HR*, 42–46; HH, "The Voice of the Negro: *The Everlasting Stain*—by Kelly Miller"; and HH, "Education and the Race" in *HR*, 122–24, esp. 123. Perhaps the experience (some thirty years after Harrison) of Theodore W. Allen, another autodidactic, anti-white-supremacist, proletarian intellectual is instructive. Allen, according to his close friend Linda Vidinha, reportedly went to college for one day and promptly left saying that "it was too confining." Like Harrison, Allen lived his life in poverty but tirelessly pursued his intellectual interests, educational work, and social activism. Linda Vidinha, telecon with author, June 28, 2007.

15. Benson, "Literary Genius of Hubert Harrison"; Hodge Kirnon, "Hubert Harrison," *Negro World*, December 27, 1927; and Ivan Lorand to author, October 22, 1983.

16. Kirnon, "Hubert Harrison," discusses Harrison's method. One the scrapbooks see HP-Sc, passim.

17. HP-Sc 11, 9, 15, 18, 29.

18. HD, September 18, 1907.

19. HD, passim and HP-Sc, passim. For a Harrison self-appraisal see the appendix.

20. HD, May 20, 1908, in which he transcribes his letter to Frances Reynolds Keyser. In a discussion following a 1912 lecture Harrison said, according to W. A. Moss, "that personally he [Harrison] was an atheist, because he had applied his scientific knowledge to religion and found it would not stand the test" (W. A. Moss to the editor, "Another Matter Now," *New York Call*, c. May 24, 1912, HP-Sc 32). Later that year Harrison described himself as an "agnostic" in HH, "In Vigorous Condemnation," *New York Call*, November 19, 1912, 6.

21. HD, May 20, 1908. Thomas Paine, *The Age of Reason* (1794), intro. Philip S. Foner (1948; Secaucus: Citadel Press, N.J., 1974), 34–36, 46, 47 ("terrify"), 50, and 190 ("forgeries"). See also Gordon Stein, ed., *An Anthology of Atheism and Rationalism* (Buffalo, N.Y.: Prometheus Books, 1980), 125.

22. HD, May 20, 1908.

23. HH, "Paine's Place in the Deistical Movement," *Truth Seeker* 38, no. 6 (February 11, 1911), 87–88, in *HR*, 40–42, esp. 40.

24. HD, May 20, 1908.

25. HD, May 20, 1908.

26. HD, May 20, 1908.

27. HD, May 20, 1908. Pat Shipman, *The Evolution of Racism: Human Differences and the Use and Abuse of Science* (New York: Simon and Schuster, 1994), 40–41, speaks of Huxley's Harrison-like "willingness to test and weigh up any and all beliefs—however sacred—on the scales of intellect."

28. HD, May 20, 1908; and Thomas Henry Huxley, "Agnosticism," *Nineteenth Century* (February 1889): v, in *An Anthology of Atheism and Rationalism*, ed. Gordon Stein (Buffalo, N.Y.: Prometheus Books, 1980), 42–45, esp. 43–44.

29. HD, November 11, 1907.

30. HD, November 11, 1907.

31. HD, October 22, 1907, indicates that over four years later he still had not finished the suicide essay.

32. HD, March 7, 1908.

33. Karl Marx, "Toward the Critique of Hegel's Philosophy of Right," in *Marx and Engels: Basic Writings on Philosophy and Politics*, ed. Lewis S. Feuer (Garden City, N.Y.: Doubleday, 1959), 262–66, esp. 262.

34. HH, "Opening the Doors," *Boston Chronicle*, April 5, 1924, HP.

35. HH, "A Negro on Lynching," *NYT*, June 28, 1903; Yohuru R. Williams, "Permission to Hate: Delaware, Lynching, and the Culture of Violence in America," *Journal of Black Studies* 32, no. 1 (September 2001): 3–29, esp. 3–4; and "Lynchings Since January 1," *NYT*, June 24, 1903.

36. Williams, "Permission to Hate," 3; "Mob Menaces a Negro," *NYT*, June 22, 1903; "Negro Murderer is Burned at Stake," *NYT*, June 23, 1903; *NYT*, May 23, 1908; and "One Arrest Made for Delaware Lynching," *NYT*, June 24, 1903.

37. HH, "A Negro on Lynching," 8; and S.H.B., "The Law's Delay," *NYT*, June 24, 1903 (the *Times* has "overflow," but it is likely that Harrison wrote "overthrow"). In the text, and in ensuing Harrison articles, "Negro" is capitalized as Harrison would have written it. It appeared with a small "n" in the *Times*, consistent with that paper's editorial policy until March 7, 1930, when it changed to capital "N" as an "act in recognition of [Negro] racial self-respect." See "'Negro' with a Capital 'N,'" *NYT*, March 7, 1930. On Harrison's opposition to the small "n," see HH, "The Real Negro Problem," in *The Negro and the Nation* (New York: Cosmo-Advocate, 1917), 30–40, esp. 35–36. Consistent with Harrison's use of the word "shock," Theodore W. Allen, *The Invention of the White Race*, 2 vols. (New York: Verso, 1994–1997), vol. 1: *Racial Oppression and Social Control*, 1:113, writes that early-twentieth-century Caribbean immigrants to the United States "experienced the 'cultural shock' of the transition from the class-based 'tri-partite social order' with its African-Caribbean 'colored' intermediate stratum, to the white-supremacist social order in the United States."

38. George E. Macdonald, *Fifty Years of Freethought: Story of the Truth Seeker from 1875*, 2 vols. (New York: The Truth Seeker Company, 1931), 2:230–31; "Anarchists are Raided," *NYT*, October 24, 1903; "Turner as a Prisoner," *NYT*, December 6, 1903; "Mass Meeting Against Law Holding Turner," *NYT*, December 4, 1903; and "H. H. Harrison, Colored Orator to Speak Here," *New Brunswick* (N.J.) *Times*, August 29, 1913. The quoted legislation is available online at http://149.101.23.2/graphics/shared/aboutus/statistics/legishist/460.htm.

39. "Mass Meeting Against Law Holding Turner"; Macdonald, *Fifty Years*, 2:230–32; and HH, "The Turner Mass Meeting: A Socialist's Defense of Opinions Expressed by Sympathizers with the British 'Philosophic Anarchist,'" letter to the editor, *NYT*, December 13, 1903.

40. HH, "The Turner Mass Meeting"; and HH, "In Defense of Anarchy," *NYT*, December 5, 1903.

41. HH, "The Turner Mass Meeting."

42. HH, "The Russian Menace," letter to the editor, *NYT*, January 4, 1904.

43. HH, "The Russian Menace."

44. HH, "The Russian Menace." HH, "Irony," December 23, 1920, HP, includes the irony quotes. See also Leonard Baskin, *Jonathan Swift: A Modest Proposal* (New York: Grossman, 1969).

45. HH, "Gov. Vardaman's Views," letter to the editor, *NYT*, February 4, 1904.

46. HH, "Gov. Vardaman's Views."

47. "Gamecocks in New Jersey," *NYT*, November 28, 1904; HH, "A Negro on Chicken Stealing: Assails the Statement That His Race Is Addicted to Vice," *NYT*, December 11, 1904; and Rayford W. Logan, *The Betrayal of the Negro: From Rutherford B. Hayes to Woodrow Wilson*, new enlarged ed., originally published as *The Negro in American Thought and Life: The Nadir, 1877–1901* (1954; New York: Macmillan, 1970), 245.

48. HH, "A Negro on Chicken Stealing."

49. HH, letter to the editor, untitled, *NYT*, July 20, 1907.

50. HD, November 25, 1907.

51. On the glamour aspect, see Mark Sullivan, *Our Times: 1900–1925*, 6 vols. (1927; New York: Scribner's, 1971) 2:95. On tensions, see Ashley L. Totten to the editor, *Amsterdam News*, August 26, 1911, HP-Sc 4, p. 346, and "Rubberneck Reviews," *Amsterdam News*, March 23, 1912, HP-Sc 4, p. 348.

52. *NYA*, December 31, 1908, 3; "St. Benedict the Moor," *NYA*, April 8, 1909, 3; "Big Church Celebration," *NYA*, November 23, 1911, 1, 2; "St. Benedict, the Moor," *NYA*, April 29, 1909, 3; and Osofsky, *Harlem*, 15, 219n. 68.

53. See HH, "One Decade of Harlem's Mental Growth" [notes], n.p., n.d., HP and "Celebrated Harlem Mass Leader Dies." See also "A S" (Arthur Schomburg) to John E. Bruce, January 17, 1917, box 2, AL, Ms. 282, John E. Bruce Papers, SCRBC; HH, "Prejudice Growing Less and Co-Operation More Says Student of Question," *Pittsburgh Courier*, January 29, 1927, pt. 2, p. 7, in *HR*, 250–53; and *NYA*, December 31, 1908, 3.

54. HH, "Politics and Personality," *Voice*, August 28, 1917, HP.

55. "Aunt Mamie," interview.

56. "A S" (Schomburg) to Bruce, January 17, 1917; and Rogers, *WGMC*, 2:439.

57. *Catholic News*, April 22, 1905, and [Announcement], June 12, 1905, both in HP-Sc 35; "Bureau of Negro Missions," *Washington Post*, May 6, 1905; and "Headed by Cardinal," *Washington Post*, November 29, 1906.

58. Anderson, *This Was Harlem*, 24; Osofsky, *Harlem*, 15, 50, 219n. 68; and "Dr. Brooks' Sermon on Race Riots," *NYA*, August 10, 1905, 4.

59. On St. Mark's Lyceum activities, see the *New York Age* on the following dates: April 13 and August 10, 1905, March 1 and 8, April 5, September 6 and 10, October 8 and 11, 1906; November 7 and December 5, 1907; June 25, July 2, November 12, 19, and 26, 1908; January 28 and April 8, 1909; December 23 and 30, 1909; January 6, February 10 and 24, April 7, October 13, November 3 and 10, 1910; June 29, 1911 and March 15, 1917.

60. "St. Mark's Lyceum Opens," *NYA*, September 14, 1905, 1; HD, September 28, 1914; "Annual Union Services of New York City Churches," *NYA*, December 5, 1907, 1; and John E. Robinson to HH, October 20, 1921, HP.

61. W. D. Howells to the editor [HH], *The Union of St. Marks*, February 28, 1906, HP; and "New York City News," *NYA*, February 22 and March 1, 1906, pp. 3, 5.

62. HD, October 27, 1907.

63. HD, October 27, 1907, and February 11 and March 13, 1908; Thomas Carlyle, "Burns," in *Critical and Miscellaneous Essays: Collected and Republished*, 7 vols. (1839, 1869: London: Chapman and Hall?, 1872) 2:395; and *The Complete Works of Robert Burns* (Boston, c. 1871), HP.

64. "New York City News," *NYA*, March 8, 1906, 3; "Dr. Bulkley Addresses St. Mark's Lyceum," *NYA*, April 5, 1906, 8; and "Manhattan and Bronx," *NYA*, September 6, 1906, 6.

65. HD, February 7, September 13, November 15 and 19, and December 10, 1908; "St. Mark's Lyceum," *NYA*, September 10, 1908, 3, and November 19, 1908, 3; and "Rev. Powell at St. Mark's," *NYA*, December 23, 1909, 2. Information on John Dotha Jones is based on Hollee Haswell, Curator of Columbiana, Columbia University, telecon with author, October 27, 1993, and Polly McLean, in-person conversation, July 25, 2007.

66. HD, October 22, 1907.

67. HD, October 22, 1907.

68. HD, February 7; and "St. Mark's Lyceum," *NYA*, September 10, 1908, 3.

69. HD, December 10 and 12, 1908; "St. Mark's Lyceum," *NYA*, December 17, 1908, 3.

70. George Young to the editor, "St. Mark's Veteran Protests," *NYA*, December 16, 1909, 4; and Marie Jackson Stuart to the editor, "Another St. Mark's Veteran Protests to the Editor," *NYA*, December 23, 1909, 2. After Harrison's death, according to his daughter Aida, Young obtained a number of his books. Young later sold many books to the New York Public Library.

71. "St. Mark's Lyceum," *NYA*, April 8, 1909, 3, and April 15, 1909, 3; "Ask Negro Women to Be Suffragists," *NYA*, February 2, 1910, 1; and "Y.M.C.A. Notes," *NYA*, December 8, 1910, 1.

72. [HH], [Notes on Marcus Garvey]; HD and Elinor Des Verney Sinnette, *Arthur Alfonso Schomburg, Black Bibliophile and Curator: A Biography* (Detroit: Wayne State University Press, 1989), 30, 247.

73. Bruce to HH, April 20, 1906; HD, November 25, 1907, September 28, 1914.

74. Bruce to Harrison, April 20, 1906; and HD, December 10, 1907. Harrison was unable to get his twenty-three-page rewrite on St. Croix published.

75. HH to the editor, *NYT*, April 13 and 27, 1907; and Hildegarde Hawthorne, "Women in All Ages," *NYT*, April 6, 1907.

76. HH to the editor, April 13, 1907, and Mary Hamlin Ashman to the editor, *NYT*, April 20, 1907.

77. HH to the editor, *NYT*, April 27, 1907. In HH, "Book-Reviewing as a Fine Art," n.p. (notes, c. 1907), HP, he cites as examples of the first three kinds of criticism: Robert G. Ingersoll's lecture on Shakespeare; Dionysius Cassius Longinus on the sublime, particularly the chapters on Sappho's poetry; and Thomas Carlyle's essay on Burns. M.U.O., letter to the editor, "'M.G.P.R.' Reviews," *NYT*, May 18, 1907.

78. HH to the editor, *NYT*, April 27, 1907.

79. HH to the editor, *NYT*, April 27, 1907; and *WGMC*, 2:617.

80. HH to the editor, "The Writing of English," *NYT*, September 14, 1907, and "On Writing English," *NYT*, September 7, 1907.

81. HD, January 29, 1908, and March 14, 1908.

82. HD, December 10, 1907.

83. HD, March 7, 1908. Later, in his personal copy of *The Essays of Arthur Schopenhauer*, trans. by Saunders T. Bailey (New York, n.d. c. 1914), HP, received on May 24, 1918, on sec. 1, p. 55, Harrison wrote: "The key will be found in the deeper fact that the I-ness of each I is only apparent and superficial. We are not individuals, but portions of a We."

84. HD, April 11, 1908.

3. In Full-Touch with the *Life* of My People (1907–1909)

1. *WGMC*, 2:432–42, esp. 433; and John E. Bruce to "My dear friend [HH] Harrison," October 16, 1907, HP. Harrison's postal records are available at "Hubert Henry Harrison," National Personnel Records Center, USPS, St. Louis, Mo. (hereafter NPRC). Florette Henri, *Black Migration: Movement North, 1900–1920* (Garden City, N.Y.: Anchor Press/Doubleday, 1975), 167, cites 175 to 180 Black New York City postal workers in 1910. While his original score on the postal entrance exam has not been found, a later score was exceptional: sorting-34, following instruction-64, general-98, total 328. See HH "Report of Ratings—Clerk Carrier Examination," September 17, 1927, HP.

2. John Walsh and Garth Mangum, *Labor Struggle in the Post Office: From Selective Lobbying to Collective Bargaining* (Armonk, N.Y.: M. E. Sharpe, 1992), 48; Sterling D. Spero, *The Labor Movement in a Government Industry* (1927; reprint, New York: Arno Press, 1971), 114; and Sterling D. Spero, *Government as Employer* (New York: Remsen Press, 1948), 122.

3. *WGMC*, 2:433.

4. HD, September 23, 1907.

5. HD, September 20 and October 15, 1907. On the strike, see "Cuba Strike More Serious," *New York Times*, October 3, 1907 (hereafter *NYT*), and on the Cuban party, see *GP*, 4:902n. 5. Serra is mentioned in Winston James, "Afro–Puerto Rican Radicalism in the United States: Reflections on the Political Trajectories of Arturo Schomburg and Jesús Colón," *Centro de Estudios Puertorriqueños* 7, no. 2 (Spring 1996): 92–127; esp. 23n. 53.

6. HD, October 12 and 13, November 25, and December 8, 1907.

7. HD, September 23, 1907. On "egotism" see the appendix.

8. HD, March 10, 1908.

9. HD, November 25, December 1, and December 8, 1907.

10. On November 15, 1908, Harrison smoked his "*last* pipe . . . and threw the pipe through the window." However, in April 1921 he admitted he was "still a confirmed smoker." See HD, November 15, 1908. On the "chronic appendicitis," see State of New York, Department of Health of the City of New York, Bureau of Records, Standard Certificate of Death, Register No. 28066, Bellevue Hospital, December 17, 1927; on the vertigo see *WGMC*, 2:437; and on the nervous condition see HD, March 25, 1919, and March 19, 1921.

11. HD, February 17, 1908, discusses the Anderson correspondence.

12. "Hubert Henry Harrison," NPRC.

13. HH, "Postal Department Is Made Goat of All Other Federal Business," *New York Call*, November 6, 1911, HP (hereafter *NYC*), and "Postal Clerks Not Protected by Civil Service From Persecution," *NYC*, November 7, 1911, HP.

14. HH, "Postal Clerks Not Protected."

15. HH, "Postal Clerks Not Protected."

16. "H. H." [HH], "A 'Cheap' Administration," *Negro World*, May 29, 1920, HP-Scrapbook B (hereafter HP-Sc).

17. On Harrison's addresses, see HH to the editor, *NYT*, April 13 and 27, 1907; HD, January 20 and 29 and June 15, 1908; and "Hubert Henry Harrison," NPRC. On Harlem, see Gilbert Osofsky, *Harlem: The Making of a Ghetto; Negro New York, 1890–1930* (1963; New York: Harper and Row, 1971), 87; "Becoming a Colored Section," *NYA*, January 19, 1911, 8; "20,000 Negroes Live in Harlem," *NYA*, May 11, 1911, 1; Ira Katznelson, *Black Men, White Cities: Race, Politics, and Migration in the United States, 1900–30, and Britain, 1948–68* (1973; Chicago: University of Chicago Press, 1976), 68–73; and Seth M. Scheiner, *Negro Mecca: A History of the Negro in New York, 1865–1920* (New York: New York University Press, 1965), 63–65. Harrison later lived at 570 and 646 Lenox Avenue.

18. Elinor Des Verney Sinnette, *Arthur Alfonso Schomburg, Black Bibliophile and Curator: A Biography* (Detroit: New York Public Library and Wayne State University Press, 1989), 28, 34, 38, 42 and Ralph Leroy Crowder, *John Edward Bruce: Politician, Journalist, and Self-Trained Historian* (New York: New York University Press, 2004), 113, 117.

19. HD, November 7, 1907; and "Organizing Race Hatred," *NYT*, October 21, 1907. Harrison's article on Fortune has not been located.

20. HD, October 13, 1907. Aida Richardson, interview by author, July 10, 1991, mentioned Forrester as godmother.

21. Booker T. Washington, "Atlanta Exposition Address," in *Black Protest: History Documents and Analyses 1619 to the Present*, ed. Joanne Grant, 2nd ed. (New York: Fawcett Premier, 1968), 195–99, esp. 196; W. E. B. Du Bois, "Of Mr. Booker T. Washington and Others," in *The Souls of Black Folk: Essays and Sketches* (1903; New York: Washington Square Press Edition, 1970), 34–48, esp. 42; and Herbert A. Aptheker, ed., *A Documentary History of the Negro People in the United States* (New York: Citadel Press, 1951), 2:900–901.

22. HD, October 13, 1907. On the craniological measurements see Stephen Jay Gould, *The Mismeasure of Man* (New York: W. W. Norton, 1981), 77–79; and Idus A. Newby, *Jim Crow's Defense: Anti-Negro Thought in America, 1900–1930* (Baton Rouge: Louisiana State University Press, 1965), 38. Harrison expresses disdain for the view "that certain craniological peculiarities would prevent them [Black people] from assimilating the learning and culture of Europe" in HH, "The Negro and Socialism: 1—the Negro Problem Stated," *NYC*, November 28, 1911, 6, in *HR*, 52–55.

23. HD, October 13, 1907.

24. HD, November 9 and 11, 1907.

25. HD, November 11, 1907. On Williana Jones (later Burroughs), see "Williana Burroughs Laid to Rest in Simple Ceremony," *People's Voice*, January 5, 1946, 9; and "Williana Burroughs," Freedom of Information/Privacy Acts, file 1060605-000, January 28, 2007, Federal Bureau of Investigation, Washington, D.C., which was kindly shared with me by Romy Taylor.

26. HD, November 11, 1907.

27. HD, November 11, 1907.

28. HD, November 11, 1907.

29. "White Rose Mission Settlement," *NYA*, July 6, 1905, 6. On Harrison at the White Rose Home, see "Special Notice" [advertisement re HH], *NYC* [c. 1912 ?], HP-Sc 32 and HD, January 29, 1908. On the home, see Floris Barnett Cash, "Radicals or Realists: African American Women and the Settlement House Spirit in New York City," *Afro-Americans in New York Life and History* 15, no. 1 (January 1991): 7–17, esp. 7–10 and 13; and Floris Barnett Cash, "White Rose Mission, New York City," in *Black Women in America: An Historical Perspective*, ed. Darlene Clark Hine, Elsa Barkley Brown, and Rosalyn Terborg-Penn, 2 vols. (Bloomington: Indiana University Press, 1993), 2:1258–59.

30. Mary McLeod Bethune, "A Tribute to My Friend and Co-Worker Frances Reynolds Keyser," in *Lifting as They Climb: The National Association of Colored Women*, by Elizabeth Lindsay Davis (The National Association of Colored Women, 1933), 213–15, esp. 213. On Keyser, see Cash, "Radicals or Realists," 7–10, 13, and 30n. 16; Charles Flint Kellogg, *NAACP: A History of the National Association for the Advancement of Colored People, 1909–1920* (1967; Baltimore, Md.: Johns Hopkins University Press, 1973), 1:47–48, 61, 304, 306; Rackham Holt, *Mary McLeod Bethune: A Biography* (Garden City, N.Y.: Doubleday, Doran, 1964), 102–4; and Elaine M. Smith, "Bethune, Mary McLeod," in *Notable Black American Women*, ed. Jessie Carney Smith (Detroit: Gale Research, 1992), 86–92, esp. 87.

31. HD, January 1, 1909.

32. HD, January 17, 1909.

33. On Harrison's involvement see "Special Notice," *NYC* [c. 1912?]. See also "Work of the Colored Y . . . Membership 10,000," *NYA*, December 30, 1909, 1.

34. HD, October 12 and 22, 1907, and January 1, 1909.

35. HD, January 30 [31], 1908.

36. "Manhattan Y.M.C.A.," *NYA*, November 12, 1908, 3; and "Y.M.C.A.," *NYA*, December 3, 1908, 3.

37. "Y.M.C.A.," *NYA*, December 10, 1908, 3; and HD, December 15, 1908.

38. HD, November 25, 1907. There is no further record of this proposed book.

39. HD, September 23, and October 13, and November 25, 1907.

40. HD, November 25, 1907.

41. A quite different approach was taken by W. E. B. Du Bois. David Levering Lewis describes how Du Bois "sedulously invented, molded and masked" his life. Du Bois, according to Lewis, "suggests he had little knowledge of the African-American community, the newcomer migrants, freed slaves from the South, in his hometown in Massachusetts." Lewis, however, "discovered this couldn't be true" and considered it "part of his [Du Bois's] adolescent self-importance and snobbism." See Lynn Karpen, "The Inventor of Himself," *New York Times Book Review*, December 12, 1993. Ralph Dumain, of the Autodidact Project, to author, June 17, 2001, writes that Harrison had very admirable traits," he was "a working class autodidact, a street agitator, organizer, educator, critic, and . . . [he was] closer to the Black working class than any other revolutionary intellectual of his time." Also see discussion of the "organic intellectual" in Manning Marable, *Black Leadership* (New York: Columbia University Press, 1998), 97–101, esp. 100; Antonio Gramsci, *"The Modern Prince" and Other Writings* (New York: International Publishers, 1957), 118–20; Antonio Gramsci, *Selections from the Prison Notebooks* (1971; New York: International Publishers, 1978), 5–11; and Anthony Bogues, *Black Heretics, Black Prophets: Radical Political Intellectuals* (New York: Routledge, 2003), 3–12, esp. 5–6.

42. HD, November 25, 1907. In the early part of 1908 he reviewed William A. Sinclair's *Aftermath of Slavery* in the *Yonkers Standard*, and he did "a longer and better" review of Henry Edwin Tremain's *Sectionalism Unmasked*. See HD, May 20, 1908, and HH, "American Slavery Past and Present," *Negro World*, August 13, 1921, 11.

43. HD, January 29, 1908. See also HD, February 7, 1908.

44. HD, November 15, 23, and 25, 1908; Aptheker, *A Documentary History*, 2:863, 874; and Eric Foner, *Reconstruction: America's Unfinished Revolution, 1863–1877* (New York: Harper and Row, 1988), xxi. Du Bois's talk was published as W. E. B. Du Bois, "Reconstruction and Its Benefits," *American Historical Review* 15 (July 1910): 781–99.

45. Mary Adams (pseud. for Williana Jones Burroughs), "Record of Revolts in Negro Workers' Past," *Daily Worker*, May 1, 1928. John Henrik Clarke, *Africans at the Crossroads: Notes for an African World Revolution* (Trenton, N.J.: Africa World Press, 1991), 371, discusses Harrison's "calling attention to the missing pages from our history" and helping in "reclaiming our African history." Pickens is quoted in "Hubert Harrison Memorial Church Booklet" (probably for Memorial Service, December 22, 1929), E. Ethelred Brown Papers, Box 1, "Harlem Unitarian Church,"

SCRBC. Williana and Charles Burroughs had four children and their son, Charles, along with his wife Margaret, founded Chicago's famous Du Sable Museum of African American History in 1957.

46. Mary Maclean, ed., *Letters and Addresses of Abraham Lincoln* (New York: Unit Book Publishing, 1903), in HP. On Maclean, see Kellogg, *NAACP*, 1:37, 45n. 66, 151; and Carolyn Wedin, *Inheritors of the Spirit: Mary White Ovington and the Founding of the NAACP* (New York: Wiley, 1998) 126–27.

47. On Harrison's disillusionment see HH, "The Grand Old Party," *Negro World*, c. July 1920, in *HR*, 51–55. See "Roosevelt the Black Man's Champion," *NYA*, February 16, 1905, 1. On the response to Roosevelt's actions see Richard B. Sherman, *The Republican Party and Black America from McKinley to Hoover, 1896–1933* (Charlottesville: University of Virginia Press, 1973), 57; Louis R. Harlan and Raymond W. Smock, eds., *The Booker T. Washington Papers*, 13 vols. (Urbana: University of Illinois Press, 1972–1984), 2:295–337, 506n. 58; Ann J. Lane, *The Brownsville Affair: National Crisis and Black Reaction* (Port Washington, N.Y.: National University Publications, Kennikat Press, 1971), 6, 70–73; and August Meier, *Negro Thought in America, 1880–1915: Racial Ideologies in the Age of Booker T. Washington* (1963; Ann Arbor: University of Michigan Press, 1987), 164.

48. August Meier, "The Negro and the Democratic Party, 1875–1915," *Phylon* 17, no. 2 (2nd qtr., 1956): 173–91, esp. 184. On Brownsville, see Lane, *Brownsville*, 6–7, 12–24, 69–130; Sherman, *Republican Party*, 57; 131; and J. D. Foner, *Blacks and the Military in American History* (New York: Praeger, 1974), 95–103, 167. On the congressional action see "Black Soldiers Finally Vindicated," *Crisis*, January 1973, 15–17.

49. On Roosevelt's unchanging stance on Brownsville, see Thomas G. Dyer, *Theodore Roosevelt and the Idea of Race* (Baton Rouge: Louisiana State University Press, 1980), 114–16. On the defections, see "A New Negro Party," *New York Evening Post*, August 8, 1910, HP-Sc 5; and Henry Lee Moon, *Balance of Power: The Negro Vote* (Garden City, N.Y.: Doubleday, 1949), 92–97.

50. HH, "The Grand Old Party," 153.

51. Maclean, *Letters and Addresses of Lincoln*, 119–21, 123, 198, 248–49.

52. HH, "As Harrison Sees It," *Amsterdam News*, October 6, 1926, 11. For Harrison's lectures on Lincoln see HH, "Lincoln and Liberty: Fact Versus Fiction, A Lecture," (notes for a lecture c. 1911), HP, and "Colored Soldiers Refused Half Pay: Dr. Harrison Honors Lincoln but Points out Expedients Adopted by Emancipator, Lauds Frederick Douglass," *Boston Chronicle*, February 16, 1924, HP-Sc 34. For his articles on Lincoln see HH, "Lincoln and Liberty: Fact Versus Fiction," in 4 parts, *Negro World*, March 5, 12, 19, and 26, 1921, and *HR*, 129–36.

53. HD, April 27, 1908. W. E. B. Du Bois, on his twenty-fifth birthday in Berlin, staged a private ritual with music, candlelight, and Greek wine. He, too, recorded the event. "Celebrating His Twenty-fifth Birthday," in *Against Racism: Unpublished*

Essays, Papers, Addresses by W. E. B. Du Bois, ed. Herbert Aptheker (Amherst: University of Massachusetts Press, 1985), 26–29.

54. HD, April 27, 1908. The "Steward" that Harrison crossed out may have been Mrs. Marie Jackson Stuart, a long time activist for St. Mark's.

55. HD, April 27, 1908.

56. HD, May 20, 1908.

57. HD, May 20, 1908.

58. HD, May 20, 1908.

59. HD, May 20, 1908.

60. HD, May 20, 1908.

61. HD, May 20, 1908.

62. Claude McKay, *A Long Way From Home: An Autobiography*, intro. St. Clair Drake (1937; New York: Harcourt Brace & World, 1970), 118. On the erotica collection, see Richard Bruce Nugent, *Gay Rebel of the Harlem Renaissance*, ed. and intro. Thomas H. Wirth (Durham, N.C.: Duke University Press, 2002), 149. On the dance see HD, February 26, 1926.

63. HD, March 3, April 29, and June 7, 1908. Special thanks to Ben Heller (to author, June 27, 2007) for help deciphering and interpreting this and other Harrison codes.

64. HD, June 9, 1908.

65. HD, April 29, 1908, December 1, 1907, June 9, 1908. In at least one, possibly related instance, Hubert attributed his moving to the "increasing indecency" of the house in which he lived (see HD, June 15, 1908).

66. "Aunt Mamie," interview by William Harrison, February 1, 1951, William Harrison Notebook, HP; HH, "Petition for Naturalization"; June A. V. Lindqvist to author, March 5, 1983; "Irene Louise Horton Harrison," photo, n.d., HP; "Marriage Certificate for Hubert Henry Harrison and Irene L. Horton," St. David's Protestant Episcopal Church, Bronx, N.Y., April 17, 1909, HP; County Clerk, New York County, Extract of State Census for June 1, 1915, No. 6747, for Hubert H. Harrison, 231 W. 134th Street, A.D. 21, E.D. 22, page 31, 32. The 1920 census reports that Irene and her parents were born in Antigua and that she came to the United States in 1908. See "Fourteenth Census," Enumeration District 972, Sheet 1.

67. HD, November 19 and 23 and December 12, 1908, and January 17, 1909 and "Why I Love You," Booklet with inscription given by HH to Irene, Christmas 1908, HP. Ben Heller to author, June 27, 2007, helped with the code.

68. HD, January 17 and February 9 and 17, 1909. Ben Heller to author, August 3, 2007, helped with the translation.

69. HD, January 31, 1909. The possibility that Lenora Larsen was the author Nella Larsen has been considered, but no final determination has been made.

70. HD, January 31, 1909.

71. HD, February 9 and 17, 1909.

72. HD, January 17, 1909, and September 28, 1914; HH, "Declaration of Intention [to Naturalize]"; and "Aunt Mamie," interview. There is no indication that John and Williana were related. In the Harrison Papers there is an absence of almost any correspondence with Lin.

73. HH, "Declaration of Intention [to Naturalize]"; "Kathryn Marion [Frances Marion] Harrison," photo, March 1910, HP; "Aunt Mamie," interview; "Marriage Certificate for Harrison and Horton." According to her birth certificate Frances was born at 307 Second Avenue in Manhattan, though her parents lived at 249 South Seventh Avenue in Mount Vernon. See "Certificate and Record of Birth," Frances Harrison, City of New York, #51631 for 1909 Borough of Manhattan. "Certificate of Marriage," Harrison and Horton, lists Hubert's address as 193 W. 134th Street and Lin's address as 26 West 136th Street. Harrison gave incorrect dates for the births of several of his children in his "Petition for Naturalization." See Charles Miller (acting chief naturalization examiner, U.S. Department of Labor, Naturalization Service), to Commissioner of Naturalization, August 21, 1922, Department of Justice, Immigration and Naturalization Service, Washington, D.C., Files 2270-P-42659 and 2270-12659. Harrison's daughter Aida Harrison Richardson provided the correct birth dates of the children in Richardson, interview.

74. HD, May 26, 1911, and April 13 and 29, 1913.

4. Secular Thought, Radical Critiques, and Criticism of Booker T. Washington (1905–1911)

1. HH, "The Negro a Conservative: Christianity Still Enslaves the Minds of Those Whose Bodies It Has Long Held Bound," *Truth Seeker* 41, no. 37 (September 12, 1914): 583 (hereafter *TS*), in *HR*, 42–46, esp. 44. On the Black church, also see Seth M. Scheiner, *Negro Mecca: A History of the Negro in New York, 1865–1920* (New York: New York University Press, 1965), 87; and E. Franklin Frazier, *The Negro Church in America* (1964; New York: Schocken, 1973), 43–44. And, on the church in the West Indies, see Ira De A. Reid, *The Negro Immigrant: His Background, Characteristics, and Social Adjustment, 1899–1937* (1939; reprint, New York: AMS Press, 1970), 124, 218.

2. Sidney Warren, "The Nature of the Freethought Movement," *TS* n.s. 1, no. 4 (September/October 1989): 47–48, esp. 47; and Joseph Jablonski, "Freethought," in *Encyclopedia of the American Left*, ed. Mari Jo Buhle, Paul Buhle, and Dan Georgakas (Urbana: University of Illinois Press, 1990), 243–44, on the labor and socialist movements.

3. "Objects" and "Political Principles," *TS* 41, no. 37 (September 12, 1914): 586; masthead, *TS* 38 (November 4, 1911): 689; and Susan Jacoby, *Freethinkers: A History of American Secularism* (New York: Metropolitan Books, 2004), 151. For a history of the movement in the United States, see George E. Macdonald, *Fifty Years of*

Freethought: Being the Story of the "Truth Seeker," with the Natural History of Its Third Editor, 2 vols. (New York: Truth Seeker, 1931).

4. David Levering Lewis, "W. E. B. Du Bois and the Dilemma of Race," *Prologue*, 27, no. 1 (Spring 1995): 37–44, esp. 43. On those attracted to the movement, see Jablonski, "Freethought," 243–44; Macdonald, *Fifty Years*, vols. 1 and 2, passim; and Louis C. Fraina, "The Socialist Movement Against the Church," *TS* 37 (April 23 and 30, 1910). On Black freethinkers and atheists, see John Ragland, "No More Ham," *American Atheist* (February 1987): 25–34, esp. 25–28; R. Murray-O'Hair, "Atheists of a Different Color: A Minority's Minority," *American Atheist* (February 1987): 17; J. G. Jackson, "Hubert Henry Harrison," 18–20; Walter E. Hawkins, letter to the editor, *TS* 53 (March 6, 1926), reprinted as "A Tantalizing Letter," in *American Atheist* (February 1987): 21; Robert A. Hill, "Introduction," in *Crusader*, ed. Hill, 6 vols., ed. Cyril Briggs September 1918–February 1922, in 3 vols. (New York: Garland, 1987), viii. On Du Bois, also see David Levering Lewis, "Two Responses to American Exceptionalism; W. E. B. Du Bois and Martin Luther King, Jr.," *Black Renaissance*, 4, no. 2/3 (Summer 2002): 8–22; Gerald Horne, *Black and Red: W. E. B. Du Bois and the Afro-American Response to the Cold War, 1944–1963* (Albany: State University of New York Press, 1986), 16; and Anthony B. Pinn, ed., *By These Hands: A Documentary History of African American Humanism* (New York: New York University Press, 2001), 211-25.

5. Hodge Kirnon to the editor, "Hubert H. Harrison," *TS* 55 (c. 1928), in HP, and "Freethought," *Washington Post*, February 22, 1919. On Harrison's favorable use of *Appeal to Reason* see HH, "The Attitude of the American Press," 17–18, HP. In "H. H." [HH], "Answers to Questions Concerning Books," *Negro World*, August 28, 1920, 9, HP-Scrapbook B (hereafter cited as HP-Sc), Harrison wrote, "Those who want good books on science, history, religion and literature at very low prices" should write to the Rationalist Press Association.

6. "Sunrise Club Would Abolish Tyranny," *New York Times*, November 26, 1905 (hereafter *NYT*). The 1905 date is from John G. Jackson, "Hubert Henry Harrison: The Black Socrates," *American Atheist* (February 1987): 18–20, which is based on Joseph F. Rinn, *Sixty Years of Psychical Research: Houdini and I Among the Spiritualists* (New York: Truth Seeker, 1950), 222–32, esp. 222–24, 230. The date appears accurate based on the fact that Rinn referred to attacks on Mary S. Pepper that are consistent with "Enemies Persecute Me, Says Rev. Mary Pepper," *NYT*, January 16, 1905. Joseph J. Boris, *Who's Who in Colored America: A Biographical Dictionary of Notable Living Persons of Negro Descent in America* (New York: Who's Who in Colored America, 1927), 87, indicates that Harrison joined the Sunrise Club in 1908. J. A. Rogers, "Hubert Harrison," in Writer's Program (New York, N.Y.), "Negroes of New York" (New York, 1940?), Schomburg Center for Research in Black Culture, New York Public Library, writes that Harrison was "one of the leading spirits of the Sunrise Club." See also *TS* 37, no. 8 (February 19, 1910): 125, on Du Bois and [HH], "Read! Read! Read!," *Voice*, July 18, 1917, HP, in *HR*, 126–28, esp. 127, on Miller.

Harrison noted in his diary that one of his talks drew the largest number of African Americans that he had seen at any of the club's activities. V. F. Calverton wrote to Harrison reminding him of their good times there: V. F. Calverton to HH, June 18, 1926, HP. See also HD, April 3, October 5, and November 2, 1922, and May 26, 1924, and handouts re HH talks for The Sunrise Club on ["The Ku Klux Klan Past and Present,"] March 19, 1923, and April 3, 1923, HP-Sc D.

7. Rinn, *Sixty Years*, title page, 222–32, esp. 222–24, 230. See also Jackson, "Hubert Henry Harrison," 19; and "Enemies Persecute Me." Whether or not Rinn had the year of the event accurate (Pepper was in the news in 1905), it is interesting to note that Harrison similarly "assisted" him in a January 24, 1920, event recorded with exacting details and accompanying newspaper clippings in Harrison's diary. At that time Hubert described it as "the most interesting dinner of the Sunrise Club" that he had ever attended. He also commented "that the ordinary person, whether a scientist or not, could not be independently relied on for a correct interpretation of the evidence of his senses." The quotes are from HD, January 26, 1920, which also included "Joe Rinn Seeks Go with Oliver Lodge," [unidentified newspaper], January 27, 1920.

8. HH, "Views of Readers: Some Further Interesting Comments Upon Moncure D. Conway and the Attitude of Virginians Toward Him," *NYT*, September 25, 1909. See also Daniel Grinnan, "Moncure D. Conway," *NYT*, September 4, 1909.

9. HH, "Erasmus Darwin and Others," *NYT*, May 29, 1909.

10. S. Reswick, "Charles and Erasmus Darwin," *NYT*, June 12, 1909.

11. Mark Pittenger, "Science, Culture, and the New Socialist Intellectuals Before World War I," *American Studies* 28, no. 1 (1987): 73–92, esp. 74–75; and Jervis Anderson, *A. Philip Randolph: A Biographical Portrait* (New York: Harcourt Brace Jovanovich, 1973), 74–75.

12. Pittenger, "Science, Culture, and the New Socialist Intellectuals," 75; Mark Pittenger, *American Socialists and Evolutionary Thought: 1870–1920* (Madison: University of Wisconsin Press, 1993), 4; HH, "Two Negro Radicalisms," *New Negro* 4, no. 2 (October 1919): 4–5, HP, in *HR*, 102–5, esp. 103; and HH, "First Principles," *Negro World*, July 16, 1921, 7. On racist implications in evolutionary thought, see Richard Milner. *The Encyclopedia of Evolution: Humanity's Search for Its Origins* (New York: Facts On File/Oxford, 1990), 380–82; Idus A. Newby, *Jim Crow's Defense: Anti-Negro Thought in America, 1900–1930* (Baton Rouge: Louisiana State University Press, 1965), 12–13; Stephen Jay Gould, *The Mismeasure of Man* (New York: W. W. Norton, 1981), 73; and Carl N. Degler, *In Search of Human Nature: The Decline and Revival of Darwinism in American Social Thought* (New York, 1991), 14–16. On Huxley, see Thomas Huxley, *Essays*, vol. 3, p. 67, cited in *Proceedings of the National Negro Conference, 1909: New York, May 31 and June 1* (New York: National Negro Conference Headquarters, [1909]), 24; and on Spencer, see Herbert Spencer to Kentaro Kaneko, August 26, 1892, cited in David Duncan, *Life and Letters of Herbert Spencer*, 2 vols. (New York: Appleton, 1908), 2:14–18.

13. HH, "World Problems of Race," c. July 8, 1926, HP, reprint, HH, "Dr. Harrison's Last Article: 'World Problems of Race': Writer Said Both Science and History Try to Rob Negro of Past Heritage; 'Ancient Egyptians' Called White Lest Negroes Get Credit for Medicine, Geometry, Religion and Architecture," *Pittsburgh Courier*, December 31, 1927.

14. Thomas G. Dyer, *Theodore Roosevelt and the Idea of Race* (Baton Rouge: Louisiana State University Press, 1980), 37; and George W. Stocking Jr., "Lamarckianism in American Social Science, 1890–1915," in *Race, Culture, and Evolution: Essays in the History of Anthropology* (New York: Free Press, 1968), 234–69, esp. 238–40, 242, 253, 255.

15. Stocking, "Lamarckianism," 255. See also Milner, *Encyclopedia of Evolution*, 325; and Jacoby, *Freethinkers*, 137. On Weismann, see Hamilton Cravens, *The Triumph of Evolution: American Scientists and the Heredity-Environment Controversy, 1900–1941* (Philadelphia: University of Pennsylvania Press, 1978), 37–38. On Boas, see Stocking, *Race, Culture, and Evolution*, 264–65. A succinct critique of the Lamarckian theory is offered in Stephen J. Gould, *Mismeasure of Man* (New York: Norton, 1981), 325.

16. Charles Darwin, *The Origin of Species by Means of Natural Selection; or, The Preservation of Favored Races in the Struggle For Life* (1859; New York: The Modern Library, n.d.), 367. Gould agrees with Darwin that natural selection is "not the exclusive means of modification" and discusses "punctuated equilibrium" in Stephen J. Gould, "Darwinian Fundamentalism," *New York Review of Books*, June 12, 1997, 34–37, esp. 34–35.

17. In a sense, Lamarckianism tried to build a bridge between the sociohistorical and the biological. Stocking emphasizes that the Lamarckian doctrine was "a behavioral theory of biological evolution." See Stocking, "Lamarckianism," 238.

18. HH, "The Brown Man Leads the Way: A Review of *The New World of Islam* by Lothrop Stoddard," concluding part, *NW*, November 5, 1921, 5, in *HR*, 315–319, esp. 317; and HH, "World Problems of Race," 1926. Theodore W. Allen, *The Invention of the White Race*, 2 vols. (New York: Verso, 199, 1997), is insightful in describing the development of the "white race" as a ruling-class social control formation that came about after Bacon's Rebellion (1676–1677) . On the back cover of volume 1, Allen comments, similar to Harrison, "When the first Africans arrived in Virginia in 1619, there were no 'white' people there; nor, according to the colonial records, would there be for another sixty years."

19. In Jean Finot, *Race Prejudice* (New York: E. P. Dutton, 1906), 310–11, Finot writes: "The science of inequality is emphatically a science of White people. It is they who have invented it and set it going, who have maintained, cherished and propagated it, thanks to *their* observations and *their* deductions. Deeming themselves greater than men of other colours, they have elevated into superior qualities all the traits which are peculiar to themselves, commencing with the whiteness of the skin and the pliancy of the hair." In his copy, received on May 7, 1925, Harrison responds,

"not so, its source is always sociologic rather than intellectual." See also HH, "The Negro and Socialism: 1—the Negro Problem Stated," *NYC*, November 28, 1911, in *HR*, 52–55, esp. 52, on "The Negro Problem's" roots in past relationships.

20. HH, "Race Prejudice—II," *NYC*, December 4, 1911, 6, in *HR*, 55–57.

21. In 1921, while discussing the subject of education in the *Negro World*, he wrote: "As we inherit our houses and lands, our arts and institutions from our ancestors, so also do we inherit our bodies and minds, our aptitudes and inclinations from thme [*sic*]. Modify them how we may, they still remain our original inheritance. Thus the social structure and purposes which determine our educational ideals and methods are in their turn determined by our social inheritance; thus the marrow of tradition is in the very bones of our being, and through the eyes of the individual soul looks out the social ancestry—the race." See HH, "The Racial Roots of Education," *NW*, May 7, 1921, HP-Sc B. On Lamarckians' belief that "complex cultural traits could be acquired, carried, and transmitted in the 'blood' of 'races' from generation to genera- tion," see Dyer, *Theodore Roosevelt*, 37–38; and Stocking, "Lamarckianism," 238–40, 244, 265.

22. In his personal copy of George A. Dorsey's 1925 book, *Why We Behave Like Human Beings*, HP, 102, after Dorsey quotes Lamarck that "all that has been ac- quired or altered in the organization of individuals during their life is preserved by generation and transmitted to new individuals which proceed from those which have undergone change," Harrison takes out "all" and writes that "*some* would be more accurate." After Dorsey writes, "Biologists have driven a hundred daggers into this [Lamarckian] theory of evolution through the Inheritance of Acquired Characteristics; [yet] the theory is as alive as ever!" Harrison adds—"And we La- marckians take comfort." Harrison's Lamarckian-like opposition to the immutabili- ty of fixed races is evidenced in his copy of Edward Wilmot Blyden, *African Life and Customs* (London, 1908), HP, 90, received on July 21, 1915, which quotes a passage from the June 1908 *Socialist Review* on eugenics and maintains that "no degenerate and feeble stock will ever be converted into healthy and sound stock by the accu- mulated effect of education, good laws, and sanitary surroundings." To this Har- rison added: "Rotten reasoning! On his own showing there could be no degenerate stock: all stocks would continue to be what they originally were. How could they degenerate at all if 'the accumulated effects . . . of the environment were not potent to transform the stock?'"

23. This approach, emphasizing social-environment influence, was consistent with early-twentieth-century Lamarckian thought. Dyer explains that "turn-of-the- century" Lamarckianism "did not stress the immutability of racial characteristics which many physical anthropologists regarded as essential to an understanding of the nature of race." Rather, it "emphasized the power of environment as opposed to the importance of heredity." Thus "the racial past of any people was a 'bio-so- cial' past" made up of "elements of biological heredity" and "characteristics acquired

through the influence of environment and culture." In this way, "racial heredity" was understood as an "implicitly Lamarckian product of social and environmental forces." Dyer, *Theodore Roosevelt*, 37–38. See also Stocking, "Lamarckianism," 243; Degler, *In Search*, 14–16, 21–23, 93; and Hamilton Cravens, *Triumph of Evolution: American Scientists and the Heredity-Environment Controversy, 1900–1941* (Philadelphia: University of Pennsylvania Press, 1978), 35–37.

24. Stocking, "Lamarckianism," 251, explains that in the early-twentieth-century "historical milieu of ascendant white civilization dominating the colored peoples of the earth, and in an intellectual milieu permeated by evolutionism and Lamarckianism, hereditarians and environmentalists had more in common than one might think." Hereditarians, anthropo-sociologists, and eugenicists "tended to assume the physical inheritance of quite complex mental characteristics," later understood as "cultural terms." But, as Lamarckians, they tended "to confuse social and physical heredity, and to assume the physical inheritance of complex cultural characteristics." There were other "environmentally oriented Lamarckians who felt that equally complex cultural phenomena were carried in the 'blood,' if only as 'instincts; or 'temperamental proclivities.'" Stocking concludes, "There was a racist potential in Lamarckianism as well—a potential whose significance depended in part on the tense of its application."

25. Historian Ernest Allen Jr., commenting on the use of the "race first" slogan by Harrison in response to the "class first" slogan used by white-race-first socialists, writes, "Characteristically, the biological aspects of 'race' and their social aspects as manifested in the structuring of social relations were constantly confused with one another." He adds, "Whereas 'class first' ignored the *special oppression* which blacks *qua* blacks suffered above and beyond that borne by white laborers, 'race first' obliterated the class aspects of the African American struggle, resulting in the ideological effacement of the class character of oppression" (Ernest Allen Jr., "The New Negro: Explorations in Identity and Social Consciousness, 1910–1922," in *1915, The Cultural Moment: The New Politics, the New Woman, the New Psychology, the New Art, and the New Theatre in America*, ed. Adele Heller and Lois Rudnick [New Brunswick, N.J.: Rutgers University Press, 1991], 66n. 35.

26. August Meier and Elliot Rudwick, "Attorneys Black and White: A Case Study of Race Relations within the NAACP," *Journal of American History* 41 (March 1976): 913–46, esp. 914; and HP-Sc 5, *The Negro American*, vol. 8: *The Negro Factions: 1. The Protestants, 2. The Subservients*, HP.

27. Harrison criticizes Washington's philosophy (though not by name) in HH, "The Negro and Socialism: 1—The Negro Problem Stated," 54. The criticism is more direct in HH, "The Black Man's Burden [I]," *International Socialist Review* 12, no. 10 (April 1912): 660–63, in *HR*, 62–67. esp. 64 and 67; and in HH, "The Black Man's Burden [II]," *ISR*, 12, no. 11 (May 1912): 762–64, in *HR*, 67–71, esp. 69. See also Louis R. Harlan and Raymond W. Smock, eds., *The Booker T. Washington Papers*,

13 vols. (Urbana: University of Illinois Press, 1972–1984) (hereafter *BTWP*), 8:542, 3:586, 3:584, and 5:386.

28. HH, "The Attitude of the American Press," 17, HP. See also W. E. B. Du Bois, "Of Mr. Booker T. Washington and Others," in *The Souls of Black Folk*, intro. Trevor Nelson (1903; New York: Washington Square Press, 1970), 38, 41–42; W. E. B. Du Bois, *The Autobiography of W. E. B. Du Bois: A Soliloquy on Viewing My Life from the Last Decade of Its First Century [1960]* (1968; New York: International Publishers, 1971), 236–53, esp. 239; and [W. E. B. Du Bois,] "The Niagara Movement: Declaration of Principles" (1905), in *Black Protest: History Documents and Analyses 1619 to the Present*, ed. Joanne Grant (New York: Fawcett Premier, 1968), 206–9.

29. Philip S. Foner, *American Socialism and Black Americans: From the Age of Jackson to World War II* (Westport, Conn.: Greenwood Press, 1977), 195–97, esp. 187. See also Charles Flint Kellogg, *NAACP: A History of the National Association for the Advancement of Colored People, 1909–1920* (1967; Baltimore, Md.: Johns Hopkins University Press, 1973), 1:9–45, esp. 43.

30. Foner, *American Socialism*, 198; and *Proceedings of the National Negro Conference 1909*, 5–7.

31. *Proceedings of the National Negro Conference 1909* (n.p.). Trotter discusses the amendments on 113–14; Stafford's comments are on 121–22; Walters discusses Ewing on 168–69 and the amendments on 172; Sinclair's presentation is on 211–13 with Baal mentioned on 212; and the Trotter resolution is discussed on 225.

32. [HH], "The Line-Up on the Color Line," *NW*, December 4, 1920, HP-Sc 33, in *HR*, 216–19, esp. 216. Wooley's published comments appear in *Proceedings*, 74–78.

33. Aptheker, *Documentary History*, 3:27; and Kellogg, *NAACP*, 1:43.

34. HH, "The Line-Up on the Color Line," 216–17; and HH, "Shillady Resigns," *NW*, June 19, 1920, 2, in *HR*, 177–78, esp. 178.

35. W. E. B. Du Bois, "Talented Tenth," in *Negro Problem*, by B. T. Washington et al. (1903; New York: Arno Press and the NYT, 1969), 33–75, esp. 42 and 75; HH, "A Tender Point," *Negro World*, July 3, 1920, HP, in *HR*, 178–80, esp. 179. Martin Luther King Jr.'s early assessment of Du Bois's "Talented Tenth" concept as expressed in his *Stride Toward Freedom* was, writes David Levering Lewis, that it was "a tactic for an aristocratic elite who would themselves be benefited while leaving behind the 'untalented' 90 per cent." See Lewis, "Du Bois and the Dilemma of Race," 43.

36. "Negroes Appeal to Europe," *New York Sun*, December 1, 1910, 9 (hereafter *NYS*), in Grant, *Black Protest*, 203–6. See also Kellogg, *NAACP*, 1:75–78, esp. 75; and David Levering Lewis, *W. E. B. Du Bois*, 2 vols., vol. 1: *Biography of a Race, 1868–1919* (New York: Henry Holt, 1993), 1:414–15.

37. "Dr. Washington Abroad: Educator Being Lionized in London," *New York Age*, September 8, 1910, 1 (hereafter *NYA*), and "Washington on Race Problem in America," *NYA*, September 22, 1910, 1.

38. Louis R. Harlan, *Booker T. Washington*, 2 vols., vol. 2: *The Wizard of Tuskegee, 1901–1915* (New York: Oxford University Press, 1986), 2:367–68, 514n. 29; "Negroes Appeal to Europe," *NYS*, December 1, 1910, 9; and William Toll, *Resurgence of Race: Black Social Theory from Reconstruction to the Pan-African Conferences* (Philadelphia: Temple University Press, 1979), 150–51.

39. "Negroes Appeal to Europe."

40. "Negroes Appeal to Europe"; editorial, *NYS*, December 2, 1910; and "D" to the editor, *NYS*, December 5, 1910, 6.

41. HH to the editor, *NYS*, December 8, 1910, 8; HH, "Charles W. Anderson," *The Voice*, October 31, 1917, 6, HP; and HP-Sc 1, pp. 363–64. His talk is mentioned in "Y.M.C.A. Notes," *NYA*, December 8, 1910, 2.

42. HH to the editor, *NYS*, December 8, 1910; and Du Bois, *Autobiography*, 240. The "N" in "Negro" was not capitalized in the newspaper version, though Harrison surely capitalized it.

43. HH to the editor, *NYS*, December 8, 1910. See also in HP-Sc 2, pp. 327, 344–46, for articles on Baltimore.

44. HH to the editor, *NYS*, December 8, 1910.

45. HH to the editor, *NYS*, December 8, 1910.

46. HH to the editor, *NYS*, December 8, 1910.

47. HH to the editor, *NYS*, December 8, 1910.

48. "L.A.W." to the editor, *NYS*, December 10, 1910, 6; and J. C. Asbury to the editor, *NYS*, December 12, 1910, 6.

49. HH to the editor, *NYS*, December 19, 1910, 8.

50. HH, "The Negro and the Newspapers" (c. 1911), in HH, *The Negro and the Nation* (New York: Cosmo-Advocate Publishing, 1917), 59–64, esp. 59–60. See also "English Writer 'Emancipated,'" *NYA*, December 29, 1910, 1, HP-Sc 7, p. 288.

51. HH, "The Negro and the Newspapers," 64.

52. HH, "The Negro and the Newspapers," 64; Daniel Walden, ed. and intro., *W. E. B. Du Bois: The Crisis Writings* (Greenwich, Conn.: Fawcett, 1972), 53. In 1944 Du Bois wrote that after the turn-of-the-century, "my long-term remedy was Truth: carefully gathered scientific proof that neither color nor race determined the limits of a man's capacity or desert. I was not at that time sufficiently Freudian to understand how little human action is based on reason; nor did I know Karl Marx well enough to appreciate the economic foundations of human history." See W. E. B. Du Bois, "My Evolving Program for Negro Freedom," in *What the Negro Wants*, ed. Rayford W. Logan (Chapel Hill: University of North Carolina Press, 1944), 49.

53. "E. T. Washington" (HH—as identified in HP-Sc 4, 347) to the editor, "The Reverse of the Medal," *NYS*, January 21, 1911; "T.A.O." to the editor, "Negro Real Estate Sharpers," *NYS*, January 19, 1911. Among the pseudonyms that Harrison used in his life are the following: Master Alcofribas, Itambe Asong, Sayid Muhammad Berghash, Caliban, Frances Dearborn, Hamlet, Hira La Ganesha, Gunga Din,

H. H., H. H. Hugo de Groot, Elbert Harborn, Herbert Harrison, A St. Croix Creole, Ignacio Sanchez, Semper Fidelis, The Taster, Nils Uhl, E. T. Washington, and Young Chen.

54. On the Afro-American Realty Company, see Gilbert Osofsky, *Harlem: The Making of a Ghetto, Negro New York, 1890–1930* (1963; New York: Harper and Row, 1971), 93–104; and Jervis Anderson, *This Was Harlem: 1900–1950* (New York: Farrar Straus Giroux, 1981), 51–56.

55. "E. T. Washington" [HH], "The Reverse of the Medal."

56. Charles William Anderson to Booker T. Washington, October 30, 1911, *BTWP* 11:351; and [HH], "Our Political Ads," *Voice*, October 31, 1917, 6.

57. "Hubert Henry Harrison," National Personnel Records Center, USPS, St. Louis, Mo.; and Charles W. Anderson to Booker T. Washington, September 10, 1911, *BTWP* 11:300–301.

58. "Hubert Henry Harrison," National Personnel Records Center; [HH], "Our Political Ads," *Voice*, October 31, 1917, p. 6 and Anderson to Washington, October 30, 1911, *BTWP*, 11:351.

59. Untitled clipping, *TS* 38 (February 11, 1911): HP-Sc 34.

60. HH, "Paine's Place in the Deistical Movement," *TS* 38 (February 11, 1911): 87–88.

61. "Hamlet" [HH], "Half A Man—the Story of the Negro," *Amsterdam News*, July 15, 1911, HP-Sc 32; "Hubert Henry Harrison," National Personnel Records Center; and Mary White Ovington, *Half A Man: The Status of the Negro in New York* (1911; New York: Schocken, 1969).

62. "Hamlet" [HH], "Half A Man."

63. HH, "Menace of Exemption: Church Property in New York, Worth $400,000,000 Plus, Evades Payment of Taxes," *TS* 38 (November 4, 1911).

64. HH, "Menace of Exemption."

65. HH, "Menace of Exemption."

66. HH, "Menace of Exemption."

67. HH, "Menace of Exemption."

68. Charles Leinenweber, "The Class and Ethnic Bases of New York City Socialism, 1904–1915," *Labor History* 22, no. 1 (Winter 1981): 31–56, esp. 43, 47; and Macdonald, *Fifty Years*, passim.

69. HH to Stoddard, November 13, 1920, speaks of "Idols of the Tribe," a book he was working on. See also "Idols of the Marketplace," scrapbook cover, HP-Sc 40. [HH], "Meditations: Heroes and Hero Worship, and the Heroic in Human History," *NW*, October 16, 1920, HP-Sc 33 ("and not"). In 1925, Alain Leroy Locke would write, in a manner similar to Harrison, "The Negro, too, for his part, has idols of the tribe to smash." See Henry Louis Gates Jr. and Nellie Y. McKay, gen. eds., *Norton Anthology of African American Literature* (New York: W. W. Norton, 1997), 964.

5. Hope in Socialism (1911)

1. Daniel Bell, "The Background and Development of Marxian Socialism in the United States," in *Socialism and American Life*, ed. Donald Drew Egbert and Stow Persons, 2 vols. (Princeton, N.J.: Princeton University Press, 1952), 1:268–69; David A. Shannon, *The Socialist Party of America* (New York: Macmillan, 1955), 4–5; and Ira Kipnis, *The American Socialist Movement, 1897–1912* (1952; New York: Monthly Review Press, 1972), 421.

2. Kirk H. Porter and Donald Bruce Johnson, comp., *National Party Platforms 1840–1968* (Urbana: University of Illinois Press, 1970), 164; and Bell, "The Background and Development," 1:269.

3. Porter and Johnson, *National Party Platforms*, 165. See also Shannon, *Socialist Party*, 11; Bell, "The Background and Development," 275; Kipnis, *American Socialist Movement*, 118 and 296; and Marc Karson and Ronald Radosh, "The American Federation of Labor and Negro Workers, 1894–1949," in *The Negro and the American Labor Movement*, ed. Julius Jacobsen (New York: Doubleday, 1968), 155–87, esp. 155–57.

4. Philip S. Foner, *American Socialism and Black Americans: From the Age of Jackson to World War II* (Westport, Conn.: Greenwood Press, 1977), xiii.

5. P. Foner, *American Socialism*, 104 ("outright"), 108 (Wayland), 111–14, 147 (Untermann); Shannon, *Socialist Party*, 50 (Berger); Nick Salvatore, *Eugene V. Debs: Citizen and Socialist* (Urbana: University of Illinois Press, 1982), 226 ("separate"); and Eugene V. Debs, "The Negro and the Class Struggle," *International Socialist Review* (hereafter *ISR*), November 1903, in *Writings and Speeches of Eugene V. Debs*, intro. Arthur M. Schlesinger Jr. (New York: Hermitage Press, 1948), 63–66, esp. 65 ("colorless"). See also Philip S. Foner, *History of the Labor Movement in the United States*, vols. 1–7 (New York: International Publishers, 1947–1988), 3:369–70; R. Laurence Moore, "Flawed Fraternity—American Socialist Response to the Negro, 1901–1912," *Historian* 32, no. 1 (1969): 1–18, esp. 2–3, 7, 9–10, 13–14; and Kipnis, *American Socialist Movement*, 132.

6. Eugene V. Debs, "The Negro and His Nemesis," *ISR*, January 1904, in *Writings and Speeches*, 66–73, esp. 68; and Debs, "The Negro in the Class Struggle," 66 ("nothing"). See also P. Foner, *American Socialism*, 95–99, esp. 98–99; Oakley C. Johnson, "Marxism and the Negro People's Freedom Struggle," in *Marxism in United States History Before the Russian Revolution (1876–1917)* (New York: Humanities Press, 1974), 74; and Moore, "Flawed Fraternity," 2, for the 1901 resolution.

7. Kipnis, *American Socialist Movement*, 133; and P. Foner, *American Socialism*, 150, 204–5, 397nn. 12–13.

8. HH, "How to Do It—and How Not," *New York Call*, December 16, 1911, 6 (hereafter *NYC*), in *HR*, 60–62; Hubert A.[sic] Harrison, "No Segregation Intended," *NYC*, January 9, 1912, 6; and "H. H. Harrison, Colored Orator to Speak Here," *New Brunswick Times*, August 29, 1913.

9. Shannon, *Socialist Party*, 44–45; and Kipnis, *American Socialist Movement*, 273–74. See also Charles Leinenweber, "The American Socialist Party and 'New' Immigrants," *Science and Society* 32, no. 1 (Winter 1968): 2–25, reprint, in *Failure of a Dream: Essays in the History of American Socialism*, ed. John H. M. Laslett and Seymour Martin Lipset (1974; rev. ed., Berkeley: University of California Press, 1984), 244–68; and Sally M. Miller, "For White Men Only: The Socialist Party of America and Issues of Gender, Ethnicity, and Race," *Journal of the Gilded Age and Progressive Era* 2, no. 3 (July 2003): 283–302.

10. Kipnis, *American Socialist Movement*, 260; and Sally M. Miller, "Other Socialists: Native Born and Immigrant Women in the Socialist Party of America, 1901–1917," *Labor History* 24, no. 1 (Winter 1983): 84–102, esp. 85. See also Mari Jo Buhle, "Women and the Socialist Party, 1901–1914," *Radical America* 4, no. 2 (February 1970): 35–55; and Bruce Dancis, "Socialism and Women in the United States, 1900–1917," *Socialist Revolution* 27, vol. 6, no. 1 (January–March 1976): 81–144, esp. 85–87.

11. Dancis, "Socialism and Women," 103, 104–14, 116. See also Miller, "Other Socialists," 87; Kipnis, *American Socialist Movement*, 263–65; Mari Jo Buhle, *Women and American Socialism*, (Urbana: University of Illinois Press, 1981), 145–75; Buhle, "Women and the Socialist Party," 39–51; and Buhle, "Women's National Committee," in *Encyclopedia of the American Left*, ed. Mari Jo Buhle, Paul Buhle, and Dan Georgakas (Urbana: University of Illinois Press, 1990), 830–31, esp. 830 (hereafter *EAL*).

12. Shannon, *Socialist Party*, 8, 9–11; Bell, "The Background and Development," 275; Kipnis, *American Socialist Movement*, 118, 296; and Mark Pittenger, *American Socialists and Evolutionary Thought, 1870–1920* (Madison: University of Wisconsin Press, 1993), 198.

13. Charles Leinenweber, "The Class and Ethnic Bases of New York City Socialism, 1904–1915," *Labor History* 22, no. 1 (Winter, 1981): 31–56, esp. 31–32, 43; and *American Labor Year Book, 1916* (New York: Rand School of Social Science, 1917?), 97.

14. Leinenweber, "Class and Ethnic Bases," 38, 43, 47; and John M. Laslett, "Jewish Socialism and the Ladies Garment Workers of New York," in *Labor and the Left: A Study of Socialist and Radical Influences in the American Labor Movement, 1881–1924* (New York: Basic Books, 1970), 98–143, esp. 109.

15. Judith Stein, *World of Marcus Garvey: Race and Class in Modern Society* (Baron Rouge: Louisiana State University Press, 1986), 44. For the 1909 date, see Johnson, *Marxism in the United States*, 80; and P. Foner, *American Socialism*, 207.

16. In J. M. Robertson, *The Evolution of States: An Introduction to English Politics* (New York: Putnam/Knickerbocker Press, 1913), HP, the Harrison quote is handwritten on the inside cover, where Harrison describes Robertson as "one of those few men whom I acknowledge proudly as 'My Master.'" Robertson was born in Scotland, mastered more than six languages, authored 110 books, was a Shakespeare and freethought expert, represented Tyneside in Parliament, was secretary to the

Board of Trade, and served as privy councillor. See Gordon Stein, ed., *An Anthology of Atheism and Rationalism* (Buffalo, N.Y.: Prometheus Books, 1980), 67–68.

17. Eric F. Goldman, *Rendezvous with Destiny: A History of Modern American Reform* (1952; New York: Vintage, 1956): 72–81, esp. 79; and "H. H. Harrison, Colored Orator to Speak Here." See also "Dr. Harris[on] Candidate for Congress on Socialist [Single Tax] Ticket," [unidentified newspaper], c. June 7, 1924, HP-Scrapbook 35 (hereafter HP-Sc), corrections in Harrison's handwriting.

18. HH, "Socialism and the Negro," *ISR* 13, no. 1 (July 1912), in *HR*, 71–76, esp. 72. See also Johnson, *Marxism in the United States*, 80; P. Foner, *American Socialism*, 207; and Bell, "The Background and Development," 283.

19. *WGMC*, 2:434.

20. "H. H. Harrison Colored Orator to Speak Here," quotes Bright. On Harrison learning from party work with foreigners and women, see HH, "No Segregation Intended," and HH, "How to Do It," 61.

21. *WGMC* 2:434.

22. Theresa Malkiel, "'Socialists' Despise Negroes in South: 'Comrades' Refuse to Allow Colored Men in Meeting Halls or Party," *NYC*, August 21, 1911, 3. See also Leinenweber, "Class and Ethnic Bases," 48; Shannon, *Socialist Party*, 52; and Moore, "Flawed Fraternity," 13. Harrison commented on Malkiel's report in HH, "Socialism and the Negro," 75.

23. "Nils Uhl" [HH], to the editor, "The Negro and His Problem," *NYC*, October 2, 1911, 7. On Harrison in Branch 5, see "Minutes of the Convention of Local New York Held Sunday November 26, 1911," "Minutes," Local New York (hereafter LNY), R2635, S V:18, Socialist Party Papers (hereafter SPP), Tamiment Library, New York University (hereafter NNYT). For similar phrasing, see HH to the editor, *New York Sun*, December 8 and 19, 1910, both p. 8; and HH, "The Negro and the Newspapers" [c. 1911], in HH, *The Negro and the Nation* (New York: Cosmo-Advocate Publishing, 1917), 59–64. "Nils" or "not" (derived from the Latin and Greek) may have been Harrison's way of indicating he was using a pseudonym in a manner similar to that used by Vladimir I. Ulianov, the leader of the Russian Bolshevik Revolution, who used the name "N. Lenin" or "not" Lenin. "Uhl" may have been a playful Harrison takeoff on "y'all" (you all). On Harrison's similar usage and themes, see, for example, HH, "The Negro and Socialism: 1—the Negro Problem Stated," *NYC*, November 28, 1911, 6, in *HR*, 52–55, esp. 54 ("touchstone"); HH, "Race Prejudice," 56 (newspapers); and "Socialism and the Negro," 75 ("Southernism"). Harrison's scrapbooks also suggest that he may have written on the Malkiel matter. See "The Negro and Socialism: 1," *NYC*, January 24, 1911, 6, IIP-Sc 6, p. 223, and "Southern Socialist" to the editor, "Racial Equality," *NYC*, January 24, 1911, 6, HP-Sc 7, p. 831, which has a handwritten reference to the "Southern Socialist" letter.

24. "Nils Uhl" [HH], to the editor. See also W. E. B. Du Bois, *Dusk of Dawn: An Essay Toward an Autobiography of A Race Concept* (1940; New York: Schocken, 1971), 230. In his scrapbook Harrison wrote over the large headlines and pictures accom-

panying the Thomas Williams article: "but when the real culprit was discovered to be a German degenerate the news didn't get six inches of space, and there were no pictures." See "Mob with Pistols and Ropes Rush Asbury Park Jail," *New York World*, November 15, 1910, HP-Sc 28.

25. "Nils Uhl" [HH] to the editor. Harrison said much more on this subject in HH, "Southern Socialists and the Ku Klux Klan" [c. 1914], *Negro World*, January 8, 1921, HP in *HR*, 76–78.

26. "Nils Uhl" [HH], to the editor; and Shannon, *Socialist Party*, 67.

27. Editor's response accompanying "Nils Uhl" [HH], to the editor.

28. Samuel M. Romansky to Julius Gerber, October 12, 1911, "Letters," Local New York, R2635, S V:21. Apparently neither Romansky nor Gerber saw anything wrong in the parenthetical description "colored" or in the spelling of "negroes" with a small "n." The historian Philip Foner, who quoted and paraphrased from this Romansky letter, used the phrase "largest population" in place of the phrase "largest segregation." See P. Foner, *American Socialism*, 206. A phrase, "greatest Negro population," does appear later in "Socialist News of the Day," *NYC*, January 20, 1912, 5.

29. Romansky to Gerber, October 12, 1911.

30. "Minutes of Executive Committee," October 18, 1911, "Minutes," LNY, R2638, S VI:5.

31. P. Foner, *American Socialism*, 204.

32. On Harrison as an editor of *The Masses*, see "Harlem Scholar Succumbs after 'Minor' Operation," *Amsterdam News*, December 21, 1927, 4.

33. HH, "Menace of Exemption," *Truth Seeker*, November 4, 1911; HH, "Postal Department Is Made Goat of All Other Federal Business," *NYC*, November 6, 1911, HP; HH, "Postal Clerks Not Protected by Civil Service From Persecution," *NYC*, November 7, 1911, HP; and Kipnis, *American Socialist Movement*, 118.

34. HH, "Postal Department"; and HH, "Postal Clerks."

35. "Dr. Hubert Harrison," handout, c. 1924, HP; "Minutes of Local New York," December 17, 1911, LNY, SP, "Minutes," R 2635, V:18.

36. HH, "How to Do It," *NYC*, December 16, 1911, 60; Sweeney to the editor, *NYC*, January 6, 1911, cites statistics from "Negroes Aided Democrats," *New York Times*, November 21, 1910. See also Henry Lee Moon, *Balance of Power: The Negro Vote* (Garden City, N.Y.: Doubleday, 1940), 84, 94.

37. HH, "How to Do It," 61. On pp. 61–62, Harrison explained that like the Foreign Language Federations, this special work required a "special literature," a "special form of address," and "a special equipment"—namely, "Negroes . . . intelligent and well versed in the principles of Socialism."

38. HH, "How to Do It," 61. On Slater, see P. Foner, *American Socialism*, 173–82; and Philip S. Foner, ed. and intro., *Black Socialist Preacher: The Teachings of Reverend George Washington Woodbey and His Disciple, Reverend G. W. Slater, Jr.* (San Francisco: Synthesis, 1983), 293–357.

39. HH, "How to Do It," 61.

40. HH, "How to Do It," 61–62.

41. Winston James, "Being Red and Black in Jim Crow America: On the Ideology and Travails of Afro-America's Socialist Pioneers, 1877–1930," in *Time Longer Than Rope: A Century of African American Activism, 1850–1950*, ed. Charles M. Payne and Adam Green (New York: New York University Press, 2003), 336–399, esp. 338, 346, 357–60, 367–69; and P. Foner, *American Socialism*, 45–59, 151–180.

42. P. Foner, *American Socialism*, 208, 397n. 21, where he cites John Burfriend to Julius Gerber, November 25, 1911, LNY; and Julius Gerber, "Report of the Executive Secretary of Local New York to the Central Committee Local New York, For the Year 1912," (February 9, 1913), 1–28, esp. 2, "Letters," LNY, R 2635, V:36.

43. "Minutes of Executive Committee," LNY, November 8, 1911, "Minutes," LNY, R2638, S VI:5.

44. "Minutes of Executive Committee," LNY, November 8, 1911.

45. LNY, SP, "Recommendations of the Committee on Propaganda among Negroes," November 22, 1911, "Minutes," LNY, R2635, S V:13; "Minutes of the Convention . . . November 26, 1911"; "To Push Agitation Among the Negroes: Local New York Approves Plan for Campaign of Organization," *NYC*, November 28, 1911, 5; and "Minutes of Executive Committee," LNY, November 8, 1911.

46. HH, *"Res Facta"* (n.p., 1911–1912), HP.

47. See, for example, HP-Sc 1 to 19; esp. HP-Sc 4; "When You Want a Book, Place Your Order with Hubert H. Harrison (513 Lenox Ave) Book-seller to the Reading Public of Harlem" (calling card), n.d. [c. 1921?], HP; and E. J. Dutton to the CC, SP, June 2, 1913, LNY, SP, "Letters," R 2636 V:61. It is quite revealing that Charles Seifert, George Young, Arthur Schomburg, and Richard B. Moore, all close enough to Harrison to be his pallbearers, were among the nation's leading Black bibliophiles. See "Lament Dream of Dr. Hubert Harrison," *Amsterdam News*, December 28, 1927, 1.

48. John E. Bruce, "The Negro Society for Historical Research," box 5, miscellaneous 13, Ms 55–13, John E. Bruce Papers (hereafter JEBP), Schomburg Center for Research in Black Culture, NYPL), contains the NSHR quotes and is in William Ferris, *The African Abroad; Or, His Evolution in Western Civilization, Tracing His Development Under Caucasian Milieu*, 2 vols. (1913; reprint, New York: Johnson Reprint, 1968), 2:863–66. A. Schomburg to "My dear [John E.] Bruce," November 24, 1911, box 2 AL/MS 289, JEBP, has the quote on Harrison. See also Joseph J. Boris, *Who's Who in Colored America: A Biographical Dictionary of Notable Living Persons of Negro Descent in America* (New York: Who's Who in Colored America, 1927), 87.

49. HH, "Lincoln and Liberty: Fact Versus Fiction, A Lecture," Handwritten Notes (1911, 1912, 1913, 1914), HP; advertisement for Harrison's Lincoln lectures, *NYC*, February 11, 1912; "Negro Lecturer Attacks Lincoln," *NYC*, February 12, 1912, HP; "Socialist News of the Day," *NYC*, December 29, 1911, 5; "Socialists Watch Night Meeting," *NYC*, December 29, 1911, 5; and HH, "Socialism and the Negro."

50. HH, "Old Age Pension Bill Is Criticized," *NYC*, November 20, 1911.

51. HH, "The Negro and Socialism: 1," 54; HH, "Old Age Pension Bill"; Porter and Johnson, *National Party Platforms*, 165; and Shannon, *Socialist Party*, 25. In HH, "Woman Suffrage," *Voice*, October 31, 1917, HP, Harrison discussed how when Black people push demands for justice the answer is "that granting of them is not 'practically expedient.'" Harrison was also impressed by the ability of the Western Federation of Miners to win the eight-hour day through militant action and "without the aid of the legislatures or the courts." See HH, "Socialism and the Negro," 68.

52. HH, "The Negro and Socialism: 1." See also HH, "The Real Negro Problem," in *The Negro and the Nation* (New York: Cosmo-Advocate Publishing, 1917), 30–40. In Harrison's Papers is a typescript: HH, "The Real Negro Problem," n.d., HP, similar to that article. On the back of p. 11 of that typescript, Harrison wrote, "The items of fact in this brief summary have been taken from a note-book which I kept from 1905 to 1912." Karl Marx, *Capital*, 1:766n. 3, similarly described capital as "a social relation of production . . . a historical relation of production."

53. HH, "The Negro and Socialism: 1." See also "HH, "The Real Negro Problem," 30–31. Like Marx, who wrote that "the ideas of the ruling class are in every epoch the ruling ideas, i.e., the class which is the ruling *material* force of society is at the same time its ruling *intellectual* force," Harrison adds (32–33) that "it is a social law . . . that whenever a certain social arrangement is beneficial to any class in a society, the class soon develops the psychology of its own advantage and creates insensibly the ethics which will justify the social arrangement. . . . the dominant ideas of any society which is already divided into classes are as a rule the ideas preservative of the existing arrangements." He then describes (33–35) how "the slave-holding section of the dominant class in America first diffused its own necessary contempt for the Negro among the other sections of the ruling class, and the ideas of this class as a whole became through the agency of the press, pulpit, and platform, the ideas of 'the American People' on the Negro." See also Karl Marx and Friedrich Engels, *The German Ideology*, part 1, sect. B, "Ruling Class and Ruling Ideas" (1846).

54. HH, "The Negro and Socialism: 1," 53–54.

55. HH, "The Negro and Socialism: 1," 54.

56. HH, "Race Prejudice—II," 55–56; and HH, "The Negro and Socialism: 1," 52–53.

57. HH, "The Negro and Socialism: 1," 52–53; A. M. Simons, "The Negro Problem," *ISR* 1 (October 1900): 204–11, esp. 206–8; Charles H. Vail, "The Negro Problem," *ISR* 1 (February 1901): 464–70, esp. 470; and Kipnis, *American Socialist Movement*, 131. On the locus of the problem in the white race, see HH, "Seeking a Way Out," *Boston Chronicle*, May 31, 1924.

58. HH, "The Negro and Socialism: 1," 54.

59. HH, "The Negro and Socialism: 1," 54–55. On December 1, 1911, four days after Harrison's article and four days before a mayoral runoff election in Los Angeles in which the Socialist Job Harriman was favored, the two McNamara brothers, working with their attorney Clarence Darrow, shocked the country by pleading

guilty (James to murder for bombing the *Los Angeles Times* building and John for being an accessory to dynamiting the Llewellyn Iron Works). See Michael Kazin, "McNamara Case," *EAL*, 463–464.

60. HH, "The Negro and Socialism: 1," 55. In 1921 Harrison wrote: "The white missionaries' function is to spread that form of religion which will soft-soap the soul of black Africa so that the business of robbing and ruling it shall become less costly and less dangerous to those who do the robbing and the ruling." He emphasized that Africans were "not quite the fool" that their white friends thought and that "after 300 years of Christian contact with Africa there are less than 3,000,000 in a population of 120,000,000 who even profess Christianity." See HH, "Africa as She Is: *Africa Slave or Free?* by John H. Harris," *Negro World*, February 19, 1921, HP.

61. HH, "Race Prejudice," 55–56; and Kipnis, *American Socialist Movement*, 131.

62. HH, "Race Prejudice," 56.

63. Theodore W. Allen, *Class Struggle and the Origin of Racial Slavery: The Invention of the White Race*, ed. and intro. by Jeffrey B. Perry (1974; Stony Brook, N.Y.: Center for Study of Working Class Life, State University of New York, 2006), 18–19n. 63; and HH, "Seeking a Way Out," *Boston Chronicle*, May 31, 1924, HP.

64. HH, "Race Prejudice," 56.

65. HH, "Race Prejudice," 56.

66. HH, "Race Prejudice," 56–57.

67. HH, "Race Prejudice," 57.

68. HH, "The Duty of the Socialist Party," *NYC*, December 13, 1911, HP, in *HR*, 58; and "Southern Socialist" to the editor, "Racial Equality," *NYC*, January 24, 1911, 6, HP.

69. HH, "Duty of the Socialist Party," 58.

70. HH, "Duty of the Socialist Party," 59.

71. HH, "Duty of the Socialist Party," 59.

72. HH, "Duty of the Socialist Party," 59.

73. HH, "Duty of the Socialist Party," 59.

74. HH, "How to Do It—and How Not," *NYC*, December 16, 1911, in *HR*, 60–62.

75. HH, "How to Do It," 60.

76. HH, "How to Do It," 62.

77. HH, "Summary and Conclusion," *NYC*, December 26, 1911, 6. See, for example, Karl Marx, *Preface and Introduction to A Contribution to the Critique of Political Economy* (1859; Peking: Foreign Language Press, 1976), 3, where Marx writes, "It is not the consciousness of men that determines their being, but on the contrary it is their social being that determines their consciousness."

78. HH, "Summary and Conclusion." Here, as elsewhere with Harrison articles, I have capitalized the "N" in "Negro" as Harrison always did.

79. HH, "Summary and Conclusion."

80. HH, "Summary and Conclusion."

81. HH, "Summary and Conclusion."

82. Thomas Potter, to the editor, *NYC*, January 11, 1911, 6.

83. George Frazier Miller, to the editor, *NYC*, December 6, 1911, 6; and "To Push Agitation Among the Negroes: Local New York Approves Plan for Campaign of Organization," *NYC*, November 28, 1911, 5.

84. Miller to the editor, 6; and "To Push Agitation," 5.

85. "Minutes of the Convention . . . November 26 1911" and "Branch 5," [notes re] "Minutes," LNY, R2636, S V:40.

86. "Help the Negroes to See the Light! Funds Needed for Socialist Propaganda Work Among Colored People. 'Appeal' of the Executive Committee of Local New York," *NYC*, December 12, 1911, 5.

87. "Help the Negroes to See the Light!"

88. W. E. B. Du Bois, to the editor, "Separate Organization," *NYC*, December 27, 1911, 6.

89. Du Bois, "Separate Organization." In the 1930s Du Bois would advocate that the NAACP pursue a "new, deliberate, and purposeful segregation for economic defense." See W. E. B. Du Bois, *The Autobiography of W. E. B. Du Bois: A Soliloquy on Viewing My Life from the Last Decade of Its First Century (1960)* (1968; New York: International, 1971), 298.

90. Du Bois, "Separate Organization."

91. "Socialist News of the Day," *NYC*, December 29, 1911, 5.

92. Harrison, "No Segregation Intended."

93. Harrison, "No Segregation Intended."

94. Harrison, "No Segregation Intended."

95. HH, "Our Professional Friends," *Voice*, November 7, 1917, HP, in *HR*, 143–47. See also Charles Flint Kellogg, *NAACP: A History of the National Association for the Advancement of Colored People, 1909–1920* (1967; Baltimore, Md.: Johns Hopkins University Press, 1973), 1:250–54; and Du Bois, *Autobiography*, 266.

96. Du Bois, *Dusk of Dawn*, 197–220, 247–51; and Kellogg, *NAACP*, 1:102–3.

97. "Minutes of the Central Committee of Local New York, . . . January 13, 1912," "Minutes," LNY, R2638, S VI:4; and "Socialist News of the Day," *NYC*, January 20, 1912, 5.

98. "Socialist News of the Day," *NYC*, January 24, 1912, 5, and *NYC*, January 27, 1912, 5.

99. "Socialist News of the Day," *NYC*, February 12, 1912, 5; and "Minutes of the Central Committee of Local New York," February 24, 1912, "Minutes," LNY, R2638, S V:4. Harrison's remarks were not located.

6. Socialist Writer and Speaker (1912)

1. "Special Fund Growing," *New York Call*, January 20, 1912, p. 5 (hereafter *NYC*). Of the approximately one hundred paid speakers for Local New York of the

Socialist Party, it appears that only Harrison and W. E. B. Du Bois were African Americans. See "List of Speakers" [c. 1912], "Letters," Socialist Party Papers, Local New York, R 2637, V:144, Tamiment Library, New York University (hereafter SPP, LNY, NNYT).

2. Frank Bohn, "Some Definitions: Direct Action—Sabotage," *Solidarity*, May 18, 1912, reprint, in *Rebel Voices: An I. W. W. Anthology*, ed. and intro. Joyce L. Kornbluth (1964; Ann Arbor: University of Michigan Press, 1968), 52, 53; [Rand School of Social Science], *American Labor Year Book, 1916* (New York, 1916), 91–92 (hereafter *ALYB*); and Philip S. Foner, *History of the Labor Movement in the United States*, 7 vols. (New York: International, 1947–1988), 4:122–46, 243–44 (hereafter *HLM*).

3. David A. Shannon, *The Socialist Party of America* (New York: Macmillan, 1955), 7–13, 21–26; Ira Kipnis, *The American Socialist Movement, 1897–1912* (1952; repr. New York: Monthly Review Press, 1972), 107, 215, 276–79, 423, 426–27; and Foner, *HLM*, 4:395. James Weinstein, *The Decline of Socialism in America, 1912–1925* (New York: Monthly Review Press, 1967), 5–16, 24–25, esp. pp. 9, 11, depicts four tendencies in the Socialist Party which were led from right to left by Victor Berger, Morris Hillquit, Eugene Debs, and Bill Haywood. He also notes that Hillquit was "sometimes associated with Berger" (9) and Debs had a "rapport" with the spirit of the Wobblies (11).

4. HH, "Summary and Conclusion," *NYC*, December 26, 1911, 6. See also Sally M. Miller, "The Socialist Party and the Negro," *Journal of Negro History* 41, no. 3 (July 1971): 220–29, esp. 222; R. Laurence Moore, "Flawed Fraternity—American Socialist Response to the Negro, 1901–1912," *Historian* 32, no. 1 (1969): 1–18, esp. 18; and Foner, *HLM*, 4:124, 127, 168.

5. Foner, *HLM*, 4:395.

6. Foner, *HLM*, 4:396, 397; and William D. Haywood, *Bill Haywood's Book: The Autobiography of William D. Haywood* (New York: International, 1929), 246.

7. It appears that all members of the Executive Committee (EC) of Local New York were "white." See, for example, "Minutes of the Executive Committee," October 18, 1911, "Minutes," LNY, R2638, S VI-5, SPP; "Harrison is Discharged" [unidentified newspaper clipping, [probably from *NYC*, February 1912], HP-Scrapbook 34 (hereafter HP-Sc); and Jean Jacques Coronel to Dear Comrade Gerber, April 29, 1912, "Letters," LNY, R2635, S V:32.

8. HH to the Central Committee of LNY (SP), February 22, 1912, "Letters," LNY, R2635, S V-31.

9. Philip S. Foner, *American Socialism and Black Americans: From the Age of Jackson to World War II* (Westport, Conn.: Greenwood Press, 1977), 213. Foner says that the report was presented on February 23, 1912. On p. 398n. 25, he cites February 28, 1912, as the date of the "Minutes of Executive Committee Meeting, Local New York." I was not able to locate this particular source.

10. "Branch 5 Lecture Tonight," *NYC*, February 28, 1912, 5; Foner, *American Socialism*, 213; and HH, "An Open Letter to the Socialist Party of New York City," *Negro*

World, May 8, 1920, 2, in *HR*, 113–16, which says Harrison's c. 1912 party work was not "awakening hostility of any sort" in Harlem (114–15).

11. In 1917 the SP in New York City recruited one hundred Black men and this, in large part, as Harrison later explained, was because of the autonomous struggles being waged outside the party and an awakened racial consciousness. To Harrison, the socialist radicals "took credit for an upsurge due to Race." Some of the ablest race leaders joined the party because they viewed it as "'good play' to encourage and give aid to every subversive movement within the white world," which sought "its destruction 'as it is.'" In 1917, autonomous struggles were led by Harrison. See [HH], "Two Negro Radicalisms," *New Negro* 4, no. 2 (October 1919): 4–5, in *HR*, 102–5, esp. 105; [HH], [Notes re "The Red Record of Radicalism"], c. 1927, HP. Richard B. Moore described the post-1917 Twenty-first Assembly District Socialist Club of which he was a member as "a unique branch of the Party—a Harlem variety of socialism made up of militant, vocal young men and one woman (Grace P. Campbell), all of African descent except for one Jewish American." Joyce Moore Turner writes that Harrison "inspired many of these members to embrace socialism." See W. Burghardt Turner and Joyce Turner Moore, eds., *Richard B. Moore, Caribbean Militant in Harlem: Collected Writings, 1920–1972* (Bloomington: Indiana University Press, 1988), 29.

12. The articles are HH, "The Black Man's Burden," part 1, *International Socialist Review* 12, no. 10 (April 1912): 660–63 (hereafter *ISR*), in *HR*, 62–67; HH, "The Black Man's Burden," part 2, *ISR* 12, no. 11 (May 1912): 762–64, in *HR,* 67–71; and HH, "Socialism and the Negro," *ISR* 13, no. 1 (July 1912): 65–68, in *HR*, 71–76. See Weinstein, *Decline of Socialism*, 95, for circulation figures; and Joseph R. Conlin, ed., *The American Radical Press, 1880–1960*, 2 vols. (Westport, Conn.: Greenwood Press, 1974), 1:15, 83 ("sharply"). An example of the journal's attention to the "Negro Problem" is the fifteen-part series, I. M. Robbins [Isaac M. Rubinow], "The Economic Aspects of the Negro Problem," *ISR* (February 1908–June 1910).

13. HH, "The Black Man's Burden," part 1, 63; and Debs, "The Negro in the Class Struggle," 65. In [HH], "The World This Month," *New Negro* 4, No. 2 (October 1919): 3, Harrison wrote that "the white man's burden is himself." In HH, "The Theory and Practice of International Relations Among Negro-Americans," *Negro World*, October 22, 1921, HP, he explained that "the theory by which" the portion of the white race that ruled the world and the world's colored majority "justify themselves to themselves is known variously as the Color Line, the White Man's Burden, and Racial Superiority."

14. HH, "The Black Man's Burden," part 1, 64–66. On the Georgia railroad strike, see Sterling D. Spero and Abram L. Harris, *The Black Worker: The Negro and the Labor Movement* (1931; New York: Atheneum, 1972), 290; "The Georgia Railroad Strike," *Southern Workman*, August 1909, HP; "Negroes Cause Strike: Georgia Railroad Engages Them as Firemen and Whites Quit," *New York Times*, May 18, 1909

(hereafter *NYT*); and "Georgia Railroad Strike Only the Beginning of It, Says Line's Manager," *NYT*, May 19, 1909. For attacks on African American cabdrivers and chauffeurs in New York, see "Negro Cabmen Not Wanted," *New York Evening Post*, February 24, 1911, HP; "Denies Auto Driver Story," *Amsterdam News*, November 4, 1911, HP-Sc 3 (hereafter cited as *AN*); and "Boycott of White Chauffeurs," *New York Age*, November 2, 1911, 1. On the painters, see "Forces Them Out," *AN*, January 1911, HP-Sc 3; and "The Labor Union's Lament," *AN*, December 3, 1910, HP-Sc 3. On the street cleaners, see "Get Into the Service," *AN*, November 18, 1911, HP-Sc 3; "A Friendly Ill-Wind," *AN*, March 30, 1912, HP-Sc 3; and "Will Retain Strike Scabs," *AN*, November 25, 1911, HP-Sc 3.

15. HH, "The Black Man's Burden," part 1, 66. In the December 1856 *Dred Scott v. John F. A. Sanford* [misspelled as Sandford] case, 60 U.S. (19 How.) 393 (1857), Chief Justice Roger B. Taney maintained that the framers of the Constitution held that African Americans had "no rights which the white man was bound to respect." See Edward W. Knappman, ed., *Great American Trials* (Detroit: Gale Research, 1994), 119.

16. HH, "The Black Man's Burden," part 2, 67–71. Harrison began his "Lynching" scrapbook in 1911. See HP-Sc 28, which has clippings from 1910–1911, 1917–1918, 1921–1922, and 1926.

17. HH, "Socialism and the Negro," 71–76. On Harrison's talk, see "Socialist News of the Day," *NYC*, December 29, 1911, 5; and "Socialists Watch Night Meeting," *NYC*, December 29, 1911, 5. Foner, *American Socialism*, p. 397nn. 12–13 discusses socialists and the capital "N."

18. HH, "Socialism and the Negro," 72, 73; and W. E. B. Du Bois, *Black Reconstruction in America, 1860–1880* (1935; reprint, New York: Atheneum, 1972), 15. Also see W. E. B. Du Bois, "Socialism and the Negro Problem," *New Review* 1, no. 5 (February 1, 1913): 138–41, esp. 140.

19. On key political debates, see Shannon, *Socialist Party*, 10–11; and Daniel Bell, "The Background and Development of Marxian Socialism in the United States," in *Socialism and American Life*, 2 vols., ed. Donald Drew Egbert and Stow Persons (Princeton, N.J.: Princeton University Press, 1952), 1:275, 277.

20. HH, "Socialism and the Negro," 73. See also HP-Sc 5, vol. 8, and HD, October 22, 1907; A. Philip Randolph and Chandler Owen, "The Negro—a Menace to Radicalism," *Messenger*, 2 (May-June 1919): 20; and W. A. Domingo, "Socialism Imperiled, or the Negro—a Potential Menace to American Radicalism," in Report of the Joint Legislative Committee Investigating Seditious Activities, Filed April 24, 1920, in the Senate of the State of New York, *Revolutionary Radicalism: Its History, Purpose, and Tactics*, 2 parts, 4 vols. (Albany, 1920), Part I, *Revolutionary and Subversive Movements at Home and Abroad*, 2:1489–1510.

21. HH, "Socialism and the Negro," 73–74.

22. HH, "Socialism and the Negro," 74.

23. HH, "Socialism and the Negro," 74–75. See "A New Negro Party," *New York Evening Post*, August 8, 1910, HP-Sc 5, p. 287. On the Douglass quotation, see Richard B. Sherman, *The Republican Party and Black America from McKinley to Hoover 1896–1933* (Charlottesville: University of Virginia Press, 1973), iii.

24. HH, "Socialism and the Negro," 75. Henry Lee Moon, *Balance of Power: The Negro Vote* (Garden City, N.Y.: Doubleday, 1949), 94, discusses the Black vote going Democratic.

25. HH, "Socialism and the Negro," 75. The Malkiel article, "'Socialists' Despise Negroes in South," *NYC*, August 21, 1911, 3, had a Memphis dateline. "Nigger Equality" (1912) called for "segregation" as the solution to the race problem; deemed social equality undesirable; and stated "we Socialists don't love the 'nigger' any better than he loves us." See Kate Richards O'Hare, *Selected Writings and Speeches*, ed. and intro. Philip S. Foner and Sally M. Miller (Baton Rouge: Louisiana State University Press, 1982), 44–49, esp. 45–46, 48.

26. HH, "Socialism and the Negro," 76.

27. HH, "Socialism and the Negro," 76.

28. Quoted in HH, "Murder as a Catholic Argument: An Interview with Father Belford," *NYC*, April 11, 1912, HP.

29. HH, "Murder as a Catholic Argument." Francisco Ferrer y Guardia was an educator, socialist, anarchist, freethinker, and founder of the Escuela Moderna in Barcelona, Spain, in 1901 and other Modern Schools throughout Spain. The schools substituted secular for religious education. He was arrested in 1909 for alleged complicity in a 1908 outbreak in Barcelona and was shot by firing squad on February 13, 1909. In 1912 the Spanish supreme military council admitted no act of violence could be traced to him and ordered the restoration of his property. See George E. Macdonald, *Fifty Years of Freethought: Being the Story of the "Truth Seeker," with the Natural History of Its Third Editor*, 2 vols. (New York: The Truth Seeker, 1931), 2:280, 297, 332, 350; and Paul Avrich, *The Modern School Movement: Anarchism and Education in the United States* (Princeton, N.J.: Princeton University Press, 1980), 3–9, 32–36. In his copy of B. L. Putnam Weale [Bertram Lenox Simpson], *The Conflict of Colour: The Threatened Upheaval Throughout the World* (New York: Macmillan, 1910), 45, HP, Harrison wrote: "the rulers of the Spanish people slew Francisco Ferrer at Montjaich in the early part of this century (abt 1909) for the sin of offering education to Spain's ignorant millions."

30. "Father Belford Raps 'Interviewer,'" (Brooklyn) *Daily Eagle*, April 12, 1912, HP; and [John L. Belford] to the editor, "From Father Belford," *NYC*, c. April 20, 1912, HP-Sc32. It is possible that Belford did not at first know Harrison's name. Previous to Harrison's interview, Bouck White, a well known Socialist Party speaker and radical clergyman in New York, had written an open letter to Belford inquiring about the reverend's proposed assassinations. It was only after being interviewed by Harrison that Belford responded to White's letter. Thus, Belford probably thought

Harrison was Bouck White when he assured him that Black socialists "would not even have their shins kicked, to say nothing of being shot" (Editor, "The Nigger in the Belford Woodpile," *NYC*, April 17, 1912, HP). Also see Shannon, *Socialist Party*, 56, 59–61; and Avrich, *Modern School Movement*, 194.

31. HH to the editor, "A Direct Issue," (Brooklyn) *Daily Eagle*, April 25, 1912, HP. See also "And When It Comes to Shin Kicking," cartoon, *NYC*, April 17, 1912, HP; and "Controversy Over Father Belford's Attack on Socialists Who Object to Being Termed Anarchists," *Daily Eagle*, April 25, 1912, 8.

32. "Invitation to Father Belford," *NYC*, May 6, 1912, HP.

33. W. A. Moss to the editor, "Another Matter Now," *NYC*, c. May 24, 1912, HP-Sc 32; "Negro Socialist Lectures," *Daily Eagle*, May 7, 1912, HP. Later in the year Harrison described himself as an "agnostic." See HH, "In Vigorous Condemnation," *NYC*, November 19, 1912, 6. On January 3, 1915, however, Harrison was scheduled to deliver a Radical Forum lecture on "A Defense of Atheism" at the Harlem Casino. See "The Radical Forum," handout, c. October 18, 1914, HP-Sc 3. A discussion between Mohandas Gandhi and Rabindranath Tagore, sheds light on two approaches to "flags." According to Rev. Andrews, when Gandhi and Tagore discussed "idols," "Gandhi defended them, believing the masses incapable of raising themselves immediately to abstract ideas." Tagore could not "bear to see the people eternally treated as a child." Gandhi reportedly cited "the great things achieved in Europe by the flag as any idol," and while Tagore found it easy to object, Gandhi maintained his position and discussed European flags with eagles and so on and his flag with a spinning wheel. See Amartya Sen, "Tagore and His India," *New York Review of Books*, June 26, 1997, 55–63, esp. 55. While Harrison exhibited a Tagore-like approach in 1912, by 1917 he would develop a tricolor flag for his Liberty League—a position more similar to that of Gandhi with his spinning wheel flag.

34. Socialist Party, *National Convention of the Socialist Party Held at Indianapolis, Ind., May 12 to 18, 1912*, stenographic report by Wilson E. McDermut, assisted by Charles W. Phillips, ed. John Spargo (Chicago: The Socialist Party, 1912), 209–10. On the convention, see Foner, *American Socialism*, 250.

35. SP, *National Convention, 1912*, 210; and HH, "An Englishman Visits America: *The Soul of John Brown*—by Stephen Graham," *Negro World*, February 12, 1921, HP-Sc 33, "the bourgeois." Berger is quoted in Kipnis, *American Socialist Movement*, 278–79. Harrison was well aware of this "response" and later cited it in HH, "Race First Versus Class First," *Negro World*, March 27, 1920, in *HR*, 107–9. In HH, "An Open Letter to the Socialist Party," Harrison adds that "The quoted passage [on immigration] cuts the very heart out of their [the Socialist's] case."

36. HH, "Race First Versus Class First," 109; and [HH,] "Race Consciousness," *BC* (March 15, 1924), in *HR*, 116–17. Judith Stein. *The World of Marcus Garvey: Race and Class in Modern Society* (Baton Rouge: Louisiana State University Press, 1986),

276, points out that for African Americans, "the feeling of racial consciousness does not exclude class consciousness."

37. Werner Sombart, *Why Is There No Socialism in the United States?* ed. and intro. C. T. Husbands, foreword by Michael Harrington (1906; White Plains, N.Y.: M. E. Sharpe, 1976), esp. xix–xxiii. Allen maintains that "'free land,' 'constitutional liberties,' immigration, 'higher wages,' 'social mobility,' 'aristocracy of labor,' to the degree they did exist, were all 'white-skin privileges,'" and "the key to the defeat of labor and popular forces" in the United States has historically been the theory and the practice of white supremacy. See Theodore William Allen: "'The Kernel and Meaning . . .': A Contribution to a Proletarian Critique of United States Historiography," n.p. [c. 1967], March 24, 1972, possession of author, pp. 1–6, 8–9, 13–14, 20–21, esp. 2 ("classical"); Theodore W. Allen, "Can White Radicals Be Radicalized?" in *"White Blindspot" and "Can White Radicals Be Radicalized?"* by Noel Ignatin [Ignatiev] and Ted Allen (New York, 1969), 12–18, esp. 13 ("key to the defeat"); and Theodore William Allen, *The Invention of the White Race*, 2 vols. (New York: Verso: 1994 and 1997), 1:136–57, 2:253–59. Among those who contributed to the "classical consensus," Allen cites Karl Marx's coauthor, Frederick Engels; Marx's U.S. correspondent and labor and socialist activist, Frederick A. Sorge; the Christian Socialist and labor historian Richard T. Ely; the Socialist party leader Morris Hillquit; the trade union organizer and Communist Party leader William Z. Foster; the labor historians John R. Commons and Selig Perlman; the labor and general historians Charles A. and Mary Beard; and the prominent American historians Frederick Jackson Turner, Allan Nevins, and Henry Steele Commager. Spero and Harris, *Black Worker*, 413, also discusses how the race problem has been a major factor serving to prevent "the development of class consciousness" among "whites."

38. Sally M. Miller, "Other Socialists: Native Born and Immigrant Women in the Socialist Party of America, 1901–1917," *Labor History* 24, no. 1 (Winter 1983): 84–102, esp. 101.

39. Foner, *HLM*, 4:406.

40. See Kipnis, *American Socialist Movement*, 336 and 418, which indicates that party membership may have dropped from 150,000 to 110,000 in four months. On the membership decline, also see Shannon, *Socialist Party*, 92. In general, see Sally M. Miller, "Socialist Party Decline and World War I: Bibliography and Interpretation," *Science and Society* 34, no. 4 (Winter, 1970): 398–411, esp. 309–405, 411.

41. Mari Jo Buhle, "Women and the Socialist Party," *Radical America* 4, no. 2 (February 1970): 50.

42. "May Demonstration [May 1, 1912]," "Minutes," LNY, R2636, S V-46. [Samuel M. Romansky], recording secretary of Local New York, to J. W. Pomarlen, March 24, 1914, "Letters," LNY, R2637, S V:117, discusses the debate; and "Flag Trampled On in Socialist Riot," *NYT*, May 2, 1912, discusses the rally.

43. HH to "Dear Comrades [of the Central Committee]," June 23, 1912, "Letters," LNY, R2635, S V:31.

44. Jean Jacques Coronel to Dear Comrade Gerber, April 29, 1912, "Letters," LNY, R2635, S V:32; and Samuel M. Romansky to Julius Gerber, September 19, 1911, "Letters," LNY, R2635, S V:21.

45. "Don't Fail to Hear Comrade Harrison," *Buffalo Socialist*, October 12, 1912, HP-Sc 34. See also "Minutes of the Central Committee," July 27, 1912, "Minutes," LNY, R2638, S VI:4; "Minutes of the Executive Committee," July 29, 1912, "Minutes," LNY, R2638, S VI:5; "Socialist State Convention Will Be Largest in History," *NYC*, June 15, 1912, 3; "Auburn Welcomes Socialist Hosts," *NYC*, June 29, 1912, 1, 3; "Socialist Meet Fairly Under Way in City of Auburn," *NYC*, June 30, 1912, 1; "State Platform of the New York Socialist Party Adopted at the Auburn Convention, June 29–30, 1912," *NYC*, July 2, 1912, 3.

46. "Minutes of the Central Committee," July 27, 1912; and, on the decision not to increase pay, see "Minutes of the Executive Committee," July 29, 1912.

47. Gabriel Kolko, *The Triumph of Conservatism: A Reinterpretation of American History, 1900–1916* (1963; reprint, Chicago: Quadrangle Books, 1967), 281 ("specific"), 285. See also Irene Diggs, "The Amenia Conferences: A Neglected Aspect of the Afro-American Struggle," *Freedomways* (Second Quarter 1973): 117–134, esp. 123; and Richard Hofstadter, *The American Political Tradition and the Men Who Made It* (1968; reprint, New York: Vintage, 1973): 266–367, esp. 297, 316, 333, 337.

48. Foner, *American Socialism*, 144, discusses Debs. See also Bernard J. Brommel, *Eugene V. Debs: Spokesman for Labor and Socialism* (Chicago: Charles H. Kerr, 1978), 72–73, 215–17; and Nancy J. Weiss, "The Negro and the New Freedom: Fighting Wilsonian Segregation," *Political Science Quarterly* 84 (March 1968): 61–79, reprint, in *The Segregation Era, 1863–1954*,ed. Allen Weinstein and Frank Otto Gatell (New York: Oxford University Press, 1970): 129–42, esp. 131.

49. "Celebrated Harlem Mass Leader Dies After Operation," *New York News*, December 24, 1927, HP; and "Enlightening Wall Street," *NYT*, September 14, 1912. See also "Central Committee Camden," *Camden County Socialist*, September 4, 1912, HP-Sc 34; "Socialist Speakers Attend Big Dinner," *NYC*, September 23, 1912, HP; "Who Is Hubert Harrison?" handout card, c. November 1920, HP; and "Must Prove His Assertion," *NYC*, June 21, 1912, HP.

50. "Don't Fail to Hear Comrade Harrison"; and Kendrick P. Shedd to the editor, "Rochester, N.Y.," *NYC*, October 13, 1912, HP. See also "Hubert H. Harrison [Lectures]," *NYC*, September 5, 1912, HP-Sc 34; HH to Irene Harrison, postcard, October 14, 1912, HP; "Colored Socialist Speaks Here Tonight," *Rochester Labor Press*, October 9, 1912, HP-Sc 34; "Superiority of Socialism or Progressivism Still in Doubt," *Rochester Herald*, October 10, 1912, HP-Sc 34; "Progressive Orator Defaults in Debate," [unidentified newspaper], HP-Sc 34.

51. "A Negro Socialist," *Auburn Citizen*, October 14, 1912, HP-Sc 34.

52. "Socialists Were Shy," *Auburn Advertiser*, October 14, 1912, HP-Sc 34. See also Kolko, *Triumph of Conservatism*, 2–3; William Osgood Aydelotte, *Bismarck and British Colonial Policy: The Problem of South West Africa, 1883–1885* (1937; reprint,

Westport, Conn.: Negro Universities Press, 1970), 2–3, 18–27; and Eric Hobsbawm, *The Age of Empire, 1875–1914* (New York: Pantheon Books, 1987), 86–88, 103, 312–13.

53. "Socialists Were Shy."

54. "Socialists Were Shy."

55. HH, "What Socialism Means to Us," in HH, *The Negro and the Nation* (New York: Cosmo-Advocate Publishing, 1917), 55–56; and Philip S. Foner, ed. and comm., *The Voice of Black America: Major Speeches by Negroes in the United States, 1797–1971* (New York: Simon and Schuster, 1972), 698. Both W. E. B. Du Bois and Karl Marx viewed slavery as capitalist and the Civil War as a conflict between contending capitalist classes. See Du Bois, *Black Reconstruction*, 29, and Karl Marx, *Capital: A Critique of Political Economy*, 3 vols. (1867), ed. Frederick Engels (1890), trans. Samuel Moore and Edward Aveling (London: Lawrence and Wishart, 1970), 1:236, 432–433, 618 and 3:351, 934.

56. Harrison, "Race First Versus Class First," 80.

57. *ALYB, 1916*, 97, 100; Leinenweber, "Class and Ethnic Bases," 33; and Julius Gerber, "Report of the Executive Secretary of Local New York to the Central Committee Local New York, For the Year 1912," February 9, 1913, 1–28, esp. 2, "Letters," LNY, SPP, R 2635, V:36.

58. [Floyd] Calvin to [?], "Extracts From Calvin's Letter of November 12th," November 12, [1923], HP; "Special Notice," *NYC* [?], n.d. [c. 1912?], HP-Sc 34; and "Special Announcement: A Course Through College Without the Expense," HP-Sc 34.

59. HH, "The Materialistic Interpretation of History," *NYC*, November 3, 1912; and HH, "Harlem's Neglected Opportunities: Twin Source of Gin and Genius, Poetry and Pajama Parties," *Amsterdam News*, November 30, 1927, in *HR*, 357–62, esp. 357. On the "New Freedom," see Arthur S. Link, *Woodrow Wilson and the Progressive Era, 1900–1917* (New York: Harper, 1954), 20–22; and Hofstadter, *The American Political Tradition*, 331–37.

60. HH, "The Materialistic Interpretation of History"; Link, *Wilson and the Progressive Era*, 22–24; and Kolko, *Triumph of Conservatism*, 2–3.

61. HH, "The Materialistic Interpretation of History."

62. HH, "The Materialistic Interpretation of History."

63. HH, "The Materialistic Interpretation of History"; and Kipnis, *American Socialist Movement*, 278, 280.

64. HH, "The Materialistic Interpretation of History." Harrison left notes on the "unconscious" in [HH], "Our Minds and How They Work," n.p., n.d., HP.

65. Bruce Dancis, "Socialism and Women in the United States, 1900–1917," *Socialist Revolution* 27, vol. 6, no. 1 (January–March 1976): 81–144, esp. 85.

66. "Harrison Lecture," *Issue* (Elizabeth, N.J.), November 30, 1912, HP-Sc 34. Weinstein, *Decline of Socialism*, 98, indicates that the *Issue*, which began in 1911 in Elizabeth, reached a peak wartime circulation of 2,800 per week. Paterson also had a weekly *Issue* that started in 1911.

67. "Harrison Lecture," *Issue* (Elizabeth, N.J.), December 7, 1912, and "Next Sunday Lecture—Hubert H. Harrison. Subject: 'The Wreckage of Religion,'" advertisement, *Issue*, December 14, 1912, both in HP-Sc 34.

7. Dissatisfaction with the Party (1913–1914)

1. Philip S. Foner, *History of the Labor Movement in the United States*, 7 vols. (New York: International Publishers, 1947–1988), 4:403–9, esp. 408 (hereafter *HLM*).

2. See the following Socialist Party, Local NY (LNY) documents in the Socialist Party Papers (SPP) at the Tamiment Library, NYU (NNYT): S. Berlin, "Statement by the Secretary of the Grievance Committee [re F. Sumner Boyd]," n.d. (c. January 1913), Letters, R2636, V:69. See also F. Sumner Boyd, ["Appeal to a Referendum vote of the Local,"] January 13, 1913, Letters, R2636, V:112; "Local New York Socialist Party Result of Referendum B. 13 Appeal of F. Sumner Boyd against his suspension by the Central Committee," [c. December 1912], Letters, R2636, V:72 ("Gerber was"); "Minutes of the Central Committee," December 28, 1912, and January 26, 1913, and "Minutes," R2638, S VI:4.

3. Berlin, "Statement [re F. Sumner Boyd]"; Boyd, "Appeal"; "Local New York Socialist Party Result of Referendum B. 13; "Minutes of the Central Committee," December 28, 1912; and "Minutes of the Central Committee," January 26, 1913.

4. Foner, *HLM*, 4:408–9; "Minutes of the Central Committee," December 14, 1912, "Minutes," LNY, R2638, S VI:4, "Local New York: Result of Vote on National Referendum D.—'Recall of Haywood,'" n.d. [1912], "Minutes," LNY, SP, R2636, VI:72.

5. See "The Meanest Game," editorial, *New York Call*, June 8, 1912, p. 6 (hereafter *NYC*); "Minutes of the Central Committee," January 26, 1913, "Minutes," LNY, Berlin, "Statement by the Secretary of the Grievance Committee [re F. Sumner Boyd]"; and Boyd, "Appeal."

6. "What Haywood Says on Political Action" [and Resolution of Protest], *International Socialist Review* 13, no. 8 (February, 1913): 622–23 (hereafter *ISR*).

7. "Queens," [*NYC*?], February 19, 1913, HP, Sc 34. On Paterson, see Steve Golin, *The Fragile Bridge: Paterson Silk Strike, 1913* (Philadelphia: Temple University Press, 1988), 1–2; Foner, *HLM*, 4:356–57, 360; and Eugene M. Tobin, "Direct Action and Conscience: The 1913 Paterson Strike as Example of the Relationship Between Labor Radicals and Liberals," *Labor History* 20, no. 1 (Winter 1979): 73–88, esp. 75.

8. Golin, *Fragile Bridge*, 12, 30, 37–38, 41, 45, 53–54, 145–146; and Steve Golin, "Paterson Strike of 1913," in *Encyclopedia of the American Left*, ed. Mari Jo Buhle, Paul Buhle, and Dan Georgakas (Urbana: University of Illinois Press, 1990), 562–63 (hereafter *EAL*).

9. "Strikers Decide to Stand Firm," *Paterson Evening News*, April 17, 1913, 1, 9; Golin, *Fragile Bridge*, 145–46, 274n. 102; and John Fitch, "The I.W.W. an Outlaw Organization," *Survey* (June 7, 1913): 358–62, esp. 360.

10. "Local Detectives Asked to Leave Haledon Meeting," *Paterson Evening News*, May 20, 1913, 1, 10; Golin, *Fragile Bridge*, 145, 146, 274n. 102; and Fitch, "The I.W.W.," 360.

11. Golin, *Fragile Bridge*, 145–46, 225, 274n. 2, 188; Foner, *HLM*, 4:356–57, 360; and Tobin, "Direct Action and Conscience," 73–88, esp. 75.

12. "Sabotage Coming in Silk Mills If Boyd Is Jailed: Negro Agitator Shouts That If Paterson Owners Want to Lose $200,000, Let Them Go Ahead," *New York World*, December 1, 1913 (hereafter *NYW*); Foner, *HLM*, 4:367. The IWW "rejected the church and the flag as dishonest tools of the exploiting class" (William Preston Jr., *Aliens and Dissenters: Federal Suppression of Radicals, 1903–1933* [1963; New York: Harper and Row, 1966], 41).

13. Steve Golin, "Defeat Becomes Disaster: The Paterson Strike of 1913 and the Decline of the I.W.W.," *Labor History* 24, no. 2 (Spring 1983): 223–48, esp. 205 ("critical" and "backs"), 223–25, 233–34, 248; *Solidarity*, June 23, 1913, 4; and Foner, *HLM*, 4:367.

14. From LNY, SPP, NNYT: "Minutes of the Central Committee," May 24 and June 14, 1913, "Minutes," R2638, S VI:4; E. J. Dutton to the Central Committee, June 2, 1913, "Letters," R2636, VI:61; Executive Secretary [Gerber] to Mr. J. O'Connell, Organizer, Branch 5, June 5, 1913, "Letters," R2636, VI:61; Executive Secretary [Gerber] to Mr. E. J. Dutton, July 16, 1913, "Letters," R 2636 V:61; and HH to the City EC of LNY, January 6, 1913, "Letters," R 2636 V:61.

15. "Meeting of the Executive Committee of Local New York," August 25, 1913, SP, LNY, "Minutes," R2638, S V:5.

16. "Meeting of the Executive Committee," August 25, 1913.

17. HD, April 13, 19, and 29, and July 6 and 13, 1913.

18. HD, August 15, 1913, and Aida Harrison Richardson and William Harrison, interview by author, August 4, 1983, New York City, which discusses Harrison's love for his children and his falling short on family responsibilities.

19. Julius Gerber, "Report of the Executive Secretary of Local New York to the Central Committee Local New York, For the Year 1912," [February 9, 1913], 1–28, esp. 20 and 21, "Letters," LNY, SP, R 2635, V:36; and "You Need English Don't You," advertisement by HH, undetermined source, HP-Sc 34. See also HH, "The Negro Question from the Socialist Point of View," *Zukunft*, n.d. [c. 1911–1913?], 129–131; HP-Sc A. The title was translated by Ethel Loboman of the Tamiment Institute, telecon, November 7, 1997.

20. "Open Air Meetings," Minutes, [June 23–September 5, 1913], "Minutes," LNY, SP, R2635, S V:9; and "Hubert Harrison Biographical File," NNYT, which lists the six lectures.

21. "H. H. Harrison, Colored Orator to Speak Here," *New Brunswick Times*, August 29, 1913; and "Russell Named By Socialists For Mayor," *NYW*, September 6, 1913, HP; Foner, *HLM*, 4:360.

22. HD, September 11, 1913.

23. "Harrison Is Discharged," [probably *NYC*], [c. February 1912], HP-Sc 34.

24. "Branch Three Street Meetings," *Citizen Sun* (Buffalo, N.Y.), September 10, 1913; "Open Air Meetings," *Buffalo Socialist*, September 13, 1913; and "Harrison, Socialist, on Green Tonight," *Evening Register* (New Haven), n.d. All are in HP-Sc 34.

25. "Police Put End to Socialist Meeting and Arrest Three Men: Hubert Harrison, Colored Orator; George Weber, Mayoralty Candidate, and University Student Taken Into Custody," *Rochester Herald*, October 27, 1913. See also "Stump Speakers on Sunday," *Rochester Evening Times*, October 27, 1913, HP-Sc 34.

26. "Stump Speakers on Sunday"; "Police Put End to Socialist Meeting." In HP-Sc 34, see also "Mayoralty Candidate Discharged," *Union and Advertiser* (Rochester, N.Y.), October 27, 1913; "Mr. Weber Wants to Know," *Labor Journal*, October 31, 1913; and "Socialists Discharged," *Rochester Post Express*, October 27, 1913.

27. See two handouts on the Harlem School of Social Science, entitled "[Harlem School] of Social Science," HP-Sc 34; HD, September 28, 1914; "Branch 5 Socialist Party, 1st Winter Session, Courses, October 20, 1913-May 15, 1914," HP-Sc 34. See also *WGMC*, 2:435 ("applied"); HD, September 28, 1914. In his personal copy of Jerome Dowd, *The Negro Races: A Sociological Study* (New York, 1907), Harrison responds to Dowd's comment: "The division of society into classes cannot take place until occupations become specialized" (97). Harrison writes: "Poor silly! Division of labor did not of itself divide society into classes. It was the division of *property* that did that—cf. [Paul] Lafargue, [Lewis Henry] Morgan, [Casely] Hayford, [and (Ferdinand) August] Bebel."

28. "Meeting of the Executive Committee of Local New York," October 6, 1913, "Minutes," LNY, SP, R2638, S VI:5.

29. "Meeting of the Executive Committee of Local New York," October 6, 1913.

30. Foner, *HLM*, 4:367; and "Sabotage Coming."

31. "The Paterson Free Speech Fight," *NYC*, November 27, 1913, 6. See also "Sunday's Protest Meeting," *NYC*, November 29, 1913, 6; and "Paterson Defense Committee Protest Meeting," *NYC*, November 29, 1913, 6.

32. "Sabotage Coming."

33. "Sabotage Coming." See also Golin, "Defeat Becomes Disaster," 224, 234, 248.

34. "Sabotage Coming." See also HH to "Dear Comrade Gerber," December 1, 1913, postcard, "Letters," LNY, SP, R 2636, V.70.

35. "Minutes of the Central Committee, Local New York, December 13, 1913," "Minutes," LNY, SP, R 2638, VI:4.

36. "Minutes of the Executive Committee, Local New York, December 29, 1913"; "Minutes of the Executive Committee, Local New York, January 5, 1914," "Minutes," LNY, SP, R 2638, VI:5; and Julius Gerber to Mr. A. De Young, Rec. Sec., 21st Assembly District Branch, 2412 Seventh Avenue, New York City, February 18, 1914, "Letters," LNY, SP, R 2637, V:87.

37. HH to the editor, "An Open Letter to the Rank and File of the Socialist Party in New York" (January 19, 1914), *NYC*, February 5, 1914, 5. In the period before the

letter was published, Harrison was scheduled to debate—see "Harrison and Wasserman to Debate on Socialism," *NYC*, January 29, 1914, HP-Sc 34.

38. HH, "An Open Letter to the Rank and File." The "knowing the reason why" phrase was likely a takeoff on the famous banner at the May 1, 1912, rally to demand freedom for the Lawrence prisoners—"If Ettor and Giovannitti Are to Die, Twenty Million Working Men Will Know the Reason Why." See Foner, *HLM*, 4:344. Harrison appears to have been the lone Black member on the SP's City Central Committee. See [HH], "The Coming Elections," *Voice*, October 18, 1917, HP.

39. "Minutes of Unemployment Conference," January 10, 1913, "Letters," LNY, SP, R 2637, V:147.

40. "Protest Meeting an Anvil Chorus," *NYC*, February 5, 1914, HP-Sc 34; "Mass Protest Meeting to Be Held Under the Auspices of the Paterson Defense Committee," advertisement, *NYC*, January 29, 1914, HP-Sc 34; and HH, [handwritten comments], HP-Sc 34.

41. A. De Young to Julius Gerber, February 14, 1914, and Julius Gerber to A. De Young, February 18, 1914, "Letters," LNY, SP, R 2637, V:87.

42. Preston, *Aliens and Dissenters*, 50, 248. Fred Merrick, editor of the left-wing Socialist, pro-IWW Pittsburgh paper, *Justice*, explained that the "Socialist Party" was "the first institution in America to make the advocacy of sabotage a crime." In this it beat "the capitalist government and the Catholic church all hollow." Merrick forecast that the federal government would soon follow the lead of the SP and use "sabotage" as a basis for imprisoning radicals. "Big Bill" Haywood similarly commented that the adoption of the antisabotage clause by the SP "gave the federal government the go-ahead signal" used "during the first World War for the enactment of criminal syndicalist laws." For such monstrous consequences, he added, the working class could "thank the traitors of the Socialist Party." See Foner, *HLM*, 4:413.

43. "The New Review," *New Review* 1, no. 1 (January 4, 1913): 1 (hereafter *NR*); Theodore Draper, *The Roots of American Communism* (New York: Viking, 1957), 49, 404n. 35; and The New Review Publishing Association to the Central Committee of Local New York, September 1913, LNY, SP, "Letters," R 2636, V:70.

44. W. E. B. Du Bois, "A Field For Socialists," *NR* 1, no. 1 (January 4, 1913): 54–57, esp. 54; W. E. B. Du Bois, "Socialism and the Negro Problem," *NR* 1, no. 2 (February 1, 1913): 138–41, esp. 140; HH, "Socialism and the Negro," *ISR* 13, no. 1 (July 1912): 66; and Mary White Ovington, "The Status of the Negro in the United States," *NR* 1, no. 9 (September 1913): 744–49, esp. 748.

45. Ida M. Raymond to the editor, "A Southern Socialist on the Negro Question," *NR* 1, no. 12 (December 1913): 990–91. See also "Socialists on the Negro Question," *NR* 2, nos. 2 and 3 (February and March 1914): 63–64 and 178–80.

46. HH to the editor of *New Review*, "Southern Socialists and the Ku Klux Klan," [n.p., c. 1914], *Negro World*, January 8, 1921, HP-Sc 33, in *HR*, 76–78, esp. 77–78. Harrison later wrote (on page 299 of his copy of Jean Finot, *Race Prejudice*, trans. Florence Wade-Evans [New York, 1906], received on May 7, 1925), "*Could he have known*

the facts as given in [James G.] Blaine & [Carl] Schurz he would have realized that the ex-rebels forced the North to give the Negro the ballot since the whites refused to take the oath of allegiance in numbers sufficient to furnish reconstruction governments and had as early as *1865* organized lawless terrorist organizations."

47. HH to the editor of *New Review*, 78.

48. "Minutes of the Central Committee," June 28, 1913, "Minutes," LNY, SP, R2638, S VI:4.

49. Joseph M. Pomarlen and W. Lembke to State Committee of the Socialist Party of New York, "Appeal from Decision of the Central Committee of Local New York, Dissolving the Decision of the 3rd & 10th A.D. of Local New York," May 5, 1914, "Letters," LNY, SP, R2637, S V:117.

50. Recording Secretary of EC of LNY to J. W. Pomarlen, March 24, 1914, "Letters," LNY, SP, R2637, S V:117.

51. Pomarlen and Lembke to State Committee of the SP of New York, "Appeal . . . ," May 5, 1914; and Anna M. Sloan to HH, March 31, 1914, "Letters," LNY, SP, R2637, S V:117.

52. Sloan to HH, March 31, 1914.

53. Sloan to HH, March 31, 1914.

54. Minutes of the Central Committee of Local New York, April 11, 1914, "Minutes," LNY, SP, R2638, S VI:4.

55. "Resolution of 3rd and 10th A.D." n.d. [c. April 16, 1914]; Reorganization Committee to Dear Comrades, LNY, SP, to Comrade, April 17, 1914; Anna M. Sloan to Local New York Socialist Party, April 16, 1914; and S. Berlin to HH, April 16, 1914. All four items are found in "Letters," LNY, SP, R2637, S V:117.

56. HH to S. Berlin, April 21, 1914, "Letters," LNY, SP, R2637, S V:117, SPP, NNYT and "Minutes, Meeting of Central Committee of Local NY," April 25, 1914, "Minutes," LNY, SP, R2638, S VI:4.

57. Joseph M. Pomarlen and W. Lembke for Socialist Party, Branch Three, to State Committee of the Socialist Party of New York, "Appeal . . . ," May 5, 1914, "Letters," LNY, SP, R2637, S V:117.

58. S. Berlin, "Report of the Grievance Comm., Central Committee, Local N.Y. vs. Hubert H. Harrison," May 6, 1914, "Minutes," and Julius Gerber to HH, May 18, 1914, "Letters": both in LNY, SP, R2637, S V:117. At the May 23 meeting of the CC, delegates from the Twenty-first A.D. reported that they were instructed to move to reopen Harrison's case. This matter was tabled. Then on June 5, M. Solomon, state secretary of the SP of N.Y. State, wrote to Gerber informing him that on June 2 the state EC dismissed the appeal of the Third and Tenth A.D. Branch against the decision of Local New York and sustained the action of the CC. See "Minutes, Central Committee of Local New York," May 23, 1914, "Minutes," and M. Solomon to Julius Gerber, June 5, 1914, "Letters": both in LNY, SP, R2637, S V:117.

59. Winston James, *Holding Aloft the Banner of Ethiopia: Caribbean Radicalism in Early-Twentieth-Century America* (New York: Verso, 1998), 126. James adds, affirm-

ing Harrison's later analysis, the Socialist Party "succumbed to the racist corruption of its American environment."

8. Toward Independence (1914–1915)

1. HD, September 16, 1918.

2. *WGMC*, 2:432–42, esp. 435–36, on book selling; and Philip S. Foner, *History of the Labor Movement in the United States*, vols. 1–7 (New York: International Publishers, 1947–1988), 4:442–43, on the weather (hereafter *HLM*). Harrison's occupations over the next few years are listed in New York City directories as painter, teacher, and porter. See R. L. Polk and Co., comp., *Trow General Directory of New York City Embracing the Burroughs of Manhattan and the Bronx*, vol. 128: *1915* (New York: R. L. Polk, 1915), 875. Also see directories for *1916–17*, 783, *1917–18*, 962, and *1918–19*, 938.

3. Harrison's family lived at 231 W. 134th St. from 1910 to at least 1920 or 1921. See HH, "Petition for Naturalization," June 22, 1922, and HH to Naturalization Examiner, July 5, 1922, both in FOIA/PA Request No. NYC840409, U.S. Department of Labor, Immigration and Naturalization Service, Washington, D.C.; "Hubert Henry Harrison," National Personnel Records Center, St. Louis; and the 1915 to 1919 issues of *Trow General Directory*. Daughter Aida Mae was born July 4, 1912. Harrison's children's birthdates were corrected from the naturalization documents in Aida Harrison Richardson and William Harrison, interview by author, August 4, 1983.

4. HD, June 15, 1914.

5. HD, June 15, 1914. Regarding the sexual double standard, Elinor Des Verney Sinnette, *Arthur Alfonso Schomburg, Black Bibliophile and Curator: A Biography* (Detroit: New York Public Library and Wayne State University Press, 1989), 36, writes, "The implicit and explicit social rule of the time was that the women, by and large, remained home attending to household tasks while their mates, gainfully employed during the day, participated at night in the events of their various clubs and lodges." Tillie Olsen, *Silences* (1965; New York: Delacorte Press/Seymour Lawrence, 1978), 12, makes the important point that "substantial creative work demands time." She adds that of the nineteenth century women "whose achievements endure for us . . . nearly all never married . . . or married late in their thirties" (16). In Harrison's copy of "Paderewski's Carload of Cuffs," *Hearst's*, January 1921, HP-Sc 11, 25, in a discussion of geniuses it is pointed out that Beethoven, Handel, Felix Mendelssohn, and Giacomo Meyerbeer never married. At that point Harrison writes, "You fool! That proved them eminently sane!"

6. HD, June 15, 1914. See also August Meier, *Negro Thought in America, 1880–1915: Racial Ideologies in the Age of Booker T. Washington* (1963; Ann Arbor: University of Michigan Press, 1987), 15 and 137.

7. HH to the editor, "New York Lecture Centers," *Truth Seeker* 41, no. 34 (August 22, 1914): 539 (hereafter *TS*); announcement re HH lectures, *Sabotage*, July 20, 1914, HP-Sc 34; and George E. Macdonald, *Fifty Years of Freethought: Being the Story of the "Truth Seeker," with the Natural History of Its Third Editor*, 2 vols. (New York: Truth Seeker, 1931), 2:350.

8. "A Splendid Offer to Young Men of Ambition," *New York News*, c. 1914, HP-Sc 34.

9. W. E. B. Du Bois, "Black Folk and Birth Control," *Birth Control Review* 16, no. 6 (June 1932): 166–67; and [HH], "The Line-Up on the Color Line," *Negro World* December 4, 1920, HP-Sc 33, in *HR*, 216–19, esp. 219. On Harrison's talks see "Victory for Harrison," *Truth Seeker* 41, no. 34 (August 22, 1914): 544; Macdonald, *Fifty Years*, 2:421, 453; and *WGMC*, 2:435.

10. "A Freethought Lecturer Arrested in New York," *TS* 41, no. 27 (July 4, 1914): 425; and *WGMC*, 2:435. See also HH to the editor, "New York Lecture Centers"; "Victory for Harrison"; and *TS* 41, no. 27 (July 4, 1914): 429.

11. "A Freethought Lecturer Arrested," 425; and [Untitled article], *TS* 41, no. 26 (June 27, 1914). The records from the Magistrate's Court show that "Herbert Harrison," a Black male age thirty-two, was arrested on the date in question. See Records of Magistrate's Court, 7th District, Manhattan, vol. 33, March 1 to August 4, 1914, 269, County Clerk of the City of New York. It should be noted that Harrison was not a citizen and was said to have been named Herbert at birth.

12. "A Freethought Lecturer Arrested."

13. HH to Joseph E. Corrigan, March 19, 1915, *Voice* 1, no. 17 (October 31, 1917): 5.

14. "Victory for Harrison"; "Open-Air Meetings," *TS* 41, no. 32 (August 8, 1914): 501; and "The Struggle for Free Speech," *TS* 41, no. 35 (August 29, 1914): 549.

15. "Victory for Harrison." See also "Negro Speaker Turns on Mob in Subway: Fells Man with Iron Bar—Angry Crowd Had Followed Him From Street Lecture," *New York World*, August 12, 1914, HP; and "Passing the First Half-Century Mark," *TS* 50, no. 35 (September 1, 1923): 553–70, esp. 567.

16. "The Struggle for Free Speech"; "Victory for Harrison"; "Negro Speaker Turns on Mob in Subway"; and "AM" [Chief Naturalization Examiner], "MEMORANDUM re Mr. Harrison, 2270-42659," July 27, 1922 FOIA/PA Request No. NYC840409.

17. "The Struggle for Free Speech" and "Victory for Harrison."

18. Henry Miller, *The Rosy Crucifixion, Book Two: Plexus* (New York: Grove Press, 1965), 560–61. "Hubert H. Harrison's Appointments," *TS* 41, no. 34 (August 22, 1914): 541 has a lecture schedule. Miller and Harrison were delegates from New York City to the June 29, 1912, New York State SP Convention. See "Auburn Welcomes Socialist Hosts," *New York Call*, June 29, 1912, 1, 3, esp. 3 (hereafter *NYC*). Richard B. Moore also heard Harrison at Madison Square and then sought him out at Ninety-sixth St. and Broadway and in Harlem. See Joyce Turner, "Richard B. Moore and

His Works," in *Richard B. Moore, Caribbean Militant in Harlem: Collected Writings 1920–1972*, ed. W. Burghardt Turner and Joyce Moore Turner (Bloomington: University of Indiana Press, 1988), 27.

19. "Open-Air Meetings," *TS*, 41 no. 32 (August 8, 1914), 501; Theodore G. Vincent, *Black Power and the Garvey Movement* (San Francisco: Ramparts Press, 1972), 40 n. The roles of Harrison and the anarchists are discussed in "A Freethought Lecturer Arrested" and in Alexander Berkman to the editor, "Anarchists and Street Speaking," *TS* 41, no. 34 (August 22, 1914): 539. Berkman points out that prior to April 1914 "no open-air meetings could be held . . . without a permit from the police, and it is hardly necessary to add that permits were not issued to organizations or individuals that were not in the good graces of the police department."

20. HH to the editor, "New York Lecture Centres."

21. HH to the editor, "New York Lecture Centres."

22. HH to the editor, "New York Lecture Centres."

23. HD, September 28, 1914. In his copy of William Henry Hudson, *Introduction to the Philosophy of Herbert Spencer* (London: Watts, 1911), 19, where Spencer claims that man has free will do to whatever he wills, Harrison writes, "Is he? The convict, the unpatriot, the Negro in America?" The Leonard Abbott–led Harlem Liberal Alliance also hosted the founding meeting of the Ferrer Association at its 100 West 116th St. headquarters. See Avrich, *The Modern School*, 35, 39, 350. Thanks to David Slavin for help with the translation and interpretation.

24. HD, September 28, 1914. HH, "Bridging the Gulf of Color," c. April 1922, HP, adds, "as late as six years ago there met every Sunday at Lenox Casino in New York a lecture forum made up of hundreds of cultivated whites who had selected as the leader and teacher a man of undiluted Negro blood."

25. "The Radical Forum," *TS* 41, no. 39 (September 26, 1914): 621; "The Radical Forum," *TS* 41, no. 45 (November 7, 1914), 717; advertisements for HH lectures, *NYC*, September 26 and 27, November 29, December 13, and c. 1914–1915, copies in HP-Sc 34; handout for "Modern Materialism" lecture of September 27, 1914, HP-Sc 34; and handout for "The Radical Forum," October 18, 1914–January 3, 1915, HP-Sc 34.

26. John T. Carroll to the editor, *New York Globe*, November 4, 1914.

27. HD, October 12, 1914.

28. HD, October 13 and December 9, 1914. Ben Heller to author, June 27, 2007, helped with the code.

29. "At Old Branch 5 Again!" *NYC*, December 13, 1914, HP; and "Removal Notice! The Radical Forum," c. December 1914–January 1915, HP-Sc 34.

30. HH, "Our International Consciousness," in HH, *When Africa Awakes: The "Inside Story" of the Stirrings and Strivings of the New Negro in the Western World* (New York: Porro Press, 1920), 96, (hereafter *WAA*); and HH, "History and Forecast of the Disarmament Movement," notes for a Lecture for the New York City Board of Education, November 16, 1924, HP, which contains the estimates. On the "scramble for Africa," see Endre Sik, *The History of Black Africa*, 4 vols., vol. 1, 7th ed. (1961; Bu-

dapest, 1970), 285–311, esp. 285, vol. 2, 2nd ed. (1962; Budapest: Akademiai Kiado, 1972), 27–28.

31. HH, "Our International Consciousness," *WAA*, 96; and HH, "Our Larger Duty," *New Negro* 3, no. 7 (August 1919): 5, in *HR*, 99–101, esp. 101.

32. HH, "The Rising Tide of Color," *Negro World* [?] (June 12, 1920) [?], in *HR*, 309–10, esp. 309; and HH, "*The Rising Tide of Color Against White-World Supremacy*, by T. Lothrop Stoddard," *Negro World*, May 29, 1920, in *HR*, 305–9, esp. 307. See also HH, "The White War and the Colored World," *Voice*, August 14, 1917, in *HR*, 202–3. In HH to T. Lothrop Stoddard, June 24, 1920, HP, Harrison wrote that he was "enclosing a copy of an article on THE WHITE WAR AND THE COLORED RACES, written in 1918 and reprinted in the *Negro World* in February of this year. The substance of it had been previously delivered in Wall St. and Washington Heights, Madison Square and other places, in-doors and out to white audiences during 1915 and 1916." Harrison also wrote "The White World and the Colored Races," *New Negro* 4, no. 2 (October 1919): 8–10, in *HR*, 203–8, in 1918 for "a certain well known radical magazine [possibly *The Messenger* or the *International Socialist Review*]; but [it] was found to be 'too radical' for publication at that time." Madison Grant, the white-supremacist author whose 1916 book *The Passing of the Great Race* was the most widely read nonfiction racist book of the year, wrote the introduction to Stoddard's book. In correspondence with Stoddard, Harrison wrote, "since I am a Negro, my sympathies are not at all with you: that which you fear, I naturally hope for." See HH to T. Lothrop Stoddard, June 24, 1920, HP.

33. HH, "The White War and the Colored World," 202–3.

34. HH, "The White War and the Colored World," 203. In Oakley C. Johnson, *An American Century: The Recollections of Bertha W. Howe, 1866–1966* (New York: Published for AIMS by Humanities Press, 1966), 81, Howe explains that Harrison said at Sunrise Club dinners that Black people, after having guns put in their hands during World War I, "will learn to protect themselves" and will "never be the same again" and that "white people had better take notice of it."

35. HH, "The White World and the Colored Races," 206.

36. Philip S. Foner, *American Socialism and Black Americans: From the Age of Jackson to World War II* (Westport, Conn.: Greenwood Press, 1977), 273; and David A. Shannon, *The Socialist Party of America* (New York: Macmillan, 1955), 81, 83, 87, 99. Harrison's emphasis on the importance of Africa and Asia in the European conflict calls to mind a similar (though discussed in national, not racial, terms) argument by V. I. Lenin. In 1914 Lenin and the Bolsheviks advanced the slogan of turning the imperialist war into a civil war. In 1915 Lenin's *Socialism and War* argued that it was the duty of the socialists to oppose their own warring governments. In 1917, in *Imperialism, the Highest Stage of Capitalism*, he extended his analysis and argued that the war was an imperialist war fought over Africa and Asia and that the imperialism of the respective home countries should be opposed by all socialists, in the interest of all working people. See Grigorii Zinoviev, *History of the Bolshevik Party*

from the Beginnings to February 1917 (1923), trans. R. Chappell (London: New Park Publishers, 1973), 182–84; and *Lenin on the United States: Selections from His Writings* (New York: International Publishers, 1970), 621n. 47.

37. Roi Ottley and William J. Weatherby, eds., *The Negro in New York: An Informal Social History* (New York: New York Public Library, 1967), 195; and Arthur E. Barbeau and Florette Henri, *The Unknown Soldiers: Black American Troops in World War I* (Philadelphia: Temple University Press, 1974), 7. See also James Weldon Johnson, *Black Manhattan* (1930; New York: Atheneum, 1967), 232–33. Theodore G. Vincent, ed., *Voices of A Black Nation: Political Journalism in the Harlem Renaissance* (San Francisco: Ramparts Press, 1973), 25, points out that positions on the war marked a major difference between "New Negroes" and older leaders.

38. HH, "The Negro a Conservative: Christianity Still Enslaves the Minds of Those Whose Bodies It Long Held Bound," *TS* 41, no. 37 (September 12, 1914): 583, in *HR*, 42–46, quotation at 43. The *Truth Seeker* used a small "n" in Negro. This was not Harrison's style, and it was not used by him when he reprinted the article in 1917.

39. HH, "The Negro a Conservative," 43–44. W. E. B. Du Bois, *Dusk of Dawn: An Essay Toward an Autobiography of a Race Concept* (1940; New York: Schocken, 1971), 132, points out that because of racism and "group imprisonment" there is a pressure for African Americans "to neglect the wider aspects of national life."

40. HH, "The Negro a Conservative," 45; and B. L. Putnam Weale (Bertram Lenox Simpson), *The Conflict of Colour: The Threatened Upheaval Throughout the World* (New York, 1910), HHP-Bo, 116. Harrison notes that Weale, who didn't believe the Christian myth himself, found that Christianity, compared to Islam, was a more efficient tool of racial subjugation. Weale wrote that "Islam gives the negro more freedom and a better welcome than Christianity" (246n. 1). Harrison agreed and, in handwritten comments on p. 257 of his copy of Weale's book, added that the Muslim "preaches the equality of all true believers—and lives up to it. The white Christian preaches the brotherhood of man, but wants 'niggers' to sit in the rear pews, to ride in 'Jim Crow' cars, and generally to 'keep in their place.'" On July 7, 1924, in his copy of T. Lothrop Stoddard, *The Rising Tide of Color Against White World-Supremacy* (1920; New York, 1922), HP, 102, Harrison wrote that "the white man fears the Black upsurgence only as the Blacks cease to be Christian—and that significant thesis was first publicly put by Putnam Weale ten years before in *The Conflict of Color*. Small wonder that Sir Harry Johnston and Sir Sydney Olivier (both non-Christians) want the Africans missionarized into that Christian Religion which they themselves have forsaken: it has such great imperialistic value in subverting the darker ego."

41. HH, "The Negro a Conservative," 45; HH, "Idols of the Marketplace," scrapbook cover; HP-Sc 40; and HH, "Harlem's Neglected Opportunities: Twin Sources of Gin and Genius, Poetry and Pajama Parties," *Amsterdam News*, April 30, 1927, HP, in *HR*, 357–62, esp. 359 ("population"). Harrison discusses the unfinished "Idols" manuscript in HH to T. Lothrop Stoddard, November 13, 1920, HP. On p. 174 of his

copy of J. M. Robertson, *The Evolution of States: An Introduction to English Politics* (New York: Putnam/Knickerbocker Press, 1913), HP, Harrison makes reference to his own book "Idols of the Tribe." In that same work on p. 2 Harrison's handwritten comments on "Idols of the Tribe" reads: "I ascribe a social imperative as its motivating cause." A similar understanding, regarding the fact that leaders often played to the masses, would later, in part, shape Harrison's attitude towards Marcus Garvey. Garvey, Harrison felt, drew power from the fact that he played to popular, though not always forward and enlightening feelings of the African American masses. Harrison, could never quite do this. Yet Garvey was able to turn his movement into what historian Randall K. Burkett calls a "a mass movement with . . . explicit and pervasive religious dimensions." The Garvey message was offered in an at times very religious sort of way—the iconoclastic and agnostic/atheistic Harrison would not offer such a religion-like vision. On Garvey, see Randall K. Burkett, *Black Redemption: Churchmen Speak for the Garvey Movement* (Philadelphia: Temple University Press, 1978), 8. In HD, "Aphorisms," started December 20, 1921, Harrison wrote, "It was a wise American that who had travelled all over the world who said that 'Human beings love to be humbugged'. Patriotism, spiritualism and the newspapers are cases in point. Wherefore, *to rule men you must fool them.* Spend your life in serving them unselfishly, and they will let you die of starvation. But fool them to the top of their bent and they will pour their wealth into your lap pockets and enshrine you in their administration. Jesus, John Brown and Father Damien died poor and despised; while Billy Sunday, Marcus Garvey and Woodrow Wilson lived in luxury and ease."

42. HD, October 8, 1914.

43. HD, October 13, 1914.

44. On Ferrer and the Modern School, see Paul Avrich, *The Modern School Movement: Anarchism and Education in the United States* (Princeton, N.J.: Princeton University Press, 1980), esp. 1–41 and 69–110; Harry Kelly, *The Modern School* (Stelton, N.J.: The Modern School Association of N.A., 1920), 2–4; Donald Drew Egbert and Stow Persons, eds., *Socialism and American Life* (Princeton, N.J: Princeton University Press, 1952) 1:716–17, esp. 716n. 184; and Kenneth Teitelbaum, *Schooling for "Good Rebels": Socialist Education for Children in the United States, 1900–1920* (Philadelphia: Temple University Press, 1993), 39–40.

45. Kelly, *Modern School*, 2–4, 7–8; and Avrich, *Modern School Movement*, 11, 112–16, 172–79, 343–47.

46. *WGMC*, 2:435. See also "*The Modern School*: A Course of Lectures in Comparative Religion by Hubert Henry Harrison," handout, and "Mr. Hubert H. Harrison Will Speak on 'Religion and Science,'" advertisement, c. 1915, both in HP-Sc 34.

47. HH, "Reading for Knowledge," *Voice*, September 1918, in *WAA*, 123–26, esp. 124; HH, "The Voice of the Negro: [review of] *The Everlasting Stain*—by Kelly Miller," c. 1924; and "Reminiscences of A. Philip Randolph," interview, July 25, 1972, Oral History Project, Butler Library, Columbia University, New York, 152–53.

48. HH, "The Negro a Conservative," 46.

49. W. E. B. Du Bois, *The Autobiography of W. E. B. Du Bois: A Soliloquy on View-ing My Life From the Last Decade of Its First Century* (1968; New York, 1971), 236; and HH, "Education and the Race" in *HR*, 122–24, esp. 123. For background on the rationalist, freethought, anarchist, and socialist influences see Avrich, *Modern School Movement*, 7, 15–18.

50. HH, "The New Knowledge for the New Negro," *WAA*, 131–34, esp. 131, 134; HH, "The World We Live In," *Boston Chronicle*, January 19, 1924, HP-Wr; [HH], "Negro Culture and the Negro College," *New Negro* 4, no. 1 (September 1919): 4–5, in *HR*, 120–122, esp. 122. See also [HH], "Read, Read, Read!" *Voice*, July 18, 1918, in *HR*, 126–27; HH, "Reading for Knowledge"; and HH, "A Few Books," *Boston Chron-icle*, March 1, 1924, HP.

51. HH, "Education and the Race," *WAA*, 126–28, in *HR*, 122–25, 123; HH, "Educa-tion and the Race" (chapter introduction), *WAA*, 123; and HH, "To the Young Men of My Race," *New Negro*, January 1919, in *HR*, 175–177, esp. 176.

52. HH, "Education and the Race," *HR*, 122–23. Judith Stein. *The World of Marcus Garvey: Race and Class in Modern Society* (Baton Rouge: Louisiana State University Press, 1986), 44–45, writes that A. Philip Randolph "recalled that Harrison thought the 'Negro's knowledge' was 'too limited to develop a vanguard in the field of revolu-tionary change.' Harrison believed that education—the attainment of enlightenment and knowledge—was a prerequisite for, not a by-product of, socialism."

9. Focus on Harlem:
The Birth of the "New Negro Movement" (1915–1917)

1. HH, "How to Do It—and How Not," *New York Call*, December 16, 1911, 6 (here-after *NYC*), in *HR*, 60–62. On p. 61 Harrison explained: "You have to know the psy-chology of the Negro, for if you don't you will fail to attract or impress him. You will fail to make him think—and feel. For many of your arguments must be addressed to his heart as well as to his head."

2. HH, "Program and Principles of the International Colored Unity League," *The Voice of the Negro* 1 no. 1 (April 1927): 4–6, in *HR*, 399–402, esp. 400; and [HH,] untitled editorial, *Voice*, July 4, 1917, HP. Frederick Douglass detailed in *Narrative of the Life of Frederick Douglass* (1845) his forceful rejoinder to his overseer ("you shall see how a slave was made a man"), and at least since that time manhood was a major concern in much African American protest and literature. Over time, male-supremacist impli-cations have been increasingly questioned and challenged. See William L. Andrews, Frances Smith Foster, and Trudier Harris, eds. *The Oxford Companion to African American Literature* (New York: Oxford University Press, 1997), 475–77, esp. 475–76. D. Hamilton Jackson, Harrison's boyhood and lifetime friend, served as educational secretary for the "Labor, Social and Reform Party (Manhood Movement)" in St. Croix. See Charles T. Magil, "Conditions in Virgin Islands Intolerable," *Chicago Defender*,

October 2, 1920, 2. Harrison's "manhood" movement was inclusionary from the beginning. The call to the first public activity of the Liberty League was addressed to those who "Believe in Negro Manhood" and those who "Believe in Negro Womanhood." See "A Mass Meeting of Colored Citizens Will Be Held at Bethel Church, . . . June 12th, . . . Under the Auspices of The Liberty League of Negro-Americans," handout, HP.

3. On the lectures, see HH, "Our International Consciousness," in HH, *When Africa Awakes: The "Inside Story" of the Stirrings and Strivings of the New Negro in the Western World* (New York: Porro Press, 1920), 96 (hereafter *WAA*); and "The Brownsville Radical Forum," advertisement, c. January 1915, HP-Sc 34. On education, see HH, "Education Out of School," *Boston Chronicle*, February 23, 1924 (hereafter *BC*), in *HR*, 125–26; [HH,] "Read! Read! Read!" *Voice*, July 18, 1918, HP in *HR*, 126–28; [HH,] "Reading for Knowledge," July 1918, in HH, *WAA*, 123–26; and *Monatlisches Zeitung Turn-Verein Vorwarts* (Brooklyn, N.Y.), July 1916, in "Praises from People and Press," c. 1920, HP-Sc D.

4. On the talks see "Who Put the Bomb in St. Patrick's Cathedral?" *New York Evening Mail*, March 24, 1915, HP; "Who Placed the Bomb in St. Patrick's Cathedral?" *New York Globe*, March 24, 1915, HP; "Some Stirring Talks on Timely Topics by Hubert H. Harrison, America's Foremost Negro Lecturer, at Lenox Casino," handout, c. 1915, HP-Sc 34. On the bombing, see Paul Avrich, *The Modern School Movement: Anarchism and Education in the United States* (Princeton, N.J.: Princeton University Press, 1980), 212–13. On the slogan, see Anthony Bimba, *The History of the American Working Class* (New York: International Publishers, 1927), 257; David A. Shannon, *The Socialist Party of America* (New York: Macmillan, 1955), 88; *GP*, 1:469–70, esp. 470n. 1; and Sally M. Miller, "Socialist Party Decline and World War I: Bibliography and Interpretation," *Science and Society* 34, no. 4 (Winter 1970): 398–411, esp. 407. Harrison's comments on Billy Sunday are in HD, "Aphorisms," started December 20, 1921

5. "Some Stirring Talks," handout, c. 1915. [HH], "The Call of Culture," n.p., c. 1914 [?], HP. Comments on the role of public speakers are based on Ira De A. Reid, *The Negro Immigrant: His Background, Characteristics and Social Adjustment, 1899–1937* (1939; New York: AMS Press, 1970), 146; and Samuel A. Darcy, interview by author, Harvey Cedars, N.J., January 24, 1980.

6. Lester A. Walton, "Street Speaker Heralds Spring in Harlem," *New York World*, March 25, 1928, p. 17 (hereafter *NYW*); "The Reminiscences of A. Philip Randolph," interview by Wendell Wray, July 25, 1972, Oral History Project, Butler Library, Columbia University, 152–153; and Claude McKay, *A Long Way from Home: An Autobiography* (1937; New York: Harcourt Brace & World, 1970), 41 and 114.

7. *WCMC*, 3:135 35.

8. "Evolution Is Discussed on Harlem Streets," *New York News*, August 28, 1926 (hereafter *NYN*).

9. [HH], "One Decade of Harlem's Mental Growth," notes, c. 1925, HP, discusses Cohen and Johnson; and [James Weldon Johnson], "An Open Air Lecture Course," editorial, *New York Age*, May 6, 1915, 4 (hereafter *NYA*).

10. [Johnson], "An Open Air Lecture Course."

11. HH to James Weldon Johnson, May 12, 1915, James Weldon Johnson Papers, Correspondence, Series 1, Folder #197, Beinecke Rare Book and Manuscript Library, Yale University.

12. HD, June 3, 1915, on the Clark meeting. On Clark's role in encouraging the publication, see Guichard Parris and Lester Brooks, *Blacks in the City: A History of the National Urban League* (Boston: Little, Brown, 1971), 171; and Patrick J. Gilpin, "Charles S. Johnson: Entrepreneur of the Harlem Renaissance," in *The Harlem Renaissance Remembered: Essays with a Memoir*, ed. Arna Bontemps, (New York: Dodd, Mead, 1972), 215–46, esp. 220.

13. HD, June 2 and 16, 1915. See "A Splendid Offer to Young Men of Ambition," *NYN*, c. 1914 and "A Course Through College Without the Expense Is What You Are Offered in The Harrison Method of Simplified Education," c. December 1915, HP-Sc 34. Arthur Schomburg to John E. Bruce, April 22, 1915, box 2, AL, Ms 286, John E. Bruce Papers, SCRBC, suggests that Harrison may not have been living with his family at this time.

14. On Royall, see "3,000 Blacks Like Attack Upon T.R.," *NYW*, July 30, 1917; Marsha Hurst Hiller, "Race Politics in New York City, 1890–1930" (Ph.D. diss., Columbia University, 1972), 188, 196, 217; Michael Louis Goldstein, "Race Politics in New York City, 1890–1930: Independent Political Behavior" (Ph.D. diss., Columbia University, 1973), 241–42, 254; Edwin R. Lewinson, *Black Politics in New York City* (New York: Twayne, 1974), 54–56; Gilbert Osofsky, *Harlem: The Making of a Ghetto; Negro New York, 1890–1930* (1963; New York: Harper and Row, 1971), 90, 92–93, 108; and Seth M. Scheiner, *Negro Mecca: A History of the Negro in New York, 1865–1920* (New York: New York University Press, 1965), 31, 156, 207.

15. HD, June 3, 1915.

16. HD, June 3, 1915. See also Nancy J. Weiss, *The National Urban League, 1910–1940* (New York: Oxford University Press, 1974), 82–83.

17. HD, June 3, 1915.

18. "Opportunity in N.Y. for Race: Thousands Attend Urban League Meetings on Sunday to Hear Washington," *NYA*, May 20, 1915, 1–2.

19. HH, "Introductory," *WAA*, 7–8; and HH, "Declaration of Intention [to Naturalize]," no. 114310, June 22, 1915, Records of Naturalization, U.S. Department of Labor, Immigration and Naturalization Service, U.S. District Court, S.D., N.Y., 172 Docket No. 42659 (which lists Harrison's address as 231 W. 134th St. and has places for information on his wife crossed out). In 1914 Harrison listed his address as 140 W. 136th St. and in December 1915 as 138 W. 136th St.

20. HH, "'They Shall Not Pass!'" *Voice*, January 30, 1919, HP-Sc 32, in *WAA*, 35–36, esp. 36; and HH, "The Negro and the Nation," "An Address by Dr. Hubert H. Harrison of Lecture Bureau, Dept. of Education, New York City, Thurs. June 21st 1923—By Radio Broadcasting of American Telephone & Telegraph Co.," handwrit-

ten notes, 1–9, HP in *HR*, 286–91, where after becoming a citizen, he writes, "The destiny of the American Negro lies in the future of America" (291).

21. HH, "Patronize Your Own," *NW*, May 1, 1920, 2, in *HR*, 111–13, esp. 112.

22. HH, "Patronize Your Own," 112–13. See also Scheiner, *Negro Mecca*, 103; and "First Black Character Doll Is Introduced," *Amsterdam News*, June 29, 1985, 19 (hereafter *AN*).

23. Osofsky, *Harlem*, 122; and Florette Henri, *Black Migration: Movement North, 1900–1920* (Garden City, N.Y.: Anchor Press/Doubleday, 1975), 88.

24. HH, "Negro Society and the Negro Stage," part 1, *Voice*, September 19, 1917, HP, in *HR*, 370–73, esp. 372; and Nathan I. Huggins, *Harlem Renaissance* (1971; New York: Oxford University Press, 1974), 9 and 139.

25. Huggins, *Harlem Renaissance*, 245, writes that "the theatrical stage itself, more than any other cultural phenomenon, opens a perspective into the pathology of American race relations."

26. HH, "Negro Society and the Negro Stage," 371. In HH to Theodore Lothrop Stoddard, November 13, 1920, HP, Harrison writes: "I am thinking seriously of perpetrating a book which I had planned about five years ago and of which two or three chapters were written; viz. 'Negro Society and the Negro Stage.'" On Harrison's difficulty in getting work because of his complexion, see HH, "At the Back of the Black Man's Mind," n.p., [c. November 1922], 6, HP, where he says that he was "'too dark'" to get employment on all but one Black paper (there were four major ones at the time) in New York. The historian Florette Henri writes that 90 percent of prominent Black leaders of the era—the kind mentioned in "Who's Who" type lists of race leaders—were light skinned. See Henri, *Black Migration*, 189, 369n. 46. For background on the Rogers book, see HH, "White People Versus Negroes, Being the Story of a Great Book," *NW*, January 7, 1922, 10, in *HR*, 301–5. On Harrison and the "'cullud' editors," see "Proud New Negro," *Clarion* 1 no. 1 (August 1, 1917), 15, HP.

27. HH, "Negro Society and the Negro Stage," 370; and Huggins, *Harlem Renaissance*, 246–249, esp. 246.

28. HH, "Negro Society and the Negro Stage," 371.

29. HH, "Negro Society and the Negro Stage," 371.

30. HH, "Negro Society and the Negro Stage," 372–73. See also Huggins, *Harlem Renaissance*, 248–51, 261, 263, 287.

31. HH, "Negro Society and the Negro Stage," 373; and HH, "Are Negro Actors White?" *NW*, March 12, 1921, HP.

32. HH, "Negro Society and the Negro Stage," part 2, *Voice*, October 3, 1917, HP, in *HR*, 373–77. On color prejudice, also see IIII, "Are Negro Actors White?"; and HH, "The Roots of Power," *BC*, June 21, 1924, HP, in *HR*, 405–6.

33. HH, "Negro Society and the Negro Stage," 373–74. See also Huggins, *Harlem Renaissance*, 285–86; and "The Return of Cole and Johnson," *NYA*, October 6, 1910, 6, HP.

34. HH, "Negro Society and the Negro Stage," 374. Harrison later explained: "For Bert Williams the way to personal success lay in flattering the white people's sense of superiority by always playing the clown. Had he done otherwise the tens of thousands of dollars which finally found their way to his pocket would have remained in the pockets of the whites. When Cole and Johnson at the Fifth Avenue Theater in the fall of 1910 appeared before white audiences in unobtrusive evening dress with an act of 'high class' singing, piano playing and clever dialogue their audiences fell off suddenly. It didn't pay. Then they made a quick change back to the standard of 'A Trip to Coontown'—fair part: Success." See HH, "Bridging the Gulf of Color," c. April 1922, HP, in *HR*, 273–77, esp. 275.

35. HH, "Negro Society and the Negro Stage," 374. See also HH, "The Art of the Theater and How To Understand It," n.p., c. January 7, 1917 [?], HP; and Doris E. Abramson, *Negro Playwrights in the American Theatre, 1925–1929* (1967; New York: Columbia University Press, 1969), x, which makes similar points.

36. HH, "Negro Society and the Negro Stage," 375; and HH, "Are Negro Actors White?"

37. HH, "Negro Society and the Negro Stage," 375. Houston Baker Jr., *Modernism and the Harlem Renaissance* (Chicago: University of Chicago Press, 1987), 25–27, 33, 37, describes how a "modern" African American narrator, developing a "liberating" "mastery of form," can use "strategies such as repetition" to "ensure attention" and "find a voice."

38. HH, "Negro Society and the Negro Stage," 375.

39. HH, "Negro Society and the Negro Stage," 375–76. Rev. Everard W. Daniel, to whom it may concern [re Mrs. Irene Harrison], January 9, 1917, HP, indicates that the Harrison children (probably because of Irene's influence) attended St. Philip's Sunday School. Harrison commented on p. 96 in his copy of T. Lothrop Stoddard, *Rising Tide of Color*, HP, "that Xtianity and race prejudice go together."

40. HH, "Negro Society and the Negro Stage," 376; and White, "The Paradox of Color," 367. Monroe N. Work, ed. *Negro Year Book, 1921–1922* (Tuskegee, Ala.: Negro Year Book Publishing, 1922), estimated that in 1920 "mulattoes" were 23 percent of the African American population (hereafter *NYB, 1921–1922*). See *GP*, 9:440n. 3.

41. HH, "Negro Society and the Negro Stage," 376.

42. Hodge Kirnon, "Hubert Harrison: An Appreciation," *NW*, December 31, 1927.

43. HH, "Our Civic Corner," *NYN*, September 2, 1915.

44. *African Times and Orient Review*, HP-Sc, esp. nos. 1 and 30, and *GP*, 1:26n. 2 and 519–21.

45. The slogan appears in HH, "Our Civic Corner," September 2, 1915, and "Join the Universal Negro Improvement Association," leaflet, c. November 1919, RG 165, MID 10218, 261-51, National Archives, Washington, D.C. The poem is in Hazel Fel-

leman, ed., *The Best Loved Poems of the American People* (Garden City, N.Y.: Double-day, 1936), 321–22.

46. HH, "Our Civic Corner," September 2, 1915. The view opposed to Harrison's is that articulated later by Gunnar Myrdal who wrote: *"only when Negroes have collaborated with whites have organizations been built up which have had any strength and which have been able to do something practical."* Gunnar Myrdal, *An American Dilemma: The Negro Problem and Modern Democracy,* with the assistance of Richard Sterner and Arnold Rose, 2 vols. (1944; New York: Random House, 1972), 2:853. See also Nancy J. Weiss, "From Black Separatism to Interracial Cooperation: The Origins of Organized Efforts for Racial Advancement, 1890–1920," in *Twentieth-Century America: Recent Interpretations,* ed. Barton J. Bernstein and Allen J. Matusow, 2nd ed. (1969; New York: Harcourt Brace Jovanovich, 1972), 52–87, esp. 53–55, 63, 66–67, 81–84 . Weiss, in discussing "black separatism to achieve racial integration," maintains that "the strategy cut them [African Americans] off from the indispensable financial resources, political power, and legal talent that only whites could supply" (53).

47. HH, "Our Civic Corner," September 2, 1915.

48. HH, "Our Civic Corner," September 2, 1915.

49. HH, "Our Civic Corner," September 9, 1915.

50. HH, "Our Civic Corner," September 9, 1915.

51. HH, "Our Civic Corner," September 9, 1915. In HH, "Addendum to the Above," *NW,* April 23, 1921, Harrison wrote, "I have never cared for such [magnificent] titles, and . . . I never shall."

52. Hubert [HH] to J. E. B. [John E. Bruce], October 25, 1915, box 1, A.L., Ms. 42, Bruce Papers.

53. HH, "Introductory," *WAA,* 5, 6; HH, "Our Larger Duty," *New Negro* 3 (August 1919): 5, in *HR,* 99–101, esp. 100; and [HH], "Two Negro Radicalisms," *New Negro* 4, no. 2 (October 1919): 4–5, HP, in *HR,* 102–5, esp. 104.

54. HH, "The White War and the Colored Races," *New Negro* 4 (October 1919): 8–10, in *HR,* 203–09, esp. 207; and HH, "Introductory," *WAA,* 6.

55. HH, "Our International Consciousness," 96.

56. HH, "U-Need-A-Biscuit," *NW,* July 17, 1920, 2, in *HR,* 149–51; and David Stivers, archivist, Nabisco Company, Parsippany, N.J., telecon, January 9, 1995.

57. HH, "U-Need-A-Biscuit," 149–50.

58. HH, "The Negro and the War," (chapter introduction), *WAA,* 25. On Harrison's use of militant language that was well understood by the Harlem masses, also see Directorate of Intelligence, Special Report No. 10: "Unrest Among the Negroes," October 7, 1919, in *Science and Society* 32, no. 1 (Winter 1968): 66–79, esp. 77–78.

59. Hans Schmidt, *The United States Occupation of Haiti* (New Brunswick, N.J.: Rutgers University Press, 1971), 6–9, 17; and *GP,* 5:643n. 2, 9:78n. 3, 181n. 8. The figure of 15,000 deaths is based on Edwidge Danticat, "Ghosts of the 1915 U.S. Invasion Still Haunt Haiti's People," *Miami Herald,* July 25, 2005.

60. [HH], [Notes re Toussaint], c. August 19, 1915, HP; and C. L. R. James, *The Black Jacobins: Toussaint L'Ouverture and the San Domingo Revolution*, 2nd rev. ed. (1938; New York: Vintage, 1963), 25, 100–101.

61. *Colored American Review* 1, no. 2 (October 15, 1915): inside cover, 1–2 (hereafter *CAR*); and HH to the editor, *CAR* 1, no. 2 (October 15, 1915): inside cover.

62. "Gunga Din" [HH], "The Black Man's Burden (A Reply to Rudyard Kipling)," *CAR* 1, no. 4 (December 1915): 3, in *WAA*, 145–46. See also *CAR* 1, no. 4 (December 1915): 1, 6, 16; and *CAR* 1, no. 5 (January 1916): 3–9, 24.

63. [HH], "Why Is Harlem Hot?" *Voice*, October 31, 1917, 6.

64. HD, June 15, 1914, with postscript dated March 27, 1916.

65. [HH], "Read! Read! Read!" 127; and HH, "The Voice of the Negro: *The Everlasting Stain*, by Kelly Miller," c. 1924, HP.

66. HH, "White People Versus Negroes," 304.

67. HH, "Leaves Torn From the Diary of a Critic—the Race in Drama," *AN*, c. July 1916, HP; and [HH], "Selling Space vs. Selling Self," *Voice*, July 10, 1917, HP.

68. HH, "Leaves Torn."

69. HH, "Leaves Torn."

70. HH, "Leaves Torn"; and Charles S. Gilpin, To Whom it May Concern [about HH], June 30, 1924, HP.

71. HH, "Leaves Torn."

72. [HH], "Selling Space vs. Selling Self." See HH, review, *The Story of the French Revolution* (by E. Belfort Bax), *AN*, July 4, 1923.

73. [HH], "A Negro for President," *NW*, June 19, 1920, 2, in *HR*, 147–49, esp. 148; and HH, "Frightful Friendship vs. Self-Defense," *NW*, June 18, 1921, 7.

74. [HH], [editorial], *Voice*, c. July 4, 1917, HP, in which Harrison wrote that it was "a year ago" that he "drew up an outline of a plan for the publishing of a Negro paper and gave it to Messrs. Randolph and Owen," but "the matter slumbered until on the 18th of June [1917]," when Harrison "again drew up a similar outline." Also see Philip S. Foner, *American Socialism and Black Americans: From the Age of Jackson to World War II* (Westport, Conn.: Greenwood Press, 1977), 268–69; Jervis Anderson, *A. Philip Randolph: A Biographical Portrait* (New York: Harcourt Brace Jovanovich, 1973), 76; and *GP*, 2:220n. 2. Years later, Randolph remembered that Harrison was "very brilliant" and "quite articulate" and "while we were interested in going to the streets," "he was already on the streets." See "Reminiscences of A. Philip Randolph," 152.

75. HH, "'Just Suppose': A Riddle for 'Scientific Radical' Liars, with Apologies to C[handler] Ow[en]," *NW*, April 10, 1920, HP-Sc 33, sarcastically and critically treats the burgeoning radicalism of Chandler Owen. HH, "Just Crabs," [*NW*, c. April 1920], in *HR*, 111, claims that "the Subsidized Sixth" held that Blacks had "no right to move an inch until the Socialist millennium dawns"; and HH, [Notes re "The Red Record of Radicalism"], [c. 1927], HP, has Harrison's reference to Owen and Randolph as "The Gold Dust Twins."

76. [HH], [editorial], *Voice*, c. July 4, 1917.

77. [HH], [editorial], *Voice*, c. July 4, 1917. HH, "Introductory," *WAA*, 8, states "that the AFRICA of the title is to be taken in its racial rather than in its geographical sense."

78. HH, "The Real Woodrow Wilson," *NW*, April 9, 1921. See also HH, "The Negro and the War," *WAA*, 25.

79. On Wilson's administration and African Americans, see Henri, *Black Migration*, 229, 248, 257; Christine A. Lunardini, "Standing Firm: William Monroe Trotter's Meetings with Woodrow Wilson, 1913–1914," *Journal of Negro History* 46, no. 3 (Summer 1979): 244–64, esp. 246, 251n. 1; Jane Lang Scheiber and Harry N. Scheiber, "The Wilson Administration and the Wartime Mobilization of Black-Americans, 1917–1918," *Labor History* 10, no. 3 (Summer 1969): 433–58, esp. 433–35; and Rayford W. Logan, *The Betrayal of the Negro: From Rutherford B. Hayes to Woodrow Wilson* (1954; New York: Macmillan, 1970), 359–70.

80. HH, "The Real Woodrow Wilson." W. E. B. Du Bois, *Dusk of Dawn: An Essay Toward an Autobiography of a Race Concept* (1940; New York: Schocken Books, 1971), 235, says that he wrote in *The Crisis* before the election that "it is better to elect Woodrow Wilson." In W. E. B. Du Bois, "Why I Won't Vote," *The Nation*, October 20, 1956, 324, Du Bois writes, "I took Hughes as the lesser of two evils." David Levering Lewis, *W. E. B. Du Bois: Biography of a Race, 1868–1919* (New York: Henry Holt, 1993), 1:523 says, "Du Bois momentarily favored Hughes." Charles Flint Kellogg, *NAACP: A History of the National Association for the Advancement of Colored People, 1909–1920* (1967; Baltimore, Md.: Johns Hopkins University Press, 1973), 1:179, says "Du Bois came out in favor of Hughes." Elliott Rudwick, *W. E. B. Du Bois: Propagandist of the Negro Revolt* (1960; New York: Atheneum, 1969), 196–97, discusses Du Bois's "floundering."

81. "Woodrow Wilson's Letter to Bishop Walters in 1912," *NYA*, July 12, 1917, 1; Herbert Aptheker, ed., *The Correspondence of W. E. B. Du Bois*, 3 vols. (Amherst: University Press of Massachusetts, 1997), 1:180; and Du Bois, "Why I Won't Vote," 324,

82. "Frances Dearborn" [HH], "The Black Tide Turns in Politics." See also Goldstein, "Race Politics," 67–68; Hiller, "Race Politics," 198; "Wrecks Wilson's Headquarters," *AN*, November 15, 1916, HP-Sc 4, 358; and "Colored Democrats Now Criticize Wilson," *NYA*, September 4, 1916, 6.

83. HD, June 15, 19, 21, 26, and 30, and on July 5, 1916, in diary code Harrison wrote: "Ella came to see me et id facimus in lite [and for that reason on the (French for) bed]." Then, the next day, "for the first time 3 coegi Nbve Mh Wboo domi sua. Deliciosa!"

84. HD, January 25, February 17, and April 24, 1917. Harrison wrote: "Ayesha enabled me to get them cz hjwjoh nfifsmpdlfu up qbxo-gpsgjuf epmmbst [Ayesha enabled me to get them by giving me her locket to pawn-forfive dollars—JP]. The glasses cost $6.00."

85. HH, "The Right Way to Unity," *BC*, May 10, 1924, HP, in *HR*, 403.

86. Du Bois, *Dusk of Dawn*, 216–17.

87. "Harlem's First and Foremost Forum," *Embryo of The Voice of the Negro: A Magazine Struggling to Be Born* 1, no. 1 (February 1927): 1, HP. See also "Infidelity Among Our Ministers: A Startling Lecture by Hubert H. Harrison at Lafayette Hall, 165 West 131st St, New York on Sunday, December 10th, [1916], at 8 P.M.," handout, HP-Sc 34.

88. HH, "Reading for Knowledge," [*Voice*, September 1918], in *WAA*, 123–26, esp. 124.

89. "Infidelity Among Our Ministers." This talk was also delivered before the Secular Society of New York under the title "Radical Results of the Higher Criticism; or Infidelity Among Our Ministers." See Joseph Silver, secretary, Secular Society of New York, to the editor, *Truth Seeker* 43 (December 30, 1916).

90. "Infidelity Among Our Ministers"; "Certificate of Incorporation of Cosmo Letter Co., Inc.," March 14, 1914, NYCC; "Cosmo Letter Company, Inc. and Brooklyn Advocate Publishing Co., Inc. Agreement to Consolidate and Sworn Copy of Proceedings," September 14, 1916, County Clerk of the City of New York.

91. "The Paterson Philosophical Society Presents Hubert H. Harrison, of New York who will speak on 'Shall the Negro Become the Dominating Race?' in Our New Hall, 202 Market St., . . . December 31, at 8 P.M.," handout, c. December 29, 1916, HP-Sc 34; "When the Negro Wakes: A Lecture of 'The Manhood Movement' Among the Negro People of America by Hubert H. Harrison at The Temple of Truth Lafayette Hall, 165 W. 131st St., Sunday December 24, 1916 at 8 P.M.," handout, HP-Sc 34; *KI*, 3:353; and Mercer Cook, to author, October 8, 1983, possession of author.

92. HH, "The Art of the Theater and How to Understand It," n.p., c. January 7, 1917 [?], HP; and "Hubert H. Harrison Lectures at The Temple of Truth, . . . Every Sunday Evening at 8:00 Free, . . . January 7th, [1917] The Art of the Theater and How to Understand It: With Especial Reference to the Lafayette Stock Company," handout, HP-Sc 34.

93. HH, "The Art of the Theater."

94. HH, "The Art of the Theater."

95. [John Edward Bruce], "Bruce Grit's Column," *Gazette*, January 20, 1917, HP-Sc 34. See also John Edward Bruce, "Color Prejudice Among Negroes," c. December 1916, in *The Selected Writings of John Edward Bruce, Militant Black Journalist*, ed. Peter Gilbert (New York: Arno Press and The New York Times, 1971), 125–28; and "Hubert H. Harrison Lectures at The Temple of Truth, . . . January 14th The Social Leadership of the Mulatto," handout, HP-Sc 34.

96. [Bruce], "Bruce Grit's Column," *Gazette*, January 20, 1917.

97. HH, "A Tender Point," *NW*, July 3, 1920, 2, in *HR*, 178–80, esp. 179.

98. "Hubert H. Harrison Lectures at The Temple of Truth, . . . The War in Europe and What it Means to the Darker Races, January 21st.," HP-Sc C; "Why Not? Spend Your Sunday Evenings with Us at The Temple of Truth, Lafayette Lodge Rooms, 165

West 131st Street, The Following Lectures by Mr. Hubert H. Harrison . . . Sunday, February 4th," HP-Sc C; and "Are You a Freethinker? . . . Lectures for the Next Six Weeks Before the New York Secular Society," c. February 4, 1917, HP-Sc C. Harrison was apparently again living apart from his family, who were at 231 W. 134th St. See Rev. Everard W. Daniel, to whom it may concern [re Mrs. Irene Harrison], January 9, 1917, HP. Harrison had published "The Black Man's Burden" in 1915 under the pseudonym "Gunga Din." After his January 21, 1917, reading, it appeared in print as Liberty League Leaflet No. 1 (c. 1917?) and it was accompanied by words attributed to Abdurrahman Es Saadi that challenge "the white man," who "insists upon his God-given right to rule" darker peoples and by lines from "America's Creed" by James Russell Lowell in his "Biglow Papers," part 1, no. 6, that talk of forcefully bringing freedom to "them infarnal Phayrisees," but quickly point out that "libbaty's a kind o'thing / That don't agree with niggers." See HH, "The Black Man's Burden: A Reply to 'The White Man's Burden' by Rudyard Kipling," Liberty League Leaflets no. 1, c. 1917?, HP.

99. "Six Lectures on Sex by Hubert H. Harrison at The Temple of Truth," c. March 17, 1917, HP-Sc; and Richard Bruce Nugent, *Gay Rebel of the Harlem Renaissance*, ed. Thomas H. Wirth (Durham, N.C.: Duke University Press, 2002), 149.

100. [HH,] "Two Negro Radicalisms," 104; [HH,] "Race Consciousness," *BC*, March 15, 1924, in *HR*, 116.

101. [HH], "The Negro in Industry: *The Great Steel Strike* by William Z. Foster," *NW*, August 21, 1920, 2, HP-Sc B, in *HR*, 81–83; and [HH], "Shillady Resigns," *NW*, June 19, 1920, 2, in *HR*, 177–178.

102. HH, "Race First Versus Class First," 109; and HD, May 24, 1920.

103. *WGMC*, 2:436.

104. Aida Harrison Richardson and William Harrison, interview by author, August 4, 1983, New York City.

105. [HH,] "Race Consciousness," 116.

106. [HH,] "Race Consciousness," 116–17. See also Work, *NYB, 1921–1922*, 53.

107. HH, "As Harrison Sees It," *Amsterdam News*, October 6, 1926, 11; HH, "The Negro and the Labor Unions," *Voice* (c. August 1917), in *HR*, 79–81, esp. 81; [HH], "Purpose of the League," *NYC*, June 5, 1921, in *NW*, June 25, 1921, 6; and "Negroes Meet Today to Seek Tulsa Redress: Hubert Harrison of Colored Liberty League Wires Oklahoma Gov. to Punish Responsible Whites," *NYC*, June 5, 1921, 1–2, esp. 2.

108. [HH], "The Negro in Industry," 82 (Foster quotations) and 83 (Harrison quotations).

109. HH, "Wanted—a Colored International," *NW*, May 28, 1921, HP, in *HR*, 223–28, esp. 226 and 228. In his second copy of Stoddard, *Rising Tide of Color*, received July 7, 1924, in Philadelphia, Harrison, on p. 169, comments on the notion expressed by Stoddard that white solidarity was a constant. Harrison writes "As in the 5th, 11th, 16th, 17th, 18th & 19th centuries? Well that is too funny!" On p. 170 he adds that "the man who wrote this waddle would say that he was not superstitious. For since the

end of the Crusades the white race has never exhibited any of this mythical solidarity. At best, there have been temporary leagues of competing conquerors and 'balances of power'. The near-record among themselves has been illuminating on this point. Spain vs. Holland, England vs. Spain, England vs. France Germany vs. Austria, Austria vs. Italy, France and England vs. Russia, England vs. America, America vs. Spain, Allies vs. Central Powers. *Some* solidarity!"

110. Huggins, *Harlem Renaissance*, 30. Harrison, the articulate proponent of the need for Black people to develop race consciousness, stressed that "before the Negroes of the western world can play any effective part they must first acquaint themselves with what is taking place in the larger world where millions are in motion."

10. Founding the Liberty League and *The Voice* (April–September 1917)

1. H. C. Peterson and G. C. Fite, *Opponents of War, 1917–1918* (Seattle: University of Washington Press, 1957), 10, points out that "many war opponents claimed that 90 per cent of the voters of the country would have opposed war if they had an opportunity to vote on it in 1917." While disagreeing with that number, Peterson and Fite add, "The American people certainly did not want war, but a vast majority was willing to accept it" (8). See also "President Calls for War Declaration," *New York Times*, April 3, 1917 (hereafter *NYT*); "Senate, 82 to 6, Adopts War Declaration," *NYT*, April 4, 1917; "House, at 3:12 A.M., Votes for War, 373–50," *NYT*, April 6, 1917; and "President Proclaims War," *NYT*, April 7, 1917.

2. J. D. Foner, *Blacks and the Military in American History* (New York: Praeger, 1974), 112–13; Peter M. Bergman, ed. *The Chronological History of the Negro in America* (New York: Harper and Row, 1969), 382; Robert L. Zangrando, *The NAACP Crusade Against Lynching, 1909–1950* (Philadelphia: Temple University Press, 1980), 6; "Police Kill Negro in Race Riot," *NYT*, May 27, 1917; "Negro Guardsmen in San Juan Riot," *NYT*, July 4, 1917; and *GP*, 9:146n. 3.

3. Judith Stein, *The World of Marcus Garvey: Race and Class in Modern Society* (Baton Rouge: Louisiana State University Press, 1986), 38, 45. See also Gilbert Osofsky, *Harlem: The Making of a Ghetto; Negro New York, 1890–1930* (1963; New York: Harper and Row, 1971), 122–23.

4. HH, "Introductory," in HH, *When Africa Awakes: The "Inside Story" of the Stirrings and Strivings of the New Negro in the Western World* (New York: Porro Press, 1920), 5–8 , esp. 8 (hereafter *WAA*); and [HH], "As the Currents Flow," *New Negro* 3, no. 7 (August 1919): 3–4 (hereafter *NN*), in *HR*, 97–99, esp. 98.

5. HH, "Introductory," 8; HH, "The Liberty League of Negro-Americans: How It Came to Be" ("From *The Voice* of July 4, 1917"), in *HR*, 86–88; and [HH], "Stop Lynching and Disfranchisement in the Land Which We Love and Make the South 'Safe For Democracy,'" handout, c. June 12, 1917, HP-Sc 34.

6. E. Franklin Frazier, *The Negro Church in America* (1964; New York: Schocken Books, 1973), 43; "Cooper Goes to Bethel Church," *New York Age*, May 31, 1917, 1 (hereafter *NYA*); and Philip S. Foner, *American Socialism and Black Americans: From the Age of Jackson to World War II* (Westport, Conn.: Greenwood Press, 1977), 85–86, 381n. 50.

7. "Announcement," *NN* 3, no. 7 (August 1919): 7. See also [HH], editorial, *Voice*, July 4, 1917, HP. Stein, *World of Marcus Garvey*, 43–44, finds that Harrison's Liberty League "seemed more promising than most [organizations] because he represented broader intellectual and political experience than the typical Harlem hopeful" and that this "Black Socrates . . . excelled at the indoor and the outdoor popular lecture."

8. "The Liberty League of Negro-Americans," 86 and 87; and "Negroes Seek Law for Mobs: Want Federal Statute to Cover Lynchings—Young Men and Women in League," *New York Call*, June 13, 1917, 4 (hereafter *NYC*). "Negroes Meet Today to Seek Tulsa Redress: Hubert Harrison of Colored Liberty League Wires Oklahoma Gov. to Punish Responsible Whites," *NYC*, June 5, 1921, has the stated purpose of the League as described by Harrison.

9. [HH], "The Liberty League of Negro-Americans," 87; [HH], "Stop Lynching and Disfranchisement"; "Negroes Seek Law for Mobs"; [HH], "Resolutions Passed at the Liberty League Meeting," *WAA*, 11 (from *Voice*, September 19, 1917), in *HR*, 88–89; and "America's Bitter Race War," "Newspaper Report from the *Brooklyn Advocate*," in *Jamaica Times*, September 22, 1917, in *GP*, 1:222–23, which gives the figure of 2,000. The Persons lynching had already led to a Harlem rally of 500 to 600 people at St. Peter's church, and it would lead to additional meetings (on June 20 and July 5, 11, 18, and 25) to plan a giant silent protest parade for July 28. See Zangrando, *NAACP Crusade*, 35–36; and *GP*, 5:188–89n. 17.

10. [HH], "The Liberty League of Negro-Americans," 87.

11. [HH], "The Liberty League of Negro-Americans," 87. On the meeting see HD, May 24, 1920, in *HR*, 188–90, esp. 190; *GP*, 1:222–23; and "Negroes Seek Law for Mobs."

12. [HH], "The Liberty League of Negro-Americans," 88. On Jewish rights in Russia, see Robert V. Daniels, ed., *The Russian Revolution* (Englewood Cliffs, N.J.: Prentice-Hall, 1972), 15–16; *GP*, 3:218n. 15, 6:48n. 1; and Zvi Gitelman, *Jewish Nationality and Soviet Politics: The Jewish Sections of the CPSU, 1917–1930* (Princeton, N.J.: Princeton University Press, 1972), 19.

13. [HH], "The Liberty League of Negro-Americans," 87. According to the *Call* more than $125 was donated and about $150 was pledged by the audience. See "Negroes Seek Law for Mobs."

14. [HH], "The Liberty League of Negro-Americans"; HD, July 1, 1918; and *GP*, 1:212n. 7, which cites the Baltimore *Afro-American*, June 30, 1917, 1.

15. HH, "Resolutions Passed," 88–89.

16. HH, "Resolutions Passed," 89. Harrison had great interest in the Irish, Russian, and Indian struggles. He often spoke on Irish affairs, and the *Boston Chronicle*

stated that he received a letter of commendation from the radical Irish leader James Larkin. Throughout 1917 and 1918 he lectured on the Russian Bolsheviks, and from about 1915 he lectured and wrote on India. See "Dr. Hubert Harrison," editorial, *Boston Chronicle*, January 26, 1924, HP-Sc 35 (hereafter *BC*); "*The Modern School*: A Course of Lectures in Comparative Religion by Hubert Henry Harrison," handout, HP-Sc 34; HH, "Reading for Knowledge" (*Voice*, September 1918), in *WAA*, 123–26, esp. 124; Sayid Muhammad Berghash [pseud. for HH], "Britain in India," *NN*, 4 no. 1 (September 1919): 9–10, in *HR*, 213–15; and Sudarshan Kapur, *Raising Up a Prophet: The African-American Encounter with Gandhi* (Boston: Beacon Press, 1992).

17. Ernest Kaiser, "The Federal Government and the Negro, 1865–1955," *Science and Society* 21, no. 1 (Winter 1956): 27–58, 43; and Charles Wallace Collins, *The Fourteenth Amendment and the States* (Boston: Little Brown, 1912) 46–47, 161, 182.

18. HH, "The Liberty League's Petition to the House of Representatives of the United States, July 4, 1917," *HR*, 93. Harrison was very interested in and supportive of Jewish struggle in Russia. In HH, "Education Out of School," *BC*, February 23, 1924, in *HR*, 125–26, he also wrote that "it is the wisdom of the weak that enables them to overthrow the strength of the strong. When the European Jews found themselves proscribed and trampled on, without rights or protection in the Middle Ages they began to specialize in two things: mind power and money power—and the first was parent of the second. They became the most intelligent people in all Europe, and although they number less than the Negroes in America . . . they have become by their intelligence more powerful than any people in Europe in proportion to their numbers."

19. Zangrando, *NAACP Crusade*, 26–27, 31, 44, and 50.

20. HH, "Our Professional Friends," *Voice*, November 7, 1917, HP, in *HR*, 143–47, esp. 146; and HH, "Shillady Resigns, *HR*, 177–78, esp. 178.

21. [HH], "Declaration of Principles [of the Liberty League]," *Clarion* 1, no. 3 (September 1, 1917), reprint as, "What It Stands For," *Voice*, September 19, 1917, HP, in *HR*, 89–92, esp. 92.

22. [HH], "Declaration of Principles," 90.

23. HH, "Our International Consciousness," *BC*, January 12, 1924, reprint, with slight changes, as [HH], "Wanted—a World Outlook," *The Voice of the Negro* 1, no. 1 (April 1927): 2. Hodge Kirnon, "The New Negro and His Will to Manhood and Achievement," *Promoter* 1 (August 1920): 7, explained, "The Old Negro was nationalistic to the extreme, even at times manifesting antipathy and scorn for foreign born Negroes," while the New Negro publications "have recognized the oneness of interests and the kindredship between all Negro people the world over." In HH, "Education Out of School," Harrison wrote: "'Knowledge is power.' . . . While we chatter about 'segregation' we segregate ourselves from that community of culture and knowledge that is as wide open to us as the winds of heaven and limitless as the eternal sea. In this respect the West Africans are far ahead of us. Let us pray for the will to follow John Mensah Sarbah, [Joseph Ephraim] Casely Hayford, E. S. Beoku-

Betts, Kobyna Sekyi and our other black brothers whom we ignorantly aspire to lead."

24. [HH], "Declaration of Principles," 90–91.

25. [HH], "Declaration of Principles," 91. See also Joseph R. Gusfield, *Symbolic Crusade: Status Politics and the American Temperance Movement* (1963; Urbana: University of Illinois Press, 1972), 102–3; and Zangrando, *NAACP Crusade*, 44.

26. [HH], "Declaration of Principles," 92; HH, "How to End Lynching," *BC*, June 28, 1924; and [HH], "Lynching: Its Cause and Cure," *NW*, June 26, 1920, 2.

27. [HH], "Declaration of Principles," 91; HH, "The Negro and the War," *WAA*, 25.

28. [HH], "Declaration of Principles," 91–92.

29. [HH], "Declaration of Principles," 92. See also [HH], "The Line-Up on the Color Line," *NW*, December 4, 1920, HP, in *HR*, 216–19.

30. [HH], "Declaration of Principles," 92; and HH, "Marcus Garvey at the Bar of United States Justice," *Associated Negro Press*, c. July 1923, 4, HP, in *HR*, 194–99, esp. 197. According to a Bureau of Investigation report, as early as November 12, 1918, Garvey explained the red, black, and green tricolor as "the black race between blood and nature to win its rights." See *GP*, 1:290. In a later interview with Charles Mowbry White on August 18, 1920, in *GP*, 2:602–4, on 603, Garvey explained that "Red showed their sympathy with the 'Reds' of the world, and the Green their sympathy for the Irish in their fight for freedom, and the Black—the negro." Harrison, "Marcus Garvey at the Bar of United States Justice," maintained that "Red, black, and green were more discordant and bizarre and appealed to Garvey's cruder esthetic sense."

31. Robert A. Hill, interview by Gil Noble, aired November 20, 1983, "Radio TV Reports, Inc., For WABC-TV 'Like It Is,' November 20, 1983," 1:00 p.m. (New York: Radio-TV Reports, 1984), 18; Colin Grant, *Negro With a Hat: The Rise and Fall of Marcus Garvey* (New York: Oxford University Press, 2008), 93; and J. W. Johnson, *Black Manhattan* (1930; New York: Atheneum, 1977), 253. See also *GP*, 1:222–23. [HH,] "The Liberty League of Negro-Americans," *Voice*, July 4, 1917, reprint, *Voice*, September 19, 1917, does not mention Garvey, but [HH], "The Liberty League of Negro-Americans," *WAA*, 9–11, in *HR*, 86–88, does.

32. [HH], "The Liberty League of Negro-Americans," 87; *GP*, quoting the *Jamaica Times* from the *Brooklyn Advocate*, 1.222–23; and HH, "Two Negro Radicalisms," *NN* 4, no. 2 (October 1919): 4–5, in *HR*, 102–5.

33. Johnson, *Black Manhattan*, 253; and John Henrik Clarke, "Marcus Garvey and the Concept of African Nation-Formation in the Twentieth Century," in *Africans at the Crossroads: Notes for an African World Revolution*, ed. John Henrik Clarke (Trenton, N.J.: Africa World Press, 1991), 197–244, esp. 230, which quotes Charles Willis Simmons, "The Negro Intellectual's Criticism of Garveyism." See also William Bridges to the editor, "Bridges Enter General Denial," *NW*, November 30, 1920; Directorate of Intelligence, Special Report No. 10, "Unrest Among the Negroes," October 7, 1919, *Science and Society* 32, no. 1 (Winter 1966): 77–78; *GP*, 1:222–23;

Hill, interview, 18; Lester A. Walton, "Marcus Garvey: His Rise and Fall," *Chicago Defender*, April 4, 1925, sec. 1, p. 1 (hereafter *CD*); HH, "Marcus Garvey at the Bar of United States Justice." On Harrison's criticism of Johnson, see HH, "Black Bards of Yesterday and Today," review of *The Book of Negro Poetry* by James Weldon Johnson, *National Star* (N.Y.), December 16, 1923, HP, in *HR*, 394–96.

34. Hill, *GP*, 1:lix, lxvi; *GP*, 3:708–13, esp. 709; and HH, "Marcus Garvey at the Bar of U.S. Justice," *HR*, 109. See also *WGMC*, 2:399–405; and *GP*, 1:210–11, 211n. 1 and 527–31.

35. Robert A. Hill, interview by Gil Noble, 18. On Harrison's oratory, see Lester A. Walton, "Street Speaker Heralds Spring in Harlem: Negro Orators Resume Soap Box Talks on Various Topics," *New York World*, March 25, 1928, 1 (hereafter *NYW*). See also "Speaker's Medal to Negro Student," *NYW*, April 5, 1903, 10; "Some Stirring Talks on Timely Topics by Hubert H. Harrison America's Foremost Negro Lecturer at Lenox Casino," c. March 25, 1915, HP-Sc 34; John T. Carroll to the editor, *New York Globe*, November 4, 1914; Hodge Kirnon, "Hubert Harrison, An Appreciation"; "Hubert Harrison," *Amsterdam News*, December 28, 1927 (hereafter *AN*); Oscar J. Benson, "Literary Genius of Hubert Harrison," *New York News*, December 24, 1927 (hereafter *NYN*); *WGMC*, 2:614; and William Pickens, "Hubert Harrison: Philosopher of Harlem," *AN*, February 7, 1923, 12. Harrison was described as "the most brilliant street orator that this Metropolis has produced in the last generation" in "The Death of Hubert Harrison," *NYN*, December 31, 1927, HP.

36. *Clarion* 1, no. 3 (September 1, 1917): 10; and *GP*, 1:25n. 5, on Garvey's August 24, 1910, failure to place. Judith Stein, *World of Marcus Garvey*, 34, states that at one c. 1915 talk in his hometown of St. Ann's Bay, Jamaica, "the audience laughed at his speech" and "Garvey burst into tears." Anselmo Jackson writes that in 1916 Garvey arrived in New York from Jamaica and soon "circularized the Negro Section of Harlem to the effect that 'Professor' Garvey, 'The World-Famed Orator' would make his first public appearance in New York City at St. Mark's Hall, 55 West 138th Street." At the talk (on May 9, 1916), Garvey "completely lost his nerve," "was obviously self-conscious," and suffered an "attack of stage fright" so serious that "he fell off the stage, much to the amazement of the audience." See Anselmo Jackson, "An Analysis of the Black Star Line," *Emancipator*, March 27, 1920, 2; and "Account by W. A. Domingo of Marcus Garvey's St. Mark's Church Hall Lecture," New York, n.d. in *GP*, 1:190–92. William H. Ferris, while a high ranking UNIA official, stated that even Randolph and Owen "were more polished speakers" than Garvey. See *GP*, 2:472.

37. HD, May 24, 1920.

38. "The Empire State," *CD*, June 23, 1917, 3

39. "Make a Drive for Liberty on Liberty's Birthday, July 4th, 1917 with the Liberty League of Negro-Americans . . . The First Mass Meeting," advertisement, HP-Sc 34; and "Urges Negroes to Get Arms: Liberty League President Advises His Race to 'Defend Their Lives,'" *NYT*, July 5, 1917.

40. On the migration and East St. Louis, see Zangrando, *NAACP Crusade*, 36; *GP*, 1:220n. 1; Florette Henri, *Black Migration: Movement North, 1900–1920* (Garden City, N.Y.: Anchor Press/Doubleday, 1975), 51–53; "Great Tide of 'Free' and Mirthful Negro Labor Brings the War to North's Industrial Centers," *New York Tribune*, January 6, 1918, HP; "Colored People Leaving South," *AN*, November 15, 1916, HP; Elliott M. Rudwick, *Race Riot at East St. Louis, July 2, 1917* (Carbondale: Southern Illinois University Press, 2005), esp. 41–58; Steven A. Reich, ed., *Encyclopedia of the Great Black Migration*, 3 vols. (Westport, Conn.: Greenwood Press, 2006), 1:271–72, 3:42–48; and "Tells Causes of Great Migration," *Richmond Planet*, February 16, 1918, HP-Sc 8.

41. Edward Robb Ellis, *Echoes of Distant Thunder: Life in the United States, 1914–1918* (New York: Coward, McCann and Geoghegan, 1975), 416; Monroe N. Work, ed., *Negro Year Book, 1918–1919* (Tuskegee, Ala.: Negro Year Book Publishing, 1919), 50 (hereafter *NYB*); *GP*, 1:220n. 1; and Zangrando, *NAACP Crusade*, 37. In HP-Sc 28, see "4 Whites, 3 Blacks Shot as Race Riot Grows in Illinois," *NYW*, May 30, 1917; "Negroes Flee Rioting Mobs," *New York Evening Sun*, May 29, 1917; "50 Negroes Hurt by White Mob," *New York Evening Mail*, May 29, 1917; "Truth About East St. Louis Massacre," *CD*, July 14, 1917, 1, 9; and "Sue East St. Louis For Big Riot Damages," *Guardian* (Boston), January 19, 1918.

42. Samuel Gompers, "East St. Louis Riots—Their Causes," *American Federationist* 24, no. 8 (August 1917): 621–26, esp. 623 and 626. See also *NYB, 1918–1919*, 8–15, 50; "Industries Welcomed Negro to East St. Louis; Labor Feared Him and Mob Butchered Him," *New York Tribune*, January 6, 1918, HP-Sc 3; "Roosevelt and Gompers Row at Russian Meeting," *NYT*, July 7, 1917; "Labor Denies Riot Blame," *NYT*, July 6, 1917; "Roosevelt Takes Gompers to Task," *CD*, July 14, 1917, 1, HP-Sc 28; and *GP*, 1:220n. 1.

43. "Urges Negroes to Get Arms"; "Make a Drive for Liberty"; "Negro Guardsmen in San Juan Riot," *NYT*, July 4, 1917; "Hayward Begins Inquiry into Riot," *NYT*, July 5, 1917; "Hayward Defends His Men," *NYT*, July 6, 1917; Peterson and Fite, *Opponents of War*, 88; and Zangrando, *NAACP Crusade*, 35–36. New York also had riots on May 26 and June 18.

44. "Urges Negroes to Get Arms." See also *GP*, 1:211n. 3. Arthur E. Barbeau and Florette Henri, eds., *The Unknown Soldiers: Black American Troops in World War I*, (Philadelphia: Temple University Press, 1974), 21, attributes this quotation to Harrison.

45. "Urges Negroes to Get Arms," 9; and [HH], "As the Currents Flow," 98.

46. Robert A. Hill, ed. and intro., "Introduction," in *The Crusader*, 3 vols. (New York: Garland, 1987), 1:xiii; Baltimore *Afro-American*, June 30, 1917, 1; and "Urges Negroes to Get Arms." Stein, *World of Marcus Garvey*, 42, explains, "In 1917, the advocacy of self-defense was a litmus test of militance, dividing old from aspiring leadership."

47. *Voice*, masthead, August 1, 1918, HP; "President Calls For War Declaration"; "Speech by Marcus Garvey," October 16, 1921, in *GP*, 4:119–22, esp. 120; and *GP*, 1: lxvi, xciii. In addition to its principal motto, *The Voice* also adopted two others. One was the quotation that Harrison had used on his *New York News* column, the four-line poem beginning "For the cause that lacks assistance" and derived from George Linnaeus Banks. The other, used on the front page of *The Voice*, was: "The Paper with a Purpose for Men and Women with Red Blood in Their Veins." See *Voice*, masthead, October 31, 1917.

48. Hodge Kirnon, "Toward One Common End," *Promoter* 1 (1920): 8; and Hill, "Introduction," 1:vi.

49. [HH], "Owing to the High Cost of Manhood THE VOICE Has Gone Up To 5 Cents: Read the Explanation," *Voice*, October 18, 1917, HP. This article cites the original price. See also, HH, "The East St. Louis Horror," *Voice*, July 4, 1917, HP, in *HR*, 94–95; [HH], "The Liberty League of Negro-Americans"; [HH], "How The Voice Took," *Voice*, July 10, 1917, HP; "Hubert Harrison's New Paper," *NYN*, July 5, 1917, HP-Sc 34; *Truth Seeker* 44, no. 29 (July 21, 1917), HP; [HH], editorial, *Voice*, July 4, 1917; [HH], "A New News Policy," *Voice*, July 4, 1917, HP; advertisement for Socialist Party, *Voice*, July 4, 1917, HP. The letter from Sir Harry Johnson, author of "The Real Roots of the War," in the June 1917 *Crisis*, was reprinted in part in *Voice*, July 4, 1917, HP-Sc 8, 25. Harrison used Johnson's comments as a takeoff in [HH], "Africa at the Peace Table," *Voice*, December 26, 1918, HP, in *HR*, 210–12.

50. HH, "The East St. Louis Horror," 94–95.

51. HH, "The East St. Louis Horror," 95.

52. [HH], "How The Voice Took."

53. [HH], "How The Voice Took."

54. Mary W. Ovington to "My Dear Mr. [Hubert] Harrison," c. July 1917, in [HH], "Our Professional Friends," 145. For more Harrison thought on Ovington, see [HH], [re "Vesey St. Liberals"], n.d. [c. 1921], handwritten, HP-Wr; HH, "*Nigger Heaven*—a Review of the Reviews," *AN*, November 13, 1926, in *HR*, 344–51, esp. 345–46; and Claude McKay, *A Long Way from Home: An Autobiography* (1937; New York: Harcourt Brace and World, 1970), 113.

55. "Hubert Harrison's New Paper," *NYN*, July 5, 1917; Nicholas [Biddle?] to Col. R. H. Van Deman, Office of Military Intelligence, Washington, September 25, 1917, MID 10218-10, National Archives, Washington, D.C. (hereafter cited as DNA).

56. [HH], "How The Voice Took"; HH, "Introductory," 8; "Liberty League of Negro-Americans: Africa First," Membership Card No. 1 issued to Hubert H. Harrison, September 2, 1917, HP-Sc 34; and "Pledge Card for Liberty League and *Voice*," n.d. [c. 1917], HP-Sc 34.

57. [HH], "A New News Policy."

58. [HH], "A New News Policy." In HH, "The Negro and Social Service," *BC*, February 9, 1924, Harrison offered that "in journalism, as in art the first necessity

is that of selection. And . . . its news selection is generally an index to the Policy of the newspaper."

59. The quotes are from [HH], "A New News Policy." Examples of "slipshod" journalism are found in [HH], "Lessons in Language: Culled from the Columns of Our 'Colored' Contemporaries," *Voice*, July 10, 1917, HP and HP-Sc 4, 359–62, which also contains Harrison's reactions.

60. [HH], "Owing to the High Cost."

61. [HH], "How The Voice Took," which includes John Edward Bruce to HH, n.d.; and [John Edward Bruce] "Bruce Grit" to "Dear Harrison," July 24, 1917, HP.

62. [HH], "Owing to the High Cost"; [HH], "Advertising in the Voice," *Voice*, July 10, 1917, HP; [HH], "The Voice Speaks to the Business Man," *The Voice*, August 14, 1917; and [HH], "Selling Space vs. Selling Self," *Voice*, July 10, 1917, HP.

63. [HH], "A New News Policy"; [HH], "Owing to the High Cost"; and [HH], "Advertising in the Voice."

64. Osofsky, *Harlem*, 122–23; Seth M. Scheiner, *Negro Mecca: A History of the Negro in New York, 1865–1920* (New York: New York University Press, 1965), 221–22; Barbeau and Henri, *Black Migration*, 88–89; Frederick G. Detweiler, *The Negro Press in the United States* (Chicago: University of Chicago Press, 1922), 6, 11–12, 15; Jervis Anderson, *A. Philip Randolph: A Biographical Portrait* (New York: Harcourt Brace Jovanovich, 1973), 146; and *NYB, 1918–1919*, 429–53.

65. Barbeau and Henri, *Black Migration*, 88–89, 167; Detweiler, *Negro Press*, 6, 11–12, 15; and John B. Wiseman, "Moore, Fred[erick Randolph]," in *Dictionary of American Negro Biography*, ed. Rayford W. Logan and Michael R. Winston (New York: Norton, 1982), 446–48, esp. 447.

66. [HH], "Advertising in the Voice."

67. [HH], "Owing to the High Cost."

68. [HH], "Owing to the High Cost."

69. [HH], "Owing to the High Cost."

70. [HH], "Arms and the Man," *Voice*, July 17, 1917, HP, in *WAA*, 16–20, esp. 16. See also "The Unruly Tongues," *NYA*, July 12, 1917, 4.

71. [HH], "Arms and the Man." See also Louis Bryan, "Brief History of the Life and Work of Hubert Henry Harrison," April 20, 1937, Federal Writers' Project, Schomburg Center for Research in Black Culture, New York Public Library (hereafter SCRBC).

72. [HH], "Arms and the Man."

73. [HH], "Arms and the Man."

74. Roosevelt is quoted in Rudwick, *Race Riot at East St. Louis*, 134. See also "Gompers Row at Russian Meeting," 1, 4; "3,000 Blacks Like Attack Upon T. R.," *NYW*, July 30, 1917, HP-Sc 34; and "Negro Speaker Scores T. R.," [source unidentified], July 30, 1917, HP-Sc 34.

75. HH to Theodore Roosevelt, R 239, July 7, 1917; Theodore Roosevelt to HH, R 417, July 11; and Theodore Roosevelt to HH, R 393, July 11, all in Theodore Roos-

evelt Papers, Library of Congress, Washington, D.C. See also "Negroes Laud Colonel," *NYT*, July 16, 1917.

76. HH, "The Negro and the Labor Unions," [*Voice*, c. August, 1917], in *HR*, 79–81, esp. 80 and 81; and Gompers, "East St. Louis Riots," 626.

77. HH, "The Negro and the Labor Unions," 80.

78. HH, "The Negro and the Labor Unions," 81 and [Chandler Owen and A. Philip Randolph], "The Negro and the American Federation of Labor," *Messenger* 2, no. 8 (August 1919): 10–12, esp. 12.

79. HH, "The Negro and the Labor Unions," 81. Gabriel Kolko, "The Decline of American Radicalism in the Twentieth Century," *Studies on the Left* (September/October, 1966): 15, points out that the Socialist Party "always maintained its primary contacts with the A. F. of L., which at this time [the WWI era] was the most conservative major union in the world."

80. HH, "The Negro and the Labor Unions," 81; and [HH], "Purpose of the League," *NYC*, June 5, 1921, in *NW*, June 25, 1921, 6.

81. HH, "As Harrison Sees It," *AN*, October 6, 1926, 11. See also "Roosevelt and Gompers," 1, 4.

82. "Bruce Grit" [John Edward Bruce] to [HH], [fragment remains]; [HH], "How The Voice Took"; [HH], "Selling Space vs. Selling Self"; [HH], "Advertising in The Voice"; and [HH], "Lessons in Language," all in *Voice*, July 10, 1917. Three later articles on police brutality were: "Policeman Brutally Assaults Colored Man," *Voice*, July 24, 1917; [HH], "A Call to Action," *Voice*, July 31, 1917; and "Ingratitude for Kindness," *Voice*, August 21, 1917; all in *Voice*, October 31, 1917, HP. On the firemen see [HH], "Negro Fireman Gets No Medal," *Voice*, July 17, 1917, in [HH], "The 'Voice' Vindicated by Fire Commissioner," *Voice*, September 12, 1917, HP. Samuel Battle was appointed New York City's first Black policeman in 1911, but by 1929 the *Amsterdam News* reported that there were only five Black firemen and ninety Black policemen in the city. See Osofsky, *Harlem*, 128, 130, and 166; "New York City Has a Colored Police Officer," *NYA*, June 29, 1911, 1; and W. Marvin Dulaney, *Black Police in America* (Bloomington: Indiana University Press, 1996), 22.

83. [HH], "Arms and the Man"; [HH], "Negro Fireman Gets No Medal"; "Fireman Woodson Gets Bravery Medal," *NYA*, July 12, 1917, 1; and *NYB, 1918–1919*, 42.

84. The response was "Bruce Grit" [John Edward Bruce] to editor [HH], *Voice*, August 7, 1917, HP. See also [HH], "Theatrical Notes," *Voice*, August 7, 1917, HP. Harrison was interested in sexual subjects and had an extensive erotica collection. He reportedly wrote *Sex and Society* [1922?], though no copy has been located. See "Six Lectures on Sex by Hubert H. Harrison at the Temple of Truth," handout, c. March 17, 1917, HP-Sc 34; and "Harlem Scholar Succumbs After 'Minor' Operation," *AN*, December 21, 1927, 1, 4. In 1921, while teaching at the Cosmopolitan College of Chiropractic, Harrison delivered weekly lectures from May 14 through June 18 on: "The Nature and Origin of Sex," "The Origins of Our Sex Ideals," "The Mechanics of Sex," "Analysis of the Sex Impulse," "Sex and Race," and "Marriage and Free

Love." See "Six Lectures on Sex and Sex Problems [by HH]," handout, c. May 14, 1921, HP.

85. [HH], "A Call to Action."

86. [HH], "A Call To Action." See also "Big Get Together Movement in Thirty-eighth Precinct," *CD*, September 14, 1918, 5.

87. [HH], "A Call To Action."

88. "Negroes Begin Move for More Recognition: Committee Will Demand More Police Captains and Health Protection Like Whites," *NYT*, September 27, 1926; and [HH], "A Call to Action."

89. On the parade, see Richard B. Moore, "Africa Conscious Harlem," *Freedomways* (Summer 1963): 315–34, esp. 321; Ottley and Weatherby, *Negro in New York*, 199–200; "Negroes in Silent Protest Parade," *NYC*, July 29, 1917, 1, 5; Peterson and Fite, *Opponents of War*, 88; "Nearly Ten Thousand Take Part in Big Silent Protest Parade down Fifth Avenue," *NYA*, August 2, 1917, 1; [a fragment of] "Protest Parade Committee Makes Report," *Voice*, August 7, 1917, HP; *Clarion* 1, no. 2 (August 15, 1917); and *NYB, 1918–1919*, 101–2. In an example of how one movement builds off another, Zangrando, *NAACP Crusade*, 35–36, 228, notes that James Weldon Johnson, one of the principal organizers of the "Silent Protest Parade," had walked in a similar demonstration for Women's Suffrage in May 1911 as a member of the Men's League for Women Suffrage.

90. HH, "The Drift in Politics," [*Voice*], [c. July 25, 1917], in *HR*, 137–39, quotations on 138.

91. "3,000 Blacks Like Attack." On independent political action in 1917, see Hiller, "Race Politics," 188, 217, 239; Goldstein, "Race Politics," 241–42; and John Henrik Clarke, "The Impact of Marcus Garvey on the Harlem Renaissance," in John Henrik Clarke, *Marcus Garvey and the Vision of Africa* (New York: Random House, 1974), 180–90.

92. "3,000 Blacks Like Attack." See also "Negro Speaker Scores T.R." and Sherman, *Republican Party*, 63–66.

93. "Negroes Resent Slur on Colonel Roosevelt," *New York Globe*, July 31, 1917, HP-Sc 34; and [HH] "Peanuts and Politics," *Voice*, August 14, 1917, HP. *NYB, 1918–1919*, 55–56, has a list of the UCL demands.

94. On Harrison as "the father of Harlem Radicalism," see, for example, Ottley, *Negro in New York*, 223; and Anderson, *A. Philip Randolph*, 79.

95. For examples of Harrison's influence see Anderson, *A. Philip Randolph*, 76, 79, 123; W. A. Domingo, interview by Theodore Draper, January 18, 1958, New York, N.Y., Theodore Draper Papers, Robert W. Woodruff Library for Advanced Studies, Emory University, Atlanta, Georgia, Preliminary listing as box 20, folder 7, "Negro Question for Vol. 1 (cont.)," Notes re: W. A. Domingo [notes re interview January 18, 1958]; Johnson, *Black Manhattan*, 253; Clarke, *Marcus Garvey*, 197; William H. Ferris, "The Spectacular Career of Garvey," *AN*, February 11, 1925, sec. 2, p. 9; Walton, "Marcus Garvey: His Rise and Fall"; Cyril V. Briggs to Oakley C. Johnson, October

3, 1961 and April 18, 1962, box 7, folder 18, Oakley Johnson Papers, SCRBC; Richard B. Moore, "Africa Conscious Harlem," *Freedomways* (Summer 1963): 315–34, esp. 320; "Garvey Arrived Here in Summer of 1916: Planned Work at Tuskegee," *AN*, July 6, 1940, L. S. Alexander Gumby Papers, Columbia University, Rare Book and Manuscript Library, 32-009; Jackson, "An Analysis of the Black Star Line"; J. A. Rogers, "Hubert Harrison," "Negroes of New York," July 30, 1939, p. 3, R 974.7-W, Federal Writers Program, SCRBC; and [Report of an interview with (Cyril V. Briggs) editor of *The Crusader* and a representative of this (Military Intelligence Division) office, June 22, 1921], in Parker Hitt to Director, Military Intelligence Division, June 23, 1921, DNA), RG 165, MID 10218-424-1, R 7.

96. "Negroes Seek Law for Mobs."

97. The sources for this list are:

Isaac B. Allen: "Garvey Arrived Here in Summer of 1916"

Henry B. Alston: [HH], "The Voice for Sale," *Voice*, September 12, 1917

Charles H. Anderson: [HH], "How The Voice Took." On Anderson, also see *NYA*, January 21, 1909, 7, and March 8, 1906, 1; and "Prof. Anderson to Open the Renaissance," *Inter-State Tattler*, September 16, 1927, 4

Mr. Armstrong: "Three-in-One Carnival for the Benefit of the Voice and the Liberty League of Negro-Americans," flyer, c. September 4, 1917, HP

Albert Banfield: [HH], "The Voice for Sale"

John Batson: [HH], "The Voice for Sale"

August Valentine Bernier: *Clarion* 1, no. 2 (August 15, 1917); J. D. Simmons, interview by William Harrison, February 23, [1951], [New York], in "William Harrison Notebook," HP

Lawton D. Birch: [HH], "The Voice for Sale"

Edward O. Boddie: [HH], "The Voice for Sale"

Mr. Bolden: "Three-in-One Carnival"

Cyril Valentine Briggs: Theodore G. Vincent, *Black Power and the Garvey Movement* (San Francisco: Ramparts Press, 1972), 78. A note indicates that this information probably came from an interview with Richard B. Moore (278n. 68)

John Edward Bruce: "The Voice Is Coming Out to Stay," flyer, c. July 4, 1918, HP-Sc 34; "Bruce Grit" [John E. Bruce] to "Dear Harrison," July 24, 1917

Charles Burroughs: "The Voice Is Coming Out to Stay"; *Voice*, masthead, July 11, 1918, HP; and HH, "Negro Society and the Negro Stage," pt. 1, *Voice*, September 19, 1917, HP, in *HR*, 370–76

James Cornelius Canegata: "The Voice Is Coming Out to Stay." St. Croix–born James Cornelius Canegata was also the father of the actor Lionel Cornelius Canegata, better known as Canada Lee (1907–1952), who won acclaim in the stage role of Bigger Thomas in Richard Wright's *Native Son* (1941), in the movie *Cry, the Beloved Country* (1950), and for his civil rights activism

James D. Carr: "The Voice Is Coming Out to Stay"

Melville Charlton: "Make a Drive for Liberty"; and Eileen Southern, *The Music of Black Americans: A History*, 2nd. ed. (1972; New York: Norton, 1983), 282

Rev. Dr. A. R. Cooper: [HH], "The Liberty League of Negro-Americans"

M. I. Daniel: [HH], "The Voice for Sale"

Wilfred Adolphus Domingo: *Clarion* 1, no. 2 (August 15, 1917); Simmons, interview

W. Clayton Dowdy: "The Voice Is Coming Out to Stay"; and *Voice*, masthead, July 11, 1918

Mr. Elkins: "Three-in-One Carnival"

Gertrude Miller-Faide: *Clarion* 1, no. 3 (September 1, 1917): 3. A copy of this issue was kindly provided to me by Nancy and Randall K. Burkett

Charles H. Florney: *Voice*, masthead, July 11, 1918; and *Voice*, masthead, August 1, 1918, HP

Lovett Fort-Whiteman: *Clarion* 1, no. 3 (September 1, 1917). For subsequent Fort-Whiteman activities, see Glenda Elizabeth Gilmore, *Defying Dixie: The Radical Roots of Civil Rights, 1919–1950* (New York: Norton, 2008), esp. 34–66.

John A. Fountain: [HH], "The Voice for Sale"; and [HH], "The (New) Voice," *Voice*, July 11, 1918, 4, HP

R. Benjamin Fray: "Garvey Arrived Here in Summer of 1916"

Marcus Garvey: Walton, "Marcus Garvey: His Rise and Fall"; HH, "Marcus Garvey at the Bar of United States Justice"; and Jackson, "An Analysis of the Black Star Line"

James A. Glasgow: [HH], "The Voice for Sale"; and Simmons interview

Mrs. Eslanda Cardoza Goode: [HH], "Advertising in the Voice"

George H. Green: *Clarion* 1, no. 2 (August 15, 1917)

Edgar Mussington Grey: Simmons, interview; [HH], "The Liberty League of Negro Americans"; and "Negroes Meet Today to Seek Tulsa Redress," *NYC*, June 5, 1921, 1–2

James Harris: [HH], "The Voice for Sale"

Hubert Henry Harrison: *Clarion* 1, no. 2 (August 15, 1917); *Voice*, masthead, July 11, 1918; *Voice*, masthead, August 1, 1918; "Negroes Meet Today to Seek Tulsa Redress," 1, 2; HH, "Affidavit of Circulation," *Voice*, August 21, 1917, HP; [HH], "The Liberty League of Negro-Americans"; "Urges Negroes to Get Arms"; and [HH], "The (New) Voice"

Cornelius A. Hughes: "The Voice Is Coming Out to Stay"

Anselmo R. Jackson: Anselmo Jackson, "Facts and Phrases," *Voice*, August 1, 1918, 2; HP and Anselmo Jackson, "The Awakening of the Masses," *Voice*, July 11, 1918, 2; DNA, RG 165, MID 10218-18-1, R 3

J. H. Johnson: [HH], "The Voice for Sale"

W. D. Jones: [HH], "The Voice for Sale"

Arthur E. King: "Negroes Meet Today to Seek Tulsa Redress"

Charles T. Magill: "Certificate of Incorporation of The Race Publishing Company, Inc.," December 10, 1917, filed December 24, 1917, Office of the Secretary of State, State of New York, Albany, no. 10366, box 658, p. 905

Rev. Dr. George Frazier Miller: "The Voice Is Coming Out to Stay"

R. B. Minor: [HH], "Owing to the High Cost"

Abbie Mitchell: "Make a Drive for Liberty"

Irena Moorman-Blackston: HD, July 1, 1918; "Negroes Meet Today to Seek Tulsa Redress"

George H. Nelson: [HH], "The Voice for Sale"

Andrew C. Pedro: [HH], "The Voice for Sale"

Rufus L. Perry, Esq.: "The Voice Is Coming Out to Stay"

Daniel E. Petersen: *Clarion* 1, no. 2 (August 15, 1917)

Miss Julia Peterson: [HH], "The Voice for Sale"

Rev. Adam Clayton Powell Sr. : [HH], "Stop Lynching and Disfranchisement"

Alexander Rahming: *Clarion* 1, no. 2 (August 15, 1917); and Simmons, interview

William H. Randolph: [HH], "The Voice for Sale"

Emil M. Rasmussen: *Clarion* 1, no. 2 (August 15, 1917)

Dr. E. Elliot Rawlins: *Clarion* 1, no. 2 (August 15, 1917); and HH, "The Negro in Industry: *The Great Steel Strike* by William Z. Foster," *NW*, August 21, 1920, 2, HP-Sc B, in *HR*, 81–83

Andreamentania Paul Razafinkeriefo: Andrea P. Razaf[in]keriefo, "Friend Jones" and "Prayer of the Lowly," *Voice*, September 4, 1917; and letter to "Dear friend Harrison," October 22, 1917, in *Voice*, October 31, 1917. All in HP

Arthur Hilton Reid: *Clarion* 1, no. 2 (August 15, 1917)

C[harles] Luckeyeth "Luckey" Roberts: "Make a Drive for Liberty"

Mrs. A. C. Schuster: [HH], "The Voice for Sale"

Auto Scott: *Clarion* 1, no. 2 (August 15, 1917)

Charles Christopher Seifert: Simmons, interview

Mr. Slater: "Three-in-One Carnival"

Mrs. Bernia L. Smith: "The Voice Is Coming Out to Stay"

Joseph Smith: [HH], "The Voice for Sale"

Arthur Sye: [HH], "The Voice for Sale"

James C. Thomas Jr. : [HH], "The Liberty League of Negro-Americans"

Julius A. Thomas: "The Voice Is Coming Out to Stay"; *Voice*, masthead, August 1, 1918, 4; [HH], "The (New) Voice"

E. Thompson: [HH], "Stop Lynching and Disfranchisement"

Orlando Montrose Thompson: [HH], "The Voice for Sale"; and Thompson, "Affidavit of Circulation"

Charles E. Toney: [HH], "The Voice for Sale"; "The Voice Is Coming Out to Stay"

William Monroe Trotter: "Make a Drive for Liberty"

A'lelia Walker: *Clarion* 1, no. 2 (August 15, 1917); and *Voice*, masthead, August 1, 1918

Madame C. J. Walker: *Clarion* 1, no. 2 (August 15, 1917); and "Three-In-One Carnival"

Sinclair Wilberforce: Sinclair Wilberforce, "Harrison Delivers Inspiring Lecture at the Harlem People's Forum," *Voice*, [August 1, 1918], HP

Dr. Reverend William: "Negroes Meet Today"

98. "Bruce Grit" [John Edward Bruce] to "H. H. Harrison, Esq.," marked "Personal" (one of two Bruce letters of that date), August 2, 1917, HP.

99. Simmons, interview; and *New Negro*, October 13, 1917, p. 6

100. HH, [unidentified article], *Voice*, August 7, 1917, HP; [HH], "Theatrical Notes," *Voice*, August 7, 1917, HP.

101. HH, "An Ode to the Dead," *Voice* (First Extra Edition), August 11, 1917, HP; [HH] "The Voice Speaks to the Business Man," *Voice*, August 14, 1917, HP; [HH], "Peanuts and Politics," *Voice*, August 14, 1917, HP; and [HH], "The White War and the Colored World," *Voice*, August 14, 1917, HP.

102. *Clarion* 1, no. 2 (August 15, 1917).

103. *Clarion* 1, no. 2 (August 15, 1917).

104. *Clarion* 1, no. 2 (August 15, 1917).

105. *Clarion* 1, no. 2 (August 15, 1917); Simmons, interview. Also see *GP*, 1:212–18, 224, 228–29, 232–34, 237–38, 305–07 and 2:552–53.

106. See *Clarion* 1, no. 3 (September 1, 1917), esp. "Declaration of Principles of the Liberty League" (3–4), and "Why Did They Prefer Colored?" (14–15).

107. "The Future of the Negro," *Clarion* 1, no. 3 (September 1, 1917): 4.

108. "Our Foreword," *Clarion* 1, no. 3 (September 1, 1917): 9.

109. HH, *The Negro and the Nation* (New York: Cosmo-Advocate Publishing, 1917), 2, 5. Also see HH, "Affidavit of Circulation," and Orlando Thompson, "Affidavit of Circulation," both in *Voice*, August 21, 1917.

110. *Clarion* 1, no. 3 (September 1, 1917): 3; and Aida Harrison Richardson and William Harrison, interview by author, New York City, August 4, 1983.

111. HH to Theodore Lothrop Stoddard, November 13, 1920, HP.

112. HH, preface to *The Negro and the Nation*, 2; Theodore Lothrop Stoddard to HH, November 1, 1920; and HH to Stoddard, November 13, 1920, both in HP.

113. *Clarion*, 1, no. 3 (September 1, 1917), 10; and Claude McKay, *The Negroes in America* [1923], ed. Alan L. McLeod, trans. from the Russian by Robert J. Weiner (Port Washington, N.Y.: National University Publications, 1979), xi and 11.

114. HH, "Affidavit of Circulation," and Thompson, "Affidavit of Circulation."

115. [HH], "Houston vs. Waco," *Voice*, August 28, 1917, HP. On Houston, see Barbeau and Henri, *Unknown Soldiers*, 26–29; Aptheker, *A Documentary History of the Negro People*, 3:184–85; Herbert Shapiro, *White Violence and Black Response: From*

Reconstruction to Montgomery (Amherst: University of Massachusetts Press, 1988), 106–9; and Robert V. Haynes, *A Night of Violence: The Houston Riot of 1917* (Baton Rouge: Louisiana State University Press, 1976), 15–46.

116. Barbeau and Henri, *Unknown Soldiers*, 28–31; Aptheker, *Documentary History*, 3:184–85; "Houston Race Riot the Result of Series of Mob Executions Says White Editor," *NYA*, August 30, 1917, 1. Haynes, *Night of Violence*, 90–139, 319, points out that race riots occurred in 1917 in East St. Louis, Houston; Chester, Philadelphia; Lexington, Kentucky; Newark; and New York City, and in all but one of these, "more blacks were killed and wounded than whites." Houston, where more whites died, was the exception.

117. Barbeau and Henri, *Unknown Soldiers*, 28–31; Aptheker, *Documentary History*, 3:184–85; *GP*, 2:428n. 1; Haynes, *A Night of Violence*, 2, 254–323; Charles Flint Kellogg, *NAACP: A History of the National Association for the Advancement of Colored People, 1909–1920* (1967; Baltimore: Johns Hopkins University Press, 1973), 1:260–62; and *NYB, 1918–1919*, 67. In Harrison's Papers, see "A Military Lynching," *Richmond Planet*, June 5, 1918, HP-Sc 8; "Colored Folks Dazed," *Richmond Planet* [from *Savannah Tribune*], January 12, 1918, HP-Sc 8; "Court Martial is Dangerous Place for a Guilty Man," *Houston Post*, c. November 5, 1917, HP-Sc 8; "2 More 24th Men Turn States' Evidence," *Guardian*, December 1917, HP-Sc 8; and "Asks Race to Aid Families of Men of 24th Hanged," *NYN*, December 20, 1917, HP-Sc 8. When the thirteen soldiers were executed in December 1917 *The Voice* had ceased publishing, and Harrison later cited the lack of a militant Black response as one reason why the paper was needed: [HH], "The Reawakening of the Voice," *Voice*, July 11, 1918, 4, HP. In 1921 President Warren G. Harding received a petition signed by 50,000 and reduced the sentences of those imprisoned. By 1924 most had been released from prison, although the last soldier was not released until 1938. See Jack D. Foner, *Blacks and the Military*, 115.

118. [HH], "Houston vs. Waco." On the Jesse Washington lynching, see Patricia Bernstein, *The Waco Horror: The Lynching of Jesse Washington and the Rise of the NAACP* (College Station: Texas A&M University Press, 2005), esp. 4, 105–18; Shapiro, *White Violence and Black Response*, 111–13; and Kellogg, *NAACP* 1:218. On the very different treatment of white soldiers in Waco on July 29, 1917, see Haynes, *Night of Violence*, 65–67.

119. [HH], "Politics and Personality," *Voice*, August 28, 1917, HP.

120. [HH], "Politics and Personality"; HH, ["Reply to Jose Clarana,"] *NW*, April 30, 1921, 5; and HH, "To the Young Men of My Race," *New Negro*, January 1919, in *HR*, 175–77, esp. 177.

121. The interview with Morton appeared in [HH], "A Square Deal to All," *Voice*, October 18, 1917, HP.

122. [HH], "The New Policies For the New Negro," *Voice*, September 4, 1917, HP, in *HR*, 139–40, esp. 139.

123. [HH], "The New Policies For the New Negro," 139; and Hiller, "Race Politics," 134, 171. On New York, also see Goldstein, "Race Politics," 78–79. On Washington's approach, see Louis R. Harlan, "Booker T. Washington and the Politics of Accommodation," in *Black Leaders of the Twentieth Century*, ed. John Hope Franklin and August Meier (Urbana: University of Illinois Press, 1982), 1–18, esp. 3, 9–11.

124. [HH], "The New Policies For the New Negro," 139–40.

125. [HH], "Why Is a Negro?" *Voice*, September 4, 1917, HP.

126. HH, "The Problems of Leadership," *WAA*, 54–55. See also [HH], "Why Is a Negro?"; and HH, "Negro Society and the Negro Stage," pts. 1 and 2, *Voice*, September 19 and October 3, 1917, HP, in *HR*, 370–76.

127. [HH], "Why Is a Negro?" On George W. Harris's change, see "Using Term 'Negro,'" *NYA*, January 30, 1926, HP. Harrison had E. S. Beoku-Betts, "The Negro: Pre Historic and Historic," *African Times and Orient Review* (August 1917): 46–48, HP, which described a February 1915 editorial in Harris's *News* urging abolition of the word "Negro" (48).

128. [HH], "News and Views," *Voice*, September 4, 1917, HP; and [HH], "Why They Call Us Niggers," *Voice*, September 4, 1917, HP.

129. "Yung Cheng" [HH], "Real Estate News from Siam," *Voice*, September 4, 1917, HP; and (on Yung-chen), see Immanuel C. Y. Hsü, *The Rise of Modern China*, 3rd ed. (1970; New York: Oxford University Press, 1983), 169.

11. Race-Conscious Activism and
Organizational Difficulties (August–December 1917)

1. On circulation, readership, and literacy, see Frederick G. Detweiler, *The Negro Press in the United States* (Chicago: University of Chicago Press, 1922), 1, 7, 12. On Garvey's financial efforts see HH, "Marcus Garvey at the Bar of United States Justice," *Associated Negro Press*, c. July 1923, HP, in *HR*, 194–99, esp. 194–96. Regarding the *Negro World*'s difficulties and how they were solved: Garvey revealed on March 1, 1919, that "for six months the Association has been publishing this paper at a great financial loss." See "Fund Raising Appeal," *Negro World*, March 1, 1919 (hereafter *NW*), in *GP*, 1:383. The Black Star Line then raised $765,130 from July 1919 to February 1922, and Garvey collected an additional $144,450 for the Liberian Construction Fund. From such money, some $46,555 reportedly went "for the good will of the *Negro World*." See *GP*, 1:xlviii–xlix; and "Negro 'Napoleon' Counts on a Loyal Million to Aid Him," *New York World*, January 14, 1922.

2. William H. Ferris, [speech, March 7, 1920] *NW*, March 13, 1920, in *GP*, 2:243.

3. J. Domminick Simmons, interview by William Harrison, [New York], February 23, 1951, in "William Harrison Notebook," HP; [HH], "Send Us the News," *Voice*, September 4, 1917, HP; "This Is the Startling Announcement Which Was Promised Last

Week," *Voice*, September 4, 1917, HP; [HH,] "The Voice Is Coming Out to Stay!" flyer, c. July 4, 1918; and [HH,] "The Resurrection of the Voice," *Voice*, July 11, 1918, 4.

4. [HH], "The Sunday Voice," *Voice*, September 19, 1917, HP.

5. Anselmo Jackson, "Analysis of the Black Star Line," *Emancipator*, March 27, 1920, 2; and Richard B. Moore, "The Critics and Opponents of Marcus Garvey," in *Marcus Garvey and the Vision of Africa*, ed. and comm. John Henrik Clarke, with Amy Jacques Garvey (New York: Vintage, 1970), 210–34, esp. 217.

6. [HH], "The Sunday Voice."

7. Aida Richardson and William Harrison, interview by author, March 16, 1984, New York City. On Harrison's disinterest in "the desire to amass wealth—to 'get on' in the ordinary sense" and on his desire to pursue his "mission," see the appendix.

8. [HH], "The (New) Voice," *Voice*, July 11, 1918, 4. Edgar M. Grey stated that in 1921 Harrison refused financial support from the Communist Party underground group (there were two Communist Parties at the time—an underground group and an exposed group) via Rose Pastor Stokes, who "put up to Harrison a proposition by which . . . the Communist Party, would finance him so that he could use the Liberty League as a branch of spreading communism among Negroes by agitation with white people—which Harrison refused." Grey added that Cyril V. Briggs and the African Blood Brotherhood accepted Communist Party financing. See "Report of Agent P-138 [Herbert S. Boulin] for July 10, 1921," July 13, 1921, National Archives, Washington, D.C., (hereafter DNA), RG 65, BS 202600-2031-6. On October 21, 1917, Harrison went before the Executive Committee of the Socialist Party of Local New York and solicited an advertisement. An SP advertisement did run, and this approach was consistent with his stated policy of accepting advertising from all parties during the election. See Socialist Party, Local New York, Minutes of EC, October 21, 1917, R 2639, SP Minutes, 1900-1936, Collection VI:5, Socialist Party Papers, Tamiment Library, New York University (hereafter cited as SPP, LNY, NNYT). In the summer of 1919 *The Messenger* reportedly had a circulation of 33,000, was capitalized at $25,000, and had 356 stockholders, half of whom were white. See "Postmaster [Albert S.] Burleson Bars Colored Monthly Harlem Magazine From Mails, Editors Protest," *Harlem Home News*, July 6, 1919 (hereafter *HHN*). In 1926 Randolph's Brotherhood of Sleeping Car Porters received some $10,000 from the Garland Fund, administered by the American Civil Liberties Union. See Manning Marable, "A. Philip Randolph and the Foundations of Black American Socialism," *Radical America* 14, no. 2 (March–April 1980): 18. Some years later, however, Randolph would resign from the Negro National Congress, citing communist influence and warning, according to John Henrik Clarke, "that you generally get your funds from where you get your control." See Clarke, *Africans at the Crossroads: Notes for an African World Revolution* (Trenton, N.J.: Africa World Press, 1991) 375. Greg Leroy, "The Founding Heart of A. Philip Randolph's Union: Milton P. Webster and Chicago's Pullman Porters Organize, 1925–1937," *Labor's Heritage* 3, no. 3 (July 1991): 24, 42n. 52, also points out

that Randolph "had no children and relied heavily upon the income his wife Lucille earned as an agent and officer of the Madame C. J. Walker Cosmetics Company."

9. [HH] "Announcement: The Voice for Sale," *Voice*, September 12, 1917.

10. [HH,] "Announcement: The Voice for Sale."

11. "To the Friends of the Liberty League," *Voice*, September 19, 1917, HP; and [HH], "Some of Our Friends," *Voice*, September 19, 1917, HP.

12. "Additions and Changes," *New Negro* 1, no. 4 (October 13, 1917): 6; and *New Negro* 1, no. 6 (December 15, 1917): 14. Copies of these issues were kindly provided to me by Nancy and Randall K. Burkett.

13. Simmons, interview; *Clarion* 1, no. 2 (August 15, 1917), names some who moved. W. Burghardt Turner and Joyce Moore Turner, eds., *Richard B. Moore, Caribbean Militant in Harlem: Collected Writings, 1920–1972* (Bloomington: University of Indiana Press, 1988), 38, also indicates that Garvey got desk space from Cosmo-Advocate publishers. Tony Martin, *Race First: The Ideological and Organizational Struggle of Marcus Garvey and the Universal Negro Improvement Association* (Westport, Conn.: Greenwood Press, 1976), 10, explains, "Shortly before, or perhaps shortly after, Harrison's meeting, Garvey began to hold weekly meetings of his own every Sunday at 3 P.M. in Harlem's Lafayette Hall." These meetings were scheduled "to continue on until October 1917," and the UNIA then moved its meeting place "to the Palace Casino where it remained for most of 1918."

14. The historian Hollis Lynch correctly emphasized that some people attended both Harrison's and Garvey's meetings in a conversation with the author. In 1920, during the high-point of UNIA radicalism, Harrison stressed the similarity between the Liberty League and UNIA when he wrote in [HH], "The U.N.I.A.," *NW*, August 14, 1920, "The Universal Negro Improvement Association in the scope of its appeal embraces and expresses the spiritual standpoint of the new Negro. The essence of the spirit is the call to racial self-help and self-sufficiency" (2). Lester A. Walton, "Marcus Garvey: His Rise and Fall," *Chicago Defender*, April 4, 1925, sec. 1, p. 12 (hereafter *CD*), explained that Garvey considered a primary objective to be "the awakening of a race consciousness and the arousing of the proper appreciation of the Negro for his own." On "race consciousness" and Garvey, see also A. F. Elmes, "Garvey and Garveyism—an Estimate," *Opportunity* 3, no. 29 (May 1925): 139–41. William H. Ferris, "The Spectacular Career of Garvey," *Amsterdam News*, February 11, 1925, sec. 2, p. 9 (hereafter *AN*), thought that fully half of the UNIA rank-and-file members were "attracted by the idea of colored people getting together and doing big things to add to the prestige and standing of the race."

15. See, for example, Major Walter H. Loving to [Brigadier General Marlborough Churchill,] Director of Military Intelligence, "Final Report on Negro Subversion," letter, August 6, 1919, [re Harrison, p. 11], DNA, RG 165, MID 10218-361-1, R 6, where Loving writes that Harrison is "a scholar of broad learning and a radical propagandist . . . [and] a very convincing speaker. I consider his influence to be more

far reaching than that of any other individual radical because his subtle propaganda, delivered in such scholastic language and backed by the facts of history, carries an appeal to reason . . . Mr. Harrison's lectures might well be considered as a preparatory school for radical thought."

16. *GP*, 1:lix–lxvi, 1:210–11, 211n. 1, esp. lix; and Robert A. Hill, ed., Barbara Bair, associate ed., *Marcus Garvey: Life and Lessons; A Centennial Companion to the Marcus Garvey and Universal Negro Improvement Papers* (Berkeley: University of California Press, 1987), xix. See also HH, "Marcus Garvey at the Bar of U.S. Justice," 196–98.

17. A Harrison effort at self-appraisal is found in the appendix. See also Jeffrey Babcock Perry, "Hubert Henry Harrison, 'The Father of Harlem Radicalism': The Early Years—1883 Though the Founding of the Liberty League and *The Voice* in 1917" (Ph.D. diss., Columbia University, 1986), xiii–xiv; "Unrest Among the Negroes," October 7, 1919, DNA, RG 28, unarranged box no. 53, file no. 398, in W. F. Elkins, "'Unrest Among Negroes,': A British Document of 1919," *Science and Society* 32, no. 1 (Winter 1966): 66–79, esp. 77–78; and Winston James, *Holding Aloft the Banner of Ethiopia: Caribbean Radicalism in Early Twentieth-Century America* (New York: Verso, 1998), 129, which states that Harrison "did not suffer fools gladly largely because he was so extraordinarily wise" and he "made powerful enemies, black and white, who harmed him." James adds that Harrison was also a "philanderer" while Garvey, "in marked contrast, had little time for anything that was not directly connected with what he regarded as the redemption of Africa."

18. Hill, *GP*, 1:lii, lviii; Perry, "Hubert Henry Harrison," 566–68; James, *Holding Aloft*, 129; and, on the religious aspect, Randall K. Burkett, *Black Redemption: Churchmen Speak for the Garvey Movement* (Philadelphia: Temple University Press, 1978), 3–18, esp. 18.

19. [J. E. Bruce] "Bruce Grit" to "H. H. Harrison, Esq.," marked "Personal," August 2, 1917, HP; and [Report of Briggs interview,] Parker Hitt, acting chief of staff for Military Intelligence Division, Washington, D.C., June 23, 1921, re Negro Activities, Interview with [Cyril Briggs] editor of the "Crusader," June 22, 1921, MID 10218-424-1, DNA. Bruce's early warnings may have been more accurate than anyone would have predicted. W. A. Domingo was said to have started Garvey selling items to the public. Cyril Briggs described Domingo as "faint hearted" and vacillating. Garvey later claimed Edgar M. Grey stole money. William Harrison also stated that his father did not trust Grey. (Richardson and Harrison, interview; Simmons, interview; and Cyril V. Briggs to Oakley Johnson, October 3, 1961, Oakley C. Johnson Papers, Box 7, Folder 18 [microfilm], Schomburg Center for Research in Black Culture, New York Public Library [hereafter SCRBC]).

20. On the move towards Garvey, see Simmons, interview; and for Moore's comments, see Turner and Turner, *Richard B. Moore*, 38. See also Bruce to Harrison, "Personal," August 2, 1917; and "Mass Meeting to Elect Officers of the Liberty League and to Discuss the Problem of 'Negro Soldiers vs. Negro Citizen,'" *Voice*,

September 19, 1917, HP. Mark Ellis, "'Closing Ranks' and 'Seeking Honor,' W. E. B. Du Bois in World War I," *Journal of American History* 79, no. 1 (June 1992): 101, points out that "the years 1917 to 1920 were hard for the editor of any publication that challenged the status quo and depended on the mail for circulation." On Harrison's wartime militance, see [HH], "A Prophetic 'Voice': The Cause of the Negro's New Attitude Toward Race Riots," *New Negro* 4, no. 1 (September 1919): 8 (hereafter *NN*), which reprints an extremely militant Harrison editorial printed in the July 4, 1917 *Voice*. Theodore G. Vincent, *Black Power and the Garvey Movement* (San Francisco: Ramparts Press, 1972), 42, points out that, because of Harrison's stance on the war, "association with the [Liberty] League was no light matter." Hill, *GP*, 1:lix–lxvi, esp. lix discusses imperial aspects of the Garvey movement.

21. Turner and Turner, *Richard B. Moore*, 38.

22. On activities of the "politicals," see Hill, *Life and Lessons*, 36 ("forced" and "beat up"), 380, and 402; "Garvey Tells Story of Bitter Struggles," *Pittsburgh Courier*, February 22, 1930 (hereafter *PC*); *GP*, 1:lxiii–lxv, 7–8, 223–25, 233–34 (which lists officers involved in the UNIA takeover), 241, and 242; Marsha Hurst Hiller, "Race Politics in New York City, 1890–1930" (Ph.D. diss., Columbia University, 1972), 285; and Michael Louis Goldstein, "Race Politics in New York City, 1890–1930: Independent Political Behavior" (Ph.D. diss., Columbia University, 1973), 241 n. 1.

23. Simmons, interview; Edgar M. Grey, "Notes on 'The Garvey Movement': A Study," *NYN*, February 21, 1925, box 20, folder 6, Theodore Draper Papers, Robert W. Woodruff Library for Advanced Studies, Emory University, Atlanta; Jervis Anderson, *A. Philip Randolph: A Biographical Portrait* (New York: Harcourt Brace Jovanovich, 1973), 80. On the relations of the above named individuals to the UNIA, BSL, and *Negro World*, see the following items: Allen: *GP*, 1:226n. 1; Bruce: *GP*, 1:200n. 2; Domingo: *GP*, 1:192, 527–31, and W. A. Domingo, interview by Theodore Draper, January 18, 1958, Theodore Draper Papers, Robert W. Woodruff Library for Advanced Studies, Emory University, Atlanta; Grey: *GP*, 1:211–12n. 3; Jackson: *GP*, 1:282n. 3; Moorman-Blackston: *GP*, 1:224n. 4, and Cleveland G. Allen, "Among the Negroes of Harlem," *HHN*, January 23, 1918; Reid: "Report of Agent P-138 [H. S. Boulin], for June 12, 1921," June 14, 1921, DNA, RG 65, BS 202600-2031, and *GP*, 3:681–82n. 1; Seifert: *GP*, 1:226n. 3, Allen, "Among the Negroes of Harlem," *HHN*, January 23, 1918, Simmons interview; Thompson: *GP*, 2:390n. 1; Duncan: *GP*, 1:224n. 1.

24. See "Argus" [John E. Bruce], "Answer, 'Professor' Garvey, Answer," to the editor of *New Negro*, c. January 1918, reprint, *GP*, 1:234–35, esp. 235; "Statement of John E. Bruce," c. January 1918," in *GP*, 235–36, esp. 236; and *GP*, 1:349–50. The figure of 100,000,000 was frequently claimed by Garvey. See HD, August 31, 1920; and *GP*, 9:161n. 4.

25. Simmons, interview; HH, "Two Negro Radicalisms," *New Negro* 4, no. 2 (October 1919): 4–5, in *HR*, 102–5; "Negroes Meet Today to Seek Tulsa Redress," *New York Call*, June 5, 1921 (hereafter *NYC*); and *GP*, 1:200n. 2, 224n. 4.

26. "Additions and Changes," *New Negro* 1, no. 4 (October 13, 1917): 6.

27. [W. A. Domingo], "Race First!" *NW*, July 26, 1919, reprint, in *GP*, 1:468–70; Ferris, "The Spectacular Career of Garvey," 9; and *GP*, 2:352.

28. HH, "Marcus Garvey at the Bar of United States Justice," 196–98.

29. HH, "Marcus Garvey at the Bar of United States Justice, 196–98, esp. 197; and *GP*, 1:lxvii, lxviii, 210–11, and esp. 3:709, on Garvey's decision to stay.

30. The sources for this list are:

Isaac Allen: *GP*, 1:226n. 1

John E. Bruce: *GP*, 1:200n. 2

W. A. Domingo: Simmons, interview; *GP*, 1:192, 527–31; and Domingo, interview

Gertrude Miller Faide: *Clarion* 1, no. 3 (September 1, 1917): 3; and *New Negro* 1 no. 4 (October 13, 1917): 6

Marcus Garvey: *GP*, 1:567–68, 2:684

Edgar M.Grey: *GP*, 1:211–12n. 3; and Simmons, interview

Hubert Henry Harrison: HH, *When Africa Awakes: The "Inside Story" of the Stirrings and Strivings of the New Negro in the Western World* (New York: Porro Press, 1920), 8, (hereafter *WAA*); HH to Lothrop Stoddard, August 21, 1920; HH, "Addendum to the Above," *NW*, April 23, 1921, 5; and HH, "Statement of Hubert Harrison," Interrogation by Postal Inspector Williamson, June 16, 1922, Federal Bureau of Investigation, Department of Justice, Washington, D.C., 190-1781-6

Anselmo Jackson: *GP*, 1:282n. 3

Irena Moorman-Blackston: *GP*, 1:224n. 4; and Allen, "Among the Negroes of Harlem," *HHN*, January 23, 1918

Dr. E. Eliott Rawlins: *GP*, 5:722n. 4, 834; and *NW*, February 24, 1923

Andy Razaf: See Andrea Razaf[in]keriefo, "Prayer of the Lowly," *Voice*, October 31, 1917; and Andrea Razaf[in]keriefo, "Friend Jones," *Voice*, October 31, 1917

Arthur Reid: "Report of Agent P-138, For June 12, 1921" and *GP*, 3:681–82n. 1

Charles Christopher Seifert: *GP*, 1:226n. 3; Allen, "Among the Negroes of Harlem," *HHN*, January 23, 1918; Simmons, interview; Robert A. Hill, interview by Gil Noble, aired November 20, 1983, "Radio TV Reports, Inc., For WABC-TV 'Like It Is,' November 20, 1983," 1:00 p.m. (New York: Radio-TV Reports, 1984), 20; HH, "Marcus Garvey at the Bar of United States Justice," 197; and Ferris, "The Spectacular Career of Garvey," 9

Orlando M. Thompson: *GP*, 2:390n. 1

31. Simmons, interview and *GP*, 1:224n. 1.

32. *GP*, 1:lvi–lix, lxvi–lxvii, lxx–lxxviii, 323–24.

33. Jackson, "An Analysis of the Black Star Line," 2.

34. Ferris, "The Spectacular Career of Garvey," 9.

35. Domingo, interview, 2.

36. *WGMC*, 2:436.

37. [HH], "The Coming Election," *Voice*, October 18, 1917, HP; HH, "Charles W. Anderson," *Voice*, October 31, 1917; Goldstein, "Race Politics," 216–17; Hiller, "Race Politics," 230–55; "3,000 Blacks Like Attack Upon T. R.," *New York World*, July 30, 1917; Cleveland G. Allen, "Among the Negroes of Harlem," *HHN*, October 17, 1917, 6; and "Patronize These Negro Enterprises," *Colored American Review* 1, no. 1 (October 1, 1915): 8–9, 15.

38. [HH], "The Coming Election"; Edwin R. Lewinson, *Black Politics in New York City* (New York: Twayne, 1974), 47, 55; and Judith Stein, *The World of Marcus Garvey: Race and Class in Modern Society* (Baton Rouge: Louisiana State University Press, 1986), 45.

39. On the change in Harlem, see Florette Henri, *Black Migration: Movement North, 1900–1920* (Garden City, N.Y.: Anchor Press/Doubleday, 1975), 88–90; Gilbert Osofsky, *Harlem: The Making of a Ghetto; Negro New York, 1890–1930* (1963; New York: Harper and Row, 1971), 122–23, 131; Seth M. Scheiner, *Negro Mecca: A History of the Negro in New York, 1865–1920* (New York: New York University Press, 1965), 8, 9, 221–22; and Charles V. Hamilton, ed. *The Black Experience in American Politics* (New York: Putnam, 1973), 3–4.

40. HH, "The Right Way to Unity," *Boston Chronicle*, May 10, 1924, HP (hereafter *BC*), in *HR*, 402–4, esp. 403; Goldstein, "Race Politics," 391.

41. [HH], "The Coming Election."

42. [HH], "The Coming Election." See also Hiller, "Race Politics," 202, 230–31; Goldstein, "Race Politics," 215; Scheiner, *Negro Mecca*, 206–7; and Charles Flint Kellogg, *NAACP: A History of the National Association for the Advancement of Colored People, 1909–1920* (1967; Baltimore, Md.: Johns Hopkins University Press, 1973), 1:162.

43. [HH], "The Coming Election." See also *GP*, 7:64n. 4.

44. [HH], "The Coming Election."

45. [HH], "The Coming Election."

46. [HH], "A Square Deal to All," *Voice*, October 18, 1917. See also Goldstein, "Race Politics," 67, 78; and Hiller, "Race Politics," 198.

47. [HH], "The Negro Candidates," *Voice*, October 18, 1917, HP. See also HH, "A Negro for President," *NW*, June 19, 1920, 2, in *HR*, 147–49

48. Allen, "Among the Negroes of Harlem," *HHN*, November 4, 1917, 6; [HH], "*Terms of Peace and the Darker Races* by A. Philip Randolph and Chandler Owen," *Voice*, September 19, 1917, HP, in *HR*, 297–99; and HH, review of *A Defence of the Colored Soldiers Who Fought in the War of the Rebellion* by John Edward Bruce ("Bruce Grit"), *Voice*, September 19, 1917, HP.

49. [HH], "*Terms of Peace and the Darker Races.*"

50. "H. H." [HH], "'Just Suppose' a Riddle for 'Scientific Radical' Liars, With Apologies to C[handler]. OW[en].", *NW*, April 10, 1920, HP-Sc B.

51. Socialist Party (hereafter SP), Local New York, Minutes of Executive Committee, October 10 and 21, 1917, R 2639, SP Minutes, 1900–1936, Collection VI:5, SP Papers, Tamiment Institute, New York University.

52. "Wilson Attacked by Negro Speaker," *New York Globe*, October 17, 1917, HP.

53. Minutes of Executive Committee, October 21, 1917. See also "Morris Hillquit," *Voice*, October 31, 1917 (advertisement for the SP ticket).

54. "New York News," *Chicago Defender*, October 27, 1917, 4.

55. Cleveland G. Allen, "Among the Negroes of Harlem," *HHN*, October 28, 1917.

56. [HH], "Negroes Hiss Roosevelt at Palace Casino—Ex-President, Speaking for Mitchel, Is Greeted with Cries of 'Hillquit and Socialism!'—Thomas, Negro Candidate, Stampedes Vast Assembly—Colonel Forced to Quit—'Fighting Jack' Is Shouted Down and Hooted," *Voice*, October 31, 1917, 1.

57. [HH], "Negroes Hiss Roosevelt." See also "Roosevelt Hits a Dusky Snag," *NYC*, October 30, 1917; J. M. Turner, *Richard B. Moore*, 31; and "Hillquit Decries Race Issue," *NYC*, November 4, 1917, 1.

58. [HH], "Negroes Hiss Roosevelt." See also Hiller, "Race Politics," 285; and "Frances Dearborn" [HH], "The Black Tide Turns in Politics," c. December 1921?, HP, in *HR*, 158.

59. [HH], "Negroes Hiss Roosevelt." See also [HH], "The Black Tide," 158. In HH, "Prejudice Growing Less and Co-Operation More," *Pittsburgh Courier*, January 29, 1927, sec. 2, p. 7, in *HR*, 252, Harrison writes that "in St. Mark's and St. Benedict's lyceums in West 53rd street they [Caribbean-born and U.S.-born] effected literary combination some years before."

60. "Negroes Hiss Roosevelt"; Minutes of EC, October 21, 1917; and HH, "Why Is Harlem Hot?" *Voice*, October 31, 1917.

61. HH, "Why is Harlem Hot?"; and "Negroes Hiss Roosevelt at Palace Casino."

62. HH, "An Open Letter to the Socialist Party of New York City," *NW*, May 8, 1920, 2, in *HR*, 113.

63. HH, "An Open Letter," 113–14; [HH], "The Black Tide," 158; and Cleveland G. Allen, "Among the Negroes of Harlem," *HHN*, January 27, 1918, 6.

64. HH, "An Open Letter," 114.

65. HH, "An Open Letter," 114.

66. The ads are in *Voice*, October 31, 1917.

67. HH, "Our Political Ads," *Voice*, October 31, 1917. See also "Morgan a Friend of the Negro," *Voice*, October 31, 1917.

68. HH, "Charles W. Anderson," *Voice*, October 31, 1917.

69. HH, "Charles W. Anderson."

70. Cleveland G. Allen, "Among the Negroes of Harlem," *HHN*, October 3, 1917, 6, and November 4, 1917, 6.

71. HH, "Woman Suffrage," *Voice*, October 31, 1917. See also Marjorie Spruill Wheeler, "A Short History of the Woman Suffrage Movement in America," in *One*

Woman, One Vote: Rediscovering the Woman Suffrage Movement, ed. Marjorie Spruill Wheeler (Troutdale, Ore.: New Sage Press, 1995), 11–19, esp. 11–13.

72. Aileen S. Kraditor, *The Ideas of the Woman Suffrage Movement, 1890–1920* (Garden City, N.Y.: Anchor Books/Doubleday, 1971), 167 and 170; Nancy F. Cott, *The Grounding of Modern Feminism* (New Haven, Conn.: Yale University Press, 1987), 68; and HH, "Woman Suffrage." See also Rosalyn Terborg-Penn, "African American Women and the Woman Suffrage Movement," in Wheeler, *One Woman, One Vote*, 135–55, esp. 150.

73. Cleveland G. Allen, "Among the Negroes of Harlem," *HHN*, November 7, 1917, 6; and Nannie H. Burroughs to the editor [of the *Afro-American*], in "Should We Vote the Socialist Ticket?" *Crusader* 1, no. 2 (October 1919): 2, where she also writes that women of the Woman Suffrage Association "in their effort to secure the ballot, they have virtually promised [t]he South to leave the Negro woman out of the equation."

74. HH, "Woman Suffrage." See also Cleveland G. Allen, "Among the Negroes of Harlem," *HHN*, November 7, 1917, 6, and January 9, 1918, 6.

75. [HH], "A Course in Languages," *Voice*, October 31, 1917.

76. "The Gary System and How It Works," *Voice*, October 31, 1917. See also Hiller, "Race Politics," 235–36; "Gary System and Mitchel Flayed by Parents League," *HHN*, October 28, 1917, 6; and Cleveland G. Allen, "Among the Negroes of Harlem," *HHN* October 3 and November 4, 1917, 6 and 6.

77. From the *Voice*, October 31, 1917, see "The Harlem People's Forum," advertisement and Milton Lehrman to "Dear Mr. Harrison," October 18, 1917, *Voice*, October 31, 1917.

78. [A. P.] Razaf[in]keriefo to "Dear Friend Harrison," October 22, 1917, *Voice*, October 31, 1917.

79. Jackson, "The Black Star Line," *Emancipator*, March 27, 1920, 2; R. B. Moore, "The Critics and Opponents of Marcus Garvey," 217; *GP*, 2:237–38n. 1; Richardson and Harrison, interview; HD, April 27, 1908; and appendix.

80. Hitt, interview with [Cyril Briggs]; and David J. Garrow, *The FBI and Martin Luther King, Jr: From "Solo" to Memphis* (New York: Norton, 1981), 12, 164–65.

81. Claude McKay, *A Long Way from Home: An Autobiography*, (1937; New York: Harcourt Brace and World, 1970), 118; James, *Holding Aloft*, 129; and HD, January 16, 1918.

82. HH, "Our Professional 'Friends,'" *Voice*, November 7, 1917, in HP, *HR*, 144.

83. HH, "Our Professional 'Friends,'" 144.

84. HH, "Our Professional 'Friends,'" 145 (which includes Ovington's letter, Harrison's August 3 reply, and his general comments), also explains that while sending his response to Ovington he rejoined the party by sending his membership dues. In HH, preface to *The Negro and the Nation* (New York: Cosmo-Advocate Publishing, 1917), 2, written in August 1917, Harrison explained that he had left the Socialist

Party in part because he held a race-first view and "wished to put himself in a position to work among his people along lines of his own choosing."

85. HH, "Our Professional 'Friends,'" 146.

86. HH, "Our Professional 'Friends,'" 146; and HH, "An Open Letter," 114. See also "Harlem People's Forum: Hubert Harrison, Lecturer. . . . This Sunday: Our Professional Friends the 'NAACP' National Association for the Acceptance of Color Proscription," *Voice*, July 11, 1918, 1; Henri, *Black Migration*, 284; and Hal S. Chase, "Struggle for Equality: Fort Des Moines Training Camp for Colored Officers, 1917," *Phylon* 39, no. 4 (December 1978): 297–310, esp. 297, 306, 309–10.

87. [HH], ["Re Vesey St. Liberals"], n.p., n.d., HP; and HH, "In Case of War— What?" *Boston Chronicle*, June 14, 1924 ("government"), HP.

88. Mark Ellis, "Joel Spingarn's 'Constructive Programme' and the Wartime Anti-lynching Bill of 1918," *Journal of Policy History* 4, no. 2 (1992): 134–61, esp. 135–37.

89. Kellogg, *NAACP*, 1:254; [HH], "Why Is the Red Cross?" *Voice*, July 18, 1918, HP; and [HH], ["Vesey St."].

90. W. E. B. Du Bois, *The Autobiography of W. E. B. Du Bois: A Soliloquy on Viewing My Life from the Last Decade of Its First Century* (1968; New York: International Publishes, 1971), 266.

91. Nathan I. Huggins, *Harlem Renaissance* (1971; New York: Oxford University Press, 1974), 37; HH, "Our Larger Duty," *New Negro*, 3, no. 7 (August, 1919): 5, in *HR*, 99–101, esp. 100; HH, "Introductory," *WAA*, 5; and Rogers, *WGMC*, 2:436.

92. HH, "Our Professional 'Friends,'" 146. See also HH, "A Cure for the Ku-Klux," *Voice*, January 30, 1919, HP, in *HR*, 266–67.

93. HH, "Our Professional 'Friends,'" 146.

94. HH, "Our Professional 'Friends,'" 147.

95. [HH], "Election Results," *Voice*, November 14, 1917, HP. On the 1917 vote, also see Charles Leinenweber, "The Class and Ethnic Bases of New York City Socialism, 1904–1915," *Labor History* 22, no. 1 (Winter 1981): 31–56, esp. 33 and 47.

96. [HH], "Election Results."

97. [HH], "Election Results." See also "Socialist Vote Smashes Record," *NYC*, November 7, 1917, 1.

98. [HH], "Election Results."

99. [HH], "Election Results"; and C. G. Allen, "Among the Negroes of Harlem," *HHN*, November 18, 1917, 6.

100. [HH], "Election Results." See also Cleveland G. Allen, "Among the Negroes of Harlem," *HHN*, November 18, 1917, 6, and January 16, 1918, 6; "Court Orders Recount of Ballots for Alderman," *NYA*, November 15, 1917, 1; and "Thomas and Johnson Are Elected in Harlem," *NYA*, November 5, 1917, 1.

101. See Lewinson, *Black Politics*, 57; and Stein, *World of Marcus Garvey*, 45–47.

102. William Monroe Trotter to HH, November 17, 1917, HP. Miller said of Harrison—"With his wonderful grasp of history, theology, the social sciences, and literature, [he is] charming ever with exquisite English." See "Who Is Hubert Harrison?"

handout card, c. November 1920, HP, which cites Dr. George Frazier Miller, pastor of St. Augustine's Church, "Reply to Bishop Nelson," 14.

103. [HH], "To Old Subscribers," *Voice*, July 1, 1918, HP; [HH], "To Newsdealers," *Voice*, July 11, 1918, 1; Simmons, interview; Cleveland G. Allen, "Among the Negroes of Harlem," *HHN*, January 20, 1918; "A December Dance," advertisement, *Voice*, October 31, 1917; "Certificate of Incorporation of The Race Publishing Company, Inc.," December 10, 1917, Office of the Secretary of State, State of New York, Albany, no. 10366, book 658, p. 905.

104. [HH,] "The Resurrection of the Voice," 4; and [HH,] "The New Voice," *Voice*, July 11, 1918, 4.

105. Robert A. Hill, "Introduction," in *The Crusader*, ed. and intro. Hill (New York: Garland Publishing, 1987), 3 vols., 1:v–lxvi, xlix nn. 4–5, and vi, which cites Hodge Kirnon, "The New Negro and His Will to Manhood and Achievement," *Promoter* 1 (August 1920): 6; and Hodge Kirnon, "Towards the One Common End," *Promoter* 1 (August 1920): 8.

106. "Knowledge Is Power and These Lectures by Hubert H. Harrison Wall Street's Famous Negro Lecturer Will Give You a Powerful Grip on the Problems of Life," c. December1917, HP-Sc 34; "Harrison and Owen Will Debate on 'Negroes First,'" *NYC*, December 22, 1917, HP; "Is the Doctrine of 'NEGROES FIRST' a Logical and Sound Socialistic Position?" advertisement, *NYC*, December 22, 1917, HP; "The Greatest Debate in Years Between Hubert H. Harrison Affirmative and Chandler Owen Negative Subject: Resolved: That the doctrine, 'Negroes First,' is sound, logical or DEFENSIBLE," c. December 22, 1917, HP-Sc 34; and C. G. Allen, "Among the Negroes of Harlem," *HHN*, October 17, October 21, and December 9, 1917, all p. 6. On Owen changing the billing, see HH to the editor, *NYC*, January 7, 1918, HP..

107. HH to the editor, *NYC*, January 7, 1918.

108. HH to the editor, *NYC*, January 7, 1918.

109. HH to the editor, *NYC*, January 7, 1918.

110. [HH], "One Decade of Harlem's Mental Growth," [c. 1925], HP; and HH, "Patronize Your Own," *NW*, May 1, 1920, in *HR*, 112.

111. Rogers. *WGMC*, 2:436 ("profoundly"); Cleveland G. Allen, "Among the Negroes of Harlem," *HHN*, December 9, 1917, p. 9 ("club"); HH, [Notes re "The Red Record of Radicalism"], [n.p., c. 1927], HP; and A. Philip Randolph to Elizabeth Gurley Flynn, Secretary, The American Fund for Public Service, Inc. [Garland Fund], January 22, 1925, in "Applications Favorably Acted Upon, I: Gifts 1922–1927," "Messenger," vol. 8, bound file no. 67, ("the first Socialist"). See also Philip S. Foner, *American Socialism and Black Americans: From the Age of Jackson to World War II* (Westport, Conn.: Greenwood Press, 1977), 286–87.

112. Leinenweber, "Class and Ethnic Bases," 47; HH, [Notes re "The Red Record of Radicalism"], [n.p., c. 1927], HP; and Randolph to Flynn, January 22, 1925.

113. HH, "Race First vs. Class First," *NW*, March 27, 1920, in *HR*, 109; and HH, "An Open Letter," 116.

114. C. G. Allen, "Among the Negroes of Harlem," *HHN*, October 3, 1917, November 4, 1917, January 2, 1918, and January 16, 1918, all p. 6; and Hill, "Introduction," 1:vi.

115. W. E. B. Du Bois, "Segregation," *Crisis* no. 41 (January 1934): 20.

12. The Liberty Congress and
the Resurrection of *The Voice* (January–July 1918)

1. See Robert L. Zangrando, *The NAACP Crusade Against Lynching, 1909–1950* (Philadelphia: Temple University Press, 1980), 6; [untitled], *Richmond Planet*, February 16, 1918, HP-Sc 8; and "Post Office Clerks Dismissed by the Wholesale in Charleston," *Boston Chronicle* (hereafter *BC*), January 31, 1918, HP-Sc 8. The May 29, 1918, *Amsterdam News* claimed that 230 Blacks were lynched in the first fourteen months of the war.

2. *GP*, 1:341n. 2. See also Alexander Trachtenberg, ed., *The American Labor Year Book, 1919–20* (New York: Rand School of Social Science, 1920), 90–95, 102 (hereafter *ALYB, 1919–20*); and David A. Shannon, *The Socialist Party of America* (New York: MacMillan, 1955), 109–10.

3. HD, April 24, 1917, January 16, March 22, 27, 30, and 31, 1918, in HP. Harrison stopped by regularly to have dinner with the children.

4. Socialist Party, Local New York, Minutes of EC, February 27, 1918, Tamiment Institute, New York University (hereafter SP, LNY, NNYT), R 2639, SP Minutes, 1900–1936, Collection VI:5; and Shannon, *Socialist Party*, 95–99.

5. HD, March 27 and September 16, 1918; Report of the Joint Legislative Committee Investigating Seditious Activities, Filed April 24, 1920, in the Senate of the State of New York, *Revolutionary Radicalism: Its History, Purpose and Tactics*, 2 parts in 4 vols. (Albany: J. B. Lyon, 1920), part 1, *Revolutionary and Subversive Movements at Home and Abroad*, 1:613–18, esp. 613 and 614. In Harrison's copy of J. M. Robertson, *The Evolution of States: An Introduction to English Politics* (New York: Putnam/Knickerbocker Press, 1913), 72, HP, Robertson writes "that it may be the last card of Conservatism to play off the war spirit against the reform spirit." Harrison adds, "perhaps this was one of the conscious imperatives of the Great War—on both sides."

6. SP, LNY, Minutes of EC, March 27 and September 16, 1918, NNYT, R 2639 SP Minutes, 1900–1936, Collection VI:5. See also "Negro Workers Get Impetus to Organize in Labor Unions," *New York Call*, June 24, 1918.

7. Marsha Hurst Hiller, "Race Politics in New York City, 1890–1930" (Ph. D. diss., Columbia University, 1972), 285–86 and 289; and Edwin R. Lewinson, *Black Politics in New York City* (New York: Twayne, 1974), 59.

8. HD, September 16, 1918.

9. "American Federation of Labor to Make Special Efforts to Unionize the Colored Workman," *New York Age*, May 4, 1918, 1 (hereafter *NYA*); Trachtenberg, *ALYB 1919–20*, 42–57, esp. 46; and Philip S. Foner, *Organized Labor and the Black Worker, 1619–1975* (New York: Praeger, 1973), 141. Marc Karson and Ronald Radosh, "The American Federation of Labor and Negro Workers, 1894–1949," *The Negro and the American Labor Movement*, ed. in Julius Jacobsen, ed. (New York: Doubleday, 1968), 157, explains: "the AFL did little in the way of appointing Negro organizers, although recommendations that this be done were adopted by the AFL Conventions of 1902, 1907, 1917, and 1918. For all practical purposes, the AFL did not even aid the unorganized Negroes in gaining entry into the segregated structure which the 1900 Convention had created."

10. HD, July 1, 1918; "Negro Workers Get Impetus to Organize"; advertisement, "A General Membership Meeting of the International Federation of Workers in the Hotel, Restaurant, Club and Catering Industry," Philadelphia, May 23, 1918, HP-Sc. C; advertisement, "'Shall the White and Colored Workers Unite for Higher Pay?' A Lecture on the Present Conditions in the Hotel and Restaurant Industry by Hubert Harrison," Washington, D.C., July 5, 1918, HP-Sc C; and Trachtenberg, *ALYB, 1919–20*, 148.

11. "Negro Workers Get Impetus to Organize"; and "Pullman Men to Organize: Three Hundred Employed in Pullman Service Hold Big Mass Meeting in New York City," *NYA*, June 29, 1918, 1.

12. Hubert H. Harrison, American Citizen to Naturalization Examiner, U.S. Department of Labor, 151 Nassau St., New York, July 5, 1922, FOIA/PA Request No. NYC840409; and William W. Boyer, *America's Virgin Islands: A History of Human Rights and Wrongs* (Durham, N.C.: Carolina Academic Press, 1983), 86. In the 1920 census Harrison claimed that he was naturalized in 1913. That was not the case. See Bureau of the Census, *Fourteenth Census of the United States: 1920—Population*, vol. 258, E.D. 972, sheet 1, line 87.

13. HD, March 27, 1918. David Kennedy, *Over Here: The First World War and American Society* (New York: Oxford University Press, 1980), 157, notes that 2.5 million "non-declared" alien men without preliminary citizenship papers were initially exempted from service. It is quite possible Harrison at first counted on this.

14. HD, March 27, 1918.

15. HD, March 27, 1918. In his diary entry of March 22, 1919, Harrison detailed how the previous night he had dictated a letter to be sent to Major Walter Loving, which was really intended for Loving's "superiors in the 'Bureau of Intelligence', War Dept. Harrison's letter explained how "the radicals of vision" might be willing to cooperate "in allaying friction and promoting goodwill," but, "we absolutely demand, as the price of our aid, the head of John the Baptist on a charger, viz: that Scott, Haynes and their ilk be dumped once and for all." In a diary entry of April 25, 1919, he noted, after talking with Loving, that Loving had gone over his letter and enclosures with

his superior and the "ferment is working." He wrote: "I shall live to see Emmett Scott paid off for what was done to me in 1911 and Geo. Haynes for—other things." Harrison subjoined in a note dated November 3, [1919,] "Read today in a newspaper that Geo. E. Haynes has lost his job as Secretary of the National Urban League." See HD, March 22, April 25, and November 3, 1919.

16. Mary Ann Hawkins, Regional Archives Branch, General Services Administration, Region 4, East Point, GA 30344 to author, July 15, 1984; HH, Draft Registration Card, Serial No. 2795, Order No. 4744, Division. No. 144, New York City, September 12, 1918. On draft classifications of Black Americans, see Arthur E. Barbeau and Florette Henri, *The Unknown Soldiers: Black American Troops in World War I* (Philadelphia: Temple University Press, 1974), 36; and *GP*, 4:1024n. On the "slacker" raids, see "Get 1,500 in 3-Day Roundup," *NYT*, September 6, 1918; H. C. Peterson and G. C. Fite, *Opponents of War, 1917–1918* (Seattle: University of Washington Press, 1957), 231; *GP*, 1:393n. 6, 400n. 6; and Kennedy, *Over Here*, 165–67.

17. Merton A. Sturges, U.S. Department of Labor, Naturalization Service, New York to Commissioner of Naturalization, re: 2270-P-426559 [Hubert Harrison], HH, July 26, 1922; Robert C. Davies, Acting Adjutant General, War Department, Adjutant General's Office, Washington, to Commissioner of Naturalization, U.S. Department of Labor, Washington, re: Hubert Harrison, August 8, 1922; Robert C. Davies, War Department, to HH, July 1, 1922, FOIA/PA Request No. NYC840409; M. Hawkins to author, July 15, 1984; and HH, Draft Registration Card.

18. "Negro Is Genuine," part 1, *New Negro* 2, no. 2 (March 1918): 15–16.

19. HH, "Africa at the Peace Table," *Voice*, December 26, 1918, HP, in *HR*, 210–12, esp. 212; and HD, March 28, 1918.

20. HD, March 28 and April 12, 1918; and Aida Harrison Richardson and William Harrison, interview by author, New York, August 4, 1983.

21. HD, July 1, 1918; [HH,] "Negroes Asking for Foretaste of Democracy," *Voice*, July 11, 1918, 1–2, 4; and William Monroe Trotter to HH, November 17, 1917, HP.

22. "Call For Colored Liberty Congress," May 11, 1918, MID-10218-153-3, National Archives, Washington, D.C. (hereafter DNA); P. F. Goodwin, Capt., to Intelligence Officer, Washington, D.C., June 14, 1918, file 9140-2222-35, DNA.

23. Mark Ellis, "'Closing Ranks' and 'Seeking Honors,' W. E. B. Du Bois in World War I," *Journal of American History* 79, no. 1 (June 1992): 96–124, esp. 103, Du Bois quoted at 105, 114; Mark Ellis, "Joel Spingarn's 'Constructive Programme' and the Wartime Antilynching Bill of 1918," *Journal of Policy History* 4, no. 2 (1992): 134–61, esp. 134, 139, 141, and 142; Ernest Allen Jr., "'Close Ranks': Major Joel E. Spingarn and the Two Souls of W. E. B. Du Bois," *Contributions in Black Studies* no. 3 (1979–80): 25–38, esp. 26, 27, 33–35; Roy Talbert Jr., *Negative Intelligence: The Army and the American Left, 1917–1941* (Jackson: University Press of Mississippi, 1991), 20–21, 22, 55; and Theodore Kornweibel Jr., *"Seeing Red": Federal Campaigns Against Black Militancy, 1919–1925* (Bloomington: University of Indiana Press, 1998), 11.

24. Lt. Col. M. Churchill to Charles H. Studin, June 3, 1918, RG 165, MID 10218-139, box 3192, DNA' and Ellis, "'Closing Ranks,'" 105–6.

25. Ellis, "'Closing Ranks,'" 99, 105, and 107.

26. Fred W. Moore to Chief Military Intelligence Branch, Washington, D.C., June 19, 1918, MID-10218-153-7: "Subject: Proposed National Convention of Negroes."

27. Allen, "'Close Ranks,'" 28, 32n. 13; and Talbert, *Negative Intelligence*, 123.

28. [Major] J. E. Spingarn, "Memorandum for Colonel Churchill, Subject: Negro Subversion," June 10, 1918, in Allen, "'Closing Ranks,'" 33–35.

29. Zangrando, *NAACP Crusade*, 43–45, states that after Dyer asked the NAACP to sponsor a bill making lynching a federal crime in March 1918, the Board of Directors explored various options in mid-May and "actually declined to make an open push . . . on grounds that the measures were not constitutional." This position "relied heavily on advice from eminent lawyer-president, Moorfield Storey, who at the time took a very conservative, traditional position" (44). By mid-1918 Storey was willing to concede that the federal government could counter lynchings through wartime powers and national emergency needs. In general, however, as Zangrando emphasizes, "The Association followed Storey's advice and muted its role as lobbyist for an antilynching bill" (45). (Trotter's proposal to make lynching a federal crime had been soundly defeated at one of the NAACP's founding meetings.) The basis for the NAACP position was articulated earlier in W. R. Harr, Assistant Attorney General, for the Attorney General, to Oswald Garrison Villard, chairman of the NAACP, on December 31, 1911, file 158260-7, RG 60, DNA. Harr wrote: "There is no authority in the United States Government to interfere [with mob violence] because the parties committing such crimes violate the laws of the State where the offense is committed and are punishable in its courts having jurisdiction of the offense."

30. "Historic Colored Liberty Congress," *Guardian*, July 16, 1918, 1; and Ellis, "'Closing Ranks,'" 105 (and on p. 124 he emphasizes Du Bois's following of Spingarn's lead and his quest for the captaincy as driving motivations). Allen, "'Close Ranks,'" 32, emphasizes Du Bois's "two souls, two thoughts, two unreconciled strivings, two warring ideals" as an aspect of the developments of May through July.

31. J. E. Spingarn for M. Churchill to Intelligence Officer, Northeastern Department, Boston, Mass., June 13, 1918, DNA, RG 165, MID 10218-153-6, R 3.

32. Moore to Chief Military Intelligence Branch, June 19, 1918; and Monroe N. Work, ed., *Negro Year Book, 1918–1919* (Tuskegee, Ala.: Negro Year Book Publishing Company, 1919), 74.

33. HH, "The Descent of Dr. Du Bois," *Voice*, July 25, 1918, *HR*, 170–72; Allen, "'Close Ranks,'" 25–29; Kellogg, *NAACP*: 1:271–74; and Ellis, "'Closing Ranks,'" 142.

34. Ellis, "Joel Spingarn's 'Constructive Programme,'" 142.

35. "Address to the Committee on Public Information, 1918," in *A Documentary History of the Negro People in the United States*, ed. Herbert Aptheker, vol. 3: *1910–*

1932 (Secaucus, N.J.: The Citadel Press, 1973), 218–22, which includes the "Address" (3:218–21), "Bill of Particulars" (3:221), and the "List of Conferees" (321–22).

36. "An Extract from the Resolutions Adopted by the Conference of Colored Newspaper Editors Held in Washington Last Week Under the Auspices of the War Department and the Committee on Public Information," *Official Bulletin*, June 29, 1918; Allen, "'Close Ranks,'" 33, 36, 37; and "Minimum Consideration Only Asked by Colored Editors," *Guardian*, July 6, 1918, 3.

37. Talbert, *Negative Intelligence*, 121; and James Weldon Johnson, "What the Negro Is Doing for Himself," *Liberator*, June 1918, 29–31, in [HH,] "Democracy Now or Later? Well-Known Colored Editor, Field Secretary of Major Spingarn's National Association, Urges Negroes to 'Cry Aloud and Spare Not,'" *Voice*, July 11, 1918, 2.

38. HH, "The Descent of Dr. Du Bois," 172. See also HH, "When the Blind Lead," *NW*, c. February 1920, in *HR*, 173–74.

39. HD, July 1, 1918. On the Liberty Congress, see [HH,] "Negroes Asking for Foretaste of Democracy," 1; "How Negroes Feel About Freedom," *Voice*, July 11, 1918, 4; "Historic Colored Liberty Congress"; and "Liberty Congress in Interesting Session," *NYA*, July 6, 1918, 1.

40. "Excerpts from Address at Colored Liberty Congress, June 24–25–26–27, 1918, Washington, D.C.," MID-10218-153-8, 1; HH, "To Our People in Washington, D.C.," *Voice*, July 11, 1918, 1; HD, July 1, 1918.

41. HD, July 1, 1918.

42. HD, July 1, 1918.

43. HD, July 1, 1918. *The Voice* reported that a committee composed of Trotter, Allen, Twine, and Lankford met with Clark regarding the request for a joint session. Then Boies Penrose (Rep., Penn.), in the Senate, and Dyer and Martin P. Madden (Rep., Ill.) in the House, took "hold of the programme of the Negro Congress in the halls of the white Congress." See [HH,] "Negroes Asking for Foretaste of Democracy," 2. See also "Negro Rights Plea Made to Congress: Delegates to Session Here Put Petition in Penrose's Hands," *Washington Post*, June 30, 1918, 8.

44. HD, July 1, 1918; "Historic Colored Liberty Congress"; and Emmett J. Scott, *Scott's Official History of the American Negro in the World War* (n.p.: Emmett J. Scott, 1919), 97–98 (on Ballou's order).

45. HD, July 1, 1918; and "Cause of Colored America Reaches U.S. Congress," *Guardian*, July 6, 1918, 1, 3. In his diary Harrison said that Dyer spoke on Wednesday while the *Guardian* correctly maintained that it was Madden and that Dyer spoke on Thursday.

46. HD, July 1, 1918; and [HH,] "Negroes Asking For Foretaste of Democracy," 4. Harrison used a lowercase "w" in whites and a capital "N" in Negroes in this article.

47. "Excerpts From Address at Colored Liberty Congress," 2.

48. [HH,] "Negroes Asking for Foretaste of Democracy," 4.

49. J. G. C. Corcoran, Report of June 29, 1918, for June 28, 1918, "In re: Harrison: Liberty Alleged Connections with Rich Anarchists," Bureau File, OG 369936,

RG 65, DNA; and HD, July 1, 1918. See also "Attention: 'Workers in War Time and Why they Should Combine'; A Great Lecture to the White and Colored Workers of Washington, D.C. by Hubert Harrison of New York, Editor of the *Voice*, Organizer of the Hotel and Restaurant Workers, Chairman of the Colored Liberty League, . . . Wednesday, June 26, 1918 at 8:30 p.m., Free," Bureau File, OG 311587, RG 65, DNA, OG 311587; and "City Briefs," *Chicago Defender*, June 29, 1918, 9.

50. Corcoran, Report of June 29; J. G. C. Corcoran, Report of July 1, 1918, for June 30, 1918, "In re: Harrison: Liberty Congress," Bureau File, OG 369936, RG 65, DNA.

51. The "Petition" appears in Aptheker, *Documentary History*, 3:215–18. On harassment and discrimination of Black troops, see Jack D. Foner, *Blacks and the Military in American History* (New York: Praeger, 1974), 118–24.

52. [HH,] "Negroes Asking For Foretaste of Democracy," 1, "Joel Spingarn's 'Constructive Programme,'" 142; and Allen, "'Close Ranks,'" 36.

53. W. E. B. Du Bois, "Close Ranks," *Crisis* no. 16 (July 1918): 111.

54. *Crisis* no. 14 (June 1917): 59. On the captaincy, see Ellis, "'Closing Ranks,'" 96, 98; Mark Ellis, "W. E. B. Du Bois and the Formation of Black Opinion in World War I: A Commentary of 'The Damnable Dilemma,'" *JAH* 81 no. 4 (March 1995): 1584–90, esp. 1590, 1587; and Talbert, *Negative Intelligence*, 121.

55. H.H, "The Descent of Dr. Du Bois," 172. Ellis, "'Closing Ranks,'" 122, notes that Elliott M. Rudwick (*W. E. B. Du Bois* [New York: Atheneum, 1969], 203) described "Close Ranks" as a "colossal blunder" and that "Du Bois was scarred by the accusations of treachery from fellow black leaders and he never forgot them." See also Allen, "'Close Ranks,'" 26.

56. Ellis, "'Closing Ranks,'" 108. Ellis, "W. E. B. Du Bois," 1590, maintains that "a day-to-day study of the events leads to the conclusion that 'Close Ranks' was a *quid pro quo*, and that the editorial and the captaincy were firmly linked." Allen, "'Close Ranks,'" 26, states, "Harrison's charges proved to be rather incisive in their overall characterization." He notes that researchers, working with declassified military documents have been able to confirm "the essence of the 'script' which Harrison envisioned behind Du Bois' call to 'Close Ranks.'" David Levering Lewis, *W. E. B. Du Bois: Biography of a Race*, 2 vols. (New York: Henry Holt, 1993), 1:555, states, "Du Bois stuck a deal, through Spingarn, with the War Department" to write "Close Ranks" in exchange for the captaincy in order "to consummate the bargain." He does not think it was done with "cold calculation." William G. Jordan, "'The Damnable Dilemma': African-American Accommodation and Protest During World War I," *Journal of American History* 81, no. 4 (March 1995): 1562–83, considers Du Bois's editorial "an understandable response to a predicament that defied satisfactory solution—the dilemma that Du Bois and other African Americans faced during he nadir of black history in the United States" (1564).

57. Ellis, "'Closing Ranks,'" 108–9.

58. Ellis, "'Closing Ranks,'" 109; and Lewis, *W. E. B. Du Bois*, 1:556.

59. The accuracy of Harrison's explanation is confirmed in Allen, "'Close Ranks,'" 26; and Ellis, "'Closing Ranks,'" 115–17.

60. HH, "The Problems of Leadership," *WAA*, 54. See also Ellis, "'Closing Ranks,'" 115–17.

61. HH, "The Problems of Leadership," 54–55. Mark Ellis, "'Closing Ranks,'" 124, states that Du Bois had a "deliberate purpose" in mind when he wrote the essay. He considers the editorial "a conscious deviation in the trajectory of his wartime writings" that "was specifically included in the July 1918 issue of the *Crisis* to help get him into military intelligence." He adds that "Du Bois's black critics, such as . . . Harrison, were equally astute" and "their charges were well founded."

62. HH, "The Descent of Dr. Du Bois," 171.

63. Lewis, *W.E.B. Du Bois*, 80; and HH, review of *Darkwater*, by W. E. B. Du Bois, *NW*, April 17, 1920, in *HR*, 319–22, esp. 320.

64. HH, "The Descent of Dr. Du Bois," 171–72; and HH, "When the Blind Lead," 174.

65. HH, "The Descent of Dr. Du Bois," 171–72.

66. HH, "The Descent of Dr. Du Bois," 172.

67. HH, "The Descent of Dr. Du Bois," 171.

68. HH, "The Problems of Leadership," 54; [HH], [re "Vesey St. Liberals"], n.d., HP. In *The Voice* of July 11, 1918, Harrison bitingly referred to the NAACP as "Major Spingarn's National Association." See [HH,] "Democracy Now or Later?" 2.

69. HH, "When the Blind Lead," 174; and HH, "The Problems of Leadership," 55.

70. Harrison commented critically on whites who sought to choose Negro leaders in HH to Lothrop Stoddard, August 21, 1920, HP. See also [HH], ["Vesey St."], HP.

71. Woodrow Wilson, "Mob Action," from the Committee on Public Information, Released for Afternoon Papers on Friday, July 26[, 1918], MID 10218-154, DNA.

72. Ellis, "'Closing Ranks,'" 118.

73. W. E. B. Du Bois, *Dusk of Dawn: An Essay Toward an Autobiography of a Race Concept* (1940; New York: Schocken Books, 1971), 257; HH, "The Problems of Leadership," 54; Kellogg, *NAACP*, 1:273–75; Allen, "'Close Ranks,'" 31, 33n. 26; and Ellis, "'Closing Ranks,'" 118 and 119.

74. [HH,] "The Voice Is Coming Out to Stay!" leaflet, c. July 4, 1918, HP; [HH,] "The Resurrection of the Voice," *Voice*, July 11, 1918, 4.

75. *Voice*, July 11, 1918, 1; and Andrea Razaf[in]keriefo, "The Voice," *Voice*, July 11, 1918, 1.

76. [HH,] "To Old Subscribers," *Voice*, August 1, 1918; [HH,] "The Voice Is Coming Out to Stay!"; [HH,] "The Resurrection of the Voice"; [HH,] "To Our People in Washington, D.C."; and Monroe N. Work, *Negro Year Book: An Annual Encyclopedia of the Negro, 1921–1922* (Tuskegee, Ala.: Tuskegee Institute, 1922), 380. Harrison sensed the potential of the South that Marcus Garvey would later develop. See Tony Martin, *Race First: The Ideological and Organizational Struggle of Marcus Garvey and the Universal Negro Improvement Association* (Westport, Conn.: Greenwood

Press, 1976), 16, which explains that within a few years "the southern United States was the most thoroughly UNIA-organized area in the world."

77. Andrea Razaf[in]keriefo, "Hubert H. Harrison," *Crusader* 1 no. 4 (December 1918): 17.

78. "Lament Dream of Dr. Hubert Harrison: Eulogized by Several Who Knew His Life and Work," *Amsterdam News*, December 28, 1927, 1.

79. Harrison speaks of "white capitalist" centers in HH, "The New International," *NW*, May 15, 1920, reprint, "A New International," in HH, *When Africa Awakes: The "Inside Story" of the Stirrings and Strivings of the New Negro in the Western World* (New York: The Porro Press, 1920), 111–13, esp. 112.

Select Bibliography

The major sources of biographical material on Hubert Harrison are in the Hubert H. Harrison Papers, which are at available at the Rare Book and Manuscript Library at Columbia University. The Papers include Harrison's diary, writings, correspondence, scrapbooks, books, and miscellany. A Finding Aid for the Papers is available online at http://www.columbia.edu/cu/libraries/inside/projects/findingaids/scanspdfs/Harrison_Hubert_H.pdf, and it will be accompanied by the forthcoming *Writings of Hubert Harrison*, edited and introduced by this author on the Rare Book and Manuscript Library Web site.

Information on Harrison's genealogical background can be found in the St. Croix Population Database of the St. Croix African Roots Project in St. Croix.

Harrison's two books, *The Negro and Nation* (New York: Cosmo-Advocate, 1917) and *When Africa Awakes: The "Inside Story" of the Stirrings and Strivings of the New Negro in the Western World* (New York: Porro Press, 1920), contain editorials, articles, and reviews. A large selection of Harrison's writings are available in *A Hubert Harrison Reader*, ed. intro., and notes Jeffrey B. Perry (Middletown, Conn.: Wesleyan University Press, 2001). Of the publications Harrison edited, there are scattered issues of *The Voice* (1917–1919), the *New Negro* (1919), and the *Negro World* (1920), and complete sets of the *Embryo of the Voice of the Negro* (1927) and the *Voice of the Negro* (1927).

The best sketches by contemporaries of Harrison are those of J. A. Rogers, "Hubert Harrison: Intellectual Giant and Free-Lance Educator (1883–1927)," in *World's Great Men of Color*, by J. A. Rogers, 2 vols. (New York: J. A. Rogers, 1946–1947), 2:611–19, which is also reprinted as "Hubert Harrison: Intellectual Giant and Free-Lance Educator," in *World's Great Men of Color*, by Joel A. Rogers, ed. John Henrik Clarke, 2 vols. (New York: Collier Books, 1972), 2:432–42; and Richard B. Moore,

"Hubert Henry Harrison (1883–1927)," in *Dictionary of American Negro Biography*, ed. Rayford W. Logan and Michael R. Winston (New York: Norton, 1982), 292–93. Geraldo Guirty, "Crucian Becomes Eloquent Harlem Protester of Injustice," *St. Thomas Daily News*, February 10, 1984; and John G. Jackson, *Hubert Henry Harrison: The Black Socrates* (Austin, Tex.: American Atheist Press, 1987), are portraits by people who knew Harrison in their youth.

An original biographical article on which most later information on Harrison's early years appears to be based is "Dr. Harrison's Rise as Orator Is Like Fiction: Educator, Writer, and Speaker Now Ranks with Best in His Line," *Chicago Defender*, January 19, 1924.

Around the time of Harrison's death, biographical sketches appeared in: Joseph J. Boris, *Who's Who in Colored America: A Biographical Dictionary of Notable Living Persons of Negro Descent in America* (New York: Who's Who in Colored America, 1927), 86–87; "Hubert Harrison Dies: Harlem Scholar Succumbs after 'Minor' Operation: Came to America in 1900 from St. Croix, Virgin Islands, Where He Was Born—Unusual Ability Forced Recognition Here," *Amsterdam News*, December 21, 1927; Oscar J. Benson, "Literary Genius of Hubert Harrison," *New York News*, December 24, 1927; Hodge Kirnon, "Hubert Harrison: An Appreciation," *Negro World*, December 31, 1927; "Garvey Aid and Author Passes Away: Hubert H. Harrison Dies in New York," *Chicago Defender*, December 24, 1927; "Hubert Harrison Dies Suddenly in Bellevue Hospital: Complications Following Operation Brings Death," *New York Age*, December 24, 1927; "Dr. Harrison Dies After Operation," *Pittsburgh Courier*, December 24, 1927; "Lament Dream of Dr. Hubert Harrison: Eulogized by Several Who Knew His Life and Work," *Amsterdam News*, December 28, 1927; "Dr. H. H. Harrison, Noted Colored Lecturer, Dies," *Survey Graphic*, December 20, 1927; "Celebrated Harlem Mass Leader Dies After Operation," *New York News*, December 24, 1927; "The Death of Hubert Harrison," *New York News*, December 31, 1927; "Hubert H. Harrison!" *Pittsburgh Courier*, December 31, 1927; and "Obituary: Hubert H. Harrison," *New York World*, December 18, 1927.

During the Depression two other biographical sketches were prepared: J. A. Rogers, "Hubert Harrison," in Writer's Program (New York, N.Y.) "Negroes of New York" (New York, 1940?); and Louis B. Bryan, "Brief History of the Life and Work of Hubert Harrison," April 20, 1937, in Writer's Program (New York, N.Y.).

A third wave of biographical sketches includes Irwin Marcus, "Hubert Harrison: Negro Advocate," *Negro History Bulletin* 34, no. 1 (1971): 18–19; Ralph L. Crowder, "Street Scholars: Self-Trained Black Historians," *Black Collegian* 9, no. 3 (1979): 8–20, 80; Helen C. Camp, "Hubert Henry Harrison, April 27, 1883–December 17, 1927," in *American Reformers*, ed. Alden Whitman (Bronx: H. H. Wilson, 1985), 406–7; and three very similar pieces by Wilfred David Samuels, all titled "Hubert H. Harrison and the 'New Negro Manhood Movement.'" These appear in Wilfred D. Samuels, "Five Afro-Caribbean Voices in American Culture, 1917–1929: Hubert H. Harrison, Wilfred A. Domingo, Richard B. Moore, Cyril V. Briggs, and Claude McKay" (Ph. D.

diss., University of Iowa, 1977), 50–77; Wilfred D. Samuels, *Five Afro-Caribbean Voices in American Culture* (Boulder: Belmont Books, 1977), 27–41; and *Afro-Americans in New York Life and History* 5, no. 1 (January 1981): 29–41. A 1983 footnote sketch by Robert A. Hill is provided on "Hubert Henry Harrison," in *The Marcus Garvey and Universal Negro Improvement Association Papers*, ed. Robert A. Hill (Berkeley: University of California Press, 1983) 1:210–11.

Very useful for the socialist period is the chapter "Local New York, the Colored Socialist Club, Hubert H. Harrison, and W. E. B. Du Bois," in Philip S. Foner, *American Socialism and Black Americans: From the Age of Jackson to World War II* (Westport, Conn.: Greenwood Press, 1977), 202–19.

The first lengthy treatment of Harrison was Jeffrey B. Perry, "Hubert Henry Harrison, 'The Father of Harlem Radicalism': The Early Years—1883 Through the Founding of the Liberty League and *The Voice* in 1917" (Ph. D. diss., Columbia University, 1986), which includes an extensive bibliography (711–809). This was followed by a number of shorter pieces by Jeffrey B. Perry, including: "Harrison, Hubert Henry," *Encyclopedia of African American History and Culture*, ed. Jack Salzman, David Lionel Smith, and Cornel West (New York: Macmillan, 1995), 1230–31; "Harrison, Hubert Henry," in *American National Biography*, ed. John A. Garraty and Mark C. Carnes, 24 vols. (New York, Oxford University Press, 1999) 10:212–14; "An Introduction to Hubert Harrison, 'The Father of Harlem Radicalism,'" *Souls* 2, no. 1 (Winter 2000): 38–54; "Hubert Harrison: Race Consciousness and Socialism," *Socialism and Democracy* 17, no. 2 (Summer–Fall, 2003): 103–30; "Harrison, Hubert Henry," in *Encyclopedia of the Harlem Renaissance*, ed. Cary D. Wintz and Paul Finkelman, 2 vols. (New York: Routledge, 2004) 1:538–40; "Hubert Henry Harrison," in *African American Lives*, ed. Henry Louis Gates Jr. and Evelyn Brooks Higginbotham (New York: Oxford University Press, 2004), 379–80; and "Harrison, Hubert Henry," in *Encyclopedia of the Great Black Migration*, ed. Steven Reich, 3 vols. (Westport, Conn.: Greenwood Press, 2006) 1:378–79.

Shorter pieces, subsequent to the lengthy treatment, include Portia James, "Hubert H. Harrison and the New Negro Movement," *Western Journal of Black Studies* 13, no. 2 (1989): 82–91; Barbara Bair, "Hubert H. Harrison (1883–1927)," in *Encyclopedia of the American Left*, ed. Mari Jo Buhle, Paul Buhle, and Dan Georgakas, (Urbana: University of Illinois Press, 1990), 292; Patrick Innis, "Hubert Henry Harrison: Great African American Freethinker," in *Secular Subjects* (St. Louis: Rationalist Society of St. Louis, 1992); Greg Robinson, "Hubert Henry Harrison," in *Encyclopedia of New York*, ed. Kenneth T. Jackson (New Haven, Conn.: Yale University Press, 1995), 530; the chapter "Hubert Henry Harrison, New Negro Militancy, and the Limits of Racialized Leadership, 1914–1954," in *Uplifting the Race: Black Leadership, Politics, and Culture in the Twentieth Century*, by Kevin K. Gaines (Chapel Hill: University of North Carolina Press, 1996), 234–60, 286–88; and the chapter "Dimensions and Main Currents of Caribbean Radicalism in America: Hubert Harrison, the African Blood Brotherhood, and the UNIA," in *Holding Aloft the Banner of Ethiopia: Carib-*

bean Radicalism in Early Twentieth-Century America, by Winston James (New York: Verso, 1998), 122–84. James has also written two pieces related to Harrison's experience with the Socialist Party: Winston James, "Being Red and Black in Jim Crow America: Notes on the Ideology and Travails of Afro-America's Socialist Pioneers, 1877–1930," *Souls* 1, no. 4 (Fall 1999): 45–63; and Winston James, "Being Red and Black in Jim Crow America: On the Ideology and Travails of Afro-America's Socialist Pioneers, 1877–1930," in *Time Longer than Rope: A Century of African American Activism*, ed. Charles Payne and Adam Green (New York: New York University Press, 2003), 336–99.

This volume on Harrison's life will be followed by the forthcoming *Hubert Harrison: Race Consciousness and the Struggle for Socialism, 1918–1927*.

Index

"Black Man's Burden, The: A Reply to Rud-
yard Kipling" (HH, poem), 261–262, 276,
484–485n98
"Black Man's Champion" (Roosevelt), 101
Black Man's Mind, 479n26
Black migration: as form of direct action, 291;
and East St. Louis, 297; the Great, 12
"Black Moses" (Jackson), 45
Black power, 13
"Black Prince" (boxer), 49
Black progress, 67, 148
Black race: and Colored, 275; consciousness of,
176, 278, 280, 364, 394; HH plea on behalf of,
231–232; intellect of, 347; Lincoln opposes
equality for, 102; and tricolor flag, 489n30
Black Radical Congress, 16
Black Reconstruction in America (Du Bois),
179–180
Black Republicans: Clubs, 54; Socialists run
against in 1918, 368; *Voice* reports on, 324.
See also Anderson, Charles W.; Republican
Party; Tuskegee Machine; Washington,
Booker T.
Black Socialists: Father Belford and, 460–
461n30; Williana Burroughs, 94; Grace P.
Campbell, 458n11; and Harlem branch of,
458n11; and HH's emphasis on African liberation, 4; HH leader among, 6–7, 204, 266;
HH offers first major analysis by, 172; HH's
race conscious approach and, 311; Peter
Humphreys, 155; Richard B. Moore, 272; oppose Black Republican candidates in 1918,
368; Thomas Potter, 166; predecessors, 154–
155, 215; Randolph and Owen, 119, 266, 268,
293, 330, 344; George W. Slater Jr., 154–155;
Thomas Sweeney, 153; George Washington
Woodbey, 154–155
Black soldiers: and Brownsville, 101; as a menace where lynchings occur, 323; and Houston, 322, 358; role in winning Civil War, 100;
in World War I, 370, 382
Black Star Line, 295, 320, 329, 336–338, 501n1
Black voters: as balance of power, 153, 340;
breaking from Republicans, 153; Citizen's
Committee report to, 312; demands of, 312,

325; and election of 1917, 340–342, 347, 359–
360; increased interest in Socialism, 155;
new mood among, 262; sold like sheep, 319
Black workers: AFL does little to organize, 369,
513n9; capitalists pit, against white workers,
144, 162, 180, 193; condition of, 54; demands
are working class demands, 180; and discrimination in defense industries, 408n33;
and Frederick Douglass at 1872 convention,
183; excluded from unions, 202, 309; HH
attempts to organize, 368–369, 380, 383; HH
calls upon to form own unions, 279, 308–309;
HH supports over racist unions, 103; hostility to organized labor, 279, 308; hurt by race
prejudice, 162; IWW seeks to organize, 174,
193; as "more essentially proletarian," 7,
147, 180–181; non-unionization of, 54–55;
in Post Office, 83, 86; Randolph says we
alienated, 364; removed from jobs, 177; in
St. Croix, 25–26, 28, 36, 41, 45; seniority
rights opposed, 129; Socialist Party has few,
146, 151; Socialists view of, as a hindrance,
180; as test of Socialism's sincerity, 181; as
"strikebreakers," 180, 202, 297; and support
of demands of labor, 92, 279; as "the ultimate
exploited," 180; wartime migration of, 369;
"white" labor opposition to, 279, 297, 298,
309. *See also* Pullman porters
Black writers, promotion by HH, 6
Blaine, James G., 84, 468–469n46
Blake, Eubie, 6, 353
bleaching, of skin, 255, 279
block clubs, 257
blocks, most densely populated, 2, 54, 87–88, 394
blood: alleged "superiority" in mixed "Negro,"
126, 275–276, 326; HH and "undiluted Negro
blood," 43, 472; Lamarckianism and, 444n21,
445n24
Blyden, Edward Wilmot, 50, 249, 372, 426–
427n81, 444n22
Board of Education, New York City: awards
HH prize, 56; William L. Bulkley and, 74;
Charles Burroughs and, 351; Williana Jones
Burroughs and, 94, 100; discrimination by,
50, 55, 89, 100; finds "genius," in HH, 56;

Board of Education, NYC (*continued*)
  Abraham Flexner and Gary Plan, 351–352;
  HH applies for lectureship, 82, 104; HH lec-
  tures for, 6, 11, 15, 97, 472n30; lecture series
  at the "Y," 96–97; Dr. Thorne praises HH, 57;
  "Trends of the Times" lectures, 11; unable
  to locate HH school records, 429n12
Boas, Franz, 120
Boddie, Edward O., 315, 331
Bohemian Federation, 145
Bohn, Frank, 202
Bolden, Mr., of Liberty League Quartet, 315
Bolden, William, 307
Bolsheviks, 189, 232, 368, 451n23, 473n36,
  487–488n16
bombings: AFL for the Steel Trust, 210; *Los An-
  gles Times* building, 210; St. Patrick's, 477n4
Booker, Henry Arthur, 347
Book of American Negro Poetry, The (Johnson),
  489–490n33
book selling, of Richard B. Moore, 273; of oth-
  ers, 157
Borinquen, 23
Boston: William Stanley Braithwaite of, 79; color
  line in, 290; HH attends meeting in, 285–286,
  299; HH elected Liberty Congress Chair in,
  286; D. S. Klugh of, 373; Fred W. Moore of,
  374; Matthew A. N. Shaw of, 379, 382; Alex-
  ander Wayman Thomas from, 89; William
  Monroe Trotter of, 89, 123, 296
Boston Chronicle, 11, 57, 487–488n16
Boston Guardian, 123, 305–306, 378
"Boston Riot," 123
Botto house, 202–203
Boudin, Louis B., 146, 202
Bough, Auguste, 48
Boulin, Herbert Simeon (agent P-138), 502n8,
  505n23
Bowery, 264
boycotts, 200, 458–459n14
Boyd, Frederick Sumner, 201, 204, 206, 209–
  214, 216
Boyer, William W., 31, 370, 410–411n2,
  426–427n81
Braithwaite, Isaac Newton, 272

Braithwaite, William Stanley, 79
Branch 3, Socialist Party, Local N.Y., 209, 217
Branch 5, Socialist Party, Local N.Y.: and charges against Boyd, 201; and charges against
  HH, 205; composition of, 156–157, 167;
  denied right to schedule speakers, 190; and
  Harlem School of Social Science, 208; head-
  quarters of, 229; HH delegate of, 156, 201;
  HH lectures for, 207; HH listed as member
  of, not of CSC, 176; HH proposed as speaker
  from, 190; and "Negro" work, 151–152, 154;
  "Nils Uhl" a member of, 149; organizer arrested with HH, 175; Margaret Sanger in,
  222; special literature in, 154, 172; supports
  referendum against Haywood, 201
Brathwaite, James, 37
Brawley, Benjamin, 263
Braxton, William Ernest, 87
Bray, Paul Henry, 92
Bridges, William, 311, 360
"Bridging the Gulf of Color" (HH), 472n24,
  480n34
Briggs, Cyril V.: and African Blood Brother-
  hood, 365; and *Colored American Review*,
  260–261; and *Crusader*, 300; on W. A. Domin-
  go, 504n19; freethought influence on, 115;
  funding of, 330, 502–503n8; HH influence
  on, 314–315; and Liberty League, 315, 368;
  as "New Negro," 2, 5, 8, 362
Bright, Leonard, 148
Bright, Mr., of Lafayette Hall, 319
"Brigit" (Ned Harrison's mother), 40, 422n55
"Britain in India" (HH), 487–488n16
Bronx, 146, 224, 334, 371; Frances Marion
  born in, 110; Lincoln Hospital of, 108; St.
  David's Protestant Episcopal Church of, 110,
  421n49; Woodlawn Cemetery of, xxiv, 12
Brooklyn, N.Y: Father Belford of, 184–186, 460–
  461n30; Black population of, 304; Brownsville Radical Forum of, 243, 296; William B.
  Derrick of, 89; Fleet Street Church, 296; HH
  speaks in, 296; John Hylan of, 339; Beatrice
  Ione-Wade, 331; of; Local Kings County,
  189; George Frazier Miller of, 167–168,
  316, 362; *Monatlisches Zeitung Turn-Verein*

Christianity (*continued*)
be a Christian nation, 136–137; Booker T.
Washington and, 123, 126. *See also* Catholic
Church

Christiansted, 24, 32–36, 38–39, 41, 46–49

Christmas, 198, 295

Chronicles, 135

Chronological History of the Negro in America
(Bergman), 414–415n17

Churchill, Marlborough, 374, 378, 385–387,
391–392

Cicero, 56

Cincinnati, 155

circulation figures: *Appeal to Reason*, 143; *Baltimore Afro-American*, 304; *Chicago Defender*,
304; *Chicago Whip*, 304; *International Socialist Review*, 176, 458n12; *Issue*, 464n66; *Messenger*, 304, 502n8; St. Benedict's *Messenger*,
70; *Negro World*, 336; *New York Age*, 304,
329; *New York Call*, 149; *New York News*,
329; other Black papers, 305–306, 328; *Pittsburgh Courier*, 304; readership of five times,
304; and the Post Office, 504–505n20; *Voice*,
9, 304–306

Citizen Sun, 207

Citizen's Union, 65

civic consciousness, and organic relationship to
community, 195

civilization: Father Belford sees threat to Christian, 185; church plays role in downfall of,
137; as code word for armed might, 357;
colored peoples and "white," 445n24; and
democracy, 357; Du Bois's "Talented Tenth"
and higher, 238; historical development of,
142, 276; race and, 65–66

Civil Rights Act (1964), 408n33

civil service, 50, 101, 348; discrimination, 269;
firings, 366; HH instructor in, 194, 222

Civil War, 67, 101, 254; post–, 115, 122, 190, 214;
pre–, 233

civil war, 473

Clansman, The (Dixon), 161

Clarion, 289, 314–315; appearance of, 318–320;
HH disavows, 331; on HH as "the Race's
most prominent agitator," 295; and move-

ment toward Garvey; 332; staff of, 331–332;
united with Liberty League and UNIA, 295;
women and, 332

Clark, James B. (Champ), 381–382, 516n43

Clark, John T., 246, 248–250, 478n12

Clarke, Ethel Oughton, UNIA officer, 332

Clarke, John Henrik, 437–438n45

class consciousness: among African Americans,
461–462n36; African Blood Brotherhood
and, 260; classical consensus on, 188,
462n37; defined, 405n16; HH challenges
idea that African Americans are hindrance
to, 160; HH's development of, 22, 63, 83, 87;
HH encourages development of, 3–4, 193–
194; HH's influence of race and, 314, 320; of
HH in relation to Garvey, 5; HH "most class
conscious of the race radicals, and most race
conscious of the class radicals," 17, 394; lack
of, in U.S. 187–188; vs. sex consciousness,
197; leading Socialists maintain that race
consciousness supersedes, 187; *Messenger*
as, 304; in postal union, 86; race consciousness compatible with, 278, 461–462n36; relation between white supremacy and, 187–188,
417n29, 462n37; *Voice*'s race and, 328

class exploitation, and racial oppression, 21, 122,
405n16

"class first": HH responds with "Race First,"
277–278, 445n25; HH urges race consciousness in response to, 278; ignores special
oppression of Black people, 445n25; and
Randolph and Owen, 266, 268, 363; white
socialists and, 187, 277, 445n25

class interest, 31, 141, 279

class radicalism, 311, 365

class solidarity, 26, 367, 369

class struggle: Black workers as hindrance to,
180; and the color line, 30–31, 149; Debs
says, is "colorless," 143; and growth of
Socialist Party, 146; HH on, 207, 227; HH
on Black workers as key to, 180; HH on
"Negro" in the, 177, 180; HH on struggle
against white supremacy key to, 280; HH,
readings on, 208; in St. Croix, 24–25; strategy, 122; theory of, 147–148

of religion is the foundation of all criticism"
(Marx), 63; of Democrats, 269; of Du Bois,
9–10, 385–390, 392, 515n30, 517nn55–56,
517n59, 518n61; Du Bois never forgot HH's,
408n34; of educational efforts, 57; elected
at St. Mark's, 76; first published theater
criticism, 263–266; four types of criticism
explained, 80–81; freewheeling atmosphere
at the "Y," 97; and function of criticism,
273–274; of Marcus Garvey, 10–11; and
higher criticism, 104, 135; illustrates Socialist philosophy, 192; insightful, 138; "inveterate," 13, 399; and "Leaves Torn from the
Diary of a . . ." (HH), 264–265; and literature
as "criticism of life" (Arnold), 251; of the
NAACP, 127; in *New York Times*, 79–81;
O'Neill praises, 2; perceptive, 239; popular,
7; public, 138; of Republicans, 102, 269; of
rigid intellectual approaches, 195–197; of
Socialist Party, 166, 214; on a subservient
critic, 265–266; of the "Talented Tenth,"
125–126; of theater, 250–255, 263–266; of
theology, 1, 3–4, 104, 135–138, 225, 233–234;
trailblazing, 6; of Booker T. Washington, 10,
129–131, 134, 245, 248
HH, death of, 12; funeral, 14; gravesite, xxiv, 403
HH, and debates: on Asian immigration among
Socialists, 186–187, 216; with Adolph Benvy,
209; among Black people on education, 238;
over "Close Ranks," 385–386; on evolutionary vs. revolutionary socialism, 142, 180–182;
on the Haywood-Hillquit debate, 175; over
the IWW, 198; with Chandler Owen, 362–363;
on the protective tariff, 74–75; on sabotage
among Socialists, 188–189, 198–200, 209–
210, 216; training for, in lyceums, 72, 76, 113,
138, 227, 323; training for, with the Socialist
Party, 191; training for, at the White Rose
Home, 97, 113, 138; training for, at the "Y,"
76, 97, 113, 138; with Frank Urban, 189, 205,
215–218; on voting rights, 75
HH, and democracy: on abuse and potential of,
4; as America's great experiment, vii; as bait
for clever statesman, vii, 258; on betrayal of,
161; on cant of, vii, 4, 258, 359, 370; on colo-

nial subjects and, 28; "Colored," 182–183;
and color line, 169, 357; as convenient camouflage, vii, 258–259, 395; demands for, 9,
285–289, 363; denial of, and race consciousness, 259; double standard of, 130; and
"downright lying," vii, 4, 357; as "dust in the
eyes of white voters," vii, 4, 258, 395; face
value is equality, 258; failure causes "great
unrest," 258; falsity of, 160; "implies a revolution," vii, 4, 158, 161, 395; international crusade for, 321; and Liberty League, 285–292,
312; majority demanded, 258–259; "Make
the South 'Safe for,'" 282, 284–285, 296;
make world safe for, 281–282, 285–289, 296,
300, 344, 373; masks imperialist aims, vii,
258, 357, 395; "Negro," and, 382; "Negro"
left out of, 258; "Negro" as "touchstone" of,
vii, 4, 150–151, 160, 395; not all it could be,
415n18; not real aim of war, 357; on "one democracy," vii; only for whites, 231, 348, 370;
Paine and, 60, 135; possible, vii; pretends
Wilson meant his words about, 259–60, 291;
and race-conscious activity, 365; radical implications of, 4, 161, 213; a right, 129; in
Russia, 307; a sham, 130, 357; slogans of,
258, 357; and social change, vii, 3–4, 17, 158,
161, 395; and social equality, 163; and Socialist Party, 190, 213, 359; speciousness of, 160;
"time to make a bold bid for," 290; "touchstone in the Negro problem," 150; and undemocratic practices, 65; and the Uneeda
biscuit analogy, 259; war for, will come
home, 279; wartime use of, vii, 258, 289, 357,
395; for whites is "impudence" for people of
color, 258; Wilson's essence of, is a voice in
government, 291
HH, diary, 22; codes in, 107, 109, 483n84;
reasons for, 59;
HH, and direct action, proponent of, 26, 184,
198–200, 291, 299, 311
HH, and "Dr.," alleged, 57, 429n13
HH, and W. E. B. Du Bois. *See* Du Bois, W. E. B.
HH, as editor: of *Embryo of the Voice of the
Negro*, 521; of *The Masses*, 152; of *Negro
World*, 5, 293, 329, 335; of *New Rochelle Fair*

115; importation of "Negro," 307; inaccessibility of records, 411n1; labor-caste schools, 179; labor party, 186; lynching of a laborer, 63; organized, puts white race first, 7, 187; and Palace Casino meeting, 305; power, 184, 186–187; race consciousness as response to "white," 395; "race riots" and white, 297–298; and racism, 162–163; relations in St. Croix, 25–26, 28–30, 32–34, 423n66, 423–424n67; slavery and, 159; Socialist Party and, 142–145, 209, 278; special oppression of, 445n25; struggle in Paterson, 202–205; struggles in St. Croix, 25–27, 45; "unscrupulous labor leaders," 312–313; and war, 369; "white," 129, 277–279, 298, 307, 395; white race and social control of, 31–32; and white supremacy, 462n37; white supremacy in movement of, 8, 277. *See also* American Federation of Labor; Black workers; Gompers, Samuel; HH, on labor

Labor Act of 1849, 25

"Labor, Social, and Reform Party (Manhood Movement)" (St. Croix), 476–477n2

Lafargue, Paul, 208, 467n27

Lafayette Hall: Garvey talks at, 319–320, 503n13; HH talks at, 271, 296, 318, 350, 352, 484–485n98, 503n13

Lafayette Players, 264, 276

Lafayette Stock Company, 251, 264–266, 296–297

Lafayette Theater, 265–266, 310; strike, 309

Lamarck, Jean Baptiste Pierre Antoine de Monet de, 119–120

Lamarckianism, 119–121, 444n21; active approach suggested by, 120; as central to understanding of race, 120; critique of, 120; HH's opposition to immutability of races, 444–445nn22–23; HH's support for, in some cases, 122, 444nn21–22; HH on "we Lamarckians," 444n22; on neo Lamarckianism, 122; racist potential in, 445n24; sociohistorical, behavioral, and biological, 443n17, 444–445nn23–24; widespread belief, 120

Langston, Ralph E., 182

Lankford, J. A. (referred to as Sandiford by HH), 381, 516n43

La Reine, Estate, 36

Larkin, James, 487–488n16

Lenora, Larsen, 110, 439n69

Larsen, Nella, 439n69

Latimer, Lewis H., 74

Latin: for "Holy Cross," 23; HH instructs in, 194; HH skill in, 56–57, 107; HH's teacher, 429n12; Nils, for "not," 451n23

La Touche, Mrs., 109–110

laughter, HH's audience convulses with, 192

"L.A.W." (letter writer), 129–130

Lawaetz, Eric J., 22–23, 426n80

Lawaetz, Eva, 425n75

Lawaetz, Herman, 49

"law of social pressure," 234

Lawrence, Mass., strike, 201, 210, 406n38

Lawton, Marie C., 313

Lay of the Last Minstrel (Scott), 156

Lea, Henry Charles., 81, 98

leaders, Black: accuse Du Bois of treachery, 517n55; Blacks should chose, 129; break from, 182–183; as chief buffering agent, 324; chosen by whites, 123; conservative, Urban League, 247; conservatism of, 232–234; and criticism, 323; demands of, 341; HH among, 1, 410n52; HH concerned about, 122; HH criticizes notion that whites should choose, 129; HH's dissatisfaction with Miller and other, 263; of HH's youth, 12; influenced by freethought or atheism, 115; and light skin, 479n26; militant wartime, 373; needs of, 324; opportunity for independent, 340; and patriotism, 232; and police brutality, 310; Republicans a harmful influence on, 102; Republican Party and, 102, 182–183; Republicans subsidized, 102; shortcomings of, 263; should be chosen by the Black masses, 129; Spingarn and Liberty Congress's, 377; and unions, 308; war position as difference between old and new, 232; B. T. Washington most powerful, 6, 127; white appointed, 324. *See also* Anderson, Charles W.; Du Bois, W. E. B.;

Race Congress, 286, 350; First National, 390
race consciousness: and activism, 243–399; and
advertising democracy, 277; and Blacks in
Socialist Party, 363–364; and "capitalist imperialism," 279; in Caribbean, 32; and class
consciousness, 278–280, 461–462n36; and
color line and, 30; and the Deep South, 10; a
defensive measure, 11, 278–279, 395; defini-
tion of, 11, 278, 405n16; and democracy, 10;
development of, and "race first," 277–280;
and draft for a paper, 266–267; and East
St. Louis, 313; and electoral politics, 360;
Garvey draws from HH, 9, 322, 337–338,
365, 503n14; and Harlem, 314; HH's class
consciousness and, 4, 9, 13, 222, 244; HH's
in relation to contemporaries, 4–5, 17, 394;
HH as leading proponent of, 17, 176, 282,
314, 365, 394; and HH's oratory, 295; and
HH's response to racism is innate, 187;
and HH's talks on the war, 258–260; and
HH's theater reviews, 265; influence on
others, 314–317; and International Colored
Unity League, 11; and international consciousness, 486n110; and labor organizing,
278–279; and Liberty Congress, 282, 375;
and Liberty League, 282, 314, 317; and
lynching, 313; and Locke's "New Negro,"
407n28; and mass emphasis, 1, 12, 389, 394;
as more class conscious than race first,
278; need for, 4, 187; *Negro and the Nation*
and, 320–322; *Negro World* and, 10; and
new leaders, 317; "New Negro Movement"
and, 8, 243; not "white hate," 280; outside
of the Socialist Party, 176; as protective
reaction, 187, 278; and provincialism, 280;
and race first, 277–278; radicalism, 311; Raz
and, 352; in response to white supremacy,
32–33, 187, 277, 279–280; and segregated
camps, 357; and Socialists, 176, 187, 364;
socially derived, 100; and strategy for radical change, 277–280, 395; and Temple of
Truth lectures, 243; in *Voice*, 304, 306, 323,
326–328, 392; on war quickening development of, 258–259, 277, 320, 372; and "white
first" attitude, 277, 279

"race first": activity, 292, 312, 318, 350; and attitude of white men, 348; and Black leaders,
325; in business, 249; challenges "America
First," 357; as defensive measure, 277;
and "The Drift in Politics" (HH), 312; "in
everything," 292; and examples of Irish and
Jews, 312; HH and, 7–9, 187, 277, 325–326,
328, 367; HH as coiner of, 336, 357; and HH
leaving the Socialist Party, 509–510n84;
and HH's newspaper plan, 268–269, 271;
HH responds with, 8, 187, 277, 348, 356; in
HH's talks, 262; implications of, 277–280,
445n25; and *Negro World*, 336; and *New
York News*, 326; organized labor putting
white race first, 7, 187–188, 277–278, 298;
Chandler Owen on, 363; and "patronize
your own," 249; political demands, 312;
principle, 302; propagandistic doctrine, 277;
and race consciousness, 277–280; replaced
by call for race consciousness, 278; replaces
"class first," 268; response to "class first"
of Socialists, 277–278; response to racism
of Socialists, 7, 187–188, 197, 277–278, 298;
response to Woodrow Wilson's "America
First," 277–278, 357; *Voice* and, 9, 302, 328;
and the war, 348, 356, 371; and women's
suffrage, 350
race hatred: capitalists foster among workers,
144; McKay on, 32; mob violence and, 323;
newspapers and, 131; *New York Times* editorial on, 89; against whites, 125, 280, 356. *See
also* race prejudice; white supremacy
race history class, 95
race prejudice: in America, 33, 150; Christianity
and, 255, 480n39; created and fostered by
capitalists, 122, 193, 159; distinct from color
prejudice, 253–254; divides workers, 193–
194; HH articles on, 161–165; HH challenges
innate theory, 69, 122; HH comments on
Jean Finot, 443–444n19, 468–469n46; IWW
opposed, 215; James F. Morton on, 118;
newspapers' role in, 163; not innate, 122,
162–163; Mary White Ovington on, 214; socialist duty to oppose, 7, 143; Socialist Party
views on, 144, 187; South as source, 150;

segregation (*continued*)
and, 9, 286–289; George Frazier Miller and, 167; NAACP and, 357; need for legislation on, 161; *New York Evening Post* on, 358; in New York schools, 50, 90; Niagara Movement and, 123; Kate Richards O'Hare and, 183, 460n25; in politics, 54; in the Republican Party, 54; "results in the vitiation of democratic faith" (HH), 161; Theodore Roosevelt works to outlaw in N.Y., 50; in schools, 50; in social activities, 53; and the Socialist Party, 7, 144, 149, 171; in the South, 393; T. McCants Stewart and, 90; in training camps, 281, 286, 355–358, 376; in travel, 269; in the United Colored Democracy, 54; in the U.S., 8, 32, 42, 366; Oswald Garrison Villard and, 358; Julius A. Wayland and, 143; Woodrow Wilson and, 269, 358

Seifert, Charles Christopher: bibliophile, 453n47; idea for Black Star Line, 337–338; with Liberty League, 316; movement toward Garvey, 317–319, 335, 338; UNIA officer, 332, 334

Sekou, Malik, 25

Sekyi, Kobyna, 488–489n33

Select Bibliography of the Negro American, A (Du Bois), 100

selected index, 347

Selective Service Exemption Board, 370

self-defense: calls for armed, 9, 266, 268, 289–291, 298–299, 357; HH and *Age* on, 305–306, 310; HH and *Amsterdam News* on, 306–307, 310; HH calls for, 266, 268; touchstone of militancy, 299, 491n46

self-determination, 258, 266

self-reliance, 4, 11, 256

Selkridge, Bishop T. Frederick, 319, 332

Seme, Pixley Ka Isaka, 73

Senegal, 290

seniority rights, for Black workers, 129, 177

sensationalized treatment of Black people, 63, 149–150

Senussi movement, 290

separate appeals, 143, 145

separate organization: by creed, 226; in NAACP, 456n89; by sex, 44; in Socialist Party, 145, 167–172, 176; in U.S. army, 281, 322–323, 356

serfs, political, 177, 179, 287

Serra, Miss, 84

Serra y Montalvo, Rafael, 84, 434n5

"Sex and Race" (HH), 494–495n84

"Sex, Sinners, and Society" (HH), 227, 243

"Sexual Appeal of Spiritualism and Some Other Religions, The" (HH), 276

sexual relations: class basis of, 196; double standard and, 196, 221; free love and, 116, 222, 236, 276; and gay dance, 107; and HH's erotica collection, 276; and HH's sexual activities, 352–354; HH speaks on, 108, 222; and men leaving home, 276; and monogamy, 276; and origin of sex ideals, 276; and sexual freedom, 237; and sexual license, 196; spiritualism and unmarried women, 276; white doctors and Black women, 108

sexual suggestiveness of plays, 310, 318

Shakespeare, William, 90, 156, 320, 433n77, 450–451n16

Shaler, Nathaniel Southgate, 69

"Shall the Negro Become the Dominating Race?" (HH), 273

Shanghai, 48, 289

Shannon, David A., 146, 462n40

Shaw, George Bernard, 16, 228, 263, 275, 410n49

Shaw, Letitia (foster sister of HH), 422n58

Shaw, Matthew A. N., 379, 382

Shaw University, 263

S.H.B. (letter writer), 63–64

Shedd, Kendrick P., 153, 192

Sheik-ul-Islam, 372

Shepard, Edward M., 65

Shields, W. M., 379

Shop-Talks on Economics (Marcy), 208

Sierra Leone, 24, 29, 48, 285

Silent Protest Parade, 312, 487n9, 495n89

Simmons, Charles Willis, on Garvey, 294, 489–490n33

Simmons, J. Domminick, 319, 333, 335, 504–505n20

London, 126; and Fred R. Moore, 255, 306; "most powerful Black man," 123; and Robert R. Moton, 377; NAACP and, 125, 357; national leadership of, 5; and National Negro Business League, 247; and National Negro Committee, 126–127; and *New York Age*, 89, 245; and Niagara movement, 123, 357; philosophy, 123, 161, 177, 182, 184; prominence of, 67–68, 97; and Theodore Roosevelt, 123; and John M. Royall, 247; and Emmett Scott, 134, 329, 392; strategy of, 271; and William Monroe Trotter, 123, 379; and Tuskegee machine, 123, 126, 130–134, 149, 246; and Urban League, 247–248. *See also* Anderson, Charles W.; Scott, Emmett J.

Washington, D.C., 275, 373, 381, 392. *See also* Editors' Conference; Liberty Congress

Washington, E. T. (HH pseudonym), 131

Washington, Jesse, 323, 500n118

Watertown, N.Y., 191

"Watergut," Christiansted, 38

Watkins, Lucian B., 6

Wayland, Julius A., 143

Weale, B. L. Putnam (Bertram Lenox Simpson pseudonym), 233, 450n29, 474n40

Weber, George, 208

Weekly Issue, 203, 464n66

Weekly People, 163

Weekly Standard (Yonkers), 92. See also *Yonkers Standard*

Weeks, W. Wesley, 87

Weismann, August, 120

Weiss, Nancy, J., 481n46

Wells, Charles E., 208

Wells, Herbert George, 25, 156, 163

Wells-Barnett, Ida B., 124

West Africa, 29, 238, 372, 488–489n23

West Africa Before Europe (Blyden), 372

West African National Congress, 290

Western Federation of Miners, 173, 184, 454n51

West Indian Abroad, 90

West Indians: cooperation with African Americans, 9; employment opportunities, 54–55; families, 46; friends, 109–110; in New York, 54–56; prejudice against, 346; presence and color prejudice, 255; tensions with African Americans, 70. *See also* Caribbean peoples

West Indies, 69, 275

Westinghouse, George, 193

Whaley, Allen W.: admires HH, 361; HH describes as faker, 75; and Liberty Congress, 373, 379, 382; speaks with HH, 314, 345, 350

"What I Live For" (Banks), 256, 480–481n45, 492n47

"What Is Conscience Worth?" 362

What Is Man? (Twain), 372

"What It Stands For: Declaration of Principles" (HH), 407n31

"What Shall the Attitude of the Socialist Party Be Toward the Economic Organization of the Workers?" (debate), 175

Wheatley, Phillis, 95

Wheaton, J. Frank, 349

When Africa Awakes (HH), 10, 293, 321, 405n17, 519n79

"When the Negro Wakes: A Lecture of 'The Manhood Movement'" (HH), 272–273, 406n27

"Where Did Man Come From?" (HH), 272

Whig, as term, 326

White, Bouck, 224, 460–461n30

White, Charles Mowbry, 489n30

White, George, 63–64

white, HH as, 424–425n73

white capitalist centers, 519n79

"white capitalists," 271

"White First": of organized labor, 277; of Socialist Party, 277

"White Man's Burden, The" (Kipling): color line and racial superiority, 458n13; HH on, 177 178, 179, 261, 458n13, 484–485n98

"white men's niggers," 380

whiteness, demystification of, 32

Whiten-Up ads, 255, 303, 305–306

white patrons, 12, 330, 502–503n8

white people: attempt to control Black activity, 377; Black lecturers and, 227; and class consciousness, 417n29; hated by intelligent "Negroes," 356; labor and East St. Louis, 297–299; and labor organizations, 297–298,

white people (*continued*)
307; racial policy of, 31–32; and science of inequality, 443–444n19; walls of racial self-protection, 280

"White People Versus Negroes: Being the Story of a Great Book" (HH), 479n26

white primary, 177

white race, 31, 230–231, 416n25, 443n18

white race first: and class after, 277; of labor, 298; HH challenges, 298; race consciousness a reaction to, 187; among socialists, 197–198, 278, 445n25

White Rose Home: background, 93–96; HH and Boys Club, 96; HH lectures at, 75, 96–97; HH literary club, 96, 98; HH's race history class, 96, 98; HH Reconstruction class, 96, 100, 113; HH seeks to get "in full-touch with the *life* of my people," 99, 113; HH's work at, 93–99, 103, 113; Frances Reynolds Keyser of, 73, 95–96, 104, 106; library of, 95; Victoria Earle Matthews of, 94–96

"white ruling class," 100

"white" support, 256

white superiority: alleged, of mulatto, 326; vs. class consciousness, 417n29; enacted it into law, 179; flawed, 230; HH talk on von Treitsche, 243; material-based, 230; taught in St. Croix, 33; and Bert Williams, 480n34

white supremacy: anticipatory nature of HH's ideas on, 5; central to capitalist rule in United States, 4, 280, 395; centrality of struggle against, 5, 151, 218–19; challenges to, necessary for class struggle, 280; as challenge to socialism, 150, 188; in church, 234; deliberately fostered, 150, 161; duty of radicals to challenge, 409; duty of white workers to challenge, 279, 409; Fourteenth Amendment challenge to, 287–288; Garvey on the power of, in the U.S., 32; HH's challenge to, 10, 150–151, 198–199, 234, 279, 394; HH's response to, 8–9; and HH's "unremembrance," 13; and intellectual life, 63; Liberty League and fight against, 243, 277–280, 287; need to challenge, 4, 121, 199, 394; need for mass-based struggle against, 394; "New

Negro Movement" challenge to, 243; and organized labor, 277; produces race consciousness, 278; race-conscious challenge to, 188, 277–79, 372, 394; rampant in New York City, 53–55; how reinforced, 198; relation to class consciousness, 187–188, 462n37; retardant of class consciousness, 188; requirements for response to, 9; revolutionary implications of challenging, 158, 409; in science, 120; and separate Black organization, 171; social action against, 121; in Socialist Party, 8, 142, 144, 163, 171, 277, 364; and understanding of "race," 121; in U.S., 32; more virulent, 34, 41, 421; and World War I, 372; and women's suffrage movement, 350

"White War and the Colored Races, The" (HH), 473n32

"White War and the Colored World, The" (HH), 230, 318

"Who Put the Bomb in St. Patrick's Cathedral? With a Word of Warning to Millionaires and the Public" (HH), 244, 477n4

"Why is there no socialism in the United States?" (Sombart), 187–188, 462n37

"Why Men Leave Home" (HH), 276

"Why Should the Negro Go to War?" (HH), 343

"Why They Call Us 'Niggers'" (HH), 326

Why We Behave Like Human Beings (Dorsey), 444n22

Wibecan, George E., 296

Wiggins, Lida Keck, 74

Wilberforce, Sinclair, 317

Wilberforce University, 89, 100

Wilde, Oscar, 81

Wilkes, Mattie, 264

Wilmington, Del., 63–64

William, Rev., 317

"William Morris," 149

Williams, Bert, 253, 311, 427n82, 480n34

Williams, Eric, 31, 417n31

Williams, George Washington, 98

Williams, Mrs. R.H., 110

Williams, Thomas, 150, 451–452n24

Willis, William H., 329, 392

Wilson, Dooley, 264

GPSR Authorized Representative: Easy Access System Europe, Mustamäe tee
50, 10621 Tallinn, Estonia, gpsr.requests@easproject.com

www.ingramcontent.com/pod-product-compliance
Lightning Source LLC
Chambersburg PA
CBHW050900050426
42334CB00052B/750